Saginaw Chippewa Tribal College
2274 Enterprise Drive
Mt. Pleasant, MI 48858

# THE MYSTIC WARRIORS
# OF THE PLAINS

# THE MYSTIC WARRIORS OF THE PLAINS

Thomas E. Mails

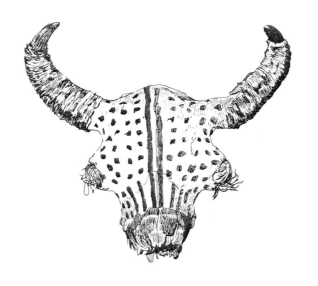

MALLARD PRESS

MALLARD PRESS
An Imprint of BDD Promotional Book Company, Inc.
666 Fifth Avenue
New York, NY 10103

To

Al Miller

and

To a People who once danced in the Sun

# Contents

# CONTENTS

# List of Color Plates

# INTRODUCTION

When I was a little boy living in Antioch, California, I suffered every winter season from wretched earaches. During some of the more trying moments, my sympathetic German grandfather, August Thomas, sought to relieve the pain by blowing pipe smoke in my ears. I'm not sure that the smoke actually helped the ache, but the warmth and attention was soothing, and as the misery began to ease, Grandfather would complete his "medication" by telling me enthralling stories of his early days among the Indians in Colorado. Sometimes he added to the enjoyment by drawing stick figures of various happenings he shared in.

Before I was five, I had begun to copy his sketches, and for years after that spent hour after hour in my room drawing cowboys and Indians on shirt cardboards saved for me by the local merchants. Thus I entered upon my life as an artist, and by this route I began to admire a race of exciting Plains Indian people without ever having met a real one. In addition to this, the boys of my generation played "cowboys and Indians," and through it all I inevitably became and remained a Western fan, preferring such books, movies, and in time television programs to any others.

The ensuing years led me to service in the U. S. Coast Guard during World War II, and after that to the College of Arts and Crafts in Berkeley, California. Then came a period of work in architecture and industrial design, and finally the seminary and a career as a Lutheran minister which was begun in Minnesota.

In 1962 I returned to California, and to the city of Pomona, from whence in 1963 our family made its first vacation trip to Flagstaff, Arizona. Here I discovered, in a small pawnshop, of all places, that one could still purchase some of the ancient Plains Indian artifacts. My first possessions were three unusual pieces, a strange pipe, a wondrous bear claw necklace, and a rawhide case for carrying coup feathers to war. Wishing to know more about these I went looking for books—and the abundance of information I assumed was readily available. My hopes were immediately dashed, for the popular books on Indians contained surprisingly few details concerning the "best-known" Indians of America.

Meanwhile, my appetite for accurate knowledge was being increased by regular additions to my "Indian collection," and it was becoming clearer with every purchase that I was obtaining the products of a deeply religious people, and of some of the finest and most sensitive artists in history. I was delighted!

By constantly prowling through the rare-book stores of many cities, I finally assembled a fairly extensive library of old Indian books—finding in these at last the comprehensive information I had not found in the popular books. Even then, I had either to buy or to read over half a thousand publications to gain the knowledge I wanted. So in the fall of 1965 I undertook the project which has become the present book. It is an attempt to offer everyone an intimate, organized, and yet comprehensive meeting with an extraordinary people and their life-way during their peak culture period, which extended from A.D. 1750 to A.D. 1875.

Rare books, old paintings, ancient drawings, museums, private collections, and a few living scholars are the only reliable sources of information left concerning the people of the Plains, yet *the best of these sources are very good.* From them one can still draw a remarkable, and I think accurate, picture.

An extensive bibliography is included at the back of the book, but since I will be mentioning certain important authorities on Indian lore throughout the material, I want to list them here—and their writings from which I've drawn my principal information. Naturally, I recommend them to all who are interested in the Indians of the Plains. The authors and their books are listed in an order of merit:

Linderman, Frank B., *Plenty Coups, Chief of the Crows,* U. of Nebraska Press, 1962. This book is in paperback, and is the extraordinarily sensitive unfolding of the chief's life story by a man who knew the chief and many other Indians very well.

McClintock, Walter, *The Old North Trail,* U. of Nebraska Press, 1968. Also in paperback. By a man who lived with the Blackfoot Indians for many years and took dozens of superb photographs.

Ewers, John C., *The Horse in Blackfoot Culture,* Smithsonian Institution, Bulletin 159, U. S. Government Printing Office, Washington, 1955. John Ewers is easily the dean of American Indian scholars, and everything he writes about the Plains Indians proves to be accurate, readable, and incisive when it is compared to Indian accounts. I also recommend the Heye Foundation books by Wildschut, which Ewers edited, on Crow Indian beadwork and Crow Indian medicine bundles.

Dockstader, Frederick J., *Indian Art In America,* New York Graphic Society, 1962. The finest work on North American Indian art to date by the eminently qualified Director of The Museum of the American Indian, Heye Foundation, New York, N.Y.

Powell, Peter J., *Sweet Medicine,* University of Oklahoma Press, Norman, 1969. If the reader wishes to understand the Sun Dance and the exemplary spiritual life of the Plains Indians, this superb work on the Cheyenne Indians is a must.

Catlin, George, *Letters and Notes on the Manners, Customs, and Condition of the North American Indians,* Ross & Haines, Inc., Minneapolis, 1965. The copious insights of this great artist who spent many years among the Plains Indians are indispensable to anyone who wishes to know the people well.

Densmore, Frances, *Teton Sioux Music,* BAE Bulletin 61, 1918. Far and away the best and most profusely illustrated treatment of Sioux customs.

Lowie, Robert H., *Indians of the Plains,* American Museum of Science edition in paperback, 1963. Lowie was a recognized authority, and gives excellent details, although he is not my preferred expert as per the information in the book just mentioned. However, his finest work, *The Crow Indians,* Holt, Rinehart & Winston, reissued in 1956, is a must for everyone.

Dodge, Col. Richard Irving, *The Plains of the Great West* and *Thirty-Three Years Among Our Wild Indians,* reissued by Archer House, Inc., New York, 1959. Here are reams of potent observations—all of which need to be tempered by comparing them to Indian accounts—but they are excellent reading.

Denig, Edward Thompson, *Five Indian Tribes of the Upper Missouri,* U. of Oklahoma Press, 1961. Denig lived as a trader among the Indians from approximately 1843 to 1854. His observations are as good as any to be found. *The 46th Annual Report of the Bureau of Ethnology,* Washington, 1930, is the document to obtain, but it is very hard to find.

Lehmann, Herman, *Nine Years Among the Indians, 1870–1879,* Von Boeckmann-Jones Co., Printers, Austin, Texas, 1927. Some fine insights by a White man who lived for a time as a southern Plains Indian.

Any book by George Bird Grinnell is a masterpiece of empathy with the Indians, as is the case also with those of J. W. Schultz. Both men lived with the Indians and were able to gather accurate information about them—and they present this exceptionally well in many of their writings. Norman Feder, Curator of American Indian Art, Denver Art Museum, is also an outstanding authority whose books and articles deserve attention.

Prince Maximilian of Wied Neuwied, 1782–1867, made a two-year journey to the Plains and returned with a detailed description of the Indian culture. He was accompanied by Carl Bodmer, a Swiss artist, who made superbly detailed drawings and paintings. No finer work can be found than *Travels in the Interior of North America,* translated by H. Evans Lloyd, London, 1843.

For extensive details, the many drawings of the *Journal of Rudolph Friederich Kurtz (1846–1852)* are of great value, BAE Bulletin 115, 1937. For outstanding and abundant photographs the twenty-volume works of Edward S. Curtis, 1907, are illustrated beyond compare.

One must, in the end, study the marvelous paintings of Frederic Remington and Charles Russell in the books edited by Harold McCracken, which are brilliantly done and are available everywhere.

A few thoughts should be borne in mind by the reader as he considers my views regarding the Plains Indians of yesterday and today.

I capitalize the word "White" throughout. This is not a common custom among those who write about the Indians, but I do it for a special reason. The word "Indian" is not a proper term for the Plains people, yet non-Indians use it offhandedly to identify them. Likewise, to an "Indian," all non-Indians are

"Whites," and so I employ the capitalization in a general sense to delineate all those peoples outside the Indian nations, and in particular all but the Spanish nationalities which settled in their area during the expansion to the west. I except the Spanish because they must be mentioned by name when the diffusion of the horse is considered.

Also, the book is about the Plains Indian warriors and their culture, and so the only references to Whites have to do with their influences upon the development and the demise of that culture. The usual references to the details of the White-Indian wars will be omitted.

I will often make reference to "bands" and "clans," since each tribe was subdivided into one or the other of these. Bands were subdivisions of a tribe which consisted in the main of different, or unrelated, families. Clans were subdivisions which were made up of relations or families; fathers, brothers, sisters, uncles, cousins, nephews, etc.

George Catlin distinguished between the titles "warrior" and "brave." A brave was a man who had not counted coup; that is, he had not touched an enemy in battle with his hand or with something held in his hand. A warrior had accomplished this act one or more times; I make the same distinction in my book.

Most of the larger Indian nations were subdivided into several major tribes, but I've forgone the articulation of these divisions in favor of a single title for each. Further subdivisions lead inevitably to complications in understanding, and to fine points which are not germane to the thrust of my material, which is to present an organized and systematized overview of the Plains culture with an emphasis upon the male warrior.

The material I offer will contain more references and comparisons to Scripture and Christianity than is usual for a book about Indians. As a Lutheran pastor, such an orientation is logical for me, yet nothing about my view is apologetic insofar as the Plains Indians are concerned, for intriguing comparisons between Christianity and the Indian religion come forth as naturally as can be. There really is no other way to approach the Indians for one who knows this. I have a profound regard for the Indian religion and no desire to convert those who practice the ancient faith to Christianity.

The bright colors of the garments in my paintings might well surprise the viewer. It should be borne in mind that the colors depict them as they actually were when they were first put on—not somewhat faded as they appear in museums today. Even now, though, a hundred years or more later, the richness of many Indian pieces is resilient enough to reveal how brilliant they were in the beginning. For further proof, one need only see dyed quills which have been shielded from the light in hide containers and so have maintained their original rich colors.

Whenever Indian artifacts are considered, it is vital to recognize that most of the older items found in books or collections today were gathered or drawn or photographed considerably later than the pieces were originally fashioned. Therefore one can only speculate broadly as to the date of origin of a certain piece or style, and absolute statements in this regard cannot be made. However, it is reasonable to assume that the first sighting of a given item or costume by exploring Whites was not an indication that the style observed was just appearing among the Plains Indians. On the contrary, whatever the newcomers saw had been in vogue for a decade or more. Also, each of the styles continued to be popular long enough to overlap succeeding phases, so that in the case of clothing several types of shirts and leggings would be in evidence at a given moment—the percentage of each type being influenced by whether it was toward the beginning or end of its evolutional phase. A good example is the tubular style of male leggings. These were in use when George Catlin was painting the Indians in 1832, yet museum files show that tubular leggings which had been worn before 1830 were still being collected from active wardrobes as late as the 1860s. In the same way styles which were popular in the 1870s continued into the 1920s, the major difference being in the newer decorative touches and in the materials from which the later garments were made; the cuts and patterns remained about the same. This is a fact which offers great advantages in the way of source material to historians and artists, since many of the photographs taken from 1875 on, and in abundance after 1900, show excellent continuations of the earlier styles. The researcher without the more recent photographs would be hard pressed to do an adequate job. In this book, a number of photographs taken after 1900 have been used as guides for illustrations of much earlier styles and events. Naturally the oldest photographs available were used whenever possible, and whenever clothing was added to a figure an authentic item from a documented collection was employed.

Since my goal has been to show the broad and accomplished scope of the Plains culture, the *unusual* in garments and customs is depicted together with the usual, or common, garments and customs. The captions will indicate which of these were unusual according to the individual case.

I have made extensive use of old photographs as sources for illustrative material. The subjects who lived during the time period of the book, 1750 to 1875, are no longer alive. Old photographs or illustrations alone reveal what actually existed and the Indians as they actually looked. Therefore, whenever possible photographs or ancient drawings were carefully followed to make the book as accurate as possible. A summary of the source photographs drawn upon is set forth at the back of the book, together with a listing of the artifact locations. When considering the use of old photographs it should be further remembered they were taken before the advent of color photography, the details were often obscured and some pictures are now faded, many of the subjects were poorly posed, and their clothing often consisted of a curious mixture of Indian and White items. To render the clothing and other artifacts in accurate color requires an exhaustive search by the artist through the collections of both the United States and Europe. Details must often be patiently researched and added. The White man's clothing must be removed from the Indian and replaced with original garments. Indians badly posed must be reposed with the pen or brush, Indian subjects photographed in the photographer's studio must be extracted and placed in an outdoor setting natural to their original environment, and often several photographs must be combined in a new composition. Hence the drawings in the book are usually adaptations rather than direct copies.

There are many reasons for writing an extensively illustrated book about the Plains Indians, but not the least of these will be to make an attempt to correct the *misconceptions* which have come into being, and to fulfill *a profound desire to give an extraordinary culture its just reward.* For despite the fact that the Plains people are thought to be the best-known American Indians in the world, less than a handful of the dozens of books written about the Plains Indians treat them as an accomplished and contributing culture. The result has been that most non-Indians have settled for an ethereal picture of mysterious individuals caught somewhere between blatant savagery and indolent pandering.

It is not difficult to determine how this tragic mistake came to pass. The Whites of the late nineteenth century and what they did to the Indian-Americans may be likened to a group of powerful, uninvited guests who were graciously accepted into a mansion, took it over by force, decimated the family, and then, in all but a few instances, locked the survivors in the mansion's most pitiful rooms. After this the guests' only contact with their prisoners was to send occasional food, to observe them as caged animals through a small, barred window, and to move them rudely to successively poorer rooms. Furthermore, the descendants of the usurper are continuing most of this treatment today!

Scholars who have studied the literature of the Plains people will know there are exceptions to this woeful "rule of remote observation." Some published works depict the Indian with great sympathy. Yet even popular Western titans of the easel such as Charles Russell and Frederic Remington portrayed him so much of the time from such a distance that only the real student and dedicated scholar could supply the details.

Quite possibly a question of some import will sooner or later arise in the minds of those well acquainted with Indian literature, and it might be best for me to answer the question now. My picture of the Indian will emerge as a wholly sympathetic one, and it will tend to cast him in a haloed light. Those who are knowledgeable will realize there is another side, a matter of naïveté and super-stition, a matter of such things as sanitation not comparable to that of the present day, and the problem of abject savagery in the treatment of captives. Nomadic groups without modern facilities on the often dusty plains were sometimes dirty, and some tribes did heap stomach-turning abuses upon male and female spoils of war. Yet there were notable exceptions to these instances. Some Indians bathed regularly year-round, most had very neat dwellings and even had excellent methods of cleaning their hide clothing, and the practice of wanton brutality was by and large minor among the majority of the larger tribes. Then too, an over-emphasis on some of these negative characteristics by those who were hardly qualified to judge them has warped the picture in the other direction so excessively as to obscure the Indian's finer qualities. Many of the White men who actually lived with the Indians saw so few of these disturbing things as to be not worth mentioning.

The worth of such a sympathetic view is to be found in the "pudding," for a comprehensive study of the Plains Indians shows that their virtues far out-weighed their shortcomings. Also, the finer religious and secular qualities of the Indians were of ancient vintage, and these qualities did not often profit from White influence. It is evident that the Indians could not have been what they were in the year 1800 without a long history of excellent progress in a material and religious life-way. Their life pattern militated against sudden—or even signifi-cant—changes. Therefore, every custom the Whites found when they arrived on the Plains was seasoned wine—though put in some ways into new wineskins because of the arrival of the horse and, accordingly, the greater accessibility of the buffalo.

Perhaps the Indians of 1750 to 1875 were not really saints, yet they achieved so much that it is equally wrong to call them primitives or savages. Neither description is accurate or adequate.

Since the White and Indian views of the Indian's customs and intents often varied to a significant degree, and since the Indians of the various tribes were quite consistent in their statements, *I have made it a regular habit to choose the Indian's view of a practice wherever it was available.* I take for granted that he understood his intentions better than others. I have also learned, in any case, to avoid dogma-tisms about the Indian attitudes, dress, and practices of the eighteenth and nine-teenth centuries, for the modern scholar, be he Indian or White, deals with a shrouded period of history.

Rather than listing the sources for my material in footnotes at the bottom of each page, I have gathered them together in a section at the back of the book. Also, while most of the Indian artifacts will be included in different illustrations throughout the book, only one illustration of a given item will be near the place where it is described in the text. To gain a broader picture, the reader can check the Index for a listing of all the illustrations of and references to a certain item.

I am deeply indebted to several museums, and to one private party, for their generous permission to examine and reproduce many of the Plains items in their collections: to the Southwest Museum in Highland Park, California, and to its fine Director, Carl S. Dentzel, for his many courtesies; to the Heard Museum in Phoenix, Arizona; to the Museum of the American Indian in New York City; to the Museum of Natural History in New York City; to the Museum of Man in

San Diego, California; to the Denver Museum of American Indian Art and to the Denver Public Library, Denver, Colorado; and especially to the Thomas Gilcrease Institute of American History and Art, Tulsa, Oklahoma. I would be very remiss not to express my gratitude for extraordinary kindnesses extended to me by Gilcrease Director Paul A. Rossi, and his assistant Daniel M. McPike, during my period of research there. My thanks also to the Harvey family for permitting me to spend a week photographing the awesome collection of Fred Harvey while it was still in the warehouses at the Grand Canyon. Most of the Plains Indian part of this collection is now on loan to the Heard Museum, and a few additional pieces were photographed there.

In my aforementioned desire to have authentic Plains faces and apparel and other items, I have drawn upon over five hundred publications for photographs and paintings from which to make my own illustrations. Since it would be impossible to thank the producers of these publications by name, I instead offer my sincerest gratitude to them as a unit, hoping they will feel that my work enhances their contributions. An extensive bibliography listing the publications I used the most is included at the back of the book.

My most heartfelt thanks are due a number of people who lent valuable encouragement and guidance during my years of working on the book: to Gordon Aasgaard; to Al Miller of the 49 Steps in Los Angeles; to Clyde Vandeburg of Vandeburg-Linkletter Associates, Los Angeles; to Steven L. Rose and Joyce Grimes of the Biltmore Galleries, Los Angeles; to Margaret Jamison and Richard Harris of the Jamison Galleries, Santa Fe; and to the members of my congregation, Christ the Victor Lutheran Church, Pomona, for never protesting the endless hours spent on this extracurricular activity. Whether or not it is the customary thing to do, I owe too much to Richard Laugharn and Harold Kuebler of Doubleday & Company, Inc., not to express my appreciation for their tireless efforts to help in every way.

I thank J. R. Eyerman for the infinite patience and craftsmanship which produced the superb transparencies for the color plates, and Glenn Harrison for the hundreds of photographs he made at considerable effort to assist me in drawing the book into its final form.

Finally, I thank my wife for her steady encouragement and for her faith in the value of the material, and also my daughter Allison, who typed redraft after redraft until at last the work was finished.

*Claremont, California*                                                THOMAS E. MAILS
*September 1, 1970*


It is with the greatest sadness I append this note regarding the dedication of the book: my dear friend, Al Miller, who owned the well-known 49 Steps

Antique Shop on La Cienega Boulevard in Los Angeles, passed away in mid-May of 1971, and will not have the pleasure of seeing the finished book. As such I feel I should say something more about him. Al was a friend of the Indians and a sensitive collector for most of his life. He also lent immediate and generous support to anyone who sincerely wished to be and to do the same. He let me have many beautiful Indian items from his shop long before I was able to pay for them all, because he knew how much they meant to me. From the moment he saw the first of my drawings he gave steady and enthusiastic encouragement to the completion of my book. It was Al who introduced me to Clyde Vandeburg, my agent, and who arranged my first meeting with Steven Rose of the Biltmore Galleries. Whatever I have accomplished herein has been due in large measure to his continuing kindness and interest. He and his equally kind wife, Lillian, who continues to operate the shop, deserve to be remembered, and especially by me. It was the most natural thing ever that I should dedicate this book to Al Miller.

*June 20, 1971*

# THE MYSTIC WARRIORS
# OF THE PLAINS

# Chapter 1

# ORIGIN, DISTRIBUTION, AND NATURE OF THE PEOPLE OF THE PLAINS

I find that the principal cause why we underrate and despise the savage, is generally because we do not understand him; and the reason why we are ignorant of him and his modes, is that we do not stop to investigate—the world has been too much in the habit of looking upon him as altogether inferior—as a beast, a brute; and unworthy of more than a passing notice. If they stop long enough to form an acquaintance, it is but to take advantage of his ignorance and credulities—to rob him of the wealth and resources of his country;—to make him drunk with whiskey, and visit him with abuses which in his ignorance he never thought of. By this method his first visitors entirely overlook and never understand the meaning of his thousand interesting and characteristic customs; and at the same time, by changing his native modes and habits of life, blot them out from view of the enquiring world for ever.[1]

GEORGE CATLIN

Neither historians nor archaeologists have progressed to the point where they can say precisely how the Indian tribes of the Plains came into being. The idea given the greatest credence today is that they migrated across the Bering Strait to Alaska, with the first of them coming as much as forty thousand years ago, and from Alaska into the Americas. Enough has been discovered to give substance to the idea, yet as one who finds no problems with divine creation, the total evidence points far more strongly to the following: Some tribes were always here in all parts of North America, while others migrated across the strait or came by sea vessel across both the Pacific and Atlantic oceans. Hence there were *four* strains or basic families which later subdivided into the tribes we now know.

Several factors can be cited in defense of this proposition: the difference in physical characteristics, which suggests multiple and diverse sources; the suspected sea routes under investigation by such modern pioneers as Heyerdahl; new pictograph evidence which reveals inward migration from the Pacific islands; the discovery that the Americas Man is of ancient vintage with a pre-White legendry incorporating all of the common creation accounts; and finally, the fact that Plains religion is of an almost uniquely monotheistic nature.

According to Wissler, certain tribes were "always" on the Plains, notably the Apache, Blackfoot, Arapaho, and Kiowa.[2] Legends are the only source of such knowledge, and thus one cannot posit the idea as an absolute, but from the evidence at hand it is a most reasonable position. The Blackfeet were in Mackenzie River country by 500 B.C. and Coronado found Apaches in present-day Texas in A.D. 1541. The other tribes migrated to the Plains from the east or west as intertribal pressures and the lure of the buffalo encouraged them.

The authors of several recent books have declared that "all" of the tribes "spilled" onto the Plains as the more powerful Eastern Woodland tribes forced them out. The forcing part is accurate, but the action was more that of steam escaping through a pressure valve, with each puff of steam pushing those emerging before it farther and farther away. Thus about A.D. 1700 the Sioux moved from the Woodlands to Minnesota, and then to the Black Hills—forcing the Crows and Cheyennes on just ahead of them. Once horses were obtained, each migrant tribe began to stand its own ground, and although contested, well-boundaried tribal areas were established. Soon, even the great Woodland tribes decided it was best to leave them alone.

From approximately 1775 on most of the shifting ceased, the various Plains domains were set, and because of the spread of the horse, a common, buffalo-and-horse-oriented pattern of life had emerged which lasted till about 1875, the end date varying somewhat according to what happened to each tribe in its contact with the Whites.

In brief, as one considers the mystic Americans beyond that date, the situation was this: While one must proceed with care in making identifications of habits, garments, trappings, and weapons, each tribe had a few customs, symbolic designs, and color choices which were unique unto itself. By making the proper associations scholars can often issue specific statements and identify selected items in collections of ancient artifacts. Beyond this, area identifications may also be made, since distinguishable differences occurred in four identifiable zones. For example, the color of clothing grades from gray-white in the far north, to creamy white in the next area, to yellow in the next section immediately south of the mid-Plains, and then to yellow-green in the far south of the present Oklahoma and Texas area. Nevertheless, so common was the general life pattern that the Plains tribes of America may be fairly treated as a whole; as long as in addition to the foregoing, it is remembered that the present tribes consider themselves distinct from one another and are, understandably, not fond of the designation "Indian," since it is a term which lumps them together and confuses the distinctions.

As the years passed and the various Plains territories were established, many of the tribes were obliged to form alliances with each other in order to survive against the elements and hostile attacks. Thus the Mandans allied themselves with the Arikaras. The Crows kept a standing relationship with the Hidatsas. The Sioux, Cheyenne, and Arapaho were close enough to combine their forces against the United States Army when circumstances demanded it.

Besides this, and even in the face of continual minor hostilities, the tribes of the Plains maintained contact with one another through trade centers, and evolved a unique sign language which made communication possible between any two tribes.

It is said that the White men built no original trails in the West, that the pathways carved out by ancient Indian traders had been there waiting for them for centuries. There were in fact literally thousands of the trails, whose crossed lines after the pattern of a gigantic web eventually covered North America. Some were short side roads, and others were main trunks that followed the main migrations of the game and the locations of water. These were the trade arteries that connected prehistoric men, and many have been retraced by the paved highways people travel today.

Because of its central location, great rivers, and flat terrain, the Great Plains became a natural storage and redistribution shed for prehistoric and historic transcontinental commerce. By the early 1700s, goods of every kind important

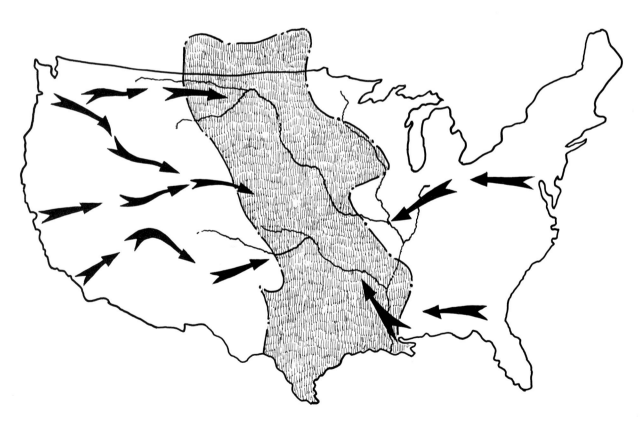

Ancient trade routes used by the Indians of North America to carry trade goods to and from the Plains tribes.

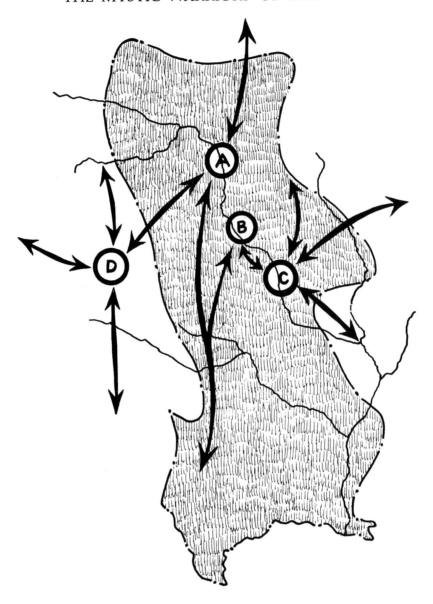

The main trade centers of the Plains after A.D. 1700 *A*, the Mandan. *B*, the Arikara. *C*, the Sioux. *D*, the Shoshone-Nez Percé.

to the Indians were being fed back and forth from the west and the east into this central dumping area and, having been deposited at certain key crossroad points, were then interchanged between the tribes; yes, even between enemy tribes such as the Sioux and the Crow, who used a mostly neutral stationary tribe like the Hidatsa and Mandan to make the exchange—at a trader's profit, naturally! In time, four main trade centers came into being, with the following tribes serving in this capacity: the Mandan, the Arikara, the Sioux, and the Shoshone-Nez Percé.

In addition to the trade center activities, peace councils and temporary treaties between unfriendly nations were often arranged for no other reason than to trade, although surely other excuses were given as a disguise—since the Plains enemies would never admit they needed each other. In fact, though, the diversities within the cultures stimulated barter. All Indians were interested in new goods and ideas, and always wanted to know what the other tribes were doing. A final point to be made in the trade feature is that it shows in an impressive way that while the tribes contested constantly with their particular enemies in raids and small battles, they had other relationships too.

Some authorities argue that the need and desire for trade, more than anything, led to the development of the sign language, which, in an amazing diversity of tribes with different and difficult languages, enabled them to converse across linguistic boundaries even better than they could have with words.

Every expert agrees that the sign language reached its highest development among the Indians of the Plains. It evolved over the years into a full-fledged method of communication, and Indians who were total strangers and from different tribes could converse freely and fluently with it on any subject, secular or religious. It may be the only universal language man has ever produced.

Those who saw it in action among the Indians have described it as a thing of grace and beauty, needing no help in the way of facial expression, for the signs were sufficient in themselves. It was a cultivated art of great practicality, and founded upon principles which could be learned by everyone. Authorities point out that it could also be used at a distance which the eye could reach but not the ear, and was an extremely helpful tool when people wanted to talk without being overheard. Everyone practices it in a simplified way whenever they clench a fist, order an item with their fingers, or signal with hand or arm for a turn.

Experts also see a strong connection between Indian sign language and their primitive picture writing, called pictography. Some have pointed out that a single picture often spoke an entire sentence, and that in many cases the shape of a hand gesture conformed exactly to the lines used in a drawing. The tree picture sign was given with the fingers upraised like branches, and a jagged lightning line was shown by zigzagging the hand.

It can be said, therefore, that the Plains Indian tribes held and practiced a great deal in common. In the same way, the Indian tribes of today seek opportunity to associate in tribal gatherings and festivals, and often work together in achieving Indian needs. Still, each tribe maintains its own rich and proud heritage, and one which it intends to preserve at all costs. Therefore, a tribesman is never an "Indian," but rather a Crow, a Cheyenne, a Jicarilla Apache. And it is truly unfortunate that the multiplicity of nations makes it impossible to refer to them by tribal distinctions in general conversations.

A close acquaintanceship with the Plains Indians soon reveals there are significant differences in physical characteristics. Facial structures vary considerably, and in time one who has studied them can often tell what area an Indian

Plains Pictography and sign language. *a*, sign for Oglala Sioux chief. *b*, Sioux warrior named Tall Panther. *c*, Sioux warrior named Afraid of Bear. *d*, sign for top man. *e*, sign for Oglala Sioux subchief. *f*, sign for light. *g*, sign and hand gesture for sun. *h*, sign and hand gesture for antelope. *i*, Indian warriors conversing in sign language.

is from. As a rule, the southern Indians were broad and stocky compared to the northern tribes, where men often averaged six feet or more in height.

The first White mountain men and artist-historians to visit the Great Plains were profoundly impressed with the comeliness and grace of the people who dwelt there. Even the designation "red man" hardly applied to the Indian. His skin was quite white, and only those parts of his body which were regularly exposed to the sun turned a coppery brown, or in some tribes an umber color. The title "red" really came from the earth-red and vermilion paints worn by almost all of the people as a sacred color.

In 1837 the artist Alfred Jacob Miller effectively summed up the physical characteristics of the Indians in his journal:

American sculptors travel thousands of miles to study Greek statues in the Vatican in Rome, seemingly unaware that in their own country there exists a race of men equal in form and grace (if not superior) to the finest beau ideal ever dreamed of by the Greeks. And it does seem a little extraordinary that up to this time (as far as I am aware) not a single sculptor has thought it worth his while to make a journey among these Indians, who are now sojourning on the Western side of the Rocky Mountains, and are rapidly passing away. Most unquestionably, that sculptor who travels here,—and models from what he sees (supposing him to have equal power and genius), will far excel any other who merely depends upon his own conception of what it ought to be.[3]

Seemingly, there are many benefits to be reaped in cultivating a deeper understanding of and broader relationships with the Plains Indians.

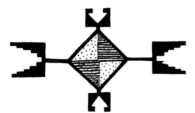

Nearly every writer opens his account of the Indians of the Plains with a detailed description of the Midwest land and elements. At first I wondered why this was so, since they did not say, and then it struck me that the nature of the country played a dominant role in the development of its animal and human inhabitants.

The sweeping heartland of America is a basin of exciting natural extremes. In the badlands of the western Dakotas there are eerie rocky tablelands etched by centuries of water and wind. In central Nebraska one discovers endless hills of sand transported there by awesome storms. Giant potholes mark the Minnesota and South Dakota terrain like the skin of a gigantic orange. Most of the area is treeless, with the few wooded areas there being found only in the hills and alongside streams.

The wind seems to blow constantly. On the central and southern Plains a dry blast of summer gale may, in a few days, parch everything in its path, while a sudden northern draft can bring a cold front deep into Texas within a few hours. In spring or summer a cooled moisture-laden air mass moving north from the Gulf of Mexico may dump an incredible ten or more inches of rain in a matter of minutes. The grassy sod seldom holds under such a downpour, as is shown by the countless raw gullies and deep-worn stream beds which cover the landscape.

Swift rivers like the Missouri, the Bighorn, the Yellowstone, the Arkansas, and the Platte cut broad paths through every part like undulating rain streaks on a windowpane.

The grasslands are the awe-inspiring birthplace of violent, screeching storms and booming thunder. Spring tornadoes regularly flatten a twisting pathway eastward in any part of the area. A bombardment of hail the size of hen eggs can maul the grass, trees, and whole flights of migrant birds. Sometimes during the winter the northern prairie is ghostly silent and somber; between the silences savage blizzards rage. In the worst winters of old they thinned even the ranks of the tough buffalo, and brought death to any living thing which was unprepared. By contrast a flow of warm air from the mountains will melt a foot of snow overnight and send sparkling freshets romping across the sand bars of dry river-beds. Late summer is sticky hot, while spring and fall are jewel-studded with royal blue skies and hills crested by a breath-taking green. The Plains are white in winter, green in spring, yellow in summer, and red-orange in the fall. Early in the morning Mother Nature coats everything with a translucent glaze of blue, at night she does the same with purple. Midday is so crystal-clear you can see a spot of color twenty miles away.

The Plains are a veritable sea of grass. Shortgrasses dominate a narrow western band running the full length of the Plains from north to south. Over-ten-inch mixed grass occupies a similar mid-belt, and tall grass, as high as eight feet, bands the entire eastern edge as far south as Kansas. Explorers said they could become lost more quickly on the Plains than in the eastern forests.

As might be expected, a land of such contrasts was the home of those hardy living communities which could adapt to all its conditions.

In the time period under consideration, two varieties of hoofed mammals were typical of the grasslands: the sixty-miles-an-hour pronghorn, called so but not an antelope, and the largest and most spectacular creature of North America, the majestic, purple-headed American bison, known to one and all as the buffalo.

No other animal ever gave so much to a people as the great, shaggy buffalo.

Tornado on the Great Plains.

For that reason, the Indian male revered, studied, and imitated it intensely—discovering in the doing some enthralling things—and that being the case, those who would know the Indian must study the buffalo intensely too. A broad knowledge of the bison's make-up, habits, and religious connotations is essential to every Plains Indian student.

Its name was given to Indian children so they would be hardy and reach maturity quickly. Social organizations were named after it, and medicine men called upon the powers of the "Spirit Buffalo" to help them perform their rituals successfully. On occasion, a chief tied the long forelock of a bull to the tip of a lodge pole as an emblem of strength and prosperity. Sometimes the entire head was placed on the ground at the rear of the lodge and sacrificial offerings were laid on top of it. Buffalo skulls were frequently painted with traditional colors and symbols, and used in such ceremonies as the Sun Dances and vision quests.

Other creatures of significance joined the buffalo on the Great Plains:

Elk made extensive use of the grasslands, but were found most commonly in the summer near forested and mountain country. White-tailed deer inhabited the wooded stream bottoms of the grass region.

Birds of many kinds were seen, dominated by varieties of hawk, falcon, and the stupendous golden eagle, which patrolled the prairie sky like a professional sentinel, its keen eyes missing not a single movement on the ground far below.

Ground squirrels and prairie dogs abounded. So did the owl, the gopher, mice, rabbits, and snakes.

Until the late nineteenth century there was the coyote and the now extinct white wolf. Along the upper Missouri River ranged a huge and powerful subspecies of grizzly bear. Farther south there was the badlands grizzly. The black and brown bear were common to all areas.

There were also badger, beaver, weasel, otter, skunk, prairie chicken, sage grouse, killdeer, and, later, pheasant.

In all, the ancient Plains were a marvelous, compelling place, full of adventure, and promising a fresh new scene with the topping of every ridge or the turning of a broad riverbend.

The famous hunter and scout Thomas Tibbles wrote in 1850 that "No more beautiful country was ever seen," and theirs was the happiest group "that could ever have ridden across the prairies," as they started off for weeks of tall timber, sweeping plains, clear brooks, and abundant wildlife.[4]

Young Count de Pourtales was simply exuberant over traveling this colossal country in 1832: "Since we left Independence eight or ten days ago [see how quickly he loses track of time], we have camped out every night, slept in bearskins, and done our own cooking. I do not think that I have ever eaten or slept so well in my life. We get a great deal of exercise . . . The weather is magnificent . . . I am wearing a leather shirt, leggings, and moccasins, which I find much more comfortable than shoes, when I am on horseback. I do not know how I shall become reaccustomed to civilization. I have given up ... all the superfluous things which turn man into a dull brute ... We do not spend one cent for food and lodgings, since our beds are on our horses' backs and our meals are supplied by our own hunter's skill. Water is delicious ... food is good ... everything is seasoned with a hellish appetite, our good humor, and long and original tales ... Our physician has become a useless piece of furniture."[5]

George Catlin, dean of the American Indian historians, described some parts of the country as "soul-melting scenery." It was "A place where the mind could think volumes; but the tongue must be silent that would speak, and the hand palsied that would write. I mean," he says, "the prairie at sunset; when the green hill-tops are turned into gold—and their long shadows of melancholy are thrown over the valleys—when all the breathings of day are hushed and nought but the soft notes of the retiring dove can be heard; or the still softer and more plaintive notes of the wolf, who sneaks through these scenes of enchantment."[6]

Here then was the wild, wonderful Plains of America when the ancient Indian civilization occupied it. And as its wildlife adapted to its extremes so too did its human inhabitants, who fitted themselves to earth and sky as a glove shapes itself

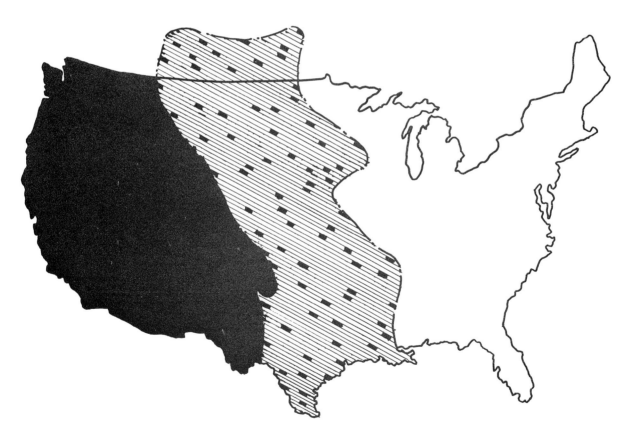

Tribal division of North America. Solid area, coastal and Southwest tribes. Shaded area, Plains tribes. White area, Eastern Woodland tribes.

to the hand. Taking their lead from the elements and their colors from the earth and sky, over the years they became a people of grand, natural extremes—and whose names, accordingly, are more legend than the country. They were a people perfectly united with their domain; a generation whose wild, free manner of life blew and basked as the wind and land itself. Obviously, anyone looking for a passive civilization on the Plains would inevitably be disappointed.

If the continental United States is divided into three irregularly shaped vertical ribbons, a black one as wide as the distance from the Pacific coast to the eastern edge of the Rocky Mountains, a gray one stretching from there to the eastern Minnesota border, and a white one from that point to the Atlantic, the result is a simplified layout of the geographic areas which the cultural types of Indian-American tribes occupied when they lived as free nations during the eighteenth and nineteenth centuries. The black ribbon would designate the Coastal and Southwest tribes. The gray central ribbon would represent the land of the inhabitants of the Great Plains area, and the white ribbon would set forth the territory of the Eastern Woodland Indians.

At their population peak, around A.D. 1800, all of the Plains tribes together numbered no more than 200,000 people, and an approximate numerical breakdown of the individual nations as of that date would be as follows:

| North | | | South | | |
|-------|------|------|-------|------|------|
| | Blackfoot | 30,000 | | Kansa | 3,300 |
| | Cree | 4,000 | | Osage | 6,200 |
| | Assiniboine | 10,000 | | Kiowa | 2,000 |
| | Gros Ventre | 3,000 | | Comanche | 10,000 |
| | Crow | 4,000 | | Kiowa Apache | 300 |
| | Hidatsa | 2,500 | | Wichita | 3,200 |
| | Mandan | 3,600 | | Jicarilla Apache | 800 |
| | Arikara | 3,800 | | Lipan Apache | 500 |
| | Sarsi | 800 | | | |

| Central | | | Rockies | | |
|---------|------|------|---------|------|------|
| | Sioux | 27,000 | | Shoshone | 2,000 |
| | Cheyenne | 3,500 | | Ute | 4,500 |
| | Arapaho | 3,000 | | Nez Percé | 6,000 |
| | Ponca | 800 | | Flatheads | 3,000 |
| | Pawnee | 10,000 | | | |
| | Oto | 1,800 | | | |
| | Omaha | 2,800 | | | |
| | Iowa | 1,100 | | | |
| | Missouri | 500 | | | |
| | Sauk & Fox | 6,500 | | | |

These were the mighty religious and artistic people of the Great Plains, whose sculptured eagle feather bonnets and fringed garments swayed with the drumbeat

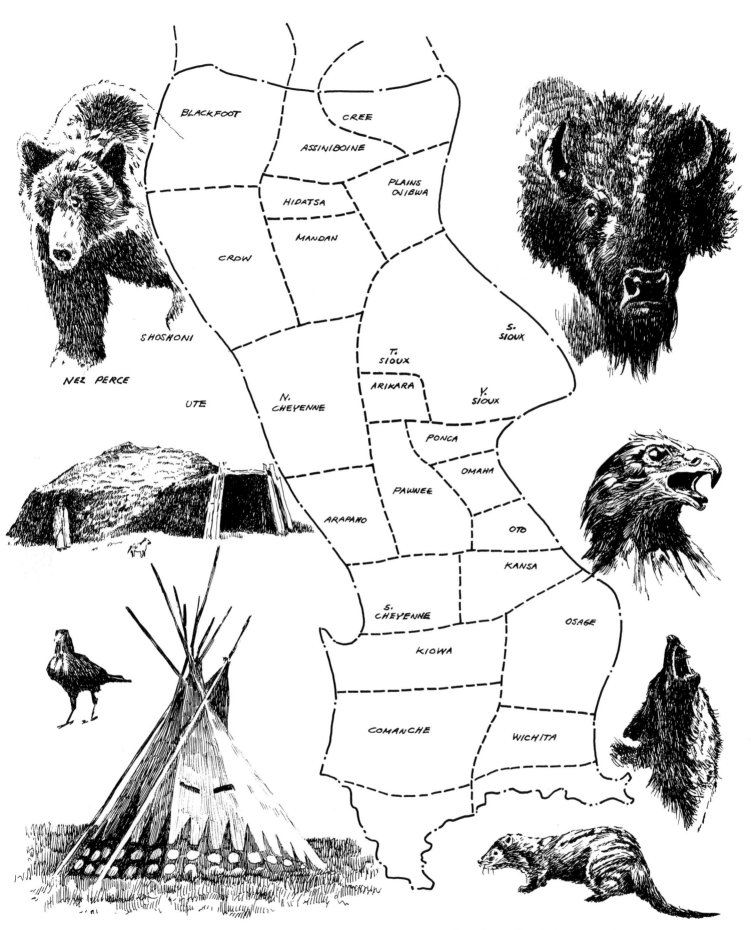

The Plains tribes as of A.D. 1800–50, and the approximate areas they claimed as their own territory. Also illustrated are the Indian dwellings and some of the principal birds and animals of the Plains: crows, bears, buffalo, eagles, wolves, ermine.

and wind as they danced and rode, and whose daring horsemanship became the equal of any the world has ever known. The colorful Plains costume under a cerulean blue sky was "a spectacular creation; a dazzling sight," and one can add that the Indian's way of life matched the glorious costume. "He has captured the imagination of the entire world; and he stands as a symbol for all American Indians."[7]

To expedite their study of these ancient peoples, ethnologists and anthropologists classified the Indian groups according to the languages they spoke. Those speaking the same languages were gathered together into a unit, and the unit was given an identifying title. Two considerations were employed to accomplish the classifications. The first step was to draw together those whose speech was so similar they were able to communicate with each other, even though there were minor differences in dialects. Such peoples were said to be speaking dialects of the same language. The second step, which was used to refine the first one, was to relate each tribe to a common root tongue, which might date back for thousands of years and to the assumed land of a tribe's origin. When the two steps were completed, the conclusion was that six identifiable family or stock languages existed on the Plains.

The Algonkian family included the three Blackfoot tribes, the Cheyenne, Arapaho, Gros Ventres (also known as the Atsinas), and Plains Crees.

The Athabaskan family was composed of the Sarsi and the Kiowa, Lipan and Jicarilla Apaches.

The Caddoan family consisted of the Pawnees, Arikaras, and Wichitas.

The Kiowan family was limited to the Kiowas.

The Siouan family was made up of the Mandans, Hidatsas, Crows, Sioux, Assiniboines, Iowas, Otos, Missouris, Omahas, Poncas, Osages, and Kansas.

The Shoshonean family, also known as the Uto-Aztecan, included the Wind River Shoshones, Comanches, and Utes.

By considering these, one may easily see which tribes, even though faced with the obstacle of interfamily dialects, could communicate verbally within their family, making the necessary compensations by the use of sign language. Communication between tribes of different linguistic families, however, was accomplished in its entirety by sign language; the exception being that a few people in each family usually learned the language of one or two other families, finding the ability to be an advantage in intertribal dialogues over boundaries, trade, and the menace of foreign intruders.

Similarities in language and the resultant family groupings do not, however, mean that all of the tribes of a given family were on friendly terms. In fact, while an exemplary harmony reigned during the pre-White days, after the advent of the horse and the intrusion of the Spanish and Whites, pleasant relationships between any tribes became more the exception than the rule. The nature of survival on the Plains made some degree of hostility inevitable as tribes contended for territory, wealth in horses, and the ever migrating and decreasing bison. Massive warfare between tribes seldom took place, but minor skirmishes and raids were so common as to be a way of life for all tribes during all but the most inclement winter days. A temporary peace between two or three tribes would be worked out as changing conditions demanded it, but it never endured for long. Indeed, this divisional factor of life on the Plains made its inevitable contribution to the downfall of the Indians, since they resisted the idea of uniting in common cause against the White armies until it was too late. One can readily see how different the outcome might otherwise have been as he considers the Custer incident.

In view of the foregoing, while an exhaustive rundown of tribal relationships would be unproductive, and indeed not exact because such relationships were always in a state of flux, a sample picture of Plains conditions about the year 1850 can be obtained from the following:

The Assiniboines were usually friendly with the Crees, but were steadfast enemies of the Sioux, Crows, Blackfoot, Mandans, Hidatsas, and Arikaras.

The Sioux made late concords with the Northern Cheyenne and the Arapaho. They traded with the Mandans but they also fought them—and every other tribe on the Plains, with the Crows and Pawnees drawing their particular vengeance.

The Gros Ventres maintained good terms with the Crows and Arapaho, but warred continually against the Blackfoot, Sarsi, and Assiniboines.

The Arapaho were hostile to the Shoshones, Utes, Comanches, Kiowas, Pawnees, Crows, and Sioux. A very-late-nineteenth-century truce was made with the Sioux, Comanches, Kiowas, and Cheyenne.

The Western Crees were somewhat friendly with the Assiniboines, but fought the Blackfoot tribes and the Sioux.

The Sarsi were the only friends of the Blackfoot, and contested regularly with the Crows, Assiniboines, Shoshones, Flatheads, and Kutenai. These last two were mountain, and not properly Plains, tribes.

The Shoshones were friendly with the Flatheads, and made an occasional peace with the Nez Percés, Utes, and Bannocks (another mountain tribe). But they battled the Gros Ventres, Mandans, Hidatsas, Arikaras, Blackfoot, Crows, Cheyenne, Arapaho, Utes, and the mountain tribes.

The Comanches were sometimes friends of the Kiowas and Apaches, but fought every other tribe they could reach to the northwest, north, and east.

The Crows were occasionally friendly to the Gros Ventres and Nez Percés, and traded regularly with the Mandans and Hidatsas, but maintained continual hostility toward the Sioux, Cheyenne, Arapaho, Blackfoot, Flatheads, and Shoshones.

Taking these relationships as a guide, it would be possible to make an interesting chart which established the various directions which raiding parties traveled as they set out from their home territories and which revealed how far they went.

Obviously, though, a complicated web would result, and with the raiding parties of each tribe almost constantly in motion along these lines the encounters between hostiles were sudden and frequent; a condition which demanded a high degree of skill in many fields from every Plains Indian, whether hunting or seeking a contest.

As their numbers suggest, the dominant tribes of the Plains were those with the largest populations, the Blackfoot confederation, the Sioux, the Assiniboines, the Pawnees, and the Comanches. Naturally too, these tribes occupied the greater territories, and a rough idea of the tribal domains is given by the dotted lines on the map on page 13. In most instances it is impossible to define the exact boundaries of the various nations since they were assumed and not marked. A territory usually amounted to that area which a given tribe could adequately control and no more. Even then the peripheral areas were often in dispute.

One naturally wonders which of the tribes produced the greatest warriors. Most Indians were convinced that their own men outshone the others by far, paying only grudging admiration to certain of their enemies. Most everyone, Whites included, considered the Blackfoot tribes to be an unrelenting terror, and the Sioux were a foe of some magnitude for anyone to take on. In the south the Comanches were clearly dominant. Size, however, was not always the determining factor, since most battles were between small parties where individual prowess held sway. Some of the smaller nations, such as the Shoshones, Cheyenne, Arapaho, and Crows, established enviable records on the fields of battle. The stationary village tribes were the least aggressive of the Plains peoples, and in most instances fought more in defense than they did on offense.

Craftwise, the Blackfoot tribes, the Crows, the Sioux, and the Mandans, in that order, outdid the rest during their golden period, which extended from A.D. 1775 to 1875. From any standpoint it was an exciting and spellbinding hundred years, no part of which should ever be allowed to pass from view.

# Chapter 2

# MANNER OF DAILY LIFE

While the ancient Plains population was not, by modern comparisons, huge, even the individual tribes were much too large to travel and to pursue their way of life as a single group. So for many reasons, not the least of which was good sense, they subdivided into small bands which were made up of unrelated families, or into clans consisting of persons related by marriage, and went their independent ways within prescribed boundaries. Usually they assembled upon notice for one or two grand tribal buffalo hunts, fall and spring, and once during the early summer for the annual games and Sun Dance. They also gathered on rare occasions for massive tribal defense. The one exception to this dispersal of the tribes was the few earth lodge groups who lived together as a single unit most of the time.

Two types of dwellings were used by the Plains tribes: the better-known ingenious buffalo hide tipi, and the more permanent earth or bark lodges of a few small and generally stationary agricultural groups such as the Arikara, Mandan, Omaha, and Pawnee. Even then, all tribes employed the tipi while on the move. The buffalo hide tipi and all of its contents easily deserve a place among the world's leading examples of classic mobile design. Averaging fourteen feet in diameter and large enough to house an average family of five to eight persons, it could be set up by a woman in less than fifteen minutes and taken down in three. The homes and furnishings of an entire camp could be packed upon horse- or dog-drawn travois and on the move in twenty minutes. The tipi, assisted by only a brush fence, carried its occupants through the worst winters using minimum fuel, and with rolled-up sides became a vented summer unbrella. During the day its translucent walls admitted a pleasant light, and at night each dwelling transformed itself into a giant candle to illuminate the camp. It required no painting, save decoration, and was repaired simply by patching.

Since most Plains Indians moved with the buffalo during all but the winter months, their camps advanced within their own territory every few days, moving ten or fifteen miles each time. In so doing, some important side functions were served. The elements disposed of the sanitation problems after they moved on, and the migration itself was a source of constant excitement and adventure.

Generally speaking, a tribe hunted within its own domain, and the territorial

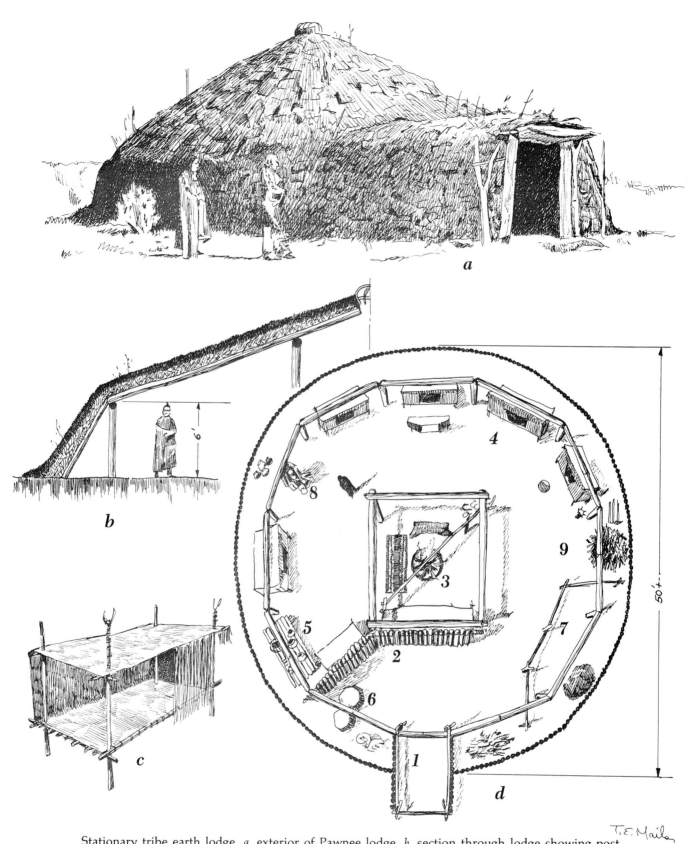

Stationary tribe earth lodge. *a*, exterior of Pawnee lodge. *b*, section through lodge showing post framework covered with thick layer of brush and sod. *c*, typical bed. *d*, Hidatsa earth lodge floor plan: *1*, entrance; *2*, screen wall; *3*, fireplace; *4*, beds; *5*, food platform; *6*, bull boats; *7*, corral; *8*, shrine; *9*, firewood.

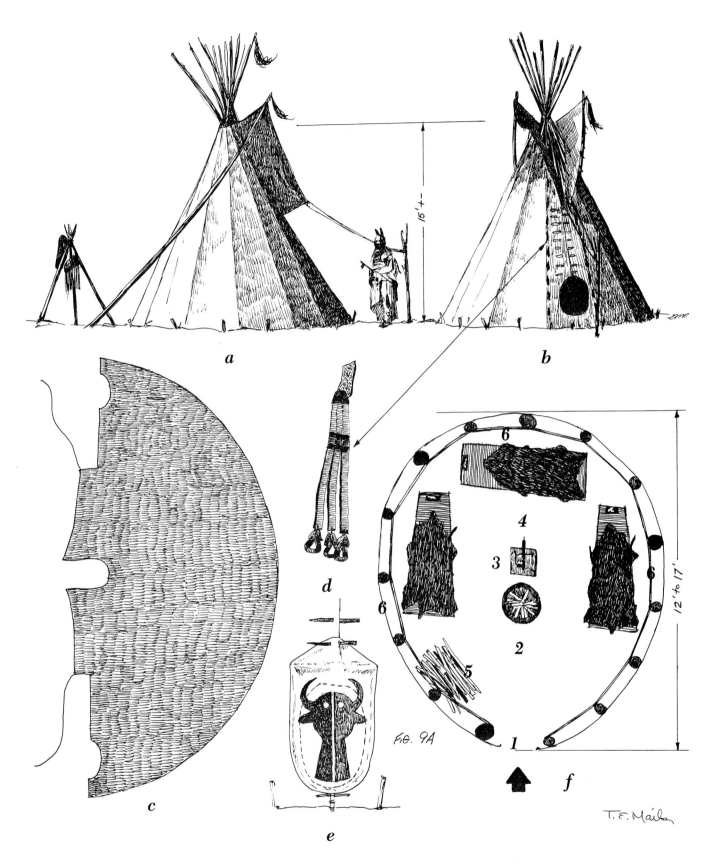

Plains Indian buffalo-hide tipi. *a*, side view. *b*, front view. *c*, tipi pattern. *d*, quilled tipi ornament. *e*, hide door cover. *f*, Sioux floor plan: *1*, entrance; *2*, fireplace; *3*, altar; *4*, beds; *5*, firewood; *6*, poles.

Tipi details. *a*, sides rolled up for summer ventilation. *b*, section through tipi wall showing outside cover and liner. *c*, buffalo-hide liner.

boundaries became the only common hunting grounds; a situation which, however, often led to some sudden and spirited engagements between tribes. Ordinarily small war and raiding parties were the only groups to invade the heartland of the dangerous neighboring areas—the exception being times when hunger drove entire tribal divisions to it.

By and large the Plains Indian-Americans lived on buffalo meat. The earth lodge tribes grew corn, squash, beans, and a few other vegetables, but the rest gathered only small seasonal amounts of wild berries, chokecherries, turnips, and later a few other items obtained in intertribal or White trade, to add to their diet. On the somewhat rare mountain trips, antelope, elk, and deer meat was obtained, but it never replaced the buffalo. Mountain sheep skins were used for clothing, and while I've not found evidence of the Indians' eating the meat, they probably did. Most tribes did not care for fish, although some tribes, such as the stationary Mandans who lived on the Missouri, Heart, and Knife rivers, and the Eastern Rockies Utes and Shoshones—who made infrequent forays onto the western edge of the Plains for buffalo—did catch and eat them. Of course, Indians ate whatever they could catch when they were hungry enough. Now and then, even dogs and horses were killed to provide their meals.

The desired village sites for the nomadic tribes were those which offered a good water supply, ample wood, grazing and forage for horses, protection from wind, and security from enemies. Level, wooded bottom lands cradled by bluffs or ridges were generally sought. At the tribal assemblies, however, they camped on the high flatter ground, pitching their tipis in a great circle with the main entrance to the east. The usual village plan was an informal assemblage of lodges, with the location of each tipi determined by family relationship, position in the previous village site, and geographical configuration. Relatives tended to live near one another, but when a new household was set up the owners were at liberty to place their lodges wherever they wished.

To select the best campground, even for a night on the Plains, required instinct, excellent judgment, and a knowledge of all the possibilities facing the camper. There were numerous questions involving the comfort and safety of the party to be decided by the camp leader as camping time arrived, and the fact that an Indian chief could constantly select a camp capable of supplying their varied wants testifies to a high degree of competence. He had to take into account the clan's own comfort and that of its stock. And, he must consider all of the dangers to which they might be exposed, either from human enemies or from the elements. A hunting party would choose a different site than a war party, and each in making its selection had to relate its objects and intentions to all the surrounding possibilities.

Colonel Richard Irving Dodge once followed a predatory party of Comanches for more than thirty days, and the camp in which he finally surprised them was the only site in all that time that could have been approached without discovery.[1]

Except in winter, the location of a camp indicated something of its occupants. A camp near water and away from all timber was probably Sioux, who had a deep respect for ambush; a camp on open prairie, but near timber, would be Cheyenne or Arapaho; a camp situated among open timber, Kiowas or Comanches; while smoke issuing from the cover of a dense thicket would indicate Osages, Omahas, or Pawnees.

Grazing buffalo.

TOP
FIG. 11

BOTTOM
FIG. 12

Horse and Dog travois. *a*, horse travois. *b*, Blackfeet women using travois. *c*, method of transporting incapacitated person. *d*, Cheyenne willow basket to protect or cover children on travois. *e*, dog travois. *f*, dog with travois—Blackfeet.

Camp leader and assistants selecting camp site.

Indian village.

Nez Percé woman making pemmican.

Cheyenne women fleshing buffalo hides.

During the spring months, tipis were repaired or renewed from new hides which had been collected during the fall and winter. Leggings and moccasins were made from the "smoked tops," and the smoking of hides for all uses began with the arrival of warm weather. The society clubs put on their mesmerizing dances, and the vital vision-seeking rites continued from late spring until the snow fell in October or November. In May the bands moved from their winter settlements to higher ground. This movement was traditional and not entirely the result of necessity. If food supplies were low, a buffalo hunt was planned to coincide with this migration. During the early summer months, individual family hunts were carried out, with men and boys hunting game for their household on a regular basis. When not occupied with this, they constructed and repaired their weapons. Meanwhile, the women were busy gathering early roots and berries. Hide painting was done while the weather was bright and warm, and at this time sweet-smelling leaves were gathered and preserved, especially during the Moon of the Ripe June Berries. Limited tribal hunts were organized whenever a herd of buffalo was sighted.

The major part of the summer was given over to ceremonial affairs. It was the master season of celebration; there was vision-seeking and cult performances, there were society elections and even such exotic occasions as female virtue feasts,

Cheyenne men making bows.

and the stupendous Sun Dance served as the monumental climax of the ceremonial season.

As the festival season ended for most tribes, a fall hunt was immediately organized. In some tribes, however, there was no formalized communal hunt as such, rather the great camp circle broke up, and the individual bands set out to hunt on their own.

Assiniboine hunter with hunting dogs.

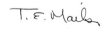

Autumn was an equally busy time of year. Women gathered their auxiliary foods and dried buffalo meat in preparation for the approaching winter. Men hunted intensely so that the supply of meat would be adequate, and when the season drew to a close underground caches were prepared as winter insurance. Wood was gathered wherever possible to provide fuel for the winter.

In addition to the activities described thus far, male war and raiding parties were conducted during all but the worst weeks of the winter. Small groups left their base camp at irregular intervals, often being away for weeks, and always had to catch up with the main migrating group upon their return.

Taking their guidance from what they saw during the reservation period, some people have decided that the Plains Indians sat around and did nothing most of the time. Yet this is a superficial judgment made when they could no longer move freely about and their befouled camps were no longer cleaned by nature. On the contrary, before this time they were a very industrious people, and their magnificent productivity and accomplishments make this abundantly clear.

In amplification of this truth, Maximilian visited a Blackfoot Indian camp, and returned with the following vivid description of its activity:

Maximilian watched the preparation of furs, the making of pemmican, the constant tailoring and dressmaking of the women. The handicrafts of the polished-stone age were going on all around him and he filled a lot of notebooks. The Blackfeet were not so good at them as some of the Plains tribes and had to keep interrupting their warfare so that they could trade, especially with their inveterate enemies the Crows, for bonnets and decorated robes and clothes and weapons and parfleches and utensils. Their ceremonies were without end; dances to bring the buffalo or to propitiate some supernatural who had indicated his displeasure, seasonal observances that had to be made at the appointed time, private magic or goopher dust that required the cooperation of neighbors, fraternity rites, lodge meetings, supplications for aphrodisiacs, commemoration of the heroes. Town criers were always summoning emergency assemblies to meet special situations and the normal death rate was always adding mourning shrieks to the bedlam and amputated fingers to the general bloodiness. Someone was always yelling and clattering rattles to scare diseases out of the sick. The beauty of Indian music, whether vocal or instrumental, is somewhat esoteric to such white men as do not live in Santa Fe and Maximilian's ears suffered from an energetic, lethally monotonous caterwauling that nothing could shut off. Day or night there was no escape from the drums, the thump of moccasined feet, and the singing that was just "hi-ya" in Indian scales. Observation of other tribes had made Maximilian a sophisticate; the jugglery of the Blackfoot medicine men, he found, was not up to Broadway.[2]

Even while the camp was moving, the tumultuous picture changed very little, as the following description of the Shoshones on their way to a celebration indicates:

About two hundred and fifty braves on their best horses—and they bought good ones from the Nez Percés—rode in full dress ahead of the village. Stately chiefs, caracoling horses, medicine men juggling as they rode, deep-voiced chants, warwhoops, muskets firing, arrows skittering across the plain. Sometimes a squad of young braves break into a gallop, angling away from the column in pursuit of imaginary Sioux, hanging by their heels on the far side of their horses, shooting arrows under their necks. Other performers do all the tricks that are still called Cossack. Others leap to the ground and take imaginary scalps, then ride on singing the scalp song. Everything is orderly again when the procession nears the Company camp—columns of files, lances and painted war shields at salute, dignity swelling the noble chests and making the noble faces solemn . . . And behind them the Snake village is strung out for well over a mile, dust from the scraping travois, from the horse herd which the boys are driving, from the interweaving horses of the women. Old men and women ride the travois atop the piled tipis and parfleches; so do young children. Stolid babies swathed to the chin in cradles stare out from their mothers' backs. The ladies who have to manage all this are shrill and profane. There is an incessant brawling of excited dogs. Reaching the river and its cottonwoods, the village breaks up into its components. Even noisier now, the women help one another put up the tipis. The horses are watered and herded across the plain.[3]

Since the Shoshones were poor in comparison to the huge and prosperous tribes, one can easily imagine what the Sioux, Blackfoot, Assiniboine, and Comanche parades or migrations were like.

When the first heavy snows were about to fall, the bands and clans gathered at a predetermined place to decide upon the permanent winter camp sites. Once selected and occupied, these locations were used until March or April.

The winter camp was regarded by the Indian as his true home. The intensity of war, hunting, and constant movement slacked off, and he settled down to a period of preparation for the more vigorous seasons to come.

When a winter site was selected, the entire tribe went to it en masse, but there was no attempt at order in the location of the lodges. The followers of a given chief might be scattered for miles, each taking advantage of the sheltered nooks formed by thickets or bluffs. The great questions facing each Indian were shelter, convenience, and feed for the ponies, though the desire to keep as near to each other as possible was obviously served.

A winter camp might occupy a mile one winter, and the next would extend as much as six miles along a stream. Sometimes several friendly tribes occupied the same stream and made an immense camp.

Indians at relative peace and with plenty of food found the winter camp a place of constant enjoyment. The prospect of rest, with its home life and pleasures, came like a soothing balm to all.

The aged warriors spent their daylight hours in gambling, their long winter evenings in endless repetitions of stories of their noble performances in days gone

*a*

*b*                        *c*

Tipi details. *a*, winter tipi with brush shelter wall. *b*, travois loaded with folded tipi. *c*, winter food caches.

by, and their nights in restful sleep. It is said by those who shared these sessions that the Indians were as exciting storytellers as ever lived. They knew how to capture the listener's attention, and how to fix a story in his mind.

There was even another, and perhaps more important, kind of storytelling going on. As the Indians had no written records, the maintenance of their historical accounts depended altogether on oral tradition. Therefore, each tribe had its historians who considered it their sacred duty to instruct selected young men carefully in the traditions of the nation, just as their own teachers had taught them. The pupils would gather in the lodges, and the old men would repeat in words and actions the captivating tales again and again, until at last the hearers had committed them to memory. In this way the sacred stories, elaborate rituals, and all the tribal history were handed down. The old men who were most learned in this ancient lore took an immense pride in their knowledge, and had a consuming desire to transmit it in the precise form in which they received it. If, among his descendants, one found a boy who manifested a special interest in the stories, or showed a marked capacity for remembering them, he redoubled his efforts to perfect him in this learning. To some he would present certain old stories as gifts, and these, thereafter, might not be related by another until the recipient passed them on.

The women enjoyed the winter too, for the hectic taking down and putting up of the tipis ended, as did the packing and unpacking of bags and ponies. The stormbound days and longer evenings of winter made it the ideal time for the women to manufacture and repair clothing, and they were forever busy with their

Village herald or "crier," who announced important matters.

rolled skins and awls. Sinew, especially that taken from alongside the buffalo's back and leg bones, was the Indian's thread. Splitting it for size was a task requiring great skill. Each of those taken from the different parts of the body had its own properties which made it best for specific uses. The women had been diligently trained in sewing from early childhood, and produced, as any museum reveals, some of the finest artwork in the world. Beads, porcupine quills, bird quills, grasses, paints, ermine tails, fringes of other fine furs, small animal and bird bones, bars of metal, bells, braided hair, and fleeces appeared as if by magic from the hide container which the seamstress had added to and repacked at every move throughout the year.

The clothes maker worked in traditions of art and craft that were old and rigid. As with the man's duties, religious rituals to guarantee quality were a part of every task; so too were certain social obligations to older women who had either taught them their skills, or sold their right to use them. A specialized item such as a chief's gift, or even some steps in the making of an ordinary item, might be forbidden to any but those who had the right, and these would perform them with the proper accompanying fees and feasts. Generally speaking, any woman at work was a skilled artisan and a happy one. She sang, chattered, made jokes, and evidenced pride in the highest degree.

The Indian woman was not, as is commonly thought, a drudge or slave. White men who lived with the Indians, such as Grinnell, Schultz, and McClintock, deride this notion as an erroneous one, and avoid the use of the demeaning title "squaw." Women did do all the hard camp work. They cooked, brought wood and water, dried the meat, dressed the robes, made the clothing, collected the lodge poles, packed the horses, cultivated the ground, and generally performed all the tasks which might be called menial; but no one thought of them as servants in this. On the contrary, their position was respected and their crafts were highly valued. A man's offer to help with the difficult female tasks would always be scorned. He had his place, and the women had theirs. Then too, wives were always consulted on intimate family affairs and often in more general matters. They also shared jointly with their husbands in sacred rituals. A few women were even admitted to the band councils, and gave advice there. Assuredly, the privilege was unusual, and only granted to women who had performed a deed comparable to those of the leading men of the tribe, but it did happen!

A wife did not hesitate to interrupt and correct her husband, and the husband listened with respectful attention, though of course the amount of it depended somewhat upon her proven intelligence. So while their lives were hard, they still found time to contribute, to gossip, and to gamble, and on the whole managed considerable pleasure in life. Seldom did an Indian wife want to trade what she had for the manner of existence she saw among wives in the non-Indian world.

The Indian ladies readily endorsed the idea of polygamous marriages. Battle deaths often left a plurality of husbandless women behind. Then too, the hard labor involved in their chores became easier as it was divided among a number of wives. In most tribes, tradition gave a woman's husband first claim on her younger sisters as his additional wives, and if there were no sisters, the original wife sometimes turned to other families to obtain a second wife for him. In any case she remained number one, there was less work for her to do, and she always had somebody to talk to when her husband was away on his hunting or warring trips.

The faulty attitudes of Whites about Indian women was often revealed by their seeming readiness to misunderstand these wonderful people. For instance, many a White person was dismayed as he saw the Indian wife trudging along behind her husband; she carrying a bulky load on her back, while he carried only his weapons. Yet Indians would explain that he was in front of her to break the trail in summer and winter, and carried just his weapons so as to be unimpeded and instantly ready to defend her against attack. By this he fulfilled the vows he made to her to do this very thing on their wedding day, and she was pleased that he did, since her life depended on it.

Men could not marry until they had *earned* the right. Among the Crows, this meant they did not marry until they were either twenty-five or had counted coup, that is, touched an enemy during combat with something held in their hand. Plenty Coups, a chief of the Crows, explained that the custom was followed because a man who had counted coup or reached the age of twenty-five was considered to be strong and healthy. He pointed out that "men breed their horses with great care, but often forget themselves in this respect. When a man breaks a traditional law and marries any woman whenever he can, imperfectly formed children are born."[4] Yet the chief had never heard of a deformed Crow child when he was a young man on the Plains, and while the old ways were still being followed.

In the ancient Crow law governing marriage, no man could wed a woman belonging to the same clan as his own. Children always belonged to the clan of their mother, and the law prevented the possibility of inbreeding, because when they married they had to mate with those of another clan. Occasionally new blood was infused by unions with members of other tribes, so that, the Indians say, "the race did not decline." Indians were high in their praises of the law that permitted men to marry under twenty-five only if they had counted coup. The rule made them strive to be strong and brave, and they believed that a man could be neither without good health through physical activity. To show how far they pursued these ideals, even though the law permitted a Crow man who had reached the age of twenty-five years and had not counted coup to take a wife, he could not "paint his woman's face," which was something every real warrior did each morning, so that even this tribal distinction was withheld from both of them, and the incentive to bravery and tribal defense was kept to the fore.

In horse parades and while moving the camp the wife often rode her husband's best war horse and carried his lance and shield, proud to be united with

T. E. Mails

Sioux warrior playing love flute.

him as one person in all they did together. Many tribes had no formal wedding service, but in some tribal marriage ceremonies, a thumb of each was cut slightly, and the two thumbs tied together. As the blood mingled, the officiant declared they were now as one, just as the blood was one, and they were commanded to live as "one flesh" ever after. Such vows were just as sincere and effective as we intend them to be when they are repeated in marriage ceremonies today.

Morally, the Indians did remarkably well at setting commendable standards for a supposedly primitive people, and at times performed better than many of what are considered to be the more civilized nations. In fact, their moral decline during the treaty and reservation period bears an almost direct ratio to the amount of contact occurring between the White and Red races.

Feminine chastity was highly prized, and a suitor would only offer expensive gifts for a virtuous girl. Likewise, certain honored tasks at the sacred ceremonies could be carried out only by a woman of irreproachable purity.

The Pawnees did some wife sharing on a temporary basis, but the practice was not characteristic of the area. Some tribes allowed a husband to disfigure a promiscuous wife. The Blackfeet and Piegans cut off the woman's nose, and thus marked her for life. A prosperous Indian male might, as previously stated, have several wives—sometimes as many as four or five. Yet most marriages by far were monogamous. As for divorce, a marriage could be dissolved without fuss, and often was. But a faithful and industrious woman was seldom cast out.

Returning, however, to the winter season, and concluding our thoughts regarding it, it brought a special and unending period of excitement ot the young. During the day there were new games, dances and feasts, visits and frolics; pleasures of every kind. At night by the flickering fires of the tipis the storytellers prepared, rehearsed, and presented their marvelous recitals. Above all it was the season for love-making, and it was said that "Winter was the time when love rules the camp."

Echoing the conclusions of all who knew them well, Colonel Dodge pointed out the numerous faults of the Indians, but also said:

These primitive people are habitually and universally, the happiest people I ever saw. They thoroughly enjoy the present, make no worry over the possibilities of the future, and never cry over spilt milk. . . . The Indian man never broods, and in spite of that dreadful institution, polygamy, and the fact that the wives were mere property, the domestic life of the Indian will bear comparison with that of average civilized communities. The husband as a rule, is kind; ruling, but with no harshness. The wives are generally faithful, obedient, and industrious. The children are spoiled, and a nuisance to all visitors. Among themselves, the members of the family are perfectly easy and unstrained. It is extremely rare that there is any quarreling among the wives. There is no such thing as nervousness in either sex. Everybody in the lodge seems to do just as he or she pleases, and this seems no annoyance to anybody else.[5]

Few can deny that the life pattern of the Plains Indians included much to recommend it to others. The Indians themselves deeply regretted its loss, and hearkened back to it in the most poignant of terms—as did sympathetic Whites who were able to live with them in such a way as to appreciate their manner and intent.

E. N. Wilson, a White boy who lived for two years with the Shoshones, states that his Indian mother "was as good and kind to him as any one could be." When he pleased her by an act or remark, her face would "light up," and sometimes a tear would steal down her brown cheeks. Then she would grab him and hug him "until you could hear his ribs crack." In fact, she did everything she could to make him happy.[6]

The Indians regularly include statements similar to the following in their stories of olden days:

"The weather was cold [as we began our war party trip], but in those days in all kinds of weather men had good times. Cold days were the same to us as warm ones, and we were nearly always happy!"

"At returning home to see the clans gathered, our hearts sang with the thought of visiting friends we had not seen in a long time."

"It was good to live in those days!"

"Those were happy days," the old warrior said softly. "Our bodies were strong and our minds healthy because there was always something for both to do. When the buffalo went away we became a changed people."[7]

Clearly, the Plains Indians of the year 1800 were an industrious, unburdened, moral, sensitive, and contented people. They had evolved a way of life which produced a healthy and productive society—devoid of disabling mental distresses and having no need for drugs and excesses to dull the senses. The very young child was free to play with reckless abandonment, but the rest of the community maintained a careful balance each passing day between industry, pleasure, and religion.

Indian religion has received but the briefest mention thus far, yet only because it was so vital and comprehensive. While religion was participated in fervently by everyone, it remained an individual and personal matter of the greatest portent. In fact, it was the source and center of each Indian's life. This being the case, the treatment of the Plains Indian religion will involve a much broader coverage as one moves deeper and deeper into the life-way of the people. Before that the tribal social life and governmental forms should be considered, with exemplary personal attributes and religion being brought in as the capstones of the total picture.

# Chapter 3

# SOCIAL CUSTOMS

The Plains Indians lived in circumstances which made them constantly aware of the capricious forces of nature, of their vulnerability to attack, and of their responsibilities, yet they loved living, and a sizable portion of their time was given over to social activities and events. A group spirit pervaded every village. People enjoyed eating and talking together, and hospitality was a norm of life. Everyone agreed that for the general good of the community as a whole it was better to give than to receive. The mathematics of such a course recommended itself highly, for while an individual watching out for himself might gain the minor securities self-trust brings, the social plan brought each person the comforting assurance that as he looked out for others, everyone in the village was looking out for him. Therefore, the village had a summary strength; the abilities of each multiplied by the number present, and the tribe as a whole developed a corresponding power.

The social life manifested itself at four levels or strata. First of all, the intimacy of the band and the clan kinship ties afforded numerous opportunities for close fellowship within each family and between families. Communal eating and conversation was a regular thing. Chores were often shared, and there was a constant interchange of gifts. Male heroes received especially warm attention from the immediate family, since the status of anyone was enhanced by his association with an acknowledged leader. Beyond this, personal fellowship carried over into tribal relationships, since friendships were engendered and matured over the years, and the annual tribal encampments afforded grand opportunities to renew cherished relationships of long standing. Indians on their way to the great tribal gatherings were usually brimming over with emotion and anticipation, barely able to contain themselves until the reunion took place and anxious to discover what had happened since last they met.

A second stratum of social life took place at the community level, since the entire village shared in an annual cycle of religious events, in the dissemination of all important news and its consequences, in some buffalo hunts, in victory celebrations, in dances, and in the frequent migratory movements. Thus while each person maintained his individuality, he never did so to the point where he considered it more important than his place in the village and tribe. Of course there were occasional frictions which divided people and altered loyalties, but for the most part, a given individual was always a vital part of a greater whole.

And so he or she sought constant opportunities to solidify the unit by creative participation in community events.

The third and fourth strata of social life were natural outcomes of the inter-dependent attitude of the individual in his community. Moving beyond the family level, community activities were played out in a heightened sense at the tribal level. Annual encampments afforded opportunities for council meetings, clothing comparisons, craft displays, trading, huge dances, horse races, gambling, rampant gossiping, games, love-making, hero adulation, and the like. Everything common to a family was also the norm for the tribe. And, all in all, it made for a very rich life.

The fourth and highest stratum of social existence will be readily understood by those who are members of present-day clubs or secret societies, since they will appreciate the social and psychological function such organizations serve for the individual, and for the public as a whole. If anything, this was truer still of the Plains Indians, since the societies played a vital and dramatic role in the life of the village and tribe.

Societies were sometimes borrowed from another tribe, but most had their beginning in the vision or dream of the man who thereafter became the founder. The vision would set forth the society's purpose, the number of its members, and at least the rough form of the society's colors, symbols, garb, dances, songs, and rituals. Once the vision was accepted as legitimate by the tribe's elders, other people were invited to join, and the society was born.

Subsequent visions might contain information which helped to enlarge the concept and costume of the club, but its initial purpose seldom changed a great deal. The order of rank in the band was usually determined by the date of origin of the club, with the most ancient society being accorded the highest rank, and after it the next oldest, etc.

While most societies were made up exclusively of male participants, many of them had women's auxiliaries. Sometimes a woman was made a member just to cook and pick berries, but neither she nor the auxiliaries participated in the truly secret rituals. A few of the tribes had societies whose membership was limited to women. The village tribes of the Upper Missouri had important women's organizations, and among the Pawnees there was a curious association of single women and widows who donned shabby clothing before they tortured prisoners of war. Among the Kiowas, a man starting out on a raid frequently appealed to an organization of forty old women, whom he feasted on his return in gratitude for their prayers. Guilds of skillful tipi cover makers and of expert quill workers existed among the Oglala Sioux.

It may be fairly said, however, that in number, impact, and magnitude the male societies prevailed over the village.

They were called Warrior Societies, and the title itself explains their main purpose. Their function, though, was really a fourfold one: they provided a club

Ermine headdress used in the ceremonies of the Blackfoot Horn Society. Members were believed to have enough supernatural power to cause death, and were greatly respected by the other members of the tribe.

atmosphere with the luxury of participation in those mysterious activities limited to the members of a given society, they preserved order in the camp and on organized hunts, they punished offenders against the public welfare, and they cultivated a military spirit among themselves and others—especially young boys—with the ultimate aim of assuring the longevity of the tribe. Often they are referred to simply as police or protective organizations, and in this aspect of life the power of the head or camp chief depended on his cooperation with the societies.

No single society was ever given a monopoly on camp police duty. The headman of the village would call upon one or more of the societies to guard the camp for a stated period, and then they would be replaced by a random selection. The rotation continued until all societies had a turn, and then the cycle would be repeated. Societies were also summoned for specific duties, but even after selection did not act until requested by the headman to do so. Since society membership had nothing to do with family ties or heritage, this, together with the no monopoly principle, tended to blunt any grasping for personal power. Further to prevent the seizure of power and the development of exclusive circles of warriors, retirements and new recruits caused society personnel to change from year to year.

This latter fact, however, did not exclude all vestiges of arrogance. A highly competitive spirit was engendered, and a society which was enjoying a season of prestige because of its brilliant military accomplishments might well assert itself in ways well calculated to make its superiority known. The Peigan Brings Down the Sun told Walter McClintock how his powerful Braves Society expected people of the village to give them whatever they wanted. Failing this, they simply took it. Often they marched through the camp shouting orders. "If people bothered us or got in our way, the bear braves shot at them with arrows." Surely they didn't wound their own people, but the intent was clear. Sometimes the Braves punished women who picked wild berries against their orders by tearing their lodges to pieces![1]

Not incidentally, it was the Warrior Societies which fostered the creation of the most marvelous and enthralling of the Plains costumes. And a society dance was an entrancing thing to see. However, with few exceptions the secret and religious aspects of the groups led them to perform for Indian audiences only. Fortunately a few White men were allowed to witness them, and thus were given the privilege of recording their apparel and rituals. George Catlin drew and painted several of the society dances—especially those of the Mandans—and Walter McClintock was able to take some extraordinary photographs of the Blackfoot divisions. Robert Lowie and John Ewers have provided excellent written accounts of Crow and Blackfoot societies, and museums have collected enough society articles that, by adding all of this information together, a rather comprehensive picture of the societies can be drawn today.

There were two types of Warrior Societies, and historians have classified them as age-graded societies and non-graded societies. Simply put, membership in the age-graded societies was determined by the age of the participants. The first or lowest grade consisted of boys approximately fifteen years of age and up who had made a successful vision quest and gone on a first successful raid. The next grade might begin at age eighteen or so, with the ages for the successive steps in all instances varying with each tribe. Membership of non-graded societies had nothing to do with age. A warrior with noteworthy accomplishments or promise might be invited to join a society regardless of how old he was.

In the age-graded scheme, each warrior passed through all of the societies in turn as he advanced in years. In the non-graded scheme, a warrior usually belonged to a single society for the period of his active warrior life, retiring from all society activities at the average age of forty or so. On rare occasions in both schemes, however, an outstanding warrior might be invited to join more than one society at the same time.

Most society groups were small, numbering from ten to twenty persons, although powerful societies with as many as sixty or more members were known to exist. Usually, the society had a "charmed maximum number" which its founder had received in the vision which gave the society birth. This meant that recruits were invited only at those times when the group had sustained losses through retirements or deaths.

Each society had its own name, and its own tipi or ceremonial lodge which was painted with symbols and colors given to the society founder in his original vision. And it also had its own special medicine bundle. On any given day some of the members gathered in the club lodge to foster their association in the accepted club manner. Each society had its traditional ceremonies and annual festivals, when the awesome medicine bundles were opened, and at such times every member was present. It should be mentioned that the apparel, etc., of a certain society was respected by all others, and exact duplications were avoided. Somehow the visions never caused the founders to violate the principle.

Society names were both descriptive and captivating. For example, the age-graded societies of the Blackfoot were named in grade order as follows: the Doves (or youths); the Mosquitoes (men who went to war); the Braves (or tried warriors); the Brave Dogs; the Kit Foxes; and the Bulls, who were the oldest in origin and held the highest standing.[2] Of these, the first four were most often called upon for police duty.

In 1833 Maximilian set forth a list of the intriguing names of the ten non-graded societies of the Hidatsa tribe: Stone Hammers, Lumpwoods, Crow Indians, Kit Foxes, Little Dogs, Dogs, Half-shaved Head, Black Mouths, Bulls, and Ravens.[3]

It is important to add that while the different tribes often had clubs bearing the same names, the rank of these clubs would usually vary with its tribe. A Kit Fox might be a first-rank society in one tribe and a fourth in another. Also, if

*a*, Black Eagle, leader of the Blackfoot Kisapa (Hair Parters) Dance. The Kisapa was a social organization composed of young men. *b*, typical society rattles.

a new society of great antiquity was borrowed from another tribe, it was often inserted into the existing scheme at whatever rank the elders of the community felt it deserved. This revised the previous sequence of rank—yet it was not a matter of great consequence since the societies competed at an equal level anyway both at home and on the field of battle.

As the years went by and death, old age, and other circumstances took their toll, some of the societies passed inevitably out of existence. Aged warriors often spoke of once great clubs which had become extinct.

Five tribes—the Mandan, Hidatsa, Blackfoot, Arapaho, and Gros Ventre— employed the age-society system. In this scheme it was customary for young Indian braves to buy the right of their immediate elders to their sets of regalia, dances, and songs, the purchase of which gave them access to the total privileges of the club. In such cases the buyers did not join the sellers as members, but displaced them. The sellers in turn became a cohesive group which jointly bought the emblems and privileges of yet an older group; a process which was repeated at age intervals until the original group of boys had reached the highest and oldest existing grade. When at last they sold their final possessions, they retired from the associational scheme. All males of the five tribes entered the age-graded system and remained within it as age-mates until retirement.

The lively barter involved in these purchases had some delectable features, and these reveal in one more way the Indian's thorough enjoyment of life. For example, the youngest Hidatsa and Mandan groups, called "sons," was always eager to advance, and their "fathers," remembering their own youthful desires, made the most of their advantage, professing the greatest reluctance to give up their beloved dances, badges, and rituals. Hence, the young buyers were obliged to arrive at the sellers' lodge with a great profusion of gifts and a smoking pipe, which would be accepted, but only as a token of the sellers' agreement to discuss the offer. Irrespective of the substance of the discussion, the seniors were sure to declare in the end that the initial offering was insufficient; so the buyers, as they knew they would need to do, held back a reserve supply of gifts, and in addition scurried around to coax more property from their relatives. The older men continued to act as if they were doing their juniors a great favor, until at last a proper tension was reached and began to show itself in the long faces of

---

PLATE 1.   SOUTHERN CHEYENNE WARRIOR ▶

The Southern Cheyenne is identified by his painted yellow shirt, adorned by twisted buckskin fringes and by painted celestial symbols. He carries in his hand a leader's eagle-wing fan and on his arm a catlinite ceremonial pipe—from which hangs his beaded pipe bag containing tobacco. He wears beaded braid ties, and his hair is wrapped in otter fur.

the sons. Finally the sellers smoked the pipe again, ordering the buyers to bring food to feast their "fathers" for four or more successive evenings. Once more the relatives helped the purchasers to collect the food; then, on the appointed evenings, the sellers received their feasts and began to teach the buyers the songs and dances unique to their society. Continuing the extortion program, the head of the club would exhort the sons to pay generously for the emblems they were to receive. He would also urge them to imitate the example of some of the distinguished fathers as warriors. As the final evening of instructions came to an end, the insignia were turned over to the new members with proper pomp and circumstance, and a public procession and dance followed in which they advertised the fact that they were now the proud representatives of the grade just entered.

Societies which were not graded in any way existed among the Sioux, Assiniboines, Cheyenne, Crows, Pawnees, Arikaras, and the Wind River Shoshones. The Plains Crees had only a single warrior society into which all worthy young men were invited. This club might buy new dances from another band or nation, and it held two sets of insignia and ceremonial privileges.

The Crow and Cheyenne societies can serve as a typical example of the non-graded type. Membership was voluntary, not dependent on age, and particular societies might hold different levels of rank at different periods of time. The Crow Lumpwoods and Foxes, who were quite similar in insignia and organization, and the Cheyenne Dogs were the most important societies in the tribes during the years 1800 to 1875. While the age system tended to eliminate the status rivalry between societies, wherever non-age-graded clubs ranked as virtual equals, serious competition often set in. Thus the Lumpwoods and the Foxes sought valiantly to outdo each other annually in striking the first blow against an enemy, and the same kind of rivalry existed between many of the Sioux groups.

Every society of either type had its own medicine, or sacred, bundle which contained the objects the founder had been directed to in his initial vision and subsequent visions. The Brave Dog Society bundle of the Piegans contained a war bridle and a whip, and the members carried it to war because of its protective power. It was also used on other important occasions. When not in service it hung from a pole in the society lodge. On another pole hung the society's special rattle, a banner decorated with ermine, an eagle feather warbonnet, and a weasel tail

---

◀ PLATE 2. DAKOTA COUNCIL

Composition developed from several black and white photographs from *Teton Sioux Music*, by Frances Densmore, BAE Bulletin 61, 1918. The left figure is Brave Buffalo, who was an elk dreamer. The center figure is Teal Duck, a Yankton Sioux who was a clan chief. The right figure is Gray Hawk, a renowned buffalo hunter. The decorated tipi is a council tent.

suit—which was itself looked upon as a medicine bundle. Most societies had their own decorated flags and staffs, which were so well known as to identify the society whenever they were carried.

Each society had its own special songs, which stressed the nature of the club and the ideal of the warlike spirit so necessary to preserve the tribe. Members sang their songs constantly as reminders; in camp, on the trail, when riding into battle, and in ringing unison at the traditional society gatherings. Such songs were considered to have a special power and were to accompany all ritual acts to make the acts effective.

Above all, a society member was expected to be very brave, and only the bravest of all were selected as club officers. Officers were distinguished from other members of the society by their superior regalia, and were deliberately to flout danger. Thus, while the rank-and-file members—or as the Indians called them, "lay members"—of the Oglala Sioux Kit Fox organization wore their dance costume of kit fox skin necklaces, a forehead band decorated with kit fox jawbones, and at the back of the head a crown of crow tail feathers and two erect eagle feathers, the officers were distinguished from the rest by their yellow-painted bodies, and four of them who carried special lances revealed by this that they were under a vow to lead in battle and never retreat. Lances such as those just mentioned, straight or curved over at the top, were common society regalia in Plains organizations.[4]

The Crow Foxes and Lumpwoods had two officers, elected for one summer season only, who each carried curved-end otter-skin-wrapped staffs. Two other officers bore long straight staffs with eagle feathers on their smaller end. The straight staff put the staff bearer in a potentially perilous place, for he was required to plant his staff in the ground during a fight. While it was in the ground it represented Crow country. If no fellow society member rode or walked between him and the enemy he was duty-bound to stand by it until either the Crows triumphed or he died; or as the Indians described it, "dropped his robe." Once "ridden between," however, he could relocate the staff in a more favorable location with honor. Staff bearer coups counted double, since their lives were always in special danger while "carrying the stick" in battle. They were self-appointed in a simple ceremony. The head of the society, after asking who would next carry the sticks, passed the pipe. The two men taking the pipe were thereby engaged to carry the sticks for the present season.[5]

The Crow Big Dog Society was led by a pair of bear-belt wearers. The belt was made of bearskin with the legs and claws still attached. Members painted their bodies with mud and bunched up their hair to resemble a bear's ears. Belt wearers did not hold an enviable position, though, since they had to vow to walk straight up to the enemy in time of danger. They were never to retreat, and were required to rescue imperiled tribesmen.

The bear-belt wearers were followed in rank by two or four sash wearers.

Society equipment. *a*, typical wooden, curved society staff or lance wrapped with otter fur and adorned with ribbons and eagle feathers. This type of staff also identified assistant war party leaders. The warrior also wears the more common version of the short soldier sash, which was about seven feet long. *b*, the neck insertion method of wearing the sash. *c*, the shoulder loop method of wearing the sash. *d*, Crow warrior carrying feathered coup stick. *e*, typical willow coup stick. *f*, Sioux warrior holding leader's flag.

*a*, Crow Big Dog Society member wearing cap of dried bear guts and sash of hide or trade cloth, and carrying rattle (Lowie reports Crow sash 12 feet long and 5 inches wide). *b*, Crow Hammer Society member. *c*, typical society staff wrapped with otter fur and topped with hawk or owl feathers (Hidatsa). *d*, society buffalo horn rattle. *e*, society leader's wand with eagle claw, beaded handle, and eagle feathers.

The distinctive sash was made of hide or trade cloth, and either hung diagonally over the shoulder by a loop at the end or had a slit to put the wearer's head through. The first style hung down the wearer's side, and the second down the middle of his back. The sash was usually over twelve feet in length and was five or so inches wide. It trailed behind the warrior while he was afoot and sometimes reached the ground while he was mounted on a horse. Its length was necessary to give the sash wearer some mobility in war, for he drove his staff through the end of it when he planted the staff in the ground. During a dance, the lay members led the officers around by their sash. Part of the Crow sash wearer's special regalia was a cap covered with dried bear guts. It was painted red and worn because wearing it would impart the animal's strength and ferocity to the warrior. Such caps were often worn into battle, as were selected other items characteristic of the society.[6]

The members of some societies earned the right to wear gorgeous feather dance bustles called "crows." These consisted of a single large bustle belted to the back at the waist, and in some cases of a second and smaller one tied to the back of the neck. These are often a part of the costumes worn by mounted Sioux warriors in old war pictographs, but while they did wear them in parades—and the crow had a split tail for that very reason—they were primarily a dance garment and never worn into battle. They were so splendid that no Indian would risk ruining one and they were not collapsible so as to be easily carried on the trail. Therefore, their main use in pictographs was to identify the wearer. The grandest ones made toward the end of the nineteenth century were constructed of pheasant feathers, but earlier ones were made of golden eagle, hawk, owl, and other feathers. In considering these, one must remember that everything the Indian used for his costume was selected for better reasons than mere decoration. The following description of the Omaha crow bears this out very well:

A man who had attained more than once to honors of the first three grades became entitled to wear a peculiar and elaborate ornament called "the Crow." This was worn at the back, fastened by a belt around the waist; it was made with two long pendants of dressed skin painted red or green, which fell over the legs to the heels. On the skin were fastened rows of eagle feathers arranged to hang freely so as to flutter with the movements of the wearer. An entire eagle skin, with head, beak, and tail, formed the middle ornament; from this rose two arrow shafts tipped with hair dyed red. On the right hip was the tail of a wolf; on the left the entire skin of a crow. This composite decoration illustrated certain ideas that were fundamental to native beliefs, namely; That man is in vital connection with all forms of life; that he is always in touch with the supernatural, and that the life and the acts of the warrior are under the supervision of Thunder as the god of war. This relation was believed to be an individual one and any war honor accorded was the recognition of an individual achievement. Such a bestowal was the outcome of the native method of warfare, for there was no military organization, like an army, in the tribe, and strictly speaking, no commanding officer of a war party;

T.E. Marlor

Mounted Crow named Shot in the Hand wearing long dog soldier sash and carrying society staff and shield—after 1880 photograph by Lothrop, "The Boy with the U. S. Indians."

when the battle was on, each man fought for and by himself. A valorous deed was therefore the man's own act and the honor which was accorded the kind of act performed was accredited by Thunder through the representative birds associated with Thunder and contained in the Sacred Pack.

"The Crow" decoration is said to symbolize a battlefield after the conflict is over. The fluttering feathers on the pendants represented the dropping of feathers from the birds fighting over the dead bodies. Sometimes the wearer of "the Crow" added to the realism by painting white spots on his back to represent the droppings of birds as they hovered over the bodies of the slain. The two arrow shafts had a double significance; they represented the stark bodies and also the fatal arrows standing in a lifeless enemy. The eagle was associated with war and with the destructive powers of the Thunder and the attendant storms. The wolf and the crow were not only connected with carnage but they had a mythical relation to the office of "soldiers," the designation given to certain men on the annual tribal hunt, who acted as marshals and kept the people and the hunters in order during the surround of the herd. These men were chosen from those who had the right to wear "the Crow" and this regalia was generally worn at that time. It was worn also at certain ceremonial dances.[7]

The Cheyenne Fox Society member carried a stringless bow and a rawhide rope and pin which was tied at the belt and was called a "dog rope." Fox members were to follow the habits of the fleet and competent fox, who was swift in retreat, but a terror when cornered.

If a Cheyenne Fox member chose, he could make a vow before a battle to drive his pin into the ground and tie himself to it with his dog rope as the enemy closed in. He would then remain there and fight until either the enemy was beaten or he was killed. Others could stand with him and try to save him if they wished to. A warrior who sided a pinned comrad four times gained the eminent right to free a friend in future wars; he could intervene when the warrior was about to be killed, pull the pin, lash him across the back with it, and by so doing cancel the vow.

The Fox (or Dog Men) became one of the leading Cheyenne military societies. Many of its members took the suicide vow each year. It even received a special nickname, and was called "the old men's charm." When the members paraded around the camp before a battle the older men would flank them and sing their praises "as men about to die in the bravest way possible."[8]

Most young boys formed imitation organizations which were patterned after the warriors' societies, although a few of their groups, such as the Crow Act Like Dogs, had no counterpart in the older men's groups. Dressed only in breechclouts and moccasins, the Act Like Dogs would go outside the camp and smear their bodies with white clay. Then they would sneak to the edge of the village, and at a given signal, scatter and run through the lodges, barking and growling like dogs while they wildly snatched at choice pieces of meat which had been hung to dry. The villagers joined in the game with great enthusiasm. The old men fell

Sioux dancer wearing crow bustle and roach headdress. The neckpiece of the bustle is on the ground in front of him. (*Facing Page*) Back view of dancer in action.

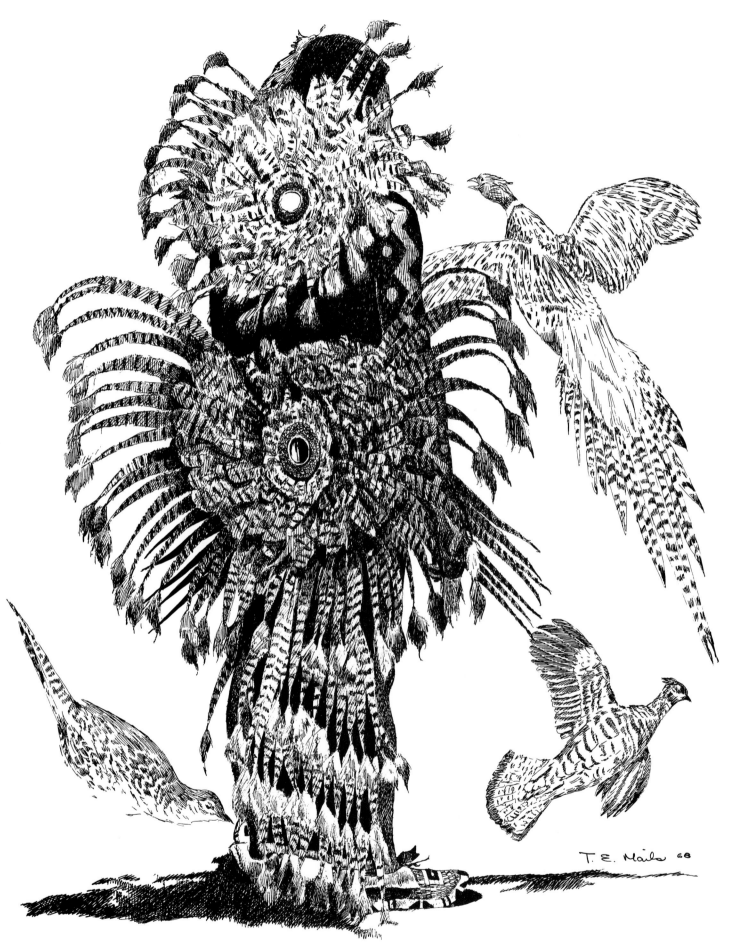

Omaha two-piece crow bustle made of pheasant feathers (circa 1890).

back in supposed fear, and the women cried out in mock alarm, running after the "dogs" with sticks and, in a playful manner, harassing them. Sometimes the women threw pieces of meat at them as they would at their own dogs. When each youth had collected enough meat, the group went back to the woods, washed in a nearby creek or spring, cooked the meat at a campfire, had a sumptuous feast, and animatedly discussed their happy adventure.[9]

A Crow society, called the Hammers, was exclusively for boys about sixteen years of age. Usually, little was required of them, but in serious emergencies the same bravery was expected of them as of the other society members. Their emblem was a small, elongated wooden (or stone) hammerhead. It was mounted on a wooden shaft over eight feet in length. Some of these were painted with white clay and decorated with a long, erect feather at the top, while at three distinct points along the pole were two other feathers and a bunch of shorter ones. Other models were adorned with yellow and red or yellow and blue paint, put on in stripes corresponding to the body colors of their owners.[10]

Mystic animal cults were numerous among the tribes of the Great Plains. Each of these entrancing groups was composed of individuals who believed they had obtained supernatural power from the same animal or bird through a dream or vision. Like the societies, they evolved distinctive ritual and ceremonial regalia associated with the animal from which the cult's power was derived.

The Bear Cult was a prime example. It was composed of a small number of men in nearly every tribe who believed they had obtained a supernatural bear power through dreams. They painted bear symbols on their tipis and shields. When a cult member died, his power went away to the great hunting ground with him. It could not be transferred to another person.

This cult performed several major functions: It conducted ceremonies in honor of the bear, it held bear feasts and ceremonial bear hunts. It participated aggressively in war expeditions, and it doctored the sick.

When participating in any of these activities, the Assiniboine Bear Cult member shaved the middle of his head and rolled some of the remaining hair at each side into a ball resembling a bear's ear. He painted his entire face red, and then made vertical bear claw marks on each side of it by scraping away some of the paint with his fingernails. After this he painted a black circle around each eye and around his mouth. He wore a bear claw necklace over a yellow-painted skin shirt, which was perforated all over in a unique way with round holes, and further decorated with cut fringes along the bottom edge and the sleeve ends. A small, rectangular flap of skin was cut in the shirt at the center of the wearer's chest, and the flap hung down the front.[11]

The Bear member also carried a glorious kind of knife. It had a broad, flat, single- or double-edged metal blade whose handle was made from a bear's jawbone. It was a piece of graceful sculpture without fault. The Blackfoot bear knife is a superb example of this ancient art.

Assiniboine Bear Cult member wearing perforated skin shirt with grizzly bear fur pendants tied on his cult staff (after Ewers, *Indian Life on the Upper Missouri*, p. 133).

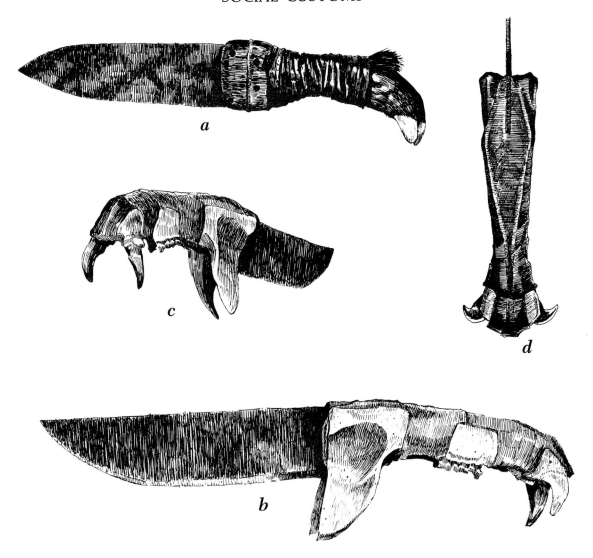

*a*, Typical ancient Blackfoot Bear Cult knife. The metal blade is double-edged stabber type and the handle is a bear's jawbone. *b*, less typical Blackfoot Bear knife dating from late nineteenth century which shows sculpture quality of knife: single-edged metal blade, jaw handle is covered with sinew. *c*, rear view. *d*, top view.

T. E. Mails

When a member of the Bear Cult went into action against the enemy he always wore his distinctive bear outfit, and since bears were noted for their ferocious attacks, a charging cult member made a grunting noise like a bear and made every effort to be as much a bear as possible!

Every warrior in every tribe had a bird or animal patron of one species or another. Each man sought to duplicate the attributes of his patrons when engaged in a war. In the Indian's mind a man did not fight another warrior, but rather a bear, a buffalo, an eagle, an ermine, or the like. And because each warrior wore some sign or a part of his society regalia into battle, if it was plain enough to be seen an enemy could size up what sort of an animal or bird he was fighting. He then adjusted his attack accordingly. Played out to its fullest extent the habit added some wonderful facets to the Plains encounters.

A delightful trait designed to break the potential austerity of an overdone traditional life was provided by societies called "contraries," which were found in each tribe. Members of these were obliged to say the opposite of what they meant and to do the opposite of whatever was demanded of them. Generally, they behaved in a way contrary to common sense. If one said "go," he really meant "come." Oglala Sioux contrary society members were seen plunging their arms into very hot water, and then splashing it over each other, complaining all the while that it was freezing cold.

When one pauses to assess the ultimate value of the societies in the social scheme of the Plains, he finds that the Indians have already done it for him. The venerable Crow chief Plenty Coups revealed how captivating and how effective societies were in the perpetuation of a Crow boy's individual responsibility to the tribe as a whole when he said:

That night the secret societies held meetings, the Foxes, the Warclubs, the Big-dogs, the Muddy-hands, the Fighting-bulls, and others. Bright fires blazed and crackled among the pines, and drums were going all night long. I wished with all my heart that I might belong to one of these secret societies. I thought most of the Foxes, and I looked with longing eyes at their firelit lodge, where men spoke of things I could not know. But I was yet only a boy.[12]

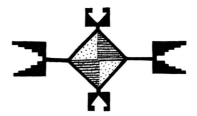

It has been seen that Plains Indian social life was carried out at four levels: the family, the community (or village), the tribe, and the society. In each of the last three levels social life expressed itself more in songs and dancing than in all other types of social activities put together.

In fact, it is impossible to refer to the Plains Indians of old without speaking of songs and dancing, for these played a continual and vital part in their life-scheme. They had dances for almost every occasion. These were seldom indulged in for exercise and amusement. Usually they were performed as integral parts or expressions of the more serious things in life. More narrowly, the dances were an activity intended to heighten and sharpen every worthwhile thought and emotion.

Sioux Omaha Dancer. Dance is better known as the Grass Dance because dancers wore braided grass in their belts to symbolize the scalps of their enemies. The dance came from the Omaha tribe and was the most popular social dance of the entire Plains. Many of the dancers carried a wooden whistle with its head carved to look like a crane.

The Indian dancer saw, heard, and felt the story he was trying to portray with a peculiar intensity, and because of this he usually enacted it so well that it was not difficult for his informed and sympathetic audience to catch the meaning of his every motion. It has often been said that in some dances the degree of acting was so intense that whole scenes of history came to life, and in the case of animal dances the dancers seemed to become the beings they were impersonating. Some important things beyond this remain to be said about the dance and religion, but because the religious association must first be clearly established, further comment along these lines will be held for the section on religion (page 87).

Many of the dances were religious ceremonials, whose intent was to gain wisdom from or give thanks to the supernatural powers. Some of the dances were associated with warfare, and these were held before a war party started out as well as on its victorious return. There were comic, healing, peace, victory, mourning, and hunting dances, dances of a purely social type, and in the more stationary villages of the Mandans and Pawnees, planting and harvest dances. Some dances were performed exclusively by men, and some solely by women. In other instances men and women danced together. Some dances were held in which anyone might take part, and others were limited to a single dancer selected for the occasion. Many dances, as was true in the case of the society songs, were private property, and could only be performed by their rightful owners. Each of the Plains Indian societies had dances that centered in the themes of mystery and war. Some dances to be used while curing the sick were owned by individual holy men, and some by societies of medicine men. However, it should also be pointed out that every ritual was not a dance, and the word "dance" has often been wrongly applied by White men to some of the great Indian rituals in which dancing actually played but a small part. This is especially true of what are commonly referred to as the Calumet, Ghost, and Sun Dances.

All Indian dances followed traditional forms. Some of the dance steps were simple, but others were complicated and quite difficult to learn. And the male style differed from the female. When men danced the heel and ball of each foot in turn was lifted and brought down with considerable force, so as to produce a thudding sound. The changes of their position were slow, but the shifts in attitude were rapid and sometimes violent. Women employed the shuffle, the glide, the hop, and the leap. Usually, dancers moved in a clockwise circle direction, "with the sun." When dancing with the men, women were usually placed in an inside circle.

Every song, prayer, and dance connected with a ceremony was to be performed according to its traditional form, for it was believed that serious misfortune

PLATE 3.  PAWNEE MORNING STAR PRIEST ▶

would come to the performers immediately upon the heels of any deliberate failure to give a strictly accurate performance. Informers report that if anything went wrong, the ceremony must either begin again or else be abandoned, although while that seems to rule out enjoyment, Indians often had a good laugh after a ceremony had ended during which there had been a humorous mistake. The value of adherence to traditional forms can easily be seen. For example, in the dances where personal experiences were portrayed the dancer was allowed some freedom of invention, yet even here the performer was compelled to parallel conventional forms or else his story would not be understood by his audience, which interpreted the dance by making comparisons with tradition. The need to perform the dances along traditional lines did not, however, interfere with the development of new dances or prevent the spread of a certain dance from one tribe to another. Nor did it prevent real happiness in dancing, for the Plains Indian appreciated, and did not regret, his place in a long line of heirs.

In order to maintain their distinctiveness, the different tribes usually varied their ways of performing dances bearing the same name. The Crows would not do a Bear Dance in exactly the same way as the Hidatsas. Society dances were also shaped until they had established a distinct identification within each tribe. Some dances originated with each tribe, and were indigenous. Others were borrowed by one tribe from another. The Crow Bear Song Dance and the Singing of the Cooked Meat—a semi-annual occasion for rock-medicine owners to open their sacred bundles—were indigenous. Other Crow dances, like the Medicine Pipe Ritual and the Horse Dance, were the products of visits with other tribes, usually their Hidatsa kinsmen. The Crow Bear Song Dance performers were known by their ability to produce from their mouths parts of a creature or object which had "miraculously" entered their stomachs during a fast. Among those things revealed were such unappetizing objects as elk chips, white clay, black dirt, owl feathers, ground moss, snails, eggs, feathers from an eagle's tail, and, commonly, parts of the bodies of bears and jackrabbits. People owning renowned horses would exhibit horse tails; and those who had proven they could doctor wounds, buffalo tails. Usually the Bear Dance was held in the fall, when the ripe berries "caused the bears to dance in the mountains."

Music for the dances would be furnished by the singing of the dancers and the playing of the instruments they carried, or else by a separate chorus and orchestra. Sometimes the dancers and orchestra combined their talents. If a chorus was used the singers either gathered around the drum, stood or sat as a group to one side, or else stood in the center of the circle of dancers. There were moments in some dances when the orchestra would cease playing while the

◀ PLATE 4. SIOUX PRAYER FOR FERTILITY

Blackfeet Elk Medicine Pipe Dance.

dancers provided their own accompaniment, after which the process was reversed or the two would combine. Drums, flutes, whistles, and rattles were the principal instruments used by orchestras and dancers to accompany the singing. Time was generally marked by the drum.

While Whites were usually gripped by the pulsating drumbeat which accompanied Indian dancing and singing, the first reaction to their songs was often a disagreeable one. To avoid this one had to learn that the Indian's mind was on the force behind the songs. He did not only sing and listen to a song, he also lived it; it was a means of accomplishing transformations within himself so that he could bring his person into accord with the Spirit, with the universe, and with his fellow man.

The throbbing of the drum, which to him was the heartbeat of the world, combined with his words and pulled his thoughts into a tangible form he could deal with. In practice, the seemingly unmelodious sounds were transformed into a series of related phrases which spoke infinite meanings to his mind and heart. Thus it is easy to see why the Plains Indian developed a song for every moment of his life, and why all of these made deep and abiding contributions to his happiness.

Gros Ventre Fly Society Dance.

Bear Dance, Arikara Medicine Ceremony.

Traditional and ceremonial songs, like dances, were considered to be the property of the tribal leaders or of an individual, depending upon which received them first, and they must be bought, traded, or given as a gift before they could be used by anyone else. Indians had an amazing facility for memorizing the songs, and some could sing hundreds of verses without a mistake. Fortunately, and perhaps not accidentally, most songs were very short; as such, a stanza or two would be repeated over and over again. Bearing the main intent in mind, one can appreciate that the repetition only increased the ultimate value received.

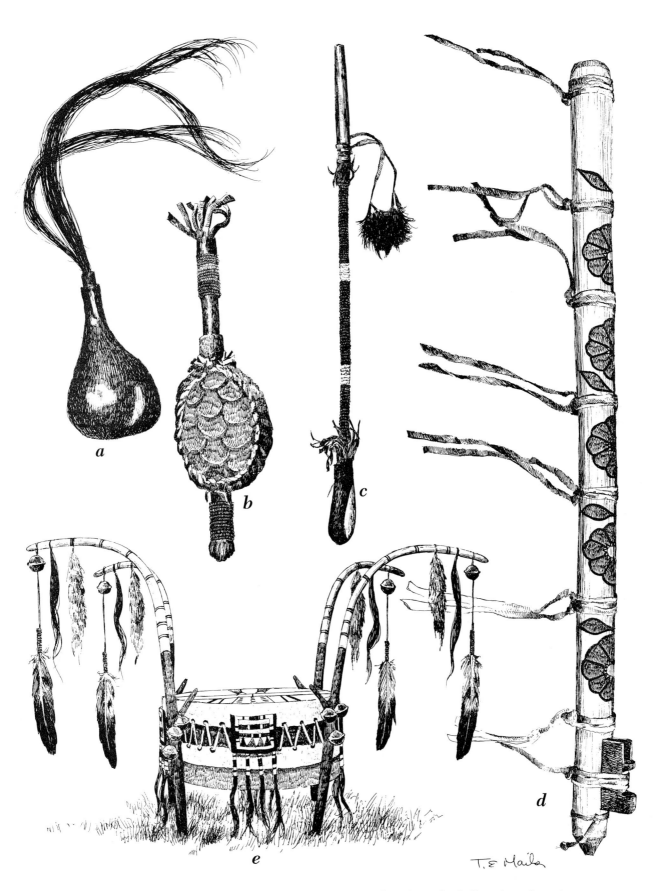

Musical instruments. *a*, deer hide rattle with horsehair pendant. *b*, turtle shell rattle. *c*, drum beater with beaded handle. *d*, wooden flute with rawhide fringes (34 inches long). *e*, four-man drum.

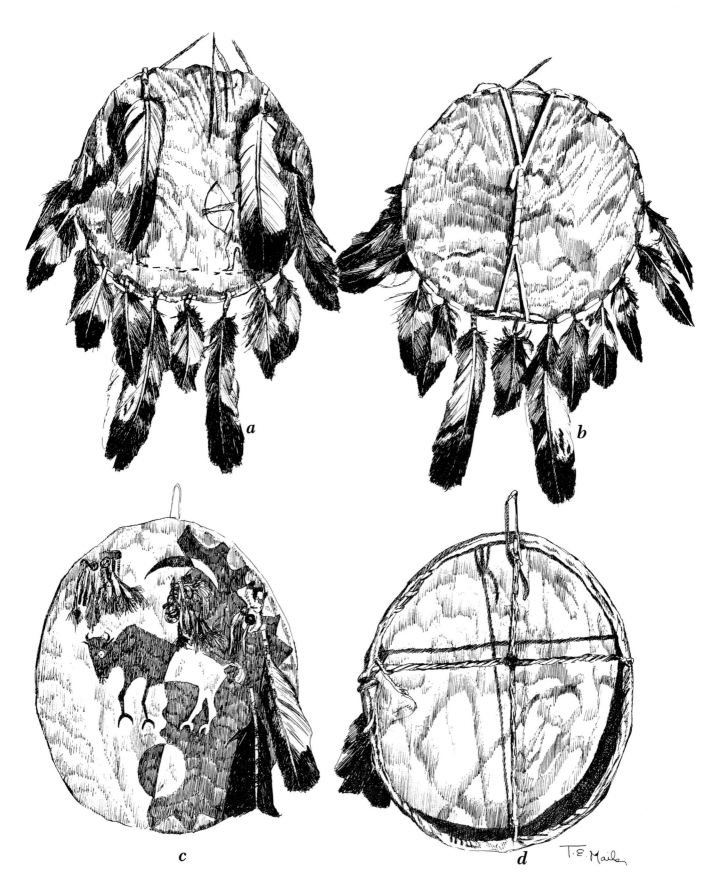

Lightweight hide dance shields: Top, buffalo hide with golden eagle feathers—*a*, front; *b*, back. Bottom, elk hide with metal bell and quill strip thumpers, very old style on wooden hoop frame—*c*, front; *d*, back. Rough diameter of both shields, 18 inches. Hides used for dance shields were much thinner than those of war shields.

T. E. Mails

Sioux victory dancer carrying hide-wrapped sacred sage and also a victory wreath, and wearing crow bustle (circa 1876).

Indeed, simplicity was the keynote for Indian songs and no attempt was made to duplicate the White man's often complicated verbiage.

Typical Plains Indian songs were as follows:

<table>
<tr><td>The Fox<br>I am;<br>something<br>difficult<br>I seek<br><br>Owls<br>were hooting<br>in the passing of the night<br>owls<br>were hooting</td><td>This honored one,<br>this honored one,<br>horses<br>I donated<br><br>sacred<br>he made for me<br>sacred<br>he made for me<br>a blacktail deer<br>sacred<br>he made for me<br>those<br>you had seen</td></tr>
</table>

In considering their brevity, several important points besides those already mentioned should be borne in mind. First, they could be brief because the circumstances of their composition and rendition would be well known to all the members of the band. It would not be necessary to include the more intimate details. Second, the songs served to emphasize the main point of a story, and were kept simple so the point would be easily understood and remembered by an audience. Third, traditional phrases were used, and as such evoked traditional responses from the audience. The phrases, then, served to promote a familiar atmosphere for each song. Fourth, the very abstraction of the brief statements provided an aura of mystery, and like an incomplete painting, a Plains song tended to draw the listener into the singer's life experience of the moment. Fifth, the words, phrases, and stanzas were repeated many times. In rituals, the stanzas were usually repeated in sets of fours or sevens, both of which were considered to be sacred numbers. The aim was to rhyme thoughts, not sounds, and as such to achieve a familiarity which brought a sense of comfort and security to both the singer and his audience.

There was no part singing or harmonizing, for harmonizing would have interfered with the basic purpose. Instead, each Indian sang his song with maximum force, following impulses rather than a melody rule book. Often the measure of the drumbeat differed from that of the song, for the drum controlled the body movements while the song was geared to the soul. In a way, this tended to draw the entire person into the dancing activity. Martin Luther once remarked upon the infinite wisdom of God, who in the sacraments gave us a material element that the body could experience, and in the Word, a spiritual element that could be absorbed by the soul. The idea, as Luther saw it, was that the activity of the ritual *involved the total man.* Apparently the Great Mystery was able to communicate such comprehensive understandings to the Indians as well, for they came to the same concept, and put it to the best of uses.

Sioux Indian women. Girl at left wears dentalium beaded dress and hair-pipe bone necklace. Mother at bottom right has hair cut short in mourning for deceased husband.

# Chapter 4

# PERSONAL QUALITIES

Once the true nature or life-way of the ancient Plains Indians becomes clear, several profound opportunities present themselves. First, there is the distinct possibility that by adopting some parts of the Indian life-way we can at last recapture a portion of that superb freedom, adventure, and happiness which characterized the Plains dweller of 1750 to 1875. Second, we can now share in certain valuable religious truths of the Indians which have been kept secret or were overlooked. Third, the charity and hospitality of the Plains Indians could easily offer itself as an ideal model for the world. Fourth, since they were a creative and inventive people of such a unique kind, that aspect of their life can now be added to the many abilities already possessed in creative areas.

The reason these opportunities have not presented themselves until now is that non-Indians have been merely spectators concerning the Indians, and so have missed the proverbial forest because of preoccupation with the trees. Nearly everything about the Indian has been considered save his greatest aspect, his superb process of mental preparation for life, and how that process affected and improved everything he did. By it, he learned to flow, not fight, with God and nature, and the rest of mankind could profit greatly by being, for a while at least, his student instead of his teacher.

Comparing them to the White race, early writers who had but scanty or hearsay knowledge of the Indians usually described them as a limited or "savage" people. Yet the comparison was a decidedly unfair one, for the Indian's life and mind was not geared to function like those of the average man of the industrial world. He was shaped by his natural religion, by his elders, and by his primitive and wild surroundings. Associating on the most intimate basis with extreme natural conditions and with only the people of his own race, his standard of wisdom and learning became that of nature, and of the wise men of his tribe who had earned their positions as teachers through practical experience.

Thus he inevitably came to act as nature did and to think as the elders thought. His reasoning processes remained much the same as those of the generations before him. Slight advances in culture were brought about from time to time by new influences, such as the horse and trade with the Whites, but except for the expansion and intensification of craftworks, the general cultural change in all parts of the Plains from 1750 to 1875 was slight, and happened at a leisurely pace. It is important, in saying this, to recognize that by "culture" I mean the Indian's life-way, and not the externals of existence. Insofar as the life-way is concerned, new influences made little difference in the Indian's developmental process. Time in particular was the least of his concerns, and he never thought to invent a gadget to measure it or to speed up the manufacturing process. Clocks are only needed by those who endorse the idea of scheduled lives or who believe that true productivity is only determined by inventories taken at the end of a day.

As a rule, the Indian remained without training in most matters having to do with what others call "civilized life." Indeed, moving in the opposite direction, he became a partner of natural existence as it was. And, in respect to things with which he became familiar, he developed abilities sufficient to astonish the Whites who came as the first visitors to his country.

Like the wild bird and beast, like the white clouds and the straight green trees, like the eternal rocks and the crystal streams, the Indian was a part of nature. He became so because he studied the whole of it until little escaped his mind or eye, and then he sought to move with it in a rare kind of conformity. Ultimately, what he received was a special kind of inner peace. It is true that he was wholly unable to reason scientifically, because his directions did not lead him to the kind of information upon which such reasoning might be based. Yet considering the total circumstances, the human product and what he produced are all the more remarkable. And in the end, one is almost forced to wonder whether the Plains life-way is not in many ways preferable to that of the non-Indian.

It is essential to pause here and to summarize the life-way characteristics which resulted from the leisurely evolution of the Plains culture, for without this it is utterly impossible to know what the Plains people were really like, and without this there can be no true understanding of why they so enthusiastically embraced the customs which characterized their day.

Among the members of a given tribe, honesty was an absolute, and lying was sure to bring the direst consequences. The straight stem of the pipe a man smoked represented the need to speak straightly (or truthfully). In matters concerning those things in which he had no positive knowledge, he was exceedingly careful to qualify his statements, so that it never might be said of him that "he had two tongues." Theft was virtually unknown in an Indian village and people could leave their goods unattended without fear. A lost piece of property was immediately delivered to the camp crier, who proclaimed the news of its discovery throughout the camp, so that the owner of the lost article might recover it. However, since it fitted his idea of proper defense, an Indian did not hesitate to take all the property he could from an enemy. Even then the usual loot was horses, and an enemy's village was seldom disturbed or ravaged.

There was universal hospitality and charity within the tribe. Food was always

The reflective pipe smoker meditating upon how the pipe connected him with God (after Olaf Seltzer). (*Right*) Sioux pipe smoker preparing to "speak straight" by smoking the straight pipe.

shared. Those who did the actual procuring of an animal, such as a buffalo, might take some small special advantage, but that was all. Except in times of great scarcity, food could be had from a successful hunting party for the asking. So long as there was any food remaining in the lodge, every visitor received his share without the slightest hesitation. Childhood friendships were likely to last throughout the lifetimes of the persons involved. In battle and in cases of special need, friends would often give their lives for each other. Tom Newcomb, a scout for General Miles in the early seventies, and who later lived with the Sioux, stated that he never saw more kindness, charity, and brotherhood anywhere than he did among the Sioux.[1]

Respect for parents and for the rights of others and self-control were natural outgrowths of the interdependent Indian community. Serious family or camp quarrels were extremely rare. In all matters of consequence children obeyed their parents and the camp leaders or police societies. It is said that once quarrels did occur, the parties to them were likely to be difficult to control. Each participant would behave as unreasonably as a child, seeing only from his own point of view, and acknowledging no justification on the part of the other. Most serious arguments resulted in the destruction of property, and only rarely in a killing. In such instances the killer might himself be killed by a police society, or he would be cast out of the village. The very least he would suffer would be a total loss of influence and social ostracism. Even a chief or principal man who killed a member of his tribe in self-defense would lose his position of influence and be avoided forever by all the members of the tribe.

People who imagine the Plains Indians to be savages would not expect to find etiquette in common practice, yet their forms of it would do credit to any nation.

There were many wisdom sayings which were addressed to the young—some of which included admonitions about eating. These had nothing to do with the use of utensils, but more importantly with promoting respect and concern for elders. For example, a boy would be told he should not eat a certain soft part of the buffalo, else his legs would become soft. But the real meaning of the admonition was that he should have the courtesy to leave the tender parts for the aged, who could not chew as well as he.[2]

The warmest space in a lodge, the one directly in back of the fire, was reserved for guests. It was the place of honor, and robes were spread there to make the visitors welcome.

An Indian never passed between the fire and another individual unless an apology was first made for cutting him momentarily off from its warmth. The same was true of passing between people who were engaged in conversation.

When a guest came he took his seat quietly and remained so for some time. No one addressed him until he had time to "catch his breath," which really meant time to avoid having any matter hastily introduced. The use of the pipe aided further in such deliberateness. Departures from a tipi after a discussion were made without ceremony. After all, the matter was finished. Why belabor it?

The Indians tell about a courtesy which was practiced between married persons and their in-laws. Direct address was avoided, and an intermediary passed information back and forth between the two. However, the rule was not inflexible, and stories are told about son-in-laws who became close companions of their father-in-laws.[3]

Now that the practice has ceased, many have speculated about the purpose of the custom, for it appears awkward at best. Some old Omaha men who were questioned about it thought it was done to show respect for elders. But there are excellent reasons beyond that. In the first place, it avoided direct confrontation over the differing opinions about life that commonly occur between newlyweds and in-laws, and in the second—assuming that the premise about their learning from the same God approximately what the Christian would is a correct one—it would have something to do with a man's "leaving his father and mother and cleaving to his wife," so that the two could live as an unimpeded "one flesh." A person can be neither a good husband nor wife until the umbilical ties with mother and father have been severed.

Etiquette also required that a person's name should not be mentioned in his presence. This practice was intended to deepen the relationship between people—strange as this may at first seem. Others were addressed as father, mother, friend, brother, etc. These were terms of relationships which express a love that is not conveyed when the personal name is used. The Indians felt that any impersonal stranger could use a name. In the same way a man of standing would be called "aged man," which granted him the status of wisdom, and which tended to bring forth a profound response.

Politeness forbade a person to ask a stranger's name or even what business had brought him into the community. These awaited the development of events. Now and then an emissary from another tribe came and went without anyone's having learned his name.

Cleanliness was a norm of Plains life, and irrespective of the problems of the elements and constant travel, it was practiced to a commendable degree. Alexander Henry II, a trader during the early 1800s, stated that the Sioux, the Crows, the Cheyenne, and the Mandans had the custom of washing morning and evening.[4] George Catlin reinforced this, pointing out that while there were many exceptions, the Plains people as a rule observed decency, cleanliness, and elegance of dress. "There are few people, perhaps, who take more pains to keep their persons neat and cleanly, than they do."[5] The stationary village tribes, who had the advantage of nearby rivers, bathed every day in summer and winter. In addition to all of this, the sweat lodge was in common use by young and old alike.

Physical health received a high priority on the Plains, since it was a requisite for survival. The Indians followed a demanding system of physical training, and the elders often advised the young to condition themselves properly for the rigors of the mature years ahead. Indulgences, in particular, were curbed. Young men were forced to exercise, and advised not to smoke. Fasting was a regular practice, as was long-distance running and winter swimming. In 1882 a young Cree carrying dispatches ran 125 miles in twenty-five hours, and the feat was so common that it received no comment among the Indians.[6] The health of the Plains people was so good that prior to contact with the Whites no plague-type infectious diseases or mental disorders were known to them.

Responsibility and loyalty were common traits in an Indian community. Every boy was continually nurtured by the admonition that he must become a brave protector of his country and his tribe, and a dependable friend. Here an incredible wrong should be put right. Many authors have stated that Indian men went to war for personal gain and glory; that it gave them wealth and an opportunity to be adored. In short, it was done for vanity's sake alone! But the Indian accounts

Part of a mounted war party carrying feathered lances and coup sticks.

do not support this contention in any way. Horse raids and warfare were defensive activities designed to keep the enemy off balance and to impair his economic base—so that he could not make massive war. The adulation which followed success in these things was simply a just reward for meeting one's responsibilities in protecting the tribe. Jonathon Carver, commenting upon his visits with the Indians, said:

The honour of their tribe, and the welfare of their nation is the first and most predominant emotion of their hearts; and from hence proceed in a great measure all their virtues and their vices. Actuated by this, they brave every danger, endure the most exquisite torments, and expire triumphing in their fortitude, not as a personal qualification, but as a national characteristic.[7]

Pride was one of the most important of the Indian's qualities, for he was proud to be an Indian, and in particular a member of "his" tribe. Moreover, he gladly took his place of responsibility in a continuing line of heirs. History was a vital thing to him. He also placed great store in achievement and its rewards. Few of his tasks were done carelessly; the greater percentage by far were executed with thoroughness, thoughtfulness, and attention to detail.

Joy was a word that belonged to the Indians. Life was rich, and the Indians were only stoical and sullen in the presence of Whites during the war and reservation period. They were really a *happy*, delightful people, so ready to laugh at an amusing incident or clever joke that they reminded the early White visitors of children at play.

A quote from Colonel Dodge puts this truth very well:

In his manner and bearing, the Indian is habitually grave and dignified, and in the presence of strangers he is reserved and silent.

The general impression is that the Indian is a stoic. Nothing can be further from the truth. Stoicism is a "put on." In his own camp, away from strangers, the Indian is a noisy, jolly, rollicking, mischief-loving braggadocio, brimful of practical jokes and rough fun of any kind, making the welkin ring with his laughter, and rousing the midnight echoes by song and dance, whoops and yells.

He will talk himself wild with excitement, vaunting his exploits in love, war, or the chase, and will commit all sorts of extravagances while telling or listening to an exciting story. In their everyday life Indians are vivacious, chatty, fond of telling and hearing stories. Their nights are spent in song and dance, and for the number of persons engaged, a permanent (safe) Indian camp is at night the noisiest place that can be found.[8]

Wisdom of a special type was also to be found on the Plains. Joseph Epes Brown, in his book entitled *The Sacred Pipe*, tells how he came after many years of study to believe there was a lofty wisdom among the central Indian people.[9] This led him to record and edit the sacred knowledge of the Sioux spiritualist

Shoshone warrior and his wife in dignified splendor on fully outfitted horses.          T. E. Mails 68

Black Elk, who could neither read nor speak English, and therefore had never read the Bible. Here he found ample evidence to support the fact that the old Indian holy men possessed qualities and degrees of spirituality rarely found in the world today—"for want of which the world is becoming impoverished, in spite of its material wealth." The following paraphrases of the wise teachings of several tribes will in themselves show that what he says was undeniably true.

Any man who is attached to the senses and to the things of this world is one who lives in ignorance and is being consumed by the snakes which represent his own passions.

Our Father has made his will known to us here on this earth, and we must always do that which he wishes if we want to walk the sacred path.

There can never be peace between nations until there is first known that true peace which is within the souls of men. This comes when men realize their oneness with the universe and all its Powers, and when they know that the Great Spirit is at its center, that all things are his works, and that this center is really everywhere, it is within each of us. He watches over and sustains all life. His breath gives life; it is from him and to him that all generations come and go.

Every step we take upon mother earth should be done in a sacred manner; each step should be as a prayer. The power of a pure and good soul is planted as a seed, and will grow in man's heart as he walks in a holy manner. The Spirit is anxious to aid all who seek him with a pure heart.

We are two-legged as the birds are because the birds leave the world with their wings, and we one day leave it in the spirit. This is one of the things we learn from the holy birds.

The breath of the Spirit is seen in the corn, since when the wind blows, the pollen falls from the tassel onto the silk surface surrounding the ear, through which the fruit becomes mature and fertile.

We should all remember how merciful God is in providing for our wants, and in the same manner provide them for children, especially those who are without parents.

The old men tell us that everything they see changes a little during a man's natural lifetime, and that when change comes to any created thing it must accept it, that it cannot fight, but must change.

Our people were wise. They never neglected the young or failed to keep before them deeds done by illustrious men of the tribe. Our teachers were willing and thorough. All were quick to praise excellence without speaking a word that might break the spirit of a boy who might be less capable than others. The boy who failed at any lesson only received more lessons and care, until he was as far as he could go.

A man should rely on his own resources; the one who trains himself is ready for any emergency.

The youth who thinks first of himself and forgets the old will never prosper, nothing will go straight for him.

A man who is not industrious will always have to borrow from others, and will never have things of his own. He will be envious and tempted to steal. He will be unhappy. The energetic man is happy and pleasant to speak with; he is remembered and visited on his deathbed. But no one mourns for the lazy man.

A thrifty woman has a good tipi; all her tools are the best, so is her clothing.

# Chapter 5

# FORM OF GOVERNMENT

As the impressive qualities of the Indians begin to mount, it is not surprising to discover that their common form of tribal government promoted the worth and freedom of the individual. Distinctions of rank were established and maintained for good order, but there were no hidebound hereditary classes, no servants or slaves. As is the case in every society, the children of distinguished men enjoyed certain advantages; a chief's son or the child of a rich family was more quickly (and perhaps prudently) acclaimed than an orphan would be. Naturally the owner of important positions or properties tried to bequeath them to his descendants, and thereby encouraged the continuance of his family's privileges, but just as often, everything a warrior had was given away at his death. Where specific public functions were exercised by a particular clan, it might, in rare cases, regard itself as socially superior. Yet since even the camp chief and village leaders exercised only a minimal power, the practical significance of social eminence was slight. It is important to establish that, in the Indian's view, supernatural favor and personal aggressiveness could bring anyone to a position of wealth and high standing. Hence to begin life as a social nobody was a special kind of challenge; a man could strive for spiritual blessings through visions and prayers, distinguish himself as a tribe-protecting warrior, gain wealth, and ultimately surpass others by the status he obtained. Any man always had hope, and he always had a worthwhile goal.

Greed, at least as it is understood in materialistic terms today, was seldom present on the Plains. Except in disciplinary instances, no Plains leader or influential group could appropriate the possessions of any villager; such an act was unthinkable. On the contrary, a leader could only receive and maintain his status by lavish generosity to the unfortunate. Charity, next to a fine war record, was *the* basis for achieving and maintaining a high standing. The Oglala Sioux had a society of chiefs enjoying superior prestige, but when a novice was admitted, he was immediately urged personally to look after the poor; especially the widows and children.[1] Among the Blackfoot tribes a man aspiring to become a leader sought to outshine his competitors by his feasts and presents, even at the cost of self-impoverishment, for, once selected, he continued to give away with one hand what he had obtained with the other.[2] The Omahas recognized two classes of meritorious tribesmen—"such as had given to the poor on many occasions, and had invited guests to many feasts," and those who, in addition, "had killed several of the foe and had brought home many horses."[3] A Cheyenne points out that the aspect of such exorbitant generosity among his people often led men to decline an offer of chiefdom.[4]

Absolute governmental power was only executed on special occasions, such as at the annual tribal hunts or a major festival. Even here, a police force consisting of one of the societies—appointed to this task for a year—and not the chiefs, would exercise coercive authority if it was required. Normally the greatest chief would not dare lay hands on the meanest tribesman, but the police appointed by him or by a festival priest did have the power to carry out a chief's order to restrain a misbehaving individual. In particular, the annual buffalo hunts required careful obedience to the leader's instructions, lest the whole people suffer; hence the police would issue orders that no one must hunt by himself and thereby deprive the other families of an equal chance by frightening the herd away. The Cheyenne police, more lenient than those of most other tribes, nevertheless whipped even eminent people who became offenders on such occasions. The Omaha police once flogged a leading man so violently that he never fully recovered.

As mentioned earlier, nearly all Plains Indian tribes divided into scattered bands for most of the year, uniting only for major ceremonies and communal hunting. Thus it was during the summer months at the great tribal gatherings that their authoritative police societies were used to the greatest extent.

The leaders of the warrior societies were often called "chiefs" by the Whites. But the Indians reserved this title for members of the tribal governing body. And a man could not be at one time a tribal chief, a society leader, or a "war chief," he could only be one or the other.

Some tribes had a head chief and many lesser chiefs for each of the tribe's small bands and clans. These came together and consulted on all tribal affairs. Others had a council of chiefs made up of the leaders of each band, and who each held equal authority. In no case could one man speak for and bind the entire tribe, especially in something so important as the making of a treaty. Understandably then, when the Whites violated this custom and obtained but a single signature, it often led to wars.

In battle, the Cheyenne camp chiefs stayed in the background until needed, and their military societies, led by temporarily elected war chiefs, did the fighting. Whenever the battle became serious, though, all chiefs were to enter the fight and must not retreat. In such instances, they either were killed or triumphed.

When the Crow council of chiefs, called "good men," thought a man's vision to be outstanding, they might permit him to lead the camp through four trial moves. If during this period he found enough food and pastureland, if war parties returned with captured horses and with no serious casualties, and if the camps

Plenty Coups, great chief of the Crows (1850–1932) (adaptation from photograph taken in Washington, D.C., in 1921).

Mandan war leader in ermine headdress with split buffalo horns, wearing ancient-style elk shirt (circa 1830), carrying captured Crow medicine ring with rock medicine on the ground. Captured war trophies were often used as goads to excite warriors in preparation for a revenge raid.

were not raided, he then joined the council of chiefs, whereupon the regular head chief resumed control. The main duties of "the One Who Owns the Camp," or Crow village head chief, were to help the other chiefs decide when and where their followers should move, where they should stop to camp, and to appoint the warrior societies needed to police the camp. There was another procedure by which a Crow man might become a chief. A warrior who had struck what his tribe considered to be the four important coups gave presents to an acknowledged chief on four different occasions, supposedly without divulging his motive. Then, after making his request to buy the chief's medicine bundle or a duplicate of it, he was either accepted or rejected.[5]

The Assiniboine tribe subdivided itself into bands, each of which lived and hunted alone, occupied a district, and had its own chief. However, if the land area occupied by one of these bands was large, there might be as many as three band chiefs and many headmen, who together formed a council for the band. At the passing away of one chief, the other council members selected his successor. This was a fairly common practice for the entire Plains area. Occasionally a medicine priest, feared for his powers, might obtain chiefdom by political maneuvering, and it is said that some of these proved thereafter to be "bad rulers."[6]

Most chiefs were experienced warriors, but relatively young. Washakie of the Shoshones was an exception. He became a chief in his early twenties and remained influential for his entire career. Yet in the usual instance, while the wisdom of the old was appreciated and solicited, there was a limit to the deference paid to old age insofar as chiefdom was concerned. An aging chief usually declined in prestige after the age of forty, and if he sought to remain in office, factions commonly contended he was "getting too old." In their view, a good tribal leader must continually be proving his ability in the hunt, war, and medicine, and an older man could not do this. Talent as an orator seems to have counted a little, but was minimal in the selection of a chief.

Autocratic chiefs did exist at times on the Plains, and an exceptionally powerful personality could exert great influence. Generally speaking, though, the spirit of the Plains culture militated against dictatorships. Even the splitting up of most tribes into small and independently governed bands or clans for the larger part of the year helped to distribute authority.

Denig points out a few things which should be included to keep our thoughts in good balance. He said that every band of Indians took its nature from its chief. In other words, if in his habits and example a chief was good, wise, and prudent, his tribe followed his lead; "he communicated to his people a like disposition." The contrary was also true, and a predatory clan was inevitably led by a predatory chief.[7]

He also states that a chief who was under recognized supernatural protection could carry out arbitrary measures and force his people to conform to whatever rules he devised for their conduct. If he was "strongly supported by family connections, decided and brave in his actions, and feared on account of his supposed supernatural protection, his word was law and his people his slaves."

However, few chiefs attained this sort of power, and since it inevitably brought a natural unhappiness to everyone, such singular authority was always terminated as soon as it could be accomplished. One despot went blind, and shortly thereafter was shot through the heart and eliminated by one of his disgruntled followers.

With or without autocratic leaders, there were sets of unwritten rules followed by all the nations, though no courts or judges existed to administer justice in the modern jurisdictional sense.

The following were the crimes which the Blackfeet considered sufficiently serious to merit a distinct punishment, and the penalties which were attached to them.

Murder: A life for a life, or a heavy payment by the murderer or his relatives at the option of the murdered man's relatives. This payment was often so oppressive as to strip the murderer absolutely of his entire property.

Theft: Simply the restoration of the property taken.

Adultery: For the first offense the husband generally cut off the offending wife's nose or ears; for the second offense she was killed by the police society. Sometimes a woman, if her husband complained enough about her, would be killed by her brothers or first cousins, and this was more usual than death at the hands of the All Comrades Society. However, if he wished, the husband could have her put to death for the first offense.

Treachery (that is, when a member of the tribe went over to the enemy or gave him any aid whatever): Death on sight.

Cowardice: A man who would not fight in defense of his tribe was obliged to wear a woman's dress, and was not allowed to marry.

If a man left camp to hunt buffalo by himself, thereby driving away the game, the All Comrades were sent after him, and not only brought him forcefully back, but often whipped him, tore his lodge to shreds, broke his travois, and took away his store of dried meat, pemmican, and other food.[8]

Among the Cheyenne, murderers were banished at once; an act which held feuding to a minimum, and which some feel gave them a better stability than was possible in other Plains tribes where such control was not achieved.

It should be pointed out that murders within the tribes were extremely rare—almost non-existent. The tremendous power of public censure and opinion

Chief's eagle-head staff with buffalo horn, and eagle feather and strap on handle. Close-up of head at right.

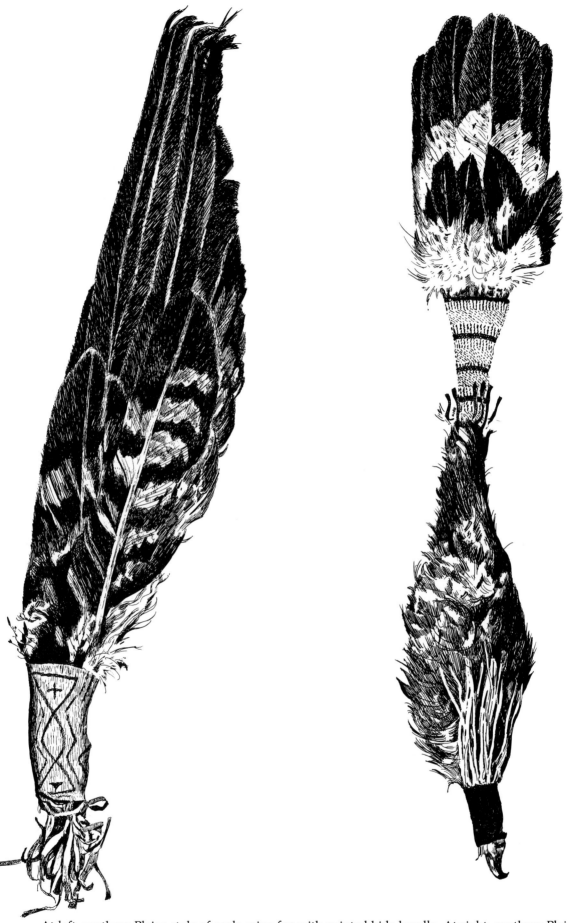

At left, northern Plains style of eagle-wing fan with painted hide handle. At right, southern Plains style of fan where tail feathers make fan and the eagle body and head are attached to the fan handle.

Cheyenne chief with his authority being questioned by one of the other leaders of the band.

did much in itself to curtail dishonor, community misbehavior, and violence. The Plains Indians were exceedingly sensitive to reactions and to gossip which would affect their social standing. A person who broke the common unwritten rules would be "held up to general ridicule amid shrieks of laughter," and the embarrassment of the victim sometimes drove him into exile or onto the warpath. The Crow and Hidatsa tribes had a definite way of exercising discipline of this order. Relatives teased each other about little things, but also had the serious duty of publicly upbraiding each other for improper conduct. A cowardly man who was exposed and jeered would feel like sinking into the ground with shame, and the wide-eyed children, whose parents made sure they saw it all, would be taught an important lesson. Therefore, it is helpful to note that while strict order and discipline were lacking in child training, the strong public censure applied to adults who broke the rules did more than enough to shape up the children and keep them in line. The Indian method of training was discipline by example!

Generally speaking, the office of chief had few compensations attached to it. It was honorary, laborious, and frequently a thankless task. There were no insignia of rank except a distinguished staff of office. A chief might carry a staff topped by an eagle head, or a beaded one with an eagle's claw at the end. He would undoubtedly be entitled to wear the usual warrior's headdress of eagle feathers and to carry an eagle wing fan. He would also own the regal ceremonial clothing worn by all distinguished warriors on ceremonial occasions and occasionally in battle; but a chief seldom dressed better than the majority of the male members of his tribe. His tent did occupy a central position, he was consulted on all important matters, he felt worthwhile, needed, and he was given many fine pieces of artwork by grateful families in appreciation of his contributions. Still, he had to secure and maintain his living and position in the same manner as the others, and he did not possess the great powers so often attributed to chiefs in fictional works.

A chief controlled the destiny of his people only so long as the correctness of his judgments were proven, and thereby supported his authority. The American Indian was a firm *individualist,* and no single person ever held total influence over any Plains tribe. Perhaps it is fortunate for the White army that most battles by far were fought as the combined efforts of small groups of individuals, each man fighting as his supernatural patron and as he pleased, for the Plains Indians constituted the best light cavalrymen the world has ever known, and had they united against our soldiers and settlers the result could have been an incredible disaster for the Whites.

Authorities are correct when they assert that *individualism* among the American Indians is as apparent now as it ever was. Many feel it is one of the reasons that the American Indian earned a reputation for being an exceptionally courageous and resourceful fighting man during World War II and the Korean conflict. They believe it also explains why foreign persuasions have never been able to establish even a toe hold among the Indian-Americans.[9]

# Chapter 6

# RELIGION—
# SUPERNATURAL BELIEFS

In the life of the Indian there was only one inevitable duty—the duty of prayer, the daily recognition of the Unseen and Eternal. His daily devotions were more necessary to him than daily food. He wakes at daybreak, puts on his moccasins, and steps down to the water's edge. Here he throws handfuls of clear, cold water into his face, or plunges in bodily. After the bath, he stands erect before the advancing dawn, facing the sun as it dances upon the horizon, and offers his unspoken orison. His mate may precede or follow him in his devotions, but never accompanies him. Each soul must meet the morning sun, the new sweet earth, and the Great Silence alone![1]

When you arise in the morning, give thanks for the morning light. Give thanks for your life and strength. Give thanks for your food and give thanks for the joy of living. And if perchance you see no reason for giving thanks, rest assured the fault is in yourself.[2]

For many and complex reasons it has not been easy for White men to understand how the Indian thought. The culture gap is enormous, and tensions have hindered communication. Nevertheless, this much is certain, everything about the Plains Indians centered in religion, and all they undertook began with and was thereafter influenced by this single base or source. It is a truth which applies to everything from child raising to crafts, from community relationships to warfare, and from philosophy to storytelling.

Even the placing of their camp lodges in a circle open to the east and the facing of every lodge entrance to the eastern side projected the idea. By this simple gesture a warrior was awakened by the dawn, and immediately reminded by the sun's rise to pray to the One-Above and to the sun and to the Four Old Men, giving thanks for his strength, his family, his village, and his tribe. Every new day came as a holy event, and he would not eat food until he had made an offering of some kind to the One-Above. If he had been unfortunate or had done some wrong, he also purified his clothing and his weapons in the incense of burning cedar or sage so that he could have a new start. Such acts of mental and physical

Sioux warrior praying to the Great Spirit as the day begins. He holds a catlinite pipe in his hand and carries his medicine bundle looped over his shoulder.

preparation gave the man confidence and strength to face the day. They also made him a thoughtful father, husband, fighter, and hunter.

The Indian frankly admitted he could only gain victory and be successful in his undertakings if he had the help of the force which ruled nature—so, literally, looking through nature up to nature's God, he appealed for divine assistance, and attempted to win the deity over to his side. Further, to show how much in earnest he was, he offered sacrifices of food, tobacco, ornaments, a small lock of his hair, or even a piece of his flesh. And whenever he received specific success or good things from God, he offered some part of these to God in thanksgiving.

Spirituality invaded and benefited every part of the Indian's life. In a communal antelope hunt a Comanche priest would try to block the escape of the game by crossing certain sticks decorated with antelope hoofs. And when the herd had been surrounded, he could supposedly kill a particular antelope by simply pointing one of the hoofs at it.

In the Indian's mind, garments made of animal skins retained the semblance of the animal, and the comfort the skin contributed to the body served to increase the warrior's confidence in the close relationship he conceived to exist between all other visible created forms and himself. Although in later times the Indian's ordinary trade cloth clothing ceased to exemplify this close relationship, a man entering upon sacred ceremonies with the desire of securing supernatural aid wore as many of his primitive garments as he could still muster. For example, in the rites preceding the Omaha tribal buffalo hunt, the priests and chiefs wore uncut buffalo robes, the hair outside, so wrapped about their bodies that as they sat together they presented the appearance of a group of buffaloes. Wearing the robes in this fashion was explained as being done in recognition of the transmission of life from the buffalo to man that the latter might live. Again, a warrior on his way to raiding enemy territory might wear a wolfskin over his shoulder or tie the skin of some swift bird of prey to his head or body. This direct coupling of the man and the living creature not only indicated an appeal for help but was believed to promote the transmission of the help and to make it more direct in the hour of need.

Much of the Indian's optimism regarding success rested on the principle that imitation of a desired event could produce it. This was even true of a complex ceremonial. At one stage of the Tobacco Dance the Crow Indians raised their drumsticks above their heads to symbolize and to promote the growth of the plant, and the farming tribes of the area placed great credence in their agricultural rites.

Religion also asserted itself in warfare. Even when he was anxious to go, no warrior ventured forth on a raid unless he had been prompted toward it by his supernatural protector in a dream or vision. Shields owed their efficacy more to the vision that had suggested the appendages and designs on their covers than to the toughness of the hide. In a ceremony for bringing about the death of tribal enemies they were about to encounter, the Crows would blacken ceremonial articles, since it was their custom also to put black paint on their faces after a killing. Many times a warrior attempted to determine whether the raid or war party on which he was setting out would meet with success; if, for example, in peering into a mixture of badger and buffalo blood he saw a resemblance of an enemy's scalp, he felt encouraged to proceed; if he saw himself scalped, he abandoned the project instantly! An owl's hoot could cause any jittery Kiowa on the trail to turn around and go home.

The Indians have always been a profoundly religious people. They never built churches or composed a book of sacred writings like the Bible, they had no prayer books, hymnals, holy days, or Sabbath. Yet all they owned and every act of their lives was bound up with their religion; which accounted for the exceptional quality of everything they produced and did.[3]

They trusted in a creative power that was higher than all people and the universe, and each tribe had its own name for Him. Because of the good which came from the sun, many felt He dwelt in the center of it, and that its radiance, light, and warmth really came from Him. The Crows called him First Maker, the Pawnees named him Ti-rá-wa, the Sioux spoke of him as the Great Spirit or Mystery, the Arapaho referred to him as the Man-Above.

A lesser power in the world called Mother Earth governed everything that grew, and the Indians also believed in the power of the sun, of the night sun or moon, of the morning star, and of the Four Old Men who directed the winds, the rains, and the seasons, and gave them "the breath of life," which they understood to consist of the wisdom necessary for existence.

Their God was eternal; He had no beginning and no end. He also provided mankind with a never ending life after death. Plenty Coups believed that because he was old, he was living "an unnatural life," a life which nobody knew all about, and he was anxious to step past it and go to "his Father," Ah-badt-dadt-deah, "where he would live again as men were intended to live."[4] Literally translated, the Crow word "Ah-badt-dadt-deah" means "the One Who Made All Things." F. B. Linderman, who studied the Indians for forty years, and seems to have obtained the best non-Indian grasp of the Indian religion, came to think of this Crow word as more nearly a term than a name, since to the Crow the actual title was unpronounceable, just as it was with other ancient peoples such as the Jews. If one spoke the name in an Indian's presence, it brought an instant silence and a profound shift in attitude toward reverence. His God was sensitive, all-powerful, everywhere present. For this reason, in crossing a very deep stream the warrior sometimes gave the water a material offering, such as a piece of meat or fine clothing. In this instance it was not only done to satisfy the evil spirits he believed lived in the water, but was also an offering to his Father, so that he might pass safely and sensibly through an element which was powerful and not naturally his own; a protective idea and practice which was extended to all elements possessing powers beyond his control.

On the other hand, if one spoke of lesser gods, such as those to whom the Father entrusted much of the work of secondary creation, the Indians would always smile tolerantly. They held these in moderate respect, but were ready to laugh at the mention of their names—because it was they who caused the seeming shortcomings in nature. Frank Linderman felt this to be "a delicious touch," since by clinging to this view, in his few faultfindings with created things like the violent storms and oppressive heat the Indian never blasphemed against his God, continuing to hold Him in the deepest reverence.[5] Linderman believed the Plains Indians to be monotheist, and so do I . . . especially since the Indian accounts fully agree.

The Indian of old knew that he could find his individual way to and/or with God apart from the community. His relationship with God was not dependent upon others. But he also recognized that his religion as a whole must be directed toward and function as a group effort; it was and remained *both* a community and an individual affair. Above all, this gave it the substance and effectiveness that only a community—a brotherhood—could muster. Individual worship and service was carried out in private acts, so that one side of the Indian's religion remained a very private thing. But group ceremonies combined their worship in such a way as to produce on the other side a functioning and harmonious community—hence their Church was never a building but people relating personally and in community to God.

If there was a significant difference between the Indian and the Christian, it was this: The Indian came, by divine providence, to know the same God as the Christian, but he knew Him only in an abstract way—leaving him prey to much wondering and superstition—while through Christ and the Bible the informed Christian can know the specific will of God in those things wherein he has made his will known. Christian missionaries ought to have recognized this, and, rather than seeking to convert the Indian should only, at his invitation, have added the specifics to the excellent religion he already had. The Christian and the Indian of old would have benefited most by simply learning from one another, each appending to his own base the new understandings of the other.

Many Indian tribes were without a definite tradition of the creation, while others had detailed oral records of it. The priests and doctors (or mystery men) were the repositories of these accounts, and only they were able to tell the legends in their fullest form.

The Indian was acquainted with all the forces of nature, but was ignorant of their origin and fearful of their causes. Furthermore, he came to recognize that the dangers which the forces threatened could not be averted by an independent act of his. Some higher power must prevent or blunt them. So he prayed continually for its help, and above all learned by this process to live respectfully and carefully.

A mental attitude such as this was fertile soil for the growth of legends or folklore, and attempts to explain the ordinary phenomena of nature gave rise to a great number of marvelous, imaginative stories. All of these had to do with the natural objects among which the Indians lived: with the heavenly bodies, the mountains, rivers, and trees, the animals, birds, and mythical people. They dealt also with a great variety of other subjects, such as history, mythology, the creation, the development of man, his emotions, his yearnings after the eternal unknown, and his fears of the elements. Out of this came a core of long-established customs, with appropriate collections of appurtenant religious articles which also passed into the keeping of priests and leaders of the tribe. It was true folklore, magnificently practiced, and it was their only historical record. Even a brief exposure to it reveals the marvelous appreciation for every created thing it gave the Indians. Their scientific knowledge will not compare favorably with the monumental insights of modern technology, but they received a reverence for life from their deductions which is most impressive!

The sun was regarded as a male person who made a daily journey from the eastern horizon to the west, there entering his lodge to pass the night. The sun's home was beyond the big water and in a pleasant country. His lodge was handsomely painted with figures of strange medicine animals, and from the tripods which stood behind it hung stupefying weapons and mysterious medicine bundles. Here, too, dwelt the moon, the sun's wife, the old woman; and in this place, according to the Blackfoot, lived also the morning star, who was the son of the sun and moon.

Among the Pawnees and a few other tribes, the evening star was the protector of fields and planting. Many tribes regarded certain bright stars as men, who started out from their heavenly lodges at sunset and made nightly journeys across the sky.

A Pawnee priest about to begin the morning star ceremony is shown in color in plate 3. The long line of gourd rattles in the background are for the others who will soon join him. An alabaster snow goose and the sacred medicine bundles were also used in the ceremony.[6]

The ancient plainsmen believed, as did the Whites until Galileo, that the earth was flat and circular, and its edges ran vertically downward. The earth was the mother, the fruitful one on whom they depended for food, drink, and a place to live. She produced the corn, the roots, and the berries, the buffalo grass, so that without the earth they would have had no food. The ground furnished a course for the water and the essential lodge pole trees, so it too was sacred. The Great Power put the earth here, and later must have put men on it. Without it nothing could live, so they prayed to it with that in mind.

The thunder, the lightning, the tornado, and the rainstorm were all of one class in the Indian's view, yet nothing else was so terrible to him as the thunder. He called it "that dreadful one," because it struck without warning, shattering a rocky crag, or felling the tallest pine or strongest animal. Usually it was described as a great bird, which flew through the air with his eyes shut, but when he opened them, the stunning lightning flashed forth. Some thought the boom of the thunder was caused by the wings of the Thunder Bird, while others thought it was his resonant call. The Thunder Bird was worshiped with elaborate ceremonials, partly because he brought the rain and made the berries large and sweet. In the autumn, the Thunder Bird went south with the other birds, but returned each spring to herald the growing grass and the blossoming flowers. There was also bitter enmity between the Thunder Bird and some of the evil underwater monsters. So thunder beings were not all bad, they brought much good, and in addition tested man's strength and endurance.

The winter was caused by the Cold Maker, whom some tribes called the Winter Man. He was as white as snow, and came from the far north riding a white horse in the midst of a snowstorm. As he passed he spread the cold and snow all over the country. In the spring the sun forced him back, so it could be seen that each one had his own power.

The wind could only be felt, but it was thought that the principal God used it as his messenger, sending it to carry his words to people, or sometimes using it to transport people to him. The Blackfeet believed the wind was caused by a great animal that lived in the mountains, and as it moved its ears backward and forward it made the wind blow in furious gusts. Wouldn't that idea bring a happy chuckle to any boy? Wouldn't the vivid image also fix itself in his mind?

The depths of the water sheltered a horde of mysterious inhabitants. Some of them had the forms of strange people, others were animals similar in appearance to those living on the land, and some were monsters! Many were lying in wait for any foolish person who ventured too far into the water, seizing and dragging them down. (Even if the monsters were actually tides or quicksand, the Indian views at least made them careful!) The bitter feud between all of them and the Thunder Bird kept them from surfacing often. If he saw one he swooped down, grasped it in his claws, and carried it aloft. Some people actually saw the Thunder Bird carrying away an underwater monster, and the Sioux believed that each of the landslips so often seen in the bluffs along the Missouri River showed where the Thunder Bird darted down to seize a water beast.

Some tribes believed that malevolent beings lived under the springs in their domain and had to be kept happy; therefore, they brought presents of various kinds and left them by the springs. Otherwise, if a tribesman should jump across a stream flowing from an unpropitiated spring, one of the evil beings might shoot him with a mysterious invisible arrow which caused some kind of disease.

Some ghosts were greatly feared. These were primarily the spirits of the scalped dead, and they often returned to the places where they had lived. There were also many untraceable stories telling of the return to life of persons who had died.

Since the Plains Indian shared his home with the animals and the birds, he acknowledged their close kinship and believed that God put them on earth to teach men valuable lessons. He accepted that all living things had a common creator, so he called them his relations—sometimes his younger brothers. He knew that in certain respects they were his inferiors, for he could usually overcome them; but he also saw they possessed God-given abilities that were sometimes keener and more to be relied upon than his own. Many were abilities which he greatly desired to possess, such as bravery, craftiness, endurance, or physical attributes. Therefore, in peace and in danger, he prayed to the animals and birds to help him, either directly by their own intervention, or by serving as instructors through which the ruler of the universe worked. Thus in the mind of the Indians animals and birds often took upon themselves a *holy* character, and in every tribe tales and traditions grew up which had for their central motif the unique powers exercised by certain creatures.

It is interesting to see how the warrior went about obtaining the help and qualities of the members of the wildlife kingdom. Some investigators have thought it amounted to no more than an Indian's superstitious belief that if he prayed or talked to the animal, it would either answer back or transmit a strange, un-determined power or ability by osmosis. This, however, is not the answer, for while the Indian did believe that the Almighty gave each of His creations some peculiar grace or power, and that these favors, at least in part, might be obtained from them by him, he knew he could only acquire them if he studied their possessors' habits and then copied them to the limit of his own ability. More broadly, once a certain animal or bird was seen as his helper through a vision, it meant studying the creature for weeks on end—until its every habit was known—and then the careful, constant practice of these same traits by the Indian for the rest of his life.[7] Accordingly, as the warrior matured, he acquired abilities for scouting, hunting, and wise living far beyond those of many other peoples.

The animals were regarded in different ways by the various tribes of the prairie, but obviously the better known a species was—whether by reason of its strength, its agility, its numbers, or its importance as food—the more likely it assumed a special character as a divine messenger.

Naturally, the buffalo headed the list. The Sioux believed that everything necessary to life, spiritual and material, was symbolically contained within the animal. The Blackfeet called it Ni-ái, which meant "my shelter and my protection," and all of the Plains tribes prayed to it. Many placed the sun-bleached skull of a buffalo bull before their sweat lodges. And upon emerging from the lodge, they lighted the pipe and offered it to the bull's head, asking it to rise from the ground, put flesh upon its bones, and run off over the prairie, so that they might have its meat to eat and its skin to use as a covering for the tipi.

The bear was also venerated, yet not so much for its strength as for its wisdom. It was believed to be invulnerable to other animals, to have the power to fend off most of the bullets or arrows shot at it, and to be able to find the herbs needed to heal itself when wounded. It could impart these same qualities

The Sioux storyteller, recalling his famed rescue of a wounded comrade (mounted warriors after
C. Russell).

to those it wished to help, and sometimes a bear restored life to persons toward whom it felt an especial friendliness. A profound reverence and respect for the bear was common to all the North American tribes.

The wolf exemplified craft in war. Scouts wore his skin when on a war party, and in Indian sign language the gesture for a scout was the sign for wolf. The animal was highly respected, and all Indians regarded it as an ally. Sometimes wolves "talked" to people, telling them what was going to happen, and informing them of the whereabouts of their enemies.

The eagle, hawk, and owl—all birds that captured their prey—typified the courage and dash needed for success in war, and were always prayed to in this wise. The raven, magpie, and chickadee were birds of great wisdom. They also talked to people, telling them of coming events, leading them to game, advising them of danger, and recommending a course of action. Certain small water birds were used as messengers by the supernatural powers. In fact, all birds were said to have some spiritual power. It was believed that the underwater people used wild fowl—ducks, geese, and swans—for their beasts of burden, and that swans often transported an Indian to the home of a principal god who had called upon that person in a dream to visit him. Fowls of all kinds were commonly placed in Blackfoot medicine bundles.

Beliefs about insects were less common; yet there was a general faith in the spiritual power of the spider. It was a wonder-worker, and it always represented intelligence. The Crows thought the butterfly imparted agility, but the Blackfeet saw it as a sleep producer and bringer of dreams. So, the Blackfoot woman would embroider a cross on a piece of buckskin and tie it to her baby's hair when she wished it to sleep, at the same time singing a lullaby which asked the butterfly to come flying about and put the child to sleep.

These and a host of similar beliefs and tales dealt chiefly with the phenomena of nature, but there were dozens of others that told of the past doings of the people, often built around a moral lesson, and showing how bravery, endurance, singleness of purpose, or some other virtue was inevitably rewarded by success.

Besides the tales and traditions which treated of the creation, nature, animals, and people, there was a class of folk story which dealt with mythical persons of great power, maliciousness, and childishness. These tales were told largely for entertainment.

Stories having a historical center described the beginnings of certain customs which had been practiced so long their point of origin was forgotten.

There was a legend to describe how the Indians, and everything they knew of, came into being.

Taken in their sum, the tales of the Indians were profound and enthralling—especially when one considers how and why they were told. To appreciate anything of their import one must move back in time and imagine he is sitting by the fire in one of the great circular lodges. Storytelling was best when it was late at night and all was still, save for muffled drumbeats and singing in the distance, and the occasional rumble of a trotting horse carrying its rider to his home. The fire flickered brightly, shedding a ruddy glow on the faces of the people who sat about it and casting their tall, swaying shadows onto the lodge walls. In the background one could just make out the sleeping places. From the lodge poles hung the awesome weapons of war. Grand costumes and saddles dangled in silent testimony from other tipi poles, and over the bed of the lodge owner hung the sacred bundle, which contained those mysterious objects which he valued the most highly of all his possessions. After a time an old man in a reminiscent mood would bend forward and refill his pipe. He lit it by a coal taken in a special manner from the fire, then uttered six prayers as he pointed the stem first to the sky, next to the earth, and finally offered it to the four points of the compass. After this the solemn words of his ancient legends flowed gravely and reverently with only the snapping of the burning wood to interrupt them. In sharing such wonderful experiences, Frank B. Linderman said he often felt "How real a thing to the believer is his religion, whatever the religion may be!"[8]

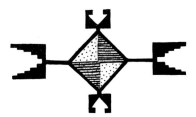

The mood and depth of the Indian can be further established by a brief explanation of how he made use of the circle and the pipe. In considering this, one is inevitably led to wonder if anyone else has ever gained as much from the daily consciousness of a circle as did the Indian.

His circular home, the tipi, was a representation of the universe, and the space outside it was symbolically the domain of the creator. Hence it is seen that he made a daily distinction between the finite world and the infinite home of God—which reminded him of the need for humility and led him to a willing dependence upon the Higher Power. Since the hair of the head was considered an extension of the soul, to release the soul of a slain enemy, he placed the victim's scalp on the end of a long pole, thrust it through the draft opening at the top of the tipi, and shook it loose; as it fell into God's domain the spirit of the slain was released to God.

When he danced, he danced in a circle—usually slowly, and employing a moderated chant. Both dance and chant were carefully paced to avoid interfering with what he was meditating upon each time he made the circle.

The sunwise or clockwise direction was almost always used, although the

Plains hand drum. *Top left,* front, with symbols for sun, four directions, and four winds (cross). *Right,* back, drum hide stretched over wooden hoop frame—15 inches in diameter, $2\frac{1}{4}$ inches thick. *Bottom,* Plains drummer (after Charles Russell sculpture).

*Top,* Sioux pipe with catlinite head carved like an eagle, wooden stem plated with porcupine quills, feather and horsehair pendants. *Bottom,* Sioux men smoking pipe socially in summer tipi.

*a*, Pawnee priest leading Calumet Pipe (Hako) Ceremony for the making of brothers, either cementing bonds within a tribe or between men from the Pawnee and other tribes. *b*, detail of the white feathered male stem—the bird parts used on the pipe are of the eagle, chief of the day; owl, chief of the night; woodpecker, chief of the trees; and duck, chief of the water. The other pipe symbolizes the female. *c*, the feather symbol of Ti-ra-wa (God). *d*, the mother corn symbol of growth. Both of these articles played important roles in the ceremony. Drawings taken from article by Alice Fletcher depicting ceremony she witnessed in 1884; also BAE Report 1904, and G. A. Dorsey, American Folklore Society Report, 1904.

counterclockwise movement was employed prior to or after a catastrophe to imitate the thunder beings who always acted in an anti-natural way. His sunwise movement always began at the south point, because the south was the source of life. From here he moved west through the joy of youth toward the setting sun. Night fell, and he saw as he approached the colder north where the white hairs were that life is made up of both night and day, good and bad. Moving on, he arrived, if he lived, at maturity, at the source of light and understanding, which taught him how to prepare for consequences, which is the east. Progressing further, he returned at last to where he began, to his second childhood, giving back his life to all life, and his flesh to the earth whence it came. Then he began the circle again. "The more you think about this," said the Sioux Black Elk, "the more meaning you will see in it."[9]

Finally, he considered all of man's lifetimes to be lived in a series of cycles, or circles. He believed there were four such ages or cycles, and concluded from the signs attending the end of the nineteenth century that we, much in accordance with current views of Jesus' Second Coming, are nearing the end of the last circle; the end of the four ages.

And now the pipe.

Tobacco was the only crop cultivated by some of the tribes. Different nations mixed it with different things, but it was often mixed with sumac leaves and the dried inner bark of either red alder, dogwood, or red willow to make a pleasant-smelling mixture known as kinnikinnick, which had none of the injurious qualities of our modern tobacco. It is said that horses would scent an Indian by this odor at a long distance. The willow bark was scraped off in long shavings, put on a piece of rawhide, and left to dry. Then, with hands greased with buffalo fat, the bark would be crushed into small particles. The grease which adhered to it helped to make it burn freely. It was rarely smoked alone because of its bitterness. They usually added, in a ritual manner, an equal part of Arikara twist tobacco and a small amount of a fragrant root or herb.

Although male Indians enjoyed smoking when they could, tobacco was in short supply. So for the most part it was saved for use in religious ceremonies, and smoking per se was practiced only on solemn occasions. There were, however, many such opportunities. The Indian smoked to arrest evil powers, to gain protection from his enemies, to bring game closer to the village, and to invoke the blessing of supernatural powers on anything of importance that he was about to undertake. Ordinarily, young men were advised not to smoke, as it would make them short-winded.

Certain spectacular pipes or pipe stems, which were seldom intended for actual smoking, were supposed to be possessed of sacred power and are known today as calumets. They derived their name from a French word meaning "reed" or "tube." Calumets were made in pairs, and were called into service by many of the tribes when peace treaties were made. It is from this custom that the term

*Top,* ancient Blackfoot ceremonial pipe with eagle head, feathers, and black hide wrapping on stem; bronze ax and pipe bowl; 40 inches long (circa 1840). *Bottom,* Blackfoot ceremonial pipe; spiral hide wrapping on stem, black horsehair in center inset with six human teeth; feathers are golden eagle; 30 inches long.

"pipe of peace" came into being. Such pipes, said to be able to compel peace, were recognized as flags of truce between warring tribes and were used by messengers as a passport. Calumets also had an important part in the adoption ceremonies and dances of the Omaha tribe. A further use of the calumet was in the Sioux sacred rite for "the making of relatives." This was a ceremony in which people were united as brothers, and was even used with members of other tribes.[10]

Ostentatious and powerful medicine pipes, kept well wrapped in sacred bundles, were regarded as powerful medicines in curing the sick, for bringing success in war, and for use with prayers for the prosperity of the people. Such pipes could only be unwrapped and put into supernatural action by their owners at certain times, and with elaborate traditional ceremonies. When not in service, they were wrapped together with rattles, paints, and other articles used in the pipe rituals in many layers of bright trade cloth or fur, and then covered by an outside wrapping of waterproof animal skin. Such bundles were hung from a tipi pole above the owner's head inside the tipi at night, and during sunny days hung outside over the lodge door or on a tripod behind the tipi. The Blackfeet believed that medicine pipes were given to them by the thunder, and spoke of them as "thunder's pipes." Theirs were perhaps the most spectacular creations of all the sacred Plains pipes, but few were made and they are hard to find today.

The preeminent ceremonial pipes are longer than other Plains pipes, ranging from thirty to sixty inches in length. Most are of the pipe-tomahawk type, with brass heads. Decorations on sacred pipes are always unusual. A special Blackfoot pipe was covered with red and green stripes, and had a cluster of black hair around the middle, which was inset with human teeth. Another had the pipe stem nearly covered with a whole eagle. A section of its center shaft was wrapped with hide and had rare, translucent white beads running in a double row along each side. The hide itself was dyed black, which dates it as having been made before 1860. Its over-all length was forty inches. The eagle was considered to be a solar bird, and a prime representative of the Great Spirit. To use his feathers and body in any ceremonial way was to bring a part of the Spirit's power down to earth for man's particular benefit.

The numerous appurtenant pieces in known Blackfoot pipe bundles included the fetus of a deer; squirrel, muskrat, mink, and bird skins; necklaces; and many other objects. The owner was expected to open a bundle at the first thunder in the spring, and when someone had vowed to make the Sun Dance with the pipestem. It was also opened when a bundle was to be transferred to a purchaser. Everyone in the tribe was supposed to profit from a bundle, but its special benefit was to the owner, giving him wisdom, status, and protection. He was, however, obliged to submit to many fanciful and demanding rules. Examples are that he was only allowed to point with his thumb and could not pick up any object that he found; he had to hold his pipe in a particular way; he must never sit on his bedding; and so forth. His wife had to make smudge every morning and shift the position of the bundle in fixed sunwise sequence, and under no condition was it to touch the ground. These seem at first to be unnecessary cautions, yet they kept the owner's mind continually on the bundle and its purpose. When about to open his pack, the owner invited an experienced ritualist to be his aide, and a few selected others to help with the singing. The ceremony itself consisted in opening the pack, in singing songs by sets of seven, and in simple dancing, each dance being a careful and impressive imitation of the actions of the animal or bird being removed from the bundle—all of which released their qualities to the group.

When a number of men met in council, they would squat on their haunches or sit cross-legged in a circle, in which position they would remain and smoke for hours. In a ring of sixty-five men, fifteen or more pipes would be going at once. Each Indian would blow the smoke toward the sky and offer a prayer—first to the Great Spirit for aid, and then to the bad spirits not to trouble him. All of this would go on for hours.

But the usual practice was to employ only one pipe for a medicine ceremony. The medicine man or host would light it with a coal from the fire and, blowing a puff of smoke toward the sky, would extend the stem heavenward as a prayer to God. Next he would point the stem toward the earth, and then to each of the "four winds," or directions—south, west, north, and east. After this he passed the pipe "with the sun" to the man on his left, who smoked in the same manner. The pipe went around until it reached the man seated at the door of the lodge. When he had smoked, it was passed back around the circle until it reached the man on the other side of the entrance, for it was traditional not to pass the pipe across a doorway. Arriving here, it was again passed to the left until it reached the medicine man or was smoked out. In this way the pipe was supposed to be constantly repeating the path of the wisdom-dispensing sun.

There were several vital thoughts which undergirded the act of smoking. The pipestem was considered to be a connecting link with the supernatural. In the very process of filling and using the pipe, all wisdom, represented by the powers of the six directions, and all things, represented by the grains of tobacco, were drawn inward to a single focal point and placed in the bowl or heart of the pipe, so that when filled the pipe contained, or really became, the universe. But it was also men, for the one who filled and smoked the pipe united himself with it and brought the wisdom and power of the six directions of space within himself. By this gathering together he ceased to be separated from them, and in another way increased in holiness. In its sum, the general approach in smoking led the assembled Indians to patient actions and considered opinions.

As he filled the pipe, the leader called upon the Great Spirit to behold it, adding that the smoke from his tobacco would cover everything upon the earth, and even reach to the heavens. He would then ask that the nation's people would be as the smoke. The pipe smoke was the bearer of a heaven-sent voice, and all the wildlife and the six directions joined with the smokers in sending it. This showed that the Indians were thinking of the soul and of death, and was a sure sign they were humiliating themselves before the Great Spirit, since they knew they were as dust before Him, who was everything and all-powerful!

Pipe smoking was also used as a solemn form of affirmation, or truthtelling. If a man sitting in a lodge told his companions an improbable story and they wanted to see if he was telling the truth, the pipe was given to a priest, who painted

Sioux warrior Standing Bear invoking wisdom of the Great Spirit by directing pipe toward heavens. He wears a splendid double-tailed eagle headdress.

the stem red and prayed over it, asking that if the man's story was true he might have a long life, but if it was false his life would end in a short time. The pipe was then filled, lighted, and passed to the man, who had seen and overheard what had been done and said. The priest then said something like this to him: "A man's mind should be straight. Accept this pipe, but remember that, if you smoke, your story must be as sure as the bowl in this pipe, and as straight as the hole through this stem. If so, your life shall be long and you will survive, but if you have spoken falsely your days are numbered." The man might then refuse the pipe, saying, "I have told you the truth; it is useless to smoke this pipe." But if he declined to smoke, no one believed what he had said; he was looked upon as having lied. If, however, he took the pipe and smoked, everyone believed him, for it was the most solemn form of oath.

Many additional customs, varying with the different tribes, were used with the pipe. A forked stick taken from a medicine bag was employed to transport a piece of burning dung or a coal used for lighting the pipe. For cleaning the pipe every man carried a slim, pointed stick about the size of a lead pencil. Ashes were carefully caught in a container and kept. Absolute quiet was to reign in the tipi when smoking was going on. Many turned the pipe in different but special ways when they received it, and some would not accept it unless it was handed to them just so. The Cheyenne thought it unlucky to touch anything with the pipe while smoking. The very old Shoshones removed their moccasins before smoking, and requested their visitors to do likewise. Some said it involved an obligation of friendship, and a wish that a disloyal smoker would always go barefoot. But the intent may have been similar to God's command to Moses to remove his sandals before approaching the Burning Bush, whereby he symbolically put the world, typified by the dirt on his footwear, behind him as he stepped onto holy ground. The narthex serves the same symbolical purpose in the church building today. It is a space that separates the worship area from the finite world. The idea is not to cut man off from the world, but for him to put it aside for a while so he can listen attentively—with an uncluttered mind—to God, who then tells him how to live wisely in his finite world.

PLATE 5.   CREE WARRIOR ▶

He wears two coup (or war honor) feathers in his fur cap, which is made of bobcat fur. Over his shoulders is a Hudson Bay blanket. The buffalo hide shirt is adorned with six porcupine quill horse tracks indicating the number of horse raids he participated in.

# Chapter 7

# RELIGION—THE PRACTICES

# OF MEDICINE

Some men among the Arapaho, and among other Indians, had special gifts. These were our priests and medicine men. They knew, each one of them, everything connected with some one of our ceremonies; they knew songs and rituals for healing the sick and for bringing success in war and hunting, for bringing rain, and for warding off storms. They performed these services for anyone in need of them, or for a whole village, and sometimes for the whole tribe.[1]

Once when I was visiting among the Osages, I got very sick with influenza. The white doctor could not cure me and I thought I might die. But the Osage medicine man performed his ceremonies for me, and boiled herbs in water, which I drank. The next day, although I was still weak, I was well again. I have known white doctors and ministers

---

◀ PLATE 6.  SIOUX WARRIOR WITH BUFFALO HORNS

The buffalo horn bonnet is one of several collected by Chief Joseph White Bull, nephew of the renowned Sitting Bull. It is assumed they were acquired during the reservation period shortly after the famous Custer battle in 1876.

Joseph White Bull, a Miniconjou Sioux, participated in the battle, and later claimed to be the one who actually inflicted the fatal shot upon Custer—a claim supported by the authority Stanley Vestal in 1934, and also by James H. Howard in a recent book entitled *The Warrior Who Killed Custer.*

According to Catlin, only a few of the most outstanding warriors in each tribe were permitted to wear buffalo horn headdresses. And so they are rare—a truth attested to by the fact that few are seen in museums and in publications.

This bonnet fur is bobcat. It has an eagle's head mounted on top, plus a quilled ring and many dyed eagle breath feathers. The side and horn feathers are hawk. The long plume at the back reveals that the wearer has made his renowned Sun Dance one or more times. The shirt in the picture is a type common to both the Sioux and the Omahas— although the shirt shown was photographed on an Omaha man in 1920 who claimed it was his grandfather's war shirt. See color plate 10.

who have special knowledge and power, and do remarkable things for the bodies and the minds of people who need their help. The work of these healers and seers is part of some overall power too great to be understood by any one people or group. No one can see more than some part of its wonder. That is why there are so many religions.[2]

The minute one moves into the realm of those areas in life which the Indian was unable to explain, he must deal with the overworked word "medicine," for the early explorers and settlers called every unusual thing the Indians did by this name—hence the priests and doctors were designated as "medicine men."

All these things which non-Indians spoke of as medicine the Indian called mysterious, which only meant that he could not explain much about them. The Indian called White whisky "medicine water," because it acted upon him in a way that he could not understand, making him dizzy, temporarily happy and drunk. In the same way he called the horse "mystery dog" and the gun "mysterious iron."

The term "medicine," as Whites used it in this connection, was derived from the French word for doctor. The early trappers referred to the man who employed healing as a *médecin*, or doctor. From calling the doctor himself *médecin*, they went on to describe his often amazing power by the same name, and the similarity in sound to the English word "medicine" made the term easy to adopt by the English-speaking peoples. So at last "medicine" came to mean an unexplainable power, and the "medicine man" the person who controlled the power. Unfortunately the notion of curing or healing became, in a measure, lost, and many concluded that Indian doctors were simply weirdly dressed "noisemakers" who actually accomplished no healing at all. This was not the case.

We should not be misled or troubled by the Plains Indian's inability to unravel questions about God and nature in scientific terms, although he surely did interpret them in superb parable form. Compared to the totality of God, the Christian likewise knows very little about Him, and must learn to live comfortably with this fact. He too does not know what God looks like, where He lives, how a being can be eternal, or how He is able to manifest His awesome powers—because man has no earthly parallels with which to compare such mysteries. All one knows about from Scripture are His qualities, and how He has acted in history on man's behalf. Actually, man ought to be pleased about this, for he would have distinct problems if he did not have a God who transcends him in every way. A God he could entirely define would not be able to do the miraculous things for him that he cannot do for himself—for example, to create him and raise him to eternal life. Thus the individual who insists upon comprehending God before he will accept Him inevitably defeats his own purposes and hopes.

Also, the word "medicine" should not be applied as a general term to describe every form of Indian mystical practice—especially since a careful examination will show there were distinct categories of practitioners; their only common bond being that they began their careers with visions and employed prayer and supplication in their approach.

It is very helpful to take a close look at the way the Indian actually understood his mysterious things, and then at the distinct categories he used to describe the men who practiced holy rites.

When used as a noun by itself, the word "mystery" or "medicine" meant something endowed with the ability to transmit power from the First Maker or his assistants to man. And when employed as an adjective-prefix, it also meant sacred, or set apart for use in religious ceremonials. Hence it compares well with the Christian understanding of the word "holy," which does not mean pure in habit or free from sin, but rather set apart by God for God's use through the rituals He has given regarding it. Thus the person or item, in spite of his or its faults, becomes, in a pictorial sense, a channel or tube through which the creator transmits His wisdom and power as He ministers to men.

Whites speak of the "Holy Bible." A consecrated Communion chalice is called "holy." Christians are described as the "body" of Christ. The sacred bundle of the Beaver Medicine of the Blackfeet was, therefore, a bundle containing many skins of birds and animals which were set apart. It was appropriately believed to have been given originally to the Blackfeet by the beavers, and was handed down from generation to generation as all holy things of all religious people are. It was only opened upon an important religious occasion, and its exposure was accompanied by a profound and traditional secret ceremonial rite.

Several channels were engaged to transmit power from God to the Indians. There were priests, who compare to Christian pastors, and whom I will often hereafter call holy men; there were doctors or herbalists, who compare to present-day physicians; there were war chiefs, who compare to White activistic prophets; and there were medicine bundles, visions, dreams, and wildlife. All of these were ways to minister to and obtain man's needs and to defeat the evil forces. For while the Indian had never heard of the Devil until "the Black-Robes" brought him to this country, he did believe there were real created things which possessed evil powers. The Kiowas, for instance, lived in great fear of the owl, and other nations feared other things, such as ghosts and thunder.

The following quote from George Bird Grinnell supports the idea of channels or intermediaries:

It is generally believed that, among the Indians of North America, the priests and the shamans, "medicine men," or doctors, are the same. This is not the case with the Pawnees. Among them the priestly office was entirely distinct from that of the doctor, and has nothing in common with it. The priest was in a sense the *medium* of communication with Ti-rá-wa; he prayed to the diety more efficaciously than could a common person, acted, in fact, as an intercessor; he knew the secrets of the sacred bundles, and when he asked anything good for the tribe, or for an individual, it was likely to be granted. His education and the power given him from above brought him into specially close relations with Ti-rá-wa, who seemed to watch over him and to listen to him when he interceded for the tribe. He was an intermediary between Ti-rá-wa and the people, and held a relation to the Pawnees and their deity not unlike that occupied by Moses to Jehovah and the Israelites.

The office of the "medicine man," shaman or doctor, had to do only with sickness or injury. He was the healer. Disease was caused by bad spirits and it was the doctor's part to drive off these evil influences.[3]

The present-day Hopi medicine men of Arizona explain their preparation for healing in a way which profoundly substantiates the general understanding by Indian holy men of themselves as "tubes." The Plains doctors may not have done exactly as they do, but the general approach was similar.

The Hopi holy men do not go immediately to a patient when called, but instead go apart to prepare themselves. The desired time is four days, but it is less when an emergency situation demands prompter attention. During the period apart they work feverishly through prayer and meditation to cleanse themselves; to get the "me" or self which impedes God out of the way so that they can be clear, clean, fit channels through which the Great Spirit can and will work. In any event it is apparent that God is seen as the healing instrument, not the man, and it's as sound a theological concept as can be imagined.

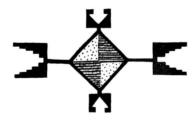

While accounts sometimes disagree about the order in which the steps of given treatments were carried out, it appears that the treatment of an illness most often began with an appeal by the individual to his personal medicine bundle. If this failed, a doctor (herbalist) was called—and then, as a last resort, the priest (holy man) was summoned.

The Blackfeet had a superstition that a doctor should not reveal his sources of inspiration, nor his methods, nor hand them down to others. But anyone could collect different kinds of herbs for their own use, and if they wanted to know the mysterious kinds of plants from which certain healing herbs were obtained, they paid a large fee to a herb doctor who showed them the "right" plants. Professional treatments with herbs followed prescribed rules. The herbalist had his method of administering them, and the patient was under strict orders during the recovery period. A doctor's fee was paid, the same as it was to the holy man. The patient's family was sometimes excluded from the ceremony, because the

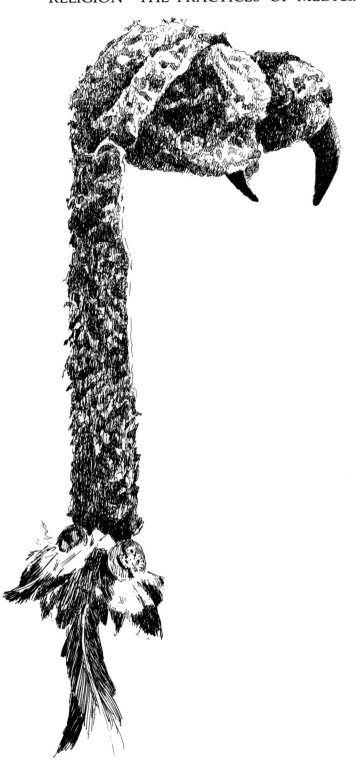

Blackfoot doctor's buffalo horn headdress dating to about A.D. 1840. The hair humps on the front of the cap are dyed in several colors. Two beaded disks are attached to the end of the tail. This is an unusual style as Blackfoot headdresses go, but it is part of a very old and authentic collection, Pasadena Museum.

presence of spectators was said to weaken the doctor's power. Yet when he was sure of success, they were quickly invited to stay!

Indians say their herb doctors obtained much of their knowledge of the different kinds of medicine plants in dreams or visions, and the informer (a being) was promised a part of any fees received. Therefore, after the herbs were dug, carefully selected offerings were deposited in the holes, and covered with dirt. Many valuable herbs were discovered by trailing sick animals to see what they ate. In particular, bears were followed, for they had "good claws for digging herbs," and they taught the herbalist many things. Wildschut spoke of the root of a plant of the carrot family which was used as ceremonial incense and a cure-all. Bears fattened themselves on it in winter.[4]

No one herbalist had all the answers. There were specialists for all the different kinds of sickness; their power being circumscribed by the limitations of their visions or dreams. And even after a man was given knowledge about how to use a certain medicine, he might have to experiment for some time to find out what it would do. A few herbs were very strong, and if used improperly would kill the victim.

In many cases of Indian medicine, the doctors often took chances and tested it upon themselves. Sometimes they died from it too!

Cheyenne and Kiowa healing included both internal medicine and minor surgery and was often highly effective, at least until the time when native practitioners ran afoul of the White man's diseases.

The doctor, in contrast to the priest, seldom wore an elaborate costume. He came to the patient's tipi in breechclout or ordinary clothes. He did have his special headdress, charms, or gadgets, which were both intriguing and spectacular. All doctors had their rattles. The plainest form was simply a gourd, but others were made of an animal bladder or more grandly of an entire eagle's head. There were also white ermine and deer claw rattles.

In a typical treatment of an ill person, the doctor built a fire, taking a coal from it and burning a twisted piece of sacred sweet grass to cleanse his hands in the smoke. Then he sang, made an application of his medicine, and, using a buffalo horn tube or applying his mouth directly to the place of the illness, sucked the evil out that was causing the pain, spitting "it" onto the ground. (One authority says that sucking drew the cleansing west wind through the patient.)[5] The patient was again sung and drummed over, put in a hot sweat bath once or twice—and usually felt better. The total time spent on the patient was determined by the seriousness of the illness. Some White informants suggest that the doctor prepared himself in advance to make a spectacular demonstration by concealing an item in his mouth that he would later spit out in public view as the evil causing the illness.

The Shoshones believed that disease was caused by a ghost that had entered the patient's body. Incantations, prayers, drums, medicine whistles, and sweat

Doctor's rattles. *Top,* rawhide rattle head with complete eagle head on handle. *Bottom,* gourd head with eagle down feathers on handle.

Blackfoot doctor sucking disease from patient's head.

lodges were used to prepare the patient, then to extract the ghost, the doctor formed a tube of his hands, applied it to the patient's mouth, and began to suck until the sick individual retched and finally belched forth the evil spirit. This was seized by the physician, shown to the spectators, sometimes in the shape of coagulated blood or some other object, rubbed between his palms, and thus killed. Cheyenne accounts mention spitting chewed herbs on the patient's bodies. Ute doctors often drove evil spirits away by stretching the patient out on the ground and scarifying (gashing) him with an eagle claw from head to heel, while a group of men sang an incantation in chorus. A Kiowa doctor learned to use wooden suction cups and melted buffalo tallow to close wounds. Part of the Blackfoot treatment involved spraying yellow paint on the ill person through eagle's wing bones.

There was no distinction of rank among doctors, only a difference in specialty. Some did extraordinary things with ailing horses. Besides aiding the sick, doctors could sometimes charm arrows for hunting and impart supernatural powers to shields. None of the doctors were believed ever to have engaged in deliberately causing the sickness or death of a fellow tribesman. Now and then a doctor's wife assisted him. Sometimes the sons or nephews of physicians followed the same profession, but as a free choice.

A prominent Sioux medicine man said that a bear told him of herbs to be used in treating adults, and that a badger revealed the remedies he employed for sick children.[6] He kept the hide of the same mink for fifty years as a container for his principal remedies. In this pouch were four small packets of herbal medicine, the packet containing the principal medicine being edged with beads. It also contained a small horn spoon without a handle for administering medicine to a child. His principal remedy was the yarrow plant. The three other remedies were for loss of appetite, headache, and for those "suffering from heart trouble or pain in the stomach." Like other medicine men, he kept a large supply of herbs at his home and carried only a small quantity on his visits to patients. In treating their patients, all doctors, at some time during the treatment, vigorously imitated the actions of their animal or bird helpers.

This Sioux doctor was also particularly successful in the treatment of fractures, in which he employed gauntlet-like splints of rawhide. The wrapping he used for a broken wrist was eight inches long. Other doctors speak of splints made of wood.

A second Sioux physician, who also received his knowledge of healing herbs from a bear, said that when summoned to treat a sick person he put on a necklace consisting of a strip of hide to which were attached two small bags of medicine, one edged with blue beads, the other with pink and white beads, and a bear's claw. He pressed the claw into the flesh of the patient in order that the medicine might enter more readily and be more effective.[7]

A third Sioux doctor's medicine pouch was made of four antelope ears and

*Left*, doctor's medicine bag made of badger skin with quilled paws. *Right*, rattle with handle wrapped in white ermine skin, with gourd at top and dangler of cut deer claws.

had a buckskin top, the whole being decorated with wrapped quill bands and done in typical Sioux colors and patterns. Inside were seven small hide packets of herbs, the entire foot of an eagle, and a small piece of elk horn. On the inner edge of each bag was a small mark by which the owner identified its contents. He used the eagle claw in treating scrofulous sores, especially on the neck. In this treatment he scraped the surface of the claw, mixed the scrapings with hot water, and applied the mixture to the skin. The piece of elk horn was said to be an effective remedy for broken bones, but the manner of its use is not known.[8]

Walter McClintock, in *The Old North Trail*, lists thirty-four herbs used by the Blackfeet in combating a dozen common ailments. They treated colds, snow blindness, eye diseases, stomach troubles, snake and rabid dog bites.[9]

The Kiowa had a renowned society of Buffalo Men, one or more of whom went on every raid. When members of a war party were wounded, the Buffalo Men would shake their rattles and their buffalo tails and sing their special song. They also painted their faces with red stripes, running horizontally across the mouth, and painted similar stripes on their horses. They not only claimed great success in healing the wounded, but in addition became outstanding war chiefs.

There are hundreds of cures set forth in literature by and about Indians, and more than enough to substantiate their superb healing abilities. It has been said that their treatments were crude and foolish; the patients either died or recovered unexplainably with no real thanks to the doctor. Yet the Indian accounts belie this, suggesting that the Plains doctors attained a high degree of competence for their limited means, and accomplished more than other isolated civilizations of their time. Both Indian and White witnesses attest to dozens of remarkable cures. In speaking of the doctors of the Plains, Catlin reports that "many of them acquire great skill in the medicinal world, and acquire much celebrity in their nation."[10]

It is true that much of the treatment by both doctors and holy men was aimed at heightening the attitude of faith already possessed by the Indians. In this sense they were also psychologists, and realized as medical people do today that a patient's healthy attitude and faith has a great deal to do with his recovery.

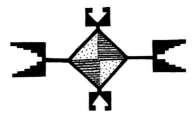

When the doctor failed, or if in the beginning it was plainly seen that the ordinary treatment would be of no avail, the priest was called. These were the men who wore the awesome costumes and performed the enthralling rites so

Indian doctor holding a number of healing instruments which were actually used, although he would probably employ only one at a time: the appropriate one for a specific disease. In his left hand is a buffalo tail switch. In his right hand is a fur-wrapped stick used as a love charm. Around his neck he wears a heavily beaded rock medicine. The quilled otter skin medicine bag on his belt is a type called a "breast hanging." On his head he wears a plumed doctor's hat. All items shown are Crow.

common to Plains literature. Unfortunately, few White men were permitted to see those profoundly sacred moments when the priests worked, and until recently the Indians, quite rightly, kept the details of these most private matters to themselves.

Plenty Coups tells of a warrior who was brought home bleeding badly and near death. After the decision was made by the village leaders to attempt to heal the man, a crier rode through the camp to give exact instructions as to what the people were to do. In other words, everyone joined in; the congregation united with its member in need.

Then the holy man, named Bird Shirt, who was also referred to as "the Wise One," took his medicine from its bundle. It was a whole wolfskin with the head stuffed. The legs of the skin were painted red to their first joints, and the nostrils and a strip below the eyes were also red. After this, Bird Shirt painted himself to look like his medicine, the wolfskin. His legs to the knees, his arms to their elbows, his nostrils, and the strips below his eyes were coated with red, while he sang steadily with the beating drums. He painted his head with clay until it looked like that of a buffalowolf, and made ears with clay that could not be told from a real wolf's ears. In his actions he imitated the wolf—and he intensified these as he approached closer and closer to the man to conduct his ritual—which was successful, for the patient recovered.[11]

The best-known priest's costume is one described by Catlin, who saw it in action on a priest in a Blackfoot camp, and painted a famous portrait of the owner.[12] A man had been shot, and was lying on the ground in a condition that offered him no hope of recovery. Yet the Bear Cult priest "had to be called." Several hundred spectators were assembled around the patient in a large ring by the time he arrived. A deathlike hush came over the crowd, "and nothing was to be heard, save the light tinkling of the rattles upon his dress, as he slowly moved through the avenue left for him."

He entered the circle with his body in a crouching position, and with a slow step. His body and head were entirely covered with the skin of a yellow bear, the head of which served as a mask, the huge legs and claws of which were dangling on his wrists and ankles.

Attached to the bearskin were the skins of many deformed animals, hence medicine beings—snakes, frogs, and bats—beaks, toes, and nails of birds—hoofs of deer and antelope—in fact some part of almost everything that swam, flew, or ran in his part of the world.

In one hand he shook a frightful rattle and in the other brandished a profusely adorned medicine spear. To all of this he added Indian yelps and the appalling grunts, snarls, and growls of the grizzly bear, and guttural incantations to the good and bad spirits, dancing around and over his patient—and rolling him about in every direction.

It lasted a half hour, till the patient died, and the priest danced off to his

Two of three pieces of the complete medicine paraphernalia of a Sioux priest. The top piece consists of a sacred flute, bow, arrows, and rattle—laden with fur and beads. The lower piece is a buffalo hide shield with painted symbols, red felt ribbons, herb pouches, eagle feathers, painted beads, and wooden bear claws.

The third piece of the Sioux medicine outfit shown left. It consists of a pouch stuffed with buffalo grass, a rawhide case enclosing a stuffed weasel or "fisher," and a paint pouch filled with sacred red paint. The beads are painted with dots and some are dentalium. The weasel is exposed for graphic purposes only. In actual use it would be either kept in the case or entirely removed for a ceremony.

tipi to hide his mysterious dress away. Catlin was so impressed that he went to great lengths to obtain the priest's outfit for his personal collection.

A truly regrettable fact is that all but a few of the great medicine garments were either buried with their owners or burned at their death. Even museums with large collections are often in short supply in such items.

There are, however, fine medicine bundles in several museums and in a few private collections. The rare and complete paraphernalia of a Sioux priest has been detailed on pages 120–21. It consists of three stupendous pieces—a sacred flute, bow, and rattle; a buffalo hide shield covered with paint symbols, red felt ribbons, bags, feathers, and claws; and stuffed medicine pouch and stuffed weasel case. Everything is adorned with spectacular trade beads, and wonderful items are appended everywhere.

Drums played such a vital part in every healing ceremony that it is important to understand why they were used. The round form, as usual, represented the entire universe, and its steady beat was its pulsing heart. It was as the voice of the Great Spirit, which stirred men and helped them to understand the mystery and power of all things; it soothed the tortured mind, and brought healing to the suffering body.

Grinnell tells us that the more serious diseases which the Indian did not comprehend, and for which they had no medical treatment, were believed to have been caused by evil spirits. These must be driven away by the dream power of the doctor, who relied for help on this power and not on any curative agents. His treatment consisted of burning sweet-smelling vegetation to purify the air, of singing and praying to invoke the help of the evil spirits, and of sucking and brushing off the skin of the patient to remove the mechanical causes of the disease. "Usually," Grinnell said, "such treatment gives no relief and the patient dies, but in wounds or other injuries these doctors have a success which oftentimes is very remarkable."[13]

---

PLATE 7.   THE VISION SEEKER ▶

A Crow youth alone in an eerie wilderness. His body is daubed with white clay, which he has applied to purify himself so as to become fit for God's use. He holds sage, a sacred plant, in his hand; and the buffalo's skull, with its celestial and longevity symbols, also rests on a bed of sage. After four days of fasting and prayer, his vision has arrived in the form of an enormous golden eagle carrying a boy in his giant claws. The eagle will henceforth be the young man's special helper, and as he seeks to become more and more like the great solar bird, he will indeed come to be a great leader and protector of his tribe.

After a great deal of research, Robert Lowie concluded that the commonest primitive theory of disease was that it was caused by a foreign object in the patient's body, "hence the physician tried to extract it, usually by suction, exhibiting to the patient and his relatives the splinter, thorn, or whatever had supposedly caused the problem." A Crow with the dubious name of Bull All the Time cured several patients by sucking at the afflicted parts with a pipestem and pulling out, respectively, a bone, a black beetle, and a morsel of meat.

Father Nicholas Point felt that treatments by Indian doctors were applied in a manner "best calculated to degrade human nature." Nevertheless he sets forth a most captivating description of the treatment process. "If, for example, the medicinal power was attributed to a bear claw, and deemed applicable to the treatment of a given wound, the medicine man hurled himself upon the poor patient as a bear upon his prey, imitating as closely as possible the roaring and the fury of the animal. If he was called upon to cure an internal malady, he sucked vigorously at what was thought to be the spot on the surface of the body directly above the internal malady. Then, like a man holding the malady in his mouth, he retired with violent gyrations, or vomited what he claimed was the malady he had just sucked from his patient. If his medicine was that of a wolf, the medicine man, to give thanks to his wolf for a cure so marvelous, but so perilous to him, began to howl like a wolf."[14] The most commonly practiced medical or surgical operation he saw was that of "breathing." This operation consisted in breathing or blowing on a wounded limb or on some part of the body thought to correspond to the internal malady. "This is done with such comical seriousness and with such violence that one can only avoid breaking out into laughter by thinking of the soul of the dying patient." He added that the reputation of a successful medicine man was rapidly enhanced, until finally "foolish credulity accords to the most dishonorable impudence the most coveted of titles, that of one 'strong in medicine,' which carries with it much more prestige than the title of a doctor." To be "strong in medicine" was to be simultaneously "a prophet, a miracle-worker, a kind of pontiff."[15]

The priests frequently moved beyond their curing rites to the realm of prophecy. Catlin knew of medicine men who foretold the arrival of visitors, the coming of storms, and the approach of enemies. Many could do astounding feats of magic and juggling. Some medicine men had the special power of tipi shaking.

---

◀ PLATE 8. THE GOOD OMEN

Three Crow warriors on their way to a council meeting sight an eagle carrying his captured game, a good omen indicating the efforts of the council and the war raid to follow will be successful. Adapted from photograph by Curtis.

Sioux priest treating patient with sacred sage brush and hide rattle.

One such man, bound and placed inside a small tipi within a lodge, sang and called upon the spirits that could tell him what he wanted to know. When the voices of the spirits were heard talking to him, the tipi shook as if a high wind were blowing, and the lodge poles creaked. After that, the thongs which bound him were found to be untied. Then he could tell where a lost child was, or, in the old days, where buffalo were and what enemy was approaching. White people, as well as Indians, saw this ceremony performed and called it too strange and wonderful to be explained.

The Assiniboines believed that the spirits of the dead journeyed toward the east, and there were holy men among them who claimed they had power to bring the spirits back. So when a sick person was in a coma, a holy man was called in and a sacrifice made, after which he worked his medicine. Stripping to clout and moccasins, the holy man painted his whole body with white clay to resemble a ghost. In each hand, he carried an awesome rattle. First he sang several songs, and then, while the drummers beat time, he ran toward the east for some distance. He returned, and if he felt what he did was successful, explained that he believed he had headed off and captured the spirit. If the patient came out of the coma, the effectiveness of the cure was proven, and the spirit was surely brought back.

Whatever struck the Indian as mysterious was considered to be holy. The word was applied to both persons and things. Thus a Crow tribesman, even though not a healer, who magically lured deer into a corral was described as a holy man, while in their legends the same title was applied to heroes and witches. Again, an inanimate object, because of its oddity, was often treated as a medicine person. A Crow who found a peculiarly shaped rock suggestive of an animal would treasure it, paint it, grease it, wrap it up with his finest beads and other offerings, and hang it around his neck as his guardian protector. Curiously shaped "buffalo calling stones" were collected by the Blackfeet, and will be considered in more detail further on. Periodically, an owner would pray to his rock medicine to grant him safety, long life, and wealth, and however one looks at it, it did, by *reminding* him to conduct himself in such a way as to ensure his chances.

The Crow warrior Two Leggings revealed that the use of a rock medicine depended on the instructions the dreamer received.[16] Some rocks were war medicines, some helped to steal horses, others were used for doctoring or simply to gain wealth and live a long life. The Crow name for rock medicine was "bacoritse." It was applied to all peculiarly shaped rocks, and particularly to all fossils (ammonites and baculites) found on the surface of the earth. All rocks to which this term applied were sacred, but they were not all considered holy. This distinction is vital, because all "rocks" that were considered to be authentic holy medicine were first seen in dreams and visions.

Taken in its totality, the practice of "medicine" was a religious act, in which the Indian herbalists, doctors, and priests understood themselves to be channels or tubes through which, after proper cleansing, the Great Spirit would work. All

*a*

*b*

*c*

T. E. Mails

healing came from God and was accomplished by Him, and the doctor's glory came from his successful association with the Wonder-Worker from above.

The administration of medicine in general had a psychological basis, with recovery based in a large sense upon the patient's faith in the Indian healing process. The Indians did discover many beneficial herbs, and they practiced some minor surgery. Yet their knowledge of the body was limited, and their skills overall were no match for modern medicine.

In the end, one must praise what they achieved with such limited means, and should also remember that present-day Indians often prefer out of experience to be treated by their own doctors and priests—perhaps because they lack understanding, or perhaps because religion and the direct association with God is so much a part of their native process.

◄

a, medicine necklace made of bear claws carved from buffalo hoofs with sacred stone pendant. b, Nez Percé doctor's rattle with beaded hide handle, eagle down feathers, and buffalo hoof clappers—dated 1887. c, extremely rare Sioux fertility pole fetish with seven beaded amulets tied to a 21-inch-long rawhide strap. From the top down they are a purse placed upside down to symbolize the tribe's goods flowing freely to all, a horse symbol for the successful buffalo hunt and horse raid, a pair of turtles and lizards to symbolize the male and female continuance of life, and a knife case to symbolize continued hide preparation and crafts. It can be seen in color in plate 4. Frances Densmore saw Sioux women in 1911–14 with many beaded turtles worn on their belts as fertility charms.

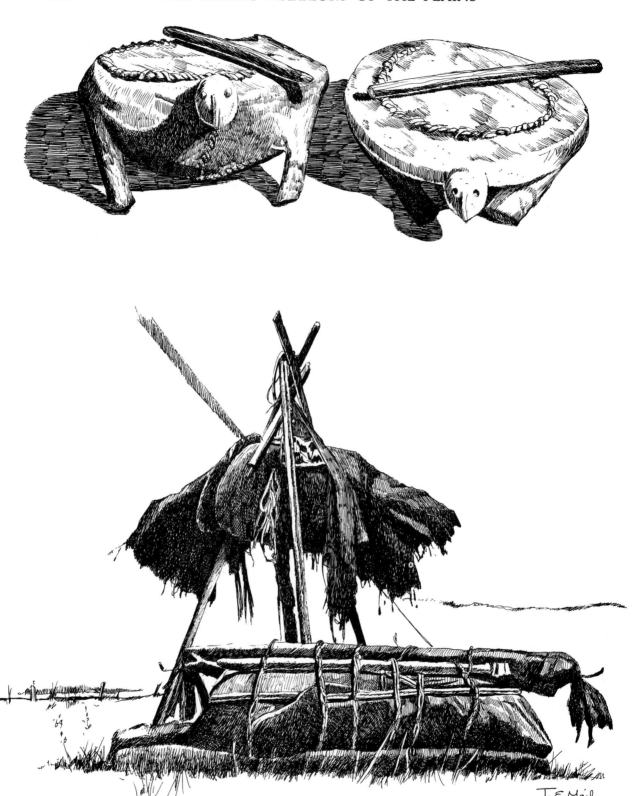

*Top,* buffalo-skin turtle drums used in Mandan ceremony given to thank God for favors granted. *Bottom,* Beaver Medicine Bundle of Blackfoot Mad Wolf used in ceremony to restore health.

# Chapter 8

# RELIGION—VISIONS AND
# PERSONAL POWER

The first hambeday, or religious retreat, marked an epoch in the life of the youth which may be compared to that of confirmation or conversion in Christian experience. Having first prepared himself by means of the purifying vapour bath, and cast off, as far as possible, all human or fleshly influences, the young man sought out the noblest height, the most commanding summit in all the surrounding region. Knowing that God sets no value upon material things, he took with him no offerings or sacrifices, other than symbolic objects, such as paints and tobacco. Wishing to appear before Him in all humility, he wore no clothing save his moccasins and breechclout. At the solemn hour of sunrise or sunset, he took up his position, overlooking the glories of earth, and facing the "Great Mystery," and there he remained, naked, erect, silent, and motionless, exposed to the elements and forces of His arming, for a night and a day or two days and nights, but rarely longer. Sometimes he would chant a hymn without words, or offer the ceremonial "filled pipe." In this holy trance or ecstasy the Indian mystic found his highest happiness, and the motive power of his existence.[1]

In commenting on the matter of inspiration from above, Indians said that while the White men had their new ideas, the Indians had their dreams or visions; thus to them anyone's inventions were not the achievement of a creative human genius after all, but the gift of a Spirit that had revealed to the "inventor" just how the apparatus was to be constructed. The human inventor deserved no praise, and works or wonder from above were to be expected as the norm of the life lived in faith. Again, the emphasis fits the Christian viewpoint very well: in all things giving thanks to God for His providential mercy!

Because they believed them to be given by God, the Plains Indians attached a crowning importance to visions. Most of the men went frequently to lonely, mystery-shrouded spots in order to obtain a divine revelation. Crow tribesmen did report that they received unsolicited favors when in danger, and that occasionally a spirit came unannounced to befriend a mortal. But the normal procedure for obtaining supernatural help was to go into solitude, to fast and thirst for from two to four days, and to beg the spirits to take pity on the sufferer. To accelerate the answer, an adult Crow seeker often cut off a small piece of a finger of his left hand or in some other way abused his flesh as a sacrificial gesture.

Although every person desperately wanted a revelation, not all were able to obtain one. Tribal tradition compelled the vision seekers to admit their failures to the camp leaders, and seekers were taught to fear the consequences if they did not, for something terrible was sure to happen to them sooner or later. So to avoid condemning such a one to prolonged anxiety, most tribes resolved the dilemma by permitting a successful visionary to sell part of his power to less fortunate and desperate tribesmen. By the sale, he adopted them just as his vision helper had adopted him. He sold them a part of his bundle or made each of his new disciples a replica of his sacred paraphernalia. He also taught them his sacred songs, and warned them against the breach of any taboo associated with his medicine. All of this was done for a fee. It was not the preferred way, yet enough for a man to make his entrance into the social pattern of his tribe. Later on the adopted one might still be blessed through a vision with his own helper and bundle.

Plains elders cultivated an atmosphere which prompted their children to seek a revelation at an early age, either directly or indirectly. A boy grew up hearing constantly that all success in life had its beginnings in visions; hence he would go away to fast, praying for a powerful benefit. A mature man or woman would also seek a vision whenever a special need arose.

One could easily question what was really seen on the vision quests, but the Indian firmly believed in the reality and tangibility of the visions he experienced. Even so, he would be the first to admit that the way for the receipt of a vision was greatly helped by the exhaustive mental and physical conditioning which preceded the trip. Actually the preparation began with the strong emotional impulse the child received from his parents as they goaded him continually about the need for a vision. Then his seclusion in a lonely and dangerous spot and his fasting and self-mutilation further intensified his emotional state. In addition to these intensifications, the legends told by his people and the accounts of the fantastic, prosperous experiences of contemporary tribesmen etched themselves on his mind and helped to shape and interpret the impressions that finally came to him in his first vision.

The Sioux called vision seeking "crying," or "lamenting." It was a ritualistic way of praying which was very important, and indeed stood at the center of their religion, for from it they received many good things.[2]

In the old days Sioux men and women "lamented" all the time. But they believed that what was received through these prayers was determined in part by the character of the person who did it, for it was only those people who were of exemplary character and were well prepared who received the truly great visions, which were later interpreted by the holy men, and which in the end gave strength and health to the nation. Therefore, it was very important for the person who wished to "lament" to receive aid and advice from a holy man so that everything would be done correctly. The great Sioux chief Crazy Horse received most of his power through the "lamenting" which he did several times a year, and even in the winter when it was more difficult than ever. As a result he received visions of many helpers, and from each of these he obtained "much power and holiness."

Some Indians received a vision when they were very young and lacked the experience to cope with it, so they went again to "lament" that they might understand it better. Warriors "lamented" whenever they wished to strengthen themselves for a great ordeal, such as the Sun Dance or the warpath. Some people did this in order to ask a favor of the Great Spirit, such as His curing a sick relative; and then they also "lamented" as an act of thanksgiving for the gifts which the Spirit gave them in response. Assuredly the most important benefit from "lamenting" was that it helped the Indian realize his oneness with all things, to know that all things were his relatives; and then in behalf of these to pray to the Great Spirit that He might give him further knowledge of the One who is the source of all things, yet vastly greater.

The following is a summary of some of the more vital details of vision seeking:

1. The all-powerful "medicine" believed needed by every young man before taking the war trail was obtained chiefly through visions, which provided him with helpers from the elements and from the bird or animal kingdoms. Medicine could also be obtained by purchase or gift, but it was never so effective as that which was personally earned.

2. Records show that vision seekers began as early as age nine, although dream seeking could go on for years before a satisfactory one was obtained. The honesty involved was of prime importance. No Indian would risk deluding himself about a vision. The result would be a catastrophe, and bad luck would plague his every step! Being so convinced of this, his thought patterns led him so as to guarantee it would be so!

3. Advance preparations sometimes included fasting, minor physical sacrifices, and sweat baths. A newly tanned robe painted with white clay, undoubtedly to emphasize purity, was usually taken along. A medicine bundle of known potency might be taken, and Sioux records tell of human and buffalo skulls being employed. This last was more common to adult quests, however.

4. Vision seeking was carried out in an area well calculated to enhance the entire purpose. It was high, thus closer to the One-Above. It was away, so as to make the seeker self-dependent. It was sought in an area with ever present risks. There must be possible contact with fierce animals or birds, there must be danger of falls, etc. These made their inevitable contribution to the mental state

necessary for a proper vision. The more rugged and mysterious the country, the more eerie the noises, the better!

5. Immediately prior to reaching the actual location where the vision would be sought, these things were done (again remembering they were common practices, but not by any means a rule): They bathed, and cleansed themselves meticulously. This included sweat baths, steam bathing, and purification in the smoke from pine needles or sage. Then they painted themselves with white clay.

6. At the spot of seeking, they built beds of flat rocks, sometimes covering them with pine branches or with sweet sage and ground cedar—all materials which had sacred qualities. They also made physical sacrifices of the flesh, which they believed represented ignorance, and began praying.

7. Vision seeking continued from one to five days (four was the standard number), during which (although violations of this are on record) neither food nor water was taken. The Sioux often set up a center post, to which offerings were tied, and four other posts with cloth flags tied to them—in the form of a cross—and between which they walked—so slowly that a "round" often took an hour or more.

8. Vision quests were not always successful, and some gave up quickly.

9. Women who "lamented" first purified themselves in a sweat lodge. They were helped by other women, but did not go up on a high and lonely mountain. They only went to a hill or a valley, for they were women, and needed protection.

10. It is imperative to recognize that, in the Indian mind, going for a vision was responding to a call from the Great Spirit. They believed that in sending information to them through a helper, the Spirit was calling them to reflection and service—just as God called Abraham and blessed him in order that he might be a blessing to others, Genesis 12:1–3. Any Christian should also know that prayer is not something he does on his own, but rather a response to God's indications that He knows the man needs to talk with Him.

The vital factors in vision seeking were found in tribal conditioning, the purification rites, and the location. In effect, the individual cleansed himself in mind and body to make himself like the priest; a fit tube through which the One-Above might work. Most importantly, the earthliness was removed by his purification, so it would not impede Him in any way.

The crowning point is that it worked! Incredibly powerful visions did come which performed wonders for the warrior, and many included predictions of the future so marvelous and accurate as to leave one in awe. The results more than justified the practice, and one can easily understand how young men embraced the method so enthusiastically as they did. And one should never forget that the preparation played as essential a part in the man's life as the ultimate vision itself.

As stated earlier, the exciting beings who came to befriend men and women in their endless vision quests varied enormously in character. Buffalo, elk, bears, eagles (sometimes conceived as birds producing thunder by flapping their wings), and other birds constantly figured in their scenes, but so did the lowly beasts such as dogs, rabbits, mosquitoes, and mice. Celestial patrons were also frequent, stars figuring prominently among the Pawnees. Fanciful creatures of more or less human shape likewise appeared in visions. Sometimes the helper came in human guise, but in disappearing assumed his true shape or otherwise gave a clue to his identity.

In his first stupendous mountaintop vision, Plenty Coups of the Crows received guidance from a certain "Dwarf-Chief."[3] The chief said that he could give the Indian boy nothing. He already possessed the power to become great if he would but use it. He was to cultivate his senses and to use the powers which Ah-badt-dadt-deah had given him. Then, he would go far! "The difference between men," said the dwarf, "grows out of the use, or non-use, of what was given them by the Divine Being in the first place."

In amplifying this, the Dwarf-Chief stated that all men have a natural power to cope with life's demands within them. Plenty Coups had a will, and he must learn to use it; to make it work for him. He should sharpen his senses as he sharpened a hunting knife, remembering, in example, that a wolf smells things better than the Indian boy does because he has learned to depend upon his nose. "It tells him every secret the winds carry because he uses it all the time and makes it work for him."

Plenty Coups would be given nothing special, not even the usual medicine bundle, because he already possessed everything he needed to become great.

In going over all this afterward, the Indian boy saw and understood that whatever he accomplished would be by self-development under God. He had a strong will and he would be successful if he used it wisely.

In a second vision, Plenty Coups was told exactly how he was to develop these powers and abilities.[4]

He was made aware of the tiny chickadee, who was least in strength but strongest of mind among his kind. This little speck of a bird was willing to work to gain wisdom, and he was an exceptional listener. Nothing escaped his ears, which "he had sharpened by constant use." Wherever others talked together of their successes or failures, the chickadee was there listening. But in all his listening he never intruded, never spoke in strange company, and never missed a chance to learn from others. He gained success and avoided failure by learning how others succeeded or failed, and thus acquired happiness without great trouble to himself. "There was scarcely a place he did not visit, hardly a person he did not know, yet everybody liked him because he minded his own business—or pretended to."

After that, Plenty Coups' helper was the chickadee, and in memory of the dream he kept the stuffed skin of one with him always, tying it beneath his left braid just back of his ear before a war party or horse raid.

Now and then just a color or a design seen in a vision became the visible embodiment of a man's power. If so, he painted it on himself, his clothing, his arrows, his horse, and whatever else he could. As in the case of other helpers, this was done to keep it alive and dominant in his mind and heart, for if he became lazy or careless he knew it would lose its power to sustain life and health. He knew that neglect caused divinely infused power to seep quietly away—like water running from a small hole in a canteen—until at last an awareness of its loss burst upon the apathetic owner, and he panicked in a belated admission of his plight!

Whatever was received in the revelation, the helper being or design acted thereafter in a father-child kind of relationship. He usually taught the seeker a sacred word power song, instructed him as to how he must dress in battle, and frequently imposed certain taboos in diet or behavior. If a man was to become a doctor, he was told what medicines or curing devices he must use. A budding prophet would be given ceremonies which would bring him special wisdom. It was evident from the past history of other tribesmen that any infraction of the rules laid down by the helper could destroy the guardian's protection and bring about a dire calamity.

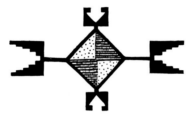

Once he received it, the Indian always carried a token of his vision with him, and he painted it in symbolic fashion on various things such as his shield cover, clothing, and tipi. But the most effective concentration of power came with the assemblage of his medicine bundle. These were utterly fantastic and captivating sets of all the sacred objects shown to the Indian in his vision or visions. A Pawnee bundle always contained as a minimum one pipe, tobacco, paints, certain birds and corn, plus the special things unique to each man. Crow bundles came to be the grandest assemblages of all, yet every tribe had sumptuous tribal bundles which, it is said, "accomplished things which would not be believed had they not been witnessed by many people." The opening of such bundles and the treatment of their contents were accompanied by scrupulously observed traditional rites, each so secret that few were ever observed by White men.

A sacred-bundle complex undergirded the entire Pawnee political organization. Each of the thirteen Skidi villages owned a bundle, which had to be opened at the first thunder in the spring, when its keeper made offerings and went through the traditional rites. Four of the bundles were preeminent, and a fifth, associated with the evening star, took absolute precedence. The priests in charge of these preeminent bundles, rather than the titular chiefs, held supreme authority over the tribe. Normally, the priests took turns in assuming responsibility for the welfare of the people for the period of a year, and specifically for the success of the tribal buffalo hunts. If these hunts went awry in any way, the Evening Star priest was asked to intervene on behalf of his officiating colleague.

A Cheyenne doctor's medicine bundle and its contents (see also next two illustrations). It remained in use through several generations, including the early reservation period—up till 1900 or so. *a,* the shiny black bag itself is made of cowskin, with the fur left on. The top edges and sides are beaded, with the top border consisting of four-pointed stars and of feathers. Most of the beads are different tones of blue. It is 12 x 8 inches, and 8 inches thick when stuffed with all its items. *b,* a 10-inch long deer tail switch used for brushing patients off, and considered very holy. *c,* a bracelet, consisting of two grizzly bear claws mounted on a German silver band. *d,* a medicine rattle made of a buffalo bladder and buffalo tail. These were the most prized type for medicine use, and are extremely rare today.

The Pawnee priesthood was strictly hereditary, passing from its holder to the next of male kin in the maternal line.

The objects within any medicine bundle were believed to be the actual dwelling places of the dreamer's helpers. In the Crow tradition certain things in a medicine bundle always meant the same: Horsehair represented the hope for horses, elk teeth or beads meant wealth, and a strip of otter skin indicated water, because the otter was the chief of all water animals. Further, some Crow warriors purchased powerful medicines from well-known holy men or renowned warriors to add to their own bundles because they wanted the proven additional power and sacred helpers. In such cases an owner would rarely duplicate all of his bundle, and even then retained a little power over his copies, as was believed to be right.

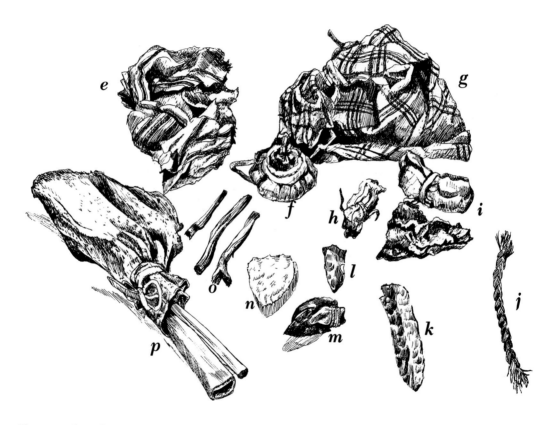

Cheyenne bundle contents continued. *e*, a calico cloth containing bits of pulverized grass. *f*, a small, greasy buckskin wrapper containing a white substance—like dried buffalo dung. *g*, a calico bag containing a large quantity of kinnikinnick. *h*, a small skin with ground root inside. *i*, two bladder skins which were tied together in the bundle. The top one holds a few sage leaves, and the bottom one powdered red paint. *j*, an 8-inch braid of sweet grass. *k*, a 5-inch stone lance point. *l*, an old stone arrow point. *m*, a fetish, consisting of an eagle claw, the fetish stone, and an old, blackened stone arrow point. *n*, a white stone arrow point. *o*, three root sticks ranging from 4 to 6 inches in length. *p*, a soft white buckskin bag containing ground leaves, a 9-inch pointed wood paint stick, and an 8-inch bone with one end wrapped with sinew—used as either a pipe or a sucking tube.

The contents of a bundle could only be replaced or duplicated according to certain rules. For example, the Indians believed that the mystic power with which a bundle was endowed did not release itself to men to its fullest extent until it was "brought to life" by the singing of songs and the performance of the appropriate ceremonies. Therefore, when a bundle was sold or duplicated, the songs and rituals were also passed on to the new owner.

William Wildschut concluded, after years of study and investigation, that it was not possible to classify the great variety of Crow Indian bundles on the sole basis of either similarity of contents or similarity of functions. Bundles that served the same general functions often differed markedly in what they contained. Other bundles containing sacred objects of similar appearance served a variety

Cheyenne bundle contents continued. *q*, a large, cotton cloth sack containing two smaller bags with bright, powdered yellow paint in them. *r*, a large cotton sack holding a small piece of brightly colored calico cloth, many large dark-brown seeds, and a 6-inch pointed stick. *s*, a red-daubed buckskin pouch containing a grayish-green pulverized wood—as from a decayed log or an anthill. *t*, a dark-red buckskin bag containing gray-green ground leaves. *u*, a buckskin bag filled with powdered red paint. *v*, a beige cotton cloth wrapped around several roots—which are broken into small pieces. *w*, a colored cloth holding the wood of a rotted log, and immersed in the wood a flat, 1-inch diameter round stone, which is translucent, and reddish brown in color. *x*, a cloth bag filled with a brownish-purple powder which turns a dull red when mixed with water. It is a plug-cut tobacco bag, with the seal of North Carolina on it—Marburg Brothers.

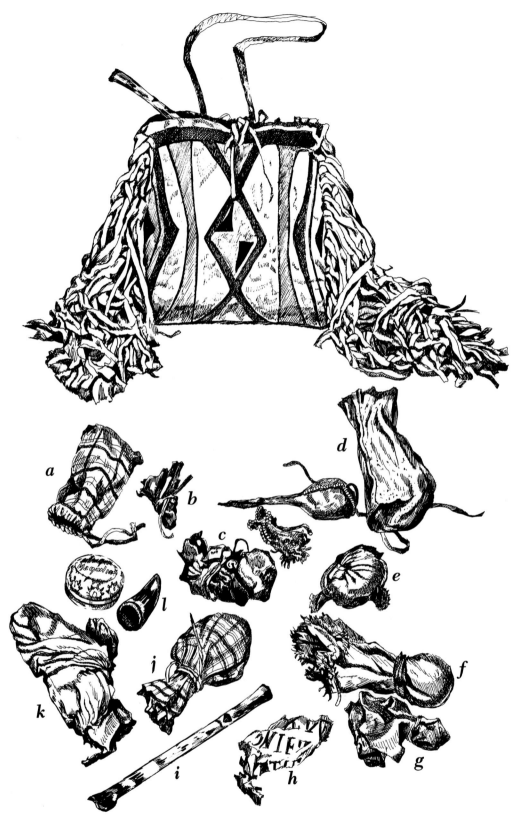

of uses. However, he was able to divide Crow medicine bundles into the following limited number of meaningful categories:[5]

1. *Sun Dance Bundles.* These were the only individually owned bundles employed in a ceremony in which the entire tribe participated. Much remains to be said about the Sun Dance, but the Crow dance was never given as a tribal act of adoration to the sun. It was essentially a ceremony in which the participants hoped to receive visions which would enable them to gain revenge upon their enemies. The Sun Dance bundle, therefore, may be considered the principal war medicine bundle of the Crows. However, unlike other war bundles, it was seldom if ever taken on war expeditions.

2. *War Medicine bundles.* These were employed to bring success in warfare and in horse stealing. They contained the material representations of the original maker's vision and were therefore of many varieties. Of these, the hoop medicines and arrow medicines could be considered subclasses.

3. *Shields.* Painted and decorated shields, at one time numerous among the Crows, were important war medicines. Some could even be used to predict the outcome of a raid or battle.

4. *Skull Medicine Bundles.* The principal article in each of these bundles was a human skull. They approximated the Sun Dance bundles in sacredness, but they were used for many purposes. At one time they were numerous, but by 1927 were very scarce because they had usually been buried with their last owners. The younger generation became afraid to handle them or to keep them in their tents or cabins.

When the wrapping on a scaffold burial wore away, a relative would sometimes take home the skull. On occasion the relative would also have a dream in which the deceased would explain certain medicine power possessed by the

◄

A Shoshone doctor's medicine bundle. *Top,* the painted rawhide carrying case. *a,* calico bag containing a round metal can of Magnolia candies, Provo, Utah, date 1900. Can contains a calico cloth which holds a piece of newspaper wrapped around a peyote button. *b,* greasy buckskin pouch which once contained powdered red paint. *c,* two very old buckskin bags tied together. One contains ground weeds and the other powdered black paint. *d,* buckskin bag covered with powdered yellow paint inside and out. Contains long buckskin thong with two brass beads in middle, medicine pouch with translucent white beads on edges, and rattle made from bladder with edging of white beads. *e,* cotton cloth containing buckskin bag soaked in red paint containing in turn a strange sacred stone worn smooth. *f,* greasy canvas cloth containing roots. *g,* buckskin pouch containing decayed wood. *h,* piece of newspaper. *i,* 8-inch-long eagle bone whistle. *j,* calico bag containing roots and small white rock. *k,* cotton cloth containing long braid of sweet grass. *l,* buffalo horn cup for sucking out diseases.

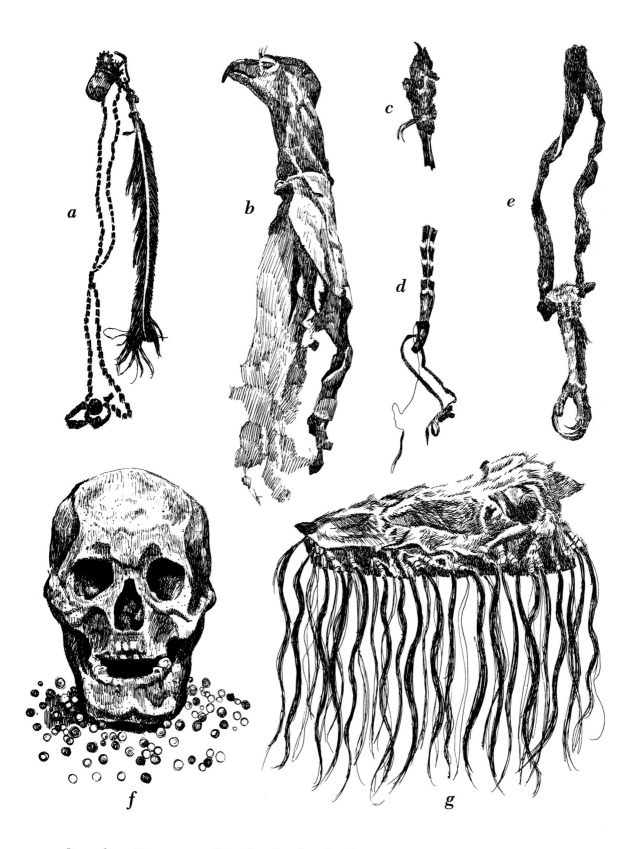

Items from Crow war medicine bundles: bundle of Crow warrior Two Leggings. *a*, herb bag to renew horse's wind. *b*, chest hanging made of eagle's head to impart bird's powers. *c*, swallow for power to evade enemies. *d*, porcupine-quill-wrapped eagle feathers to tie to horse's mane to impart swiftness. *e*, otter skin and eagle claw necklace to impart eagle's swiftness in pouncing on victim. *f*, skull from skull medicine bundle of the Crow Braided Tail. *g*, coyote's head with hairlocks from war medicine bundle of the Crow Sees the Living Bull.

Crow war medicine ring with hide-covered hoop, shown on both sides, two stuffed parrots, war whistle of eagle bone, eagle feathers, and mountain lion skin pendant.

skull and would prescribe the skull's care and give associated songs and rituals. Usually these were the skulls of great medicine men or of people who had the ghosts as their medicine.

The skull of Braided Tail, one of the most famous Crow medicine men, became an oracle to its successive owners, informing them on raids of the location of an enemy and telling them how many men would be killed at a certain place. In time of famine it instructed the owner where to find game. It could even tell a sick person whether he was going to die or if he could be cured, and it could locate lost property.

5. *Rock Medicine Bundles.* These bundles each contained as their most vital object some kind of sacred rock. They served many different purposes. Some were used as war medicines.

6. *Medicine Pipe Bundles.* The principal articles in these bundles were pipe-stems, or stems and bowls. As mentioned, some of them were employed in the Medicine Pipe Ceremony, and others were carried by the leaders of war expeditions.

7. *Love Medicine Bundles.* These bundles, described in a general way in the next few pages, contained sacred objects which had the power to attract members of the opposite sex.

8. *Witchcraft Bundles.* Although rare, revenge bundles were pressed into service to do harm to the personal enemies of their owners. Great secrecy surrounded their use.

9. *Healing Medicine Bundles.* These contained the various articles already detailed in the section on doctoring.

10. *Hunting Medicine Bundles.* These bundles held sacred objects used to bring success in hunting buffalo or other wild game.

Besides his medicine bundles, each warrior carried or wore a smaller and more convenient personal medicine—to remind him that his helper was always close at hand. These were fashioned to function as neck and hair ornaments. Those amulets worn around the neck might be a buckskin bag containing herbs, a sea shell or bone disk to represent the sun, a sinew rosette with golden eagle breath feathers (soft white feathers taken from under the eagle's tail), a weasel skin for swiftness of movement, or an assemblage of small bags containing several med-

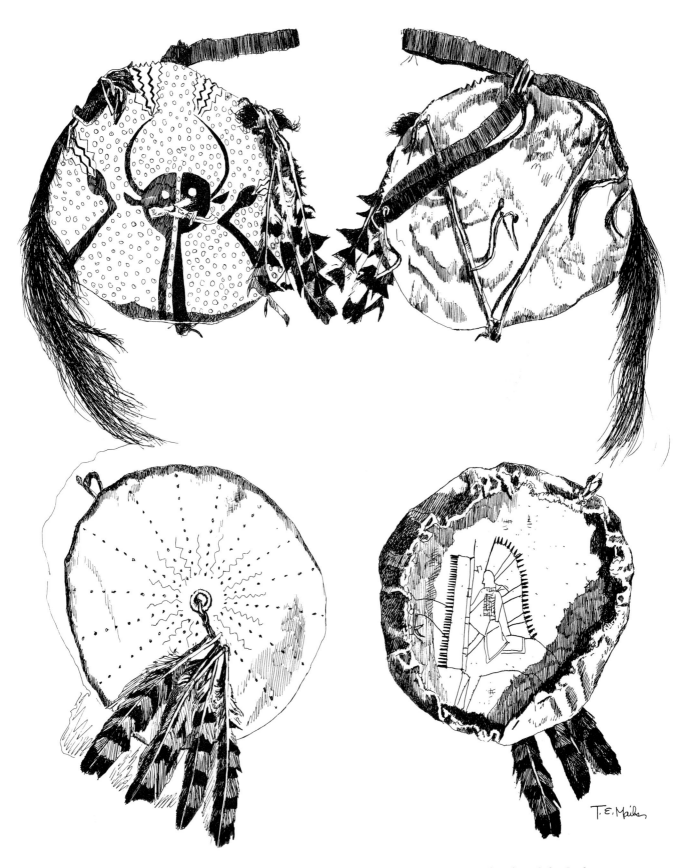

Medicine shield of Owl, Cheyenne medicine man. Made at Fort Marion, Florida, while Owl was a prisoner there from 1875 to 1878. The canvas cover is particularly interesting, since there is a pencil pictographic drawing on its inside, suggesting it was cut from a larger scene. The words "Fort Marion" are inscribed just below the horse's hind legs (not shown). *Top left,* front view of shield, with buffalo, hail, snake, and lightning symbols, cut owl feathers, and buffalo tail switch. *Right,* back view of shield with buffalo-hide loop, hair left on. *Bottom left,* front of shield cover with sun symbols and owl feathers. *Right,* back of shield cover.

The Cheyenne Little Wolf, wearing a silver cross medicine symbol. The cross was always worn so as to be standing on one foot; with one bar vertical and the other horizontal. The cross represented the four winds which helped the holy men dream and speculate about life beyond icines. Ornaments made of assembled medicine helpers were worn on top of the head, at the back of the head, or tied to a braid. Sometimes it was simply the skin of a helper bird which was tucked behind the ear before going into battle. Other times it was a bird made of rawhide, a large brass button, a piece of bone, or beadwork, each with a tie string for fastening it to the hair. At the center of many hair ornaments was a long buckskin thong or a woven disk of sinew decorated with bone or trade beads, an ermine skin, a hair lock, or a large eagle plume.

A Sioux warrior named Jaw, who had fought many battles against the Crow Indians, said that he always carried, attached to his war whistle, two little bags containing the same medicine; one for his horse and one for himself. The medicine was curative and also had power as a charm. He said, "If the horse had a headache I might chew a little of the herb and put it in his mouth." Jaw was skilled in stealing horses from the enemy, and he often chewed this medicine as he went to the windward side of the horses, at which they "pricked up their ears," being attracted to it.[6]

Because they were a proven healing agent, spruce needles were often powdered and placed in a buckskin bag somewhat resembling a tapered awl case in shape, to be hung around an infant's neck as a safeguard against illness. Adults used white weasel skins, the foot of a white weasel, unusual stones, buffalo horns, tails, and names for similar purposes. Bear claw medicine necklaces were in common use by all tribes. One very old woman kept two small, irregular pieces of obsidian in a bag as a preventive against eye disease; occasionally she scratched her arm with the stones. Some men had their medicine enclosed in a little piece of buckskin and tied to the middle of either the front or back of a beaded necklace, Southern Cheyenne warriors carried spear grass about in small bags which were tied to the laces of their shirts.

A rarely used kind of evil charm was prepared by placing rattlesnake heads on hot coals in a hole in the ground and covering them with the fresh liver and gall of a wild animal. During the process of steaming, the liver absorbed the poison from the heads. It was carefully preserved in a little buckskin bag, and when its owner wore it he believed he could, by looking intently at his desired victim and murmuring evil incantations, effect his death.

---

the grave. The top of the cross, marked by an arrow, represented the north wind and was worn nearest the head, where intelligence rests. The left arm covered the heart; it was the east wind, which sent life and love. The foot was the south wind, indicating fiery passion, illustrated by a sun symbol. The right arm was the west wind, covering the place from which the breath goes out at death. A star design denoted this. A circle was placed at the center of the cross to represent the earth and man.

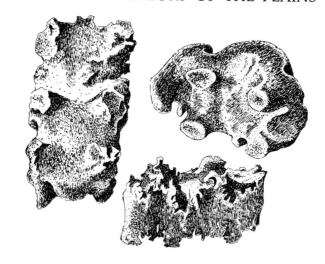

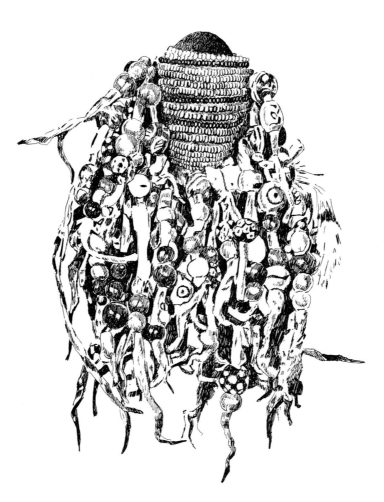

*Top,* Blackfoot buffalo stones used in calling buffalo. *Bottom,* Crow rock medicine hung on thong around neck.

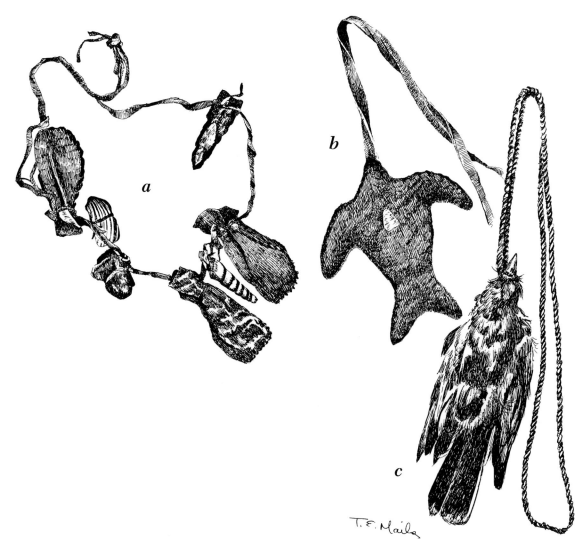

*a*, necklace of personal medicines consisting of medicine pouches, stones, and shells. *b*, necklace with rawhide Thunder Bird. *c*, necklace with stuffed bird representing personal helper encountered in vision.

Love charms were extremely popular, and it takes very little imagination to appreciate the fun the Indians had with them. One man wore a weasel foot on his hat as a woman medicine; he expected that it would help him in "catching a woman." Woman medicine in the shape of shavings of wood or bark was rubbed on the neck, tied up in a bag or piece of cloth, and attached to the belt. A certain passionate Sioux warrior was once seen putting spruce needles in his mouth. He then chewed them thoroughly, spit the moistened substance in his hands, and rubbed it on his head for woman medicine. This fellow also knew of a small inedible root which could be dug up and employed for the same purpose. The root was glued to a small stone, and the smitten lover crept up behind the woman he desired and threw the charm at her. Perhaps three or four nights later, she came to see him. If she looked into his eyes and laughed the charm had worked. The warrior said he had repeatedly used this charm "with success!" In fact, it gained such eminence that a desolate Ross Fork Shoshone visited him and paid a dollar and a half for some roots. The following spring the Sioux saw him married to a woman.[1] There was yet another root which was said to cause disastrous consequences. If dropped in a woman's path, it would cause her immense problems in about ten days; apparently it was used to get even for the first medicine's failure to work properly!

Elk horn headdress from Crow warrior Long Tail's love medicine bundle.

Crow love medicines included a number of engrossing items, such as painted wooden flutes, full-sized painted and quilled robes, charming belts of prized animal fur, and elk horn headdresses.

The Sioux also had beautiful painted wooden flutes which were used to woo young ladies. It is said that the love flute had an entire language all its own, and White visitors reported that their mournful sounds were often heard at eventide in the Indian camps.

Young men who coveted certain maidens went to herb doctors and paid them large fees to charm the girls so that they would return their affection. Depending upon the passion's urgency, the resulting love medicine prepared by the doctor was administered either with or without a ceremony. There were many kinds of intriguing charms designed by doctors for this purpose, although most consisted of a mixture of herbs and objects placed in a small beaded or painted bag, which was carried by the amorous male whenever he was courting. Again, the doctor's rules for the charm's use must be followed to the letter, else the charm would not work.

Surely, love medicines had their serious aspects, for marriage was vital on the Plains. Yet a good deal of humor accompanied their use, and helped to make courting a memorable and desired experience.

The northernmost bands and clans of the Assiniboine tribe were renowned for their possession of a charm which increased speed and gave stamina to male runners. The medicine was made from herbs, but the mixture and directions for its use were "known only to certain herbalists." Aspiring runners paid them high fees, and obtained the medicine for use whenever they competed against another tribe. Since this was not exactly a secret, the Assiniboine runners were always vigorously accused of having used such medicine if they won a competition where the other bands had entered their best men. Yet despite the purposely overblown arguments which followed, the Assiniboines could not be disqualified, because no one ever *proved* that any such medicine was used.

Of course, the northern men did everything in their power to encourage suspicion. Runners made every effort to display the medicine bags, which obviously contained some mixture, and hung them prominently on their belts. But since, however, other kinds of medicine were often carried in the same way, other tribes could not prove the bags contained the medicine swift runners used. Nevertheless, anyone watching closely would see that just before a race the owner chewed some of the herbs and deftly smeared a little of the juice on his feet. Then when the race started, he deliberately ran just behind the other runners so that the medicine would cast its spell upon them. As they approached the finish line he simply trotted past the hypnotized competition and won!

Naturally, suspicious runners sought to prevent a northern clan man from dogging their footsteps. It was hard enough to race him, let alone his herbs. So they attempted to keep far to one side or the other, for it was well known that the medicine worked only when the keeper ran in someone's tracks. It's wonderful to imagine this subtle psychological contest taking place, and it would be delightful to share in such pleasures today.

Horse racing was a cherished pastime of every tribe, and included the aspect of gambling as well. Charms to speed up horses were made from parts of fast animals and swift-flying birds, such as tail feathers from hawks or falcons, the tips of the tails of foxes, or the short prongs from the horns of antelope. It was generally accepted that wolves' tails always made horses long-winded! They were hung around the necks of horses on buckskin thongs or beaded bands so that the medicine lay between the points of the shoulders. However, bird feather charms were always tied to the horse's tail.

While runners made much ado about their personal medicines, there was no secret about the charms used for horses. Even when horses ran in a race where the betting was heavy the charms were publicly applied and attached to the animals. Naturally, to win over a medicine-toting horse was an achievement bringing grand acclaim, and it is known to have happened many times.

The Cheyenne Stands in Timber said with a wry face that "If you wanted a horse to play out you could imitate a bobwhite, as the cry of this bird causes instant exhaustion." With great delight he told of an auto trip in Oklahoma during which a bobwhite was heard singing and the car immediately broke down![8]

Since herbalists dealt with horses, owners often paid them to locate animals which were lost, as well as missing horse-gear objects.

The Cheyenne tell of a certain medicine for horses which would help them win races and be excellent performers in warfare, and heal them when sick. It was made from plants obtained in trade from the Southwest Indians, and especially used for distemper and other sicknesses. They also had a powdered kind of medicine which was blown into the horse's nostrils a ritualistic number of times and worked absolute wonders.

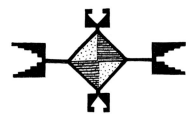

"Lamenting" for a vision was a sacred thing to the Plains Indians, and it was practiced by them as far back in time as their memories could transport them. Most tribes considered the "lamenting" rites as being at the very center of their religion. Everyone, men and women alike, was expected to seek at least one vision, both for the power they received personally and for the cumulative power which came to the tribe through the totality of all of the visions.

Without a vision, a man was next to nothing, since he had no source of power, no special wisdom, and no protection. He could, through purchase of some of the produce of another man's vision, live a tolerable existence, but that was all. Any Indian who failed to achieve a clear and successful vision would constantly express his wretchedness over his situation. He remained like one in a desert without water, and unable to find peace or rest.

Once the vision was achieved, however, and its content explained by the camp leaders and holy men, the boy, often no more than nine years of age at the time, had his "power," and could proceed with the regular steps toward maturity and a life of service for his people. He gathered some tangible part of every thing of the earth seen in his visions into a sacred medicine bundle and painted his possessions with his revealed symbols in the colors which had also been designated. Smaller bits of these things were placed in bags or assemblages of a size small enough to be worn at all times, and especially on excursions into enemy country. It is of some consequence to note that medicine bundles told much of the story of a man's life.

Holy men and doctors were given the guidance needed to provide the added medicine items so vital to tribal and social development. Most tribal medicine bundles came into being as a result of famous and unusual visions by those who practiced medicine, as did smaller tokens to implement courtship and marriage and tribal enjoyment such as games and racing.

The exception to this would be the great tribal bundles which were prepared after some of the earliest tribesmen of each nation had unexpected visitations by mystery people who came down to earth as messengers from God, and who established the customs among the tribes which were considered vital to their survival. "When the earth was young" a White Buffalo Maiden came to the Sioux and presented them with a sacred pipe, which became a symbol of a covenant between the Buffalo tribe and the Sioux, and it was also to be used for healing and as an instrument of peace between nations. In a slightly different approach, the Cheyenne's prophet was a human being named Sweet Medicine, who was blessed with a special vision which provided guidance for the tribe for all of its lifetime. The prophet also returned from his vision trip with four sacred arrows which became the core of the tribe's principal medicine bundle.

The essential thing to bear in mind is that in their quest to reach an accord with all things, the Indians assumed that invisible presences existed to answer every need, and that all they required was a means of making them visible so as to deal with them on a man-to-man basis. The ultimate process which evolved brought them into close contact with the supernatural and the natural worlds and enabled them to live in harmony with these in all their extremes.

Miracles became the norm for the people who walked so intimately with God. They were the usual, for the Spirit had promised them through his intermediaries, and astonishment would only have come if they had failed to take place; the truly amazing thing would have been their not happening.

In this way the Indians learned to accept miracles as the commonplace thing for those who, in a manner of speaking, held the hand of the One-Above. Yet they knew His gifts were graces, and not earned, so fitness, sacrifice, petition, and thanksgiving also became daily pursuits in their life, and the nature of these activities is just as engaging as the visions and medicines themselves.

# Chapter 9

# RELIGION—PURIFICATION

Grandfather, Great Spirit, you have been always, and before you no one has been. There is no other one to pray to but you. You yourself, everything that you see, everything has been made by you. The star nations all over the universe you have finished. The day, and in that day, everything you have finished. Grandfather, Great Spirit, lean close to the earth that you may hear the voice I send. You towards where the sun goes down, behold me; Thunder Beings, behold me! You where the White Giant lives in power, behold me! You where the sun shines continually, whence come the day-break star and the day, behold me! You where the summer lives, behold me! You in the depths of the heavens, an eagle of power, behold! And you, Mother Earth, the only Mother, you who have shown mercy to your children!

Hear me, four quarters of the world—a relative I am! Give me the strength to walk the soft earth, a relative to all that is! Give me the eyes to see and the strength to understand, that I may be like you. With your power only can I face the winds.

Great Spirit, Great Spirit, my Grandfather, all over the earth the faces of living things are all alike. With tenderness have these come up out of the ground. Look upon these faces of children without number and with children in their arms, that they may face the winds and walk the good road to the day of quiet.

This is my prayer; hear me! The voice I have sent is weak, yet with earnestness I have sent it. Hear me![1]

While medicine and visions became a source of power for the Indians, and while they supplied those who received the visions with constant reminders of their power source and direction, there was still the matter of the adequate preparation of one's self to receive the daily guidance which God and the helpers wished to bestow.

Put simply, it was a matter of purification, of becoming fit to abide in a constant relationship with the Great One-Above. Most especially, since they recognized that certain acts such as warfare and friction displeased God, it was necessary for them to have a means of revitalization, or of being born anew, with the acts of ignorance being forgiven and put behind.

The sweat bath, which was a rite performed in a traditionally constructed sweat lodge, served the purification purpose. It purified the body and the soul for free communication with the Spirit. Some tribespeople performed the purification rite daily, and during times of special need or danger several times a day. It was always enacted before any undertaking of major importance to the tribe, such as a war party or the making of a treaty.

In and around every village stood small shelters, shaped like the rounded upper half of a ball. Their frameworks were made of bent willow branches and they were covered with hide robes, or later with trade blankets. In these shelters the Indian warrior purified himself, using all of the created and intermediary elements of the world, rocks, fire, water, earth, and air. He heated the rocks, which represented the eternal Mother Earth, in a sacred fireplace, and poured water over the rocks to make steam to cleanse his body and to carry messages up to God. Chanting sacred songs, he rubbed sage and sweet grass over his body to make it give off an acceptable fragrance. And finally he was in a proper condition to be forgiven, and to look forward to life as though it were all new and well and good.

The sweat lodge was a much used item, and it played a central role in the Indian scheme of life, for it was a vital link in their relationship with God. The Crow tribe believed that it was the original medicine which God, or First Worker, and his two boy servants who came as messengers, gave them. In the old days it was their most sacred medicine, and it ranked before all fasts and important ceremonies. It healed and cleansed their bodies, and when they burned incense inside the sweat lodge while praying to First Worker, it cleansed their souls.

The Crow sweat lodge can serve as an approximate model of the lodges of most Plains tribes. It was oval in shape, an oblong framework dome made of intertwined willow branches about six feet long, five feet wide, four feet high, and always oriented on an east-west axis. When in use, it was covered with overlapping layers of hides or blankets. The number of willow branches used to build the framework of the lodge varied according to the occasion; fourteen was a common number for the daily bath lodges among the Crows and the Blackfoot, but in the most auspicious ceremonies a hundred or more would be used. A small pit was dug in the middle of the lodge. A large fire was built at the end of a path a few yards from the eastern entrance of the lodge, and round stones were laid in it to heat.

As a rule, at least four bathers joined in the sweating. When bathers were inside for ceremonial purposes, a helper passed four red-hot stones into the pit, one at a time, carrying them on forked sticks. Then the remaining stones were put into the pit in the same manner, and a hide container of water and a wooden cup were passed inside. After the door flap was dropped, one of the bathers, called the "water chief," said a prayer and poured four cups of water on the stones. Hot steam filled the darkened interior, and the participants sweated profusely. After a while the flap was raised to let in fresh air. When it was closed a second time, the water chief emptied seven cups on the stones; following another cooling-off period he poured ten cups. After a final breather, an indefinite number

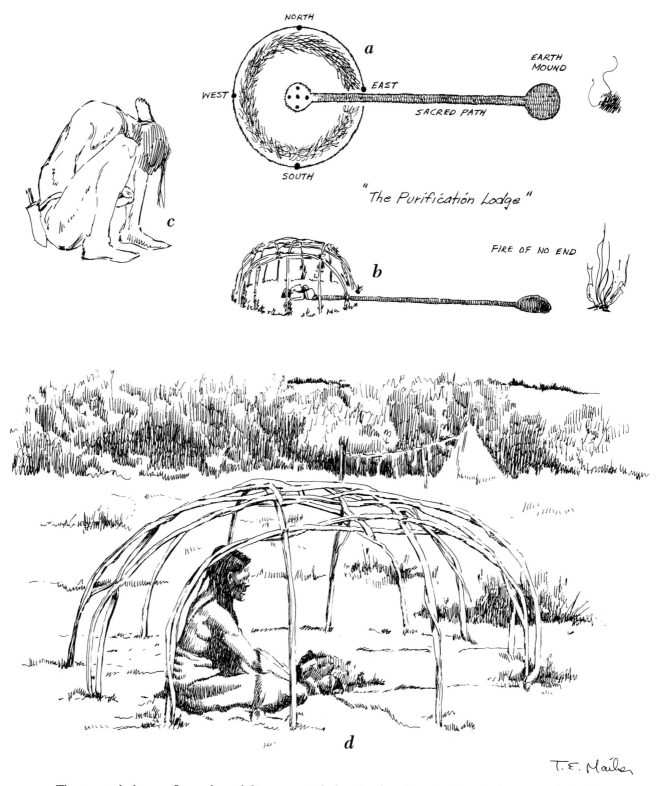

The sweat lodge. *a*, floor plan of Sioux sweat lodge. *b*, elevation of Sioux lodge. *c*, method of sitting within lodge. *d*, Cheyenne sweat lodge showing willow-frame structure.

of cupfuls were poured, called "million wishes." In general, the heat was intense, and the bathers sat with their heads between their knees in order to endure it. When the bathers had had enough, the door flap was raised a final time and they all ran and plunged into the nearest creek or river. In the wintertime they rolled in the snow. Sometimes long switches of sage or buffalo tails were used by the bathers to draw heat to their bodies. On the highest ceremonial occasions live coals were taken inside before any water had been sprinkled. Pine needles or bear root shavings were laid on them as incense, and many prayers were spoken.

Every part of the lodge and the ceremony was replete with meaning. Some White authorities state that the Crows conceived of the bath as an offering to the sun. But the Crows themselves put it differently. To them, the sweat lodge itself represented First Worker's body. The steam from the heated stones, and the smoke from the incense when it was used, was His image. The first four cupfuls of water symbolized First Worker's arms and legs, as did the four main supporting willows of the sweat lodge. The next seven cupfuls became the Big Dipper. The ten cupfuls represented the cluster stars, and the indefinite number turned their minds to the Other-Side-Camp, where the Indians lived on after they died.[2]

When Indian men and boys were preparing for a vision-seeking fast they terminated the sweat bath ritual by carefully washing their bodies in a stream and scrubbing their nails. Then they purified themselves further in a sacred smudge of burning pine needles. After that, they applied a coating of white clay to remove as much as possible of their human smell. The helpers which came in visions were believed not to like the smell of men, and since one fervently wished to obtain their favor, everything possible was done to please them. Broadly understood, the sum of the acts fostered a mental and a physical involvement which greatly benefited the total man in his daily life.

The Sioux symbolism of the sweat lodge was even more impressive than that of the Crows. As they saw it, the rite of the sweat lodge called all the powers of the universe into play; earth, and the things which come forth from the earth such as water, fire, and rocks, and also the sky and its celestial dwellers. The water represented the thunder beings who came in a breath-taking way, yet brought a paradoxical kind of goodness, for the bubbling stream which came from the hot mountain rocks, within which was fire, was frightening, yet when duplicated in miniature the lodge, the heat and fire and steam coupled with prayer purified them so they might strive to live as the Spirit willed. And, if through many rituals they became very pure, He might even send them an especially powerful vision.

As they used the water they thought of Him, who is always flowing as a stream giving His power and life to everything. The willow branches used to construct the lodge also taught the bathers a lesson. In the fall the leaves of the willow tree died and returned to the earth, but in the spring they came to life again. So too, men died but lived again in the real world of God, where there is nothing but the eternal spirits of deceased things. A foretaste of this true life could be known here on earth if they purified their bodies and minds, thus coming closer to the Great Spirit who is all-purity. Furthermore, the willows were set up in such a way that they marked the four quarters of the universe. Thus the entire lodge became an image of the universe, and everything of the world and sky above was contained within it, so that being purified, it could serve as a messenger to carry man's voice up to God.

The rocks were used to represent Grandmother Earth, from whom all fruits came, and thus the eternal nature of the providential Spirit. The fire used to heat the rocks was a ray from the sun, and represented the great power of the Spirit which imparts growth and enlightenment through the sun to all things.

The shallow hole which was excavated at the center of the sweat lodge to receive the rocks designated the center of the universe, where the Great Spirit Himself dwells. All the things employed in the sweat rite were holy to the Indian, and must be thoroughly comprehended if he hoped really to purify himself, for the true power of a thing or an act was found in the meaning and the understanding.

Like the tipi, the sweat lodge was always oriented with its door facing toward the east. About ten paces out from the doorway, a sacred fireplace which was called the "fire of no end" was built to heat the rocks. To make this, the lodge builders placed four sticks running east and west, and on top of them four more sticks running north and south. Around these they leaned a cone of sticks. Rocks were then placed at the four directions, and more sticks were piled on top. As they kindled the fire, they prayed in such a way as to acknowledge the creative and preservative power of God, now to be made manifest through the sweat bath.

In constructing the shallow rock-receiving "altar" within the sweat lodge, where the heated rocks would be placed, they drove a stake into the earth, and used it as a compass point to draw a circle with a rawhide cord. During the establishment of this "holy" center, they again prayed, this time for their ritual prayers to be heard, and for a final resurrection of the soul to be with Him in the heavenly places. Through the total purification act they fervently hoped to make themselves worthy of this ultimate blessing.

The earth taken from the round hole, which was now dug at the point of the stake, was used to form a narrow sacred path leading out of the lodge to the east, at the end of which a small mound of dirt was built. Once again they prayed, for the path was called "the sacred path of life," and as they walked it, their steps represented their plea for mercy and protection throughout the days of their life.

The Sioux leader of the purification rite entered the completed lodge first with his sacred pipe. He "made an altar" of the central fireplace hole by placing pinches of tobacco at its four corners. Then he burned sweet grass, rubbing his entire self and the pipe with the smoke—which drove all evil things from the lodge. Following this, pinches of tobacco were offered to all of the visible and invisible powers, and the leader left the lodge to place the pipe on the earth mound at the end of the sacred path, with the bowl on the west side and the stem slanting to the east.

All of those who were to share in the rite now entered the lodge through its low door, "in recognition of their finite nature." Once inside, they moved sunwise around the lodge and sat on a ring of sacred sage which bordered its perimeter. At first, the men all kept silent, and remembered the Great Spirit's goodness. Then the leader's pipe was passed into the lodge by an outside assistant—usually a man, but sometimes a woman. Each participant smoked it, accompanying each puff with appropriate prayers. Then the helper closed the door flap and plunged them into darkness, which symbolized man's ignorance. During the course of the sweat ritual which followed the door flap was raised four times to permit the light of wisdom received in each of the four great ages of mankind's evolution to enter and sweep away the ignorance.

The continual prayers which they offered centered in their request to be able to see with the eye of the heart as well as with their two physical eyes. Leaving the lodge at the completion of the ritual was the equivalent of leaving ignorance and darkness behind. They were, in effect, born anew . . . to walk in the light which had now been given them. The final prayer was that they had done good for the entire nation, and that the generations to come would also walk in this sacred manner.[3] Sioux leaders were so convinced about the importance of bathing that most believed that as the custom fell into disuse during the reservation period a proportionate loss of power came upon their nation, and made their decline inevitable.[4]

# Chapter 10

# RELIGION—THANKSGIVING

Because hardships and the unexpected were so much a part of their life, the belief came to pass among the Plains Indians that personal suffering was involved in the receipt of supernatural power and favor. Suffering and testing were also their forms of thanksgiving, since they proved, beyond any doubt, the sincerity of their gratitude to God for His response to their pleas. A simple and easily given thank-you was not enough for the Indians of the Plains.

The vision quest was one of their modes of sacrifice, since it required exhaustive preparations, danger, self-mutilation, and fasting.

Indeed, limited self-mutilation was a regular means of propitiation and thanksgiving, and while it seems brutal and risky, it appears not to have done them any permanent harm.

Men about to go on the warpath, and in particular on a revenge raid, would sometimes slice bits or narrow cross strips of skin from their arms from the shoulder to the wrist, and from their legs. An even greater sacrifice was made by cutting a spiral strip, as large as a dinner plate, from the skin of the chest. The Crows often cut horseshoe-shaped strips from their arms. A common form used to deepen the attitude of suffering necessary for a successful revenge raid was to scarify (gash) the arms and legs.

Men who felt they would be in unusual danger on a war party often promised the lesser spirits who served as their helpers that if they came through safely they would suffer in thanksgiving.

Now and then the pledge was fulfilled in the form of a vision quest in which suffering was increased by a significant amount. A young warrior who wished to make his sacrifice in this way cut a stout limb from a tree, tying a hide rope to the top, to take up on the hill with him. At daylight the next morning he filled a pipe and went to the lodge of a man who had already done what he now intended to do. If he took the pipe and smoked, the young man would ask him to go to the hills with him, and the sympathetic elder man would agree to be his sponsor. When the reached a good place, the sponsor dug a hole in the ground and planted the pole there. He then tested the pole to see that it was firmly placed, and made certain there was plenty of room for the young man to "swing."

Then the young man sat down facing the east, holding his shoulders well back and his arms at his side. The older man pinched up the skin of the breast on either side, ran a knife through it, and then took two wooden skewers, each about a quarter of an inch in diameter and three and a half inches long, and pushed them through the cuts on each side of the breast. A knot was tied in the end of the pole rope, and a long flat strip of hide was attached to it by its middle so as to be bent like branches in a forked shape. He then slit the terminal ends of each branch with openings like buttonholes, and the holes of each end were slipped over the ends of the skewers. Then the old man stepped behind the young man, helped him up, and pulled him back hard to see if the rope was tight and the strain on it was even. Finally the sponsor told him to begin walking back and forth in a half circle. A pipe was left at the southern limit of his walk, and there he paused to smoke three times during the day. As he walked the young man sagged back on the rope, and strove mightily to tear the skewers loose from the skin of his breast.

Meanwhile, the man who had given the instructions returned to a camping place. At sundown he came back again. If the sufferer had failed to tear out the skewers, the older man cut the skin behind each skewer and freed him. Any skin removed in the process was placed on the ground at the foot of the pole, prayed over, and left there. The rope was removed from the pole, and both men returned to the camp.

Sometimes the same kind of torture sacrifice was made at night, in which case the assistant had to be a man who had sacrificed in the nighttime. The sufferer was secured to the pole while the sun was setting, and was set free as the sun rose.

Another form of sacrifice involved the use of several buffalo skulls, which were attached to slits in the warrior's chest and/or back by ropes. In this case the thanksgiver would drag the heavy skulls back and forth over a prescribed course. Once again, an older man served as an assistant, and after an agreed-upon time removed any skulls the supplicant failed to free himself of. As he released the skulls, the helper cut off the drawn-out skin, held each piece up to the sun, down to the ground, and toward the four directions. Then he buried the pieces in the ground. Naturally, the young man always gave his assistant a liberal payment!

What has been considered thus far is impressive, but the spectacular Sun Dance, since it was a tribal ceremonial event, ranked above all other forms of sacrifice and thanksgiving. It was practiced by the Arapaho, Arikara, Assiniboine, Cheyenne, Crow, Gros Ventre, Hidatsa, Sioux, Plains Cree, Plains Ojibway, Sarsi, Omaha, Ponca, Ute, Shoshone, Kiowa and the three Blackfoot tribes.

As was the case in all other matters, tribes varied somewhat in their approaches to the Dance, and in so many ways that all of the variations cannot be included here. A generalized form which includes the more noteworthy features of each tribe follows:

Ordinarily the Dance was performed during the reassemblage of all of the bands of the tribe following the winter dispersal; either in the late spring or early summer. As a rule, the performance was annual, although it always depended upon a tribesman's vow to "build the lodge," and to have it held for one of many possible reasons. A common Crow incentive for the Dance was the gaining of revenge upon a tribe that had killed a close relative.

The Blackfoot Indians insisted that the Sun Dance was far more than an occasion for the self-torture of youths who were candidates for admission to the full standing of warriors. It was their great annual religious festival, their holy sacrament, the supreme expression of their religion. Accordingly, their annual Dance always had its beginning in a woman's vow, made to the Sun God for the recovery of the sick. The entire tribe gathered to fast and pray for the recovery of the sick, while individual warriors came to inflict torture upon themselves in fulfillment of vows made to the sun at a time when they needed deliverance from peril.

The Sioux warriors believed that by suffering at the pole at the center of the Sun Lodge they took upon themselves much of the agony of their people. This tribe attributed their Sun Dance custom to an ancient vision, in which they were given the ceremony as "a new way of worship." It was an offering of body and soul to God, and as such was very holy, so when they danced they raised their heads and their right hands "up to heaven." The Sioux also believed that both the flesh and the paint they used represented ignorance, and that dancing in such a way as to tear the skewers loose freed them from human darkness. Going further, it was intended for mature people who wished to *deepen* their humility before the Spirit. And one who saw them in later years could always tell how deep their humility was by the scars on their chest and back.

The Crows were taught that sacrificing one's flesh and going through severe trials softened the heart of First Worker's animal mediators, making them want to help mankind.

The Sun Dance was always held at that part of the month when the moon was full, for then it was as if the eternal light of the creator was shining down upon the whole world. Then everyone gathered upon notice at a great encampment where the huge Sun Lodge was to be built. The clans and bands converged like lines of ants coming in a splendid parade from all directions, winding over the prairies, visiting, laughing, and singing as they came. The tipis were arranged in a great circle around the place where the Sun Lodge would be built. It was a time to wear the finest apparel, to ride the best horses, and to bring all the food that could be had for feasting. The encampment itself soon took on the aspect of a mammoth carnival grounds, and there was friendship and kindness in everyone's heart. Many people came to seek special favors, such as the healing of a sick child or the settling of a quarrel between a husband and his wife. Each of these brought offerings and prayers for the graces they asked. Other people fasted

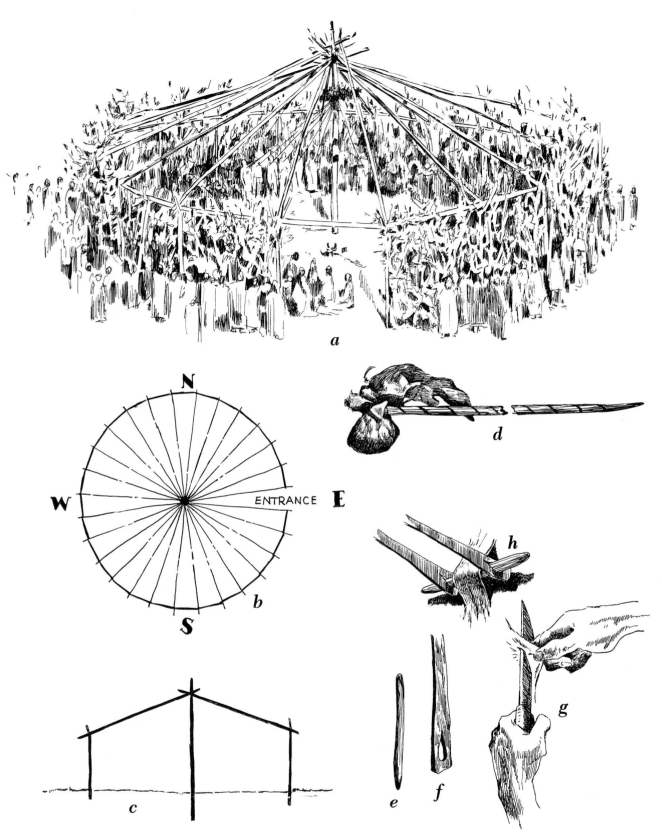

*a,* Arapaho Sun Dance Lodge; perspective. *b,* plan of lodge pole framework. *c,* section through lodge structure. *d,* stick with tobacco offering bag. *e,* wood skewer. *f,* eyelet in thong ends. *g,* cutting chest to insert skewer. *h,* method of inserting skewer.

and offered prayers and danced, or took part in the special ceremonies of the society to which they belonged. Even the children had special kinds of games which they played during the Sun Dance encampment.

A renowned priest or "lodge maker" acquainted with the awesome ritual conducted the entire ceremony, instructing the individual pledgers in a preparatory tipi while other tribesmen followed his guidance in collecting the special items which would be needed for the great lodge. All tribes had traditional ceremonies associated with the procurement of the huge central (or first) pole to be set up for the lodge. Men chosen for their eminence scouted in war dress for a suitable tree with a fork at its top, had a specially qualified person chop it, and treated the fallen tree as an enemy on whom coup was to be counted. The Sioux always used the cottonwood tree for this, because they considered it to be very sacred. According to legend, it was the cottonwood tree which taught them how to make their tipis, for the leaf of the tree was an exact pattern of it. They explained that some of their old men had learned this lesson by watching little children make play houses from the leaves. It was, they said, a good example of how much grown men could learn from little children, "whose hearts were pure."[1] Therefore, the Great Spirit would show children many things which older people missed. Also, if a person cut an upper limb of the tree crosswise, the grain revealed a perfect five-pointed star, which the Sioux took as a representation of the presence of the Great Spirit. Even in the very lightest breeze they could hear the voice of the cottonwood tree offering its prayer for men and for all things to the Great Spirit. After all, it was accepted that all created beings were alive and prayed to Him continually in their own ways.

Before raising the pole, the Sioux builders put a bundle of brush, a buffalo-hide human effigy, a buffalo-hide effigy in the shape of a buffalo, long slender sticks with small tobacco bags attached to them, and other carefully fashioned religious offerings into its fork. The finished "bundle" was called an eagle's or Thunder Bird's nest. Around this center pole and bundle they built a circular framework wall of posts and covered it with green tree branches. The Sioux saw this arrangement as a universe. The Crow Sun Dance structure was shaped like a tipi.

Within the enclosure a cleared area was established as an altar, and traditionally painted buffalo skulls were placed upon it. Most of the figures used on the skulls were black, but colorings of yellow were used to fill in areas of an eagle's feet, and purple for the spots of a turtle. A sun on a skull was painted in red with yellow radiating lines, and a quarter moon was done in half yellow and half blue. Dark red lines were placed where each horn met the skull. Balls of sacred sage were placed in the eye and mouth holes, a little bag of tobacco was tied on the tip of the south horn, and a piece of deer hide was tied to the north horn.

A coal which served as an eternal light was kept burning throughout each

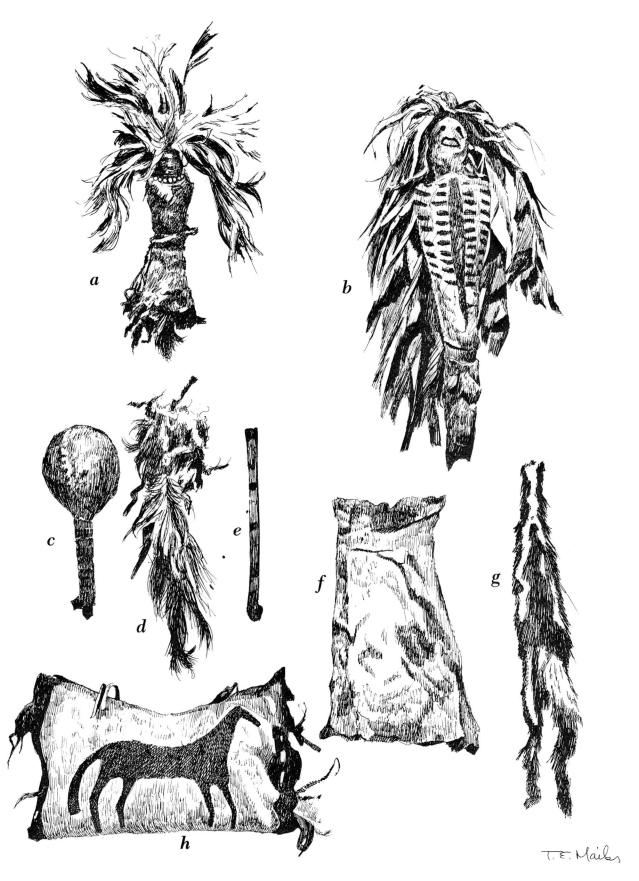

*a*, Sun Dance doll. *b*, Sun Dance doll—lines and dots represent powers owner needs, such as visionary abilities and long life. *c*, buffalo-hide rattle. *d*, hairlock symbolizing fog which could magically descend to protect a raiding party. *e*, eagle's wing bone whistle. *f*, deerskin apron. *g*, skunk skin necklace rubbed with white clay and hung with owl feathers. *h*, painted rawhide container for items.

night of the Dance. But it was allowed to go out during the day, since the sun was then present as a reminder of the creator.

Before the main celebrants did their Sun Dance, the great warriors of the tribe gave a public dramatization of their military exploits. Then the young braves and warriors who had vowed to do the Sun Dance itself entered the lodge. Purified, and painted in special ways by their sponsors, or "grandfathers," having fasted and gone without water in preparation, they were now ready to dance and to

Cheyenne Sun Dancers in medicine lodge in 1902, adapted from Grinnell photograph.

blow their special eagle bone whistles for hours on end until all of the demands connected with the Sun Dance had been fulfilled and they greeted the sun of the final morning. As in the case of the lone suffering vision swingers mentioned earlier, most of the Sun Dancers were attached, at breast or back, by skewers and thongs to the top (or bundle area) of the center pole, and they danced and pulled until they tore themselves loose or were released by the Dance leader.

The pledger usually danced, fasted, and thirsted for several days, gazing steadily all the while at the sacred bundle at the top of the central pole and praying for power. The Crow pledger was given a specially prepared sacred doll by his priestly mentor. It was placed on the center pole and he was expected to stare at it until it granted him a vision of a scalped enemy. The basic design or pattern for these dolls was obtained in an interesting way. While a certain warrior was in mourning over the killing of his wife and son, he received a vision of his next wife and of a Sun Dance doll. A year later, at a ceremony attended by men only, the first doll was constructed from the center piece of a white-tailed deer's skin stuffed with a mixture of sacred sweet grass, white pine needles, and hair from the temples and chin of a mountain sheep. This doll, a kilt from a male black-tailed deer's skin, a skunk-skin necklace, a buffalo-hide rattle, a hairlock attachment, and a whistle carved from an eagle's wing bone were all enclosed within a boat-shaped medicine bundle which was painted on the outside to represent the mountains, the earth, the sky, and the rainbow. The bundle became famous for its power and it was used in several Sun Dances.

The Sun Dance step itself was extremely simple, with the attached performers merely rising on their toes while blowing their whistles and pulling back on the thongs. There was, however, no physical torture in the Ute, Shoshone, Arapaho, and Kiowa Dances; they simply fasted for a long time, and needed great strength and endurance to complete the ceremony.

Sun Dance costumes were fairly standardized, including wreaths of sage on the head, rings of sage held in the hand, sage or some other sacred plant tied to the wrists, the special eagle whistle, and a skirt of painted hide or beaded blanket cloth reaching from waist to ankles. The Ponca Sun Dancer wore chains of beads over his shoulders and a plume feather in his hair. In other tribes rabbitskins were occasionally worn on the wrists to represent humility, and some-times breechclouts replaced the skirts. Handsome quilled falls were often worn on the back of the Dancer's head.

Blackfoot Dancers and those of a few other tribes also wore special Sun Dance necklaces made with bone beads on a hide band, with a hank of braided hair attached at the center. Some Blackfoot Dancers wore a beaded rosette necklace with a full white weasel skin hanging from the center of the rosette.

The eagle bone whistles used by the dancers of all tribes made a noise which they believed was always heard by the Spirit, and an eagle's white plume was always attached to the end of it in such a way that it extended forward when

Sun Dance items. *a*, painted buffalo skull. *b*, eagle's wing bone whistle. *c*, Blackfoot necklace with scalp lock and dentalium beads. *d*, quilled and beaded hair plume with horsetail dyed dark red—hung from scalp lock on back of dancer's head.

the whistle was blown. Each whistle was painted with red, green, blue, and yellow dots and lines which represented the remarkable perception of the eagle.

The Sioux body paint used for the dancers was as follows: Red represented all that was sacred, so the face and body were made red from the waist up. A black circle was painted around the face to represent the Spirit, who has no end. Four vertical black lines were drawn on the chin. These symbolized the powers of the four directions. Black stripes were painted around the wrists, elbows, upper part of the arms, and ankles. These were the bonds of ignorance which tied the Dancers to the earth. They went only as high as the breast skewers, for the thongs were as rays of light from the One-Above.

Because it was called a Sun Dance, some who have considered the Dance have believed that the Dancers stared constantly at the sun, but if that were the case they would have gone completely blind in a matter of minutes. They gazed at the sacred bundle at the top of the pole. And, to ease the pain, sometimes a young woman friend of a dancer was permitted to put a herb, which she had been chewing, into his mouth to ease his thirst and give him strength.

Most tribes had many supplicants dancing at once, but the Blackfeet had only one man dance at a time. Each man had an experienced helper who prepared him for the ordeal, pierced his breasts, inserted the wooden skewers, and attached the thongs leading from the fork or top of the center pole. The assistant began the pledger's actions by telling him to embrace the center pole and to pray for the successful fulfillment of his vow. Then he watched and encouraged him closely until the sufferer freed himself from the ropes. After this he trimmed off the ragged edges of flesh from the man's torn chest and instructed him to place these at the base of the center pole as an offering to the sun. With the completion of this act, the vow was fulfilled. The Blackfoot assistants were always men well advanced in years, and men who had been through the sun torture many years earlier. There could be more than one assistant for each man, and the number usually depended on the age of the sufferer and his family's confidence in his ability to take the punishment. Often the assistants were members of the pledger's society.

The Sioux had a concluding ceremony for the Sun Dance in which the Dancers wore deer heads and horns on their heads. They also had a more rarely used Sun Dance form which employed four short posts. The pledger stood in the center of these, four rawhide thongs were secured to his breast and back, and he pulled back and forth until they were all torn loose.

Toward the close of the Sun Dance ceremonies, a period of time was set aside for those who wished to make public gifts to the poor or to reward someone for special kindness. Sometimes the chiefs gave new names to men who had earned them in battle, and new chiefs were chosen to replace those who had died or could no longer carry out their duties. In one of the final acts of the Sioux and Crows, parents offered the outgrown clothing of their children up to God, hanging them from the center lodge pole with prayers for the health and growth

Gives to the Sun, Blackfeet woman dressed for her central role as Sacred Woman in the Blackfeet Sun Dance. She wears the sacred ermine and eagle medicine bonnet and an elk skin medicine robe over her dress, which was made from the skins of antelope and black-tailed deer. The Sacred Woman was a giver of the Dance, but accepted only on the basis of her purity and spirituality. During the Sun Ceremony she was the object of honor and veneration from the entire tribe. At the moment shown in the illustration she has fasted for four days and uses a cane for support (from photograph by W. McClintock).

of the children. By the time the encampment broke up, there was always a spirit of happiness and good will among all the people, and great hope for the year that lay ahead.

The entire ceremony, from pole cutting to the final events, usually lasted about ten days. When it ended, the sacred objects which had been used were wrapped and taken home by their keepers to be kept in readiness for the next Sun Dance gathering. The offerings lodge and all the sacred bundle offerings were left as they were for the elements to dispose of in time. Long afterward, when they passed the places where medicine lodges had been, people remembered the vows and the blessings and the Dancing and the feasting there, and their hearts were touched with the thought of how they had been lifted up and strengthened at those holy sites.

Until recently so little was known by Whites of the remarkable symbolism of the Sun Dance ritual and the elevated religious ideas and teachings contained in it that far too much stress was laid upon the aspect of self-torture, and the high morality it inculcated and the kindnesses it engendered were overlooked. Therefore, the Sun Dance and all other self-torture rites were prohibited by the Whites wherever possible during the 1880s, and banned outright from 1904 to 1935. Since then the Dance has been permitted in milder forms. Perhaps now it can be seen that it was not actually a Sun Dance, but rather a Dance in the Sun, by a very happy and a very spiritual people!

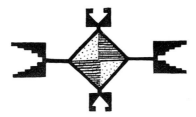

In searching out the elements of Plains Indian ceremonialism, one discovers that Indian rites were performed in single acts or, if the situation required, as parts of a larger and more complex ceremony. They included offerings and prayers, the solemn unfolding of and meditation upon the packs containing sacred objects, the painting of the celebrant's face or body, sweating, suffering, sacrificing, and the singing of sacred songs.

Prayers and offerings were the common means of obtaining divine favor, and more of the same followed in thanksgiving for wishes fulfilled. The Arapaho tribe evolved a prayer and gift pattern for all major ceremonies, including those of the military societies. In effect, it made their life itself a living covenant experience with God.

Tremendous importance was attached to songs which were received in visions, and a Blackfoot doctor's power was set in motion by the chants he had received

a

b

c

d

from above. All Plains Indians repeated the stanzas of songs in accordance with a mystic combination of numbers. The most prominent number was four, but seven might also be used. The Blackfeet sang some ritualistic songs in groups of seven, though the number four was used when they picked up ceremonial objects after three feints.

Spaces were set aside in painted ceremonial lodges where sacred objects were arranged in ritual groupings and smoked with incense. These spaces were called altars. The Blackfeet removed the grass and surface soil to form a dirt plot behind the fireplace of a ceremonial lodge, and smudged their sacred bundles there. Sometimes the plots were made in the shapes of celestial figures, such as the moon or stars, and then were coated with colored earth. The favorite incense of most tribes was an olive-colored sweet grass, and braids of it were placed in every medicine bundle for use in rituals.

As mentioned, buffalo skull altars were used in the Sun Dance lodges. The important Tobacco Order of the Crow tribe had an Adoption Lodge. A rectangular space was cleared at its center, and the members put their medicine bags on the ground at the head of the area. Each of the longer sides of the lodge was bordered by a row of willow arches resembling croquet wickets, and outside each row there was a parallel log of equal length. Four rows of juniper sprigs were laid within the rectangle. When it was finished, it was an altar which represented a tobacco garden, and the juniper signified the tobacco itself while it was in its green state. Logs used for the garden were considered sacred, and could not be burned afterward for firewood. Animal droppings were placed on the altar and lighted to serve as coals to light the ceremonial pipes and incense.

Plains Indian ceremonial masks were rare, but not wholly absent. The Bull Dancers of the Sioux wore impressive buffalo head masks, and the Fool Society of the Assiniboines, who acted like clowns in obedience to a Spirit revelation and wore grotesque fun masks of a truly fanciful nature.

The Crows used sacred dolls in their Sun Dance ceremony, the Sioux had

---

◄

*a*, Sioux Sun Dancer showing typical method of attaching rawhide rope to chest incisions. Dancer wears juniper wreath on head, has sage tied to wrists, wears beaded Sun Dance apron, carries sage wreath in right hand and his personal medicine eagle in left hand. *b,* Cheyenne Sun Dance altar built in 1902. The straight branches surrounding the small rectangular altar were brush, chokecherry, and cottonwood. The hoop was made of four cornel twigs and represented the rainbow. *c*, Cheyenne medicine lodge sun pole with sacrificial offerings attached. *d*, Arapaho Sun Dance painted buffalo skull. The Blackfoot sun skull was painted in approximately the same way. It had black spots on the north side to represent stars and red spots on the south side for the sun. Buffalo grass was stuffed into the nose and eyes to symbolize the feeding of the buffalo.

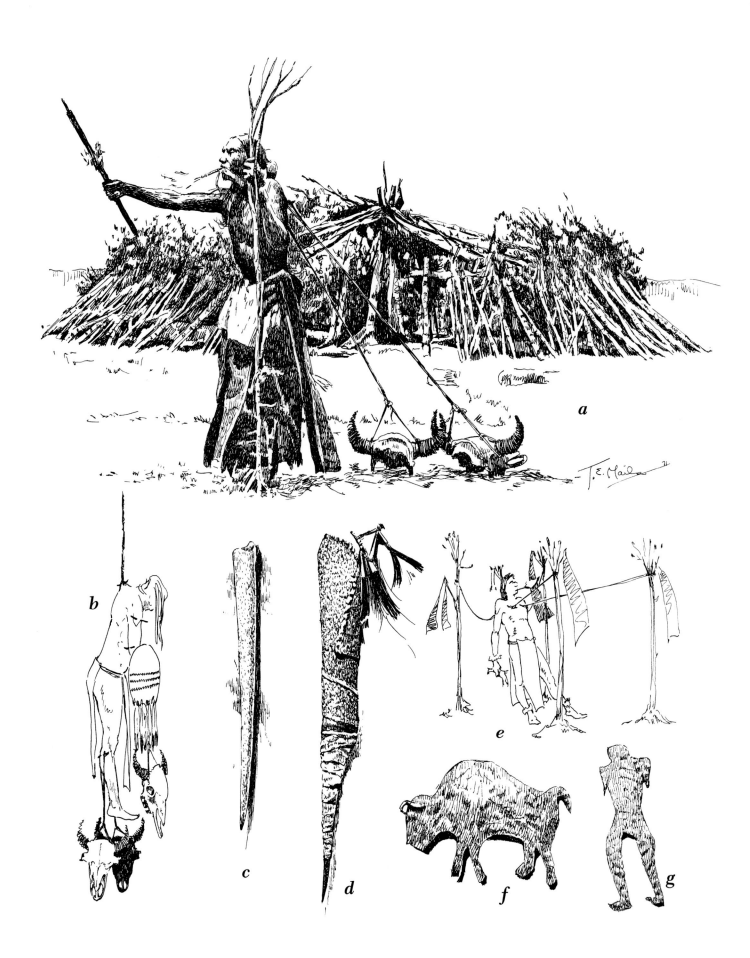

a

b

c

d

e

f

g

special dolls which were used in spirit-release ceremonies, and the Arapaho had a sacred Tai-me ceremonial doll which was carved of wood and wrapped in ribbons and furs. The doll is detailed on page 252, and its scale is shown in plate 31, where it is being held by an Arapaho warrior who is dressed in a splendid Ghost Dance shirt and is standing before a Sun Dance Lodge.

The primary purpose of all Plains ceremonials was to seek the aid of God through His intermediary supernatural powers, which were the celestial beings, the elements, and all that was a part of and lived on the earth.

Ceremonials could be complex, or they could be simple and very personal. In their most profound forms they served to gather the people into an inter-dependent community. Together with the ancient legends told by the storytellers, the ceremonies served to perpetuate the traditional values of the culture of each Plains tribe. From childhood on, the Indian was constantly exposed to the sacred rituals which dramatized and explained his heritage, even more he participated in them and thus was able to *feel* his place as well as to understand it intellectually. Thus in a culture without a written literature, the ceremonies became living dramas which kept the good things of old alive by renewing their memory in an annual cycle of ceremonial rites. To put it as simply as possible, they told the Indian who he was, and what he had to do to preserve the culture for future generations.

With but one exception, the Plains Indians did not resort to victim sacrifices or the orgies so often found in the practices of other peoples. In their earliest history, the ancient Pawnee tribesmen had a sun worship ceremony and a related star clan, which performed an annual Morning Star Ceremony.[2] At this ceremony, a captured maiden was sacrificed. The captive might have been taken at any time of the year. She was well treated, and told nothing of her fate. Three days before the great day, she was stripped of her clothing, painted all over, and treated as a sacred person. Every attempt was made to keep her from discovering what was coming.

Before the morning star rose on the fourth morning, she was led to a raised scaffold. It was considered a lucky sign if, in her innocence, the girl mounted the scaffold without resistance. Then she was tied. Priests symbolized the torture of her, but did not actually hurt her. Then a man shot her through the body from

---

◄

*a,* Cheyenne pledger dragging skulls secured to back before medicine lodge, 1902. *b,* Mandan method of suspending sun pledger in mid-air weighted with buffalo skulls weighing up to 25 pounds each. *c,* bone awl used to pierce pledger's skin. *d,* Sioux knife used in actual Sun Dance Ceremony. *e,* sufferer secured between four poles, *f,* rawhide buffalo effigy tied to Sioux sun pole. *g,* rawhide human effigy tied to Sioux sun pole. Judging from old pictographs, these effigies were made in various sizes, some being life-sized. See color plate 31.

*Front figure*, Assiniboine Fool Society clown wearing painted hide mask. *Rear figure*, Mandan Buffalo Dancer.

in front, just as the morning star rose, and at the same moment another struck her over the head with a club. Death was instantaneous. Her heart was cut out as a sacrifice to the star, and every male in the tribe shot an arrow into her body, older relatives doing this in the name of boys too young to draw a bow themselves.

At the beginning of the nineteenth century, a young Pawnee warrior of high reputation rebelled against this rite. At the critical moment he cut the girl free from the scaffold, threw her on his horse, and ran off with her. He set her free near her own tribe. When he returned, he was not punished, but admired for his courage. The people seem to have been relieved to drop a cruel practice, and it ended there.

The Morning Star Ceremony was still celebrated annually without the human sacrifice feature, however, and a Morning Star priest is shown in color together with his sacred objects in plate 3. He wears a buffalo robe painted on the treated side with celestial symbols, and holds a gourd rattle with a blue line of life painted on it. His hair is allowed to fall in the traditional Plains manner used to show humility before God.

# Chapter 11

# RELIGION—DEATH AND
# THE LIFE AFTER

I am old and am living an unnatural life. I know that I am standing on the brink of the life that nobody knows about, and I am anxious to go to my Father, Ah-badt-dadt-deah, to live again as men were intended to live, even on this world.[1]

Near Pryor I met Chief Bell-rock, who is eighty-five, and alert in both mind and body. He leaned far from his pony to shake my hand and tell me that his heart sang because of our meeting. "I shall not see many more snows," he said, his kindly face almost happy. I experienced the feeling, which always comes to me when an old warrior speaks of leaving this life, that Bell-rock believed he had lived here wisely and well, and that plentiful reward awaited him beyond. There is never any shadow of doubt in these expressions by old Indians concerning death and a future life. They do not merely imply belief, but carry the positive declaration, "I know!"[2]

The Plains Indians believed in the immortality of the soul. To them the future life was very real, and sometimes, in dreams or visions, glimpses came which they felt were insights into the life of another world peopled by the ghosts of the departed. Their understandings about the future life were vague and hazy, yet this troubled them little, for they accepted the fact that a finite being cannot understand much about an infinite person or place. Besides this, the Indians were not accustomed to deal with abstract conceptions.

Nevertheless, a general picture of their beliefs can be gathered from the accounts which they gave of ghosts and the ghost country, for all the tribes had tales which dealt with the inhabitants of the spirit world. Some of the stories were said to have come from those who died and were restored to life again, while others came from living persons who, while in a vision trance, were taken by helper animals to visit the country where the spirits dwell, and then returned to their tribe to report the condition and ways of the departed.

The views of the world of the dead differed widely. With some tribes, the Other-Side-Land appeared to be a "happy hunting ground," a veritable Garden of Eden. With others, the faraway country was a land of unrealities, where the ghostly shadows of the departed endured an existence which was only a mockery of earthly life. Grinnell attributes such melancholy beliefs to the Blackfeet and the Gros Ventres.

The deceased always took on the form of ghosts. That is, the soul or spirit became ghostlike in substance. The spirits of the dead were said to be able to return at times in various forms, but they were always thin as air, though to the eye they might appear real. They were frequently glimpsed for a moment by living persons, but were likely to vanish just as quickly. The tiny whirlwinds of dust often seen moving about on the prairie on hot summer days were believed by the Pawnees to be ethereal human beings, and some tribes thought owls were reincarnated ghosts. On occasion, spirits took the form of skeletons, which might be able to walk about; or else appeared as ordinary people. In fact, it seems these spirits could freely take whatever human or animal forms they wished. Briefly put, Indian ghostology can be explained as follows: A scalped or strangled ghost remained at earth level, able to haunt and injure the living, sometimes causing illness and even death. An unscalped ghost was free to make his way toward the eternal country, living there, but also returning as he wished from time to time.

The Indian creed held by most Plains tribes about life after death was a broad one, for excepting the conditions regarding spirit-keeping ceremonies to be discussed later, all persons of all colors or beliefs who died unscalped and unstrangled would proceed immediately to a heavenly place. One went there just as he was, with the same passions, feelings, wishes, needs, and enmities. Therefore, since he would meet enemies, every warrior strove to reduce their number by scalping as many as possible in this world and forcing their ghosts to live at ground level.

The Indians understood perfectly well that the dead did not actually take the material articles buried with them to the Great Hunting Ground, for some of the items were hung in plain view around the burial place. They did believe, however, that if the articles were allowed to remain with or near the body until the soul reached its paradise, the spirit of the dead man would have the use of a "spirit model" or duplicate of those articles. Accordingly, any article considered necessary in the future state, and which the dead man did not possess in life, was gladly supplied by relatives or friends, and often at considerable sacrifice.

Consideration and/or fear of the state of the dead eliminated grave robbing entirely. There is no known instance of the violation of the burial place of one Indian by an enemy or one of his own tribe, although he might be without weapons and starving in the midst of game, and surrounded by a dozen burial trees or scaffolds containing warrior's bodies, each of which were attended by a bow and arrows, or a gun, gunpowder, and lead which had been burned with them.

The physical misfortunes and peculiarities which an Indian had in this life remained with him in eternity. Time was no more, and everyone continued forever at the age at which he entered the new life. Those who died quickly by wound or disease took with them no reminders of the injury; but some thought a body which had been emaciated and distorted by chronic disease released a soul which always suffered in the same way.

The soul of a warrior killed in battle but not mutilated further retained no sign of the wound that actually killed him, but every mutilation inflicted on the body after death was thought to disfigure the soul. This accounts for the (reasonably) common habit of shooting arrows into an unscalped body. It was a vindictive desire to torment the enemy's soul forever. Even though the head had already been scalped and the worst damage had been inflicted, additional shooting or mutilation was done on occasion in sheer wantonness, and out of a desire to put one's enemies "in their places." Some of it can also be explained by the fact that a few of the Plains tribes believed that slaying an enemy effected the release from torment of the friends or relatives they were avenging.

Colonel Dodge spent a great deal of time trying to discover how the Indians reconciled their odd beliefs with the idea of happiness in the future state. He concluded that the Indian did so to his personal satisfaction by his abundance of faith. "His belief as to the effect on the soul of certain previous conditions of

*Left*, woman mourning husband with hair cut and finger tips cut off. *Right*, painting warrior's face with his society designs in preparation for burial.

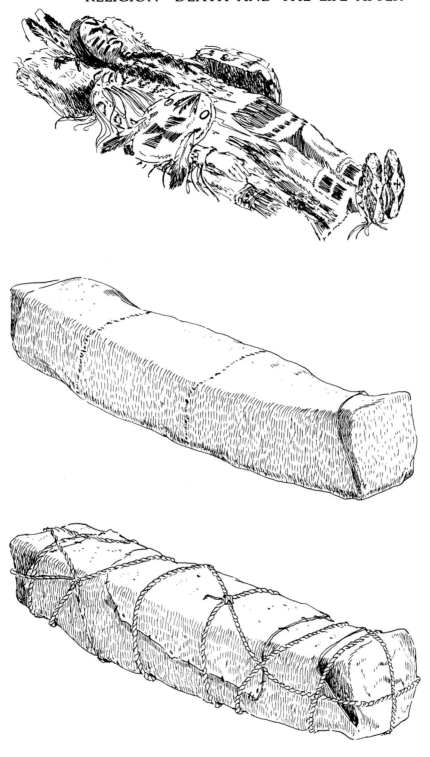

*Top*, warrior dressed and equipped for burial. *Center*, first wrapping of buffalo skin. *Bottom*, second wrapping of water-soaked hides. (Bodies were wrapped in many ways.)

life and death are, according to his ideas, solidly founded on reason. His belief in the perfect happiness of his Paradise is purely a matter of faith."[3]

Tribes varied in their choice of those who cared for the body at death. When death occurred at home, the Sioux family postponed the burial for twenty-four hours to make certain the person was dead. Once it was decided, all the relatives assisted in preparing the body. The Blackfoot body was cared for by the nearest female relations.

In no case was there anything resembling an embalming procedure. A warrior's face was painted with his well-known symbols, and especially those of his society. The eagle feathers he had earned were placed in his hair, and he was dressed in his finest clothing. Mandan and Sioux accounts reveal that his weapons, pipe and tobacco, fire-making tools, and enough provisions to last him a few days on his coming journey were placed alongside the body. Some tribes used a magnificent type of burial moccasin which was beaded all over, including the sole. Some also used an entirely beaded burial war club.

A fresh buffalo skin, still moist, was then wrapped around the body, and tightly bound and wound with thongs of rawhide from head to foot. After this, other robes were soaked in water until soft, and then wrapped in layers around the body. These too were carefully wound with thongs, until at last all air was excluded from the corpse. A great warrior's horse was painted with red "mourning" blotches. The deceased was placed on a travois, and then carried in a grand parade to the burial site.

The most common form of burial was a scaffold, which was constructed of four upright poles, each a little taller than human hands could reach and beyond the height which any of the wild animals could jump. On the top of the poles a number of smaller branches were intertwined to make a raftlike platform to hold the body. All of this was securely lashed together, the deceased was laid on it, his feet turned toward the rising sun, and then he was tied down. (An Assiniboine scout states that the feet were always turned to the west.)

A second method was the tree burial. Whether this was considered equal to the scaffold is not known. But it was often used in winter when the ground was hard, and especially by Indians living in the northern areas. In tree burials the body was prepared in the manner already indicated, and lashed to a fork in the tree. Brambles were often placed at the base of the tree to keep wild animals away.

Most of the Indian tribes believed that a body above ground had no covering to separate it from the creator, and they avoided earth burials whenever possible. The Shoshones, however, did inter their deceased in caves and under rock piles, as did the Kiowas and other southern tribes. But the elevated scaffold or tree burial was preferred, since, as time and the elements decayed and eroded the body, it was free to return to where it had come from. "Each of the elements," they said, "absorbed a part."

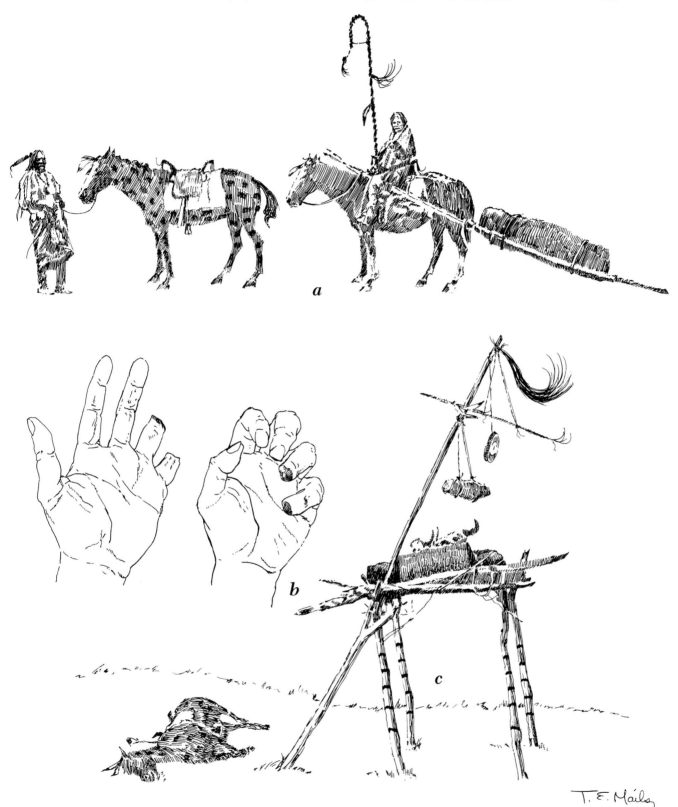

*a*, burial procession. *b*, fingers cut from woman's left hand in mourning. *c*, burial scaffold with warrior's favorite horse executed and special items suspended from pole—medicine bundle, shield, lance, and horse's tail.

Scaffold burial.

There were also lodge burials, usually reserved for the most important personages of a clan. Some of these were dressed and laid on beds, while others were put on a platform which was sometimes suspended by ropes from the lodge poles.

At times, when a great Blackfoot chief or warrior died, his lodge would be moved a short distance from the camp, and then set up in a brushy place. It was carefully pegged down, and stones and brush were piled around the bottom edge to make it secure. Inside, one end of an anchor rope was fastened to the top of the lodge poles, and tied at the other to a peg in the ground at the center of the lodge. Then the beds were made up all around the lodge, and the corpse was placed on one of them "as if asleep." The man's weapons, pipe, war clothing, and medicine were placed near him, and the door and smoke flaps were closed by sewing. No one ever again entered such a lodge. Sometimes a number of his horses were killed and left outside, so that he might have them to ride on his homeward journey. Following this, the village moved to a new location.

Tree burial.

The custom of killing horses at the grave is thought by many writers to be a standard one, but Indian accounts fail to bear this out. For example, mention is made in a Blackfoot account of a live horse with its tail and mane cut short to show it was in mourning for its master. It still had blotches of paint and decorations left over from the mourning parade. It was not killed.

A few early explorers were told of spectacular burials of great warriors and holy men mounted on their war horses, but such methods were rare and it is most difficult to substantiate them today.

If a man died in a lodge, it was never lived in again. The people were afraid of the man's ghost. So the tipi cover was sometimes used as the outer wrapping for the body.

After a death, a "giveaway" might be held to distribute some of the deceased's possessions. The name of the person was never mentioned again, unless it had already been given to another and thus had become public property.

Mourning began immediately upon death, and it was rendered in the severest possible form. Women lamented for deceased relations by cutting their hair short, and looked awfully grim during the mourning period. At the loss of a husband or son they also cut off one or more joints of their fingers. They always scarified the calves of their legs, and sometimes they gashed their faces too. Besides this, for a month or so they went daily to a place near the camp, generally a hill or little rise of ground, and there cried and lamented, calling to the deceased over and over again. Catlin said that "Anyone hearing it for the first time, even though wholly unacquainted with Indian customs, would at once know that it was a mourning song, or at least was the utterance of one in deep distress," and he was greatly moved by the sincerity of their lamenting.[4] There was no fixed period for the length of time one must mourn. Some continued a daily lament for a few weeks, and others went on much longer, even for months and years. Men mourned by cutting a little of or unbraiding their hair, by going without leggings, and for the loss of a son scarified their legs. This last, however, was never done for the loss of a wife, daughter, or any other relative. Sioux families were usually visited by their holy men, who gave them comfort and advice as to how they might best turn their misfortune into good.

Stationary tribes had scaffold cemeteries near the village. Others placed scaffolds at many places in the Plains. If there were holy burial grounds, few have come to light in Indian accounts.

When the scaffolds decayed and fell to the ground, the nearest relations buried the bones of the body. Often the skulls were buried too, but the custom of many clans was to lay them out in circles of a hundred or more on the prairie, placed some eight or nine inches apart with the faces all turned toward the center; where they were diligently protected and preserved in their precise positions from year to year, as objects of religious and affectionate veneration.

Several of these circles of twenty or thirty feet in diameter were seen on the

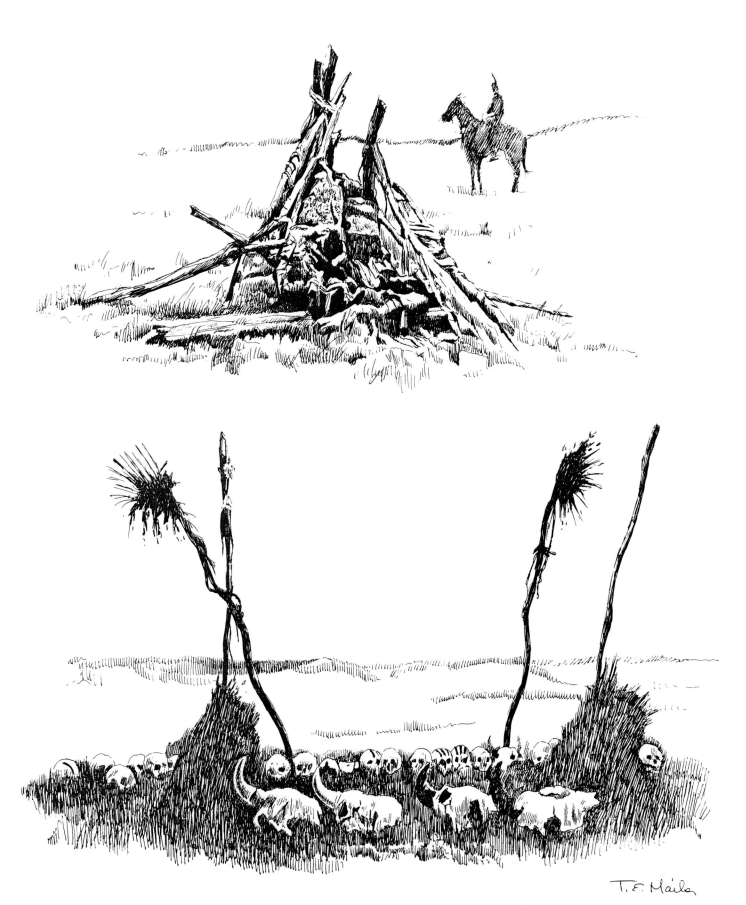

*Top,* fallen Crow Indian scaffold burial. *Bottom,* Mandan skull circle.

Plains by Whites. In the center of each ring was a mound some three feet high, on which rested two buffalo skulls, a male and a female; and in the center of the little mound was a "medicine pole" about twenty feet high, which bore many curious articles of mystery and superstition, which they supposed had the power of guarding and protecting the sacred arrangement. The people returned to the skull circles often to show their lasting affections for the dead. At these reunions fond affections and endearments were renewed, and animated conversations were held between relatives and the dead almost daily when the clan was in the burial area. Every skull was placed upon a bed of wild sage which was freshened at the reunion. A wife always knew the skull of her own husband or child by some mark or her vivid memorization of it. Considering the deep attachments of the Plains people, when the Whites moved the Indians away from their lands and onto reservations in the Indians' view they literally tore them away from those they loved, and forced them to leave their deceased alone on the Plains forever.

PLATE 9.   COMING RUNNING—BLACKFEET MOTHER ▶

Coming Running, young Blackfeet mother, 1899. W. McClintock wrote that in spite of her cares and labors, she was always smiling and in a good humor. He did not once hear her complain or speak an angry or impatient word. Her bright and cheerful disposition radiated sunshine to all around her. Adapted from photograph by W. McClintock.

# Chapter 12

# THE BUFFALO AND
# THE HORSE

Then the advisor said: "At what place have you stood and seen the good? Report it to me and I will be glad."

One of the scouts answered: "You know where we started from. We went and reached the top of a hill and there we saw a small herd of bison." He pointed as he spoke.

The advisor said: "Maybe on the other side of that you have seen the good. Report it." The scout answered: "On the other side of that we saw a second and larger herd of bison."

Then the advisor said: "I shall be thankful to you. Tell me all that you have seen out there."

The scout replied: "On the other side of that there was nothing but bison all over the country."

And the advisor said: "Hetchetu aloh!"

Then the crier shouted like singing: "Your knives shall be sharpened, your arrows be sharpened. Make ready, make haste; your horses make ready! We shall go forth with arrows. Plenty of meat we shall make!"

Everybody began sharpening knives and arrows and getting the best horses ready for the great making of meat.

---

◀ PLATE 10.  LOUD THUNDER—OMAHA WARRIOR

Loud Thunder was photographed at an Indian Hill Pageant at Kilbourn, Wisconsin, many years ago—wearing the spectacular war shirt of his grandfather.

The shirt is painted from the original. It is beaded with broad shoulder and arm bands, and hung with one hundred and four hairlocks, commonly called scalp locks by early traders and writers. However, see color plate 6 for special notes regarding the shirt.

The Plains Indians believed that the hair was an extension of the soul, and wearing such locks was another example of the Indian's profoundly religious nature.

Then we started for where the bison were. The soldier band went first, riding twenty abreast, and anybody who dared go ahead of them would get knocked off his horse. They kept order, and everybody had to obey. After them came the hunters, riding five abreast. The people came up in the rear. Then the head man of the advisors went around picking out the best hunters with the fastest horses, and to these he said: "Good young warriors, my relatives, your work I know is good. What you do is good always; so to-day you shall feed the helpless. Perhaps there are some old and feeble people without sons, or some who have little children and no man. You shall help these, and whatever you kill shall be theirs." This was a great honor for young men.

Then when we had come near to where the bison were, the hunters circled around them, and the cry went up, as in a battle, "Hoka hey!" which meant to charge. Then there was a great dust and everybody shouted and all the hunters went in to kill—every man for himself. They were all nearly naked, with their quivers full of arrows hanging on their left sides, and they would ride right up to a bison and shoot him behind the left shoulder. Some of these arrows would go in up to the feathers and sometimes those that struck no bones went right straight through. Everybody was very happy.[1]

If God was the creator and overseer of life, if the morning star, moon, and Mother Earth combined their talents to give birth and hope to the Indian, if the sun was the dispatcher of wisdom and warmth, then the buffalo was the tangible and immediate proof of them all, for out of the buffalo came almost everything necessary to daily life—including his religious use as an intermediary through which the Great Spirit could be addressed; and by which the Spirit often spoke to them. In short, the buffalo was life to the Plains Indians until the White man's goods and ways first eliminated and then replaced the animal.

Understandably, then, a major part of Indian life was oriented in and around the buffalo herds. They moved with them during all but the winter months. The buffalo's habits and kinds were studied intensely, and in time the Indians put virtually every part of the beast to some utilitarian use. In fact, it is almost astounding to see a graphic breakdown of the uses made of him—of his hide, of his organs, of his muscles, of his bones, and of his horns and hoofs. It is slight wonder that the Indians reverenced the buffalo, related him directly to the Great Creator, and believed that he would respond to religious persuasion. The Sioux thought him to be a natural symbol for the universe, and no doubt the other tribes accorded him a like honor.

There are several matters of magnitude to be considered about the Indians and the buffalo:

First, there is the matter of the buffalo's place in the sphere of Indian religion. Unfortunately, since this function is connected to so many aspects of the Indian life-way, mention of it must be made in many places, and to cover the entire subject here might cause a vital connection to be missed in another chapter. Therefore, the remarks made at this point will include only what is necessary to round out the total picture.

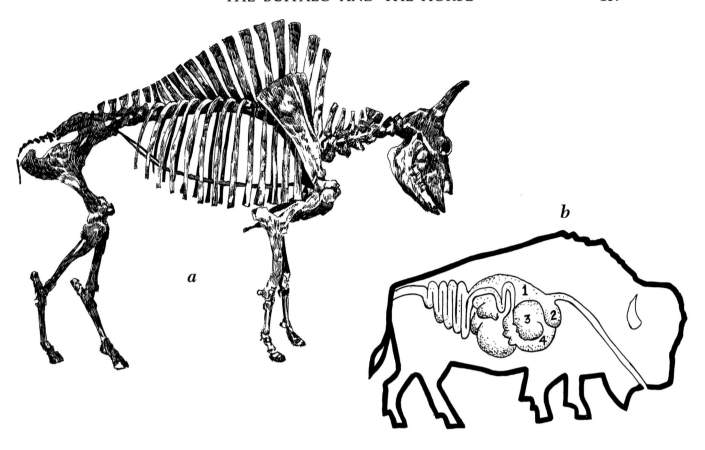

*a*, buffalo skeleton and chart of uses made of bones. *b*, diagram of four-chambered stomach of buffalo.

Second, a visual display of the infinite uses made of the buffalo is essential, for it shows the true importance of the buffalo, and also helps to draw a sharper impression of the creative talents of the Plains Indians.

Third, as one ponders the uses made of the bison, he inevitably wants to know how the Indians themselves were able to make so much of it. The answer is found in ferreting out what the Indians learned over the years about the intriguing types and habits of the buffalo. Ultimately it becomes clear that the buffalo's sex, age, seasons, and varieties offered advantages to the Indian which were so profuse as to be amazing, to say the least.

Fourth, the buffalo hunting and procurement methods used by the Indians need to be set forth.

And finally, a summary of hide preparation methods will complete the vital picture of Indians and buffalo living in what can only be called an "interdependent" state. After all, the Indians trimmed the excess from the herds season by season, and thus made it easier for their vast remaining numbers to exist. The Indians also provided fresh and succulent grass for the herds by burning off areas

HIDE

*Buckskin:*

moccasin tops
cradles
winter robes
bedding
breechclouts
shirts
leggings
belts
dresses
pipe bags
pouches
paint bags
quivers
tipi covers
gun cases
lance covers
coup flag covers
dolls

*Rawhide:*

containers:
  clothing
  headdresses
  food
  medicine bags
shields
buckets
moccasin soles
rattles
drums, drumsticks
splints
cinches
ropes
thongs
saddles
stirrups
knife cases
bull boats
quirts
armbands
lance cases
horse masks
horse forehead ornaments
bullet pouches
belts

HAIR

headdresses
saddle pad filler
pillows
ropes
ornaments
halters
medicine balls

HORNS

cups
fire carrier
powderhorn
spoons
ladles
headdresses
signals
toys

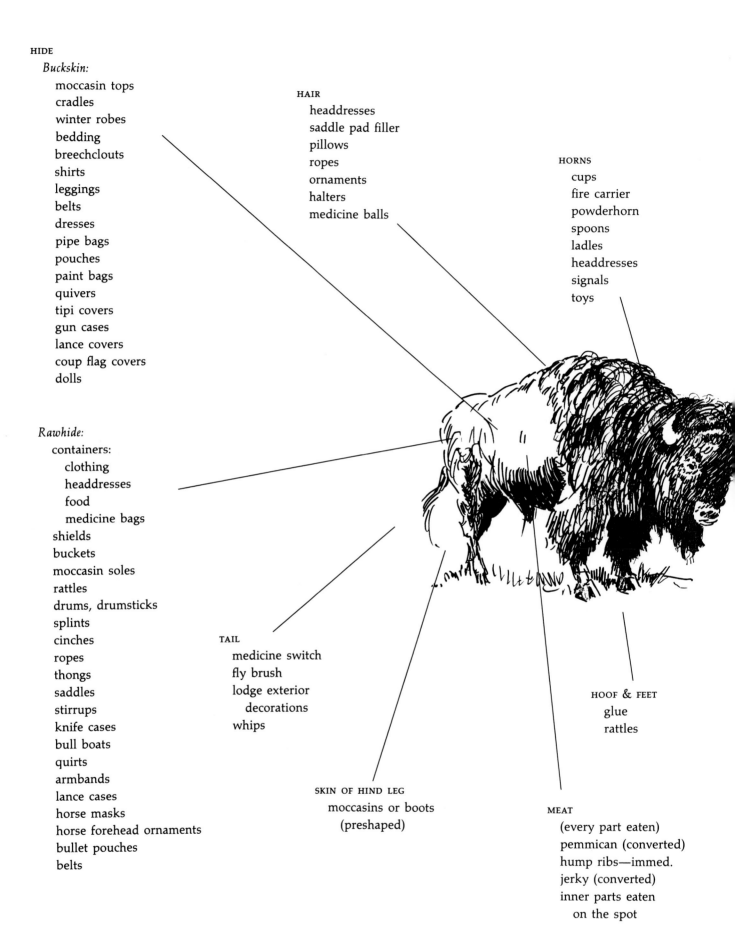

TAIL

medicine switch
fly brush
lodge exterior
  decorations
whips

SKIN OF HIND LEG

moccasins or boots
(preshaped)

HOOF & FEET

glue
rattles

MEAT

(every part eaten)
pemmican (converted)
hump ribs—immed.
jerky (converted)
inner parts eaten
  on the spot

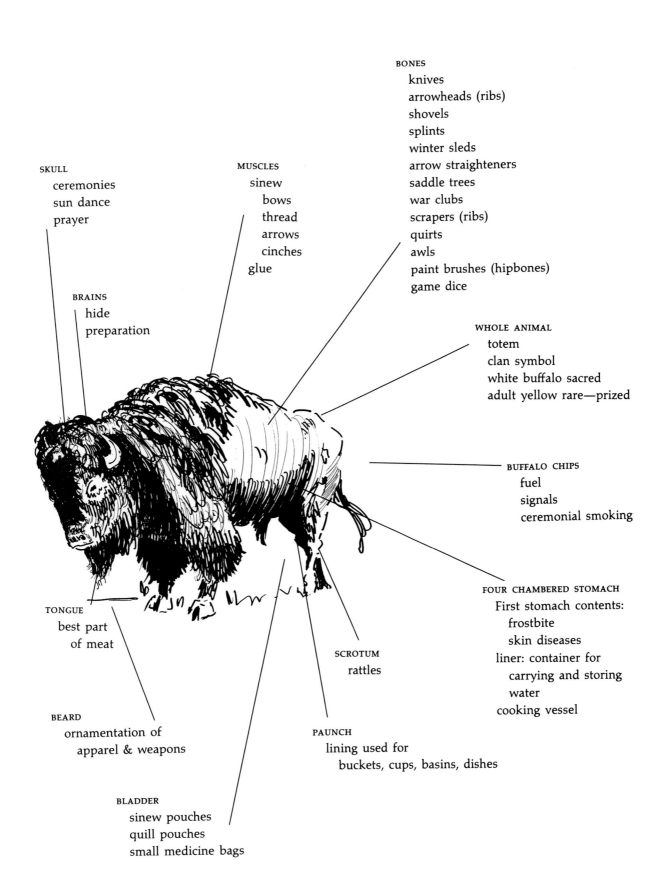

BONES
knives
arrowheads (ribs)
shovels
splints
winter sleds
arrow straighteners
saddle trees
war clubs
scrapers (ribs)
quirts
awls
paint brushes (hipbones)
game dice

SKULL
ceremonies
sun dance
prayer

MUSCLES
sinew
bows
thread
arrows
cinches
glue

BRAINS
hide
preparation

WHOLE ANIMAL
totem
clan symbol
white buffalo sacred
adult yellow rare—prized

BUFFALO CHIPS
fuel
signals
ceremonial smoking

FOUR CHAMBERED STOMACH
First stomach contents:
frostbite
skin diseases
liner: container for
carrying and storing
water
cooking vessel

TONGUE
best part
of meat

SCROTUM
rattles

BEARD
ornamentation of
apparel & weapons

PAUNCH
lining used for
buckets, cups, basins, dishes

BLADDER
sinew pouches
quill pouches
small medicine bags

VISUAL CHART OF THE USES MADE OF THE BUFFALO

of prairie at regular intervals to promote new growth. New grass was always an inducement to the herds, and it was common for some of the tribes in the north to burn off certain sections of the plains each spring.

If a child's name included the word "buffalo" in it, the Indians believed that the child would be especially strong and would mature quickly. And, though a name in itself is not the guarantee of an automatic transformation, a "buffalo" child usually fulfilled the expectations of others by striving to accomplish what his name implied. If a warrior was renamed after a vision or great hunting or war accomplishment, and his new name included the word "buffalo," it meant that the buffalo was his supernatural helper, or that he exhibited the strength of a buffalo, or that he was an extraordinary hunter. In other words, the name described the powers of the man.

Societies named after the buffalo had the animal as their patron. The founder's vision would have featured the buffalo in a prominent way, and quite probably, all or most of the society members would also have seen buffalo in their dreams or visions.

Holy men who saw buffalo in the vision during which they were called to the practice of medicine would seek thereafter to commune with the Great Spirit through the buffalo. This might be done by prayers spoken to living buffalo—and thus sent through them to God—or by the ritualistic use of buffalo parts such as the skull. Then too, their medicine bundles would always feature parts of the buffalo and/or stones associated in the mind of the holy man with the buffalo.

Buffalo calling was a constant and essential practice on the Plains. Since the Indians believed that buffalo existed for their particular use, it followed that the migrations of the herds were according to a divinely controlled pattern. Whenever, then, the season came for the great herds to approach their area, the Indians of each band sought to assist the process by "calling" the buffalo. Any delay in their appearance would, of course, intensify the calling procedures and amplify the medicine rites.

Buffalo often licked themselves, and in the process swallowed some of the hair. Over the years the hair sometimes formed itself into a perfectly round ball two inches or more in diameter. Such a ball was a great find, and it immediately became a buffalo calling item for ritual use.

The Blackfeet had special mystic rites for calling buffalo herds into their area. The medicine person employing the rites had the good fortune to own one or more of the unusual stones called "buffalo stones." These were small reddish-brown rocks from two to four inches long, and naturally shaped something like a buffalo. At least, to an Indian, they looked more like a buffalo than they did anything else. The stones were very rare, and the few that existed were only discovered now and then in the stream beds by searchers.

All that is known about the rites themselves is that the owner of a stone would invite a group of renowned hunters to his tipi to participate in the calling

Sioux warrior calling buffalo back in spring of year. Depiction based on ancient Sioux pictographic drawing done in 1890.

ceremony. There was no dancing in the preliminary rite, but the group did dance in thanksgiving at the conclusion of a successful hunt.

All of the Plains tribes had special songs which they believed would make the buffalo approach their camp areas. And all the tribes had dreamers and holy men who would conduct secret rites and then prophesy where the buffalo were most plentiful. The Mandans, after completing a meal, would present a bowl of food to a mounted buffalo head in the belief that it would send out messages to living animals, telling them of the Indians' generosity, and thus inducing them to come closer. They also prayed constantly to the Great Spirit to send them meat, and sometimes pleaded with a mystic "Spiritual Great Bull of the Prairie" to come to them with his cow, and with the herd close behind, naturally!

The holy men of the Sioux, Assiniboines, and Pawnees used buffalo skulls in rituals designed to entice the herds, and the carcass of the first animal slain in a large hunt was always sacrificed to God. On occasion, Comanche hunters would find a horned toad and ask it where the buffalo were. They believed the toad would scamper off in the direction of the nearest herd. Or the same hunters would watch a raven flying in a circle over their camp and caw to it, thinking it would answer by flying off toward the animals closest to them. They also held a nighttime hunting dance before the men left the main camp to look for buffalo. After the hunt there was a buffalo-tongue ritual and feast which they celebrated as a thanksgiving ceremony. Some of the tribes had a unique hoop game which "called" the buffalo as it was played.

In a time of great scarcity, the Mandan White Buffalo Cow Women Society held a special dance to draw the herds near the village.

George Catlin gives a vivid description of the buffalo calling dance of the Mandan men.[2] The dance lasted three days, with new dancers constantly taking the places of those who became exhausted. About fifteen men danced at a time, each wearing a huge mask made of an entire buffalo's head—the only change being the insertion of wooden eyes and nosepieces with slits in them to admit air to the dancer. Painted bodies and a buffalo tail tied at the back to a belt completed the costume. Each dancer imitated a buffalo, and when exhausted, sank to the ground. In moments another dancer took his place while he was dragged from the circle of dancers by the bystanders, and ceremonially skinned and butchered.

The Hidatsa tribe had a calling dance in which six elderly men played the parts of buffalo bulls. After dancing for a time in imitation of the bulls, they tasted dishes of boiled corn and beans. Following this, empty bowls were given to them, and each man acted as though he was eating the wonderful buffalo meat which would shortly fill the bowls when the buffalo responded to the rite and came into hunting range.

Speaking generally, when considering the energy put into buffalo calling, it should be recognized that there were many reasons to want the herds to come close to the camps: First, the transportation problem was a monumental one, since

Mandan Buffalo Dancer dancing to call buffalo.

the enormous quantities of meat and the heavy hides were not easy to carry from the hunting areas to the camp sites. Second, it was much safer to hunt in one's own domain. In particular, the penetration of enemy territory or even of contested areas was extremely hazardous. A Ponca spokesman, in describing the plight of his tribe to George Catlin, tearfully stated that the Ponca warriors, who were few in number, were being cut to pieces by the more numerous Sioux because they had to go into Sioux territory to obtain buffalo.[3] And third, without the ever present buffalo all of the Indians could not have survived—at least on the Great Plains.

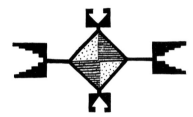

No one knows how many buffalo there were in North America before the White men came. Most estimates for the peak period of Plains Indian occupation range from sixty to seventy-five million head. As late as 1830, White hunters guessed that forty million were left.

Although the larger herds lived on the Plains, smaller ones also ranged from northern Georgia to Hudson Bay and from the Appalachians to the Rockies and beyond.

The buffalo of North America were not all the same color or size. The Plains type, with which everyone is familiar, was not the largest. The wood buffalo, found in small herds in the eastern parts of the United States and Canada, which some called the Pennsylvania buffalo, was slightly larger. Although it grazed on the open prairies in the summer, it generally sought the protection of the woods in the winter. Another type was the less common mountain buffalo of the Rockies and the Pacific coast region. It was smaller, but more fleet than the Plains bison. Unfortunately, both the wood and the mountain buffalo became extinct before scientists could learn much about them.

The need for grass and water kept the buffalo on the move most of the time. After a herd had consumed the grass on one part of the range, it was forced to move on to fresh forage. With luck, about every third day the animals would come to water, and did their drinking mostly at night. Hunters said that when a herd left a river and started up a canyon, the sound was like distant thunder and often could be heard for miles.

Some early explorers believed that the herds made long seasonal migrations, moving from south to north in the spring and returning in the fall. Others maintained that the herd movements were more local. George Catlin, who went west in 1832 to study and paint the Indians, decided that the buffalo seemed to enjoy travel, but were not truly migratory. "They graze in immense herds and almost incredible numbers at times," he wrote. "They roam over vast tracts of country, from east to west and from west to east as often as from north to south."[4]

An early writer named J. A. Allen supported Catlin's view. He noted that, while most of the buffalo abandoned the hot Texas plains in the summer for those farther north, "it is improbable that the buffaloes of Saskatchewan ever wintered in Texas. Doubtless the same individuals never moved more than a few hundred miles in a north and south direction, the annual migration being merely a moderate swaying northward and southward of the whole mass with the changes of the season."[5]

Apparently, there were at least two, and probably three, herds moving in smaller circles within their own areas—north, south, and central. This took some of them in and out of each tribal area more than once during the year, whereas if the single herd idea applied they would have passed through many tribal domains but once.

Ordinarily the herd moved at a leisurely pace, with each animal nibbling at tufts of grass as it went along. Yet the buffalo was easily frightened, and sudden movement, sound, or unusual odor could cause a terrifying and crushing stampede. A wind-blown leaf, the bark of a prairie dog, or the passing shadow of a cloud could put the entire herd into headlong flight. Even a small grass fire could send them running for many miles. The smell or sight of a man would do the same, and for this reason the Indians evolved some careful and strict regulations to govern the great annual hunts.

The size, appearance, and grazing habits of the buffalo help us understand why early explorers referred to it as a cow. To them, its only difference from cattle lay in its having a hump on its back, a larger head and front legs, and a mat of purple shaggy hair over its foreparts.

The color of the buffalo's coat varied with his age, and from one geographical area to another. Some southern buffalo were tawny, and others were almost black. Farther north, one might find an occasional blue- or mouse-colored buffalo, or even a pied or spotted one. Rarest of all was the albino, of which few existed, and even they varied from dirty gray to pale cream.

The Indian warriors set a high value on a white buffalo robe and were reluctant to part with one. A certain Cheyenne war chief wore a white robe when he led his warriors into battle, and believed that it would shield him from all harm. Some of the holy men used white robes in their medical curing rituals.

To an unschooled person, all buffalo in a herd looked alike. But there were many kinds and sizes, and their hide qualities varied considerably with the seasons. In fact, one had to know a great deal about them to utilize their fullest capabilities.

Mating time was in July. Throughout the winter the bachelor breeding bulls,

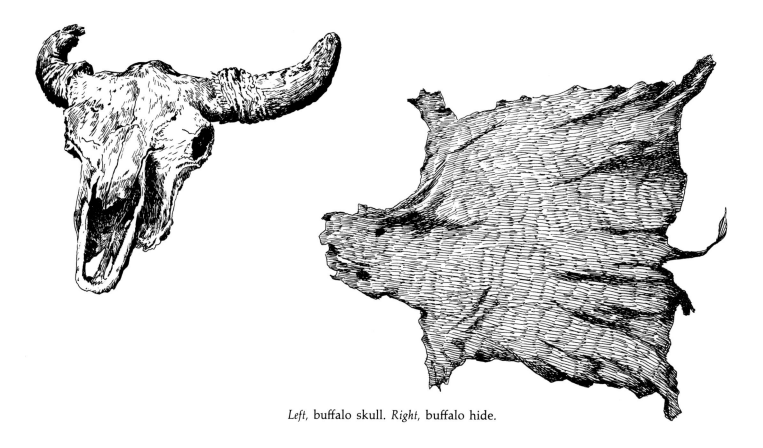

*Left,* buffalo skull. *Right,* buffalo hide.

grouped in small and large herds, roamed peacefully by themselves. But about mid-July, when the running season began, they joined the cows. During this period the bull buffalo became exceedingly vicious toward one another, and toward any Indians foolish enough to approach them. Any cow in breeding condition would be closely followed by a pugnacious bull, and "tending" pairs would be a common sight on the outskirts of every band until late August.

Whenever bulls contended with each other for the right to a cow, the rest of the herd circled restlessly around the two antagonists. Other bulls would be pawing dirt and bellowing deep down in their throats, while the cows looked on as avid spectators. Battles were often to the death, and the larger and stronger animals were usually the victors. Bulls fought forehead to forehead, roaring, heaving, and seeking to push each other backward. Much of the fighting was ritual, but the moment one gave up the jousting and turned away he was promptly gored. A swift move and a quick turn of the head left a long, deep gash in his side. The intestines immediately came out, and the loser died. The victor paid no attention to the victim after the fatal hook was made, and the cow in question was calmly escorted away. Such battles were so intense while they were going, though, that bulls would ignore human beings. Even though the main herd fled at the approach of a mounted Indian, the titanic gladiators fought on. So Indian onlookers frequently saw these herculean contests at close range, and were able to tell about them later on.

Strangely enough, old bulls mated with young cows, and young bulls with the matured cows. In the early part of the mating season, perhaps to avoid fighting, a bull with one or more cows would stay in deep coulees which were some distance from the large part of the herd.

From late summer to early fall, the buffalo grouped together in small and large herds. Bull fights at this time were rare. With grass at its plentiful best, the buffalo became fat and robust. Long lines made their leisurely way to water and back again to the feeding grounds. Usually they traveled single file, and the primary buffalo trails became three or more feet deep in places.

In late summer the animals were at ease. As the heat of the day increased they would lie down a great deal. The hunting days of the Indian tribe had not yet come, and the warriors only disturbed them on rare occasions for a supply of fresh meat.

When a herd crossed a large river, such as the Missouri, they swam in small groups, one group after the other. Because of the vast size of the herds, the leaders were already across and on their way to new feeding grounds before the last of the groups had moved up to the river. Often several hours had passed before the last group was across. When buffalo were swimming they occasionally blew water through their nostrils. This made a peculiar noise which could be heard underwater for amazing distances. The bellowing of the bulls was itself a sound which could be heard for as much as ten miles!

By October of a good year, all the buffalo were fat and the bulls were still moving with the herds, and it was the best time for tribal hunting. The first days of the hunt were devoted to obtaining all the meat needed for the winter. The chase for robes came later.

In November the bulls left the herds. They gathered in small groups and remained away from the cows until breeding time. During this period the hides from four-year-old cows were taken. The hair was not prime, but the hides were just right for new lodges.

Buffalo calves, weighing from twenty-five to forty pounds at birth, started to drop about April, and continued to appear till May. As far as is known there were no twins, but an Assiniboine named Crazy Bull claimed he saw a two-headed unborn calf while butchering a cow which he killed in March. In a chase, calves never ran close to their mothers. All of them fell to the rear, so even if there were twins, they were not discernible as such by the Indians.

The hair of the calves was of a yellowish or reddish color, and remained so until they were from three months to a year old, when they shed this wool and assumed the darker color of the adult buffalo. Calves were called Little Yellow Buffalo. Robes for children were made from these beautiful skins, and they were always tanned with the hair intact.

After an early fall hunt, a large number of motherless and deserted calves were left on the hunting ground. Cows always abandoned their calves as soon as hunters gave chase, and usually they were in the lead of a stampeding herd. The bulls ran just behind the cows and the yearlings and calves brought up the rear. Some hunters claimed that the cows could run faster than any of the other buffalo in the herd, and for this reason were always in the lead. Others said the bulls ran just behind the cows to protect them, and so were behind by choice. They always were right at the heels of the cows.

If a chase took place near a camp and calves were left, boys mounted on yearling ponies and using their small bows and arrows staged exciting miniature chases, to the delight of the warriors who looked on. Very young calves left motherless or deserted after a chase were even known to follow the hunters back to camp.

By fall a healthy buffalo youngster would have increased in size to four hundred pounds, and its coat was long, shaggy, and thickened with heavy wool against the rigors of the cold season soon to come.

The coat of a year-old calf turned from its yellowish color to a dark shade. By now he was so fluffy that he looked big for his age. The Assiniboines called them "Little Black-haired Ones," or "Fluffed-haired Ones."

Two-year-old buffalo were called "Two-Teeth," having two full teeth at that age. Just before they reached the second year, their horns emerged beyond their thick hair and commenced to curve. At that age the tips of the horns were blunt, so they were also called "Blunt-Horns."

As they passed the second year, their horns continued to curve, and three-year-olds were known as "Curved-Horns," because of the short, small, curved horns.

"Small-built Buffalo" was the usual name applied to the four-year-olds, but they were also called "Four-Teeth." Robes taken from these in January and February were considered the best of all hides. They were not too thick, and the hair was fluffed out, silky, and thick.

Boys were taught that when the robe hunters rode into a herd, they were to look in particular for the "Small-built Ones," both males and females, with trim and neat bodies, whose coats of hair were like fine fur.

At the age of six, cows were known as "Big Females," which meant they were mature animals. The bulls of this vintage were called "Horns Not Cracked" because of their fine polished horns, which resulted from hours spent in polishing them by rubbing against low-cut banks or trees. Sometimes the bulls pawed down the upper sides of washouts and used the newly exposed and harder surface as a polishing material.

Bull hides were skinned only to the shoulders and cut off, leaving behind the parts that covered the humps. To skin a mature bull, the Assiniboine boy learned how to lay the animal in a prone position and then make an incision along the back, starting a little above and between the tips of the shoulder blades and ending at the tail. When this method of skinning was completed, the hide was in two pieces.

Buffalo bull, cow, and calf.

In the more usual way of removing the buffalo hide, and a task ordinarily carried out by the women, the cow buffalo was placed on its side. Shoshone women sliced them along the back from the head to tail. Then they ripped them down the belly and took off the top half of the hide, cutting away all the meat on that side from the bones. After this they would tie ropes to the feet of the carcass and turn it over with their ponies, proceeding then to strip off the skin and the flesh from the other side in the same way.

The heavier bull, being more difficult to move, was sometimes heaved onto his belly, with his legs spread. The women would slash him across the brisket and the neck and then fold the hide back so they could cut out the forequarters at the joints. To complete the removal they would split the hide down the middle.

Fat from matured animals, when rendered, was soft and yellowish in color. The tallow from young buffalo was always hard and white.

When buffalo became old, some living beyond the age of thirty years, they shrank in size. The horns, especially those of the bulls, were cracked, craggy, and homely. Old bulls congregated in lonely groups. They remained away from the main herds and usually died of natural causes because no one cared for their meat or hides.

There were some unusual buffalo, and the strange kinds which were noticed during the hunt were the source of animated discussions at gatherings afterward.

As stated previously, the color of the hair on all calves was yellowish, and by the end of the first year had turned almost black. However, a few retained their original color through their lifetime. They were called "yellow ones," and most of them were females. They were natural-size buffalo with an odd color. Robes made from the yellow ones were rare, and a hunter was proud to be able to present one to a prominent person.

White or albino buffalo were rare, and the number taken by the different bands was so few it became a matter of historical record to be handed down from generation to generation. Only three were known of by the Assiniboine tribe. The hide of one was brought back by a war party, but the heirs did not know whether the party killed the animal or took it from an enemy tribe in a raid. Another was owned by a northern band, who, whenever a momentous occasion arose, used a piece of it to fashion a sacred buffalo horn headdress for a new headman. The third, a heifer, was only seen by several hunters who were returning to camp after a chase. Their horses were tired and no attempt was made to chase it. However, one of their number, whose name was Growing Thunder, followed the herd for some time but finally returned to the group and told how the herd seemed to guard the white one. He tried to get within shooting range of the animal but was unsuccessful. It remained at all times in the middle of the large herd.

Another kind, known as "spotted ones," had white spots on the underside and on the flanks. Some had small white spots on one or both hind legs, usually near the hoofs. Only females were marked in this way.

The "small-heads" were also females. They were of ordinary size, but had small heads and very short horns.

PLATE 11.   THE BISON HUNTER ▶

In demonstration of his tremendous horsemanship skill, the hunter guides his horse with only his knees—both hands being free to operate the bow. A long hide rope trails out from the horse's neck for the unhorsed rider to grab in an emergency. The ears of the horse are notched to indicate that he is an elite pony—one especially trained and qualified for hunting and warfare. Such horses were valued above all else, being carefully cared for and guarded.

"Curved-horns" were both male and female. The bulls of this variety had short horns with accentuated curves, while the cow horns were thin, long, and curved. The tips, which curved out of sight into the hair, made curved-horn cows look as if they wore earrings.

A certain old buffalo group was called "narrow-cows," because of the narrow-built bodies. From the side they looked like the rest of the females, but in a chase one was easily detected. In spite of their shape they were usually healthy and the meat was good.

Some females had forelocks, and sometimes hair around the horns, which were short and looked shorn. Since they resembled Indian women who had their hair short in mourning, they were known as "mourning-cows." These cows were more vicious than other kinds for some reason, and would charge mounted hunters if they came too close. Their meat was good, but it was seldom eaten because of a belief that if anyone who knew the facts ate the meat from a mourning-cow, there would be a death in the family.

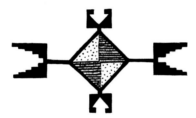

Weather permitting, hunting in winter was a fairly simple task. The Indians could either hunt on horseback or use snowshoes, which enabled them to run over soft drifts. Although the buffalo's thick, coarse hair protected them from the extreme cold, their awesome weight worked against them in the snow. They frequently became exhausted, or were mired down in the drifts and unable to move. With little danger to themselves the Indians could run up to the buffalo, caught in the sea of white, and drive their arrows or lances into their diaphragms, lungs, or hearts. Much the same approach was used when animals were caught on frozen lakes or in summer when the hunters came upon a herd swimming across a wide river.

The most ancient method of capturing buffalo in large numbers was the "piskin." Large piles of rocks, tree stumps, and buffalo dung were placed at

◄ PLATE 12. MEDICINE CROW, CROW WAR LEADER

Buffalo bull caught by hunters in winter snow.

intervals to make two converging lines, each over a mile in length. When completed they formed a long V-shaped pathway. The broad open end of the lines began at a natural grazing area, while the narrow end led into a small draw and up to a low hill about twenty-five feet in diameter. The hill would have a smooth slope on the approach side and a sharp drop on the far and hidden side. Around the far side the Indians built a large corral of horizontal logs and vertical posts. Sharpened stakes were angled across the bottom log with their points projecting in to prevent a trapped herd from jamming against the fence and pushing it over.

Once a herd moved into the vicinity of the open end or entrance of the funnel-shaped path, a "caller" wearing a buffalo robe over his head and imitating a buffalo calf sought to lure the herd toward the trap. When the buffalo started in, a line of Indian drivers upwind and behind them made noises and frightened the herd into a run. Other band members, who had already taken their hiding places behind the heaps forming the funnel, leaped up as they passed and shouted to keep them running, until at last they raced over the hill and were trapped in the corral. Here the hunters closed in to kill the milling animals with clubs, arrows, and lances.

The piskin method was not always successful, since many things could go wrong, causing the herds to veer off at the entrance or even between the piles along the pathway. A large kill also left the place in an offensive mess. In summer the buffalo herds could smell it and steered clear of the area. But wind, sun, rain, and scavenger animals purified the corral, and in two or three months it was suitable for use again. The winter snow was a perfect cleanser too.

A variation of the piskin was the "buffalo jump." In this method, the funneling pathway was employed again, but it ended at a sheer cliff some twenty or more feet in height. The best jumps were at the edge of a good pasture which sloped gently into a shallow draw and toward the rim. Hunters ran the herd in the direction of the cliff, with band members assisting again at the piles along the way. Shortly, the thundering herd plummeted into space and ended in a mass of dead and crippled beasts at the foot of the cliff. There the hunters finished them off, and the women set immediately to skinning them, since any meat not cut off, sliced, and placed on drying racks before the next morning would spoil.

Many of the buffalo jumps used by the Blackfeet and the Crows have been located in Montana. At some of these the bones and refuse cover an area several acres in width and are many feet deep, indicating their use for hundreds of years. Collectors still search through them for stone arrowheads today.

A successful piskin or buffalo jump hunt was an exhausting effort for the Indians, but it could supply each family with fresh meat for several days, with a reserve supply of dried meat, and with bones and several hides to tan.

The buffalo had poor vision, a keen sense of smell, and surprising speed when aroused. With their short tails sticking straight up and their shaggy manes shaking, they ran with a roll in their gallop which easily deceived the spectator

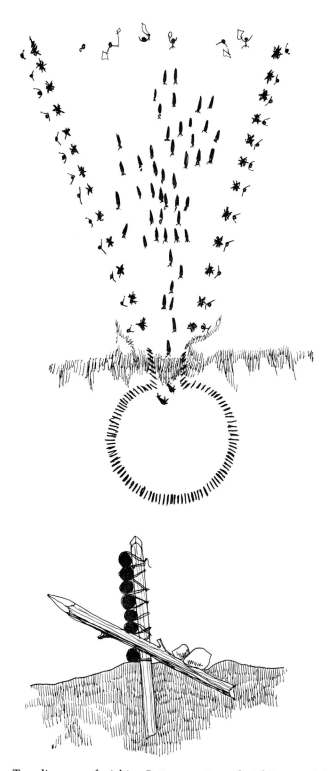

*Top*, diagram of piskin. *Bottom*, section of piskin corral fence.

as to the real pace they were going. The earth shook as they thundered over it, and not every horse could match their speed.

"Blind fury" was an exact description of a charging buffalo bull. Its momentum was fantastic. And although its eyesight was poor, once its keen ears and nose had homed in on an enemy, its tenacity and agility was astounding. Even

at a standstill, shoulder muscles tensed for action, head down, horns thrust forward, eyes bloodshot with anger, and quick hot breath steaming out of his nostrils,
the aroused bull buffalo was an awesome sight and challenge. In addition to weight
and speed, it had impressive height—a mature bull stood six or seven feet at the
shoulder hump. Beyond this there was a tough hide, a battering-ram skull with

Buffalo jump.

a thick hair pad, and a nervous system that sometimes kept it moving long after the beast was technically dead.

Against these teeming mountains of muscle, the Indian boy or warrior, until he obtained a gun, had only the bow and arrow, the lance, the long two-edged knife—and, of course, the horse, which was really the weapon that finally sliced the odds between hunter and hunted. Skillfully used, it alone enabled its master to catch up with and get away from a stampeding herd.

Accordingly, the buffalo hunt became, in addition to a source of supply, an ideal training ground for military duty on horseback, for the two-thousand-pound goliaths of blind fury and thrust were excellent tests of anyone's competence and valor as a warrior.

In the minds of the Plains Indians of 1750 to 1875, the classic buffalo hunt was the summer chase. Hunting then was close to warfare in its demands upon horsemanship and courage. Cool nerves and sharp reflexes were required of horse and rider in both hunting and war, so the young brave trained his finest horses in the buffalo hunt until they became like extensions of the lower part of his body.

It took months of hard work to ready a horse for use in hunting and warfare, and not every steed could meet the requirements. Any buffalo in good condition could outrun a mediocre horse. An acceptable mount must be able to run down its quarry in a mile or less. Since an untrained animal would shy and buck whenever it came close to buffalo, it had to be taught to race through a confusion of beasts and up to an enraged bull while guided by knee pressure alone. The hunter needed both hands free in war and in the chase, and in both instances he either let the reins drop on his horse's neck, tucked the loose ends in his belt, held them in his teeth, or locked them in the crook of his right arm.

Each warrior had to have at least one horse which was trained to a fine point for buffalo hunts and warfare. It became his best and favorite, and was usually too valuable to sell or trade. He guarded it like a treasure and picketed it just outside his tipi at night. After all, his existence and future depended upon it to an amazing degree. A buffalo and war horse was trained to stop instantly at a nudge of the knees or a tug from the rawhide thong, called a "war bridle," which was tied to the animal's lower jaw. But more than that thong was necessary, since racing through thundering herds over rough ground that was riddled with bushes, rocks, and hidden burrows portended frequent collisions and spills for the rider, so during battles and hunts a fifteen- to twenty-foot rope was ofted tied around the horse's neck so that its free end would drag behind the horse. When a falling rider seized the rope, his horse came to a sharp stop, and in a moment the man was on his feet and mounted again. Often one who had an especially valuable buffalo horse cut V-shaped notches in his ears.

Buffalo hunters stripped to a clout, or to clout and leggings at most, to reduce their weight and to free their movements. Frame saddles, shields, and other extra gear were left behind at a selected site. Some hunters used pad saddles or buffalo robes tied on with a buckskin cinch. A hunter carried six or seven arrows and his bow in his hands, or when using a gun, a few bullets in his mouth. Quivers were carried at the hunter's left side so that arrows could be quickly drawn. A heavy quirt was used to prod the horse.

A bow's length away was the distance the hunters had to try for, and the preferred targets were the intestinal cavity just behind the last rib, and just back of the left shoulder and into the heart. At that narrow distance their powerful bows could sink an arrow into the buffalo's body up to the feather, or even pass it clear through him. A foot closer brought them into hooking range, but a foot farther away meant losing power and accuracy. Unless the buffalo was hit in a vital spot, he died slowly, or often recovered altogether. In either case, he would race away and was lost to the tribe. Hunting skill was also encouraged by the fact that if two or more arrows from the same hunter were found in one of the carcasses, the women returned them to their owner with scalding compliments about his shooting ability and courage. To avoid this, many a hunter would risk his neck a second time to ride in close enough to grab his badly placed arrows and yank them free. Either that or he might try to reach a fallen animal, dismount and seize his extra arrows before the others could see them. Success in this always resulted in a private chuckle by the hunter.

To the victors belonged the buffalo's liver, and when the chase had run its course, they jumped from their horses, cut it out, and ate it raw, seasoned with gall and still steaming with body heat and dripping blood.

These were bizarre but triumphant moments, and every boy remembered to the last detail that first, crowning day when he dropped a buffalo to the ground and ate its liver. If his adulthood and capabilities had been questioned until then, such doubts moved a long ways away. Surely he was a man—and ready to assume his place in the tribal scheme!

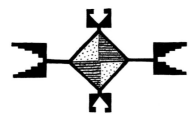

The Indian women of the Plains hold a place among the finest craftspeople in the world in the art of skin dressing. Before cloth was obtained from the Whites in trade, the nomads of the Plains made everything they lived in and wore from the hides of buffalo and other large game animals.

Prepared skins are classified either as rawhide or buckskin. To make rawhide, the hide was first staked out on the ground with the hairy side down. Then the female worker hacked away the fat, muscle, and connecting tissues with a toothed flesher, originally made of bone, but later of iron pipe. After several days' bleaching in the sun, the woman scraped the skin down to an even thickness with an antler adz. If she wanted to remove the hair, the hide was turned over and treated again with the adz. If an unusually thick hide was desired, the skin was alternately soaked and dried over a slow, smoky fire.

Rawhide, which could be bent without cracking, served primarily for binding things together and for the manufacture of waterproof receptacles.

Buckskin was required for pliable items such as clothing, quivers, bonnets, thongs, and soft pouches. To produce it the skin dresser had to tan the already prepared rawhide. Approaches varied somewhat in different areas of the Plains, but the following describes a common treatment: The tanner rubbed an oily mixture of fat, together with buffalo or other brains, into the hide, using first her hands, and then a smooth stone. After this, the hide was sun-dried and rolled up in a bundle. At this point it would shrink, and it then had to be stretched back to its proper size. Next a rough-edged stone was rubbed over the surface, and the skin was run back and forth through a loop of sinew attached to a pole. This process dried and softened the skin, and made it pliable. The hair was left on some robes, especially those intended for winter wear. The hairy surface of deerskins was honed down with a rib as a "beaming" tool before being pulled through the softening loop.

Some skins were browned, yellowed, or otherwise colored by smoking. To do this a smoldering fire was built in a small pit, and the skin was wrapped around an assemblage of poles set up in the form of a small cone or tipi. Various roots and kinds of bark were placed in the fire to make certain colors, with the amount of color being regulated by the length of time the skin was smoked. Catlin said this operation made the skin capable of remaining soft and flexible irrespective of exposure to moisture.[6] This is why most Indians smoked the skins which were to be made into moccasins, and why the smoke-saturated tops of tipis were popular for rawhide moccasin soles. In considering the over-all quality of Indian tanning, it is interesting to note that some of the skins were so perfectly tanned they are as soft and pliable today as they were a hundred years ago.

Buffalo hide was by far the most important material available for tanning, but it was much too heavy for many uses. So from time to time the hunters also brought in deer, elk, moose, mountain sheep, beavers, antelopes, mountain lions, coyotes, badgers, ermine, muskrats, and even rabbits.

Elk and deer skins were, in the main, used for clothing, a whole skin serving for the dress of a small girl, two skins for the dress of a woman, and two skins for a man's shirt. The leftover scraps of elk and deer skin were sometimes used for soft moccasin uppers, while other scraps were cut for fringes or fashioned

*a*, bone scraper with metal point. *b*, Sioux woman scraping hide. *c*, Blackfoot woman softening hide. *d*, hide formed into cone for smoking. *e*, section through cone showing fire.

into small bags. Even old dried pieces of skin were softened and used again and again. Hides of the furry animals were tanned with the fur on and used for bedding. Hides of medium-sized animals like the mountain lion and coyote were sometimes used whole for bags or quivers. Soft fur like that of rabbits and ermine was used in strips for the decoration of clothing and medicine objects.

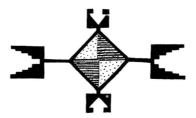

Articles made of skin soiled easily, but Indian women were able to clean a well-tanned skin satisfactorily by using chalk, porous bone, native clay, or porous rock. Wet, white clay was rubbed on the skin and brushed off when dry. The Sauk tribe mixed white clay with water until a saturated solution was obtained. Dirty deerskin leggings were worked in this with the hands, and then were wrung out, dried, and kneaded till soft. The white clay remained in the leggings and imparted a beautiful white color to them. The Blackfoot Indians cleaned tanned skins with a piece of spongelike fungus. Lice on clothing were removed by leaving the article on an anthill for a day or so. Furs and pelts were preserved by drying the marten or the fisher bird, pounding it into a powder, and then sprinkling it over the fur.

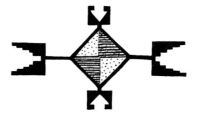

As long as the buffalo lasted, the Indians sewed with sinew thread, using an awl made of a sharp splinter of bone from two to six inches in length or a thorn of the buffalo berry bush to puncture holes in the material to be sewed. Later, a steel awl or a nail, ground to a point, was substituted. Sinew is always one of the best indicators to any collector of the date or origin of an item, and the first thing he does is to feel an old garment in search of stiff sinew thread. A good awl was a prized item to be kept close at hand. They were carried in beaded cases, most of which were long, tapered, and round. The case top had a loop to attach it to the Indian's belt. Some had a cleverly designed cap which slid up on the thongs while the loop was still attached to the belt so the cap would not be lost.

Sinew was obtained from buffalo, elk, moose and other animals. There was usually an ample supply in camp after the hunts, since every part of the animal was preserved for its special use. The prime sinew for sewing was taken from the large tendon which lies along both sides of the buffalo's backbone, beginning just behind the neck joint and extending in length for about three feet. It was removed as intact as possible to obtain the greatest length. The short piece of tendon found under the shoulder blade of the buffalo cow provided an especially thick cord of sinew, several lengths of which were sometimes twisted together for use as a bowstring.

To prepare the string, the still moist tendon was cleaned by scraping it thoroughly with a piece of flint or bone. Before it was too dry, it was softened by rubbing it together between the hands, after which the fibers of sinew could be stripped off with an awl or piece of flint. It sounds simple, and the experienced Indians did it with precise skill, but it was no task for a novice. If the tendon

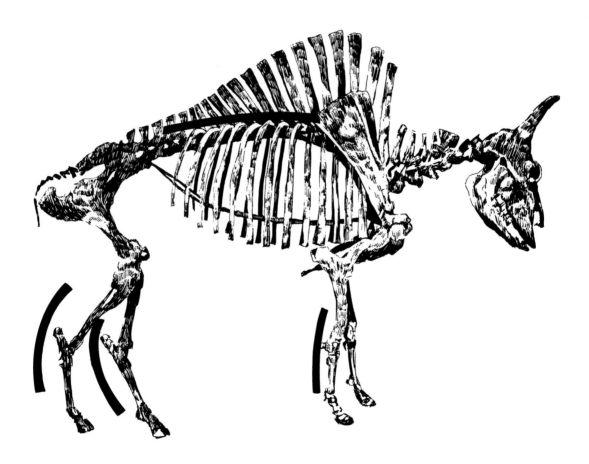

Skeleton of buffalo showing locations of sinew.

was not prepared soon after it was taken from the body, or if the natural glue was not removed by immediate soaking in water, it became stiff and dry and had to be soaked until freed from the glue which clung to it. Then it was hammered and softened until the fibers could be stripped off readily.

As the fibers were peeled off in lengths of from one to three feet, they were moistened with saliva and twisted by rubbing them against the knee with a quick motion until they acquired the proper degree of elasticity. The experienced worker often stripped off enough of the sinew to make a braid in a loose plait, from which a fiber could be drawn out as needed. The sinew was always carefully wrapped in a hide cover until it was to be used.

In sewing, the soft end of the sinew was wet with saliva, twisted to a fine point, and allowed to dry stiff and hard so that, like a needle, it might be pushed easily through the awl holes in the skins. Several pieces of sinew would be prepared in this way before embroidery work began. While working, the women kept the rest of the strip of sinew moistened by applying saliva with their finger tips or by keeping the unused end of it balled up in their mouths. Thus the mouth served as a spool from which the sinew thread was fed.

Sinew could be kept indefinitely, and the thrifty beadworker usually had a large supply on hand, although it was easier to use when fresh, as the remaining natural glues became brittle when dry. Even if it became too dry, however, it could be soaked in warm water until its flexibility returned.

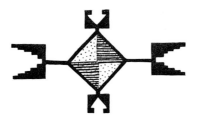

Skin dressing was intensified and facilitated by the introduction of iron blades and the White fur trade. Whereas the Indians had only killed game for their own needs, some of them now hunted on a much larger scale than before, trading the hides for beads, utensils, guns, and finally whisky, and thus playing a small part in the rapid killing off of the buffalo. Once the buffalo became virtually extinct, and deer and elk scarce, hide preparations and use came to an end, and so abruptly that it has not been possible for scholars to reconstruct in complete detail all of the old ways of dealing with hides. Before 1850 the Indians were using woolen and cotton trade cloth in addition to skins, and from 1890 on, trade cloth was almost exclusively used to make clothing.

Summing up the material on the buffalo, it is seen that the Indians were so dependent upon the animal that their entire culture came to be interrelated with

Woman sewing with sinew holding end of sinew in mouth. Back rest is Crow, made of willow branches.

it. It was their storehouse, their source of industry, their main topic of conversation, and one of the prime intermediaries between God and man. Its swift destruction by White hunters, beginning about 1870, and ending about 1880 in the south and 1886 in the north, left the Indians destitute and confused. Life itself as they knew it had been taken suddenly and cataclysmically away. Little wonder they fought so furiously for their hunting grounds, and in the end were so slow to convert to an agricultural society, although the reasons for their reluctance to be converted are exceedingly complex, and go far beyond the buffalo itself.

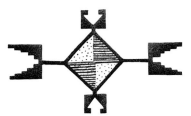

The advent of the horse revolutionized the life-pattern of the Plains Indians in a particular way. It did not begin a new culture wherein the Indians did things they were not already doing in some form or other, but it enabled the people to break forth into a nomadic life on a full-time basis. Before this they were semi-nomadic, with small bands of Indian families moving out at intervals from fairly stationary villages to hunt buffalo at piskins and buffalo jumps. With the horse to carry them, their tipis, and their other possessions, they could follow the roving buffalo herds throughout the good-weather months, and they could raid the enemy's horse herds at greater distances in shorter periods of time. This does not mean that raids on foot were no longer made, for many warriors continued to walk into enemy country so they could steal horses and get them home without the added burden of bringing their own back too. The horse led, then, to a period of great prosperity, and to what might be called the golden age of the Plains Indians, which lasted from 1750 to 1875—or perhaps to 1886, when virtually the last buffalo was killed by White hunters.

While many of the Indian tribes acquired horses before their first recorded contacts with White explorers, an absence of documentation has made it impossible to say precisely what the first sources for Plains tribes were, at what dates they first obtained horses, how quickly they spread from tribe to tribe, and precisely how that dispersion took place.

Recent findings indicate that the Spanish stock-raising settlements of the Southwest, and particularly those in the neighborhood of Santa Fe, New Mexico, were the original sources for the horse's diffusion to the Plains tribes. The Indians who worked at these settlements learned how to handle the Spaniard's horses and mules, and soon realized the superiority of their use over foot travel and for the

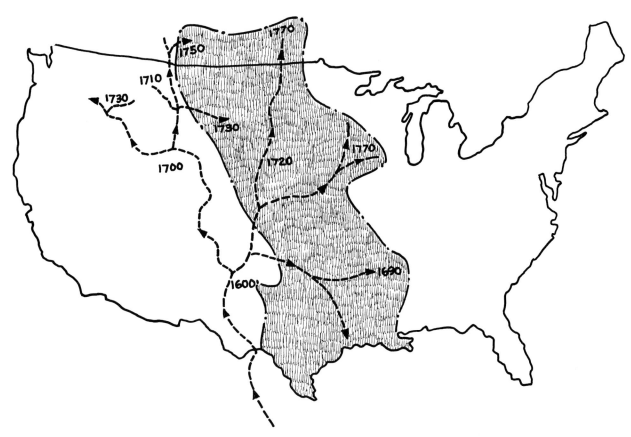

Map showing the spread of the horse into the Plains.

transportation of camp equipment. The first few horses and mules were obtained by the settlement Indians in trade for goods about 1600. Trade like this was continuous thereafter, and the Indians also stole horses whenever they could. Yet it was a development which proceeded very slowly, and none of the Plains tribes could properly be called "horse Indians" before 1650. The Ute, Apache, and Kiowa tribes were the first to put the horse to extensive use, next were the Comanches, and through the Spaniards and these original tribes the horse was diffused to the northern Plains Indians.

At the beginning of the nineteenth century there were two main routes by which horses were spread to the tribes of the northern Plains. One route led from the Spanish settlements and Indian tribes of New Mexico and Texas to the Black Hills in South Dakota, thence eastward and northeastward to the Arikara, Hidatsa, and Mandan villages on the Missouri. The other route led from the upper Yellowstone eastward to the Hidatsa and Mandan villages. Both routes, then, put the Hidatsa and Mandan trade centers at the very hub of the horse diffusion. Other tribes came to this hub from every direction, and traded goods of every conceivable kind for horses and mules. In time, as the herds began to abound, horses and mules became the measure of a warrior's wealth, and were the favored medium of exchange.

Those who have studied the horse-diffusion problem extensively believe that the first horses were spread through peaceful contact between tribes, since Indians who were unacquainted with the animals would need to be taught to ride and to manage them. Ten years or so after they learned these things, a tribe was familiar enough with the horse's value to begin the pattern of raiding from other tribes which would characterize Plains life for a century or more. During the golden age period a few warriors and some tribes remained "horse poor," but most warriors owned ten or more at any given time, and some of them had herds numbering several hundred head.

Due to an inbreeding process begun in Spain, the Indian stallion had become a much smaller animal than the larger United States Cavalry horse the Indians were to encounter in the post-Civil War days, although in the late nineteenth century many large horses which had been bred by the westward-moving White population joined their herds by various means.

The Indian pony had a large head in proportion to its body, had strong features, weighed approximately seven hundred pounds, and stood about fourteen hands in height. It exhibited a wide range of solid and mixed colors; the most familiar was the pinto.

As it developed on the rigorous Plains, the little pony came to have amazing speed and stamina. It won many a race against the White man's larger horses, and could often double the distance other laden horses could travel a day, sometimes, say some authorities, covering as much as sixty or eighty miles.

Except for the worst months of the winter, the horse herds were cared for by the young boys. Hobbles were used, at least on the lead mares, when the herds were pastured on all but snowy nights. These were ingeniously made of twisted rawhide or of rawhide rope ties. Not all of the horses were pastured, however. The best buffalo- and war-horses were picketed outside the tipis of their owners from dark till dawn—being tied to a stake or else to something inside the tent; sometimes even to the owner's wrist when he suspected that enemy raiders might be near.

Once they had become accustomed to the horse, the Indians practiced horse breeding to a remarkable degree, breeding for size, task, swiftness, and color. They developed a fair ability with horse medicines and general care, and were excellent trainers of buffalo- and war-horses. Naturally, they employed many of their personal holy items as aids in this. One learns that many a warrior loved his buffalo- and war-horse as his most dependable friend. Indeed, much of a warrior's success depended upon how closely the two worked together.

Indian accounts reveal that most Plains boys learned to ride unattended by their fifth or sixth year. They mounted their ponies from the right side—until the late nineteenth century when White saddles were obtained. They practiced with their horses until they could make them move or stop on verbal commands, and continued beyond this until they were so skillful they could ride and steer the horse by knee pressure alone, and so were seldom thrown when the horse came to a sudden, twisting stop.

White spectators were regularly awed by the riding abilities of the Plains boys and older warriors. At full gallop they could drop to either side of their horse with the greatest agility, sometimes holding on only by their heel. They were even able to ride hanging under the horse's belly. Boys learned to lean down and pick up small objects from the ground while riding at full speed, and how to ride by and lift up a fallen comrade alone or with the help of another warrior as a team effort. A practiced rider could pick a rope up by flipping it into the air with the tip of his bow while moving at full gallop. Some warriors could spring to the ground and back again while riding full tilt, so as to disturb the enemy's aim. George Catlin believed the Plains warrior to be the greatest horseman the world has ever known. He said that while some of them were less than graceful while on the ground, the moment they laid their hand upon a horse they "flew away like a different being!"[7] In fact, it can be said that the Indian's favorite horse became, in many ways, an extension of himself.

A warrior often painted his favorite war horse with the same pattern and colors he used for his own face and body. And when he was preparing for ceremonial events or for journeys into enemy territory, he painted his horse at the same time as he painted himself. Society members usually employed designs which emphasized the nature of their society, although their symbols could include depictions of their own vision helpers and war exploits. The main thing to bear in mind is that a painted horse always carried a message about his owner, hence sometimes about the quality of the horse bearing the marks—although a painted horse might not always be the one the owner had ridden on the raids described.

The total effect of a painted warrior and horse upon those who saw them was often stunning, and many Indian accounts mention the striking impression they made. One aged Crow warrior still carried the picture of a Sioux rider he had encountered a half century before, whose entire body and horse were covered with bright blue paint and white dots.

Naturally, the different tribes evolved a few exploit symbols which were uniquely their own, and they sometimes used symbols common to the Plains but which were painted with different colors. For example, the Sioux used red paint for hand prints, and the Crows used white. Nevertheless, while unique symbols and colors were employed, there were eight standard marks which were painted on Plains horses to indicate specific war achievements. A rectangle explained that the owner had led a war party. A hand print revealed that an adversary had been killed in hand-to-hand battle. A circle meant that the warrior had fought the enemy from behind a breastwork or rocks or logs. A cluster of large dots would

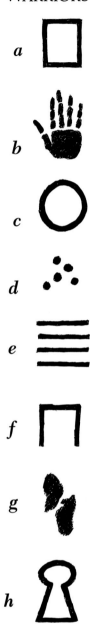

Painted exploit symbols used on horses. *a*, war party leader. *b*, enemy killed in hand combat. *c*, owner fought from behind breastworks. *d*, hail. *e*, coup marks. *f*, horse raids or number of horses stolen. *g*, mourning marks. *h*, medicine symbol.

be applied in the belief that, because a dream had revealed it, hail would fall at just the right time on a pursuing enemy. Short horizontal lines placed one above the other were coup marks, as were horizontal stripes on the horse's front legs. Each rounded or squared hoof track marked a successful horse raid, and blotchy or abstractly shaped marks indicated a horse which had been painted as an expression of mourning on the death of his owner. Any individual symbol beyond these was probably a medicine marking, such as was indicated by a keyhole-shaped line. Horses were painted on both sides, but each side told the same story. One did not add both sides together to count a warrior's achievements.

Fig 111B

Blackfoot warrior on painted horse.

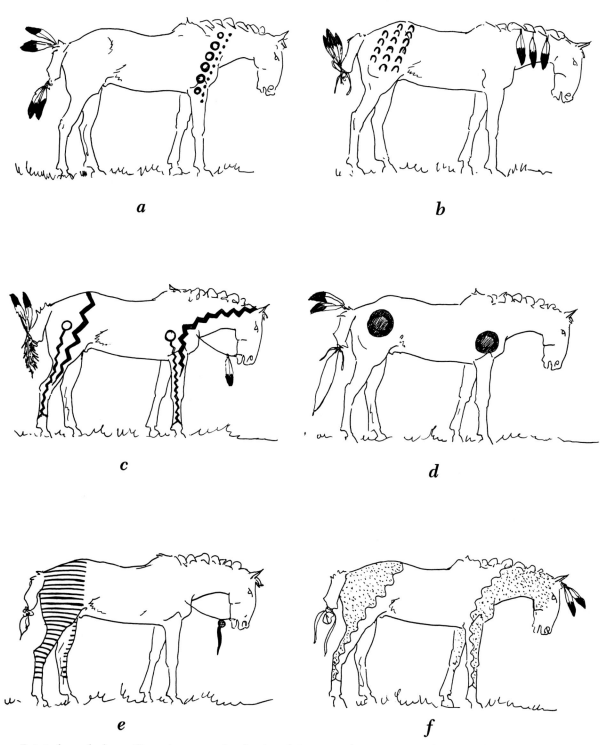

Painted symbols on Sioux horses. *a*, battles involving use of many entrenchments. *b*, horse raids. *c*, lightning marks to impart speed and power. *d*, breastwork battles in which enemies were killed. *e*, society markings. *f*, society markings.

During the early days of the reservation period, several Sioux warriors made pictographic drawings of their horse-painting styles, and these enable one to interpret the meanings of some of the symbols the Sioux used.[8] A long line of circles and dots showed that the owner of the painted horse had participated in a large tribal battle which involved the use of many entrenchments. A string of horse tracks recorded the number of horse raids a man had been on. Long zigzag lines were lightning marks whose intent was to speed the warrior and his horse on their way into battle—and to terrify a man's foes, since they would also recognize that his vision had given him lightning power. The enemy's problem of the moment would be how to cope with lightning power. Thick circle lines with the center of the circle painted red explained to viewers that battles had been fought from behind breastworks in which enemies were killed. Straight horizontal lines like long stripes and large areas of paint specks on the horse's chest and flanks were society markings. Blackfoot, Crow, and Sioux warriors painted red or white coup lines on the noses of their horses, and also red or white circles around the horse's eyes "to improve the animal's vision" in hunting and warfare.

Golden eagle tail feathers were often tied to the mane and/or tail of the war horse when the owner was about to go on a mounted war party. A common Plains custom was that of tying up the horse's tail when preparing for battle. The Indians believed it sensible to get the long tails out of the horse's way. Sometimes the tail itself was simply tied in a knot. Other times it was folded and bound together with buckskin strips, or in trade days with red blanket cloth. Feathers and fringes were often added to the ties for a more spectacular effect.

Taking their guidance from the Spanish and then the White settlers, the Indians employed the available materials of the Plains to develop a comprehensive array of horse gear. Understandably, the first pieces were extremely simple. The earliest ropes were made of rawhide, cut in a concentric spiral from one piece of buffalo bull hide. A single such cut would produce a rope seventeen or more feet in length. Later on, ropes were fashioned of braided buffalo hair, and after that of horsehair. Such ropes were done in three- or four-ply braids. Old Indian women twisted and braided the long hair taken from the brows of bison bulls, achieving ropes nine or ten feet in length. The usual hair rope ends were either tied with buckskin thongs or pasted with clay, but the Crows sometimes put a beaded buckskin cover on the ends. A few rings for use in rope ends were painstakingly worked out of stone—presumably beginning with a stone with a hole already worn in its middle.

There were a few other rope uses. Indian men used lariats in the well-known cowboy style, and for climbing purposes. They also developed a drag line which was tied around the horse's neck so that an arm could be thrust through its loop while the rider swung below the animal's neck to shoot either a gun or a bow, and the rest of the line was sometimes played out behind the horse as an additional

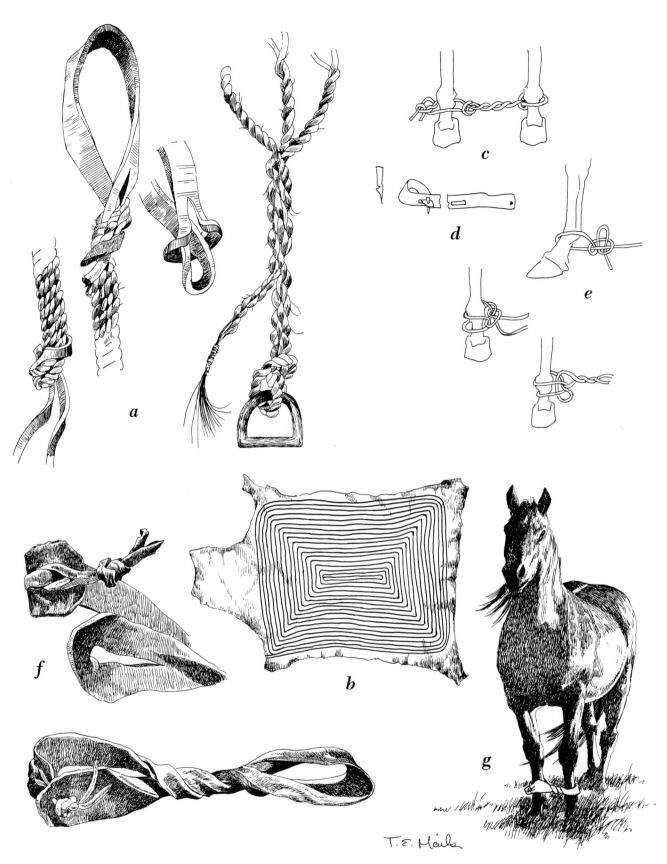

*a*, buffalo hair ropes—method of braiding and tying off rope ends. *b*, buffalo hide showing spiral cut used to make rawhide rope. *c*, rope horse hobble. *d*, rawhide hobble with wood pin to lock. *e*, methods of tying rope hobbles. *f*, rawhide twisted hobbles with close-up of hobble detail. *g*, horse wearing twisted rawhide hobbles.

Rope bridles, ancient type. *a*, war bridle tied to provide double reins. *b*, war bridle tied for single rein. *c*, halter tie for breaking horses.

safety line for accidents. George Catlin shows many of these drag lines in his paintings.

Bridles were developed in the same way as ropes. The earliest models were single-strand rawhide or braided hair, and about three quarters of an inch in diameter. Later, improved models were made of three- or four-strand braided rawhide. The standard Indian bridle was known as the "war bridle." It was tied through the horse's mouth and around his lower jaw, then looped to achieve a double rein, although an alternate method of looping produced only a single rein. The excess length of the rein or reins was usually coiled and then tucked under the rider's belt. Hide reins were often spliced to achieve a length of twenty-five or more feet, so that if the rider were thrown, he could grasp the uncoiling line and stop his horse. A war bridle could also be tied in such a way as to make a halter. Cheyenne Indians report that the simple war bridles were used until 1870, and that the more elaborate bridles patterned after the Whites and Mexicans were of later vintage. Once they adopted the newer styles, however, some spectacular beaded and quilled bridles were fashioned, and bridles were often decorated with mirrors and silver dollars. A few warriors obtained beautiful Spanish bits and bridles, but these were always a luxury item.

Several types of saddles were made by the Indians. As a rule, these were a team creation, with the man fashioning the basic wood and/or horn frame, and the woman covering it with hide and beadwork. Everyone used saddles for general travel because other items could be hung on them fore and aft, but the men usually removed theirs and rode bareback or on a robe when hunting or going into battle so as not to be impeded. Since the combination of bareback riding and the perspiration of the horse could cause chafing, the men toughened their legs and rear for such riding by standing in salt springs or in very cold water. After this, they said, even hard riding would not rub the insides of their legs raw.

The commonest form of riding cushion in use on the Plains was a pad saddle, and several types of these were produced. The basic model was nothing more than a buckskin bag which was carried empty to the place of a horse raid, filled with grass or horsehair or buffalo wool, and used as a saddle for the homeward trip. Slightly fancier models with touches of quilling or beading were also made for more regular use, and finally some pad saddles for dress parade purposes were literally covered with trade cloth, quills, beads, and fringes. Before the Indians began to use cinches similar to those of the White horsemen, the pad saddles were secured to the horse with a simple hide strap which passed over the pad and under the horse's belly.

Indian saddles were seen by Whites on the Plains as early as 1833. These were made of carved wood, or of a combination of wood and deer or elk horns which were tied together with thongs, the whole of which was covered with wet rawhide that was stitched on. Once it dried, the entire affair was bound together as if it had been done up with metal straps. Cottonwood was preferred for the

*a*, crafted pad with typical beaded targets. *b*, pad shaped to fit horse. *c*, crafted bag with beaded edge. *d*, Blackfoot pad ornamented for festival use. *e*, simple rawhide bag taken on raids and filled with buffalo hair or grass. *f*, Blackfoot pad in most highly developed festival form with quilled fringes and red cloth seat. Scale of pad saddles can be seen in drawings showing saddles mounted on horses. Generally speaking, pad saddles were quite small. *g*, alternate style of fitted pad with full rigging.

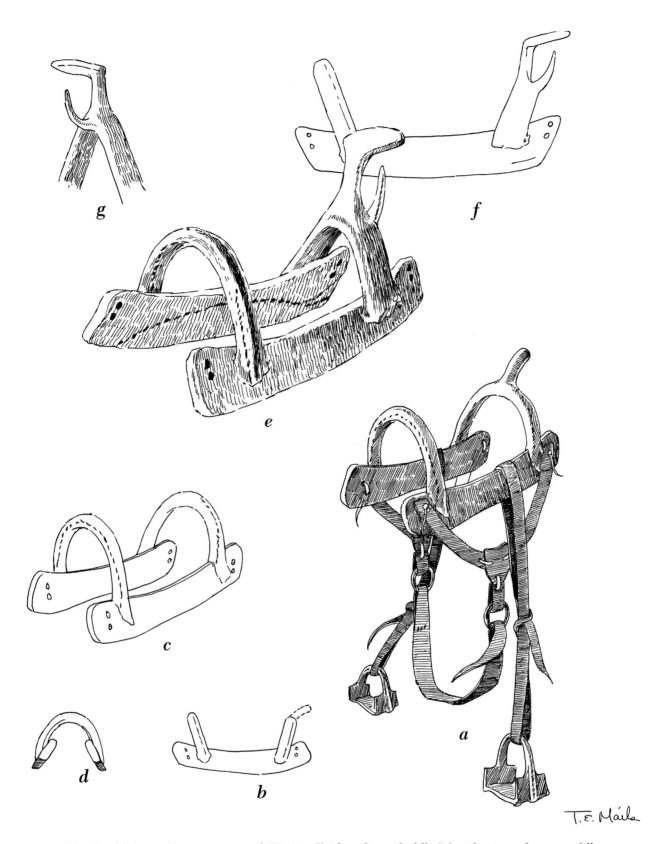

Wood saddles—male. *a*, top view of "Prairie Chicken Snare Saddle." *b*, side view of same saddle. *c*, top view of variation of snare saddle. *d*, end view of same. *e*, top view of snare saddle with pommel. *f*, side view of same. *g*, front view of pommel with horn for hanging articles from saddle. All wood used to make saddle frames was entirely covered with wet rawhide, stitched on with sinew.

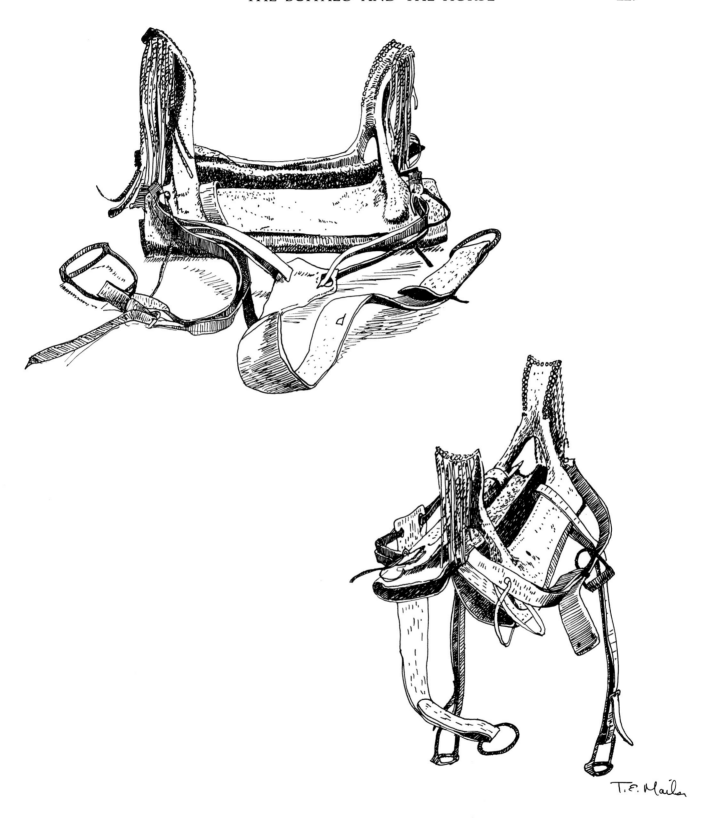

*Top,* side view of male saddle, Northern Plains style. *Bottom,* top view of male saddle.

woodwork because it was easy to carve and was very light. One of the earliest types of wood saddle was known as the "prairie chicken snare saddle." It was made of a combination of elk or deer horns and wooden sideboards, and was quite popular for long rides. A further development of this saddle employed the use of a wood pommel with a spur on its front. This was the standard type of saddle hook, upon which were hung cases and items of every sort. The fully developed male wood saddle had its pommel and cantle shaped the same and about the same height. It had rows of brass tacks as decorations on the pommel and cantle, and long fringes hanging from the points of the pommel and cantle to sway in the breeze. Southern styles were the same as those in the north, except that the fringes were twisted.

The Indian stirrups designed for everyday use were quite simple. Cottonwood or poplar branches were bent in a U shape and attached to a flat wooden base. The entire assembly was then covered with wet rawhide. Later on, metal stirrups were obtained in trade with the Spanish and White Americans.

The Indian wood-frame saddles were often padded with buffalo hair pads, which were tied to the top and to the undersides of the saddle boards. To provide additional paddings for both horse and rider comfort, a large doubled buffalo hide with the hair on was thrown over the horse, the saddle was placed on top of it, and then another doubled robe served as the actual pad which the rider sat on.

Saddles were rigged with rawhide straps tied to the sideboards by thongs inserted through holes burned in the ends of the boards. The first cinch rings were rawhide rings, or rawhide disks with holes burned in them for ties. Later, large metal rings were obtained from the White traders and settlers. The earliest cinches were simply rawhide straps about four inches wide which went around the horse and were tied in a knot under the horse's belly. Some of the later models were made of woven buffalo hair, and some were made with twisted sinew strings. The rings used for these cinches were metal, and one should note that even the cinch, which would be lost from sight under the horse's belly, was beautifully shaped and decorated.

Simple cruppers which looped under the horse's tail and were tied to the back of the saddle frame gained early use to brace the saddle, and later these too were marvelously beaded and fringed, with dewclaws or bells being attached to them in such a way as to jingle when the horse moved.

While wood saddles were primarily a woman's item, and intended for uses such as hangers on which to transport goods, museums have acquired such a tremendous variety of male saddles as to indicate a broad employment by men, and Indian accounts themselves constantly mention the use of saddles by warriors. The woman's saddle had extremely high pommels and cantles, some measuring two feet or more in height, while the man's saddle had much shorter pommels and cantles. Women's saddles were usually decorated with beading to a greater

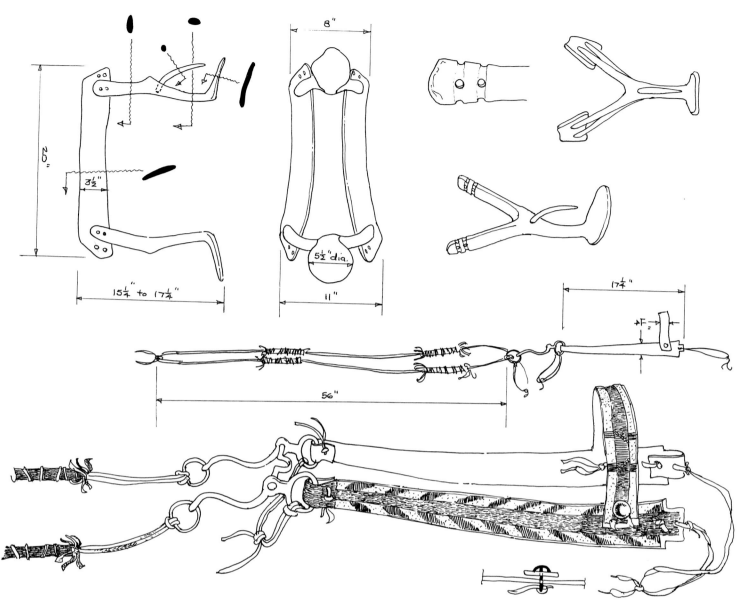

*Top,* details of wood frame assembly of Crow woman's saddle. The southern Plains style was similar, but usually had twisted rawhide fringes which were attached to pommel and cantle. *Bottom,* details of beaded Crow bridle of rawhide type which succeeded the earlier rope tied around horse's jaw. Where not beaded, the rawhide was painted a dull red. The reins are plaited trade wool, and are wrapped at intervals with bright red trade cloth.

extent than men's, some being entirely beaded, and others having pommel and cantle flaps which were very beautiful. They also made beaded stirrups to complete the saddle. However, men did use these extravagant decorations. Old photographs of Blackfoot, Assiniboine and Crow warriors show them mounted on horses which were decked out with beaded saddles and other regalia. Of course, the use of beads in such profusion dates any such item after 1840, and the more elaborate horse decorations came into vogue during the reservation period.

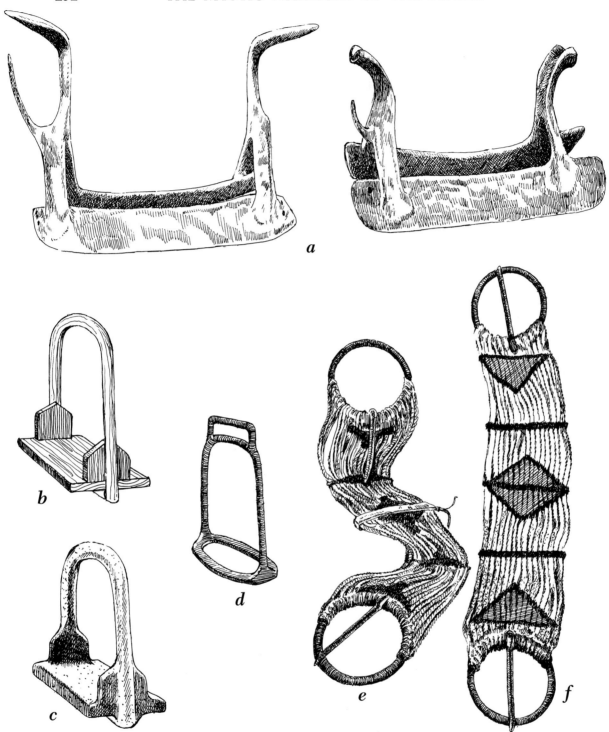

*a*, comparison of female (*left*) and male saddles. *b*, wooden stirrup frame. *c*, same frame covered with rawhide. *d*, metal trade stirrup. *e*, cinch made from woven buffalo hair. *f*, cinch made with twisted sinew strings. The rings of both cinches are trade iron. (See fully rigged saddle for scale relationship of saddle and stirrup.)

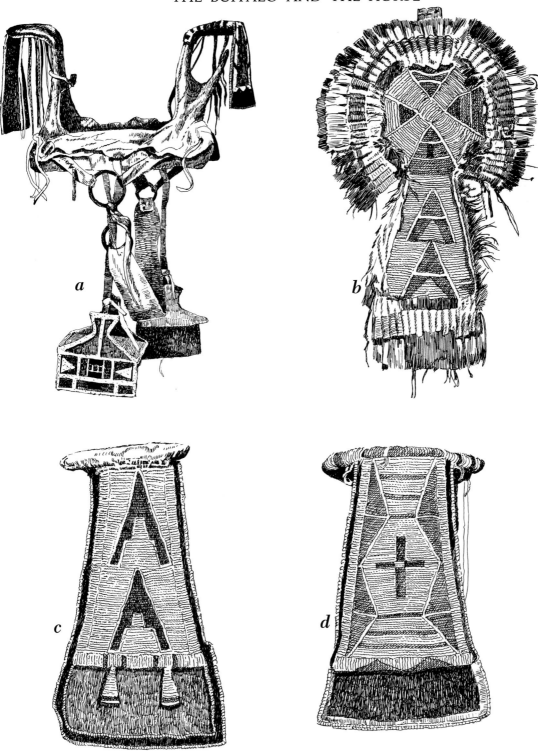

*a*, Crow woman's dress saddle. *b*, beaded Crow forehead ornament. *c*, beaded Crow pommel flap. *d*, beaded Crow cantle flap.

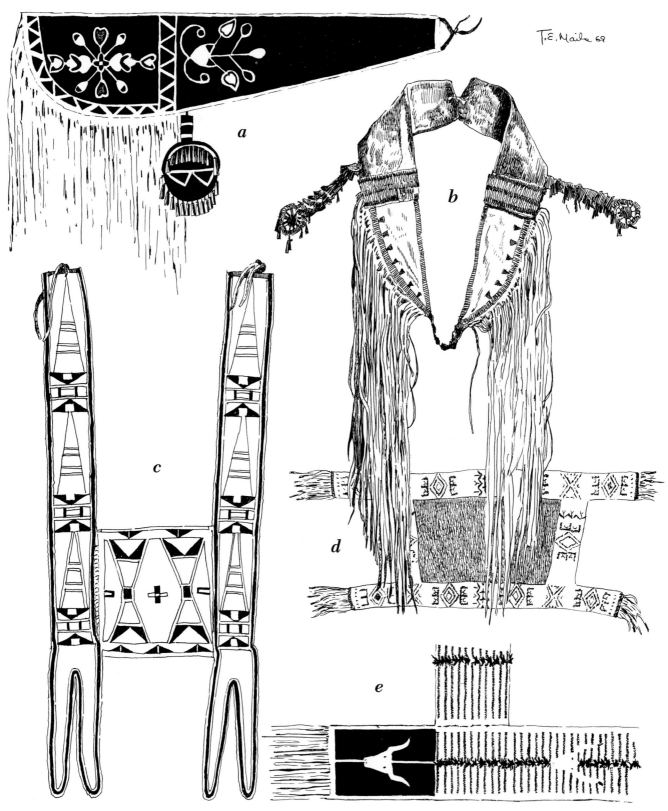

*a*, beaded Blackfoot crupper. *b*, beaded Crow crupper for a man's horse. *c*, beaded Crow martingale chest ornament—used mostly by women. *d*, beaded Sioux saddle blanket. *e*, corner detail of quilled and beaded saddle blanket.

*Right,* Crow mountain lion saddle blanket, red trade cloth ends and eagle feather ornament, backing cloth of trade calico, length 7 feet, 4 inches. *Left,* drawing after Bodmer showing Blackfoot warrior with lion skin on horse.

*Left,* horse with pad saddle and buffalo-hide blanket. *Right,* horse with Crow pad saddle, painted hide blanket, and crupper.

*Left,* horse with painted and fringed robe for saddle cover (saddle after Grinnell photo, blanket after Kurtz drawing). *Right,* horse with warrior's own trade blanket used for saddle covering (blanket style after photo by Wilson Driggs, before 1900, of mounted Shoshone warrior at Fort Hall, Idaho).

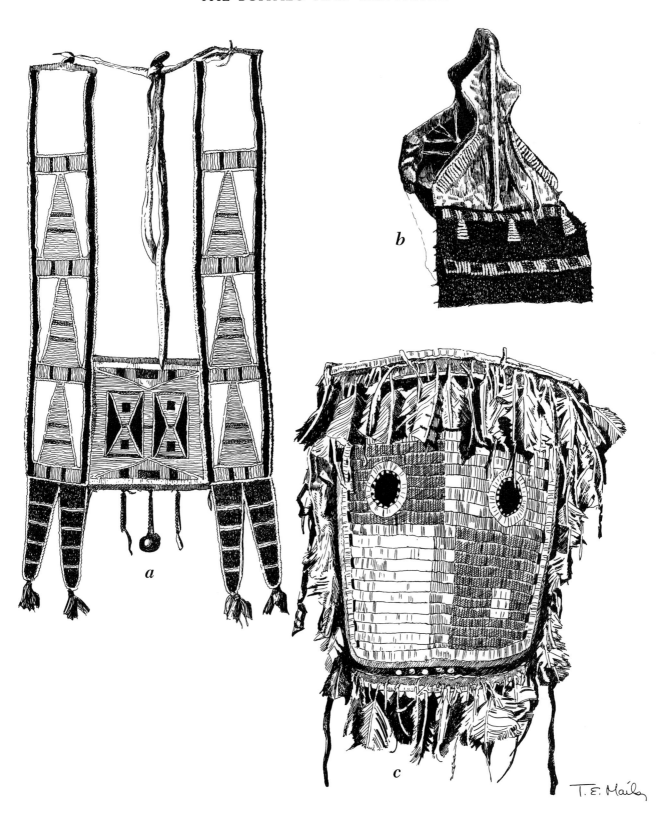

T. E. Mails

*a*, beaded Crow martingale. *b*, beaded Crow woman's stirrup. *c*, quilled and feathered mask for horse's head.

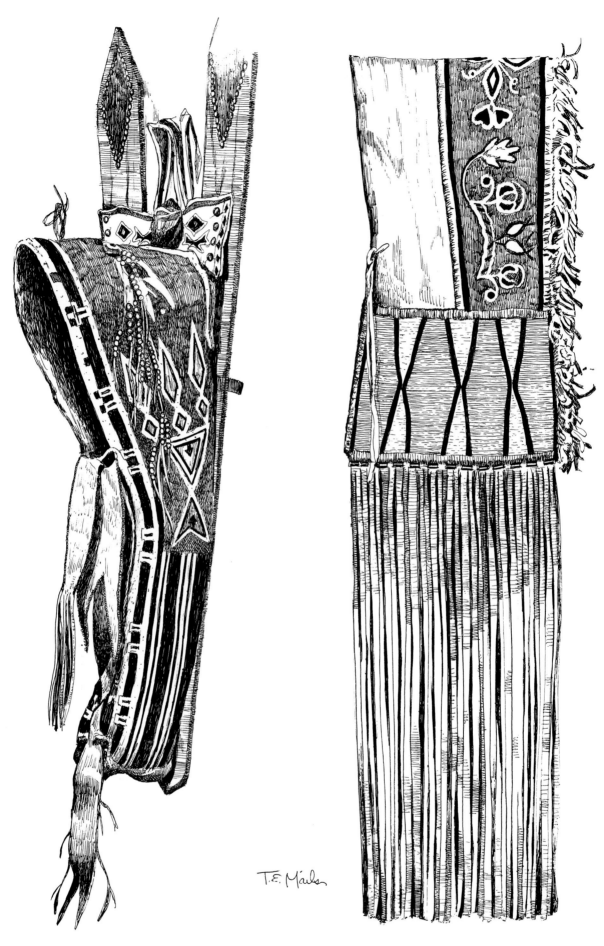

*Left*, beaded southern Plains cradleboard showing how support boards were extended above cradle and pointed to protect child in case cradle and child fell from mother's back while she was riding. *Right*, beaded pair of saddlebags with rawhide fringes. Length unfolded, 10 feet.

Crow warrior with horse fully outfitted with highest development of beaded horse gear for ceremonial and festival use.

Very old and unusual Blackfoot quirt from museum collection. Painted red and blue wooden handle with carved horse tracks and brass tacks. Length of handle 17 inches. Pendants are black horsehair, strips of otter skin, woven wool wrist loop; green, orange, and blue ribbons and golden eagle feathers. The lash is braided rawhide, beaded at the top, and with quill-wrapped fringes. Probably not a society quirt, although a Curtis photo of an old Arapaho society member shows a quirt notched on both sides like this one.

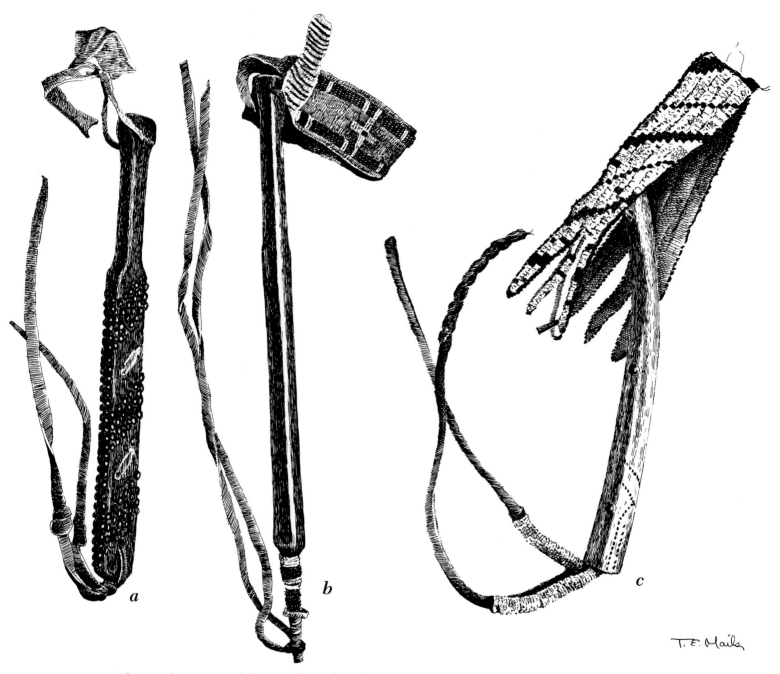

*a*, flat wooden quirt with brass tacks and rawhide wrist strap. *b*, round wooden quirt with beaded wrist strap and rawhide lashes. *c*, bone quirt with engraved design, beaded wrist strap, and plaited and beaded lashes.

that they were living in an atmosphere of divine favor, and they pressed ahead to make the utmost use of their blessings. The arts began to flourish as their opulent ceremonials to celebrate their joy and thanksgiving called for finer garments and vessels. Soon, what they produced would be able to take its place in history alongside that of the most spectacularly dressed and equipped nomads of the world.

Early explorers reported that Plains Indian warriors displayed superb horsemanship abilities. Shown here is the common custom of dropping to the side of the horse for protection in battle. Note that a rope whose ends were woven into the horse's mane was used for support.

# Chapter 13

# AN OVERVIEW OF ARTS
# AND CRAFTS

The feeling of the Plains Indians toward their God was one of deepest reverence. They did not speak of loving Him, yet they looked to Him at all times, and in this sense lived in an atmosphere which was infused with the divine presence, which *is,* after all, a love relationship in itself!

Therefore, it is of some import to recognize that the Plains Indians' craftworks, including their weapons, were a result of what they had been shown in dreams and visions, and as such were in themselves a link with the Supreme Being. Something about the form and decoration of each piece always moved its owner beyond its earthly purpose. In a sense, considering the attitude and care employed in making any object, it may be said that he prayed his creations into their finished form. Thus it was inevitable that the piece he produced always enshrined a bit of each man in his heaven-earth relationship. And by the time he died, much of the story of his life could be read in the sum of the pieces he left behind.

Indian products, although greatly influenced in time by exposure to Anglo-Saxon materials and ways, were an indigenous form of American art. Long before the entrance of foreign leaven, the Indians were well advanced in simple but diversified handicrafts. Most every piece they would ever use came into being in a simplified state early in their history and these items were only modified in form by the environmental needs and resources of the group as time passed. The skills acquired over the years and new possibilities which arose as they learned from and traded with the Whites only served to improve what already existed. The reason for this is plain. Their arts and industries utilized the mineral, vegetable, and animal products of nature. They copied directly from the plains over which they roamed, and from the sky under which they lived. Therefore, what they created was an imitation of nature, and it was usually done in an attempt to understand and adapt to the powers of the objects they were duplicating. Thus they reduced the items of heaven and earth which surrounded them to functional symbols. For example, many of their creations were what would be called textured collages today, as they were grand assemblages of wondrous items such as nuts, berries, bones, teeth, furs, skins, human and animal hair, feathers, and quills. Such items were not, however, assembled in a helter-skelter way. A dream or vision person told them what to use and where to put each piece. Every item had a special purpose, and played its part in the telling of a personal story.

Accordingly, while we find general resemblances to the primitive arts of other races, the art of the Plains Indian is so unique as to be worthy of extensive study. Naturally some people were more talented than others, but the spiritual way of life tended to produce the natural artist and craftsman. He, meaning both male and female, attained a mature reserve and dignity which endowed him with an unusual capacity for discipline and careful work. Upon examining his crafts today, one discovers that the Plains artist had innate taste, a naturally fine sense of line and rhythm, and a grand sense of texture and color; from it all evolved an art form peculiarly his own.

The approach precluded assembly line techniques. No two pieces were alike, and every item still in existence today is rare in that it is one of a kind. Mass production would have been an alien thought, for the Indian's work was really himself and for use in his daily life. It was never a piece of unnecessary bric-a-brac which would only be admired from a distance on occasion. It was a carefully formed and functional personal object of daily usefulness, and which, by its form and decoration, gave additional meaning to everything he experienced. In effect, Plains art was reverently coaxed, not forced, into being. The vital point was this: Every object served a threefold function. The first was to intensify the artist's spiritual feelings, the second was to play a utilitarian role in personal and community life, and the third was to be both mobile and durable.

All art, from forming to finish, was done in such a way as to bring the inanimate object to life in the mind of the artist. Animals and humans were drawn with their structure and life lines showing. Every piece the Indian made was detailed to show best against a blue sky or firelight, and when in motion; it was not for static showcase display. Sound too was made a part of most items. Tin cones, bells, and bags of loose stones were added to nearly every product, and the preferred sounds were those which came closest to being an echo of nature. In fact, the comparatively recent idea of achieving vision in motion was a natural part of the artist's approach on the Plains a hundred years ago. Therefore, the mobile quality of Plains art must be given its due, for not only did the finished piece itself have parts that moved, it was all easily movable from one place to another. The migrating civilizations of most other lands were forced to leave their cumbersome creations behind, but the Indian took his along with a minimum of effort and in a matter of minutes. No art has ever possessed a less static quality.

Many desirable features are found in Indian painting. If done by women it was similar to contemporary geometrical designs in form, and if by men, was realistic. They did this superbly well with pure vegetable and earth colors, painting on hides, wood, horses, and themselves!

One commonly reads that Indians were poor artists—that the Indian's ideas of art were "rude"; that he had an eye for bright colors, but no notion of drawing; his figures of men and animals were grotesque, and were as grotesquely painted in staring hues of red, yellow, and black, his paints being burned clays and charcoal.[1] It is also said that "among the Plains Indians stone sculpture was absent and wood carving as a craft too little developed to foster artistry, as demonstrated by some ceremonial objects."[2]

Such views reveal a failure to understand the Indian's artistic purpose. Modern man lives in a billboard age wherein advertisements must be simple enough to be read at a distance by a passing motorist. It was precisely so in a mobile Plains society, since clothing and other objects had to be read and appreciated while people were on the move. It made no difference whether the village was shifting its location or encamped for the night, for once the caravan stopped, the people went into a more personal kind of motion—working, dancing, joining in society activities, or telling their animated stories. Therefore, Plains art evolved as a simple form, and remained so because it was perfect for its purpose! It was billboard art, the very art form of today's rapid reader, and a parallel to the history-changing art of the French impressionists in its intent.

For centuries the women dyed the quills of the porcupine, sewing them on garments, robes, and bags, wrapping pipestems with them, and weaving them into belts and arm bands. This was an art practiced nowhere else in the world, and so marvelously done it mystifies the one who sees it for the first time as to how they accomplished it.

Beads are not often thought of as valuable gifts, yet when traders and explorers brought them to the Plains, the women urged the men to trade for them, and then used them in spectacular ways on items which they had formerly done with quills. Sometimes they used them in combinations with quills. Each region, since nature was viewed through slightly different eyes by the individual tribes, developed its own style, color combinations, and sewing methods, so that an expert could sometimes tell the tribe it came from, and the approximate date it was made.

Indian artistry exhibits a sense of color, texture, mass balance, and sculptural form. It is a mistake to attempt to relocate any part of an Indian's design or object, for one soon finds that in doing so he has thrown it out of balance. Whether by rule or intuition, no one color overwhelms anything. A small spot of bright red paint on the right is compensated for by a large mass of gray feathers on the left. The color and mass selections were thus because they were made with great patience, and women were seen to spend hours experimenting with a single design.

Plains art included sculpture, and the Indians were masters in the use of natural roots and branches for society club emblems and medicine objects. To appreciate their sculptures, though, one must recognize that true sculpture results from the completed forming of any natural object—a matter in which the Plains

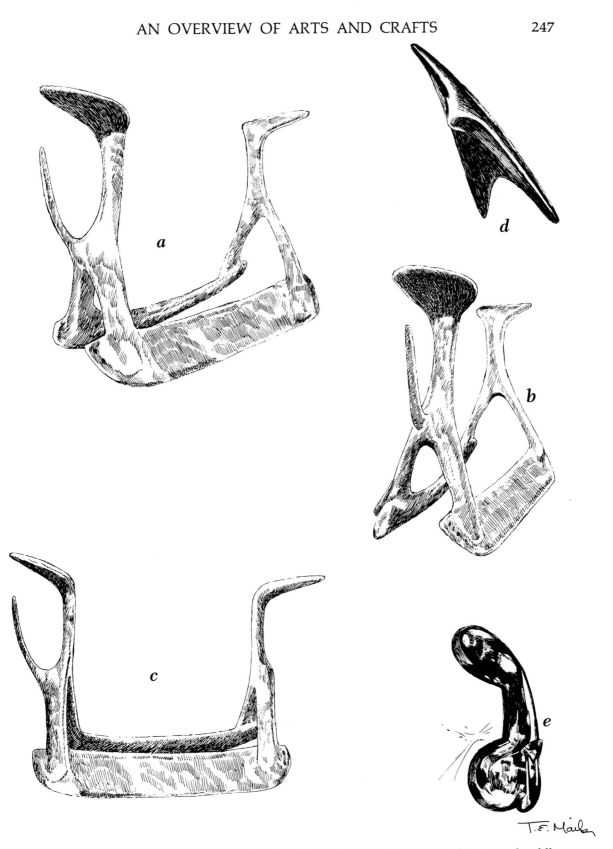

Plains woman's saddle as sculpture. *a*, *b*, and *c*, three views to show graceful design of saddle. *d* and *e*, contemporary metal sculptures for comparison with woman's saddle.

*Above,* side and back views of man's warbonnet. *Below,* warbonnet reduced to simple form for graphic illustration of sculptural qualities of bonnet.

artisan excelled. For example, if a woman's saddle is compared with pieces of contemporary sculpture, it is seen that such a saddle, or a man's headdress, if it were cast in bronze, would grace any museum's collection today, and it would look as if it were done by the finest modern sculptor. Since tactile qualities also made everything a delight to hold, it becomes even more evident that only an intensely sensitive being could have produced these, his wartime ferocity not in any case obviating the point. Besides the medicine and society club items, there were well-carved wooden musical instruments and stone pipes.

The quality of Plains Indian taxidermy was the highest, being not in the least excelled by modern methods.

Sewing with an awl and sinew, as executed by the women, was also a rare art in itself.

After the mid-nineteenth century the old techniques of horse painting were continued, but they were accompanied by beautiful pieces of horse gear. Beaded saddles, beaded martingales, cruppers, beaded stirrups, quilled head masks, quilled head decorations, and fancy bridles would sometimes nearly cover an animal. When a parade took place, the entire entourage was a splendid, mobile coronet, and in the early reservation period, horses and riders were so stately as to dazzle the imagination!

Clothing design itself was truly something, for not only the color and appendages, but also the cut of every part accommodated itself to the immediate actions and flamboyance of the Indian. War shirts were roomy and split on the sides to facilitate arm movements, or to permit sitting and riding with legs folded or bent. The absence of trouser seats eliminated binding. Fringes were placed so as to cause mobile shadow patterns as arms were raised. Split-tailed warbonnets and crow bustles hung magnificently down the horse's sides behind a mounted warrior. With a few exceptions, everything the Plains Indian made was featherlight, could be packed in a jiffy into an unbelievably small case, and then unfolded again in perfect shape and unharmed. Every part of his costume was pleasing and colorful, with this further quality—it was designed so that every angle presented something new. It follows, then, that any item in a museum should be on a rotating stand and exposed to steady breezes like those of the great prairies and plains.

After 1890, when the Indians were placed on reservations and materials were in short supply, crafts deteriorated in quality. In recent years the tendency has been toward the use of excessively gaudy colors and materials for costumes. It is only sensible that today's Indian dancers should be using today's materials. Yet the ancient products were harmonious, creative, reserved, and gracious to a fault, as any comparison will show, and the Indians themselves appreciated this no end. Many a warrior expressed his overwhelming admiration for an enemy's grand appearance; pausing, as only an Indian would do, to take this all in before engaging him in battle. Once, when moving onto a battlefield, Plenty Coups said,

Mounted Nez Percé warrior illustrating artistic unity of warrior and horse.

"I have never seen a more beautiful sight than our enemy presented . . . a young Sioux dashed from their line . . . his feathered war-bonnet blowing open and shut, open and shut in the wind, as he swung his body from one side to the other on his horse. He was riding a beautiful bay, with a black mane and tail, and fast."[3]

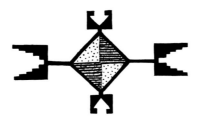

Prior to the receipt of metal tools from the Whites, all Plains implements were made of bone, wood, and stone. Many of these ancient pieces have been found, and others have been described by early travelers, yet we have only a limited knowledge of their suspected total variety. Much of the Plains style can be traced to the Eastern Woodland tribes, although the Plains type became distinctive in time, and a collector can learn to distinguish Plains items from those of other areas.

Indian women pounded chokecherries on a flat stone slab with a stone hammer called a "berrymasher," which was grooved round the middle of the stone and secured by wet rawhide passed around the groove and then wrapped and shrunken over a wooden handle. Mashers were also used to break up bones to extract the marrow. These were not war clubs. The stone heads of war clubs were sometimes mounted in a similar fashion, but as a rule they were thinner, oval or pointed at both ends. Large berrymashers were sometimes used for killing a wounded buffalo at the buffalo jumps, but that is as close as they came to contact with living things.

Water-worn pebbles and small shale slabs served as effective scrapers. Arrow shafts were smoothed between two grooved stones. Knives were of stone or bone; Coronado saw buffalo hunters cut meat with flint knives in 1541. In ancient times beautifully shaped arrow and lance heads were fashioned of stone, sinew, bone, and animal horns; although by the period under consideration metal points had been obtained in trade and stone points were no longer being made.

Pipe bowls were sculptured out of stone, especially of red catlinite. The Arapaho made black stone pipes, and the Blackfeet carved some of their bowls from a dark greenish stone which was found in their own territory.

Sharp and graceful bone awls were used to punch holes and then to push the sinew through them as the women sewed. Coronado's men also saw many of these in use. Investigators of old Pawnee dwelling sites have found fragments of perforated buffalo and elk ribs of a type known to be used for straightening arrow shafts. They have also found picks made of deer and buffalo bone which

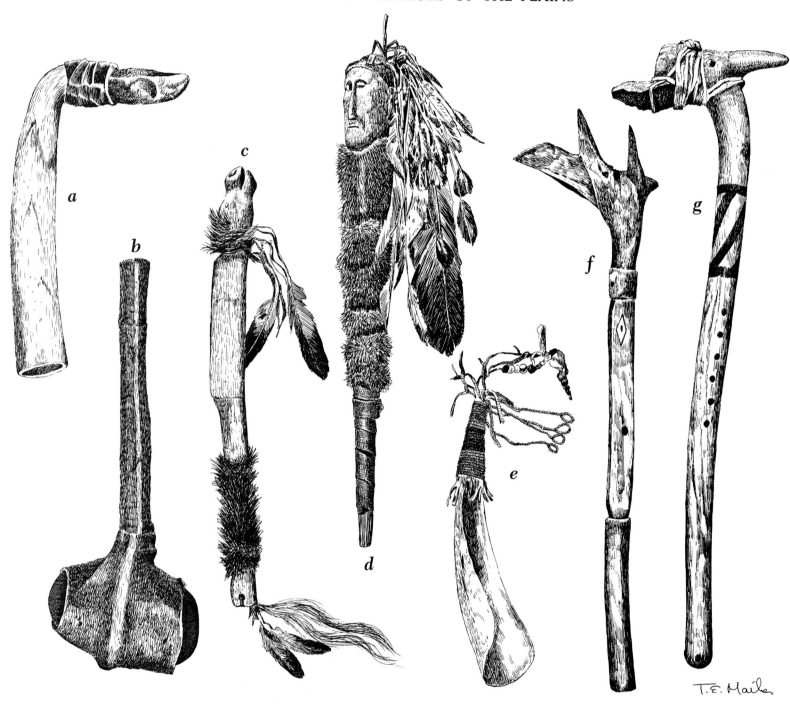

Examples of Plains sculpture. *a*, bone flesher. *b*, woman's berrymasher hammer. *c*, ceremonial wooden carving of Crow Lumpwood Society. *d*, Arapaho ceremonial doll. *e*, horn spoon with beaded handle. *f*, Sauk-Fox ceremonial stick utilizing natural root. *g*, Tobacco Society sacred hoe made from root or branch with stone blade—24 inches long.

were used for digging. Very strong hoes were made from the shoulder blades of buffalo. Skin dressers employed several implements of bone, horn, and antlers, such as the gracefully shaped fleshers made from the foot bones of large game animals. Buffalo skins were scraped with adz-shaped, classic antler tools which were fitted in the historic period with iron blades.

Not many textile crafts were practiced on the Plains. With the buffalo and other animal hides so readily available they were not needed. Even most ropes were made of hide, although the Blackfeet twisted the tough bark of a certain shrub into rope, and the Omaha tribe pounded the fibers of a nettle until it was freed from the woody part, then braided it into rope. For storage bags, Omaha women doubled plaited fiber scarves and sewed them together at the sides. The men also used them to stow away their ceremonial articles. The Iowa tribe made loosely twined rectangular storage bags and floor mats from a basswood or nettle fiber. The Pawnees made woven fiber mats for floors, bedding, beds, curtains, and corpse wrappings. A Pawnee burial site was found to contain remnants of matting which showed a simple twining technique with narrow-leaved grass or rush fibers. The same excavation revealed bits of buffalo-hair cloth.

Soft, twilled buffalo-hair wallets were made by the southernmost Sioux, but the well-made twined woven pouches of the Blackfeet were imported from the marginal Plateau tribes.

Only the stationary villagers and the peripheral groups, such as the Utes, Shoshones, Mandans, Hidatsas, Arikaras, and Pawnees, made woven carrying baskets. Small, shallow basketry gambling trays made by the coiled technique were produced by the Pawnees, Arikaras, Mandans, Kiowas, Comanches, Cheyenne, and Arapaho.

The problems involved in the maintenance and transportation of earthenware pottery made its production undesirable for the migratory tribes. Recent archaeological findings reveal that the villagers of the upper Missouri did manufacture a few clay pots. But compared with the abundant ceramic ware of other areas there was little Plains pottery to be found, and what there was, was unadorned and undeveloped. Moreover, even the villagers lost their interest in the craft when the traders' metal utensils became available. As to construction, all Plains pottery was hand-molded. Cooking vessels were of one piece, as were the clay pipes of the Mandans. An identifying Pawnee feature was a collarlike rim on the pots with an incised ornamentation consisting mainly of isosceles triangles enclosing chevrons or lines parallel to one of the sides.

Some carpentry was practiced among the Plains Indians, and the skill shown in the fitting of the posts and beams of the Pawnee and Mandan earth lodges was commendable. The Plains tribes also made some unusual wooden carvings, such as three-dimensional representations of supernatural patrons.

In their sculpturing the Indians were particularly adept at utilizing the natural shape and grain of the wood. The stationary village men manufactured a number of wooden kitchen articles, including mortars and bowls. The Omahas shaped a one-by-three-foot grinding mortar from a section of a tree trunk, chipping one end to a point for insertion into the ground, and hollowing out the opposite end. Coals placed on the hollowed surface were fanned until they burned a basin in the wood. This was followed by smoothing the mortar with sandstone and water. A huge pestle, larger at the top than at the tapering end, completed the mortar and pestle working unit.

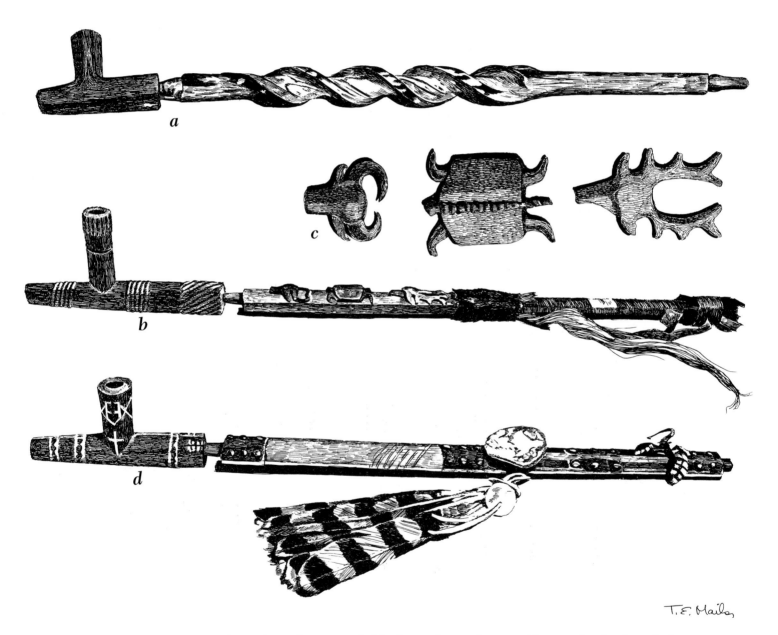

Pipes. *a*, carved spiral wood stem, probably Sioux. *b*, wood stem with carved animal symbols. *c*, enlargement of symbols. *d*, wooden stem with carved diagonal ridges and further adorned with brass tacks and sea shell.

*a,* Sioux beaded and quilled pipe bag. *b,* cross-section view of most common Plains bag showing compartment for stem and how pipe bowl and tobacco were kept. *c,* cross-section view of less common two-compartment bag—bag shown is Ute. *d,* L-shaped catlinite pipe bowl—oldest style.

The Omahas made their dinner bowls from black walnut burs, the hollowing process being the same as that just given for the mortars. Plains ladles in general were made so that the handle could be hooked over the rim of the bowl. Spoons were gracefully shaped of wood and horn and the handles were quilled or beaded. Wooden bowls were made for mixing tobacco seeds, for holding paint, and for throwing dice in games. Ladders were made of notched logs, and a Hidatsa woman ascended to the top of her corn-drying racks on a notched cottonwood tree trunk which had been pointed and driven into the ground at the butt end.

Smoking pipes were carved in many different shapes and were made from various materials. The oldest were straight tubes of animal legbone or stone and were wrapped with sinew for added strength. Later models were curved, and some had their bowls set in an L shape at right angles to the stem. A T-shaped pipe bowl made of stone was the type most commonly used on the Plains. Many stone pipe heads were carved in the shape of geometric designs, or of animals or birds. The Osage pipe had a disk-shaped head, and the northernmost tribes used a unique stubby head called the Micmac. As the years passed, hardwood, bone, clay, and stone were all used for making pipe bowls. To make a clay bowl, blocks of hard, tough clay were carved out to make the outer shape and rubbed with fat or tallow. Then stone bow drills were used to make the holes. After this the bowls were hardened over a fire, and as they were smoked hardened further.

Stone pipe bowls were made from steatite, argillite, shale, limestone, serpentine slate, and catlinite. The last named was a soft red stone found in the well-known pipestone quarries of the southwestern Minnesota area. These quarries were sacred ground to the Otto tribe as early as A.D. 1600, and the Sioux began using them about 1700. Tradition has it that the quarries were regarded as neutral ground by all of the tribes. Catlinite stone could easily be worked with flint or knife. White traders took advantage of the Indian's beliefs and the catlinite's soft, shaly deposits, and turned out thousands of pipes on lathes for the Indian trade. The stone and quarry received its name from George Catlin, who was the first White man to describe it to others in writings.

Most pipestems were made from ash or sumac, which had a soft pith in their center that could be easily removed. In the oldest method of making a stem, the wood was split, the pith scraped out, and the split pieces were glued and bound together. An elaborate plating of quillwork and wrappings of hide and fur were often added for decoration, and they helped to hold the two parts together. In trade days the pith core was removed with a red-hot wire. Another method said to have been used in the old days was to drill a small hole in the pith at one end of the stick, into which a wood-boring grub was inserted and the end sealed. The stick was then heated over a fire, and the grub, following the line of least resistance, would bore his way through the pith to make his escape.

The length of the average wooden pipe including the bowl was thirty inches, although some great ceremonial pipes were five feet long. Most wooden stems were broad and nearly flat in section. The catlinite stems were either round or oblong in cross section.

Beaded and/or quilled pipe bags were among the finest items made by the Indians. Their tobacco was carried in the bottom of the bag. The pipe bowl was separated from the stem when it was carried in the bag. Some bags had a stitched separation to provide a narrow side pocket for the stem. Ute bags had an entirely separate compartment for it. A thong drawstring tie was attached to the top of all pipe bags to secure the contents of the bag.

The Indians made an incredible variety of small pouches for every conceivable purpose. There were medicine bags which were easily identified as such by their long legs. There were small beaded amulet bags to be worn on a cord around the neck. And there were beaded belt pouches of many kinds. There was a beaded type known as a strike-a-light bag, in which flint and steel were carried—tin bells on the bottom and flap were standard decorations for these—and there were flat ration card bags used during the trading post days. Medicine bags could always be recognized by their scalloped and beaded top or bottom edges. Other bags were cut straight across. Small bags were often left plain on the back, although some of the better ones were beaded on both sides. In the latter case the two sides always had entirely different designs—but using the same colored beads or quills.

The variety of Plains musical instruments was very limited, and once again because of the mobility requirements. However, the ones that were made were gracefully done pieces of art.

The smallest musical instrument was the eagle wing bone whistle. It was sometimes left plain, yet often decorated with paint, quills, beads, beaded pendants, and eagle down, and worn suspended by a cord from the neck or the shirt front. A variation mentioned by Catlin was a turkey leg bone war whistle, but eagle bones were also used for that purpose. The tone was something like the cry of an eagle, and either end could be blown to produce a different tone for battle commands.

There was also an instrument called a flageolet which could produce a single sharp note. These were long tubular flutes of ash, the lower end carved, shaped, and painted to portray a crane's head with opened beak, and they were often carried by grass dancers. Men who dreamed of buffalo carved a larger and more elaborate twisted flute made of two grooved cedar halves glued together and bound by rawhide lashings. These were equipped with five finger holes and an air vent covered with an adjustable block for changing the pitch. They were decorated with a red paint stripe around each of the holes. A plainer version was embellished with floral symbols. Both types were used as love medicines, whose main purpose was to woo young maidens. However, men also played them in their lodges in the evening, and it is said they had a pleasant minor, lilting, whistling tone.

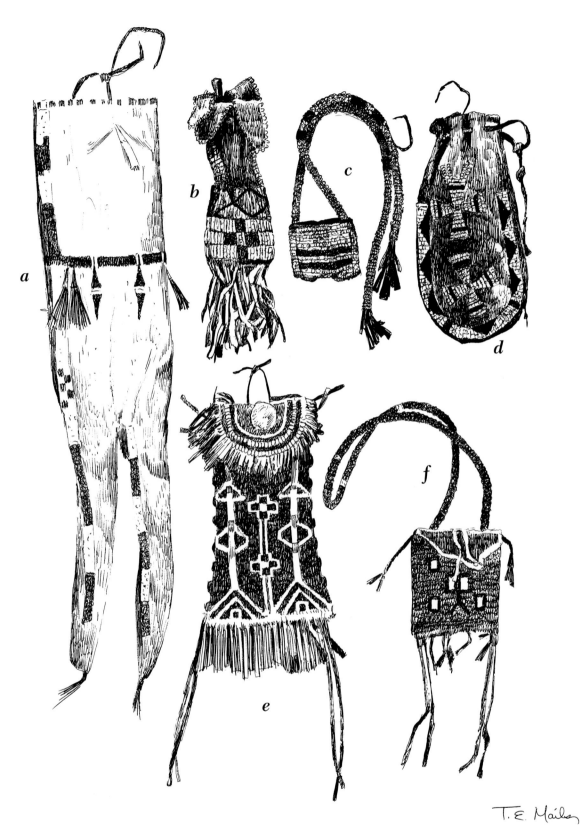

T.E. Mails

Typical small beaded bags. *a,* medicine bag, 15 inches long. *b,* small medicine bag of type worn on thong around neck. *c,* beaded top of awl case. *d,* southern Plains pouch for general purposes. *e,* strike-a-light bag to carry flint and steel. *f,* ration ticket pouch used during reservation period.

All societies had their rattles. A favorite type had two small buffalo horns separated by a hollow hide tube, in which loose stones were placed. One horn was painted black and the other was painted red. Black horsehair was tied or glued to each of the horn tips. The most common type of rattle was made of deer hide. The hide was soaked, filled with sand, and left to dry. The sand was then emptied out, and the hide was filled with round pebbles collected from an anthill. A wooden handle was inserted and it was decorated with paint, symbols, and feathers. The buffalo scrotum made an excellent rattle which was used by holy men and doctors. Gourds made fragile and short-lived rattles, but they had a good tone. Tortoise shells with deer dewclaws tied to them as knockers were used for dances, and were strapped to the dancers' legs. A stick wrapped with deerskin, to which was attached, in rows, the cut and carved claws of a deer, was also used for society ceremonial purposes. Claws like this on a rawhide bandoleer were worn over the shoulders of dancers.

The Crows, Hidatsas and Utes, as well as other tribes, made rasps out of long flat boards by cutting deep notches along the top edge. A stick made of wood or bone was drawn backward and forward along the notches to make a rasping sound to accompany dances. Some of the rasps had snake or animal heads carved at one end and were trimmed to a point at the other.

To make a drum, flat willow boards were bent and shaped to make a circular frame. Then a piece of wet untanned deerskin was stretched over this and laced on, after which carrying straps were added. Men often painted symbolic designs, such as the sun or the four directions, upon their drums, though in some cases drumheads were undecorated. A type of large double-headed drum peculiar to the Plains was built by cutting a section of a hollowed log, putting a hide head on it, and suspending it from the ground by four gracefully bent and decorated sticks. It was used for public ceremonies and dances since as many as four men could play it at once. To make even larger drums a full buffalo hide was stretched between wooden pegs a few inches above the ground. Drum beaters were made by covering the end of a short stick with a stuffed deerskin pad. The Warrior Societies decorated the handles of theirs with porcupine quillwork or with beads. Before they were played, drums were warmed over a fire to tighten the hide and to give them a richer tone, since damp weather loosened the head and affected the tone a great deal.

It is apparent, as one moves into the field of Plains Indian arts and crafts, that art forms of considerable significance are being encountered. Their creations, while primarily utilitarian, actually played roles in every area of personal and tribal life. They literally grew out of dreams and visions which resulted from the Indian's contact with God, with the ground, the trees, the air, and the visible and invisible creatures of the heavens and earth. Thus they were formed, indeed sculpted, with emotion and with a rare sensitivity to their ultimate purposes. Beyond this they were mobile in the highest degree, and when it came to garments, many were breath-taking in form, texture, color, and grace. The range of creations was broader by far than that for which the Indians are usually given credit, and a creativeness is revealed which deserves the world's highest respect. Above all, each piece was one of a kind, deeply personal, and when one advances to the point where he can read their shapes and designs he finds that a segment of an Indian's life has been enshrined in each of the things he or she has made. Discovering Indian art is, to say the least, an experience!

# Chapter 14

# PAINTING

Next to the dressing and sewing of skins, painting was probably the oldest of the major Indian arts or crafts. Certainly it dated back to prehistoric times, for Coronado learned of skin painting in 1540, and early traders and explorers found the Blackfeet already living in painted lodges and wearing painted buffalo robes.

The materials used in painting could be readily obtained anywhere in the Plains country. Native paints were derived from animal, vegetable, and mineral sources, with earth paints being the most common kind. An object can be dated by the color of its paint, for the earliest colors included only brown, red, yellow, black, blue, green, and white. Other colors indicate a later, nineteenth-century date. The Blackfeet discovered a half-dozen different reds, which provided them with colors of several hues and intensities. The base for red paints were crimson-colored earth and a crushed, pale, reddish-yellow rock. A reddish brown could be obtained by baking gray or yellowish clay over ashes until it turned red. In the spring of the year the buds of the pussy willow were picked, kept overnight, and made into still another red paint. A yellow-colored earth was found beside the Yellowstone River. Yellow was also obtained from bull berries and the moss on pine trees. Buffalo gallstones provided yet another yellow. For blue the Indian artists used a duck manure from the lakes of country where wild ducks were plentiful. It was dried in the sun and then mixed with water. The early Indians were inclined to use the same color names for both blue and green, although they readily recognized the difference between the two colors, and affirm that their people used both "in the old days." Green came from copper ores, from a colored mud, or from plants growing near lakes. Some Indians reported they also knew how to mix a native blue mud and yellow to make green. White paint was obtained from white earth and from grinding down white clay. Lewis and Clark named the present Beaver Creek near Helena, Montana, which they passed in 1805, White Earth Creek, because they learned the Indians were accustomed to dig white paint beside it. Authorities say that white was obtained from selenite stone, which was heated and formed into a fine white powder. It was mixed with water to whiten buckskin garments and skin tipis. Powdered, charred wood and black earth provided black paint.

Of all the colors, red was used most in painting. Red earth was applied liberally to the surfaces of sacred objects used in ceremonials and to the Indian's face and body. Ceremonial bundles often contained a number of sacred objects which were completely covered with red paint.

Some powdered paints—one a dark-brownish red—were even used as a remedy for eczema, for eruptions of the skin, and for protection of the skin in frosty weather.

A variety of dyes were obtained from vegetable juices and roots.

Vermilion paint was one of the articles which was eagerly sought from the White traders, and the Indians paid nearly any price to procure it for ceremonial uses.

The trader Alexander Henry listed ten different pigments employed by the Piegan division of the Blackfeet in "painting and daubing their garments, bodies and faces" in the early years of the nineteenth century.[1] It is possible that some of them were colors obtained from the traders. During the reservation period commercial paints gradually replaced most of the original earth and vegetable colors.

To prepare them for use, the native pigments were baked to a powder over a fire, then ground in small stone or wooden mortars and mixed with tallow (Lowie speaks of mixing with a "gluey material").[2] When the grinding was finished, each color was kept separately in a small buckskin bag closed at the neck by a buckskin thong or drawstring. When the artist was ready to use the paints, he mixed them with hot water, or with glue extracted by boiling in water the tail of a beaver or the white, clean underscrapings of a hide. The standard mixing bowls were very small turtle shells, clam shells, sherds, wood or stone cups.

Truly to appreciate the Indian artist's talent, one must consider that he worked with limited tools. His kit contained a number of straight, peeled willow branches of different lengths which served as rulers for painting straight lines. Some outfits included one or more short, flattened sticks for marking guidelines on a hide by pressure alone. Every toolbox had a number of chewed cottonwood or willow sticks for applying color, and the most preferred brushes were cut from the porous edge of a buffalo's shoulder blade or the end of his hipbone. The honeycomb composition of the bone brushes enabled them to hold the paint and permitted it to flow smoothly onto the hide surfaces. Thin, sharp bones were used for outlining and for painting fine lines, while other bones were rounded for spreading color over larger areas. Either the sides of the large bone brushes or else hollow bones which were loaded with paint and then blown were used for filling in the larger masses. The painter's fingers were also used for this purpose. In the last part of the nineteenth century a tuft of antelope hair was mounted on a stick in imitation of the White man's brushes. Then a separate brush was employed for each color.

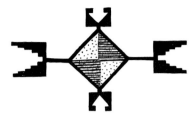

Indian artists used no sketches or patterns. They organized their designs as they proceeded, measuring the outlines with peeled willow sticks of different lengths. Once, when asked how she selected her color combinations, a woman held up a yellow flower with a purple center, saying, "See, that is how the Great Spirit does it!"[3]

The Hidatsas pressed the entire design into the hide, spread the paint over the impressions with the brush, and finally set the paint with a sizing of glue. Glue was also employed to outline the patterns, and could be used without colors on the various parts of a hide.

Early Dakota informants said that patterns were originally scraped into the skin. To accomplish this, the artist would scrape away portions of the pigmented layer of the buffalo skin, leaving sections of lighter or darker shading. Rare specimens of this technique can be seen today in some museums.

Most sizing consisted of thin glue made from beaver tail or skin scrapings boiled in water, but it was also obtained in the southern plains from the juice of crushed prickly pear leaves. After the Blackfeet obtained rice from the Whites they made a glue of it as well. The buffalo hides, having been scraped and treated with brains until they were smooth and soft, were also bone-white, and the application of the transparent mordant allowed the white to show through.

In the ordinary approach, the hide to be decorated was stretched and pegged hair side down on the ground, and the artist crouched or kneeled over it to work. Sometimes he or she was aided by one or more colleagues, especially on large surfaces and in pictographic drawings. A big hide might be placed on a vertical frame to facilitate the task. In painting a robe, a Sioux woman was seen to ply a creasing stick on the stretched and dampened hide. First she marked the outline of the border. Then, using tiny bone brushes, she applied her border color. Ordinarily, a single color was used for this. When the border was completely filled in, she painted the central portion with larger bones, creasing the outlines first and then coloring. In frescolike technique, she kept the robe damp while painting. Mixing the paint with hot water alone cause it to soak into the damp hide and permanently fixed it after it had dried. Sizing the painting helped to

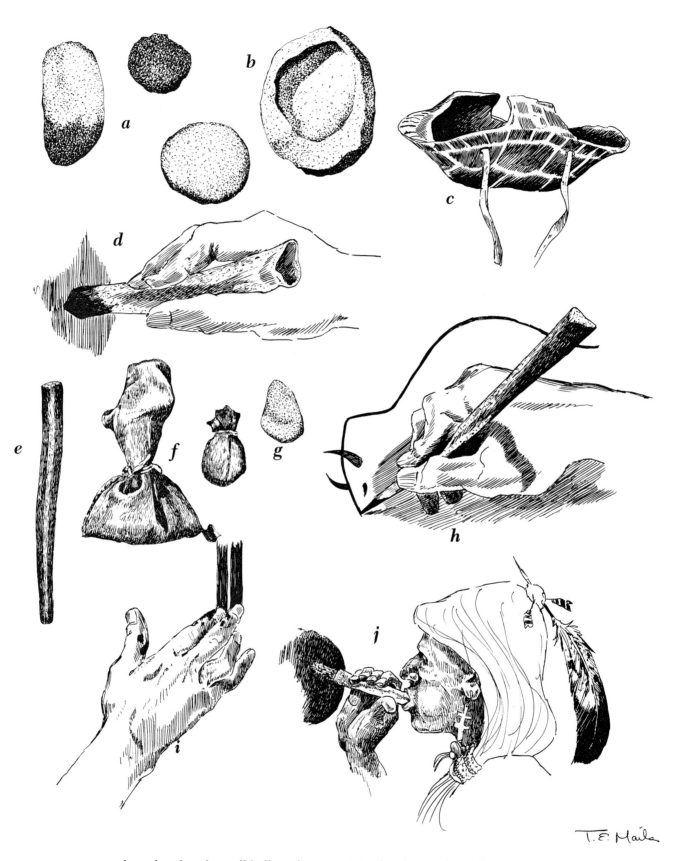

*a*, porous bone brushes. *b*, small hollowed stone mixing bowl. *c*, turtle shell mixing bowl. *d*, bone brush for laying in large areas. *e*, willow branch for painting straight lines. *f*, buckskin bags for paint. *g*, small bone brush. *h*, pointed stick for sharp lines. *i*, using fingers for broad lines. *j*, hollow bone used to blow paint on large areas.

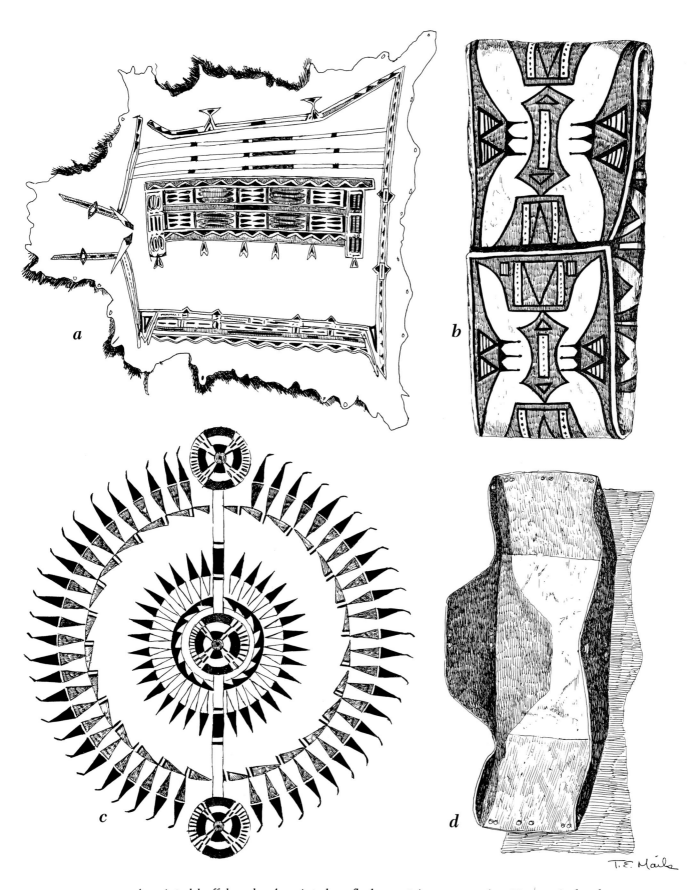

*a*, woman's painted buffalo robe. *b*, painted parfleche container—averaging 30 or so inches long when folded. *c*, man's "black warbonnet" robe design. *d*, method of folding parfleche.

preserve it further, gave it a gloss, and moreover had the pleasing effect of out-lining the designs in white. One could pour water over it after the glue dried and the paint would not run.

The most favored articles for painting by women were their rawhide parfleche storage and carrying cases, which were usually made in pairs. The hides were painted before the cases were cut out—when completed, the pair was suspended lengthwise on the horse at each side by rawhide cords passed through burned holes in the margins of the cases, and then over the pommel and cantle of the packsaddle. The contents of these remarkable cases remained dry even when the Indians were traveling in the hardest rain.

A number of smaller, rectangular or tubular cases were made from a single piece of rawhide and painted in the same manner as parfleches. As a rule, these cases were rounded or folded twice, stitched up the sides, and closed by a round or triangular flap over each end. The top was fastened in a clever manner by a thong passing through holes in the front of the case and tied. Cases intended to hold sacred medicine objects and bonnets can be identified by the long fringes at their sides or bottom. Others, without fringes, were used to carry such common household articles as skin dressing tools or the stone-headed berrymashers. Usu-ally, cases were painted only on the front side, and with a geometric design.

Buffalo robes were the next most painted items, and easily the most glamor-ous pieces of work. In certain instances the decorative designs painted and/or quilled on the robe proclaimed the status of the wearer. They also designated the sex, to a certain degree the age, and whether the wearer was married or single. All clothing, as a matter of fact, served, in addition to its decorative and protective function, to distinguish one person from another. Unmarried women's robes were often embellished with a row of medallions and pendants across the bottom, while young, unmarried men wore robes with horizontal bands of quilling with four large medallions, the first medallion being placed at the left or head of the hide.

The Indian women painted geometric figures on their robes. A typical woman's robe employed horizontal quill stripes or a frame around an oblong field, which in turn enclosed many minor figures, and was in a characteristic position above the center. Buffalo were popular symbols with women, as were two facing E's, each with four bars.

The characteristic man's robe of northern Plains tribes was painted or quilled with a stunning "black warbonnet" pattern which consisted of concentric circles with numerous small radiating figures each composed of two isosceles triangles and designated by the Indians as "feathers." The Comanches and their southern

PLATE 13.   WAR PARTNERS  ▶

neighbors used a frame with a central hourglass pattern enclosing minor designs.

In addition to what was called the "marked male robe," every warrior of note had a "war record" robe on which he pictured his accomplishments in raiding and war. In doing war robes, all Indian men painted what are best described as naturalistic or realistic figures of warriors, horses, buffalo, and other animals. The figures were always bold, simple, shown in profile, and without background. Sometimes a man added a few geometric designs to his naturalistic figures.

A man either decorated his own robe or secured the services of a more skilled painter to do it for him. By tradition, when painting war history robes, only hot water was mixed with the paint and the figures were made freehand with a bone brush. Some artists painted the robe figures in outline alone, others worked in solid monochrome, and some used many colors. Red was the favored hue, but yellow and blue were also very popular. Careful study reveals that the figures were placed on the surface of the robe in an orderly composition. The Indian mind was incapable of unharmonious relationships, and balance always resulted. If one attempts to shift or remove just one figure from any robe it is soon seen that this is resoundingly true! Again, while robe painting has been called "more properly picture writing than art," it should be remembered that simple pictorial shorthand served marvelously to tell those who were familiar with the language of the painted figures exactly what a brave man's claims to distinction were; it indicated, with great economy and force of line, the number of horses he had stolen from enemy camps on each war party, the number of enemy weapons or other personal equipment he had taken, the number of the enemy he had killed or wounded, and the number of times he had served in the responsible position of leader of a war party or as a scout. Still, aesthetics is surely central to their work, for Indians were deeply impressed with the grace and beauty of their decorated robes, and they commented frequently upon them in their recollections. Indeed, they are noteworthy both for their informative and their aesthetic qualities, and the influences of White artists did not improve them. Critics have declared that compared with the semi-realistic, decorative figures painted by Cheyenne and Teton Dakota artists during the latter part of the nineteenth century, most earlier figures are but crude suggestions of living forms, human or animal. Yet the added

◀ PLATE 14. WYOMING ENCOUNTER

A Sioux and two Crow warriors locked in a furious struggle, while others of the tribes battle in the background. The Sioux horse wears a medicine bag on a cord around his neck. The wounded Crow carries a coup stick in one hand and a mink-handled club in the other.

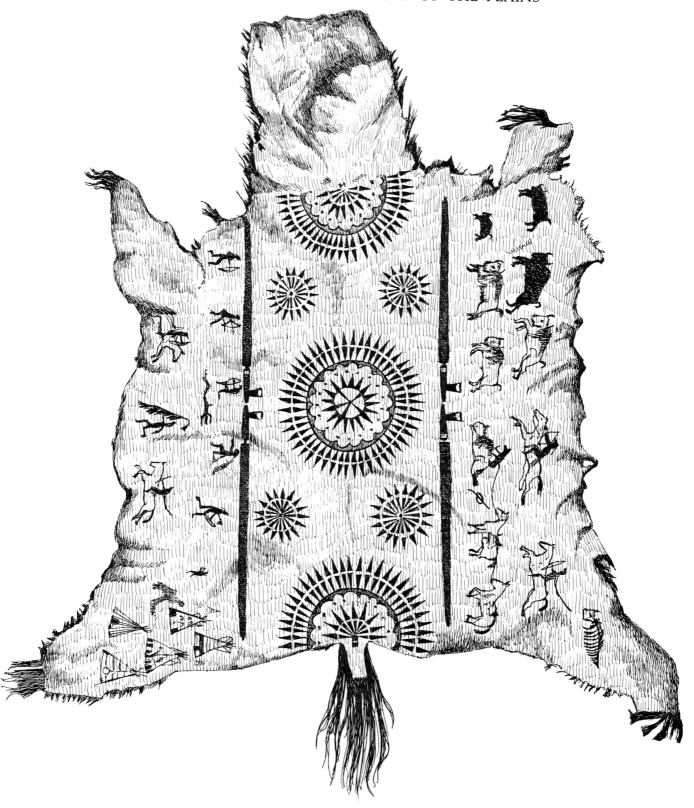

Man's painted war record buffalo robe.

Pictographic drawings used on war shirt of Mandan warrior (after Catlin).

detail actually tended to blunt the visual impact of the older work, for one cannot "read" a complex drawing while its wearer is in motion.

Robes were worn or carried in traditional ways, and had a language all their own. A speaker wore it one way when he was addressing an audience, another to show a change of attitude, another to indicate meditation, and another to display anger.[4] By tradition the head of the buffalo was worn to the left when the robe was wrapped around its owner, and all paintings were done with the "lay" of the robe in mind. Young men often wore their robes over their heads if they were courting, while older men placed one end under their right arm and held it with their left hand, leaving the right arm free. Women wore them over their heads at ceremonies.

The most remarkable and awe-inspiring of all Plains Indian paintings were the larger-than-life-size murals of animals which they painted on the conical outer walls of their lodge covers. Those of the Blackfeet were first mentioned by Alexander Henry, the fur trader, in 1809.[5] He stated that both beasts and birds were represented in the paintings, and that buffalo and bears in particular were frequently delineated. A study of photographs and older paintings by White artists reveals that little or no change in the figure styles for lodges took place over the years.

Lodge paintings were more than decoration. Those who were versed in the traditions of their people found each painting to be more replete with religious and historical symbolism than a large stained glass church window is today. There were only a few gloriously painted lodges in each camp, since these were the residences of the leading men and of societies, or the places of tribal ceremonial functions—but of those so decorated, each had its fascinating legend to explain how its owner obtained the symbols and colors. According to the legends, all of the designs were given to their first human owners in dreams or visions. In these, the original animal owner of the lodge appeared to the sleeper and promised to give him his own painted lodge and the other sacred objects—which together were to be the sources of his supernatural power. The animal owner told the sleeping or transfixed man how to paint the lodge and how to assemble and shape the other sacred objects which would be associated with it. When he awoke, the man always followed these instructions to the letter. Therefore, each painted lodge became part of a complex of religious objects belonging to its owner. So long as he possessed it, he had certain rituals to perform and taboos to recognize. Whenever he sold his painted lodge to another, an elaborate transfer ritual had to be performed. And although Blackfoot painted lodges were frequently trans-ferred from one owner to another within the three tribes, Blackfeet, Piegans, and Bloods, only the rightful owner was permitted to make use of the animal figures that belonged to his lodge. No other man dared copy them.

When a painted tipi cover became old and worn, the paintings on it were duplicated on a new one. Ordinarily, this was done in the fall of the year, just

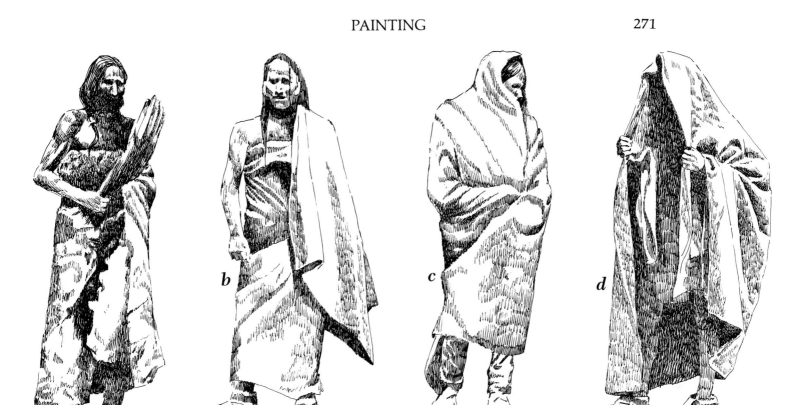

Language of the men's robe. *a*, manner worn to address audience. *b*, manner employed to illustrate change of attitude. *c*, manner used to indicate meditation. *d*, manner of illustrating anger. Additional traditional forms were used to illustrate other attitudes.

after the last tribal hunt when all the new lodge covers of the village were made. For the preliminary work the new lodge cover was stretched into shape around the lodge poles. Usually the owner employed the services of a skilled artist and told him what to paint as he drew the outline of the forms in black paint, using red willow sticks for rulers and bone paintbrushes. All outlining was done while the lodge was standing, and the old painted lodge was set up nearby so the size and arrangement of its paintings could be referred to. When the skilled artist was finished, the new lodge cover was taken down and spread out flat on the ground. At this point the owner invited a group of people of "good reputation" to his lodge for a smoke. Working in a leisurely fashion, they helped him finish the painting, using buffalo tails or handfuls of long buffalo hair to apply the paint to the larger masses. The paint for lodges was mixed with hot water and rubbed onto the cover with considerable pressure. When the painting was finished the new lodge was erected again, and all of the ornaments which had hung on the old lodge were transferred to it. Then the owners of the other painted lodges in the camp were invited to gather inside the new lodge. Everyone prayed for

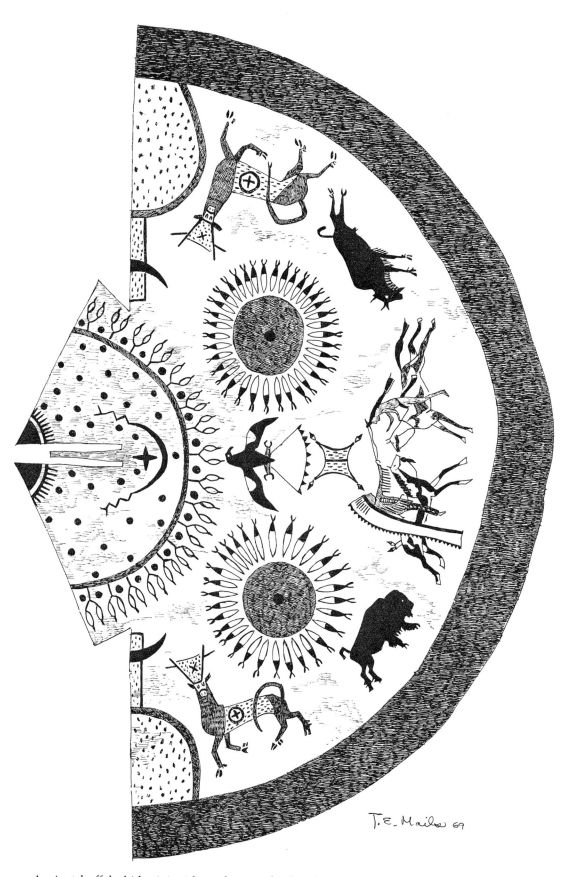

Ancient buffalo-hide tipi with warbonnet, bird and animal figures resulting from vision.

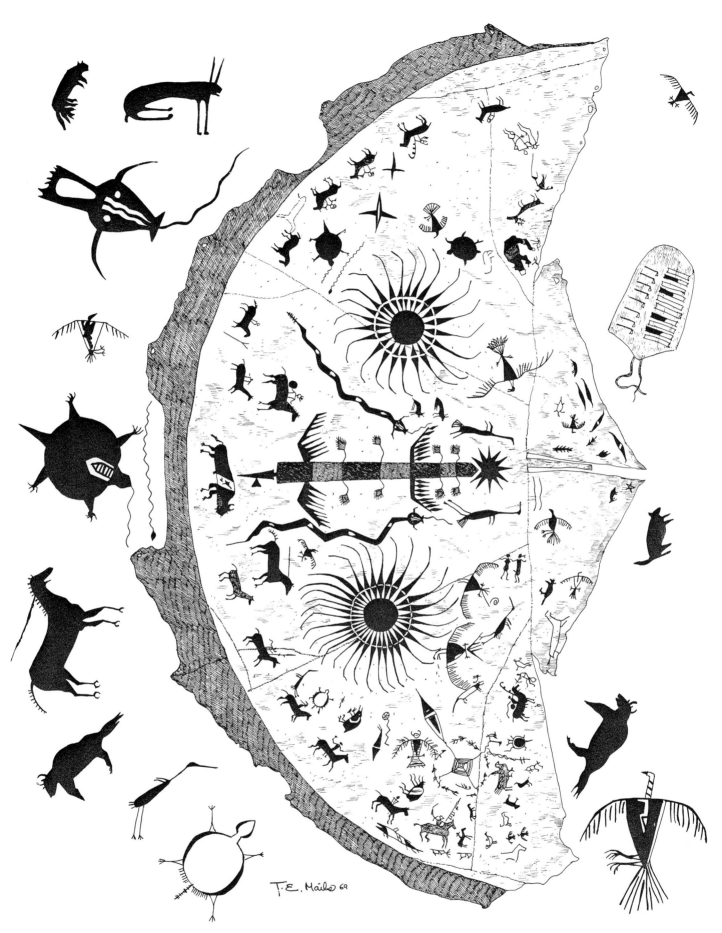

Ancient buffalo-hide tipi showing exceptional grace and creativeness of designs employed.

God's blessings upon the lodge, and then they assisted the owner in the building of a purification sweat lodge nearby. When he had completed the sweat rite the ceremony of transferring the sacred symbols from the old to the new lodge cover was considered finished.

The old painted cover was disposed of either by taking it to a lake and weighting it with stones so that it would sink, or by spreading it out on the open plains. In the first instance the cover was given as an offering to the water spirits;

*Left,* Blackfoot artist laying in outlines of tipi painting. *Right,* Blackfoot artist painting buffalo hide stretched on frame rack.

in the second, it was an offering to the sun. Unpainted covers were simply cut up to make clothing and storage items.

Wild animal figures were stylized and decorative in form. Usually the body was a plain solid color; either black, blue, red, or yellow, but some of them were further detailed with representations of the throat, heart, and kidneys, which were believed to be the sources of energy of the animals depicted.

Many professional lodge painters employed what is best described as a straightforward composition of the upper and lower portions of the cover. At the bottom, a banded area two or more feet in height was often painted red to represent the earth. Within this area were one or two rows of unpainted circles to depict fallen stars. A row of triangular or rounded projections upward from the band appeared on a number of lodge covers, and these represented rounded hills or sharp mountain peaks. A banded area at the top of the cover, including the projecting ears or wind flaps, was sometimes painted black to symbolize the night sky. Arrangements of unpainted ovals within this area represented the constellations of the Great Bear and the Pleiades. A Maltese cross placed on the west side of the top was said to indicate the morning star, or butterfly, and was believed to bring powerful dreams to the lodge owner.

Painted tipi covers often had geometric borders at the top and the bottom with naturalistic pictures in the middle to show the exploits of the owners. Chief Satanta of the Kiowas had an entirely red tipi with red streamers at the end of poles atop it. Tipis with battle pictures were known as heraldic tipis. A spectacular Sioux tipi of particular note had its north side ornamented with battle pictures, while the southern half was painted with alternating horizontal stripes of black and yellow.

The Indians used large, buffalo skin draft liners that circled the inside of the tipi and provided an air barrier to insulate the lower portions of lodges. Most of these were painted with bright geometric designs by women. Among the Blackfeet, liner paintings were confined to a long, narrow, horizontal band near the top of the item, and to additional vertical bands projecting downward from the top band at intervals of about fifteen inches. An exception to the above was that men with outstanding war records were permitted to paint their lodge linings with pictographic representations of their deeds of valor, and in so doing used them for personal historical records.

Another painting use of real significance was the pictographic signature which served to identify an individual by name. When a scout was separated from his war party or camp, he could draw his signature, couple it with other pictographs indicating his recent actions, and add a small arrow indicating his direction of movement, leaving the depiction on a rock, a piece of bone, skin, or cloth in a place where others of his tribe could find it, and thus learn what he had done and where he was going. Most tribes also kept pictographic calendar hides on which were set forth the outstanding tribal events of successive years.

Painted tipis and designs. *a*, Blackfoot. *b*, Cheyenne. *c*, Sioux. *d*, Crow. *e*, tipi liner designs. *f*, pictographic styles used for figures employed on liners and tipi walls.

However they were employed, the commonest figures in all male paintings were those of horses, men, and weapons drawn as they appeared in war or hunting. Next came religious symbols and a few buffalo. It should be mentioned that while war pictographs often show men regally dressed, that was usually done to identify the warrior. Except for premeditated engagements, warriors wore the lightest and plainest clothing possible while traveling so as not to be impeded by the weight.

Except for the huge tipi paintings, composition involved relatively small scenes. If the idea of perspective drawing ever occurred to the Plains artist, he deliberately put it away. Distant figures were frequently placed behind or above closer ones without a reduction in size, since in the artist's mind all of the figures were equally important.

It is apparent that composition was employed, and that the artist made every attempt to unify all of the scenes of a hide. In fact, they are very well balanced, and there is every reason to conclude that religious harmony led the Indian artist to employ by intuition the same rules as are used today for color and layout. Considering the Indians' educational and technical limitations, many of the pictographs displayed an enviable dynamic quality. The work was exciting, to say the least, and as good for its purpose as that which an enlightened nation has conceived of since. Old Plains painting was the epitome of visual contact, simultaneously calling into play communication, religious expression, and beauty.

The study of Plains painting is only complete when self-painting has been considered. For when an Indian was fortunate enough to have a multitude of colors, he painted his face in stripes and spots, in any style to please his individual but Spirit-guided attitude. A common face paint method was to use the finger tips or pointed sticks to paint cheek stripes from an eighth to a quarter of an inch in width vertically, or horizontally by starting at the nose, then running across to the ears, using red, yellow, blue, green, and as many other tints as one could procure. The forehead was striped in the same manner, with the lines running up and down. When the face was painted with spots, the pigments were daubed on with the fingers or paint tools. In all cases the paint was applied with forethought and purpose.

Men painted their faces regularly for protection against wind, sun, snow, and insects. When painting for this purpose the Indian first rubbed grease made from bear or buffalo back fat onto his face. Then he would dip his greasy fingers into a bag of powdered paint and rub the paint evenly over his face. Afterward, his whole body might be painted, and his fingernails might be drawn through the paint to produce a peculiar barred appearance.

Painting one's face and body was also a favorite way of mental conditioning. Indian warriors always painted themselves with their personal protective designs when they went to war (which also helped the war chief tell them apart), yet one must remember that all Indian paint cannot properly be called "war paint" since it was frequently used for purposes in no way connected with war. Designs of various kinds were used to designate membership in societies, when participating in ceremonies, as marks of achievement, and in mourning for the dead.

Bodies were painted in much the same manner and colors as faces, except that the lines were larger and more often wavy. When mixed with grease, the paints would remain on the body for a long time, for the Indian was often in a situation wherein he could not wash himself, or preferred, after a great victory or a ceremonial event, to leave the paint on as a reminder.

It might be assumed that face and body painting was done without reference to a particular design, and in fact early travelers often decided that the sole intent

Crow scout White Man Runs Him showing typical method of applying face paint.

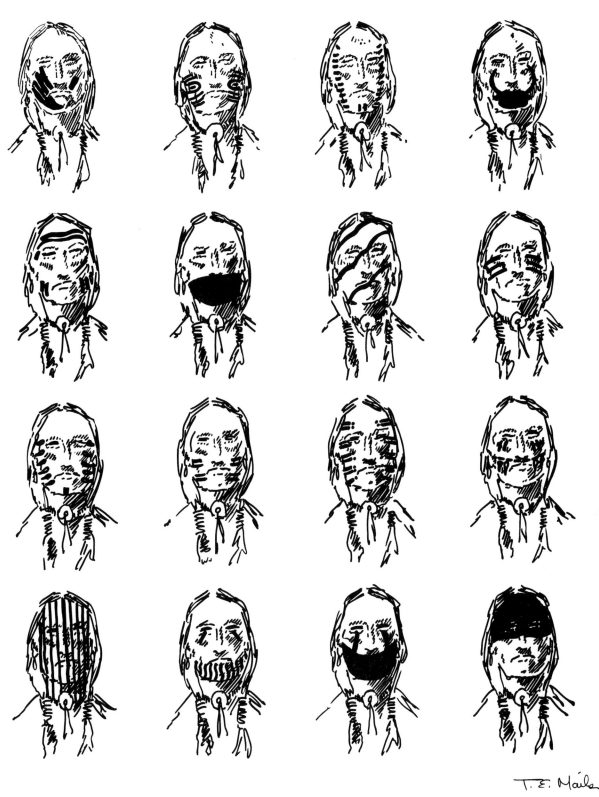

Typical ways of applying face paint, taken from the paintings and drawings of George Catlin, 1830s.

seemed to be for Indians to make themselves "as hideously ugly as possible." Yet such an approach would have been contrary to the Indian's nature, and indeed it is contradicted by better-informed authorities. With few exceptions the Indians' colors and patterns were harmonious, balanced, beautiful, and exciting. And it would be helpful if the Indian self-painting displayed in public ceremonies today was as well planned, executed, and explained. This is adequately borne out when one considers ceremonial self-painting in terms of the ancient Sioux attitude. They believed that by being painted, people had been changed.[6] The painted ones had undergone a new birth, and with this had assumed new responsibilities, new obligations, and a new relationship. Therefore, ceremonial painting was to be done in a place hidden from the people, so that those painted would come forth as they did from the sweat lodge, pure, free of ignorance, and parted from the troubles of the past. For the moment they were one with the Spirit, and a new relationship had been made.

In speaking of the use of blue paint, Black Elk said it was "very important and very sacred."[7] Like Linderman, he explained that the power of a thing or act was in the understanding of its meaning. Thus by placing blue, the color of the heavens, upon tobacco, which represented the earth, he united heaven and earth and made them one. The red line every woman placed in the part of her hair tied her in with the earth, where everything lives and increases. Once again, one is greatly impressed with the spiritual depths of the Indian mind.

As the practice continued to evolve over the years, Plains painting became absolutely spectacular. In describing a meeting with some splendid Cheyenne who were in search of adventure, Father Nicholas Point reported that their hair was dressed with a sort of red earth; faces were painted blue, red, white, yellow, or even black; garments were decorated with porcupine quills and glass beads; hair was spread fanwise on the shoulders, flat on the brow, and hanging in long braids. And their heads were adorned with two feathers, extending vertically above the eyes.[8]

Among the Omaha people, a leader of a war party painted diagonal lines on his face from the bottom of the eyes to the neck. The lines represented the path of his tears while "crying for the success of the expedition." Indeed, all war paint was applied after the nature of an appeal or prayer. Returning warriors of tribes who had taken scalps painted their faces black before entering their home village. The Crows said that black indicated the fires of revenge which had burned out with the completion of the raid. Pawnee scouts painted their faces white to symbolize the wolf, whose medicine was considered to be of the greatest help in scouting. The Kiowas often painted their body, horse, and shield with the same color either as an over-all pattern or as a more concentrated heraldic design. One Sioux warrior painted his body and his shield sky blue overlaid with large red dots! Red paint was generally applied to the face of persons taking part in ceremonies or who were being initiated into societies. Animal figures were sometimes

Tattoo designs. *Left,* Omaha warrior. *Right,* Cree warrior.

drawn on the body to indicate the main helper of the clan or society to which the person belonged. Warriors returning from a victorious battle sometimes daubed their robes and blankets with buffalo blood, yet even this was so carefully done it would tell a story the entire camp could read. St. Clair discovered some very important things about the complexity of the body painting of the Wind River Shoshones.[9] He found that Wolf Dancers had realistic representations of bears or snakes below their breasts which stood for Bear or Snake Medicine, while a Sun Dancer had a similar chest painting of a buffalo. Right angles or angular horseshoes represented horse tracks; wavy lines extending along the entire length of the arms and legs symbolized the rainbow; short lines, horizontal, curved. oblique, or vertical, indicated people killed; and painted hands recorded hand-to-hand encounters with the enemy.

Tattooing was also a common practice on the Plains. The Wichitas did a great deal of it, and so did the other southern tribes. An Omaha leader could gain prestige for himself and for a daughter recently come of age by having her tattooed in the center of the forehead with a black circle representing the sun, and with a four-pointed star on her chest to symbolize the night. These designs symbolized his own war honors. An Osage man who had distinguished himself in war could also tattoo himself and his wife with a standard V-shaped design. An old Hidatsa man of the northern Plains was seen with a tattoo on one half of his chest. The Crows sometimes tattooed both sexes; and the Crees commonly tattooed both men and women. The men did this on their face, arms, and chests, while the women were only marked in the space between their lips and chin. Osage information reveals that the custom had ritualistic and social aspects in addition to its aesthetic purposes.

PLATE 15.   WHITE BULL—MINICONJOU SIOUX WARRIOR ▶

The painting is a depiction of the famous White Bull, who claimed to be the one who killed Custer. He wears one of the great Sioux buffalo horn bonnets he collected, and a *Crow* war shirt, which would be strange were it not for the fact that warriors who were girding themselves for battle sometimes donned garments or carried weapons or medicines captured from enemies in past battles. They did this to heighten their excitement, to show their prowess to others, and to build up their own courage. It was believed that the victor in battles gained the added strength of the victim's own captured medicine by donning the garment or carrying the item. Sometimes warriors wore captured enemy clothing while in enemy territory to deceive the foe.

# Chapter 15

# QUILLWORK AND BEADWORK

Quilling, which was the ancient forerunner of Plains beadwork, was found to be in complete harmony with Indian design attitudes, and it became the highest attainment of the female arts. It demanded a maximum in sensitiveness and great dexterity, but once applied, the sewn quills presented a smooth, strawlike surface, and were well suited to the popular geometric art of the Plains. The finest porcupine quills were used for amazingly delicate work, such as on special ceremonial moccasins, and some of the Indian women's achievements with these were so exquisite they resembled the sublime moose hair embroidery done by the Indians of the north and east, and from which they could only be distinguished by the shiny surface of the quills. It is generally conceded that the Sioux, Cheyenne, and Arapaho were the best quillers, and that most of the extreme southern tribes did not use quills at all. The Sioux explained the origin of quillwork by a legend of a mythical "double woman," who came in a dream to some woman who was a twin, to teach her the use of quills. She in turn taught other women how to use the quills, and associations of quillworkers or quilling societies were formed. They met at regular intervals to exhibit and talk over their work and explain how they did it. Feasts were held and gifts were distributed. The quill designs made by each were considered her personal property and were not copied; for her designs were those which she was supposed to have dreamed and to which she could claim ownership.[1]

The American porcupine made his home in parts of Canada and Alaska, and the mountainous country of the northern and eastern United States. In the east he inhabited parts of Vermont, New York, and Pennsylvania, but porcupines were not found at all in most of the Plains country. The border line of their range followed the western edge of the Great Lakes country, swung up into Alberta, Canada, and then down through eastern Montana and Wyoming. Therefore, the majority of the Plains tribes had to obtain their quills by trade with the northernmost tribes.

---

◀ PLATE 16.   TWO ELK—OGLALA SIOUX

Map showing approximate area of northern Plains where tribes employed porcupine quillwork. Adapted from "Quill and Beadwork of the Western Sioux," Department of Interior, 1940.

T. E. Mails

The quill of the porcupine is a smooth, round, hollow tube with a sharp, barbed point at one end. It is white for about four fifths of its length, ending in a brownish-gray tip. Quills differ in length, thickness, and stiffness, being from one to four inches long, and from one sixteenth to three thirty seconds of an inch in diameter. The Plains quillworkers graded them into three sizes: the largest, which were those from the back; the slender, which were delicate quills from the neck; and the finest, which came from the belly. The medium-sized and coarser quills were used on the larger pieces. Quills were sorted as to size and color, and kept in small oval containers which were made of the intestines of an elk, of a buffalo bladder, or of rawhide. The waterproof bladder cases were usually decorated in a simple way with quill embroidery and later with beadwork.

Dye colors and hues for the quills were obtained by boiling roots or berries. Red came from the snakeberry root, the buffalo or squaw berry. Yellow came from the huckleberry root, wild sunflower or coneflower petals—boiled with decayed oak bark or cattail roots. A purplish black was derived from the fox grape or black walnuts. Green dye was secured from a root, but the exact root is not known today. Later on blue was obtained from a clay procured through trade

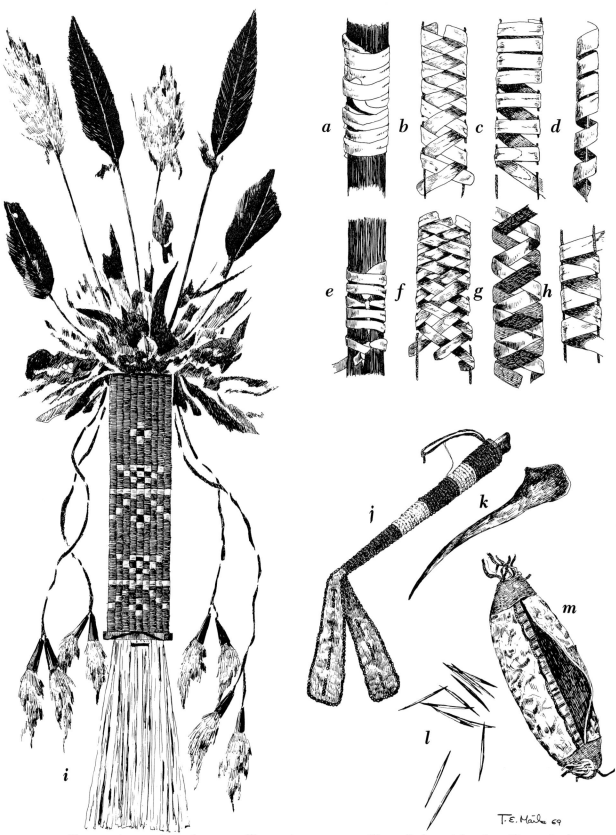

*a,* quill wrapping on hair. *b,* two-quill weaving. *c,* one quill applied straight. *d,* quill on single thread. *e,* quill wrapping without thread fastening. *f,* quill splicing. *g,* two-quill diagonal. *h,* quill on two threads. *i,* quilled hair ornament worn on back of warrior's head. *j,* beaded awl case and bone awl. *k,* bone awl. *l,* quills. *m,* bladder bag used for storing quills.

with the Whites. The quills were soaked briefly in clear water before they were immersed in the dye. The quills were boiled in the dye, then allowed to remain in the dye for only a short time, since if the quills remained in the dye too long the core of the quill would be soaked out. When the color was satisfactory, the quills were removed and placed on a piece of wood to dry.

Quills were washed well before the actual quilling began. For embroidery work the quillworker moistened and softened them by holding them in her mouth. She kept a number in one cheek, with the points protruding from her lips, and pulled out a quill as it was needed. It seems the saliva contained some special property which made the quills more pliable. After they had been softened in this way, the quills were flattened by drawing them between the fingernails or the teeth. The Sioux and the Arapaho smoothed the sewn quills further by rubbing them with a "quill flattener," which was a special tool made of a smooth, flat bone. The quiller's simple outfit included only the flattener, wood or bone awls, sinew, and a bone marker for tracing designs.

Quills were used in four principal ways: wrapping, braiding or plaiting, sewing, and weaving.

Wrapping was the simplest method of applying quills. It was used to cover long, slender objects like pipestems and leather fringes, and to bind strands of hair together. The method was to wrap the moistened quills around the item to be decorated, beginning with several overlapping rounds. As new quills were added, their ends were twisted around a previously applied quill with a half turn, and the turn was then concealed by the next quill.

Plaiting produced a more elaborate quill covering for such things as pipestems and ceremonial staffs than wrapping did. There was single-quill plaiting and two-quill plaiting. Both methods resulted in an overlapping and intertwined pattern looking like a series of small diamonds.

Since holes could not be made in quills without splitting them, quills were attached to buckskin or cloth by working a sinew thread back and forth through the material, and then winding or folding the soft, moistened quills over the exposed part of the thread. Once the quills dried, they remained firmly in position. The quills covered the thread, and when the work was completed none of the threads could be seen.

Weaving was accomplished by interweaving the quills in an over and under fashion each time they crossed. Once again a diamond-shaped pattern was produced.

The shortness of the quills led to designs which were made up of narrow bands. In a single strip the colors were varied according to a regular formula, and larger designs were made up by placing a number of bands side by side. Most quill patterns consisted of straight lines, but disks and flowers were also made for decorations on shirts, leggings, moccasins, and tipis.

Insofar as the four techniques were concerned, each Plains region had its

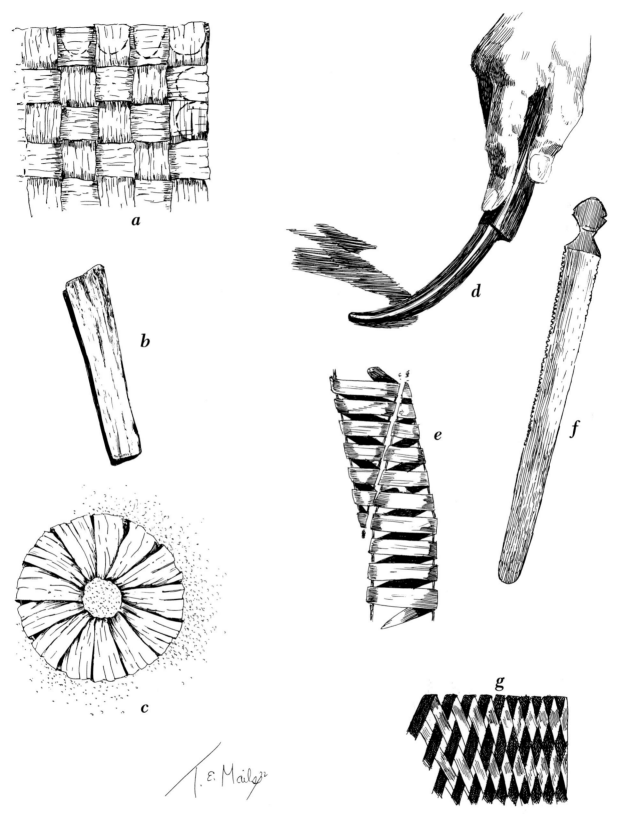

*a*, checker weave quill pattern. *b*, bone marker for incising pattern lines. *c*, rosette quill work. *d*, Blackfoot bone quill-flattener. *e*, method of butting two-thread quill patterns together. *f*, Arapaho bone quill-flattener. *g*, plaited quills.

own methods and selections of ways. For example, the western Sioux employed only the first three ways, and weaving was practiced chiefly by the Canadian Woodland Indians to the northeast of the Sioux.

With the advent of the brightly colored trade beads, quillwork gradually disappeared from many parts of the Plains. Along with it went the specific knowledge of the source and methods of preparation of many of the native vegetable dyes. Aniline dyes, carried west by the traders, were substituted for native dyes beginning about 1860, and the Indians of the reservation soon forgot how to make the native ones. Looking at the quilled pieces in museums today, one marvels at how these ancient dyes have weathered the ravages of time, for most are still so bright that they must have been radiant when they were first used. Collectors seek diligently for the relatively few quilled pieces still in existence, and even a small strip of the exquisite quilling brings an astounding price!

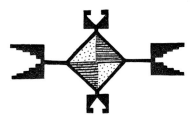

T.E. Mails

Before the European traders came to the Plains country with their glass beads, a relatively few crude native beads were fashioned out of shell, stone, bones of fish and animals, deer hoofs or toes, teeth, and seeds. There was also a tubular bone bead which was used for earrings and in making breastplates.

Most of these ancient beads were so difficult to make, however, that beadworkers were delighted to replace them with the abundant, bright, manufactured beads of glass and metal which were first brought into this country from Venice and Bohemia.

Sometime between 1800 and 1840, a large, opaque, irregular china bead was brought to the Plains. It was known as the pony bead because it was carried in by the pony pack trains. It was made in Venice, and was about one-eighth inch in diameter, or about twice as large as the beads used later. White and medium sky blue were the most used colors, but black beads also appeared in the old pieces, as did a few deep buff, light and dark red, and dark blue beads.

The beads were usually sewn onto skin strips, which were in turn sewn to the larger items to be decorated, but they were also applied directly to the item. The dominant technique employed was "lazy stitch" sewing, which affected the style since it virtually eliminated curved patterns. The straightforward designs worked out in this period were common to most of the tribes. They included narrow triangles, generally standing on or hanging from a horizontal bar; soldier-like rows of right-angled triangles; bands and rectangles; and assemblages of

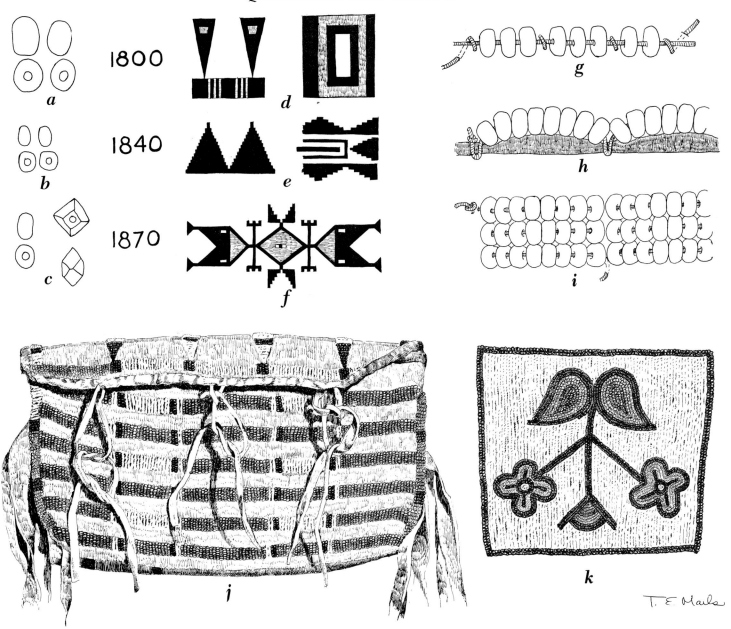

Types of beads introduced at certain dates on the Plains. *a*, pony beads, 1800–40. *b*, seed beads, 1840. *c*, medium-sized beads—richer colors, translucent, faceted, 1870 on. Typical Sioux designs which accompanied the bead periods. *d*, 1800–40. *e*, 1840–70. *f*, 1870 on. Types of bead stitches employed. *g*, the overlay. *h*, section through lazy stitch. *i*, top view of lazy stitch. *j*, beaded Crow saddlebag. *k*, example of Sioux overlaid stitch.

rectangles or straight bands. The impression conveyed was one of geometric simplicity. The beaded areas were quite narrow, with even six-inch-wide bands being infrequent. Examples of original work with pony beads were among the articles collected by Lewis and Clark in 1805.

A smaller, round, opaque Venetian bead known as a "seed" bead reached the Indians about 1840. These were traded in a great variety of colors in bunches of five or six strings each, the strings varying in length from four to six inches. Seed beads were from one sixteenth to three sixteenths of an inch in diameter. In each case the delicacy of the pattern to be embroidered determined the size of the bead chosen. Because seed beads were partly made by hand they were somewhat irregular in shape, and the beadworkers found it necessary to exercise great care in selecting those of equal size. The colors of the first seed beads were richer and softer than the colors of subsequent batches, although the latter became more regular in size. The first seed bead period brought a design shift which emphasized simple triangles, often edged with steps.

When White settlers began to crowd into the Sioux country around 1860, beadwork became a major industry. Women began to cover their possessions with huge all-over patterns. They also did beadwork for the Whites, who sometimes supplied the garment to be decorated and dictated the style. Later, the traders imported Czechoslovakian beads, which were a trifle darker than the Venetian beads and inclined toward a slightly bluish tinge. One acquainted with both types of beads can recognize this coloring and guess very close to the date of the article. About 1870 translucent beads arrived, and toward 1885 beads which were colored with silver or gilt and faceted throughout. By now there was a huge variety of colors and sizes flooding into Indian country from Venice, Bohemia, France, and England.

What is called "the modern style" of beadwork came into being between 1870 and lasted till 1900. Its involved design character easily indicates the age of the decorated pieces. Truly individual tribal approaches manifested themselves in this period. The Sioux, Cheyenne, and Arapaho confined themselves to the lazy stitch; the Blackfoot, Sarsi, Plains Crees, and Flatheads made exclusive use of the overlay. The Crows, Assiniboines, Gros Ventres, and Plains Shoshones employed and combined both techniques. In the south, where beadwork was used only for trimming, the lazy stitch was in vogue among the Pawnees, whereas the Omahas preferred the overlay.

The ornamentation style of long, narrow strips, such as those used on leggings, remained somewhat uniform throughout the area, but observable differences continued to evolve in the decoration of items. For instance, Crow beadwork often had a narrow white border and checker patterns, and employed favored subtle colors such as violet. Sioux work emphasized large white or blue backgrounds, together with designs which had four or six points. Blackfoot designs had few white backgrounds and were very bold and simple with strong color contrasts. Southern Cheyenne garments had little of the usual beadwork on them and could often be identified by the large berry beads which were used. Floral patterns are usually Crow, Sioux, Blackfoot or southeastern tribes, and are of late-nineteenth-century vintage. The Shoshones were fond of blue-gray beads. A feature of northern beading which was easily recognized was that of coating

*a*, beaded Sioux blanket strip. *b*, Sioux quilled shoulder and arm bands for warrior's shirt. *c*, beaded feather and morning star designs on front and back of same shirt. *d*, quilled design used on front and back of man's war shirt. *e*, beaded designs used on Sioux pipe bags. *f*, Blackfoot warrior wearing blanket with beaded blanket strip.

the beads on clubs and targets with glue, so that they were firmly fixed to the item which was beaded. This was a custom followed by the Blackfoot and the Cree tribes.

Sioux beadworkers named their designs after natural objects which they resembled, and frequently used a design to symbolize some mystic idea or tribal scene. Hence designs had a general meaning, but there was no "language in beadwork" which told a story so legible the average Indian, apart from its owner, would understand it. A design that signified arrow points to one woman could be tipis for another—or anything else which had a triangular shape.

Some designs were used for male objects only, while others were used for the female. Carefully selected designs were used on articles provided for ceremonies and societies. Beaded designs were always distinct from the types of symbols painted on rawhide or buckskin.

Most articles were decorated with a design which bore a close relationship to the owner and use of the article. Pipes indicated a pipeholder, a warrior who had led one or more raids, and thus "carried the pipe." A feather embroidered on a warrior's pipe bag revealed his right to wear a real eagle feather in warfare. A horse track, patterned after the hoofprint of a horse, would be used to show that a man had captured horses from the enemy. The track was usually constructed of straight lines, although sometimes the connected end was curved like the regular hoof of a horse. Turtle emblems were placed on the small "Sand Lizards," bags which held a piece of a child's umbilical cord, and also on the yoke of a woman's dress and leggings and on baby cradles. The U-shaped design below the yoke of the woman's dress represented the breast of a turtle, while the winglike extensions corresponded to the sides of his shell. Used in this way the turtle design was believed to have power over the diseases peculiar to women, and also control over birth and infancy. Some have believed that turtle designs were only worn by women, but many male garments carry the design. Buffalo headdresses often had turtle designs painted on them or had small beaded turtle effigies appended to them. A spider web design placed on the robe of a child by a medicine woman invoked supernatural protection for the wearer. Some tribes regarded the spider as a mythological instructor of women in the art of embroidery.

A special design might be composed and adopted by any person as the result of a vision or of some important event or exploit. For example, an eagle design might be chosen to indicate proven leadership, while a tomahawk or bow and arrow would represent the fearless feats of a great warrior.

As symbolism often dictated the choice of designs, so too it influenced the selection of the colors which made up the design. Accordingly the colors came to have their own meanings, although the meanings did vary somewhat from tribe to tribe. White might signify winter. But white was also related to personal qualities such as purity, and to animals which were consecrated, such as buffalo, deer, rabbits, and birds.

Sky blue might represent a body of water in which the sky was reflected. It also meant sky, haze, smoke, distant mountains, rocks, and night. Navy blue and black sometimes indicated victory or enemies killed. In ceremonial use, blue represented many things: the sky, clouds, wind, the west, lightning, thunder, the moon, water, and day. Black often portrayed the night.

Red beads on a weapon might symbolize wounds inflicted; on a coat, wounds received. One or more horizontal red lines in the design of an eagle feather whose quill was wrapped with beads depicted the number of battles in which its owner warrior had taken part. In ceremonial use, red might indicate sunset, thunder, lightning, or forms of plant and animal life. Red lines often meant longevity, for red was commonly known as the life span color, or "trail on which woman travels," and was especially symbolic of that portion of a woman's life during which children might be born. Red was used for the ownership of property, and figured prominently in the Tobacco Societies.

Yellow was used for sunlight, dawn, clouds, or earth, and the Cheyenne loved it.

Green portrayed summer, vegetation, and new life. The Cheyenne were fond of it too.

By 1900 the great period of beadwork was over, and the technical skill which had been engendered and handed down from generation to generation virtually disappeared for a time from view. This period ended with some truly sensational creations, all of which are avidly sought after by museums and collectors. Some of the finest pieces of the last days were women's belts and dresses, bags, war clubs, beaded tomahawks, and items of horse gear. No other culture has ever matched the Indians' skill in beading, and without the deep spiritual approach and purposes to guide their hands even the later Plains Indians failed to equal the quality of the ancient work, although heartening signs of a renaissance can be seen in the products found in a few contemporary trading posts and stores.

# Chapter 16

# ACHIEVEMENT MARKS

It is from observance of a thousand little and apparently trivial modes and tricks of Indian life, that the Indian character must be learned; excepting that the system of civilized life would furnish ten apparently useless and ridiculous trifles to one which is found in Indian life; and at least twenty to one which are purely nonsensical and unmeaning.

The civilized world looks upon a group of Indians, in their classic dress, and their few simple oddities, all of which have their moral or meaning, and laughs at them excessively, because they are not like ourselves—we ask, "why do the silly creatures wear such great bunches of quills on their heads?—Such loads and streaks of paint upon their bodies—and bear's grease? abominable!" and a thousand other equally silly questions, without ever stopping to think that *Nature taught them* to do so—and that they all have some definite importance or meaning which an Indian could explain to us at once, *if* he were asked and felt disposed to do so—that each quill in his head stood, in the eyes of his whole tribe, as the symbol of an enemy who had fallen by his hand—that every streak of red paint covered a wound which he had got in honourable combat—and that the bear's grease with which he carefully anoints his body every morning, from head to foot cleanses and purifies the body, and protects his skin from the bite of mosquitoes, and at the same time preserves him from colds and coughs which are usually taken through the pores of the skin.[1]

In this perceptive statement George Catlin captures an idea that is vital to everyone who wishes to understand the Plains Indian warrior's clothing and gear. Everything he wore grew out of his national and religious orientation, and because of this it served to accomplish his fervently held goals—which were to ensure the longevity of his clan and tribe and to live the kind of life that would assure his happiness in eternal life.

It follows that his clothing would become more than simple clothing; more than just a covering for his body or a costume. Ideally, it would prepare him for war and raiding by serving as a constructive prod to his mental process, and once he accomplished something it would be decorated in such a way as to become a reminder of his (hopefully) great achievements. Seeing how all this worked out is an immensely fascinating experience.

An expression often used in Indian literature is the phrase "to count coup," pronounced "coo." Writers borrowed it from the French trappers and traders, who used it to describe a blow inflicted on an enemy. Ordinarily it denoted the touching of an individual, and not an attack upon a large body of people.

In time, it came to be the most positive way in which a man could show that he was skillful and brave and conscious of his responsibilities. In practice, a coup was registered by approaching near enough to an enemy to strike him with something held in the hand. To kill an enemy was praiseworthy, and the act of scalping rendered benefits of a certain kind, yet neither of these approached the status of a coup, which could be administered without either killing or scalping. This is not to say that killing and scalping could be avoided. Horse raids and wars were engaged in at considerable risk. The stakes were high and the hazards were great. So men did die, and men were scalped. This meant that a man had to be emotionally prepared to assume the ultimate costs of selflessness, else he would never count the coups which enabled him to share in the tribal rewards of praise, respect, wealth, and leadership. Actually, the warrior in the field risked his life in order to win it for himself and others, and thus the economics of existence always hung in an interesting balance. The wonder is, the warrior came to like that balance very well.

The proudest day in the life of any young warrior occurred when he counted his first coup. And, every one that followed thereafter established a chain of indelible accomplishments. At dances and ceremonies he was expected to join the other warriors in recounting each coup which had been leveled in tribal defense; while others, particularly the young boys, listened wide-eyed, spellbound, and turning green with envy.

Most Plains tribes gave their highest tribal honors to the man who, in counting coups, consistently captured his enemy's weapons, horses, or ceremonial equipment. Believing his medicine to be especially powerful, they requested his counsel and leadership. Parents asked him to perform the naming ceremony for their newborn boy. He was selected to lead and share in tribal rituals and social affairs. Such acts as these added enormously to his prestige and wealth, since he was also given expensive gifts such as fine horses and painted buffalo robes. Eventually a successful coup counter would be one of the few who lived in painted lodges. Understandably, then, an Indian warrior sought to outshine everyone else in warfare and raiding. The better job he made of it, the greater became his personal reputation and opportunity. When he had scaled the heights, his protective medicine received the highest esteem of everyone, and his vision helpers became the desire of every vision seeker. Above all, he was expected to shun the company of those who were less aggressive, for in being rebuked they hopefully would be challenged toward service of a higher kind.

A countable coup could be struck with a whip, coup stick, club, lance, the muzzle of a gun, a bow, riding quirt, or anything else held in the hand. It could be performed on a woman enemy, who might then be captured, or even on a

Warriors striving to count coup in battle.

male child. Any such blow registered as a positive mark in tribal defense. Not incidentally, most women and boys learned to defend themselves rather well, since the choice in battle was always to be victim or victor. Still, it was the administration of the coup on an enemy warrior that called for real courage and counted the most. It was accepted that the enemy would be defending himself desperately, and trying his own best to coup and/or kill. A trained and resolute foe was patently dangerous. Even a downed man could still retaliate in remarkable ways, for Indians with a history of desperate struggles in territorial survival were well schooled in defense. They were ready and willing, and men were seldom taken as captives. Once the battle was joined, a warrior neither expected quarter nor gave it. He either fought to the death and died mute, or fled, striving even then to the last to inflict some injury on his enemy. When captured, warriors knew what was coming, and did not complain. All their lives they prepared themselves to accept capture and torture without flinching.

While the coup was primarily a blow with something held in the hand, other dangerous acts in warfare were also reckoned as coups. A Blackfoot horseman who rode over and knocked down an enemy counted the act a coup, even if his foe was on foot. After all, the downed man might still shoot the horseman or plant a lance in his middle. A certain Pawnee registered one of his coups when he simply ran up to a fallen enemy and jumped on him with both feet. Some tribes counted the stealing or capture of horses as coup, but this was not the common case. Stolen horses often counted as war deeds only.

All Plains Indian tribes shared certain types of coups, yet each held its own views as to special ones. An act of daring was, in itself, seldom deemed a coup. The Assiniboines said, "Killing an enemy counts nothing unless his person is touched or struck."[2] The Cheyenne permitted three men to count coup on the same enemy, with the first who touched him gaining the greater fame. The Crows, Assiniboines, and Arapaho allowed four men to count coup on a victim. The four important Crow coups ranged in this order: First came the striking of an enemy with a gun, bow, or riding quirt; then came the cutting of an enemy's favorite horse from a tipi door; next, the recovery of an enemy's weapon in battle; and finally, the riding down of an enemy.

The Assiniboine first coup by touching was considered a higher honor than that which was gained by the use of an arrow or bullet which killed an enemy from a distance. Sometimes an enemy, knowing their coup scheme, feigned death and drew a careless warrior within range of his hand weapons—with fatal results to the ambitious Assiniboine coup counter. The first warrior to take a scalp kept it, but if more hair was left on the victim's head and another took it, that person was also eligible to join in a scalp dance. The first Assiniboine warrior to sink a tomahawk or club into an already scalped head counted it a minor war deed, but it was considered an act of little consequence—except as one remembers what has been said concerning putting one's enemies in their places and avenging one's relatives. The Crees believed that killing a man while both combatants were out in the open was more honorable than killing him from ambush. The Kiowas gave abundant credit for charging the enemy while the rest of one's party was in retreat, and for rescuing a comrade under the same circumstance.

In some tribes, if a warrior killed his enemy after he had touched him while alive, and then finally scalped him, he could count three coups. In those tribes where stealing a horse from an enemy entitled a warrior to count one coup, he could also go on to count an additional minor coup by entering the enemy's village and, before witnesses, touching a tipi or lodge. He was said to have "captured" the tipi, and whatever design or symbol was painted on it the warrior could paint on his own when he returned home. Should a warrior count coup on an enemy tipi and then go on to enter and touch a live enemy, finally killing and scalping him, and on his way out of camp steal a horse, his rewards would be endless! On the other hand, an individual might mortally wound a man from a distance, yet not gain a single coup because four of his fellow warriors beat him to the touch. To have an enemy count coup on one's self and live was a signal dishonor, and this embarrassment was testified to before the council as well as one's victories!

Taking risks and becoming a hero would have been but a passing thing in the Indian scheme without something to single out or "mark" the distinguished warrior. So specific decorations were created and awarded for these accomplishments, and since the golden eagle was the solar bird and a favored emissary of God, one is not surprised to find that its feathers became the item most preferred for recording coups. A tail feather was awarded by the tribal leaders for each countable deed, the exception being the "grand coup," which rated more than one feather.[3] Feathers were either used to make headdresses or were inserted singly or in groups in the hair at the base of the scalp lock. Secondary uses of feathers were to ornament shields, lances, and other weapons. Besides this, the wing, or pinion feathers, of the eagle were used for buffalo horn bonnets and ceremonial fans, and for the fletching of arrows. It is claimed that an Indian warrior would rather part with his horse, his tipi, or even his wife, than lose his eagle feathers in battle, since to have this happen would be to invite dishonor and loss of status in the eyes of the entire tribe. Great Indian warriors sometimes earned enough honors to wear a double-tailed bonnet with a tail so long it would have, had they let it, dragged on the ground as they walked, and besides this they were entitled to carry a feathered lance or flag to display additional feathers. A bonnet in the famous Harvey Collection has a tail ten feet long, and could only have been worn hanging at full length while its owner was mounted on horseback.

An Indian warrior was not allowed, according to tribal law, to wear golden eagle feathers until he won them by acceptable war deeds. He had to appear before the tribal council to tell and reenact his exploits. Witnesses to the deeds were then examined, and if in the eyes of the council the deed was thought worthy

Sioux warrior Running Antelope wearing three marked coup feathers.

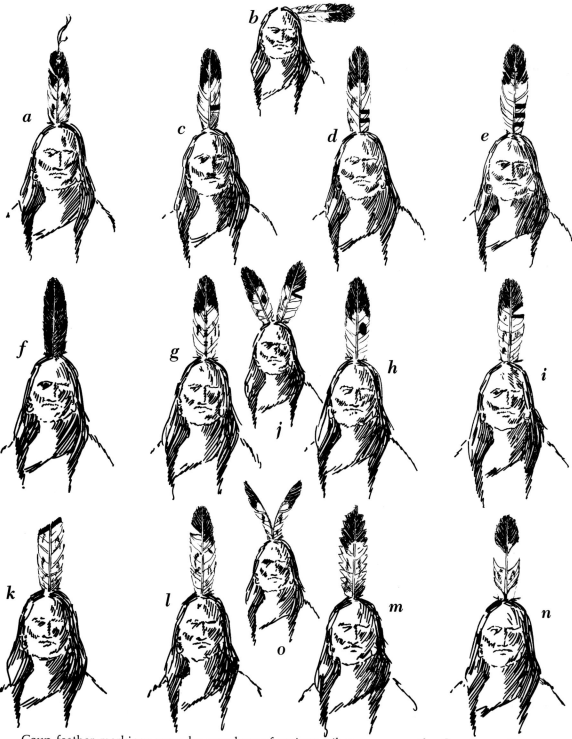

Coup feather markings worn by members of various tribes. *a*, among the Omahas, a first coup was marked by a single feather worn upright. With the Sioux, Hidatsas, and Gros Ventres, first coup marking was a single upright feather with a horsehair tuft. An upright Assiniboine feather dyed red indicated the warrior had killed an enemy. For other victories he added more feathers, stuck separately in the hair. When a warrior killed a woman, two feathers from the ring-billed gull were added to the red feathers. *b*, Omaha second coup feather worn horizontally for striking of a coup, the warrior was authorized to wear his first feather. The same method was repeated for all of the feathers he would eventually wear in his hair or headdress.

In a typical instance, when a warrior had earned enough feathers to make a warbonnet, he invited his most trusted friends to his tipi. After enjoying a meal and smoking the pipe, the friends ceremoniously laid out the feathers and sorted them according to size and pattern. As each feather was selected, the story of the coup performed by the warrior in earning it was retold. Then each feather was fastened to its place on the bonnet base, and when they were all attached the last steps in finishing the headdress were carried out.

Sometimes a tuft of horsehair, either white, yellow, or red, was added to the tips of the feathers to designate additional honors. Small feathers tipped with down from under the eagle's tail were also used for this purpose. They were attached with a glue made of boiled buffalo hoofs and white clay that holds incredibly well—even better as far as feathers are concerned than some of our modern cements. Once the right to wear one was earned, bonnets could be obtained in other ways—as a gift, or in trade with a tribe of great bonnet makers such as the Crows.

The Indians of the Plains could read the feathers of another tribe as well as they could read their own. This meant they had a ready means of identifying the enemy's outstanding warriors, who, because they wore their feathers into battle, always posed a daring and deliberate challenge. Thus a warrior who wanted

---

a wounded enemy. Third coup was awarded to the first two men to strike a dead enemy, and was shown by a single feather hanging down.

*c*, Sioux, Hidatsa, and Gros Ventre second coup, an upright feather with one red bar, or a feather tilted slightly to the left. *d*, third coup, an upright feather with two red bars, or a feather worn horizontally. *e*, fourth coup, an upright feather with three red bars, or a feather hung vertically.

*f*, a wounded man wore a feather dyed red. *g*, a wounded warrior who had killed an enemy wore an upright feather decorated with bands of quillwork, each band indicating a kill.

*h*, Sioux feathers with a red spot indicated the wearer had killed an enemy; several spots, several enemies. *i*, notched feathers explained that the wearer had cut an enemy's throat and taken his scalp, or that a man's horse had been wounded. (In some tribes a red spot indicated the wearer himself had been wounded.) *j*, a man might wear both kinds at once.

*k*, a feather with diagonally clipped top also showed that its owner had cut an enemy's throat. *l*, a notch at the top of the feather indicated a third coup. *m*, serrated edges indicated the fourth coup. *n*, sides removed leaving only a tip indicated the fifth coup. *o*, a split feather meant that the warrior had been wounded many times. Successful scouts were given a black feather ripped down the center. For battle purposes, one Kiowa warrior wore the longest wing feather of a crane in his hair.

to make a name for himself could easily choose an enemy equipped to test his mettle to the limit.

Perhaps the most flamboyant piece of feathered equipment carried by the coup counter was the "flag," which has erroneously been called a coup stick. The flag was a long pole, ranging from six to nine feet in length, which was decorated with a single row of eagle feathers, the feathers either being mounted individually on the stick with thongs or assembled on a band of buckskin or felt. Some tribes used broad stripes of color on the band. As a man accumulated his coup feathers in some tribes, they were gradually added to his pole until twenty-eight or thirty, enough for the average warbonnet, were assembled. Then new feathers, representing those on the original flag, were used to make his warbonnet. If he went on to earn more coups, the war flag remained intact and could be used together with the bonnet. When the warrior was at home he sometimes planted the prestigious flag in the ground to the right of his tipi door. Not only chiefs, but any man with enough honors might possess both bonnet and flag.

The true coup stick was only a long, slender branch which was sometimes pointed, and to which were usually attached one, or at most a few eagle feathers and/or fur or flannel streamers. However, an amazing Crow coup stick of particular note was laden with feathers from end to end, and there were probably many others like it. Every warrior had a coup stick, and many can be seen in old photographs. The Cheyenne claimed that "an old woman in a cave" told them long ago how to make a medicine coup stick. When they carried one into war, it was believed that the enemy could not hit them with bullets or arrows, yet the man who carried the coup stick could easily touch his enemy with it. Such a stick was often handed down from father to son.[4]

It has been stated that "The coup stick was a long stick, bent on one end and decorated with otter fur, used by a warrior to count coup on a live enemy."[5] But bent sticks like this were either a society symbol or a staff used on raids to identify those who were elected to assist the "pipeholder" or war party leader.

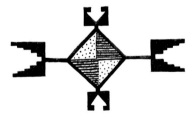

In the mind of the Plains warrior of the eighteenth and nineteenth centuries the male golden eagle flew above all the creatures of the world and saw everything. Nothing matched his courage and swiftness, and his talons had the strength of a giant's hand. The eagle was very holy. He was the solar or sun bird, and his feathers were regarded as the rays of the sun. When one or more were worn on an Indian's head or carried as a fan in his hand they established a connection between the man and the Great Mystery. Indeed, they brought God's presence as the sun sends shafts of light to earth, and in the union of the eagle and the man, the man became, he thought, as holy as the bird.

The golden eagle was easily the finest bird to be found on the Plains of North America. He measured from thirty to forty inches in height, and at maturity achieved a wing span of seven or more feet. The thirteen spectacular tail feathers of the immature bird, which are a sepia-toned white with dark-brown tips, measure from twelve to fourteen inches in length. The wing feathers, which are called pinion feathers, were used for buffalo horn bonnet tails and for various other important ceremonial regalia. The first coups were counted in single feathers. But since a bonnet without a tail needed at least twenty-eight feathers, the Indian could not make an entire warbonnet from one eagle, often needing to capture as many as six birds before he could make a well-balanced headdress. A single-tailed bonnet required several more birds, and a double-tail called for from ten to a dozen birds. The right tail or wing feathers were used on the right side of the bonnet, and the left tail or wing feathers on the left side.

When making a headdress, the plumes or fluff feathers which grow at the underside of the base of the bird's tail were used as a foundation for the larger feathers. The plumes were called "breath feathers," because of their delicacy and lightness, and the slightest air movement would cause them to sway as though they were breathing. Some of the plumes were eight inches long, and two in particular were valued as highly as brown-tipped tail feathers, since they were used at the end of the Sun Dance plume which was placed in the center of the bonnet.

Always a wise and cautious bird, the eagle could seldom be caught with a snare or shot with a bow and arrow. In fact, due to its religious significance, the Indian warrior who wanted to use an eagle as a holy medicine or to make a bonnet was not permitted to kill it with a weapon anyway. So the capture of eagles became a sacred act in itself.

Dangerous as it was, warriors caught eagles with their bare hands in eagle pits, and the way of doing this was a common one throughout the Plains.

The Cheyenne began by performing a minor religious ritual to ensure success in building the pit and capturing the eagles. Most of their pits were built near places where eagles lived, such as on a high hill, and often along the side of a divide. Since Cheyenne tradition ruled out the use of metal knives, the holes were dug with sharpened sticks by two men. The approximate dimensions were four feet wide, deep enough for a man to sit up in, and six feet long. The excavated dirt was scooped onto a buffalo robe and dumped and hidden under some brush where the eagles could not see it from the air.

*a*, the golden eagle. *b*, eagle talon. *c*, diagram of eagle bones. *d*, wing (pinion) feather. *e*, down feather. *f*, tail feather.

Eagle-hunting pit. *a*, Sioux warrior digging pit with knife. *b*, top view of pit. *c*, cross section through pit showing position of hunter in pit and stuffed wolf. *d*, hunter reaching for eagle.

When the hole was completed, tree branches as thick as a man's wrist were laid lengthwise across it. Then three long sticks were laid the other way, and all were laced together to make a kind of lid. (Custom dictated that four days were to be consumed in building the eagle trap.)

Finally bait, such as part of a young deer or antelope, was laid on top of the lid and tied fast.[6]

The Sioux did their eagle hunting in the fall of each year. Men who had earned the right to catch them set up base camps in secluded, wooded areas, and some distance away from the places where eagles were known to be. The camp consisted of a tipi or brush dwelling, and a purifying lodge. Then at a (prayerfully) chosen spot in the eagle area, the men marked out a rectangle about six feet long and three feet wide, with the axis north and south. After dividing this into smaller squares with their knives, they carefully removed the sod and placed it off to one side. They then dug their pit with only their knives, loading the earth onto a robe with large mountain sheep horn spoons. To deceive the eagles, the loads of loose dirt were dumped some distance away from the pit, and piled so as to simulate gopher hills. When the depth of the pit reached approximately three feet, a nest of sacred sage was placed at the bottom of the hole at the south end. After this a latticework of poles was laid across the top to serve as beams, leaving an opening, however, at the north end, large enough to allow the hunter to climb in later on. A rawhide rope was then stretched over the beam ends and secured with stakes to make the roof structure firm. Finally, the men replaced the sod, and brought rocks, sticks, and bunches of grass to plant and place around the lid in order to camouflage the trap further.

Once the trap was completed, each warrior returned to his tipi and prepared an altar. He stuck ten sacred tobacco offerings, each hung from a small stick, in the ground behind the fire pit. These must not be disturbed by anyone while catchers were in their pits seeking eagles. Others must neither touch them nor make a sound as they passed them.

Long before the sun arose the next day, the trapper went to the purifying lodge and took a sweat bath. After this, he and a companion proceeded to the pit, carrying with them the dismembered carcass of an animal, such as a jackrabbit. Once the catcher had climbed into the hole, his helper readjusted the camouflage, set the bait securely, and left, while the anxious catcher, lying on his back in the trap with his head near the open end, sighed deeply and awaited the eagles.

By sundown, if he was fortunate, he would catch several birds, although on some days he might not catch any. As they lighted, the eagles were seized by the legs, drawn into the pit, and killed by twisting their necks. Then they were placed on the bed of sacred sage at the foot of the pit. At the end of a successful day the happy warrior left the trap and returned with his eagles to the purifying lodge. Placing the birds in a row, he took a sweat bath in thanksgiving, "for this was the custom when one killed so many eagles."[7]

A Blackfoot warrior who wished to catch eagles moved his entire family to an area where the birds were known to be plentiful. Several miles from his camp he dug a pit like those already mentioned.

His preferred bait was a piece of the bloody neck of a buffalo, since it could be seen or smelled a long way off. His second choice was a smaller animal. Often the stuffed skin of a wolf or a coyote was placed alongside the bait in such a way as to appear to be eating it.

Like the Sioux, the Blackfoot hunter rose before it was light and after smoking and praying left his camp. He arrived at the pit while it was still dark, and stretched out in it, taking with him a slender stick about six feet long, a human skull, and a little pemmican.

When an eagle saw the meat from afar he would "boldly" descend to wrest it away from the wolf. Finding it held fast by the rope, and apparently being so engrossed as not to be disturbed by a wolf who neither moved nor complained, the bird would begin to feed on it; and while he was pecking at the bait, the trapper would seize it by the legs, draw it into the pit, and kill it either by strangling it, twisting its neck, or, it is claimed, by crushing its body with his knees, although how he did that with a furious and powerful bird in such a shallow recess I haven't figured out![8] Then he laid it to one side outside the pit, opening its bill and putting a little piece of pemmican in its mouth "to make the other eagles envious." As long as he remained in the pit, the hunter neither ate, drank, nor slept. Until he either acquired the number of eagles he needed or otherwise decided to quit, the hunter prepared a sleeping place not far off, to which he sneaked off each night after dark, and there ate, drank, and rested.

The skull was taken into the hole as a curious kind of self-protection. It was believed that the ghost of the person to whom the skull had belonged would serve a threefold purpose: It would protect the watcher against harm from the eagle, keep him edgy and awake, and would even make the watcher invisible. The eagle could not possibly see him! This may seem a farfetched idea, but it brought the hunter a strange peace of mind which assured his diligence and vigilance.

The six-foot-long stick was used to drive away hungry smaller birds, such as magpies, crows, and ravens, who might decide to take the bait. It was also used to drive away the white-headed bald eagle, which the Indians did not care to catch. Their feathers were not as attractive, and it had been learned by sad experience that they were especially powerful birds—one could "almost kill a person."

The Blackfoot warrior must not, of all things, eat rosebuds! If he did, the eagle, when he alighted, would immediately begin to scratch himself and would not eat the bait. Didn't everyone know that rosebuds would make an eagle itch? And his wife and children must not use the sewing awl, because if they did the eagles would invariably scratch the catcher. Everyone knew that too.

Blackfoot accounts insist that despite any questions as to whether an eagle would approach such a large animal, the skin of a wolf, coyote, or fox was stuffed with grass and made to stand erect and look as natural as possible. A rope was then tied to a large piece of meat for bait, which was placed by the stuffed animal skin, and the end of the rope was passed through the roof and into the pit to be held by the hunter. Then the man returned to his base camp dwelling. During the night he sang eagle songs and burned sweet grass in supplication to the eagles, all the while rubbing the smoke over his own body to purify himself, so that while he was in the pit he would give out no man scent.

The Indian hunter could always hear the sound of an eagle coming. When the bird finally came down, it did not alight on the bait, but off to one side of it, "striking the ground with a heavy thud." Once he had heard it, the warrior never again mistook that sound for anything else.

After sundown of the first or whichever day he had caught enough eagles, the successful Blackfoot warrior left his hiding place for good and proudly took his eagles, averaging from six to ten pounds in weight each, home. He carried the birds to his "eagle lodge," already prepared at the edge of the camp. Here he placed them on the ground in a row, and raised their bodies, resting each one at an angle on a long log. Pemmican was placed in their beaks so they would not be afraid of the people, and so that their spirits might tell other eagles how well they were being treated. The eagle lodge contained a human skull, and the entire family prayed to it, asking its ghost to help them lure more eagles to the pit.[9]

One Blackfoot account reveals that on a certain occasion forty eagles were killed in a single day. Sometimes the larger hawks were also caught. In the north, five eagles were considered an even trade for a good horse; a fact which shows that either eagles were more plentiful or horses were more valuable than they were farther south, where two eagles would purchase a horse.

One Indian informant explains that once the bird was pulled into the pit, its back was broken with the foot. Killing it this way allowed the wings to fall to either side and the feathers were not injured.

Some historians have believed that eagle pits deep enough to stand in were dug, yet this would be an incredible task with a knife or bare hands.

When grizzly bears were about, eagle hunting was extremely dangerous. Once an Indian was in his eagle trap when a big grizzly started to drag the bait away. The warrior had a thong attached to the meat and with this drew it into the pit. The bear turned back to investigate. With a sweep of his heavy paw he tore off the brush covering and, finding the man, dragged him out and killed him.

A Kiowa hunter sat for two days in an eagle pit. On the third day he saw an eagle light on his stuffed coyote. He reached up, but caught the bird by one leg only and pulled him down. The bird was quiet at first, but quickly got over his fright. He stuck his talons through the man's wrist, cutting an artery. The blood gushed out as they fought and struggled "like two men" in the pit. Finally,

Hunter with captured eagles at eagle's lodge, where prayers were offered in thanksgiving.

the Indian, though weak from loss of blood, managed to choke the bird to death. He tied up his wrist and took the eagle back to camp. When he got there, his arm was badly swollen. It was as big as the calf of his leg. It was very slow in healing. Those feathers, one can be sure, brought him a double remembrance—and gave a richer meaning to the marking of his every coup.[10]

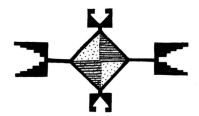

Many designations besides feathers were used as evidence of brave acts. Killing an adversary in hand-to-hand battle permitted the Sioux victor to paint a red hand on his horse's shoulder, neck, or flank. Saving a friend in battle entitled a man to paint a cross on his clothing, and if a rescuer saved more than one person he could wear a double cross. Sioux coups were indicated by painting blue or green vertical stripes on war shirts, or black horizontal stripes on leggings; red stripes always explained that the wearer had been wounded. The Blackfoot used brown vertical lines. A Kiowa named Black Hawk went to war in a shirt painted red to indicate his battle honors on one side and yellow to show his horse raid accomplishments on the other. If Assiniboine leggings were painted or quilled with pictures of hoofprints below the knee, it indicated that the person had taken horses in the summer season. Those stolen in winter were designated by white weasel skins worn as fringes on their shirts and leggings.

Horse hoofs painted on a Sioux coup feather, upon leggings, or upon a man's horse indicated the number of animals a warrior had taken, and some warriors colored each hoofmark to represent the color of the horse. One authority states that "A man's prowess and wealth were shown by the wearing of a miniature rope and moccasins at his belt to signify his capture of ten or more horses; the rope alone was worn when less than ten horses were brought back."[11] The symbols for coups varied among the Sioux tribal divisions, and individual badges were occasionally employed. Thus the Sioux High Bald Eagle carried a small wooden knife, painted red, on the end of his walking stick, and a lock of horsehair to indicate the Pawnees whom he had killed was attached to the knife.

The Crow winner of all four coups could adorn his prestigious war shirt with four porcupine-quilled or beaded bands, one running from shoulder to wrist on each sleeve and one over each shoulder from front to back. Merely earning the first coup enabled a man to attach a wolf or coyote tail from one moccasin; from both if he performed the feat twice. Eagle feathers tied to a man's gun or coup stick revealed the number of scalps he had taken. A knotted rope hanging from the neck of a war horse told of the cutting loose and successful theft of an enemy's picketed mount. The number of horses captured in a raid was indicated by stripes of white clay painted under or around a horse's eyes, on its nose, or on its flanks. A white clay hand on the flanks explained that the Crow owner had ridden down an enemy.

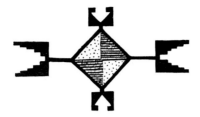

The shirts of Crow, Blackfoot, Mandan, and Sioux coup counters often bore beautiful white weasel skins, some of which were black-tipped. A gun snatcher of these tribes was allowed to put the skins on his garments. In other instances shirts, leggings, and moccasins could be decorated with the locks of an enemy's hair. Such shirts were called "scalp shirts," although toward the last half of the nineteenth century men sometimes used their own hair or the hair of family members for such purposes. Looking at a shirt in a museum now, it is difficult to tell which is the case—unless other marks on the garment show that the owner was a warrior of some renown, for this would indicate that enemy hairlocks were used. It should be noted that several hairlocks could be made from a single scalp. A shirt with 104 locks on it probably represented no more than twenty victims.

White authors expressed different opinions as to why the Indian scalped his fallen enemy. Francis Parkman believed that it represented only the meaningless act of a barbarian.[12] George Catlin decided that the Indian, like anyone else, had to do everything he could to establish his position in society, and he used the scalp as one of his certificates of achievement.[13] The majority of the Indian tribes ruled that the scalp belonged to the first coup counter—to the one who first struck an enemy with something held in his hand. And in this wise, Charles Goodnight attributed the scalping custom to the warrior's desire to prove that he was in advance of all the others in the battle, and therefore the bravest in defense of his tribe.[14]

It is often thought that scalping was only practiced by the Indians, but records show that White men and Mexicans took as many of the Indian scalps as the Indians did of theirs. In fact, it was the custom among Whites and Mexicans in the early days to offer a bounty for Indian scalps, and no distinction was made between the scalps of adults or children.

Once again, it is surprising to learn the difference between the White man's opinions of an Indian's purpose for a certain act and the Indian's own ideas regarding it. For while it is true that the custom had its ghastly nature, even making some warriors sick to their stomachs when they did it, and while Indians did agree that one reason for taking scalps was to gain status in the tribal award scheme, the real reason for scalping was a spiritual one. The act of scalping was a part of their religious view, and it was a view which prevailed throughout the Plains.

Their acceptance of the custom began with their ideas concerning the hair itself. Because the hair was the only part of the body which continued to grow significantly throughout the lifetime of the individual, the Plains people came to believe—perhaps with the help of someone's vision in the earliest period of a certain tribe—that the hair was an extension of the person's soul (or spirit). In accordance with this view, the hair became visual evidence that the soul was a

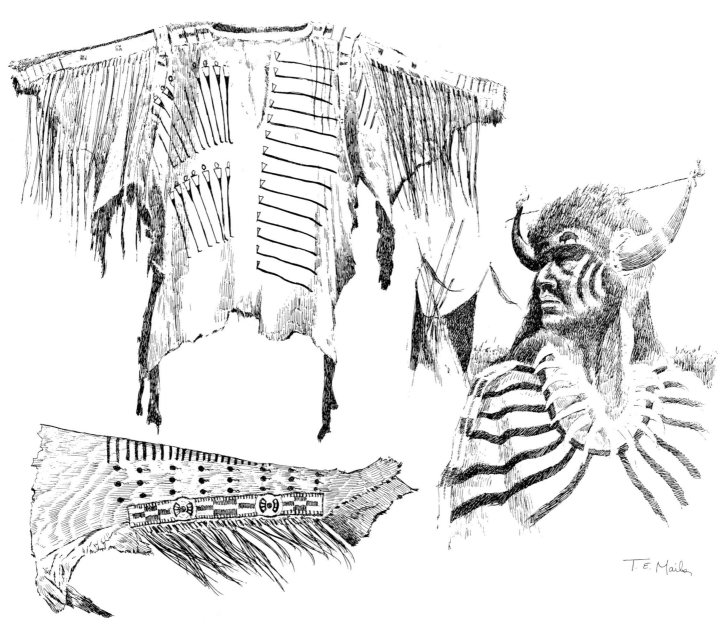

Coup markings on garments. *Top,* marked war shirt, probably Mandan, with pipes to denote leadership of raid expeditions and figures which probably indicated victims (circa 1830). *Bottom,* marked Blackfoot legging, with horizontal lines to mark raids and hairlock fringes. The meaning of the round spots is not known (style before 1845). *Right,* marked war shirt, probably Mandan. Bodmer (1833) painted Assiniboine and Crow shirts with similar markings.

War exploit indications on male garments. *Left,* Ute clothing with beaded bands on shirt and leggings, and leader's sash indicating status in war achievements. *Right,* Assiniboine clothing with coup marks and hairlocks on sleeves. The chest ornament is a quilled target.

living thing, for it was constantly growing, constantly revealing itself. Therefore, the hair was groomed and shaped with especial care, and the third task carried out in the morning, after prayer and eating, was the combing and greasing of the hair. Wives helped their husbands with this, and husbands helped their wives. And they did so with infinite patience since the care and consideration of the soul was involved.

One immediately sees why, in some tribes, the hair was encouraged to grow as long as possible. Some Crow warriors attained growths so long that the ends dragged on the ground as they walked. Others saved any pieces of fallen hair, glued them together in thick cords of assembled strands, and then pasted the cords together with globs of pitch and clay to make a kind of fall which was attached to the back of the head. Long hair was a sign of extreme humility and spirituality, and in religious ceremonies of the highest order, such as the Sun Dance, the hair was combed loose and hung free down the backs of both men and women.

Some tribes even had spirit-keeping ceremonies which involved the use of locks of the hair, hence the keeping of the soul. In the old days a Sioux, filled with grief for a near relative, might prolong his period of mourning by "keeping the spirit" for several months or a year, and then "letting it go" by means of a certain ceremony. This was a custom which demanded a great deal, for once begun it had to be carried out to the end, either by the man who undertook it or in the event of his death by his nearest relative. While the keeping rite was in process the person involved had to withdraw from all other tribal activities and must devote himself entirely to the keeping ceremony. Naturally, a man who did this successfully was considered to be one qualified to fulfill large responsibilities in the tribe.

The spirit of a child was kept more frequently than that of a grown person. The first step, taken at the death of the person whose spirit was to be kept, was to cut off a lock of the person's hair (more rarely a hair ornament might be removed) and wrap it in cloth—such as a felt of the sacred color. When this step was completed the spirit keeper rode through the camp lamenting the person's death, carrying the hair in his arms as if it were the body of the deceased and announcing to the tribe that he had taken upon himself the responsibilities of a spirit keeper and how long the keeping ceremony would last.

After this the hairlock, sweet grass, and the shed hair of a buffalo were placed in a special wrapping—the whole of which was called a spirit bundle. The bundle was then tied to a pole just outside the tipi door and left there for four days. At the end of this period the bundle was taken down and placed upon a specially prepared tripod inside the tipi. No one was allowed to pass between it and the fire so long as the spirit was kept. The keeper and his wife wore no ornaments during the keeping period, and their faces were painted all of the time. The atmosphere in the lodge was always quiet and reverent, as though the relative whom they mourned was in the lodge. It was expected that those who kept a spirit would hold charitable thoughts toward everyone in the tribe, and all unkind or harsh words were forbidden in the spirit lodge. Over the months of mourning the spirit keeper exchanged feasts with the various societies, and his lodge possessions were considered to be the property of the tribe.

At the expiration of the keeping time a final feast and ceremony were held. All the band gathered for the event and the societies had their special tipis. The societies took a prominent part in such features of the spirit releasing as took place outside the lodge, but their members did not enter the lodge unless they were men who had kept spirits.

On the appointed day the keeper and his wife laid aside all signs of mourning and put on their finest attire. A man who had kept a spirit was selected to prepare a "spirit post." This was a post about thirty-five inches long, sharpened at one end and with a face carved or painted at the other, and adorned with pieces of clothing belonging to the deceased. It was carved and dressed in the spirit lodge and set in the ground. Food was placed in front of the post, and at this time any orphan in need of help might appear and ask for help, that it be fed and cared for. Such a request was never refused. Others in need might also ask for assistance. When this was done, gifts which had been accumulated by the spirit keeper, such as clothing and beadwork, were distributed to the people in the camp. There was much feasting, and this was an occasion on which families announced publicly the names they had given their children, or had the ears of their children pierced in the same manner as at the Sun Dance.

During the day of the final ceremony the spirit bundle lay beside the spirit post, and the actual release of the spirit came when the bundle was opened at the end of the day. The spirit keeper kept the lock of hair, and the other contents of the bundle went to those who had assisted in the ceremony—such as the friend who made the spirit post.[15]

Another spirit-keeping custom was that of keeping the spirit of an enemy who had been slain and scalped in battle. Since the hair was an extension of the soul, and since souls assumed a ghost form at death, it was believed that the soul of an enemy could be forced to remain at ground level so long as the hair was kept and subjected to a certain ceremony. Keeping it in this fashion prevented the enemy's soul, and especially that of a very great warrior, from threatening those of the keeper's tribe who had gone on to the Mystery Land above, so keeping the soul rendered the deceased of one's tribe a special service. Of course, the manner of keeping an enemy's soul was far less demanding than what was required for the keeping of a relative, and no feasts or sacrifices accompanied the keeping period. At the end of the keeping period, which was usually a year, the enemy's scalp was hooked over the end of a long pole, pushed up through the smoke hole at the top of the tipi, and shaken loose. When it fell outside the tipi the spirit was considered released and free to go where it pleased. The scalp was then disposed of in the more regular ways such as burial in the ground.[16]

Sioux spirit post. *Left,* carved and painted post. *Right,* post adorned with articles of clothing which belonged to the deceased. The top of the dress is covered with beading and elk teeth.

Sioux Victory Dance.

This custom was not observed in all instances, it was only employed when the prowess of the enemy in battle had gained the profound respect of those who finally did him in. Other scalps were either used as appendages to mark the conquests of those who took them or else disposed of in less consequential ways than that of spirit keeping.

Sometimes a warrior returning from an engagement presented a scalp to the relative of a man who had died in battle. When he did so, he was returning a substitute for the spiritual essence of the lost warrior. Again, while such thoughts might be considered odd, one must remember that any tragedy becomes more endurable as the mind is put at ease. The facts may not have been changed by the presentation of the enemy's scalp, but the attitude of the mourning relative was altered, and he was able to continue on in an environment so demanding it might not otherwise have been managed. Current funeral practices have much the same thought in mind as questionable sums of money are spent in a final attempt to make up for what should have been done for the deceased while he was still alive. It's really not the preferred way, yet psychiatrists and medical doctors often recommend it as a positive means of lessening the mourner's grief.

Adding all of the foregoing together, it is clear that a strong and direct relationship existed between the hair and the soul, and thus between the soul and the act of scalping. There was nothing trivial or wanton about the removal of an enemy's hair, and it was not carried out in orgy fashion.

Because of the soul-scalp relationship, and because scalps were a tangible proof of victory in battle, a war party returning with fresh scalps was cause for a great celebration which always terminated in a scalp or victory dance, which the Indians called the "Hair-Kill Dance." Both the new scalps and those taken in previous engagements were used for the celebration. Women brought forth as many as had been kept of the old enemy scalps and added them to the freshly captured ones. It was in this dance alone that the women led the tribal ritual and sometimes put on what might be called warrior's apparel.

The preferred time for the Hair-Kill Dance was at night, when an exciting light could be furnished by a huge log fire. The faces of the girls were either painted with a brilliant vermilion or made menacingly dark with a black soil mixture. Dresses were literally covered with beads and porcupine quillwork. Arms and fingers were laden with brass bracelets or rings. Glittering shells of various kinds dangled from the girls' ears. As the drums began to throb, hundreds of women and men joined together to form a huge circle, and marching in the opposite direction inside the large circle might be twenty-five drummers and other musicians. Around the dance group stood the rest of the tribe. The pace and volume of the dance accelerated rapidly as the scalps of the slain were borne aloft on poles and shaken wildly for all to see. In a sense they were like powerful battle pennants. And scalp dances were especially tumultuous if, in addition to scalps, the war party had secured a large amount of booty in the way of horses and mules.

When an Indian scalped a foe who had one or more eagle feathers affixed in his scalp lock, which was a small braided lock of hair worn on the back of the warrior's head, these feathers were fastened to the section of scalp removed, and the entire arrangement was hung on a trophy pole. Such a scalp gained the special admiration of the dancers, for the feathers were evidence of the high status of the slain, and accordingly of the even greater bravery of the one who slew him.

In the Shoshone scalp dance, a small pole was stuck in the ground and all of the captured scalps were strung on it. As they danced around it singing and yelling at the tops of their voices, the leaders of the different bands would take the inside, the warriors would circle about them, and the women and children would dance around the perimeter. As many as five hundred Indians are known to have danced in this way at one time, and they kept at it without rest for hours on end. Sometimes the singing and dancing would continue for a week or more.

Having served their victory dance purpose, the scalps which were not to be kept in spirit ceremonies or for other purposes were disposed of. Sometimes they were buried after a series of public exhibitions, which burial was accompanied by mournful songs which were howled or sung for the benefit of the victims. Some warriors returned to the battleground where the scalps were taken, placed the scalps on buffalo chips, and left them there as a sacrifice to the sun and ground. In such cases the scalp was held toward the sun while a short prayer was offered, then placed on the chip. Other times they were cast into a stream and sacrificed to the water spirits. However, not all scalps were disposed of. Many locks were kept to adorn the warrior's clothing and horses, and some became permanent parts of sacred medicine bundles.

If a scalp was retained it was preserved on a specially formed hoop. A twig was used to make a circular loop five or six inches in diameter; then thongs of rawhide were put through the scalp around the edges and it was fastened to the hoop. The thongs stretched the scalp tight, and it was left to dry. The skin side of the scalp was painted in various colors, sometimes gray, sometimes entirely red, or one half red and one half black. The hair of a scalp lock was usually braided. Some scalps were suspended from a pole over the tipi, and others were used in numerous ways. Scalps were used for medicine and status symbols on shields, lances, robes, and as pendants on bridles. The Arikaras hung scalps in their Medicine Lodge as a sacrifice to God.

Some writers have said that the Plains Indians did not wear scalp-lock braids, but a close examination of old photographs will show that to the contrary they surely did. That "braid" was the old "knock the chip off my shoulder if you can" story, and any lack of it would have shown a man to be a coward, whose weakness multiplied out would have destroyed the clan and tribe.

After the period of trade with the Whites began, scalping was usually performed with a tool of White manufacture. The most widely used weapon was simply an ordinary butcher knife. The method of taking the scalp was simple, but bloody. Indians took one by grasping the braid of the scalp lock with one hand, and cutting a circle two or three inches in diameter around the base of it with a knife held in the other. A quick jerk would then tear it from the skull with a characteristic "flop!" If the battle was over and there was plenty of time, the warrior would cut around the entire scalp, tearing all of it from the head. The large quantity of hair was usually divided into numerous small locks, which were used in ornamenting war shirts or other personal belongings. There were known cases of scalping survival, and in these the only permanent damage was to the victim's appearance and pride. The brain itself was so well protected by its bony skull enclosure that scalping created but minor damage unless the head had been struck so heavily that a fracture or concussion occurred. Scalping was clearly *not* an act or method of killing, although unknowingly or accidentally an Indian might finish the job of killing by taking a scalp from an unconscious victim who had been mistaken for dead.

Methods of displaying scalps. *a*, scalp stretched on willow hoop, wrapped in red trade cloth with bead and shell ornaments attached (after Remington). When items such as this were attached they were usually taken from the enemy at the same time as the scalp. *b*, warrior returning from raid with scalps hung on lance (after Remington). *c*, stretched and unbraided scalp lock. *d*, drawing of scalp held in hand to indicate usual size. *e*, scalp hung on horse's bridle. *f*, scalp locks hung from war club. *g*, scalps hung from tipi flap poles.

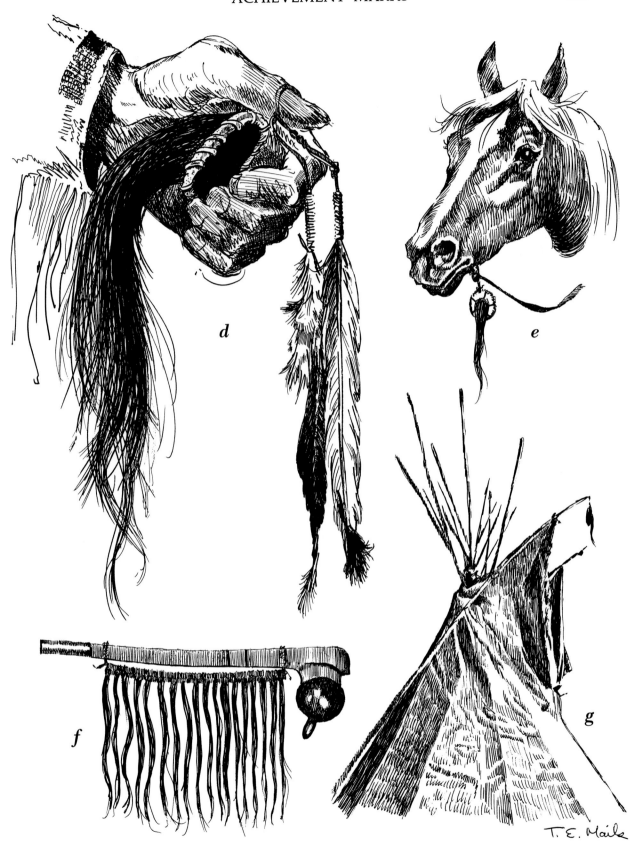

Trade butcher knife of type often used for scalping.

Considerable evidence supports the fact that in the beginning of the White-Indian struggle, Indians had no desire or reason to take White men's scalps, preferring the hair of other Indians, because an Indian scalp was worth something in honors, while the White scalp had no coup value whatsoever. It is claimed that after Custer's historic last stand on the Little Bighorn River, White scalps were thrown away "like so much horse skin."[17] Nevertheless, not all White scalps were likewise discarded. Colonel Dodge has drawings of several in his books which were made from actual items which had been kept and processed into intricate trophies, and many a war club was seen with a blond and obviously White scalp on it.

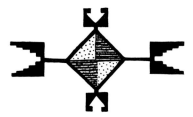

Since a boy was groomed from childhood on to be a defender of his band and tribe, it was only right that an award system would evolve to honor those who fulfilled their call and responsibilities.

The coup or "war count" system served this purpose admirably, because it provided specific goals to aim for, and once they were achieved it offered a set of decorations, like medals, to mark the achiever and to attest to what he had done.

Considering the spiritual views of the Indians, it was logical that the feathers of the solar bird, the great golden eagle, would be chosen to serve as the warrior's medals, and that further explanations by way of symbols and appendages would be added to a warrior's costume to make certain the nature of his war deeds and spiritual powers were well known to all who saw him.

After capturing the eagle in a sacred way through the eagle pit method—so as not, in their minds, to bruise or damage the bird's abilities to continue to serve as a special messenger and power transmitter from the One-Above—the warrior cut or painted the feathers in different ways for different war deeds, and placed them at specified angles in his hair to explain fully each coup which the tribal leaders had considered and then agreed he was entitled to.

In concluding this section it is important to remember the role scalping played in tribal life. Scalps, more usually just the scalp locks, were frequently taken from victims during the horse and buffalo days as proofs of accomplishment, but the underlying purpose for removing a scalp, or scalp lock, went far deeper than its being a proof. The Indian's hair was believed to be an extension of his soul, and removing it from an enemy by the scalping process could cause the soul, which became a ghost at death, to remain at earth level rather than to ascend to the Mystery Land above. The same thing could be accomplished by cutting a lock of hair from a beloved relative and subjecting it to a very holy spirit-keeping ceremony. In the latter case the hair retention was a process of devotion, and the spirit keeping was done to make the mourning time as profound and heartfelt as possible.

With an understanding of the coup in hand, one can turn to an examination of the Plains warrior's costume and general adornment, being able to recognize that the form and decoration of any garment or hair dressing or headdress would bear a direct relationship to the tribal defense and war count system.

# Chapter 17

# CLOTHING

When Indian clothing and items of personal adornment are considered, it should be remembered that everything the Indian produced was carefully formed and remarkably functional. Furthermore, the form and decoration gave heightened meaning to everything the Indian experienced—past, present, and future. Because of this garments were reverently coaxed into being. Each step was carefully thought out and patiently done. The mobile quality of their clothing deserves special emphasis, since Plains garments incorporated a kind of free motion which was so marvelous that it should not be overlooked. To miss this is to miss the entire point of their design approach and attitude. Plains clothing was *mobile* clothing in every respect. Its dangling parts moved as the person moved, creating different light patterns and aspects with every turn of the body. And the movement created pleasant sounds to accompany the motion, since the fringes scraped the garment surface, and bells and large beads appended to the garment jingled or clapped. In addition to their inherent mobility, garments were designed in such a way as to be packed quickly and transported with ease—a matter of no small consequence in a nomadic society.

From 1750 to 1875 nearly all Plains warriors dressed neatly, and some of their costumes were absolutely splendid. The garments they wore had so much beauty and personality they even inspired songs.

The original Plains clothing was made in its entirety of the skins of the different animals which abounded in the Plains region. In trade days, trade cloth added to their source of supply. As a general rule, the method of manufacture and the form of the male costume for all the Plains tribes was the same, yet there were slight differences in color, stitching, and embroidering which *might* enable a person familiar with their differences to associate a given item with its proper tribe. This "might" is important since a number of things happened to confuse the issue. Many of the tribes copied each other in dress and ornaments. Also, when items of clothing and weapons fell into the possession of victors in battle, the victors wore or used them on certain occasions, and the rest of their tribe would copy what they saw. Then too, it was the custom at intertribal peace councils to exchange fine articles of dress and other choice gifts. These factors led to the adoption of common styles, and ultimately to a broad similarity in the

Illustrations of mobile aspect of Indian clothing. *a*, Blackfoot (Piegan) warrior with shirt and leggings covered with ermine tails which dangled from garments. *b*, warrior in motion. *c*, illustration of fringes to depict how they cast shadows. *d*, illustration to emphasize tactile aspect of garments. *e*, Calder mobile sculpture illustrating how same mobile principle of Indians is employed by today's leading artists.

The breechclout. *Left,* beaded hide dress clout with fringe. *Center,* hide clout with painted ends. *Right,* trade blanket clout hung on thong belt in way it was worn by men and boys.

dress of the Plains tribes. In substance, though, the garments which evolved deserve a place among the world's finest and most natural costumes.

On anything but a very cold day, the Indian warrior in camp dressed simply—and so retained great freedom of body movement. He was the epitome of the boy who loves to strip down and run pell-mell through the woods. All the man of the Plains wore during a usual day was a breechclout, moccasins, and paint. His face and body paint completed his outfit.

The regular workaday clout was a piece of buckskin about a foot wide and ranging from five to eight feet in length, depending upon how much the owner wanted it to swing and flap as he walked or rode. The workaday clout might be painted, but it was seldom decorated to any extent. To put it on, the man tied a quarter-inch buckskin thong around his waist, tucked the middle of the clout between his legs, and pulled the ends front and back up under the thong, letting them hang over like an apron at each end to swing free. He might wear it longer in front than in back, or vice versa, depending on how he felt. It gave him all the cover he needed, and his exposed body, which was ordinarily quite white, became brown and hardened to the elements. The clout worn longer at the back and tucked under also made an excellent cushion for bareback horse riding.

For dress and formal purposes the plain clout was exchanged for a decorated one. Clout ornamentation was done in paints or dyes in bold patterns, such as stripes, squares, and dots. Some were beaded and some of the late models had sequins appended. Dress clouts were usually quite long, and especially so when used for dances—so that the maximum dramatic effect would be obtained. By the 1880s most clouts were being made of red or blue trade flannel or blanket cloth. Some tribes, most notably the Crows and a few southeastern tribes, wore a dress apron instead of a clout. These were wider than the clout, and were beautifully beaded with intricate floral designs.

To enhance his costume, for insulation in cold weather, and to protect his legs against brush and boulders while riding, the warrior added a pair of leggings. Leggings were what the word implies—they covered only the leg, and had no top as trousers do. The top of each legging was cut off at a slight angle, so as to form a V shape when the two leggings were placed together or worn. At the highest point of the angle on each legging two long straps of buckskin or cloth

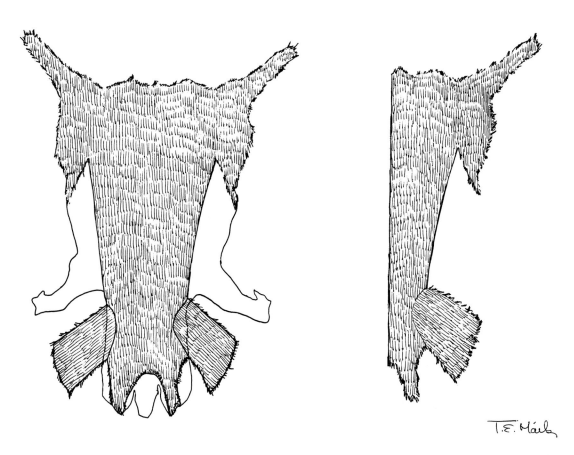

*Left,* pattern showing how old-style tubular legging was cut from elk or deer hide. *Right,* cut hide folded to make legging.

were sewn to the legging, and the loose ends of these were tied around the waist thong to hold the leggings up. They made a bulky and probably not too satisfactory knot. All Plains leggings were made in this way, but not all leggings were shaped the same. The oldest style was tubular in form and fitted the leg somewhat after the manner of spiked trousers. Even when the styles changed, the Indian fitted his leggings closely to avoid their catching on things as he went about his business.

Leggings for work purposes were made of buckskin and were often undecorated, although the Indian was not likely to go without decoration on anything for too long a time. Some work leggings received a touch or more of quillwork, such as a horse track or two, to mark war honors, and also edgings of buckskin fringe to tell those passing by as the owner worked at making arrows or whatever that he was a man equipping himself to maintain a high place in life.

Not all of the old leggings were tubular in shape. Some were made with wide, angular flaps on the lower half, the flap itself being beaded or quilled and heavily fringed. The shape of the flap could easily be seen, for it was always a different and deeper color than the rest. The mid-Plains men liked this style, as did the Kiowas. A vertical stitch line running the full length of the inside of the flap fitted the legging closely to the leg.

A characteristic of Cheyenne and Kiowa leggings was a small, triangular two-piece flap near the outside top of the legging. Sometimes it was cut as a part of the legging. Other times it was sewn on. In either case the inside surface was covered with bright red or orange—painted or cloth—and as the owner moved about the triangle opened up to show a sparkling touch of color.

Dress leggings were profusely decorated with beading or quillwork strips or bands of varying widths, and also with paint, bells, shells, and long fringes. Most leggings were smoked over a low fire to obtain a warm yellow color. It should be noted that quilled or beaded bands were applied at an angle to conform to the shape of the leg, and they were placed so as to show best when a man was sitting on the ground or on his horse. Every aspect of good showmanship was taken into consideration.

In the last half of the 1800s leggings were made of blanket cloth, and were trimmed according to the traditional methods. The preferred trade cloth colors were red, green, dark blue, or black, all of which made the white background beading stand out. A pair of black "dance leggings" of this type reputed to have belonged to Sitting Bull were obtained from his granddaughter in 1924, are well authenticated, and probably were his last pair of dress leggings. The flap edging is of material taken from American army uniforms and flags. The bead design is the tipi shape, which was the most commonly used pattern on leggings. While it was not their only method of design, Crow leggings could often be identified by a rectangular beaded patch which was applied to the bottom of the legging only. The rest of the legging was a brightly colored blanket cloth—red, blue, black,

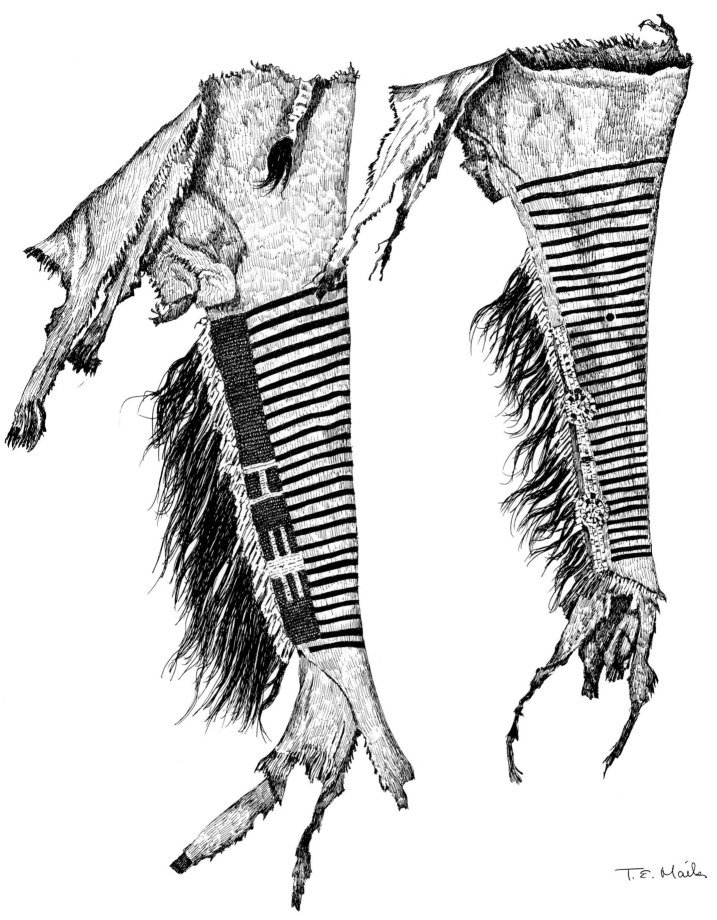

Oldest-style tubular leggings with painted coup markings. *Left*, Crow, collected 1842. *Right*, Brûle Sioux, circa 1800–45. Length approximately 36 inches.

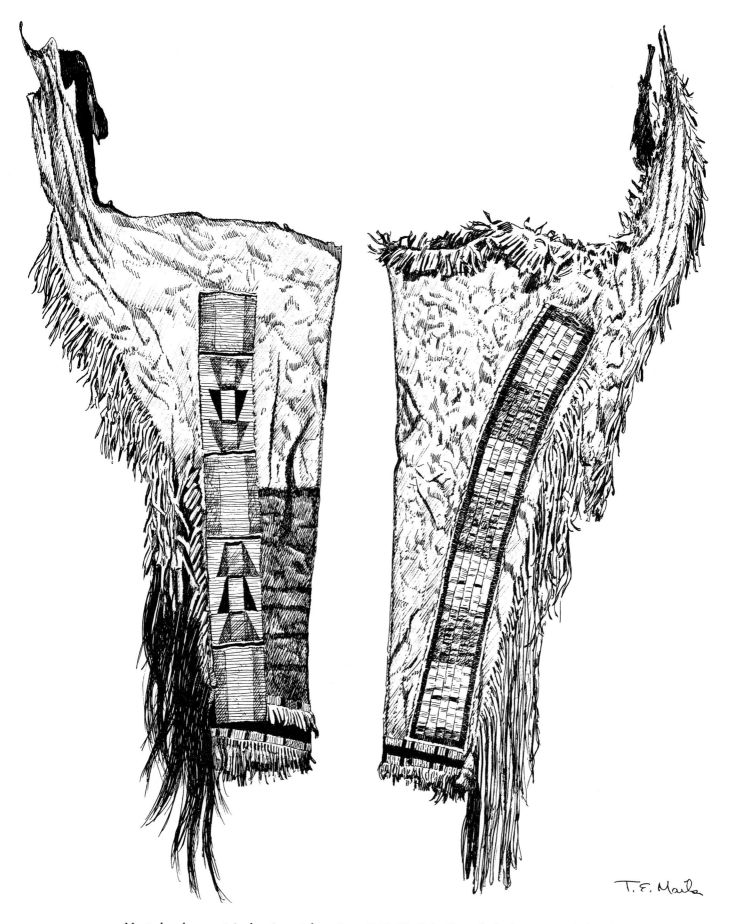

Next development in legging styles, circa 1830–70. *Left,* Crow hide legging with beaded band, hide fringe, and hairlocks. *Right,* hide legging with cut fringe, quilled band, and beaded cuff.

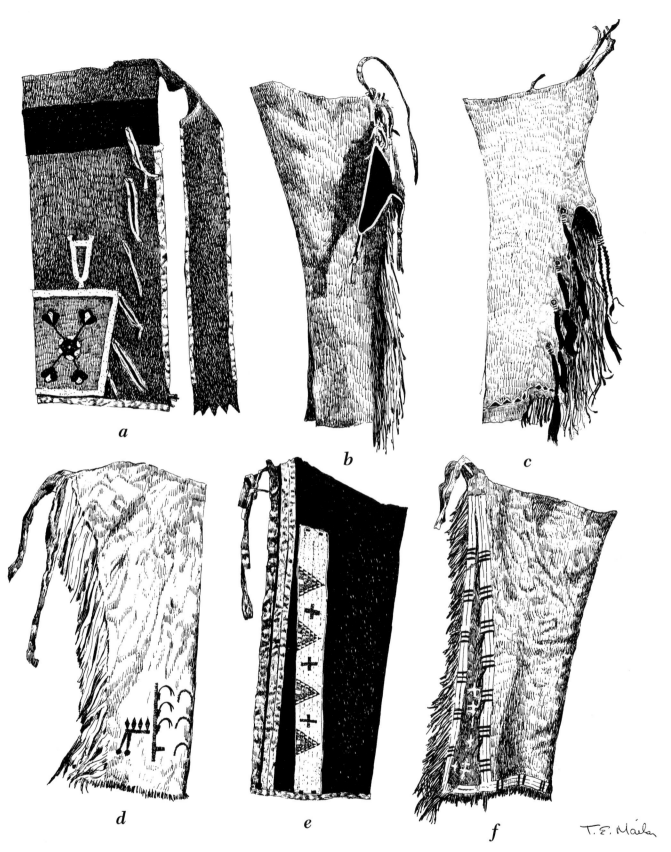

Late-make leggings, 1860 or 1870 on. *a*, Crow, green trade cloth. *b*, Kiowa, hide. *c*, Comanche, hide. *d*, Sioux, quilled hide. *e*, Sioux, trade cloth, dark blue, belonging to Sitting Bull. *f*, mid-Plains style, hide.

or green, edged with red. The Blackfoot, Flatheads, and a few other northern tribes sometimes used the same kind of patch, but with their own beaded designs.

Buckskin fringes on leggings might be plain or twisted strips, with the twisting being a more southern trait. The most successful warriors were permitted to fringe their leggings with hairlocks or ermine skins according to the honors they earned. The northern warriors who had access to the animals used more of these than the southern warriors, although some ermine skins did appear on southern garments.

War honors were also shown by painting a series of horizontal stripes, usually blue or black, on both legs of the leggings. The stripes on one leg were usually broader than those on the other leg, and sometimes the legs had different numbers of stripes, which indicates with certainty that each stripe accounted for a war or horse raid, the larger stripes probably being war records. Horizontal or vertical straight lines like these were also used on shirts, and for the same purpose.

Legging and shirt colors also explained something about the general area of their origin, since they graded in color from south to north. The southern tribes preferred a yellow and green combination, those just north of them liked lemon yellow, the next area preferred creamy white, and the northernmost tribes favored pure white or else a reddish purple tone. Naturally there were exceptions to the color rule, so traveling Indian groups approached one another with caution, and did not commit themselves until another party's identity had been firmly established.

Leggings were very functional for a people who either sat flat on the ground or were seated on horseback. A pair of modern trousers would have bound him up intolerably, so whenever a Plains warrior received a pair of pants from an agency store he immediately cut the legs off and threw the rest away. It is interesting to note that the open-seated leggings worn by the Indians provided the exact pattern for chaps worn later on by the western cowpunchers.

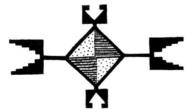

The man's dress or ceremonial shirt, often called the "war shirt," was easily the most splendid part of his apparel. Most of those seen in museums today are dress shirts, and they are extensively decorated. The usual workaday shirt was quite plain. In fact, shirts were not often worn for the ordinary tasks done around the camp. Men put workaday shirts on at times in the winter, and occasionally on bright days to prevent sunburn. The dress shirts received even more limited use. Most of them were very heavy when they were beaded, and were a considerable burden for the wearer when worn over a period of several hours.

Entire dress outfits were taken along in rawhide storage cases on what were intended to be war parties. If time permitted, these were put on with due ceremony after the enemy was sighted. Indian accounts reveal that dress or war shirts were worn in battle. The reason is obvious. A good deal of medicine had been fused into the shirts—some were festooned with medicine bags and other appendages—and they were believed to be "strong" protection. A few White authors have indicated that the Indians believed war shirts invoked their medicine even while they were still in the carrying case, but the Indian authorities do not confirm this. The stripes and appendages which the shirts bore upon their outer surface were visual aids, and they did a great deal to assist the warrior's personal attitude. And they also helped his enemy size him up and properly respect him as a foe. Warriors wore their war shirts in battle whenever they could, the weight notwithstanding!

One can estimate the age of a shirt by the way it is cut and sewn together. The older shirts were made much like a Mexican poncho with sleeves. If a blanket was folded in two along its shorter dimension and a hole was cut for the head and two short sleeves were attached, the result would match the style of an older-style Indian shirt—except that they sloped the shoulders and used two mountain sheep, antelope, deer, or elk skins to make the front and back. Two skins made an entire shirt, with every part of the skin being used in some manner to finish all of the shirt's parts.

Museum collections indicate that the more ancient Plains shirts were left completely open on the sides. They were sewn only along the shoulder, where the shoulder attached to the sleeve, and for a few inches on the underside of the sleeve to make a cuff. Even in later days, when most of the Plains shirt's parts were being stitched together, the lower half of each side was "split" or left open so as to facilitate sitting and riding. It also let air in, which was no small consideration for a thick, heavy shirt. Again, it is evident that function was a primary part of every garment's design.

The early shirt makers left the legs and tail of the animal on their shirt skins. In doing this they took advantage of these natural, decorative, and mobile appendages. Only the late-model shirts were without them, and were uninteresting by comparison. As one discovers in the case of leggings, the sumptuous shirts of the leading warriors were trimmed with rich, free-swinging animal skins, or with long buckskin fringes and/or locks of hair. Some warriors had their wives trim the hem and cuffs of their shirts with buckskin fringes and thongs, while warriors in certain tribes, mostly northern, were entitled by their high war honors to use a profusion of long white ermine skins—either all white or black-tipped—to indicate their prowess. Southern buckskin shirt fringes were often twisted into a long spiral. A further noteworthy difference between geographic areas was that

Oldest-style war shirts. *Above*, pattern and reconstruction of poncho-style shirt collected by Catlin, 1833, painted with buckskin fringes. *Bottom*, back view of poncho-style shirt drawn by Kurtz, circa 1851.

Blackfoot shirt with ermine trim, circa 1830 (after Catlin).

northern fringes ran the length of the sleeve, while southern fringes were gathered in small bunches or wrapped around the arm like a band or a skirt fringe. All thongs served as a handy repair kit while a warrior was on the trail. When something broke, he just cut off a thong, punched a hole with his awl, and fixed it!

In addition to the fringing material, the warrior's shirt of the northern Plains was usually adorned with quilled or beaded rosettes, some of them being of huge diameters. They also used four long, quilled or beaded bands, each some two and a half inches wide, one of them being placed on each sleeve and one over

*Center,* painted Blackfoot war shirt with quilled bands, hairlocks on right arm, and ermine skins on left, collected 1845. *Left* and *right,* illustration of how entire old-style shirt was cut from two hides.

Typical war shirts with beaded bands and hairlocks. *Top,* Crow. *Bottom,* Omaha. Experts viewing this shirt often differ as to whether it is Omaha or Sioux. However, it was photographed on an Omaha man in 1920, and was said to be his grandfather's war shirt.

each shoulder. The shoulder bands took their angle from the slope of the shoulder, and passed over the shoulder so as to show front and back. The very old sleeve bands did not cover the seams, since the seams were on the underside of the arm. One notes that every Plains garment was as tastefully and completely decorated on the back as it was on the front. These mobile warriors presented a spectacular appearance from every angle, and in this wise showed a talent for design which deserves the attention of fashion experts of every age.

It is said that the long, beaded or quilled bands were evidence of specific war honors, yet except for a few Crow statements there is little substance for the idea to be found in Indian accounts. Instead, it seems that the bands were given in sets to outstanding warriors as tokens of a general appreciation for their roles in tribal defense. If the bands had designated exact war honors, their designs would have told a story. The symbols used for band embroidery tell virtually no story, and indeed are somewhat uniform in concept among all the tribes. The most that can be said for them today is that they help collectors establish the age of their origin by the type of beads used, and that some patterns and colors are types unique to certain nations. Even then the embroidered or painted neck yoke used on the fronts and backs of shirts does more to help an informed person identify a tribe by its designs than the bands do.

Shirts were often painted with important history lines or pictures. A vision or a noteworthy conquest might lead an eminent warrior to paint his shirt with jagged lines to represent lightning, or with straight lines to depict the number of his war trips, or with pictographs to provide a readable, billboard record of his war history, or with broad areas of color to indicate the society he belonged to. The Warrior Societies of the Sioux tribe painted their shirts in four different ways: the upper half bright blue and the lower yellow, the upper red and the lower green, all yellow, or yellow with vertical green stripes.

The Arapaho, Cheyenne, and Kiowas often painted celestial symbols on their war shirts.

All in all, Plains shirts were glorious creations. They were very long, falling at least a foot or more below the waistline and sometimes to the knees, and they were graciously styled. Catlin simply itched to obtain many he saw, and a fine shirt is a treasure for any collector. Many a museum wishes it had collected more and handled what it had better than it did.

The Mandan, Crow, and Blackfoot shirts were easily the most beautiful, the Sioux next, and except for the Kiowa leggings and a few Comanche garments, clothing styles became progressively plainer as one moved south. Southern Cheyenne shirts often lacked the quilled or beaded shoulder and arm bands, but their shirts did have beautiful dark-green fringes. In fact, the southern tribes relied more on color for effect than on ornamentation. Many of their shirts also had powerful medicines and other appendages attached, such as twisted thongs and berry beads, amulet bags, eagle feathers dyed red, and eagle bone war whistles.

Comanche man's clothing. *Left,* front view. *Right,* back view. Legging detail in Fig. *c* on page 331.

One can easily understand why the garments of the northern Indians were more detailed than those of the Indians of the extreme south, such as the Comanches, Kiowas, and Kiowa Apaches. Winters were milder in the south, and the people who lived there did not have the winter break which gave the northerners some respite from war and the precious time needed to pursue their finer

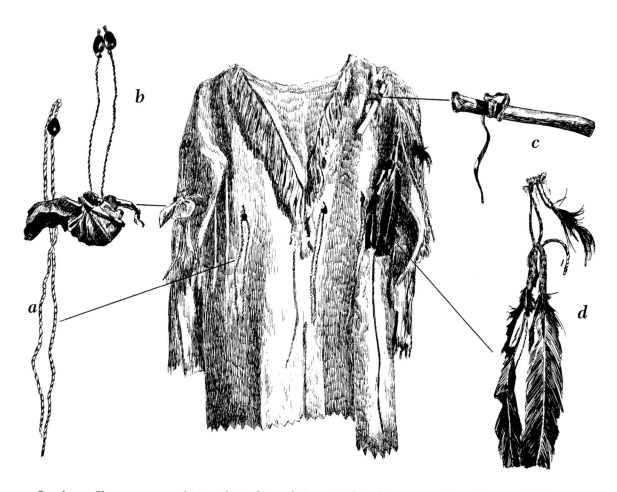

Southern Cheyenne war shirt with traditional items tied to fringes. *a*, twisted laces with berry beads. *b*, buckskin medicine bag. *c*, eagle bone war whistle. *d*, cut eagle feathers dyed red.

crafts. The southerners continued to move year round, and the tensions engendered by their general insecurity as to what they might encounter kept them in a surly mood. This was surely proven by their flagrant brutality to captives. As a general rule, the rituals of the extreme south were less exotic, their garments were plainer, their possessions were fewer, and the more barren and demanding land lent less encouragement to cleanliness. Perhaps what the southern people did accomplish under their trying circumstances is all the more to be praised.

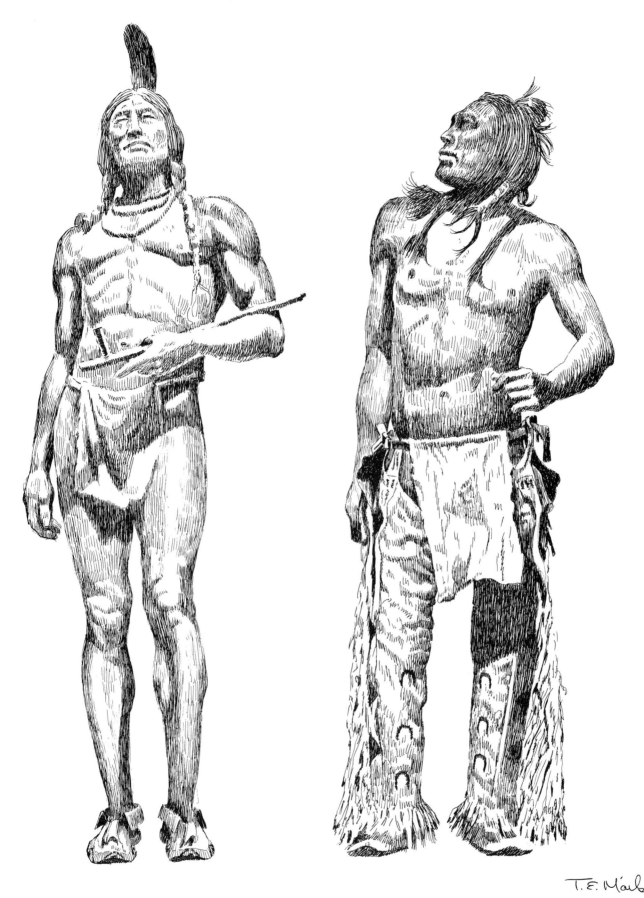

Warrior wearing breechclout.                    Sioux warrior wearing breechclout and leggings.

T. E. Mails

Sioux warrior wearing buffalo robe.          Crow warrior in full dress with double-beaded apron.

Cheyenne warrior wearing trade blanket with beaded strip.

Sioux warrior wearing double-tailed headdress to complete outfit. Tail is not most usual style, but is after copy of old headdress done by Seton, *American Indian Arts*. See pages 105 and 386 for the more common types or styles.

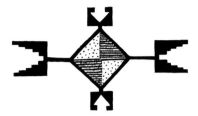

Ordinarily the men's shirts hung loose. They were not belted, and even the magnificent dress belts, which were beautifully beaded or ornamented with silver disks, were always worn underneath the shirts when a man had both on.

Actually, the Indian man used two belts. One was the "inside" thong which held up his clout and leggings, and the other was his broad dress belt, which was made of very thick hide. It was heavy for several reasons: The dress belt was put on over the thong and clout and the leggings might be tied to it. It usually carried the knife and case, and his tomahawk, gun, and whatever else he used as weapons might be inserted under it at any time. He would also tuck his pipe bag under it and tie his numerous bags to it, such as the awl case, whetstone case, and strike-a-light bag.

Metal belt buckles became available in the White trade days, but the earliest make of "outside" belt had no buckle. It was secured with thongs which were attached to each end, and then the two ends were tied together. It is not known whether the Indians preferred to wear the ties in front or back, but they probably tied the belt in front and then shifted the tie to the back so as to make the best use of the beaded designs. Dress belts are conspicuously absent in most old photographs, but many of them are included in the paintings of Charles Russell and Frederic Remington—which may be another indication that they are a late addition to the Plains costume.

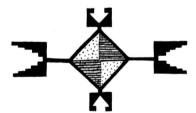

The buffalo robe has been considered in the art section. Every male Indian had one, however, and kept it nearby to throw over his shoulders or around his waist so as to be properly dressed when a visitor arrived. It has been said that no one could wrap a robe or blanket around himself as graciously and naturally as an Indian could. In all cases, the head of the buffalo was worn to the left, which meant that all robe decorations were horizontal.

Southern Indians used only robes or blankets for additional warmth in the winter, but during the trade days the northern men had their wives make them a heavy coat or "capote" out of the White man's blankets. The coat was usually white with one or more broad, bold, horizontal stripes in various colors. The capote had a marvelous peaked hood attached to it, with a long pendant dangling from it that hung down the back like a pony tail. The hoods were particularly spectacular, and Charles Russell was especially fond of them, including many in his paintings and drawings. A number of these coats can be seen in old photographs of Blackfoot and Cree Indians. The Plains Indians also made a type of buckskin coat which was cut very much like the White man's overcoats, but it was decorated in the traditional manner with quills or beads.

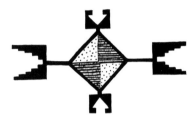

The comfortable and easily made two-piece Plains moccasins were the first part of the Indian costume to be adopted by the White man, for they were admirably suited to life in the woods and on the plains. Even today they are recognized as one of the best types of footwear for campers and outdoorsmen, although one soon learns to walk "toed-in," Indian-fashion, just as Catlin did to keep his feet from hurting in them.

---

PLATE 17.   THE COLORS OF VICTORY—BODY PAINT STUDY NO. 1 ▶

After a revenge raid, the victorious warriors would stop and paint themselves in an informative manner before entering their tribal camp for the customary and tumultuous victory celebration.

The warrior depicted here is a Sioux who has adorned himself with several significant marks. His face has been covered with grease and charcoal—the black indicating that the fires of revenge in his heart have burned out and he wishes now to purge the event from his soul. On his side is a wound, circled with a black line and surrounded with solar radiating lines which are prayers for the warm healing which comes from the sun. The red lines on his arms mark the number of his conquests in war, and the yellow lines his successful horse raids.

His single feather reveals that he has counted a significant second coup in battle. Around his neck hangs the vital medicine pouch containing small bits of each of his special helpers which were revealed to him in his visions.

Each tribe had its own footwear shape and method of decorating its moccasins, so that a trained Indian scout could often tell a man's tribe by a glance at his moccasins or his moccasin tracks. To deceive his enemies a warrior sometimes wore the captured moccasins of another tribe while on the war trail. Some made their trail moccasins with a heavy fringe or animal tails at the heel. This was an addition which was supposed to obliterate or obscure the tracks as the wearer walked along. From a design standpoint the fringes were superb additions, but one suspects that the fringe was not much help in removing tracks.

During the cold winters and the wet springs, everyone wore moccasins with both the soles and uppers made from the well-smoked tops of old lodges. Footwear made from these was not perfectly waterproof, but they never became hard or cracked from continuous use during the wet season as unsmoked hides did, and furthermore, they dried smooth without stretching. Winter moccasins either were made with the hair turned in or else cut extra large so as to fit over heavy inner wrappings which were used on the feet. During the coldest seasons, buffalo hair, leaves, or sagebrush bark was matted into insulation pads of different thicknesses which the Indians wrapped around their feet before donning their moccasins. Cold-weather moccasins were also made with high tops to protect the ankles, and with very long laces to wrap and tie them tightly about the ankle. Since they were designed only for service, they were seldom decorated in any way. In addition, the men sometimes put several applications of grease on the soles to make them more waterproof. During the summer, men and boys wore low-cut, close-fitting moccasins with stiff rawhide soles and soft buckskin uppers. Work and travel footwear was mostly left plain and made in considerable quantity, although some workaday moccasins received a little beading or quilling. On the other hand, decorations often covered the entire top, ankle, and tongue of moccasins intended for ceremonial and festival use. The soles of wedding and burial moccasins were

---

◀ PLATE 18.   CHEYENNE SUN DANCERS—BODY PAINT STUDY NO. 2

The three men in the painting wear the paint styles of different stages of the Cheyenne Sun Dance, which was a religious ceremony of tribal supplication and thanksgiving. The round spot on the chest represents the sun if red or blue—the moon if black. The long lines across arms and legs are trail lines, to help the dancer concentrate his thoughts upon the pathways of life he and his tribe must pass through if they are to survive and prosper. White spots signify hail—thus winter. Red spots are for summer. The marks on the dancer at the right are the tracks of the swift hawk.

All paint was applied with care and for a specific purpose. It was instructive and had definite associations which the person focused upon as it was worn. Its ultimate purpose was educational. It was an aid to personal growth and development.

Winter blanket coat (capote). *Left,* front view. *Right,* back view.

also beaded. Women's and girls' moccasins, although always made with high buckskin tops and rawhide soles, were left plain for daily wear and decorated for ceremonial use in the same manner as male footwear. The Plains Indians never wore stockings.

The older styles of festival moccasins were magnificently quilled. Broad scallops in the design revealed that the moccasins were southern Cheyenne. Sioux moccasins often had the top quilled in long red and green triangles, while the edges of the moccasin were beaded in white, with red-, blue-, and yellow-stepped

Man wearing capote in winter. Drawing shows typical way of carrying articles on horse. Lance is hung on saddle cantle after method shown by C. R. Russell.

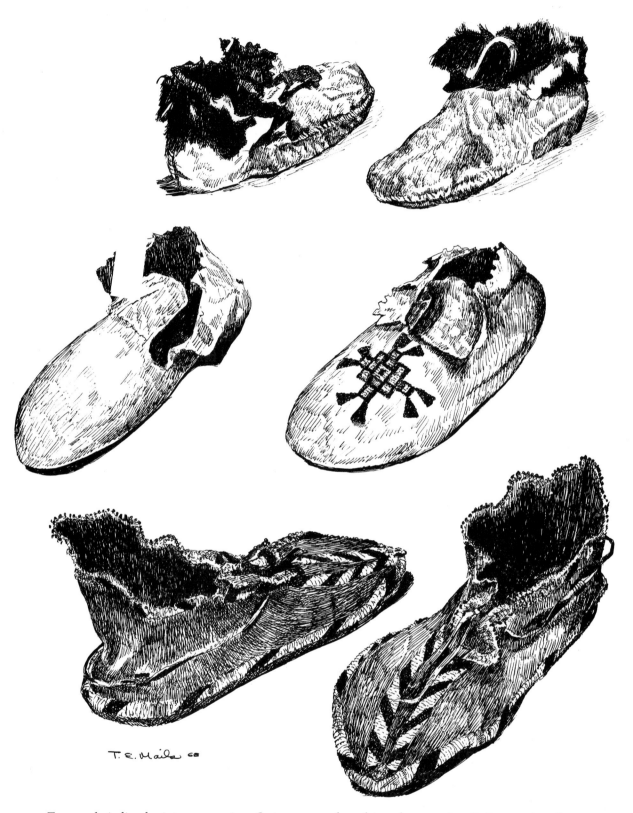

*Top row,* hair-lined winter moccasins. *Center row,* work and travel moccasins. *Bottom row,* southern Plains beaded moccasins; note strong diagonals in pattern.

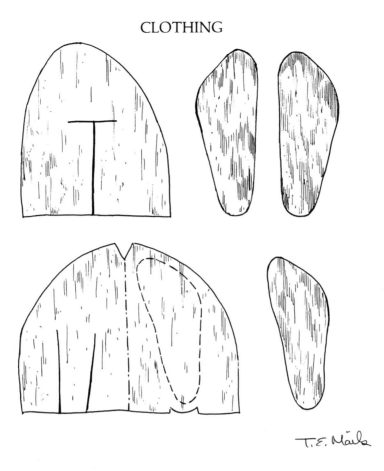

T.E. Mails

*Top,* pattern for two-piece moccasins without tongue. *Bottom,* pattern for two-piece moccasins with tongue.

triangles. Many Crow beaded moccasins had a U-shaped beaded area on the top, or red and green bands running across the top. The Kiowa and Comanche moccasins had a toe which was quite pointed, and often included a pattern of strong diagonal lines in the beading.

Moccasins always fitted the feet they were made for, and were decorated with designs that suited the line of the foot. There were two ways of, or patterns for, cutting the moccasins from pieces of hide. One made a moccasin with a tongue, the other had no tongue. The women did this without the use of measuring tools or patterns, and in the right proportions for children or grown people for generation after generation. White people, amazed at the Indians' craft and design capabilities, often asked them where they obtained their patterns for the many designs they used on leggings, arm bands, moccasins, etc., and how they transferred the patterns to the skins. It was a question which always puzzled the Indian women, for the designs were simply in their own minds; they never had patterns. They just worked them out as they went along, and always in perfect balance

*a*, ancient-style Cheyenne quilled moccasins. *b*, Sioux moccasins—quilled tops and beaded edges.

c, Crow beaded moccasins. d, Sioux beaded moccasins.

Women's clothing—included for comparison with male attire. *Left,* southern Plains woman's dress after figure in Heard Museum—hair braids wrapped with otter fur. *Top right,* beaded yoke for Sioux woman's dress. *Right,* Ute woman's dress. (Women did not usually wear fur wrappings on their braids, but Winold Reiss painted several Blackfoot women so adorned, and old photos of Shoshone and Kalispel women also depict this.)

Girls' clothing. Sioux girls wearing hide dresses with beaded yokes and edges, and also beaded female leggings, circa 1880. *Top left,* female legging for festival attire. Leggings for daily wear were left plain; neither beaded nor painted.

and proportion. "It is given to me," was about the only answer they gave when asked this question. Sometimes a woman would point to her forehead and smile; it was like asking a bird how it flew.[1] Indians in general felt the White man's shoes were terrible for walking. One said, "Our feet, in moccasins, moved as softly and freely as if they were bare, and were beautiful in motion!"[2]

The matter of hair styles, jewelry, and headdresses is still to be considered to complete the picture of the Indian's costume and grooming, but it will be helpful here to include a brief quote from George Catlin, who described his awed feelings as a great Mandan leader came before him in full costume to be painted:

No tragedian ever trod the stage, nor gladiator ever entered the Roman Forum, with more grace and manly dignity than did Mah-to-toh-pa enter the wigwam, where I was in readiness to receive him. He took his attitude before me, and with the sternness of a Brutus and stillness of a statue, he stood still until the darkness of night broke upon the solitary stillness. His dress, which was a very splendid one, was complete in all its parts, and consisted of a shirt or tunic, leggings, moccasins, head-dress, necklace, shield, bow and quiver, lance, tobacco-sack, and pipe; robe, belt, and knife; medicine-bag, tomahawk and war-club.[3]

Something should be added about their superb color work with paints and dyes, for it was so brilliant that it still glows after a hundred years, or about the softness of the tanned hides, which still remains after constant wear by the Indians and countless handlings by those who collected and preserved them.

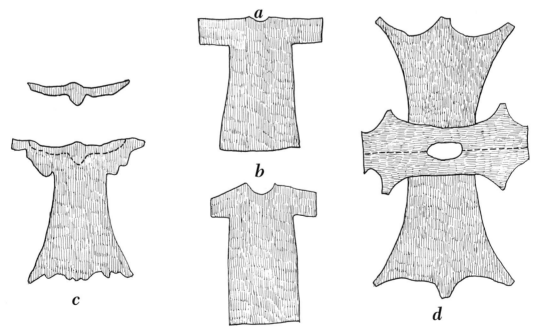

Patterns for women's dresses. *a* and *b*, two-piece dress with seams on shoulders. *c*, one-piece dress with hole cut to slip head through. *d*, two-piece dress with separate yoke sewed in place.

# Chapter 18

# HAIR STYLES, JEWELRY, AND HEADDRESSES

Since their hair was directly related to their soul, the people of the Plains treated and groomed it with special care, and unique ornaments, most of which were medicine items, were worn on the head. Added to these to enhance one's appearance was an imposing assortment of necklaces, earrings, and arm bands. Then topping it all for the men was an endless range of sumptuous headdresses, each of which either followed a tribal pattern or else was the result of a vision, and so the wearing of it heightened the spiritual atmosphere in which the warrior walked.

No one ever saw a Plains Indian who was bald-headed. Their hair was luxuriant, black, and straight. Sometimes it gave off a bluish cast, and now and then the extreme ends of the strands turned a reddish brown. Only the hair of the very old was touched with gray, and white hair was a rarity.

The usual style for both men and women was to part their hair in the middle and then to make a braid on each side which hung down on the chest—although there were exceptions to the center part which will be considered shortly. The custom for male and female alike was to paint a red line in the part with a pointed bone or wooden stick. The braids were left plain for daily wear, but for dress occasions, the men wrapped theirs with strips of red or blue felt trade cloth, or with the rich fur of the otter or beaver, the fur being cut in strips from one to two inches wide. Usually the lower ends of the fur strips were left hanging below the ends of the braids, so as to make the braids look as long as possible. Some hung almost to the warrior's knees, and presented a very handsome appearance. The otter fur was supposed to impart swiftness and cleverness to the man who wore it on his braids.

The part on the man's head terminated at the crown, where strands of hair were drawn into a bunch and braided to make a scalp lock some twelve inches or so in length. Sometimes the lock was coiled to make a small bun, and eagle feathers were inserted in it. Other times the braid hung free down the back or else was pulled forward to hang over the forehead. A warrior never cut his scalp

Hair styles. *Left,* Shoshone, Uriewici, a chief, about 1880. *Right,* Sioux, Kills First, a Sioux warrior, about 1893.

Hair styles. *Top*, northern Plains, unbraided. *Bottom left*, southern Plains, head shaved. *Bottom right*, Crow style with hair full length.

lock, as it was a symbol of his challenge to an enemy to take it if he could, and cutting it would have been considered an act of cowardice. Indian male children wore a scalp lock from the first time their parents began to dress their hair, but Indian women did not wear the scalp lock at all.

The Plains Indians did not have beards. A few straggling hairs might appear now and then on their faces, but they would immediately proceed to pluck them out with a pair of clamshells held between their thumb and fingers; or if they could secure a pair of metal tweezers in trade they would continue the operation for weeks until the beard was entirely eradicated.

The eyebrows and eyelashes of both sexes were sparse and thin. In fact, it was a rare thing to find any hair of consequence on the body of either sex. They were, as a rule, a hairless people, yet when hair made its appearance on any part of their bodies except the head, they continued to extract it until the roots were destroyed.

Actually, the man's hair was worn in as many different ways as could be conceived of, and fortunately most of these styles have been illustrated in George Catlin's wonderful paintings.

The Sioux, Mandans, and Blackfeet often wore their hair in a free-flowing style, and particularly so for ceremonials, since wearing it this way was considered to be a sign of humility and spirituality before the Great Mystery.

The men of the Blackfoot, Mandan, Sioux, and Shoshone tribes often let a flat, rectangular-shaped lock hang in the middle of their forehead, and they cut the lock off square just above the eyes. The rest of the hair was loosely combed to each side.

In an extreme departure from the usual Plains style, the southeastern tribes, the Omahas, Osages, Pawnees, Iowas, Sauks, and Foxes sometimes shaved their heads as close to the skin as possible, leaving only a tuft about two inches high and the size of the palm of the hand on the crown of the head. Often the tuft was shaped in a special way as a society or religious symbol. In the center of the tuft they left a small lock for a scalp lock, which was braided and encouraged to grow as long as possible. A small hollow bone was placed in the center of the tuft, the scalp lock was pulled through it, and another toothpick-sized bone was inserted through the braid as a key to hold the larger bone in place. Most Plains men made some use of the type of headdress called the roach, and all southern warriors wore it. The roach was made of combinations of deer tail hair, porcupine hair, and/or horsehair. The Southern tribes usually dyed their roaches red, and one or more of their war honor eagle feathers were suspended in cleverly designed bone sockets which were placed on carved bone spreaders. The feathers would spin whenever the Indian danced or rode, and presented a dazzling appearance.

Catlin reports that the southern, tuft-weaving tribes generally painted the upper part of the head and a considerable part of the face as red as they possibly could.[1] Before they obtained scissors in trade, they removed their hair with knives or burned it off with red-hot stones, and it was a very slow and painful operation.

All other tribes, Catlin says, cultivated their hair to the greatest possible length, letting it flow over their shoulders and backs, and being unwilling to spare the smallest lock of it for any consideration[2]—although some of the earliest explorers found a number of Sioux warriors had shaved heads.

The princes of the long, straight hair styles were the Crows, who considered

Crow warriors showing fall ornament made of hair assembled into broad strands with gum balls.

braids to be a departure from ancient usage for either sex. Some Crow and Blackfoot Indians employed a traditional method of cutting the front hair short and holding it straight up in pompadour fashion by packing it with bear grease or coating it with red or white clay. However, it was the hair on the back of the Crow Indian's head that received the primary attention, some of it being cultivated until it literally dragged on the ground as the owner walked about. Considering the idea of the soul-hair symbolism, such a warrior evoked considerable envy.

The Crow warriors also added fallen or cut human hair, or strands of horsehair, to their own to make a majestic fall or tail ornament. They assembled the individual strands into eight or ten cords, each about as thick as a finger, and placed the cords vertically in parallel lengths about three quarters of an inch apart. Fine gum was then mixed with red ocher or vermilion paint and used as a glue to attach the cords of hair until they had constructed an assemblage which almost reached the ground. About every four inches or so they affixed a ball of the red or white gum, and then added horizontal cross strands, weaving the whole of it into a stable ornament which was attached to the back of the head by a piece of ornamented buckskin. These made a grand sight when Crow warriors were riding across the plains with the stupendous tails hanging down their backs.

Some of the Mandan men combed their hair backward from the forehead, taking care to keep it above and resting it on the ear, and then letting it fall down over the back to their calves or to the ground. Like the Crows, they also divided it into slabs or cords—but those of the Mandans were two inches in width and filled with a profusion of glue and red paint at intervals of an inch or two. Then the entire assemblage, hair and all, was painted red. Their hair became very hard,

---

PLATE 19. MONARCHS OF MONTANA

The trade-cloth leggings of the Crows can often be identified by rectangular beaded trim patches at the bottom. Those shown are styles taken from actual leggings. The Blackfeet and some mountain tribes also used such patches, though.

The painting shows three types of articles commonly carried by Plains tribesmen. The left figure carries an eagle feather flag. Such flags were usually carried by the man who flanked the war leader, so that the war party in battle could locate the leader to obtain his commands. The center man carries a coup stick—simply a willow stick with eagle feathers attached—to use in touching an enemy and thus counting coup, or a war honor. The warrior at right holds a staff. These, in shorter editions, might be society emblems, but the longer ones were cut from trees by war expedition members who were chosen in the field to second the leader. The limb was cut green, bent over and tied in place, then wrapped with fur—sometimes wolf, but preferably that of otters since doing this would impart that animal's swiftness and agility to the bearer.

and it remained unchanged from year to year. Some of these falls were so large as to conceal the whole figure from the person walking behind them.

Blackfoot and Cheyenne warriors sometimes rolled their hair into a topknot which extended up and forward like a large horn. Sometimes it was wrapped with red felt strips or otter fur.

Most of the Indians took excellent care of their hair, oiling it and keeping it smooth and shiny, although when water was in short supply it was sometimes not clean. Herman Lehmann tells how he obtained bear grass and love vine and boiled them in water till they became a strong ooze, which he then used to wash his hair.[3] All Indians washed it when they could.

Toilet appliances were few, consisting of paint sticks and a hairbrush. The paint stick served a double purpose. It was used to part the hair and to put a red paint line in the part, including the part around the scalp lock. It was made of wood and was about eight inches long, one end tapering to a blunt point. The case in which the stick and paint bag were kept was generally ornamented, and sometimes it had a painted flap which served as a cover to protect the stick and keep it from dropping out.

One type of hairbrush was made of a "stiff grass" called by the same name. The end of the brush was tightly wound about with hide or cloth strips to form a sort of handle, and on occasion it was beautifully beaded. Other brushes were made of a porcupine tail tied to a stick with rawhide thongs. Some of them had strips of ornamental beading running up the sides. The Crees were known to use the rough side of a buffalo's tongue for a comb.

Feathers which were to be worn in the hair or inserted in the scalp lock were first bound to a small wooden pin which stiffened the quill, and if more than one feather was to be used, they were tied to a split stick or else slipped into a rawhide or bone holder which was then attached to the scalp lock. Large hair decorations of many kinds, such as those made with cut feathers and down feathers, were in common use. The feather hair decorations were very personal, with each man constructing his according to what he had seen in dreams or visions, and as such they always had a religious significance. Besides feathers, whole skins of birds, shells, beads, ribbons, claws, and bone were worn for religious reasons.

◀ PLATE 20.   BLACKFEET WARRIOR IN WINTER DRESS—
            CLOTHING STUDY NO. 1

The warrior wears a trade blanket in the traditional style for winter wear. A beaded medicine bag captured from a Crow warrior has been attached to the blanket at the right shoulder.

Some of the more interesting and significant hair ornaments consisted of celestial symbols such as a morning-star cross cut from rawhide, and to which were fastened beautiful eagle-down feathers. Rawhide hoops wrapped with dyed porcupine quills were worn on the side of the head and various medicine items were attached to these. In all instances the hair ornaments would be placed on the head with great care so as to make a balanced composition of everything the warrior had on.

Sometimes the scalp lock was further emphasized by the addition of a long, narrow rawhide strap that might hang down to the ground. Silver disks, called "hair plates," made of trade silver, hammered tin or coins were added at intervals to the strap as conches are to a belt. The Kiowas, Utes, and Comanches were particularly fond of this kind of decoration. A Shoshone was seen wearing an arrangement of linked brass rings hanging from his scalp lock after the manner of a huge chain.

*Top,* buckskin container for brush and stick. *Center,* willow paint stick and buckskin pouch containing red paint. *Bottom,* stiff porcupine hair brush.

A commonly used ornament for the front of the head was the beaded hair bow. Long strings of brass or bone hair-pipe trade beads were added to these in various combinations. Sometimes a short beaded wooden stick with various assemblages of down or cut feathers placed at its peak was secured to the top of the bow. The Crows were very fond of these ornamented plumes, and many of the old Crow photographs show them.

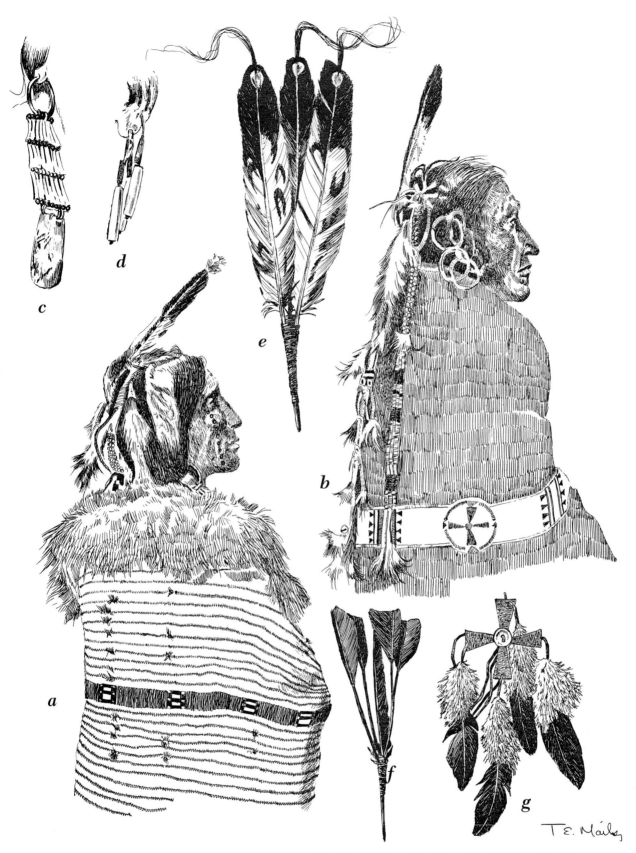

*a*, No-Flesh, Sioux, wearing plume ornament made of quills, brass beads, and eagle down feathers (he also wears quilled buffalo robe). *b*, Chief Stinking Bear, Sioux, wearing brass bead chains with quill-wrapped danglers on ends of chains and with danglers terminating in tin bells with red horsehair tufts. (*a* and *b* after paintings of Burbank from life, 1898, 1899.) *c*, dentalium shell earring (male). *d*, bone bead earring (male). *e*, eagle tail feathers bound to split wooden stick. *f*, cut feathers, usually dyed red. *g*, rawhide morning star symbol with down feathers attached.

Crow warrior in full dress. *Top left,* beaded hair bow, front and back view—hair-pipe bone beads with brass bead separators for bow chain dangler. Top right, front and end view of sun symbol cut from center of large sea shell.

Crow warrior, Long Otter, wearing complete eagle on head.

Now and then a long string of small glass or brass beads was attached to the side of the head or to the scalp lock base, and it was then draped forward to hang in a casual way down across the forehead and side of the face. Sometimes a long braided scalp lock was wound with brass wire and pulled forward in the

Sioux warrior, Spotted Eagle, wearing bound eagle on head, 1874.

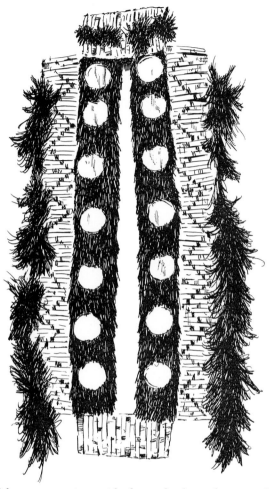

Fur and quilled breast covering with down feather edges, used by dancers.

same way. The Sioux and the Crows often did this. Beaded tubular cases and bone and metal rings were also used to slip the side hair through and to hold it neatly together when it was not braided.

Warriors often wore either parts of birds or entire birds on their heads. Once in a while a warrior would be topped with an entire golden eagle.

The bone breastplate was a popular chest ornament. The long bones, called hair-pipes, were manufactured by the Whites, and the Indians assembled them into breastplates. The bones were ingeniously held in place by the use of thick hide straps and beads which fixed them together like a lattice-type window blind. Ornaments such as sea shells and colorful trade ribbons were attached to the front of the breastplates. The top of the plate was tied around the neck with a thong, and other thongs at the bottom secured it around the waist. Since the hair-pipe bones were difficult and expensive to obtain, the number of bones in the plate

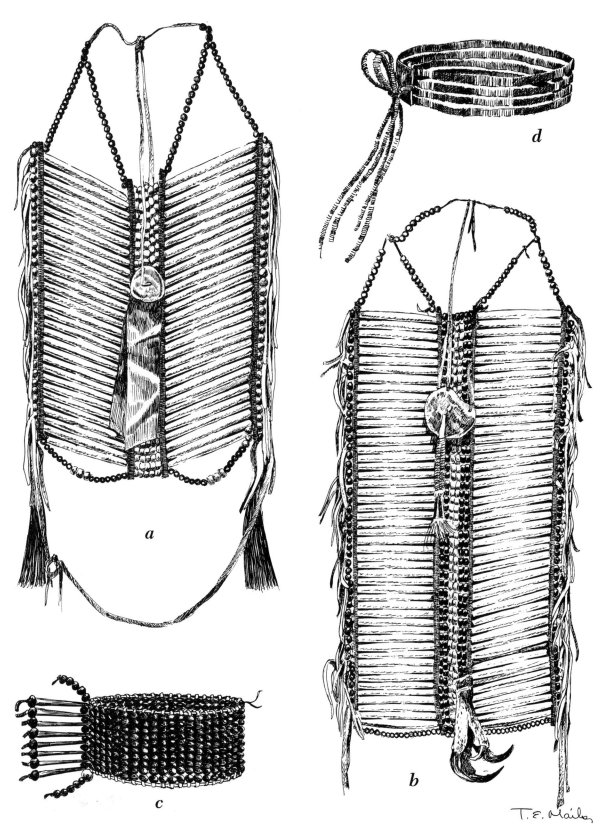

*a*, hair-pipe bone breastplate with brass beads top and bottom and red horsehair danglers.
*b*, hair-pipe bone breastplate with brass beads, quilled ornament, and eagle talon, length 34 inches.
*c*, arm band made of brass beads. *d*, quilled arm band with quill-wrapped danglers.

often indicated the wealth of a warrior. Such breastplates were worn on occasion in battles, but since they could be penetrated easily by an arrow or a bullet they were mainly a decorative or medicine item. Plush breastplates of otter skin which were covered with mirrors and gorgeously quilled breastplates were made for use in dances.

Chief Painted Horse, Sioux, wearing hair-pipe necklace and chest ornament with bones arranged vertically.

Necklaces of every kind were worn by plains warriors. Some wore a choker type made of beaded or fur-covered strips, with the fur being bear, weasel, or otter. A fond addition to any of these was a disk cut from a clamshell, and which represented sun power. The largest shells were obtained in trade from coastal Indians. They were exquisite items, since the sun would shine through them and make subtle changes in their delicate tones. The combined otter skin and bear claw necklaces of the Plains were simply magnificent. They were made in many ways. The most popular southern types were made with broad bands of otter skin, and the long tail of the swift and cunning otter was arranged to hang down the center of the warrior's back. Sioux and Blackfoot claw necklaces were made in much the same way as the southern models, but lacked the hanging otter tail. The huge, curved grizzly bear claws were the most sought after for bear necklaces, because the grizzly was powerful medicine, and a terror to kill. Sometimes the grizzly claws were only mounted on a string of large, beautiful beads, and the fur strips were not used. Eagle claw necklaces were also made, and sometimes an entire eagle's foot would hang from the center of a beaded string.

Last, but by no means least, the warrior wore a sumptuous array of earrings. In fact, everyone's ears were pierced, and it is said that the number of holes— because the process was done by people hired for the purpose and was expensive—revealed something about the wealth of the person in question. Ear piercing was a part of the religious scheme, and all children had their ears pierced during the first year after birth in a ceremonial rite of great significance. Earrings of shell, stone, and beads were made in so many ways it would be impossible to describe even a fraction of them. The shell types were the most common. Sinew string and brass or silver trade rings were used to attach the earrings to the ears.

The woven garters which are seen in some of the old photographs were only worn by the Indians of the southeast Plains, and they reveal that the man wearing them is an Omaha, Osage, or Ponca. Some of these garters had strings of brass bells attached to them for use in dancing. Headbands of any kind were seldom worn on the Plains by men or women, and when they are used today it is usually because it's an easy way to keep a wig and feathers on one's head. Also, the Plains Indians did not wear rings in their noses. The ancient Nez Percé men did do this, but they were not, properly speaking, a Plains tribe. An authority reports that Omaha tribesmen used perfumes.[4] Braids of sweet grass were worn about the neck under the robe, and columbine seeds were pulverized, mixed with water, and sprinkled over robes to give them a pleasant odor. It is not known for certain whether other tribes used similar perfumes, but since they all recognized the several values of incenses, it is reasonable to assume that everyone made use of sweet-smelling substances for personal hygiene.

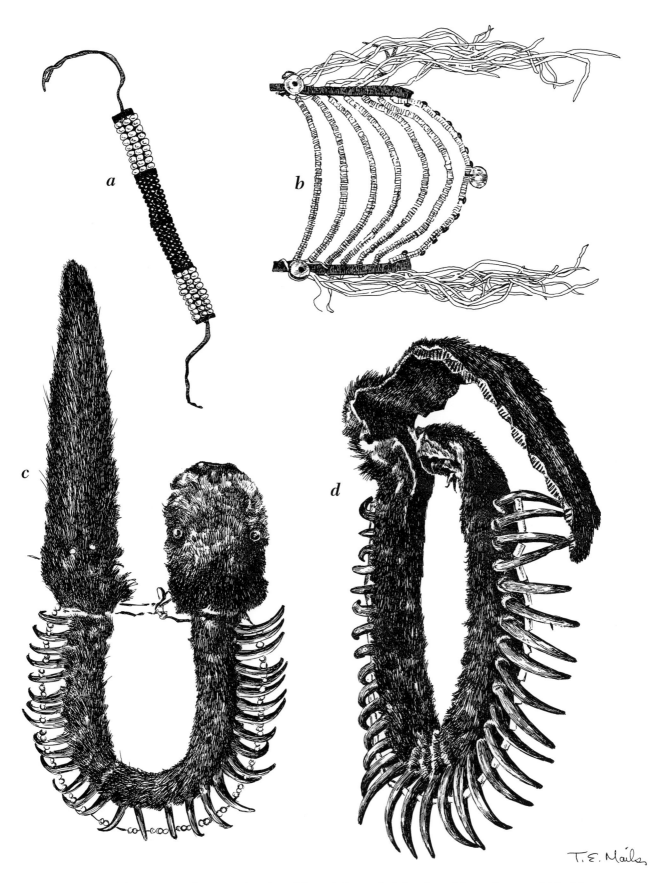

Plains necklaces. *a*, choker-type bead necklace. *b*, bone disk bead necklace, Crow and Blackfoot style. *c*, southern-style otter skin with grizzly bear claws. *d*, northern-style otter skin with grizzly bear claws—otter tail hung down back.

Eastern trade silver came to the Plains as early as 1740, and by 1830 was receiving an enthusiastic response from all Indians. Some items were finished by the Whites, and in other instances the Indians shaped the silver themselves. *a*, silver pectoral ornament with Indian engraved bird symbol. *b*, Arapaho warrior wearing pectoral ornament. *c*, silver hair plates on hide strap attached to scalp lock and small roach, Big Mouth, southern Arapaho, 1872. *d*, Blackfoot hair ornament with brass disk in center.

*e*, silver-mounted headstall and iron bit. *f*, Osage silver hair plates on hide strap. *g*, Osage hair plates on otter fur strap. *h*, Kiowa warrior wearing silver hair plates (those with holes in center are oldest types) and with silver-mounted headstall on horse. *i*, front and section of silver conch plate.

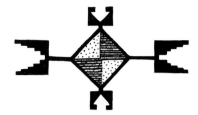

Generally the Indian loves everything that flutters in the wind. Thus he wears his hair long; his horse's tail and mane are long. He loves to have hides fringed and uses colored ribbons. Every kind of fringe and feather, but especially eagle feathers, please him so much that very often he would not relinquish things of this kind for a whole world of useful goods. And it must be admitted that in the eyes of a vain man the costume of an Indian riding through camp at full gallop is not without its charm.[5]

Because he considered it to be an extension of his soul, the Indian warrior groomed and cultivated his hair with infinite patience. To embellish it further he added pieces of personal medicine and ornaments, and topped it all off with a selection of breath-taking headdresses. Of course, in accordance with the Indian's spiritual attitude, a headdress had to be more than an adornment. It, like all of the other things he used and wore, had to be an expression of his beliefs. It must assist him in the accomplishment of his goals and it must do so by the employment of the most powerful helpers of the One-Above. To repeat what was stated in the material on Indian religion, it was believed that a person acquired the powers of other animals, birds, objects, and of the elements, by taking some part of them unto himself; by wearing or carrying these things, by reflecting upon them, and by imitating their manner of life, he gathered added wisdom and was able to duplicate their most important qualities. It followed that the shape of a headdress must also seek to express its purpose, and it did so in a marvelous way—as a study of headdresses shows.

Four types or styles of headdresses were worn by the mystic warriors of the Plains. There was the horned headdress, the golden eagle feather headdress, the hat or cap which was a smaller type of covering than the horned and feather bonnets, and the animal-skin type which employed the animal's skin in something akin to its natural state. All other varieties could be placed as subdivisions in one or the other of these categories.

The buffalo horn headdress is less well known today than the regal eagle feather bonnet, yet it held the highest position in the eyes of the Indian warriors. According to George Catlin, only a few of the highest-ranking warriors in each band were given the right to wear one by the village leaders.[6] The accuracy of this statement is supported by the small number of horned bonnets which were collected by the Whites for museums and private collections. Furthermore, only a relatively few are to be seen in old photographs in comparison to the feather style. And in each instance they are worn by eminent leaders of the tribes.

The general style of the horned bonnet was the same in all cases. There was a buffalo hide skullcap with a tail hanging from its back side, but its tail was made in two lengths. There was a short length which consisted of a buffalo hide tail—with the hair left on—reaching about to the middle of the back, and a full-length tail which hung from the bonnet to the ground. Short-tailed horn bonnets had only a few feathers appended to their tails, and these hung flat against the cap. Most of the long-tailed models had thirty or so eagle pinion (wing) feathers—and in rare instances eagle tail feathers—placed at right angles to the tails so as to extend back or out from the tails. Some of the horned bonnets were made with hawk or owl feathers—especially those of the holy men whose vision helpers were the hawk or the owl—and some were made with a combination of feathers taken from eagles and other birds. The horned bonnet cap of an outstanding warrior or a medicine man might also be entirely covered with something other than buffalo hair, such as ermine or bobcat fur, although buffalo or antelope horns would still be employed."

It was also customary for a horn bonnet wearer to append items to the skullcap which marked the significant moments in his life. Several bonnets collected by Whites had beaded turtles tied to them which contained a part of the owner's navel cord which had been placed in the turtle at birth. A horn bonnet belonging to a Sioux warrior named White Bull had a piece of the bone and tail of a buffalo bull which was covered by a quilled and beaded case and tied to the cap. Sea shells were commonly appended to the caps, as well as clusters of split and/or whole feathers. Also added were braided and dyed horsehair tails, quilled or beaded headbands, white ermine skins or tails and groups of buckskin or felt fringe. All of the horned bonnets had a long plume, some twenty-four inches or so in length, extending back from the peak of the bonnet. This was the Sun Dance plume, and it explained to all who saw it that the owner had participated in one or more Sun Dances.

Once a warrior had been given the great privilege of wearing the horn bonnet by the band leaders, he constructed it in the following manner: He made a skullcap of buffalo hide with the hair left on the outside. To this he appended the tail, making it perhaps ten inches wide and from twenty-four to thirty inches long if he wanted a short tail, and five or more feet long for the full-length style. When these were sewn together, he added the buffalo horns, placing one on each side of the skullcap. Sometimes he used the complete horn, in which case he hollowed out the center to reduce the weight. Other times he split a horn into quarters and used a much lighter piece of split horn on the bonnet. The horns were polished, and sometimes painted with symbolic lines and colors. Holes were drilled through the horns at the base and the horns were tied to the cap in very ingenious ways, so as to be secure, yet free enough to sway a little when the warrior moved. Dyed tufts of horsehair were often tied to the tips of the horns,

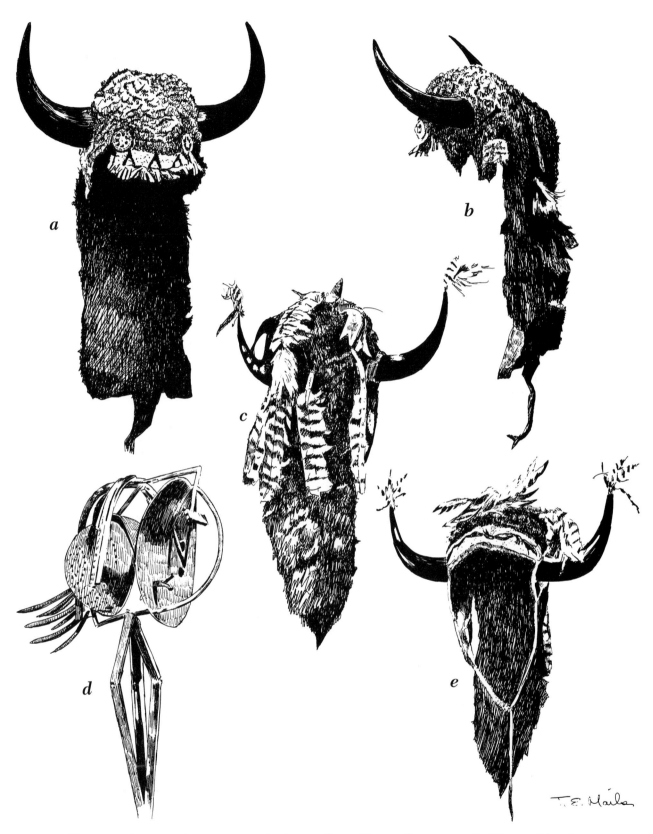

Buffalo horn bonnets from 1870s with short tails. *a*, Kiowa, front view. *b*, Kiowa, side view. *c*, Sioux, back view. *d*, modern metal sculpture showing how same design principles employed by Indians are used by contemporary artists. *e*, Sioux, front view.

Buffalo horn bonnets from 1870s with long tails. *Top,* Bonnet with pinion feather tail, eagle tail feathers on horn tips, hawk feathers on crown sides, Sun Dance plume. *a,* back view of Sioux bonnet. *b,* front view of Sioux bonnet. *c,* Calder mobile to compare mobile quality of Indian and contemporary art. *Bottom, d,* front view of Sioux long-tailed bonnet with split buffalo horns and piece of buffalo tail wrapped with quills. Belonged to White Bull, nephew of Sitting Bull, who fought against Custer. *e,* back view of same bonnet. *f,* section through split horn.

and sometimes to hold the horns in an upright position a taut buckskin thong was strung between the horn tips or angled from each horn tip to the center of the cap. Once the horns were in place the beaded headband and other appendages were added to the cap, the feathers were put on, and the bonnet was complete.

Four of the renowned horned bonnets which were collected by Chief Joseph White Bull, the nephew of Sitting Bull, and who himself fought against General Custer in his historic last battle, are shown in color in PLATE 5, PLATE 6, PLATE 15, and PLATE 29. The Sioux warriors who owned these would believe they had the dignity, the strength, the toughness, and the stamina of a bull buffalo. It was expected that they would conduct themselves accordingly as leaders of the tribe and in raids and wars in defense of their people. A unique design feature of the horned bonnets with long tails was the fact that the upper half of the feathers on the tail were turned one way, and the lower half were turned just the opposite. It gave them a balance in composition.

The man who was permitted to wear a buffalo horn bonnet would also be entitled to wear an eagle-feathered headdress. The regal golden-eagle-feathered headdress so closely associated with the warriors of the Plains was made in three styles: the simple headdress, the headdress with a single tail, and the headdress with a double tail.

The simple headdress was itself made in two ways. Most by far were fashioned with from twenty-eight to thirty-two eagle tail feathers placed in a circle around a skullcap base, and these flared back in a cone shape from the cap. However, the early Blackfoot and Cheyenne chiefs sometimes made theirs in the form of a tube with the feathers standing straight up from the cap. The tail headdresses were different only in that a long tail, sometimes extending for eight feet or more, was added to the simple headdress.

Every part of the feathered headdress had a special meaning which would be understood by all of the members of a tribe. In their view, the feathers which encircled the cap, and which radiated out from it, were not just feathers, they were—because the great golden eagle flew so close to the sun and had so much solar power—the radiating shafts of light which brought the enlightenment of the One-Above, who dwelt in the sun, down to man. From the center of this circle of light extended the long, gracious Sun Dance plume which constantly reminded the warrior of his thanksgiving vow and dance. The tail of the bonnet which hung down from the cap to the ground, and along which were spaced twenty-eight to thirty tail feathers (twice that in a double tail), was the buffalo's back—because it looked so much like the back part of a buffalo's skeleton. The eagle's soft white breath feathers, which were tied to the base of each tail feather at the point where the quills were secured to the cap or tail, were put there as reminders to the warrior that he should ride into battle like the breath feather, swaying to and fro as if with every breeze, so that the enemy's arrows and bullets would pass by or through him without permanently harming him.

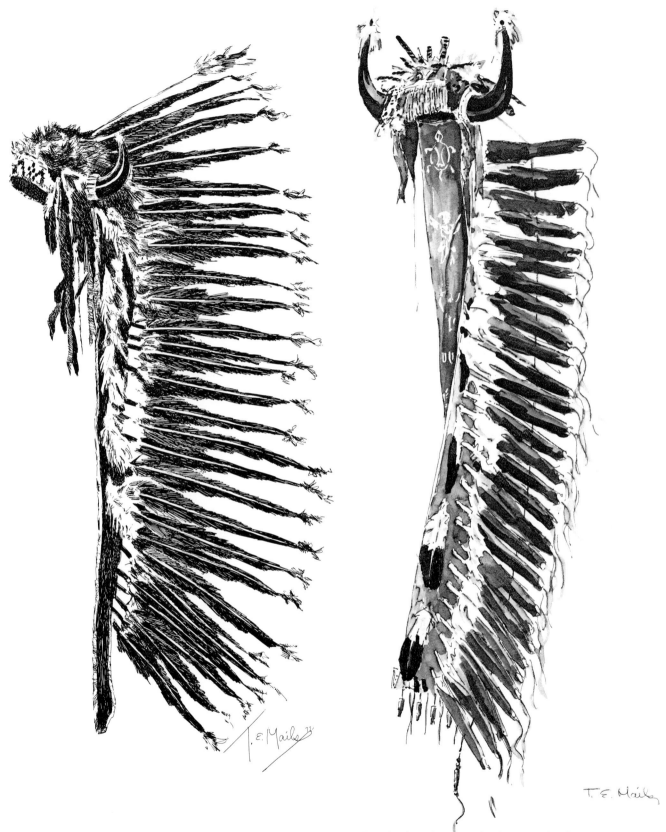

*Left*, Southern Cheyenne buffalo horn bonnet with full tail of eagle wing feathers. *Right*, Sioux bonnet with full tail of eagle wing feathers. Inside of tail is painted with symbolic designs telling life story of warrior, circa 1870.

Cheyenne warrior, Hubble Big Horse, 1898, wearing stand-up-style bonnet common only to Cheyenne and Blackfoot.

Goes Ahead, Crow warrior, wearing typical Crow eagle feather headdress with top angling almost flat back.

Sioux golden eagle feather headdress with single tail, circa 1870 and after. *a*, side view. *b*, front view. *c*, back view. *d*, perspective view. Bonnet is similar to one worn by White Whirlwind, Oglala Sioux, AMNH photo, also type shown in photos in *The Fighting Indians of the West* and in *The Vanishing Race*, Doubleday, 1890 photographs.

In making a feathered bonnet the warrior began with a hide skullcap—in trade days a felt one—and then bent a short piece of half-inch-wide rawhide around each feather's quill, leaving an open loop to pass a thong through. The rawhide was bound to the quill with a strip of flannel cloth, the preferred colors being red and yellow, and then a thong was stitched around the cap to secure the feathers at about one-inch intervals. Each time the thong emerged on the surface of the cap it was passed through a rawhide loop and then down under the cap. Holes were drilled in the feathers about six inches out from the point of the quill, and another thong was passed through the holes to aid in holding the feathers in place.

The tail feathers were attached and fixed in place in the same manner, and horsehair or breath feathers were glued to the tips of the eagle feathers with a mixture of glue and white clay. The amazing thing is that despite their size when fully opened and extended, the feather bonnets could be folded into a roll with a diameter of eight inches or less, and then reopened to fall into perfect position. Once the feathers were all in place, a quilled or beaded headband was added, as were the side pendants of ermine tails or horsehair, or ribbons or feathers, etc., and the bonnet was finished. A warrior might make four or more bonnets during his lifetime, and each one would be a little different than the others.

The cone shape of the simple headdress was sometimes an indication of the tribe to which the owner belonged. Looking at the bonnet from the back, if the top middle feathers angled up rather sharply and the whole circle had a wide flair to it, the owner was probably Sioux, and in the late nineteenth century perhaps a Blackfoot. If the top middle feathers sloped back at a low angle and the whole group of feathers was formed in a tight oval shape, the owner was probably a Crow. If the top middle feathers were absolutely flat, the owner was an Assiniboine. If the feathers stood straight up in a cylinder form, the owner was probably Blackfoot, maybe a Cheyenne.

The Sioux, Cheyenne, and Blackfoot sometimes dyed all or a few of their bonnet feathers red. This was the sacred color, and it indicated something about the owner's accomplishments in war.

The tails of both the horned and the feathered headdresses were now and then further decorated with painted symbols, which on occasion spelled out the main events in the owner's life, or with breath feathers or hide targets placed at fifteen- to twenty-inch intervals. The tails were often weighted at their ends with metal cartridge cases which the warrior had picked up on a battlefield.

The most common type of cap in use on the northern Plains was a wide band of otter fur which encircled the head like a crown. The top was left open, and if a warrior wished he could place an eagle feather in his scalp lock and let it stick up through the cap. The tail of the otter was attached to the rear of the cap in such a way as to hang down the warrior's back. Sometimes the edges of the cap and tail were beaded, and a tuft of dyed horsehair was appended to the

Sioux golden eagle feather headdress with double tail, circa 1870. *Left,* front view. *Right,* back view.

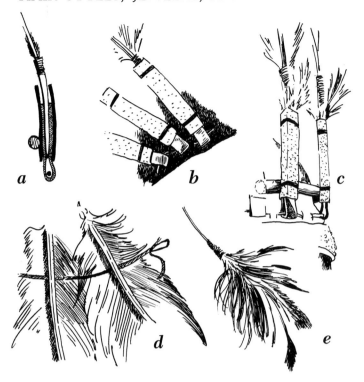

Details for attaching feathers to crown of headdress. *a*, cross section showing quill, rawhide cover, and cloth wrapping. *b*, front view of finished attachment. *c*, perspective view showing thong which secures feather to crown. *d*, thong through quill shafts for holding feather in place. *e*, end of Sun Dance plume.

end of the tail. Four round, beaded targets were also attached to the wide band of the cap for decoration.

While some of the southern tribes wore a slight variation of the cap just described, the hat most unique to the southeast had a huge hide triangle, with beaded or painted symbols on it, which extended out to the left or right side of the wide headband. These were really stunning creations, and the bold symbols, which depicted many of the warrior's accomplishments, were arranged in excellent compositions. Such hats were worn by the Pawnee, Ponca, Osage, and Oto warriors.

The roach headdress was, for the most part, an ornament worn by dancers, but the Omaha warriors wore a roach made of a deer's tail and turkey neck hair, dyed red, to designate one who had won first-coup honors. The warriors of other tribes made their roaches with stiff moose hairs, porcupine hairs, and the white hairs from a deer's tail, and when finished they stood erect, like a trimmed horse's mane, on the top and back of the warrior's head. Some were dyed in splendid colors such as orange and purple, and the Sioux dance roach was usually white and yellow with black tips.

Fur cap, northern Plains style favored by Sioux, Blackfoot, and Crees.

Fur cap, southern Plains style favored by Poncas, Omahas, Otos, Pawnees. Note huge, painted-hide triangle extension.

To make a roach, the Indian warrior gathered the strands of hair, which were about twelve inches long, into bunches about one eighth of an inch in diameter. He folded each bunch in half and tied it just above the bend, leaving a small loop at the base. Then he sewed the bunches onto the edge of a foundation, side by side in three or four rows. The foundation was made either of skin or braided cloth, and was long and oval-shaped at the front, and rather pointed at the rear end.

In the center of the foundation, the Indian placed a piece of thin carved bone or rawhide called a spreader, which kept the roach from drooping inward. He attached bone sockets to the spreader and inserted in each socket one or more feathers, which twirled in the slightest breeze.

He then made an opening or slit near the front of the foundation through which he pulled a lock of his hair. He tied the hair in a knot to hold the front of the roach in place. At the back, or pointed end, he fastened long buckskin thongs and tied them around his neck.

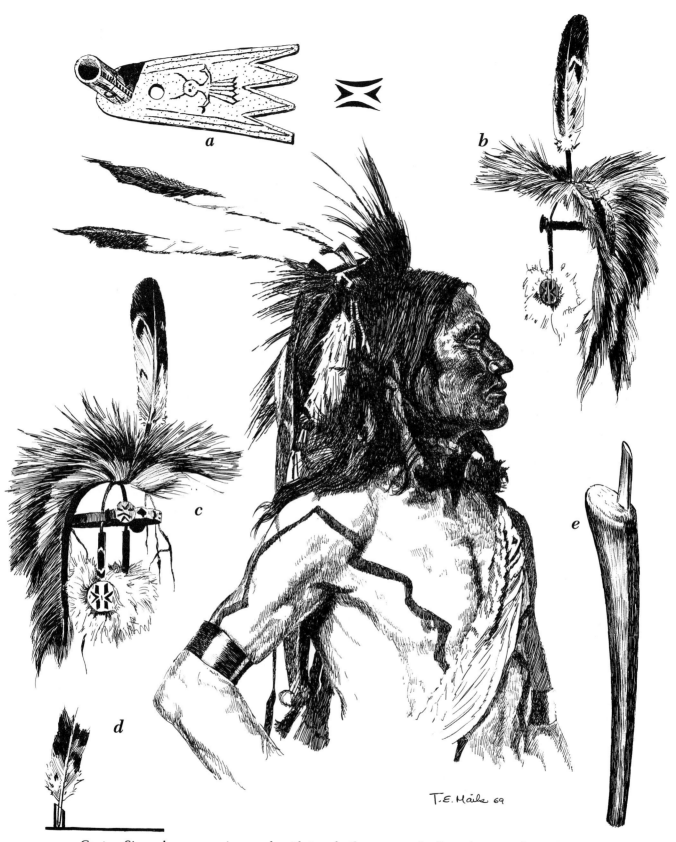

Center, Sioux dancer wearing roach with two feathers. *a*, roach elk antler spreader with engraved design. *b*, back view of roach. *c*, beaded head band of type often used by dancers after 1870 to help hold roach on. Barry photos show Sioux wearing version of the band in the 1870s and 1880s. Bands also seen in Shoshone photos taken around 1890, 1900, and 1915. However, support bands like this only became broadly popular after 1900. *d*, section through bone socket which held feather. *e*, carved wooden stick used to hold roach when not in use.

Bonnet and feather carrying and storage cases. *a*, detail of thong tie at side of case. *b*, method of attaching carrying loop. *c*, detail of lid tie. *d*, detail of lid tie. *e*, method of securing bottom cover to case. *f*, detail of bottom fringe. *g*, painted Blackfoot rawhide case. *h*, Blackfoot rawhide case for carrying selected coup feathers. *i*, case for feathered hair ornament. *j*, Kiowa bonnet case with bonnet inserted. *k*, disk top for same.

Animal headdresses. *Left,* grizzly bear headdress with head worn upright and complete bear's body hide left attached. *Right,* grizzly bear headdress worn by Bear Cult member in more traditional fashion.

Animal headdresses. *Left,* wolf, front view. *Right,* timber wolf, side view. Animal headdresses like these were usually, though not always, held on with straps which tied under the chin.

Animal headdresses. *a*, buffalo hair headdress taken from hump of animal, front view. *b*, side view.

▶

*Page across. Left,* Buffalo head bands. Head bands were not in common use on the Plains, and were worn mostly by holy men. This one, with a quilled plume and eagle tail feathers attached, is worn by Elk Head, ninth keeper of the Sacred Calf Pipe Bundle of the Teton Sioux. Note that he also wears a Christian crucifix. *Right,* Animal head bands. Weasel Head (ca. 1863–1943), Black-foot warrior, wearing head band of weasel skin and owl feathers which originated in a dream when he was a young man. He was a renowned medicine man.

Some of the Indians wore a type of beaded headband when their heads were shaved to hold the roach securely on during dances. The roach was tied to the part of the band which crossed the head.

The manner of storing the Plains headdresses was as clever as the head coverings themselves. The roach was wrapped around a sculptured wood form, with a knob on top which was inserted through the hole in the roach just as the hair was inserted when the roach was worn on the head. A piece of bright trade cloth was then wrapped around the roach and the wood form to hold them together in a neat package. Feather bonnets were folded and rolled together into a cylindrical shape as small as six inches in diameter—or eight for a bonnet with a tail—and then inserted in long, round rawhide carrying cases which were hung on the saddle while traveling.

The fourth type of head covering in use on the Plains was the skins of animals in their natural form. Some of the societies, whose vision helpers were powerful animals such as the buffalo, would make a head and back covering of the long hair and skin taken from the buffalo's brow. The horns were then attached to the gracefully formed headpiece, and the completed head covering was worn at society functions—and sometimes to war. Bear Cult members often made head coverings of entire bear heads, wearing these in accordance with the ways they had seen them in their visions. The wolf was a superb hunter, and on the other hand very difficult to catch. Therefore, his skin became the ideal covering for scouts serving as lookouts for raid and war parties. Ordinarily, the Indians did not line their animal head coverings with trade cloth.

Taken as a whole, the headdresses of the Plains warriors were meaningful and splendid creations. Moreover, their mobile qualities were equal to those in the best work of this kind being done by contemporary artists. The Indians employed the identical principles of motion seen in metal sculptures today, for their bonnets swayed and turned with every move and breeze. Again, the entire piece was carefully balanced in mass and texture and color. Really to appreciate these spectacular products, however, one must take them in his hands and pore over them like a detective searching for clues, for when he does, he discovers that the owners have added secret bits of beautiful beading and symbolic paint marks in places so hidden that the casual viewer would never know they were there. The point is, that they treated their headdresses as holy things, and so with the greatest reverence.

# Chapter 19

# BOWS, ARROWS, AND QUIVERS

Popular opinion had regarded the Indian bow and arrow as something primitive and well enough for the pursuit of game, but quite useless in a contest with the white man. This idea would be excellent if the Indian warriors would calmly march up in the line of battle and risk their masses so armed among others armed with the rifle. *But the Indian comes as the hornet comes,* in clouds or singly, yet never trying to sting until his ascending is assured and his own exposure is slight. At fifty yards a well-shapen, non-pointed arrow is dangerous and very sure. A handful drawn from the quiver and discharged successively will make a more rapid fire than that of the revolver, and at very short range will farther penetrate a piece of plank or timber than the ball of an ordinary Colt's navy pistol.[1]

The bow and arrows became the most natural weapon imaginable for the Plains Indian warrior. It was the first childhood plaything of which he had recollection. Proud fathers placed a miniature bow and a few blunted arrows in their sons' hands before they were four years old, and from then on they practiced constantly until shooting with them became an instinctive part of their nature. Since he seldom shot at stationary targets, the Indian boy's only method of aiming was what might be described as a conditioned "feeling" for direction and distance; or perhaps one could say a sensitivity which had been developed by diligent practice. Yet witnesses declare that these little fellows were uncannily accurate with their weapons as they shot at rolling hoops or birds in flight, and they could even spin around and hit pennies inserted in a split stick which was placed fifteen or more feet away from them.

In his earliest forays for scalps and plunder the would-be warrior was always armed with this weapon, for unless his father was exceptionally rich and generous, a boy could never hope to own a gun until he either obtained the means to pay for it or was fortunate enough to count coup on a man who was carrying one. Most Indian warriors did not possess firearms before they were twenty-five, and even when they became talented with the new weapon, they were never as thoroughly at home with it as with their first love, the bow and arrows.

In their first battles with Indians, Whites were often astonished to discover that retreating Indians invariably kept their bows and arrows while they abandoned their guns. Guides would then explain that the Indians had little confidence in guns in a close fight. And it was not until after the Indians obtained repeaters, like the Winchester 66 carbine and the Sharps .50-caliber carbine, that the bow was, to a great extent, put aside.

By 1875 almost all of the older warriors had obtained guns and pistols from the Whites, some of which were the very best kinds of breech-loading arms available. This greatly diminished the use of the bow, but it did not eliminate it. The supply of ammunition was scarce, or else the gun itself could break down and the Indian lacked the proper tools and the mechanical ability to repair it—which meant that the owner had to use his bow and arrows again until he could persuade a White man to mend the gun for him. The young men and the poor warriors continued to use the bow exclusively, and those who possessed firearms still used the bow occasionally, so that however rich and well-armed a band might be, the bow remained an indispensable possession of every male Indian.

No one knows for certain how the Indian bowman of the Plains held his bow and released his arrow. In fact, it appears as though several methods were used. Some investigators claim that most northern and southern Plains Indians used the "tertiary release," which consisted of holding the nock end by pinching it between thumb and forefinger, with the forefinger and the second finger hooked over the string.[2]

Another asserts that most Plains Indians released their arrow by holding the nock with the ends of the index and middle fingers, while the first three fingers were hooked on the string.[3]

A Southwest Museum leaflet points out that the release is more effective when shot from the right-hand side of the bow. "If one tries to shoot from the left-hand side, the arrow will lift off the bow unless held down by the first finger of the bow-hand and will fly wild. When an arrow is held down against the side of a bow ever so slightly its flight is retarded."[4]

The Crow Indian method was to grip the bow firmly with the left hand and then deftly to place an arrow with the right hand; the index and second finger straddling the shaft and, with the third finger, pulling the bowstring. The thumb's end was against the arrow where it was notched into the string. Chief Plenty Coups explained that "Both hands and both arms must work together—at once. The left must push and the right must pull at the same time if an arrow is to go straight or far. The left hand, palm toward one, its fingers straddling the arrow, must know and keep the center of the bow-string without the eyes having to look."[5]

It was an axiom that any kind of bow, no matter how crudely made, would shoot an arrow. It was the arrow that counted. Crooked arrows could never be used, since one could not tell where such an arrow would go. Therefore the Indians took great pains to make them perfectly straight, and they checked them again and again before and during their use on a war party.

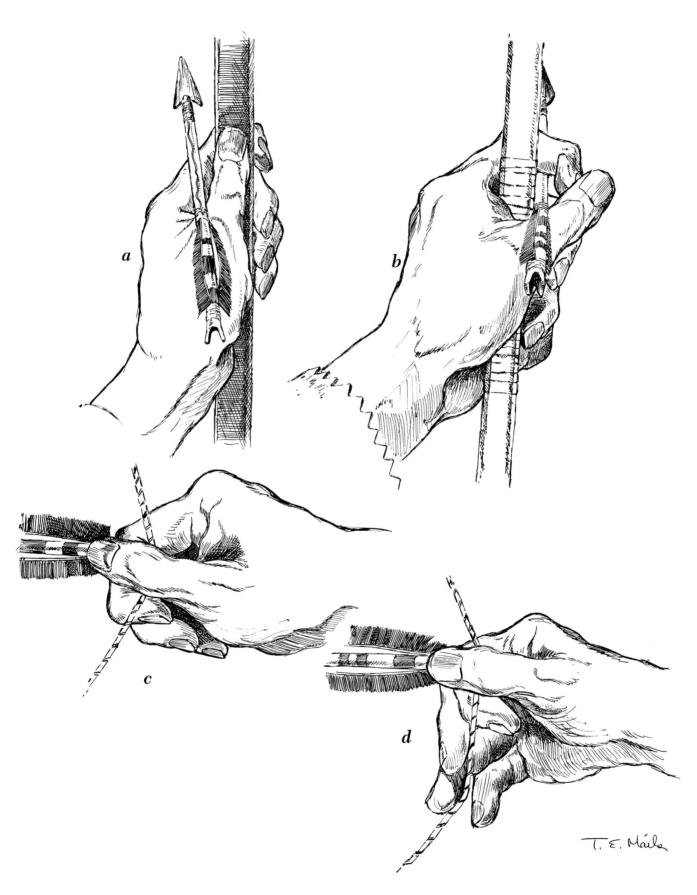

Methods of holding arrows. *a*, careless way of letting arrow rest on hand at bow. *b*, secure way of guiding arrow at bow. *c*, primary release used by beginners. *d*, secondary release used by adults.

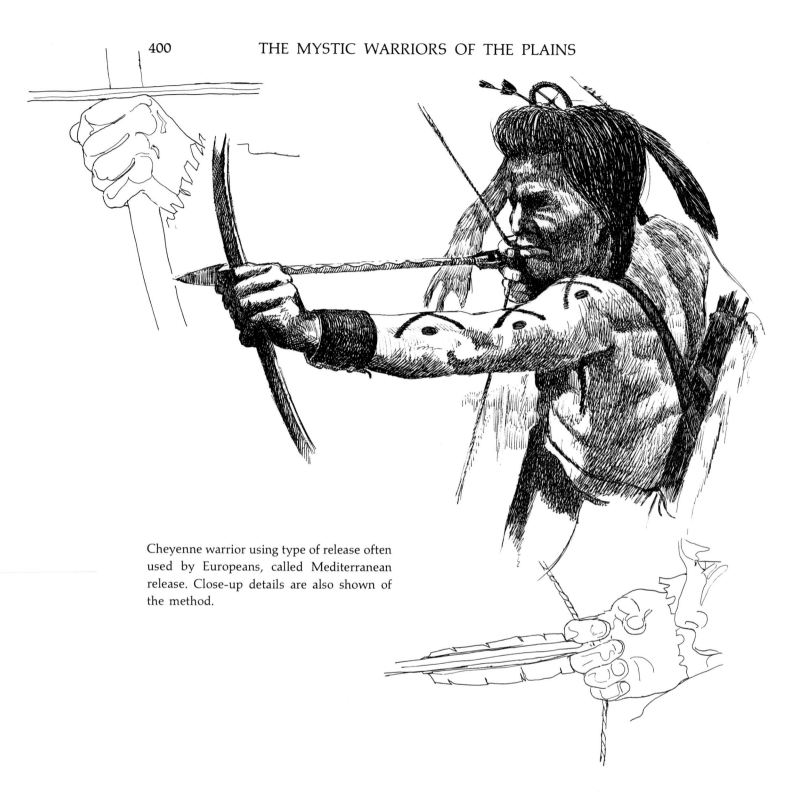

Cheyenne warrior using type of release often used by Europeans, called Mediterranean release. Close-up details are also shown of the method.

Boys first shot for distance. No particular care was given to accuracy until the required distance was reached. Then they were taught to shoot with precision. This demanded even more practice than shooting for distance. Acting as teachers, the father, uncle, or grandfather would place a buffalo chip at some distance as a stationary target. When the boy could put an arrow through its center in three out of every five shots, the instructor would roll the chip for a more demanding test. The boys considered this an exciting game, and sometimes their teachers heightened the enjoyment by trying a shot themselves.

Although a number of boys often shot at once at the same target, there never was an argument as to whose arrows finally pinned the chip to the ground, since all arrow shafts were marked with stripes of colored paint. Each boy knew which were his own arrows, and those of the other boys as well. The custom continued into adulthood, for the men of the tribe also recognized each other's arrows by their crests. This marking of arrows had both an individual and a tribal aspect, as did the selection of the feathers used to fletch the arrows. The Crows called the Cheyenne "the Striped Feathered Arrows," because of the barred feathers of the wild turkey used on their arrow shafts. Even the sign name for the Cheyenne was conceived from these feathers. It was made by drawing the right index finger several times across the left, as though making marks upon it.

The remarkable thing about a mature Indian and his bow was the rapidity and force with which he could send his arrows. He could seize from five to eight arrows in his left hand, fire the first of them in a high arch, and then discharge the rest so rapidly that the last would be in the air before the first had struck the ground.[6] In the midst of a furious battle he could launch his arrows with such force that each could mortally wound a man at twenty yards. In fact, a warrior's strength with the bow was such that the blow of the string was so severe on his left forearm that he usually had to protect it by a shield or gauntlet made of stiff deerskin. Speed in the launching of arrows was a vital concern, since in war and in hunting a man had to be quick to send a second arrow after his first. Therefore, boys were taught to hold one and sometimes more arrows in the left hand together with the bow, points down, feathers up, so that when the right hand reached and drew them, the left would not be wounded by their sharp heads. Sometimes men carried an extra arrow or two in their mouths, for this was quicker than pulling them from a quiver over the shoulder, but it was a method which was only used in especially dangerous situations.

Arrows were not easy to make, and the warrior never risked wasting them by shooting at outlandish distances. He always sought to get as close to his target as possible. Understandably, then, a boy spent many hours learning and practicing tricks and devices designed to get him close to his game. Once he was sufficiently expert with his weapons he was furnished with arrows with iron points. It was accepted that at that moment he suddenly grew up. He quit the companionship of smaller boys, and in company with young men similarly armed, he began to make long excursions after sizable game, sometimes being gone from his camp for several days.

Since the favored game of the Plains, the buffalo, had to be caught, the Indians chased it on horseback and shot it from their mounts. However, it was nearly impossible to handle a long bow on a galloping horse. A long bow was also

Warrior ready for battle with one extra arrow in mouth and several extra arrows held in bow hand.

exceedingly dangerous in case of a fall, for one could easily impale himself on it. So a shorter and more maneuverable bow was the obvious answer. As the years passed the Indians made their bows shorter and shorter until at last the Plains bows were so short they often snapped. After this new models were backed with sinew and curved to shorten them further—until at last the average bow in common use was only forty inches long or less. The stubby bow and consequently shorter arrows meant a shorter draw, but since the Indian preferred to move in close anyway, his true effectiveness was not diminished, and the bow could at last be rapidly handled from the back of a running horse. A spill no longer carried the threat of impalement, and Indians said there was a distinct side benefit—the short weapon could be easily concealed under one's buffalo robe together with a couple of arrows when a treaty council was attended whose outcome was uncertain.

An Indian warrior was able to shoot an arrow completely through a buffalo. George Grinnell reports instances where two buffalo running side by side were killed by the same shaft.[7] On the other hand, Colonel Dodge declared that he had never seen such feats.[8] He frequently saw arrows imbedded in the body of the buffalo to the feather, but said it only happened when no bone was touched. He believed that the strongest Indian, with the best bow, could not, even at a few feet, drive an arrow through a rib of the buffalo so as to inflict an immediately fatal wound. The Indians disagreed, however, and stated that the bow was the best of weapons for running the buffalo, that even the old-time White men, who had only the muzzle-loading guns, were quick to adopt the bow and arrows in running buffalo. They admitted that a powerful arm and a strong wrist were necessary to send an arrow deep into a buffalo, yet they often saw arrows driven through buffalo.[9]

Experts who have conducted tests with ancient Plains weapons have determined that the average arrow cast from a bow travels at about 150 feet per second as compared to a pitched baseball at about 60 feet per second. At a short distance, its striking weight is about 25 pounds, as compared to 3000 foot-pounds for a high-powered rifle. And they admit that within its range the Plains arrow was capable of killing a large animal as quickly and cleanly as a rifle bullet.[10]

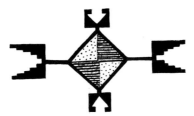

Indians have not recorded their names for bow parts nor their words used to describe the bow's action. But the archers of more recent times have coined terms to describe its use, and these will be adapted herein to simplify the discussion of the bow.

The parts of the bow consist of upper and lower limbs, a center handle or handgrip, and the upper and lower nocks or notches which hold the string. The belly or front is the part of the bow facing the archer—the back is the part which is curved away from the archer when the bow is strung.

When a bow is "braced" or strung up, the average taut string is five and a half to six inches from the inside of the handle of the bow. The height of the curve is adjusted by twisting or untwisting the string.

The ends of the bow are called wings.

An unstrung bow which reverses its curve when braced is called "reflexed" or "recurved," while one which maintains some conventional curvature is described as "following the string."

The distance a bow can shoot is called its cast.

The strength or pull of a bow is measured by the number of foot-pounds required to pull it. Smooth-pulling and well-balanced bows are called "soft" or "sweet" bows.

The Plains Indian made two types of bows, a self-bow, made of a single long piece of wood, and a compound bow, made of several layers of wood, bone, or horn, glued and lashed together. Either of these can have the word "backed" added when sinew backing has been added to them.

Horn bows, probably always sinew-backed, were used by Shoshone, Crow, Blackfoot, Nez Percé, Cheyenne, and Gros Ventre tribes. In 1875 James S. Belden, a trapper, published this description of them:

They take a large horn or prong, and saw a slice off each side of it; these slices are then filed or rubbed down until the flat sides fit together, when they are glued and strapped at the ends. Four slices make a bow, it being jointed. Another piece of horn is laid on the center of the bow at the grasp, where it is glued fast. The whole is then filed down until it is perfectly ornamented, carved and painted. It takes an Indian about three months to make one.[11]

Colonel Dodge described the horn bow as follows:

A good bow takes a long time and much care and labor in its construction. Those most highly prized among the Indians of central North America are ingeniously fabricated by carefully fitting together pieces of elk-horn, the whole glued together, and tightly wrapped with strips of the smaller intestines of deer, or slender threads of sinew, used wet, and which, when dry, tighten and unite all the parts into one compact and homogeneous whole, said to be stronger, tougher, more elastic, and more durable than a bow of any other materials. The great difficulty of its construction, the fact that it is liable to become useless in wet, or even damp weather, and the more general use of firearms, have rendered obsolete this particular make of weapon, and it can now scarcely be found,

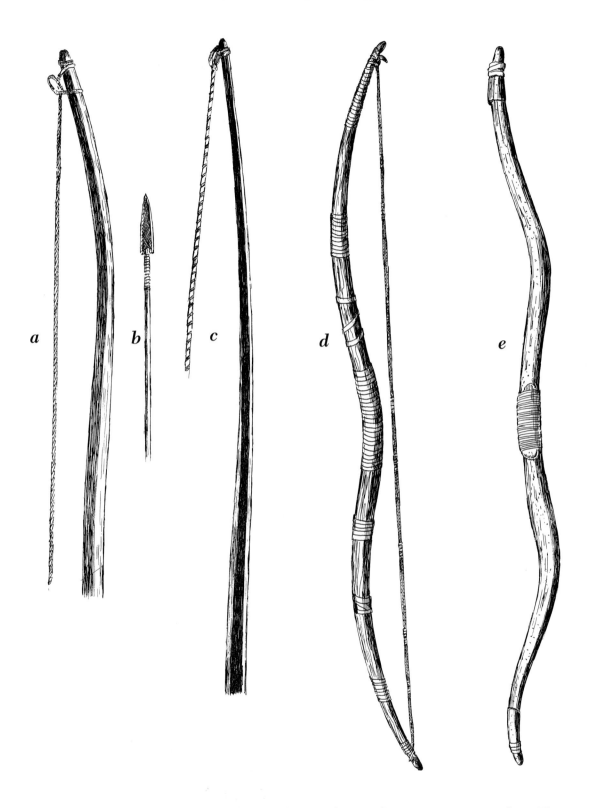

Bow styles. *a*, northern Plains curved bow. *b*, size of arrow for comparison. *c*, northern Plains straight bow. *d*, sinew-backed and -wrapped bow. *e*, horn bow.

except in museums, or kept as heirlooms, handed down from father to son in some principal family.[12]

Catlin insisted that horn bows were made of one piece of an anonymous material, probably obtained in trade from coastal Indians.[13] Horn bows were usually recurved. Alfred Jacob Miller stated that the smartest Yankee there was could not even find it convenient to attempt to make such a bow; that they were so good each one brought two fine horses in trade.[14]

The Crow, Blackfoot, and Gros Ventre warriors sometimes covered their bows with the skin of a rattlesnake. In this case the skin was glued to the bow, and served as waterproofing.

The bow in most common use by far among the Indians was made of wood. The preferred wood was Osage orange, called the "bois d'arc" by the French trappers, and commonly called "bow dark" by White frontiersmen. This wood grew in a comparatively limited area of the north country, however, and long, perilous journeys were required to obtain it. So those who made the trip brought back whole ponyloads of the valuable commodity, and made a good thing of the risks involved by trading off the surplus. Whenever Osage orange could not be obtained, the Indians used ash, white elm, ironwood, cedar, 'willow, dogwood, mulberry, indeed almost any wood; for even the most brittle kinds, when cut into layers, fitted, glued, backed, and wound with sinew, made a bow of service-able strength, though lacking in elasticity. The White traders sometimes sold the Indians straight, well-grained pieces of oak, hickory, and even yew wood for use in making bows.

Blackfoot bows were generally made of ash, which grew east of their mountains "toward the Sand Hills." When they could not obtain ash, they used the wood of the chokecherry tree, but this did not have the strength or spring to be of much service. In an emergency they even used hazelwood for bows.

Ash and ironwood are said to have been preferred by the Omahas, and the Osage orange by the Comanches; the Chicago National Museum has several Crow bows which are made of hickory and one of ash.

The Indians determined the length of their bows in a number of ways (bow length was usually determined as the distance between nocks):

1. "Each man determined the length of his bow by his own measurements. He made it as long as the distance from his right shoulder across his chest and outstretched left arm to the tips of the fingers on his left hand. The average Plains bow was from 35 to 48 inches long."[15]

2. "The proper length of an Indian bow was sometimes determined by holding the bow-stave diagonally across the body, with one end of it held in the right hand at the hip and the other just touching the finger tips of the left hand when held straight out to the side, shoulder high. This made a bow about four feet long."[16]

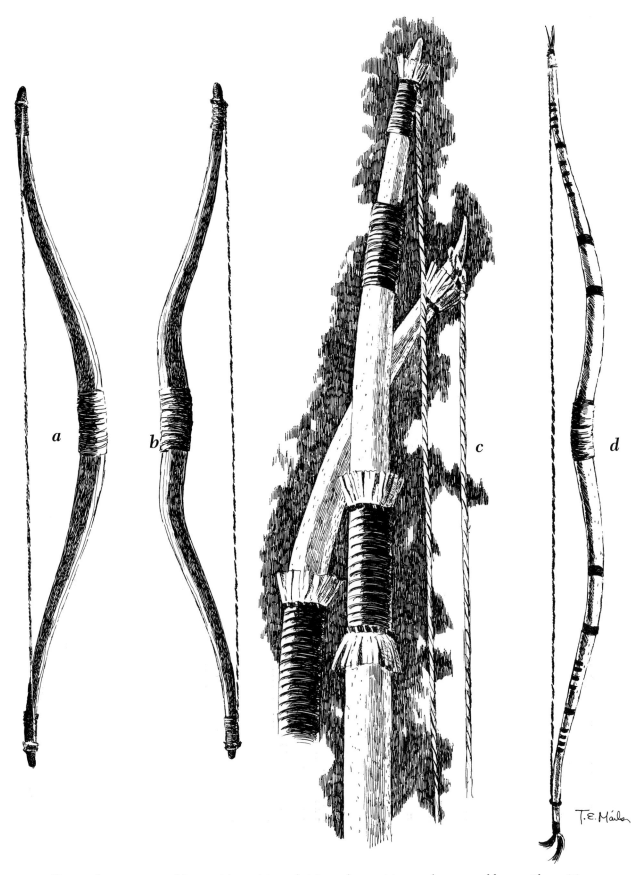

Bow styles. *a*, recurved bow with position of string when not in use. *b*, recurved bow with position of string when bow was ready for action. *c*, two Crow horn bow limbs and wings. *d*, Assiniboine horn bow.

Steps in manufacturing bows. *a*, cutting bow from limb. *b*, measuring length of bow. *c*, shaping bow by bending over knee. *d*, method of determining grip thickness and cross sections through limb. *e*, method of measuring wing tips. *f*, typical northern Plains notches. *g*, sinew-wrapped wing

tip. *h*, shaping bow by heating and bending. *i*, grooving bow in preparation for sinew. *j*, roughing bow with sandstone in preparation for sinew. *k*, applying sinew. *l*, sprinkling powdered clay between sinew layers. *m*, glue stick of type carried in quiver for repairs.

3. "The bow-length of the Plains Indian measured from the front inside point of the left side of his pelvis diagonally upward across the diaphragm to the tips of the fingers of the extended right arm and hand. Roughly this was about 4 feet. If it seemed too long he closed his hand and still violated no rules; and then he frequently heated it, and bent curves into it to further shorten it."[17]

4. "The bow was cut to a length equal in height to the distance from the owner's waist to the ground."[18]

As examples of length, a Blackfoot bow collected in 1870 was 3 feet 5 inches long, and Catlin gives 3 feet as the standard length among the Crows and the Blackfeet in the 1830s.[19] However, several bows in different collections are longer than those Catlin mentions. A Blackfoot bow measures 40 inches, a Cree 44 inches, an Osage $47\frac{1}{2}$ inches, a Cheyenne 45 inches, and another Blackfoot $47\frac{1}{4}$ inches. Some ancient Plains bows I've measured are $47\frac{1}{2}$ inches, 42 inches, and 40 inches.

The northern Indians cut wood enough to make several bows in late winter when the sap was still down. Winter wood did not split while drying. But the Omahas preferred February, when the wood was green and the sap was down. Once the staves were cut and the bow maker had trimmed off their outer bark, he rubbed them with animal fat, wrapped them in a hide bundle, and hung them at the top of the lodge, directly over the fire where the lodge poles crossed. (The Sioux say they dried them by the fire as the bow was carved over a two-week period.) The rising heat and the smoke seasoned the wood, and when the stave was at last ready, the warrior carefully shaped it from the grip out with his knife until it was ready for a final smoothing with a piece of sandstone. A young ash killed by a prairie fire was also considered an excellently seasoned bow wood.

Most Plains bows were straighter and flatter than one usually thinks when unstrung, but some craftsmen, considering them more powerful, preferred to make their bows with graceful curves. To obtain these curves they rubbed the tapered limbs with buffalo fat, and then heated one limb of the bow at a time over the fire. When it was quite hot it was either bent over the knee or else the end was placed on the ground, a foot was put on the heated part, and it was slowly bent to the desired curve. The bow was held in this position until the wood cooled and the curve became permanent. The other limb or wing was then bent in the same manner, but it took great patience and frequent reheating to make the second curve exactly like the first.

It took a month or more to make a first-class bow, and since they did break on occasion, the warriors usually kept several on hand. On war trips they always carried more than one bow, although a man could make a temporary one of most any wood to shoot game in an emergency.

The thickness and stiffness of the bow at the handle was of considerable importance. If the handle was thin and weak, and bent ever so slightly, the bow would "kick," and the string would lash the wrist. This was always more noticeable in a bow made of heavy wood. Some bows were covered at the grip area with a piece of hide or wound with sinew, but most of the handgrips were left plain. Limb ends were much smaller than the grip, being tapered to the thickness of the little finger. Some Plains bows were of the recurved type; that is, their mid-sections curved inward toward the archer, and the bow reversed its curve then strung. The members of some Sioux societies added a bone, stone, or metal spear point to one end of a straight bow so that the bow would double as a lance, but bows were not often employed in this way in battle.

Sinew-backed bows were found among the Ute, Crow, Blackfoot, Sioux, Cree, Cheyenne, and Hidatsa tribes, but not among the tribes of the southeast areas. The sinew which was used for backing bows is a smooth animal muscle of irregular width, long and flat in its cross section. The preferred piece was taken from both sides of the buffalo's backbone, although deer and elk back and leg sinews were also used. A piece of buffalo sinew measured about three feet in length, while those of other animals seldom measured more than eighteen inches. The sinew was soaked in water, pounded, and finally stripped thin and shredded. When shredded it looked very much like a yellowish, somewhat mangled telephone cable, and it is a marvel that the Indians could do the wonders they did with it.

Every Indian, male and female, carried a supply of sinew—either in a flat piece or in a braid. When they were ready to apply it they wet it again, and placed the shredded pieces in their mouth.

It was applied along the back of the bow in overlapping layers, interspersed with sprinkled layers of powdered white clay, which were stuck on with glue. After the gluing, the bow and its reinforcement were wound about with additional bands of damp sinew that shrank tight as they dried.

Some bow makers roughened the back of the bow limbs by scraping them with a piece of sandstone or flint, or else they made diagonal cuts at regular intervals. Then they smeared the bow with glue obtained by boiling either the scrapings of buffalo hoofs, buffalo horns, or rawhide in a small amount of water. On top of this glue they laid successive layers of overlapping narrow strips of deer or buffalo sinew. Since the single sinew strips were not long enough to run the full length of a forty-inch bow, two pieces were butted together at the handle and extended out to the ends of the wings. The number of sinew and clay coats determined how strong the bow would be in resisting snapping, but it should be borne in mind that the addition of sinew did not help the "cast" or distance a bow would shoot.

In a slightly different method of manufacture, when a bow was nearing completion, sinew was applied in layers in a thick coating of warm glue, then bound with strips of bark or canvas or rawhide, after which the bow was set to season for a while. After seasoning, the wrapping was removed, the glue was smoothed by scraping, a handle of soft hide was applied, and the bow was painted.

By the time several coats of the glue and clay mixture had been applied the bow coating was a dull, transparent, and grayish color, so the back and front were decorated in different designs with paint. The Sioux often painted the back blue and the front yellow, or else used alternating stripes of red and green. Then the bow was coated once more with transparent glue to preserve the colors. Usually a tuft of colored horse mane, or of human hair taken from an enemy, was tied to the top of the bow, which was, in theory, always to the right of the Indian's hand when held horizontally, and above it when held vertically.

The Comanches made their glue from bull hide shavings or from horns and hoofs. These materials were boiled in water, and when very thick were gathered on a wooden stick about the size of a pencil which was carried in the bow case. Whenever glue was needed for repair work, the end of the stick was softened in hot water and the glue was ready for use.

The final step before painting was to notch the bow, and there were various methods of doing this. Northern bows usually had a single notch at each end and southern bows employed a double notch at the end where the string would be slipped down to release the tension when the bow was not in use.

Most bowstrings were made of several pieces of sinew, stripped down to filament size and twisted together. A good string melded so smoothly, though, that when it was finished it looked like a single piece. Usually either the buffalo's sinew or the long strips from the leg of a deer were used for bowstrings. A man split off two strands from the large piece with his teeth, wet them, and started to roll them together on his leg. A third piece was placed slightly below and between these, and all three were rolled together with the palm of the hand. Pieces were added as the rolling continued to make a cord about three times the length of the bow. This was then folded in thirds and twisted to form a three-ply bowstring. The string was then stretched and put out to dry, with the ends tied in knots to prevent unraveling. When placing the string on the bow, the bow maker wound the string tightly and fast to the bow at one end—the end to be kept in the lower end of the bow case—and he fastened the other end with a half-hitch loop which could be slipped loose and down when the bow was not in use. The Kiowas made a second and lower notch or "nock" in the top end of the bow which the string could be slipped into. A bow kept taut for too long a time became more bent. Also, the sinew would stretch and lose its spring. In fact, a taut bowstring needed constant attention, for it stretched when the weather was wet, and if, on the other hand, it was not moistened a bit now and then, it shrank and would snap when the weather was dry. So the warriors kept their bows and strings well protected in a case and always had several extra strings on hand.

While most bowstrings were made from sinew, they were also made from rawhide strips and twisted vegetable fibers. Bear's guts made strong bowstrings, and some southern Indians used squirrel hide.

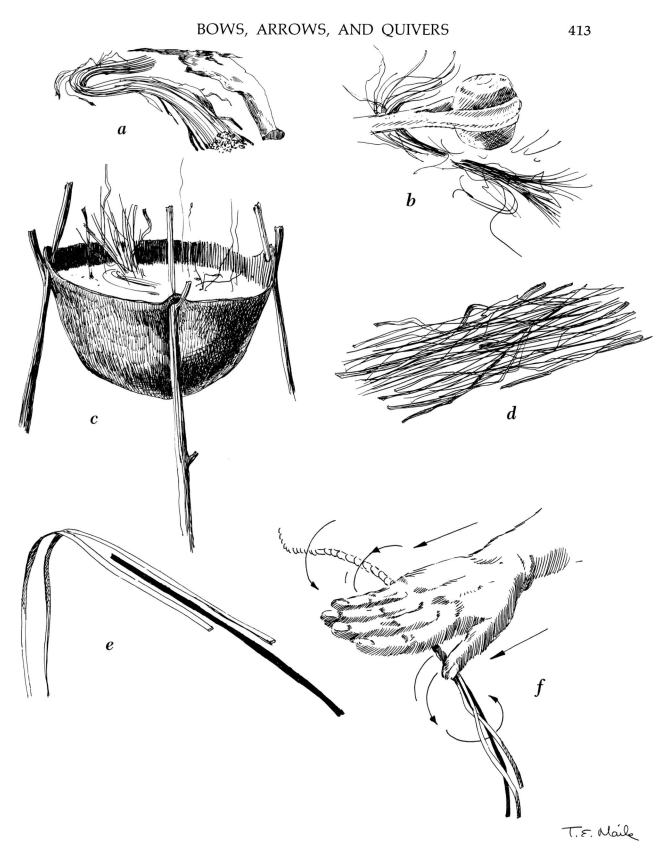

Sinew. Methods of preparation. *a*, raw sinew. *b*, pounding to soften with berrymasher. *c*, boiling in water. *d*, shredded sinew. *e*, method of splicing. *f*, rolling pieces together.

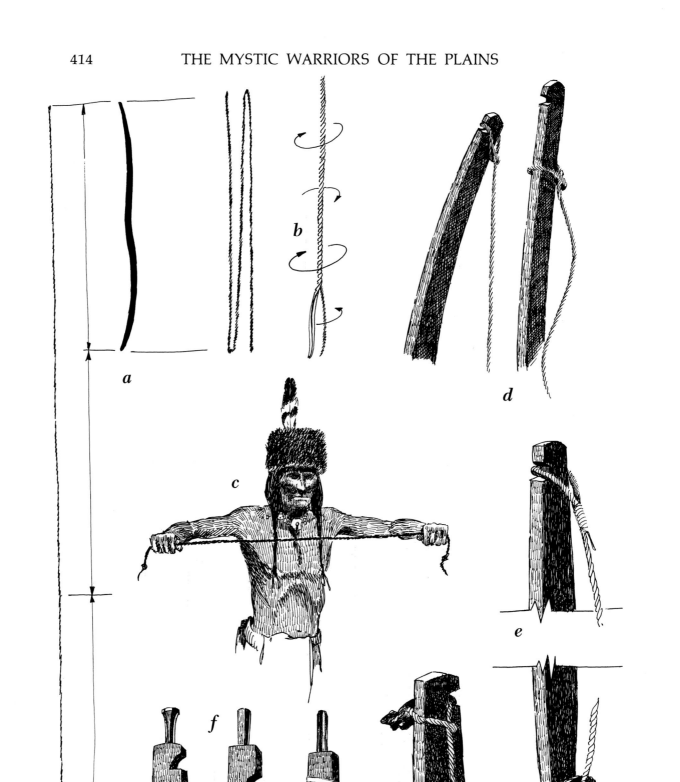

Bowstring. *a*, means of determining length of string. *b*, string folded twice and twisted to make finished string. *c*, stretching for final preparation. *d* and *e*, methods of tying bowstrings to bow. *f*, types of notches used by Indians of southern Plains.

Every Indian warrior was capable of making his own arrows, but there were also specialists who excelled in their manufacture. These arrow makers gathered unto themselves special tools and devices for use in their art. Indeed, some authorities believe that the making of the ancient stone arrowheads was a factory job, because finishing sites have been found in large numbers near the places of supply where the roughing out was done.

As in the case of the bow, the Indians did not employ the sophisticated names for the parts of the arrow which are used today. Still, the modern names are very helpful as one considers the arrow.

The wooden stick itself is called the shaft. The notch cut in the shaft to hold the bowstring is called the nock. The process of adding the feathers to the shaft is called fletching. Putting the long impression lines in the shaft is called grooving. The part of the shaft which receives the arrowhead is called the head. The process of marking the arrow with colored bands of paint is called cresting.

The woods used by the Plains Indians to make their arrows were gooseberry, Juneberry, chokecherry, ash, birch, cane, dogwood, currant, willow, and wild cherry saplings. The Sioux preferred gooseberry, with cherry and Juneberry as second choices. The Blackfoot used shoots of the sarvis berry wood, which was straight, very heavy, and not brittle.

There were three methods which were used for measuring the length of an arrow:

1. The length was determined by the distance from the elbow to the finger tip, plus the length of the small finger.[20]

2. The stick was grasped so that the butt was even with the bottom of the left hand, then the arrow maker measured hand over hand six times, a length which averaged twenty-four inches.[21]

3. The Indian measured the length of his arrows by placing one end of the shaft against his breastbone and stretching his arms out in front of him with his fingers extended. The length of the shaft was determined by the point where the tips of his middle fingers touched when he put his hands together.[22]

As compared to the other Indian tribes of North America the Plains Indians used a short, sturdy arrow with long fletching feathers. Arrow dimensions always include the arrowhead. Generally speaking, arrow shafts were proportionate in

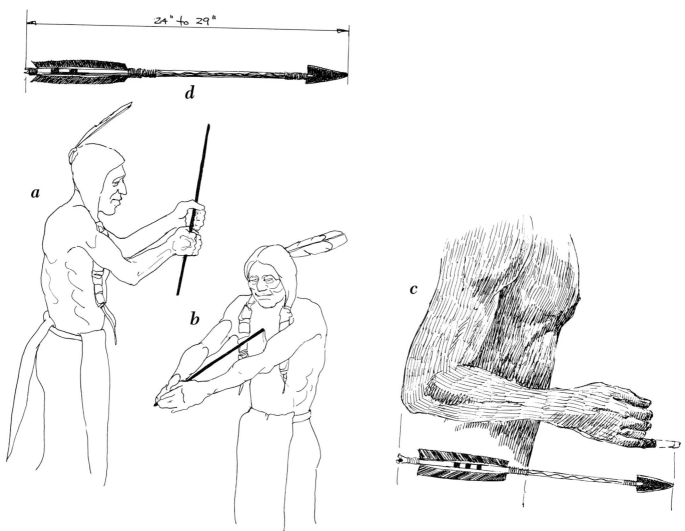

Steps in manufacturing arrows. *a*, *b*, and *c*, methods of determining length of shaft. *d*, length of average Plains arrow.

length to the bows. Blackfoot arrows in the Chicago Museum measure an average of twenty-five and a half inches in length, approximately the same as Sioux and Cheyenne shafts. As a rule, museum arrows range in thickness from five sixteenths to one half of an inch in diameter, with war arrows being heavier than hunting arrows. The average Plains arrow weighed about an ounce, therefore a full quiver weighed scarcely more than twenty ounces!

Arrow sticks were cut in late winter, about February, when the sap was down. In this condition the wood did not split while drying. Second-growth wood was the best.

Straight, knot-free saplings were hard to find. The arrow maker selected sticks which were free of branches, as smooth as possible, and about the thickness of

Arrow manufacturing continued. *a*, green sticks wrapped in hide. *b*, bundle hung in tipi to cure.
*c*, bark removed from sticks. *d*, greasing and heating to shape shaft.

his little finger. After he had cut them to the proper length, he tied them into bundles of twenty or so each, wrapped them with a hide cover, and, like the bow staves, hung them at the top of the tipi, where they would be smoked by the lodge fire for several weeks. This process seasoned the wood of the shafts and killed any insects that might be in them.

Once the shafts were well seasoned, the warrior took them down, removed them from their wrappings, and peeled the bark carefully away from each stick. Then he scraped them smooth. To give the arrows a uniform thickness he pushed them back and forth through a tubular groove in the center of two pieces of sandstone, some of which carried a special mark to identify their owners. The hole, like a little tunnel, was formed by holding the two pieces of stone together. If a curve or crook was in the shaft, the warrior rubbed it with fat, heated it, and then straightened it out in one of three ways: Either he bent it with his hands and held it till it cooled; or else he drew the heated shaft through a hole in a stone or rib or horn, such as a ram's horn; or else he had a wooden, bone, or stone wrench he could use. Any method was tedious and time-consuming. After each straightening, the sanding would continue.

The nock to fit the bowstring was then cut at one end. The nock was V-shaped for a fiber bowstring, and U-shaped for a sinew or rawhide bowstring. The type and size of the arrow nock suggested a number of things about its owner. If it was a deep cut, the fingers of the drawing hand hooked around the string with the arrow being held between two of the fingers. In this case the string, rather than the arrow, was pulled back; the arrow simply rode along because it was pinched between the fingers. It has been said that Sioux Indians used this release. Shallow nocks usually indicated a child's arrow. The wide, flaring nock meant the owner pinched the end between his thumb and finger, and the pinch was the weakest of all holds. Even with the large nock, a twenty-five-pound pull would still be about maximum.

After this the arrow maker cut a thin slit, perhaps three quarters of an inch deep, at the head of the arrow shaft in which to insert the arrowhead. The slits varied in depth according to the owner's preference and the type of arrowhead to be used. The arrowhead was then placed in the slit and secured with glue and a binding of sinew. Arrowheads made for different purposes were attached in different ways, and these will be considered shortly.

Once the head was attached, the arrow was grooved. This is a curious but almost universal characteristic of the Plains arrow. The shallow grooves, sometimes one, sometimes two, usually three of them, often run the length of the shaft from head to feathers. Occasionally they are straight, but more often they are unevenly wavy, or roughly zigzag. It has been said they were intended to represent lightning, hence power and speed; that they were thought to prevent warping and make the arrows fly straighter; and that they were intended to make game bleed more freely, and thus to leave a trail for the hunter to follow. The choice between opinions is always said to be "an open one." Surely the Indians thought them exceedingly important, for it must have taken considerable labor to put them on an arrow.

It will be helpful to think about this for a moment, and in making a decision, the following should be weighed: Even a cursory examination shows that the grooves were too shallow to help in preventing warpage or in bleeding an animal. Some Plains arrows had short grooves and a few had no grooves at all. Then too, hunters discovered that the animals died more from internal hemorrhage than anything else. One hunter mentions he shot a buffalo and found the animal to be full of blood from internal bleeding. Likewise shots through a bear's chest

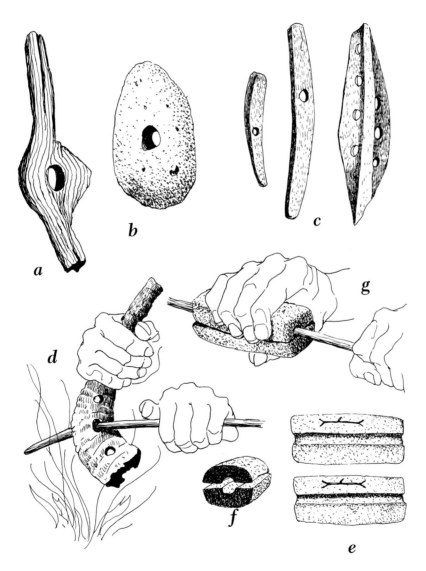

Arrow shaft-straightening wrenches. *a*, horn. *b*, sandstone. *c*, ribs. *d*, horn wrench in use. Sanding stones. *e*, marked pair. *f*, end view of pair placed together. *g*, sanding stones in use.

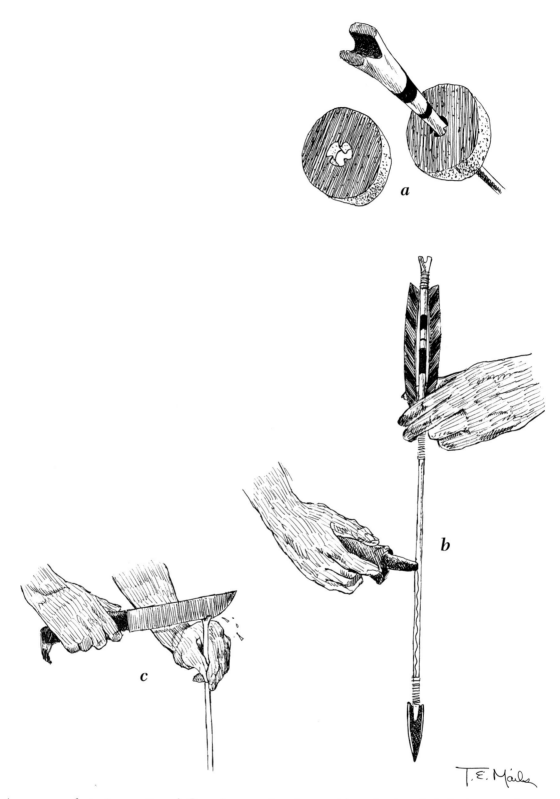

Arrow manufacturing continued. Grooving. *a*, using stones with projections in hole. *b*, using sharp stone stylus. *c*, notching arrow for nock.

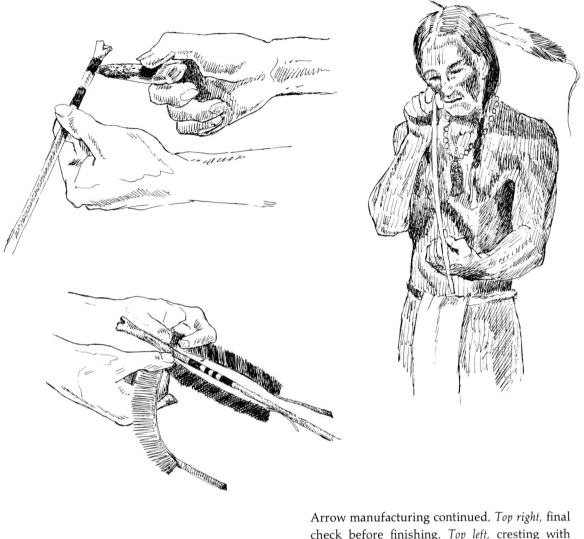

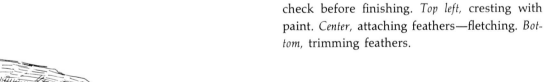

Arrow manufacturing continued. *Top right,* final check before finishing. *Top left,* cresting with paint. *Center,* attaching feathers—fletching. *Bottom,* trimming feathers.

and body caused a tremendous flooding of the entire chest cavity and abdomen with blood. Therefore, an experienced Indian hunter would not be concerned about the small bit of external bleeding there might be if the animal ran and worked the vibrating arrow back and forth. I have come to the conclusion that the grooves had a religious purpose. They were added while the arrows were bathed in prayers and incantations designed to enable them to strike unerringly and bring down their targets. The size and variety of grooves admit to almost no other purpose, and a religious conclusion truly fits the Indian mood. An Indian did not need a few spots of blood to trail a running animal which left abundant and incisive tracks.

Some have believed that the grooves were made in the arrow by passing it through a rib or bone or stone in which had been made a round hole with one or two projections on the inside. However, if this is so, only a single line at a time could have been made. The groove lines are not parallel, and one always zigs where the other zags. The grooves also vary greatly in depth, whereas they would have been uniform had they been made by a fixed projection. This probably means they were pressed into the wood by running a sharp piece of bone or stone along the shaft. There are other possibilities too, such as pressing the arrow down on a upright point while drawing it under the hand—which would be easier, and more reliable still. The idea was expressed that grooves were put in with the teeth. It could be done, but the method lacks verification by the Indians as a usual technique. The grooves were usually put on before the arrow was fletched and before the arrowhead was fastened on—since they often run under the sinew wrappings at both ends of the shaft.

After grooving, the arrow was crested with the owner's identifying bands of color. These were of an endless variety in style and colors since each man had his own easily distinguishable pattern. The paint was applied with porous bone brushes after the manner explained in the chapter on paints and painting. Sometimes the entire arrow was painted in one or more colors. Sioux war arrows were now and then colored a dull, sacred red except for the head, which for a length of some four inches was yellow. Wide blue and red bands were used in combinations too, and some arrows had paint rubbed in the grooves.

The final step in arrow making was the feathering or fletching. Arrow feathers came from the wings of various birds, chiefly from the eagle and the wild turkey, although hawk, owl, and even parrot feathers were also used. Feathers from a given wing were used on the same arrow. When split and fastened to the arrow these feathers gave it a twisting or spinning motion like that of a bullet fired from a rifle.

Some bird and fish hunting arrows received no feathers and some knob-headed hunting arrows had two. But most war and buffalo arrows were fletched with three feathers, set an equal distance apart around the circumference of the shaft. The Cheyenne used rather short feathers, but most tribes used feathers from six to eight inches long and at least one fourth the length of the shaft. Fletching feathers were fastened with glue and then lashed with sinew. In most cases the middle sections of the feathers were bowed to a slight curve and left free, with only the ends being glued and tied down with sinew. All Plains arrows were trimmed to about half an inch at the forward end, and to about one inch at the

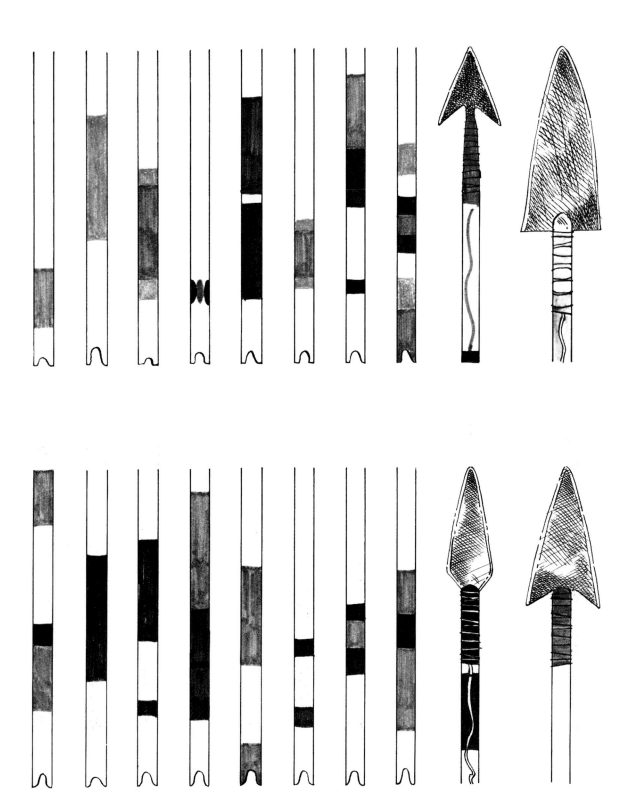

An assemblage of actual crests and markings used on Plains arrows.

Sioux chief Standing Bear putting sinew wrapping on arrow and holding sinew in mouth in traditional manner.

rear. There was a little-used method of fletching whereby one or two very long feathers were themselves spiraled around the arrow shaft to make it spin better.

The glue used for arrows was the same as that employed in putting sinew on the bow. Arrow glue was often colored with ocher. It was usually collected and stored on short sticks, then softened for use by boiling it in water or heating it over a low fire. The arrow maker chewed his sinew to soften it before use.

His mouth served as his spool to hold it as he wound the sinew onto the arrow. When it dried, it was as hard and fast as an iron band—with the advantage of not rusting but the disadvantage of loosening when exposed to continual wetness.

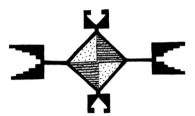

The arrowhead is about as intriguing a part of the Indian arsenal as one could possibly consider. Frank Linderman declares that the Plains Indians of the eighteenth and nineteenth centuries neither made nor used stone points—that some other earlier people fashioned them. About 1886 he began to make careful inquiry among very old Indians, and he did not discover a single tribesman who had ever heard of his own people making stone arrow points. The old men told him that before the White man came their arrow points were fashioned out of bone.[23] Adding this to what others have said, it appears that the Plains Indians of the horse-nomad period did not make stone points, although, they did use them. They found those which were used on their arrows lying on the ground as they traveled about. Herman Lehmann tempers all this a little by telling how, when he lived with the Comanches, he employed their method of making "flintstone arrow spikes."[24] Except for such stone points as were found, the usual nineteenth-century war arrowhead was made of iron or steel, furnished by the Whites—and the references herein will be to that type *only*, the exception being the rarer bone and sinew hunting points, and the wooden bird and small animal points.

The White traders manufactured quantities of sheet iron points for trade purposes, but the other point sources for Indians were the metal tie bands of barrels and the bottoms of frying pans. When a wagon train was captured, these were considered prime booty. The barrel bands were easily cut into shape and sharpened with files obtained by trade or capture, with each band delivering twenty or more heads.

The shape of the iron arrowhead indicated the use to which it was put. Hunting arrows had long, tapering blades which were firmly fastened to the shaft and could easily be withdrawn from the wound. The war arrow had a sharp blade, like a lancet, with the rear shoulders angled forward, forming barbs; their attachment to the shaft was very slight, as it was intended that the head should come off and remain in the wound, killing eventually, if not immediately.

The war arrowhead can easily be distinguished from the hunting point. If one looks at the design of the head and sees that it would resist being pulled back out of the wound, it's a war point. Some have triangular points pointing back, but others are simply cut straight across the rear end of the point. A war arrowhead could not be extracted by pulling it back out. To remove the war arrowhead, the victim had to suffer the excruciating pain of having the head either cut out or pushed on through his body. If an arrowhead could be pulled back out, the victim had been shot with a hunting arrow. Also, arrowheads often caused war arrow shafts to split on impact, further loosening the point. Since the head ends of the arrow shaft were deeply notched to receive the points this most assuredly happened on occasion, and made withdrawal, or even the pushing of the point, impossible. The back of the hunting arrowhead was rounded and glued and tightly lashed so that it could be withdrawn and used again. To facilitate withdrawal further the iron hunting head was filed sharp on its round back edges as well as on the point.

The arrowhead varied in length and shape, and the shaft itself was altered slightly according to the tastes of the different bands or tribes; and yet so constantly were arrows exchanged in gambling or barter that the character of the arrow used did not invariably determine the tribe engaged. The head was generally from two to three and a half inches in length, made of iron, and filed to a double edge. Some vicious-looking barbed points are amazingly small, though, measuring an inch or less in length.

The few southern Plains Indian tribes who lived where they could get reeds used these on rare occasions for arrows, and considered them very good because they were so much lighter than solid wood. However, the reed was much too fragile to hold a stone or metal tip, and it could not be notched, so the Indians had to insert short pieces of hardwood in both ends. They cut the reed shafts

---

PLATE 21. SIOUX APPAREL—CLOTHING STUDY NO. 2 ▶

Typical Sioux clothing worn by the foremost men of a given band.

The man on the left wears a painted men's society shirt, green on the upper half and yellow on the lower half. Around his neck is a metal cross symbol of the four winds fashioned from silver obtained from the Whites. His shirt is fringed with hairlocks. In ancient days these came from scalps taken from enemies—but later the hair came from tribal members who donated it for the wearer to use to symbolize the people who were his responsibility.

The man on the right wears a vertical hair-pipe necklace made of large bone beads. His pipe bag is covered with dyed porcupine quills. His leggings have beaded strips down them and his shirt has quilled bands on the sleeves and over the shoulders.

Eagle feather bonnets reminded the wearer of the solar bird—and they were arranged to symbolize the radiating shafts of light which brought wisdom from God, who some tribes thought dwelt in the center of the sun.

longer than wood, since they were lighter. The cut at the end near each tip was made just beyond one of the joints of the reed, so there would be a hard ring where the joint was, and the shallow cup which always began the next section of the reed received the hardwood pieces. The arrow maker pushed a six-inch stick of hardwood into the cup. He tapered its ends so that it would just fit. Then he gummed it where it emerged from the reed with pinion gum, and wrapped sinew around the outside of the reed to hold it tight. The head of the hardwood stick could be sharpened like a pencil to a self-point, or it could be notched to hold a stone or metal tip. At the back end of the reed the arrow maker inserted a small plug of hardwood. Then he cut the traditional kind of nock in it. However, most reed arrows seen in museums today are not Plains arrows, they are those of Navaho or California tribes.

The Sauk arrow makers frequently made antler-tip arrowheads. The antler was boiled in plain water for several hours until it softened so that it could be easily whittled into shape. The prongs were detached by scoring with notches and then breaking, and a conical opening was made in the porous base to receive the head end of the arrow shaft. The gluey substance which had been removed was then replaced, and the shaft thrust in. As it cooled, the joint itself became very hard and firm and the arrowhead stuck tenaciously to the shaft. When this

---

◄ PLATE 22. CLOTHING DECORATION—CLOTHING STUDY NO. 3

The man on the left wears the old-style Crow shirt of the early nineteenth century. Note the length, and particularly how the animal's leg skins were left to dangle, providing detail and motion. The shirt has quilled bands and a triangular bib. The leggings are adorned with quilled bands also, and the moccasins are covered with bright red porcupine quills. Quilling was a craft in which the Plains Indian women excelled, and they did it better than anyone else in the world. The man's head covering is a unique type—probably Assiniboine. It has split buffalo horns on it, and a tail of eagle feathers. He has a quirt in his left hand, and the type of lance used in war in the other. War lances were short, usually no more than seven feet in length. It has an iron point—of the type often obtained from the Spaniards.

The man on the right wears a shirt which has been painted green—with dark blue stripes placed over the green. Zigzag lines such as these indicated lightning, and infused its power and sudden speed into the warrior who wore them. The arms of the shirt are fringed with human hairlocks, and there are porcupine quilled bands on the sleeves and shoulders. Orange dye was often used for such bands. The legging strips are beaded in a geometric design common to the Sioux from 1800 to 1840.

Both men wear typical trade-cloth breechclouts, which were tucked between the legs and over a thong belt front and back.

The two costumes shown are in the Southwest Museum in Highland Park, Los Angeles.

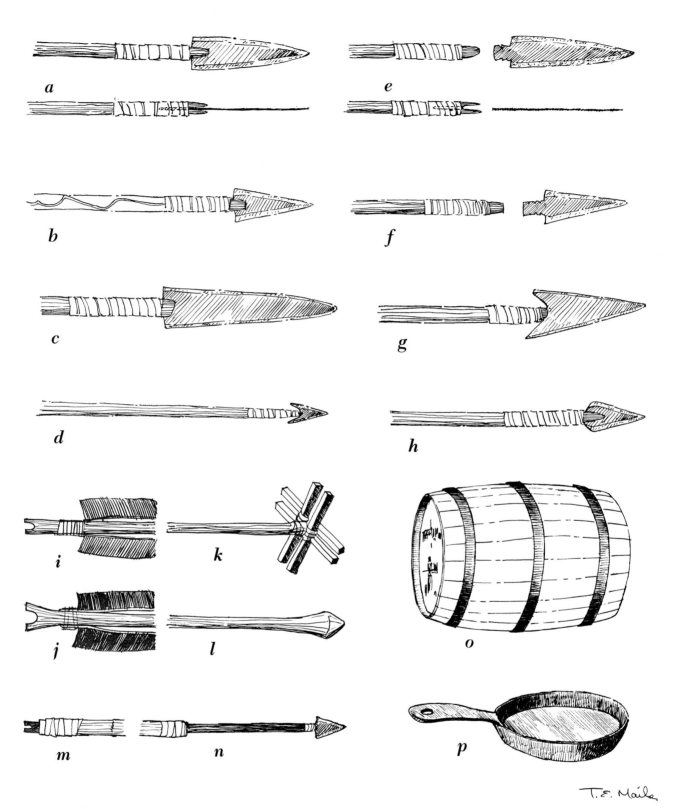

Plains arrowheads. *a, b, c, d, e, f,* and *g,* trade metal war arrowheads. *h,* steel hunting arrowhead. *i,* nock used by hunter and warrior. *j,* flanged nock of type used by boys. *k* and *l,* wooden bird and small-game points. *m,* hardwood plug nocked for reed arrow. *n,* reed arrow with hardwood tip. *o,* barrel hoops used for arrowheads. *p,* frying pan bottoms used for arrowheads. Stove parts were also desired by the Indians as arrowhead material.

was done, the dried and hardened prong was usually sharpened by grating it on a rough stone.

A few tribes used poison on some of their war arrow points, employing dried rattlesnake poison or some special concoctions made of boiled herbs and rodent skins. More probably, however, it was the rust or dried matter on the arrow points which caused infection damage, although the Comanches declared that they never used an arrow a second time which had killed a man, enemy, or friend, for it was stained with human blood.

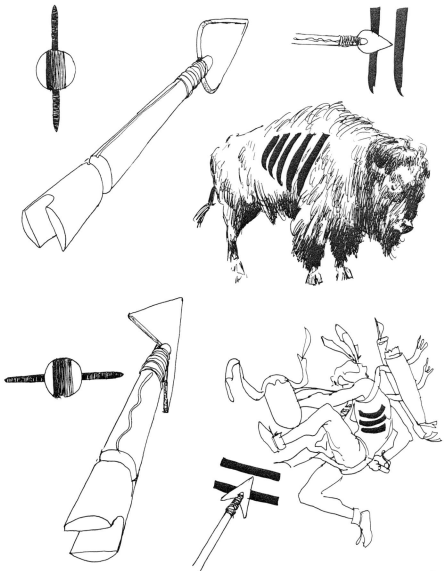

*Top,* placement of arrowhead in same plane as nock for hunting buffalo and other large game animals. *Bottom,* reversing plane to right angle for war arrow used in fighting against men. While these details are often described in Indian literature, their actual use has not been proven. They do, however, fit the Indians' religious approach to hunting and war, a fact which reinforces the possibility of head placement in relation to nock by at least some warriors.

The Comanches and some other tribes placed the blade of the hunting arrow in the same plane with the notch for the string, so that it would more surely pass between the ribs of the animal, which are vertical. For the same reason, the blade of the war arrow was placed perpendicular to the notch, the ribs of the human enemy being horizontal. However, since the arrow rotated in flight, it is doubtful that an arrow hit precisely as the warrior imagined it would.

Some Plains Indians used stiff buffalo sinew points on their buffalo arrows. The sinew point would bend around a bone instead of breaking when it struck it. The arrows used for birds and very small animals had blunted wooden points carved something like the shape of a top. Other small game points were split into prongs, and still others had small sticks set crosswise in the end.

The Assiniboines used six kinds of arrows, with the principal difference being found in the points. Some of their arrow points were of flint, bone, or iron, there was an arrow that tapered to a sharp point, a dull-pointed target arrow, and finally a knob-headed arrow used for either targets or game. Their boy's first bows were usually made of chokecherry wood. Tall slough grass, dried and cut to suitable lengths, served as their arrows, with the hard butts or joints being held against the bowstring. The Assiniboines said that a full quiver for a warrior on a war party was thirty arrows—far less than the hundred it is often claimed warriors carried. Most Indian accounts for all tribes mention taking only twenty or so arrows per warrior on a war party.

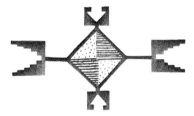

To transport their bows and arrows, the Plains Indians evolved a tapered, somewhat tubular case known as a quiver, and later added a bow case which was coupled with the quiver. This combination of cases became a model of efficiency for their purposes, and it's a pleasing experience to discover how they worked.

The earliest Plains quivers were very simple. Most were an unornamented bag of rawhide or buckskin, closed at one end and open at the other, which carried both the arrows and one or more bows. It was similar to the Woodlands type of case used by the eastern Indians. As the years went by, many of these bags were made of more luxurious skins such as that of the otter. The tail of the otter was appended to the open end of the bag in such a way as to hang like a huge pendant, and the pendant was highly decorated with porcupine quills, and later

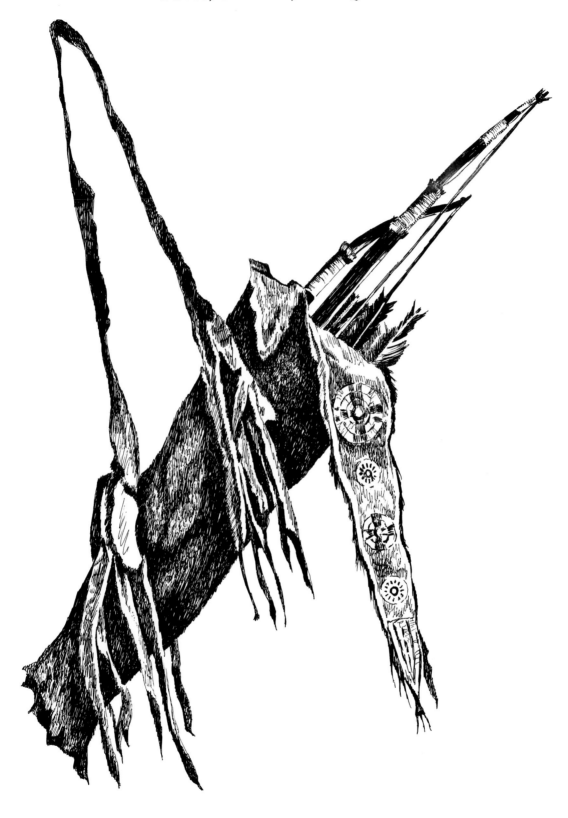

Old-style Crow quiver of otter skin which held both bows and arrows.

on, beads. Usually the legs were left on the animal hides used for quivers, and they hung free to dangle and move with the motion of the warrior as he carried the bag. Long fringes were added at both ends of the case, and a long buckskin thong or loop was attached for carrying it at the warrior's back or side.

Some of the southern Plains tribes, such as the Kiowas, continued to make a single case for both bow and arrows into the nineteenth century. However, the style of the case changed from a huge bag to a trimmer model, somewhat longer and flatter than the earlier editions. To make these, a rectangular piece of rawhide or buckskin was folded in half and stitched along the open edge. A wooden stick about a quarter inch in diameter was then secured with a looped buckskin thong to the stitched edge, and served as a stiffener to hold the case straight. A broad hide band around the middle of the case added further strength, and created a pocket to slip things through—like wooden fire drills and gun-cleaning sticks. To complete the case, a shoulder loop and some decorative flaps and fringes were attached to the stitched edge. Southern cases were easily recognized by their diamond-shaped cutouts which were used for decorations, and by the V-notched edges of the flaps. Black or red wool inserted under the diamond cutouts gave off a rich touch of color.

While they continued to make the single case, many of the southern warriors adopted what became the more traditional Plains style, which consisted of a quiver and a separate bow case. The arrow quiver remained about the same size as the early single-unit model, but the bow case was a narrow tubular case longer than the quiver and almost as long as the bow itself. Ordinarily the end of the bow extended no more than four inches beyond the case—and this was also true of the arrows in the quiver—for moisture could quickly loosen their sinew wrappings and render them inoperative.

The workaday hunting cases in the double-bag model were often made of deer hide, and their only decorations were a few fringes or the dangling legs of the animal's skin.

Inevitably, because the quiver was so much a part of the hunter's and fighter's equipment, thus exhibiting along with his other attire his status and prowess, quivers became more impressive in their make-up. The favored quiver material was the skin of the mountain lion, taken in wintertime when the pelt was thick and rich and soft. An entire skin was consumed in the making of the two cases. The body made the quiver, the pendants, and the shoulder loop, and the long, round tail made a perfect case for the bow. The pendant edges were beaded and patches of bright red felt were added to the pendant and to the ends and middle of the carrying loop. When completed, such quivers were an absolutely majestic sight. The Kiowas and Comanches produced the finest mountain lion quivers and bow cases of all the tribes, for they made many trips into the Rocky Mountains to obtain the pelts. The Sioux warriors made some fine ones too, although they did their best work on buckskin quivers which were decorated with superbly done

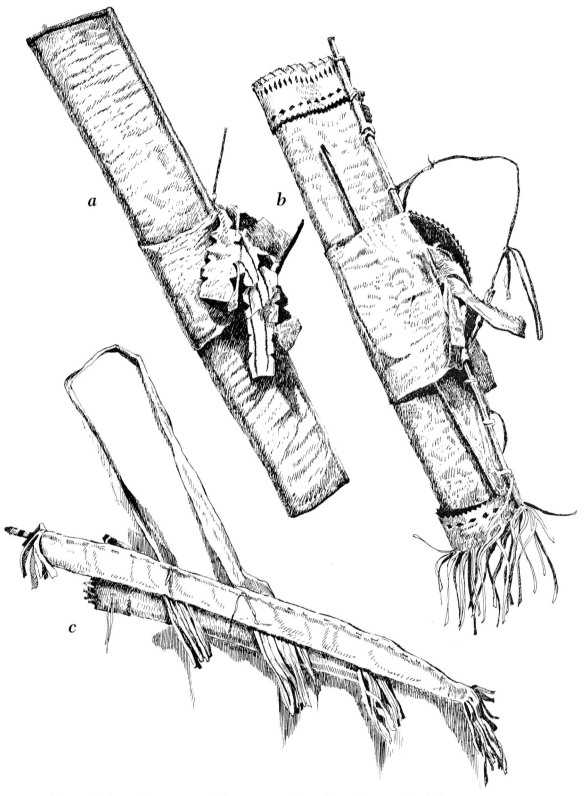

*a* and *b*, rawhide single quiver and bow cases of southern Plains. *c*, buckskin two-piece hunting quiver of northern Plains.

*Top*, mountain lion. *Bottom*, Kiowa mountain lion quiver—red trade cloth patches and beaded edges.

Details of quiver shown in previous figure. *Top,* closed ends with cut fringes and dangling paw skin. *Bottom,* open ends with beading and dangling paw skin.

porcupine quill strips, or with beaded ends on the cases. Some of theirs, where the shoulder loop was also quilled, are truly beautiful pieces of art.

The Crows were never outdone in the adornment of any piece of equipment, and while they did not equal the Kiowa creations on an average basis, some of their quivers and bow cases were simply extraordinary. A double case in the Buffalo Bill Historical Center in Cody, Wyoming, is made of rich black otter skin and has grandly beaded pendants hanging from both the quiver and the bow case. Besides this the closed lower ends of both cases are beaded, and the shoulder loop is a broad red blanket cloth band with a narrow strip of otter skin running the length of the loop and beaded at intervals. Even more, there are several bunches of long, soft fringe. It must be one of the finest quivers ever made!

The quiver and bow case combination becomes even more interesting as one sees its functional aspects. It was extremely lightweight and easy to shift about on the shoulder loop—which made it ideal for long hunting trips and war parties. The ends of the shoulder loop passed between the bow case and the quiver, so that they could also be tied to and fixed in place by their attachment to the stiffening stick which was on the stitched side of the quiver. The stick held the quiver straight so that the arrows would not bend in the case, and as long as the bow was in its case the bow case remained straight too. When the warrior went into action, however, he withdrew the bow, and the end of the bow case dropped out of the way of the quiver and did not restrict his access to his arrows.

The bow case was round, but a sectional cut through a quiver revealed it to be a teardrop shape. This allowed the arrows to fall in a somewhat loose arrangement to the bottom of the case, and they were easier to extract. At the same time the tapered smaller end of the lengthwise dimension of the soft bag tended to hold securely to the arrow points so that they would not fall out.

As stated earlier in the discussion of arrows, the average number taken along in the quiver for hunting and war purposes was twenty. This seems to be a small amount, but others could be made in the field if necessary, or picked up on a battlefield. Besides, more arrows than this would have made a bulky bundle and a heavier one—and thus one more difficult to carry.

Ordinarily the quiver was carried at a slight angle on the warrior's back. When he was on horseback he tied a knot in the loop to pull it up snugly, sometimes dropping it down around his waist so that the quiver rested on the horse. When he hunted the buffalo he let the loop out and carried the quiver at his left side, from whence he could extract the arrows swiftly by simply reaching across his body. This was much easier to do than reaching back over the shoulder and far more certain—so the same technique was often employed in warfare. The notion of an over-the-shoulder draw is a popular one, but the side draw was more positive by far. This method is seen in several of Charles Russell's paintings of Indians hunting buffalo. Since there was not much difference in the nocked ends of his arrows, a warrior, who carried both war and hunting arrows, could not

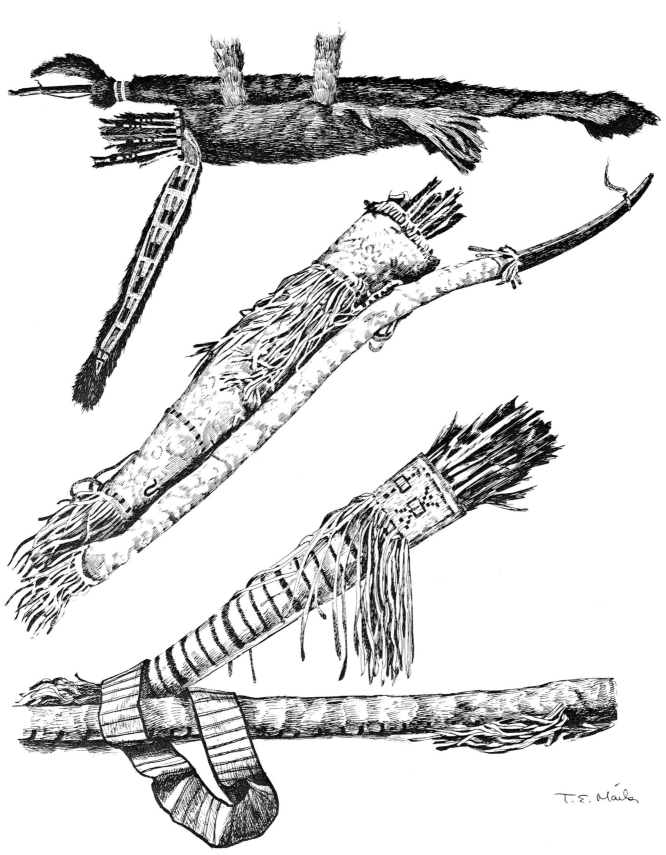

Northern Plains two-piece quivers. *Top,* mountain lion skin with quilled pendant. *Center,* buckskin cases for curved bow. *Bottom,* quilled and beaded quiver and shoulder loop—Sioux.

*Left,* a splendid Crow quiver of otter skin with two beaded pendants and otter strip running full length of shoulder loop. *Right,* Cheyenne warrior with bow case and quiver, taken from drawing by Howling Wolf, 1877.

▶

Details of the functional quiver in action. *a,* bow in bow case. *b,* bow case with bow removed, front view. *c,* bow case with bow removed, back view. *d,* method of attaching shoulder loop to quiver and bow case. *e,* cross section of same. *f,* top view of stiffening stick used to hold quiver straight. *g,* cross section of above, also showing how far bow and arrows were inserted in cases. *h,* side and cross-section views of quiver and bow case to illustrate actual shapes.

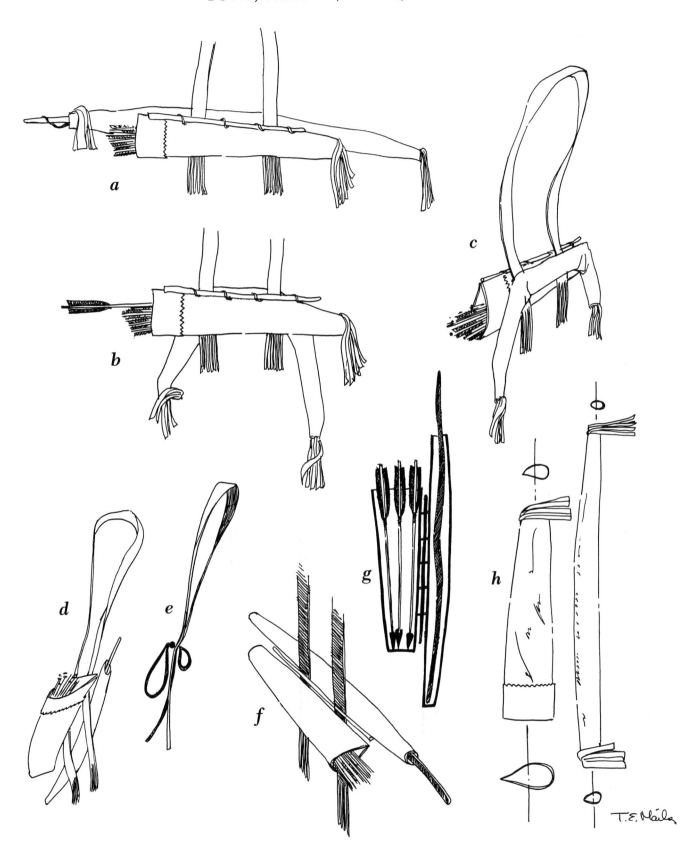

Warrior carrying quiver in traditional manner resting partly on horse.

be sure what kind he was drawing, so depending upon what he was doing he put one group or the other on top. To be more certain still when a fight was about to take place, he extracted several war arrows in advance, holding perhaps five in his bow hand and two in his mouth.

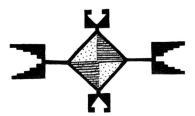

The wooden or horn bow and arrows of the Plains, carried in a lightweight but often splendidly designed and ornamented quiver or bow case and quiver combination, proved to be an ideal weapon for a nomadic people. The shortened bow which finally evolved after years of experimentation, and which was often strengthened against snapping by the addition of sinew strips, forced the Indians to move in close to their game, yet they managed to do this remarkably well—and it probably caused the hunters to sharpen and develop hunting skills they might otherwise have neglected.

The quality of the arrow was more important than that of the bow, for a slightly crooked limb and bowstring would cast an arrow fairly well for a short distance, but a crooked arrow would inevitably miss its mark. So except for the horn bow, the arrow received the greater care in manufacture.

With a well-constructed bow and arrows in his hands, the Plains Indian proved to be a match for anyone in hunting and warfare where the engagements took place at a relatively short range. His ability to fire the arrows rapidly offered a considerable advantage over the early single-shot guns, and this remained true until the repeating rifles came into vogue. Even then the Indian lacked the tools and the skills needed to repair the rifles he obtained, and so the bow continued to be a necessity throughout the nineteenth century.

Since, however, the bow and arrows were not sufficient for every situation and need, other weapons were developed and put into service. The Indian warriors made lances, knives, hatchets, and clubs—with each weapon being designed for a particular use. When these were added to the bow and arrows, a formidable arsenal was formed, and an experienced warrior employed it all with consummate skill.

# Chapter 20

# LANCES, KNIVES, CLUBS, HATCHETS, AND GUNS

Arapaho lances, too, were bright with decorations. Made of highly polished wood, they were sometimes ornamented with a bunch of eagle feathers mounted on a strip of deerskin in such a way that they streamed on the wind as the warrior carried the lance, and yet were not easily bent or broken. Other lances had a kind of narrow banner of buckskin ornamented with quillwork and feathers and with tassels of dyed horsehair hanging from their whole length. These gave the rider a grand look when his horse was running.[1]

The bow and arrow was the Indian warrior's primary weapon. But it was not the best answer to every need, and the warrior always required other weapons when his arrows were gone. To back up the bow and arrow, he developed commendable skills with the lance, the knife, hatchets, clubs—and finally in trade days some ability with guns.

Two types of lances were used on the Plains, the hunting lance and the war lance. Hunting lances were generally thicker and longer than war lances, and they were often undecorated. Some buffalo lances had rows of brass trade tacks along their sides, and a few crow feathers were attached to them on occasion because the crows were always the first birds to find food. Now and then a buffalo lance

---

PLATE 23.  BLACKFEET WARRIOR  ▶

Set against the painted background of his tipi liner, the warrior wears his hair in a typical sweep—packed with buffalo or bear grease to keep it there.

He also wears an otter fur and grizzly bear claw necklace and a beaded vest. Around his neck is a bone-bead and shell necklace. The shell represented the sun, understood as the dwelling place of the Great Spirit. From its center He sent forth warmth for growth, and light—to indicate the one wisdom able to penetrate the darkness of man's ignorance.

was painted with alternating broad bands of red and green and black. The buffalo lance point was quite long, being ten inches or more in length. The earliest points were made of stone or bone. To fashion a bone point, the leg bone of a large animal was cut in half, and the hollow of the bone served as a natural duct to bleed a punctured buffalo. In trade days iron points were obtained from the Spanish, Mexicans and the Whites.

On the whole, buffalo lances ranged from one to three inches in diameter, and from seven to nine feet in length, including both the wooden shaft and the point. As in the case of the arrow, the prime targets on a buffalo for the lance were the areas just behind the last rib and just behind the shoulder. The mounted hunter approached on the left side if he could, and holding the lance with his right hand with the shaft also firmly secured under his armpit, he lunged forward from the closest possible range and drove the lance home. He did not leave the lance in the buffalo unless the animal pulled it away from him. Instead he stayed with the impaled beast as long as he could and then pulled the lance free so that he could go after another buffalo. The large, deep wound in itself would cause the wounded animal to drop after a short distance. A Crow warrior of note had a lance with an enormous stone head which he used to slice the tendons of a buffalo's hind legs. This disabled the buffalo, and it was unable to run. His method was to cut the tendons of several buffalo and then return to finish the disabled beasts off one by one.

War lances were usually quite slim, ranging from five eighths of an inch to one and a quarter inches in diameter, and from six and a half to seven and a half feet in length. The shorter the war lance, the greater the courage of the warrior who carried it. An exception to this was the early Crow lance, which was sometimes twelve feet long, and the Comanche lances, which often measured fourteen feet.

Unlike the plain buffalo lances, war lances were decorated in every conceivable way. Many were wrapped from end to end with strips of rich animal fur, such as otter, beaver, mink, and weasel, for all of these were swift and powerful. It was thought that a lance wrapped with their fur would manifest the same abilities in impaling a foe. Some of the war lance shafts were wrapped with red blanket cloth strips, and were banded with strips of beads. Besides the wrappings, fringes were added, and golden eagle feathers were tied in clusters or at intervals, and there were clusters of feathers from other birds. The Pawnees placed owl feathers on their lances to represent the North Star, which watched over the camp

◀ PLATE 24.   ASSINIBOINE PIPEHOLDER

at night. Swan feathers held a relationship to the Thunder Bird, and gave a lightning- and thunderlike force to a lance. Long tails of horsehair were often tied to war lances and extended out from them like streamers. Some warriors tied one or more stretched scalps to their staffs, and on occasion a long string of either braided or loose locks of human hair. Multicolored ribbons were also a favorite lance decoration. It is important to recognize that whatever was added to the lance, a balanced composition was maintained.

War lances were most often employed by mounted men engaged in battle in the same manner as the buffalo lance was in hunting, with the shaft locked in the armpit between the arm and the side. The warrior attempted to get as close as possible to his enemy, then leaned forward and drove the lance home. An alternate method was to hold the lance above the head with both hands, and then to apply it with a downward-stabbing motion. Lances were also thrown, and boys played a game which sharpened their abilities to do this. A hoop was rolled, and the boys threw small lances at it until they could put the shafts through it more often than not. The throwing lances of mature warriors had a long spiral of feathers running the full length of the shaft. The lance made an excellent defensive weapon against the hatchet and club. Even a broken shaft held in both hands could be used to ward off blows.

Most war lances had a wrist thong to slip the hand and/or arm through, and another loop at the butt to use when the owner wanted to hang it on his horse. Most lances had at least one buckskin handgrip placed near the head, and sometimes two grips spaced about three feet apart for the downward-stabbing application.

Lance staves were cut in late winter when the sap was down. The wood cut in this season would not split while drying. Second-growth wood was the best. The preferred woods were ash, white elm, ironwood, oak, and hickory. Several staves were cut at the same time and smoked by the lodge fire for several weeks. This seasoned the wood and killed any insects that might be in it. Shafts were then straightened by greasing them with fat and heating them over a fire. The final shaping was done with a knife. Sometimes the carving marks were left, but if a smoother finish was desired, the shaft was rubbed with sandstone. Then the lance point was added and the decorations and grips were put on.

Several types of lance points were used. The oldest kinds were stone and bone, shaped like large arrowheads and inserted in a slot cut in the shaft head. These were then bound with a wide band of wet sinew or with a wide strip of rawhide. The Blackfoot tribes made an excellent bluestone point of huge dimensions for war purposes. Its weight made it an awesome club as well as a lance.

In trade days, knife blades were used for lance points, and White blacksmiths forged huge iron points for the Indians. Now and then a warrior who found an abandoned piece of metal filed it and pounded it into a rough lance point. The best iron points came from the Spanish and Mexicans, for they used lances

Methods of using lance. *a*, overhead stabbing method. *b*, shaft held in hand and locked in armpit. *c*, throwing lance. *d*, lance as a defensive weapon.

Warrior wielding lance in preferred fashion in battle.

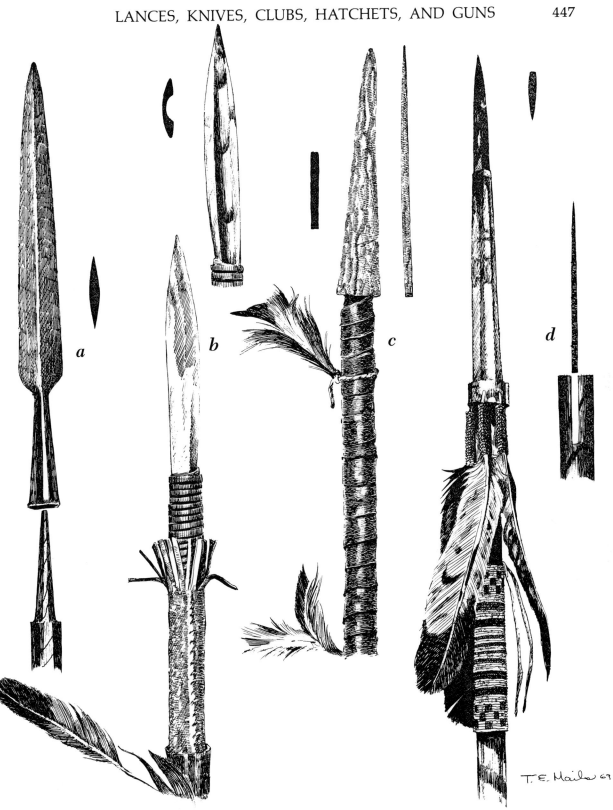

Lance points and sections. *a*, metal point obtained from Spanish and Mexicans. *b*, front and back of bone point, Blackfoot. *c*, front and edge of bluestone point, Blackfoot. *d*, knife blade used for point.

Lance points and shafts. *a*, hammered metal point and buckskin grip on shaft. *b*, hammered metal point with feathers spiraled down shaft, used for throwing. *c*, Sioux warrior with lance illustrating average length of lance.

Methods of carrying lance. *a*, butt resting on thigh. *b*, butt carried in crook of arm. *c*, butt hung from saddle by a thong loop like those used on war club handles—no boot was used to carry the lance. (Examples after C. R. Russell.) *d*, butt resting on stirrup. *e*, carried on back by shoulder loop.

Beaded carrying cases used by Crow women to carry husband's lances on parade. The cases were either hung from the saddle pommel or inserted at an angle under the cinch strap so as to point upward behind the mounted rider.

Blackfoot warrior with lance in position for charge.

themselves and forged a number of styles. Some were more than fourteen inches long and had a tapered, funnel-shaped end to receive the shaft head. A metal cotter pin was driven through to secure the iron point to the shaft. Glue was also used, and if necessary a wrapping of wet sinew or rawhide.

The lance was carried in a number of ways when the warrior was mounted. Sometimes the butt was rested on top of the thigh, and other times it was rested on the stirrup or foot. Now and then a warrior carried his lance in the crook of his arm, and he also used a sling manner of transporting it, quiverlike, across his back. The hand loops were used to tie it to the saddle when the warrior was off his horse, and by tying the butt loop to his cinch strap and the head loop to his saddle cantle, the horse could carry the lance in an upright position behind the warrior when he was riding.

In the reservation period, the Crow Indian women carried their husband's lances during camp moves and festivals in beautiful beaded and fringed scabbards. The lance head was inserted in the scabbard's pocket, and the top of the scabbard was tied to the pommel of her saddle. Warrior's wives also made buckskin bags to cover their husband's lance heads when the lances were in the tipi.

When war parties were in the field, the party leader sometimes appointed one or two men to assist him in leading the group. The usual insignia to designate those chosen was a green tree limb bent over at the top like a shepherd's crook and then wrapped with fur or cloth. Sometimes the points of their staffs were sharpened so they could be used as lances. This has led to the belief that the bent society staffs were actually lances, but they were not so in the literal sense.

Generally speaking, a large portion of any raid or war party, whether on foot or mounted, carried lances in addition to their other weapons. Old paintings and photographs show a profusion of these, and they made a superb addition to a swirling group's appearance.

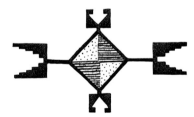

For sheer utility, the knife was the most serviceable weapon employed by the Plains warrior. He used it constantly at home, while hunting, and in warfare. As with other items, the knife was carefully crafted and often imaginatively designed. Knives were carried in highly ornamented sheaths which, in my opinion, rank among the finest cases ever made by any people.

The earliest knives of the Plains Indians were made of stone or bone. Bone knives were fashioned from the larger flat bones of the buffalo, and could be honed with sandstone to quite a sharp edge. Hunters carried large bone skinning knives, while more delicate bone sheath knives were used for carving and warfare. The custom was to wrap the knife handle with rawhide strips or with a buckskin cover.

Metal knives were vastly superior to the bone instruments, however, and the Plains warriors eagerly welcomed the new blades as traders brought them into the area in the last half of the eighteenth century.

The first knife blades they received from the White men were of English origin, although American knives followed close behind. The traders brought two types of blades—a single-edged butcher knife and a double-edged dagger. Dagger blades were very broad, and they were finished with large wooden handles made by the Indians.

It is said that the Indians favored the dagger for hand-to-hand combat. Some White authorities have felt that truly skilled knife fighters would reject these daggers as clumsy and inefficient weapons. But the Plains Indian, forced to sweep his knife in all directions while on foot or horseback, developed his own techniques. He held his knife with the blade below the hand and concentrated on two principal blows—a powerful downward-chopping motion aimed behind his opponent's collarbone, or a sidewise stroke aimed at the ribs or stomach. One should bear in mind that he used his knife against other Indians, and they fought in the same manner as he. Then too, the knife was not the preferred fighting implement in any case.

Accounts by Indians reveal that warriors were expert at throwing the knife, and one warrior tells how he brought down an enemy by this means as the enemy attempted to escape.

Before 1840 American butcher and carving knives began to displace the English blades. The famous John Russell Company's "Green River" knives and similar types produced by such firms as Lamson & Goodnow found their way onto the Plains in abundance until the fur trade ceased shortly after the Civil War.

Some of these came complete with wooden handles, and are little different from the butcher knives found in kitchens today. When blades came without handles the Indians made their own, fashioning them of wood or bone. Horn handles were cut from a section of deer or elk antler which fitted the hand almost perfectly. Some bone grips were adorned with carved figures of men and animals, while others were etched with a simple crosshatched pattern. A few knives with handles decorated with inlaid silver or pewter bands were brought to the Plains by traders and were given as gifts to favored Indians.

After 1825 the Indians were able to make a few metal knives themselves, fashioning their blades from files or saws, and adding handles of antler or other bone. The finished products were more graceful than most of the American and English knives, which again establishes the Indian's intuitive feeling for design,

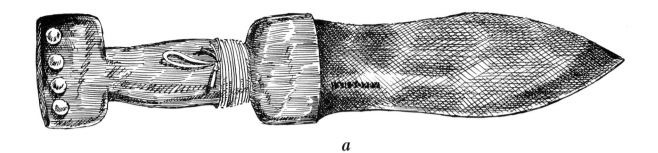

*a*, ancient Blackfoot double-edged dagger, 13 inches long. *b*, large bone skinning knife. *c*, Cree skinning knife, wooden handle, metal blade, 10 inches long. *d*, old-style beaded dagger sheath. *e*, old-style painted rawhide knife sheath showing how deeply knife was inserted in case. *f*, bone sheath knife.

Warrior using knife in traditional downward-stabbing motion of Plains.

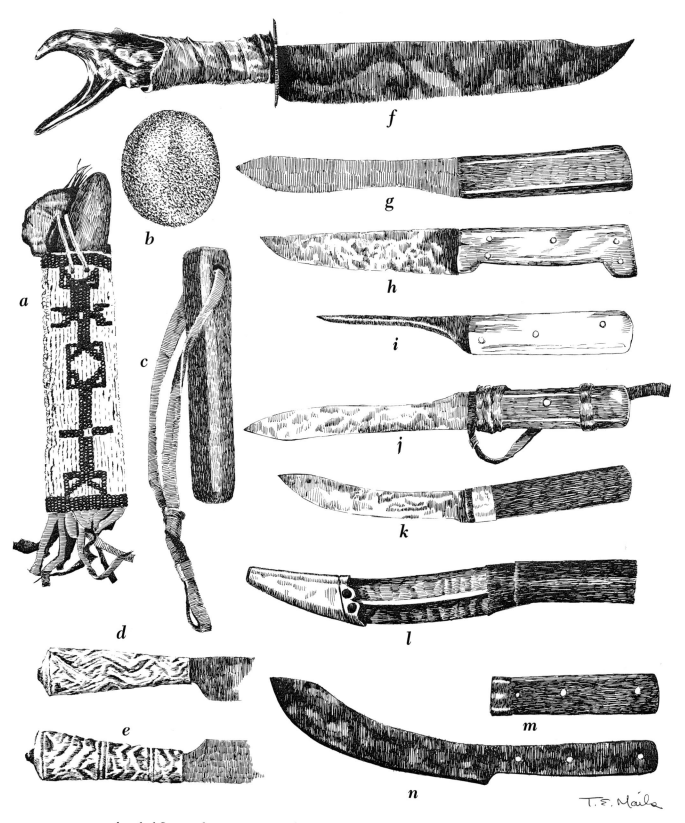

*a,* beaded Sioux whetstone case with stone inserted. *b* and *c,* whetstones used for sharpening knives. *d* and *e,* carved bone handles crafted by Indians. *f,* metal trade blade with antler handle added by Indian. *g, h, i,* and *j,* typical knives with wooden handles. *k,* knife with inlaid silver in wooden handle. *l,* presentation sheath with silverwork. *m* and *n,* detail of knife handle and metalwork.

balance, and texture. Even a very small knife with a handle made of a deer's foot and wrapped with a small piece of red wool became a superb composition. The Bear Cult knife illustrated in the society material was as marvelous a knife as anyone will ever see.

The warriors sharpened their knives with whetstones. They used round or longer cylindrical stones, and drilled holes through them for wrist straps. Whetstone cases were made of buckskin, and were beaded and fringed. As to the grinding method, Indian skinning knives had one characteristic which always revealed the fact they were Indian; the maker ground off the original edge and then beveled only one side, since it was better for skinning that way.

The Indians prized their metal knives and used them until the blades were worn down to a mere sliver.

A warrior kept his knife in a large sheath or case. In most instances it was big enough virtually to swallow up the knife. This protected the handle and blade against moisture, and it kept the knife from falling out during the owner's more hectic activities.

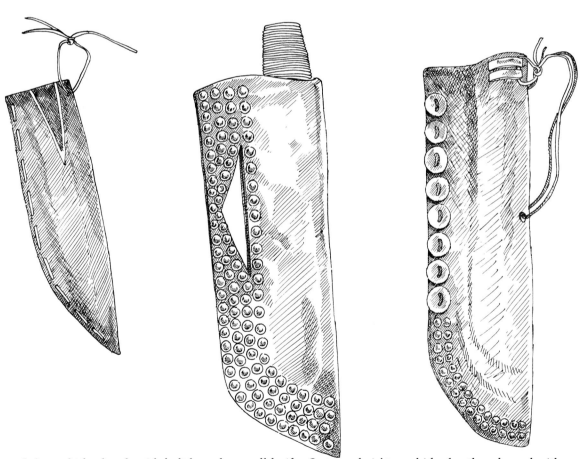

*Left,* rawhide sheath with belt loop for small knife. *Center* and *right,* rawhide sheaths adorned with brass tacks, length 9 inches.

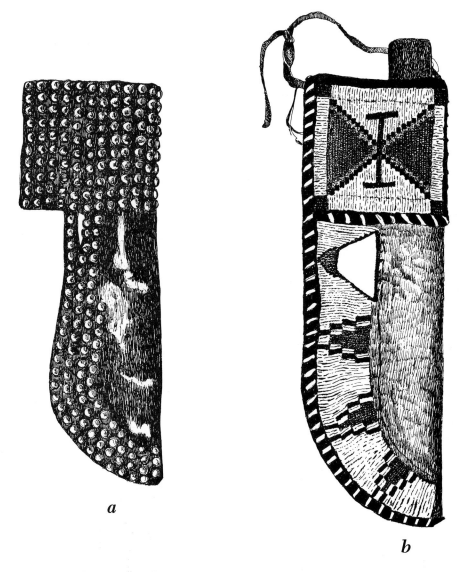

*a*, most advanced design of rawhide sheath with brass tacks. *b*, beaded Sioux sheath.

The case was made of heavy rawhide, sometimes simply folded over and stitched and other times having an insert for additional spacing and strength along the stitched edge.

The workaday case was left fairly plain, but was sometimes painted with geometrical designs.

Some of the larger sheaths were absolutely spectacular creations with beautiful patterns of brass tacks and beads added to them in many ways. Often they were twelve or more inches long, and their form was nothing short of a sculptured work of art. As such, the case always enhanced a warrior's costume.

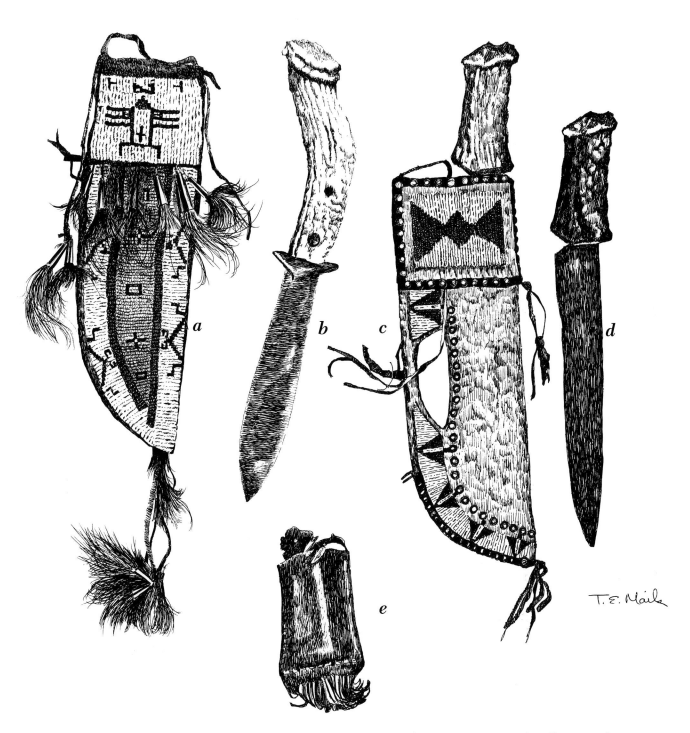

*a*, 12-inch-long Sioux fully beaded knife sheath with tin bells, horsehair tufts, and quill-wrapped danglers. *b*, dagger with antler handle. *c*, Sioux knife case with combination of beads and brass tacks. *d*, knife with antler handle from same sheath. *e*, rawhide whetstone case.

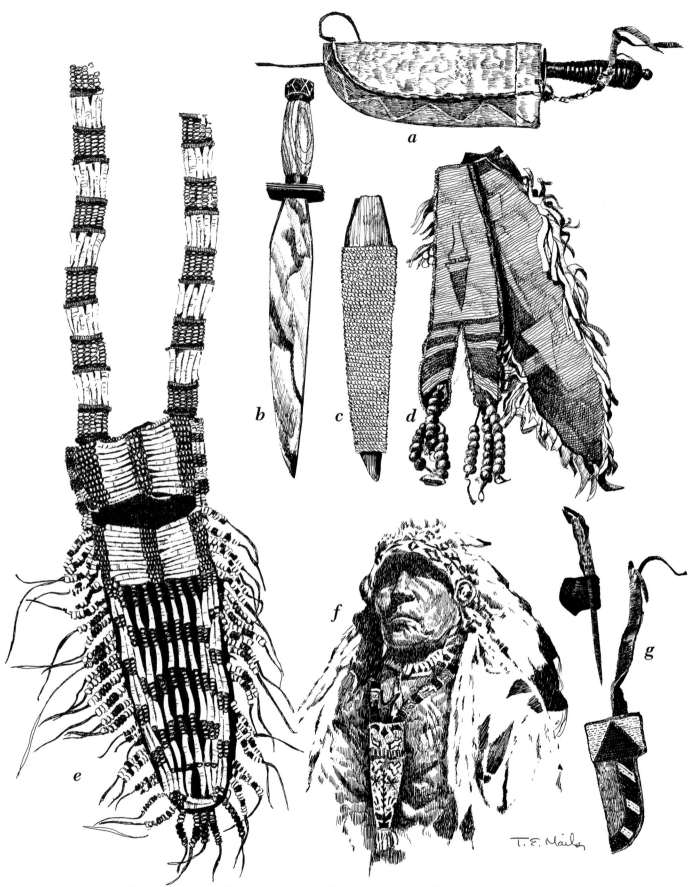

*a*, small knife in painted rawhide case. *b*, blackfoot knife with brass guards on wooden handle. *c*, cord-wrapped wooden inner sheath for knife. *d*, beaded outer case for knife b with huge pendant flap. *e*, ancient Blackfoot knife case of type carried on beaded loop around neck, covered with costly dentalium shells. *f*, warrior wearing neck-type case. *g*, tiny knife with deer's foot handle and its beaded rawhide case.

Methods of wearing knife sheaths (after drawings by C. R. Russell).

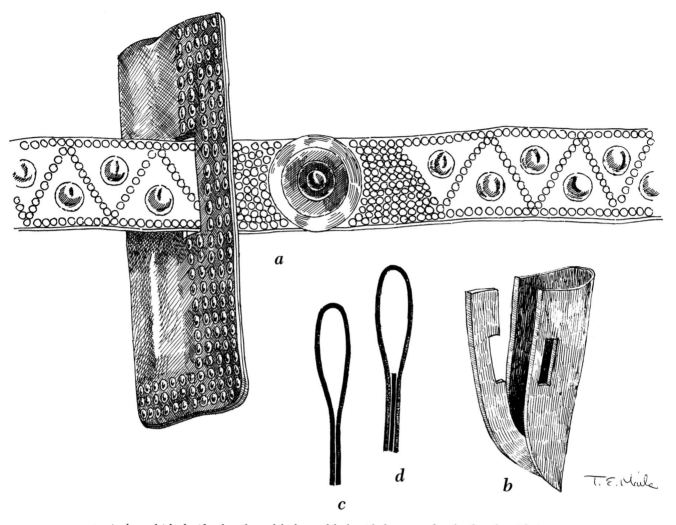

*a,* typical rawhide knife sheath and belt studded with brass tacks. *b,* sheath with insert to space out case. *c,* cross section showing sheath without insert. *d,* cross section showing sheath with insert.

More exquisite than the brass tack models were the ceremonial beaded cases. The Sioux and the Blackfoot tribes in particular excelled at making these. The typical beaded case had several long pendant strings hanging from its point, some ending in dyed breath feathers or clusters of dyed horsehair, and some with the strings beaded or quilled. An old Blackfoot knife had a brass guard and tip on its handle, and it was first inserted in an interior wooden sheath which was wrapped with twisted string. The outer case or sheath had a huge, beaded flap and fringes all around its edges. The handle and wood sheath indicate they were made in Alaska, and were obtained by the Blackfeet in trade—who then made the case for them.

The earliest method of carrying a knife was to suspend it in a decorated case on a beaded loop around the neck. The early Blackfoot models of this type were festooned with priceless dentalium beads and fringes. Later on the knife was attached to the belt. The most secure way of doing this was to provide a V-shaped or rectangular slot in the case. The belt was then threaded through the slot, and

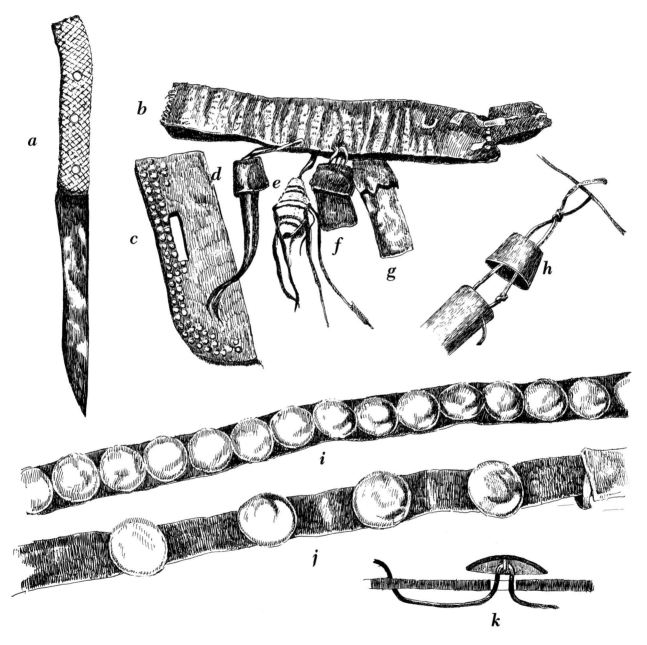

*a*, knife with crosshatched bone handle. *b*, heavy hide belt with traditional equipment attached. *c*, knife sheath. *d*, awl case. *e*, beaded rock medicine. *f*, whetstone case. *g*, sinew pouch. *h*, detail showing how awl case top slides. *i* and *j*, silver conch belts. *k*, method of attaching late model conches.

when pulled tight held the knife and case firmly in place. The advantage of a large, flat case can be readily seen in the comfort it offered, since it would not press into the side as a small case would do when the owner was walking or riding.

Some belt cases were merely suspended by a loop attached to the top of the case which the belt passed through, and more rarely in the late 1800s by belt loops such as the White hunters used on the backs of their knife cases. Some sheaths with long top loops were also pushed under the warrior's belt for added security against loss.

Belts, in this instance properly called outside belts, were decorated too. Popular styles employed patterns of brass tacks driven into a very heavy hide, the belt being three or more inches wide, and conches, which were silver disks obtained in trade or made by the Indians themselves of hammered coins. The conches were fastened to the belt by a thong lacing which passed through holes in the belt and then through holes in or rings on the conches.

Belts intended for daily use were left fairly plain, and were drilled with numerous holes for attaching a considerable amount of the warrior's traveling gear. A belt in the Fred Harvey Collection holds a knife case, an awl case (with a clever sliding top), a beaded rock amulet case, a flint and steel case, and a whetstone case. The belt has no buckle, as was the way with all early belts. Thongs attached to each end were simply tied together—which meant that belts were made to an exact fit.

As one might expect, the bead period led to elaborately decorated belts, and some, when beads were applied in combination with brass tacks, were simply marvelous creations. Here again, the intuitive design sense of the Indian crafts-people led to beading and paint patterns that conformed precisely to the shape of the item. Knife case designs usually repeated the shape of the knife, and belt patterns followed a repetitive motif.

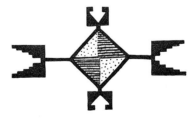

Every Plains warrior carried some kind of club when he went raiding or to war. Usually it was thrust under his belt, but when fitted with a wrist strap it could be hung from the pommel or cantle of his saddle.

The oldest types had stone heads with short wooden handles, since they were carried by footmen. The head styles varied, and the decorations were limited to paint, usually a dull red, and fringes.

Once men were mounted on horseback, the handle was lengthened for striking at greater distances. Some of the earlier forms employed the use of knife blades or hatchet blades which were inserted in sculptured wooden handles. Often several blades were used in a single club, and long horsehair tails were attached to the club handle as a decoration. A wooden ball-type of club was used on the Plains, but it received broader use by Woodland tribes. There was also a type of weapon shaped like a gunstock and known as the "gunstock club." The familiar brass tacks were often applied to these in symbolic designs.

The warrior selected the club head with great care, choosing smooth and colorful stones from stream beds that would not split on impact. One beautiful Blackfoot club had a dark-gray stone head, a shaft wrapped with a rawhide strip which was painted in alternating bands of red and dark green, a horsehair tail attached to the butt, and a White blond scalp lock with beaded strips appended. Another had a dark-green stone head with eagle feathers attached to the handle and an end ornament of rabbit fur and horsehair. From head to tip it measured thirty-four inches.

Generally speaking, the stones used for club heads weighed anywhere from two to eight pounds.

By 1800 the warriors were producing clubs in great variety, with each man fashioning his according to visions or fancy. They continued to make the ancient short-handled type, but also fashioned superb instruments with handles as long as thirty inches. Some clubs had mink- and bead-covered handles, and sling-type heads with symbolic painted lines on the head straps. Some of the stones used were almost perfect balls in shape, and were as heavy as iron. Clubs were often exquisitely quilled, with the quills covering both the handle and the head. An effective war club could be simply a huge leg bone with a hide wrist strap. Some models had a rawhide-covered shaft and a stone head which was pointed on both ends. Other club heads were made with two sharp buffalo horns, and were wicked weapons.

A popular type of Plains club is known to collectors as the slingshot variety. The head was attached to the handle by a twisted piece of flexible rawhide, which tended to catapult the stone head forward as the weapon was swung, and also kept the head from breaking off on impact. It was a testy weapon, and when a long, twisted rawhide sling was used, it could tolerate a somewhat shorter handle than the fixed-head clubs. Some of the slingshot clubs had the head attached with two flat straps placed side by side. Other clubs were made with a rawhide- or buckskin-encased rock head which was attached loosely enough to the handle to allow it to bend a little to give it slight slingshot effect. All of these clubs were given a horsehair appendage which was carefully sized and shaped to balance the club head and to enhance the club design.

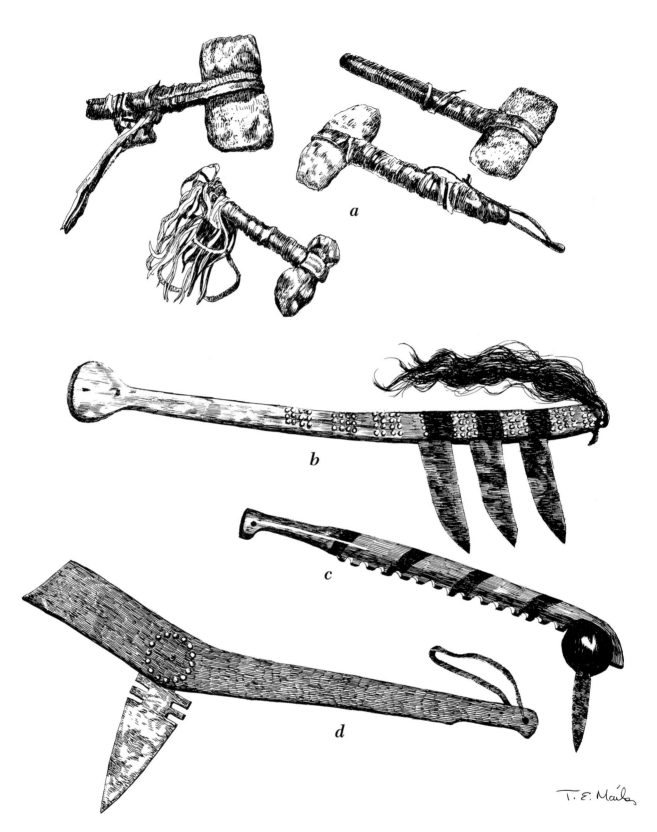

War clubs. *a*, pre-horse-period clubs with stone heads. *b*, club inset with three knife blades, decorated with brass tacks and horsehair. *c*, wooden club with serrations carved in handle, wood ball at end for weight, and knife blade inset in ball. *d*, type known as "gunstock" club, inset with metal lance blade.

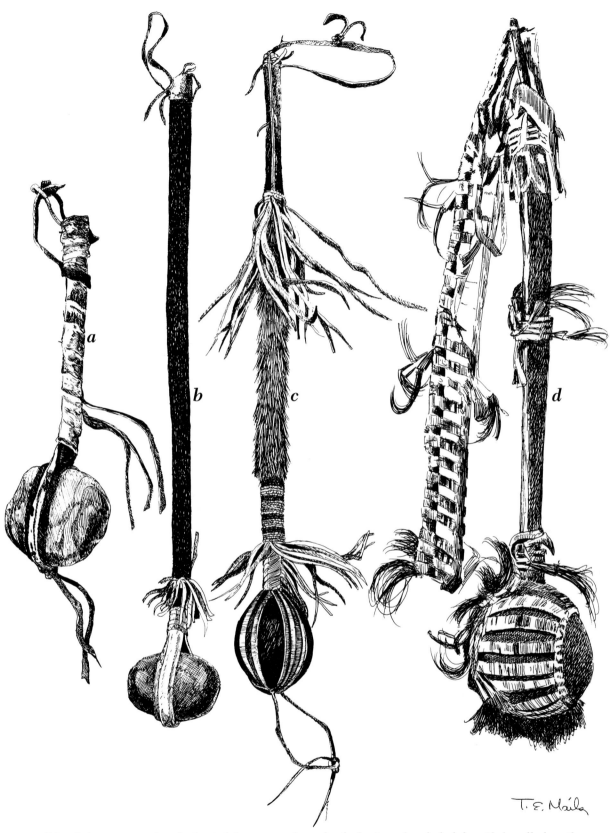

War clubs. *a*, stone head adapted for use on horseback. *b*, stone-headed club with handle lengthened for use on horse, blue wool-covered handle, 30 inches long. *c*, club with flexible sling head, bead- and mink-covered handle. *d*, very old and exquisitely quilled club with quilled pendant.

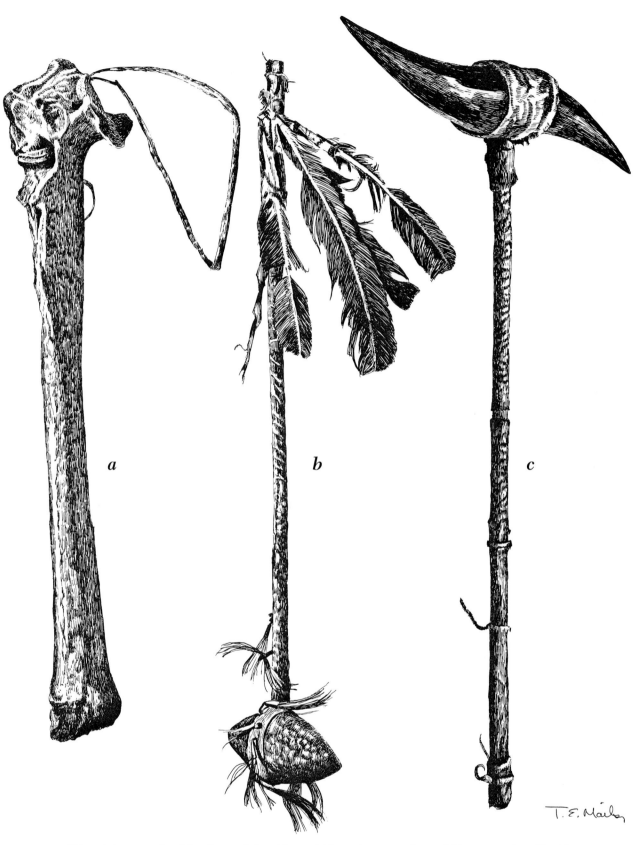

War clubs. *a*, animal leg bone club with rawhide wrist strap. *b*, rawhide-covered staff with stone head pointed on both ends, decorated with eagle feathers, 34 inches long. *c*, rawhide-covered club with buffalo horn head. Horn clubs like this were usually ceremonial rattles, but this one is solid, very heavy, and was used for war.

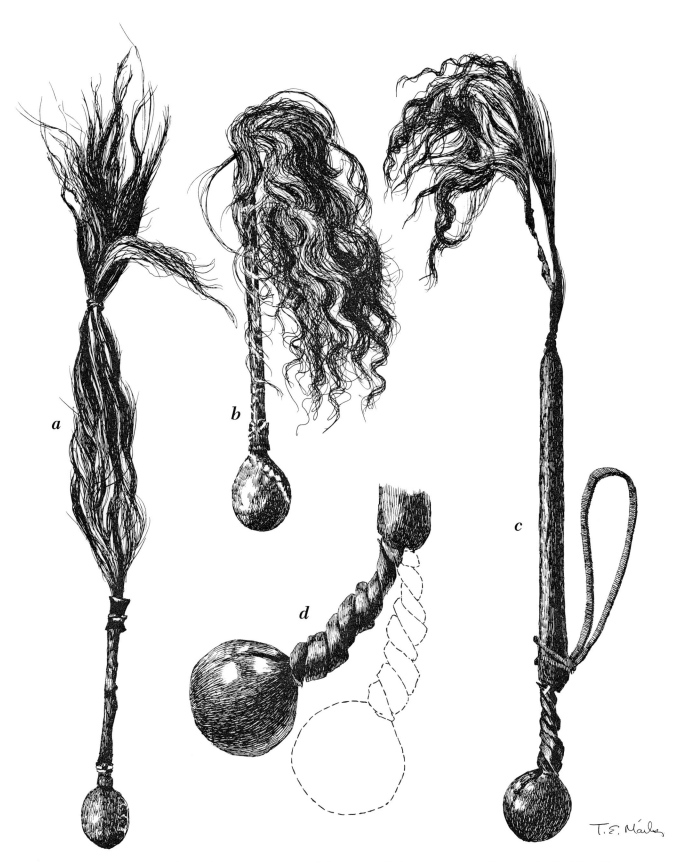

Slingshot war clubs. *a*, *b*, and *c*, varieties of the club with horsehair appendages at butt of handle. *d*, detail of head and flexible rawhide or sinew sling in action.

War clubs. *a*, Blackfoot club with hide-wrapped handle, blond White scalp lock attached to handle, horsehair pendant on butt. *b*, beaded Sioux burial club made to be placed beside great leader, black horsehair pendant. *c*, Blackfoot club with wolf fur and horsehair pendant, total length, 34 inches.

There was also an extraordinary and very rare type of burial club which was entirely beaded and was prepared in advance to be placed beside the body of a great leader. The usual model measured twenty inches in length plus its jet-black horsehair tip.

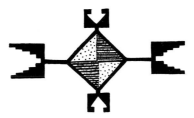

Even better known than the clubs are the famous Indian hatchets and tomahawk pipes. Except for the complete, elaborate silver inlaid presentation models which were brought to Indian leaders as gifts, only the tomahawk heads were manufactured for the Indian trade. Each nation producing tomahawk heads used its own pattern and marking. The English blade resembled a straight ax, the French was shaped like a fleur-de-lis, and the Spanish was in the shape of a broadax. However, it was the Indian artisan who gave the tomahawk its crowning glory with his beaded, carved, fur-covered, and painted handles, and stately beaded tabs and appendages which were in perfect proportion and attached to the handle ends. Plate 28 illustrates a Shoshone tomahawk in all its regal splendor, with beads, brass tacks, blazing red blanket cloth, and a white ermine. Each appendage is in perfect placement and scale to balance the head and other decorations. Since the blade was small, the Shoshone artist added an eagle feather to it to enhance the composition. Also in the plate is a typical Hudson's Bay Company pipe head, with a carved, beaded, and copper-wire-wrapped stem which was added by the northwest Indians.

Simple hatchet heads, without pipe bowls, were traded to the Plains Indians first, but by 1750 the metal pipe bowl types were also available. Neither replaced the club as a weapon, however, although George Catlin states that Plains warriors could throw the tomahawk and embed it in a person or other object with exceptional skill.[2]

Because of its portent and grandeur, the tomahawk eventually became a symbol for both war and peace. Indians meeting to arrange treaties often buried the head of one in the ground to show their peaceful intent, or smoked it together to express the same thing. Yet it spoke of other attitudes if necessary.

The tomahawks which were highly ornamented came finally to be ceremonial objects, and nothing more, for no one wanted to damage such magnificent craftworks in a battle.

Tomahawk Pipe Clubs. *a*, English trade blade. *b*, French trade blade. *c*, Spanish broadax blade. *d*, Blackfoot model with beaded pendant. *e*, Sioux model with beaded pendant. *f*, Crow model with beaded pendant.

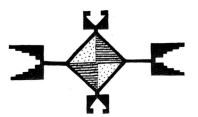

White traders began furnishing Indians with guns as early as the last part of the seventeenth century. The first types were matchlocks, flintlocks, muskets, and pistols. In Canada the Hudson's Bay Company devised a special firearm for the Indian known as the "trade gun." By 1800 it had become a lightweight, short-barreled, and cheaply constructed musket, .66 caliber or thereabouts, with a large trigger guard so that it could be fired with a winter glove covering on the hand.

Early trade guns almost invariably had a serpentlike brass figure, known as "the dragon ornament," on the left side plate, and often there was a seated fox in a decorative circle elsewhere on the gun. These ornaments appeared on Indian guns well into the nineteenth century. And the distribution of "Hudson's Bay

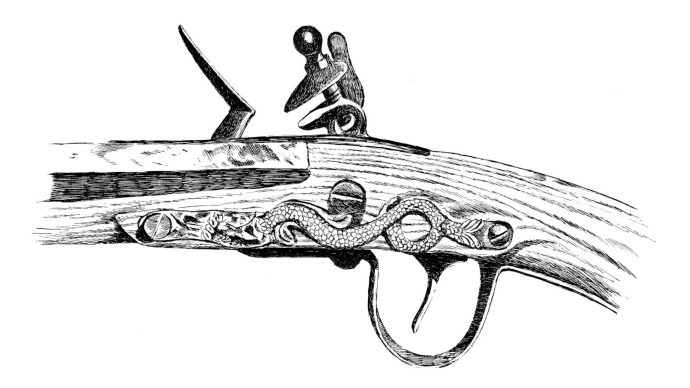

Early trade flintlock with dragon ornament.

guns" or "fusees" was so extensive that Lewis and Clark found them in the hands of Indians on the upper Missouri and at the mouth of the Columbia.

After the American Revolution, both the American government and private firms made a thriving business of manufacturing and trading British-type guns to Indians. By the early 1800s American guns were being manufactured and distributed by private American firms as well. In any case, the dragon ornament still appeared on all guns. The average cost to the Indian at that time was seven dollars per musket at government trading posts on the frontier. When the government factory system was discontinued in the 1820s, private trading companies and individuals continued to sell the same guns, and by 1840 the retail price to the Indian had increased to as much as twenty-eight dollars.

United States trade rifles, with their spiraled inner barrels to improve accuracy, paralleled the production and distribution of the trade smoothbore musket. The trade rifle, originally a flintlock, was about .52 caliber, and had a relatively short barrel, which in turn was apt to be shortened still further by the Plains Indian, who wanted a handier weapon to carry on his horse. The Indian frequently shortened all his guns by filing from four to six inches off the barrel—and sometimes cutting the stock—deliberately or by necessity after it split as it often did through overloading, falls, or other causes.

The trade rifle was usually well made, thoroughly tested by the government or trading companies, and produced by a number of American manufacturers, including some of those who produced the trade musket and Kentucky rifle.

Though the trade rifle was a more accurate and longer-ranged weapon than the smoothbore musket, many Indians still preferred the musket. The musket was less expensive to buy, it could kill a buffalo at the close range common to the Indian horseback method of hunting, it was easier to load, and it shot almost any kind of ball. In time, the Indian was able to pour his own balls with materials and molds obtained from traders or as spoils of war.

English and American trade rifles and muskets were not the only firearms which reached the western Indian. Many types of guns came into his hands in various ways, by capture, trade, smuggling, or gift. The Pueblos captured several hundred Spanish muskets during their 1680–93 wars against the Spanish. Later on, the Cheyenne said that wagon trains passing up the South Platte River between 1858 and 1865 were largely armed with American Sharps military rifles and carbines, and their people obtained many in trade and also some cap-and-ball six-shooters. The Cheyenne warriors captured their first American Spencer repeating rifles in the late 1860s by derailing a railroad handcar in Nebraska. In 1862 Bear Ribs, a Sioux chief, came into possession of a double-barreled shotgun. Canadian and American traders specializing in liquor were the first to trade breech-loading firearms and cartridges to the Blackfeet in 1869. Both the North and the South armies enlisted Indian regiments in the Civil War, and these recruits retained many of their weapons after discharge, as was customary for all soldiers.

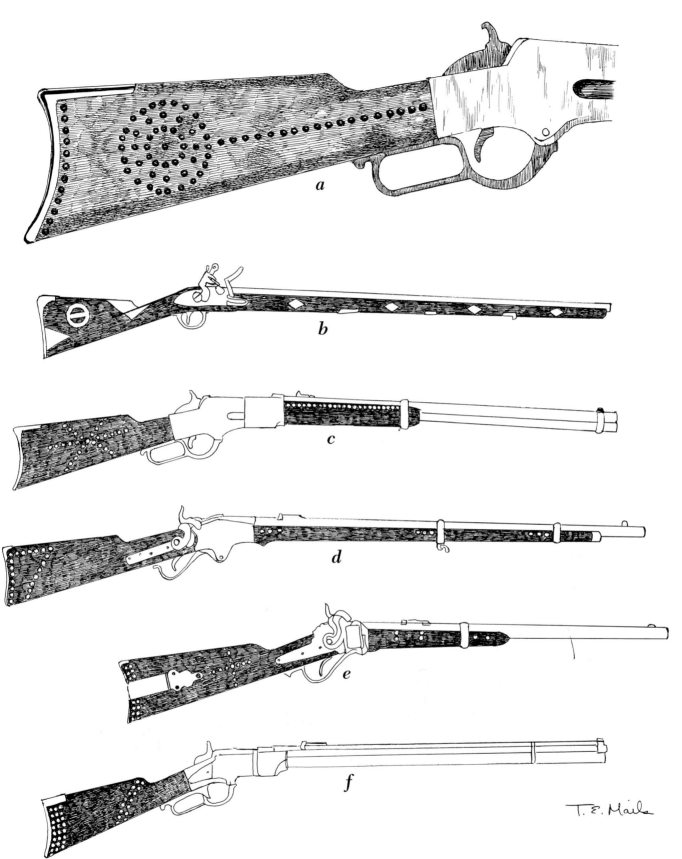

Guns used and ornamented by Indians. *a*, Winchester 66 gunstock. *b*, trade flintlock musket decorated with silver inlays (all the other guns are decorated with brass tack symbols). *c*, Winchester carbine. *d*, Spencer repeating percussion rifle. *e*, Sharps carbine. *f*, Henry rifle.

Warrior loading muzzle loader by spitting balls into barrel while riding full tilt. Some authorities have questioned this as a common loading technique, but it was illustrated by F. Remington and by others.

Some of the guns used by the Sioux in their wars against United States soldiers were identified as those given them by the Indian Peace Commission at the conclusion of the Fort Rice treaty signed in 1868. Furthermore, reservation Indians were often issued guns to hunt for food, and this was even done during the period of the Indian wars. In 1805 only about 5 per cent of the Indian men had guns, but by the late 1800s almost all warriors had them, although the guns were an odd assortment of some magnitude. Now and then, in a given battle, they might even be better armed than the White soldiers.

Most White authorities felt the Indian warrior's marksmanship left much to be desired, yet all agreed that their performance on horseback with a gun was nothing short of remarkable, especially with the unwieldly trade musket. Racing full tilt, a warrior could fire and reload his muzzle-loader at will, shooting with one hand or both hands over the back or under the neck of his horse. Taking four or more balls in his mouth, he simply spit them into his gun's muzzle after first sloshing in an estimated charge of powder from his powder horn. In this reckless manner a dozen warriors fighting at close range could send a deadly hail of fire toward an enemy.

Some of the Indian's deficiencies in marksmanship were due to a lack of cartridges, or in earlier days of powder and shot, for practicing. An Indian often traded a buffalo robe for as few as three cartridges. At such a price every round which was fired became a wealthy man's luxury. This does not mean that all Indians were mediocre shots. Indians displayed excellent shooting ability on a few occasions. Their proficiency absolutely baffled United States troops in the Modoc Wars of 1873, and Chief Joseph's Nez Percés' managed the same result in several skirmishes with White soldiers.

Of more interest is the matter of the warrior's over-all attitude toward the problems connected with reliance upon guns. The early flintlock was risky because wet weather could put it out of operation just when it was needed most. And the later percussion-cap models presented the hazard of losing all of one's caps at once, and thus being put entirely out of commission. Then too, it took about thirty seconds to patch-load, aim, and fire a musket or rifle, whereas in thirty seconds an Indian could shoot from eight to ten arrows. It was also true that the bow could kill over *almost* the same range as an early gun could manage. Maintenance was a greater problem still, for the Plains Indian knew nothing of forges or molten metals—these were not natural things—and he seldom was able to do more than patch up a broken gun in the crudest way. Many of their guns came to be covered with rawhide bindings as stocks were broken and then repaired.

A happening worth remembering is how the warrior's cleverness was brought to bear in a special way. Since there was no uniformity of make or caliber of gun, necessity led the man who was fortunate enough to procure a mold that would fit his rifle to develop an ingenious method of reloading his old shells. He took a box of the smallest percussion caps, made an opening in the center of the base of the shell casing, and forced the cap in until it was flush. Powder and lead was then obtained by breaking up cartridges of another caliber that didn't fit his gun, and using these to reload the shells—which worked about as well as the right shells would have, had he been able to obtain them. Some of his shell casings were reloaded as much as fifty times. And White soldiers who never assumed the Indians would think of such a clever thing were dismayed to discover the Indian practice—just when they believed them to be running out of ammunition and a White victory was inevitable.[3]

An Indian gun could always be recognized by some common features. Usually the barrel and/or stock had been shortened. Religious power was added by placing brass tacks on the stock in the symbolic designs obtained by the warrior's visions. The last indication would be its state of repair, for every gun showed extensive signs of patching and remodeling.

*Top,* 1866 Winchester repeating carbine with stock decorated with brass tacks, and stock and barrel patched and bound in two places with shrunken and stitched hide. *Center* and *bottom,* closeup of binding of barrel and stock. Patches are stitched along top edges in both cases.

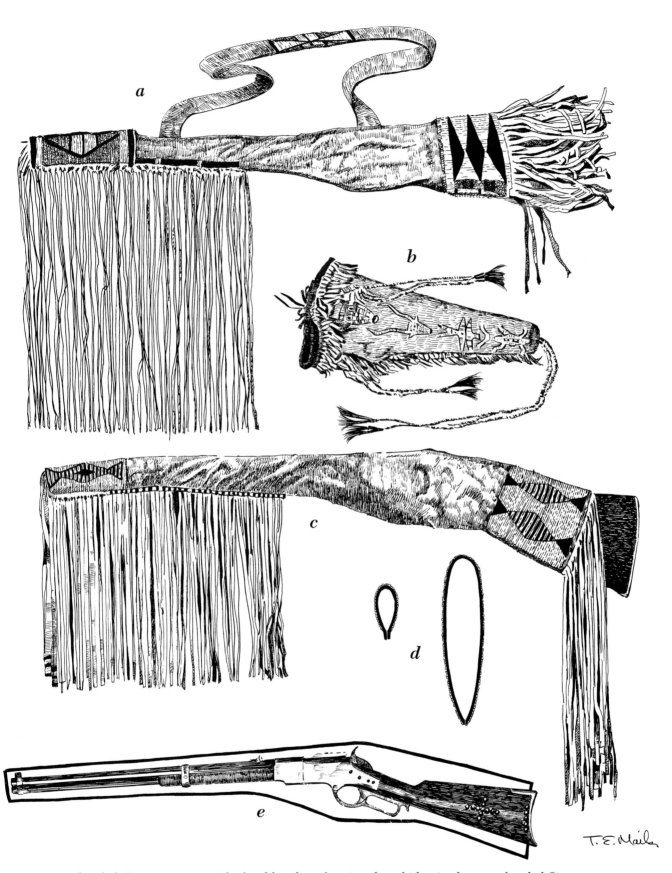

T. E. Mails

*a*, beaded Crow gun case with shoulder sling. *b*, painted rawhide pistol case. *c*, beaded Sioux gun case with typical buckskin fringes. *d*, cross section showing shape of case front and rear; *e*, section through gun case showing gun in place.

Assiniboine warriors carrying guns by shoulder sling method (adaptation after Kurtz).

From 1860 on the Henry and various types of Winchesters, Sharps, Spencers, Springfields, and the Remington Rolling Block were the guns most desired by the Indians. They also obtained flintlock and percussion pistols, but the preferred handguns were the repeating Colt and the Remington. The Indian warriors fell immediately in love with the lightweight, short-barreled Winchester carbine, and once it appeared in 1873, they would give most anything to obtain one. It was light, a repeater, and relatively easy to repair. It, at last, did replace the bow as the primary weapon.

Crow warrior carrying gun in crook in arm in traditional Crow fashion.

Methods of carrying carbines while on foot. *Left,* Blackfoot warrior with carbine in belt. *Right,* Blackfoot warrior with gun in crook of arm (after C. R. Russell).

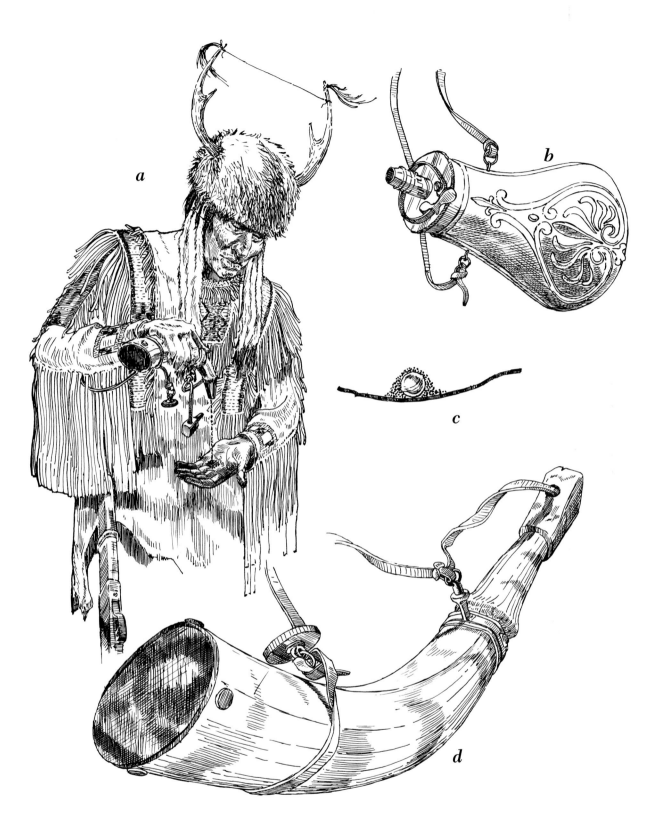

*a*, warrior pouring powder into hand to measure amount. *b*, metal trade powder flask. *c*, amount of powder poured in emergency—just enough to cover ball. *d*, buffalo horn powder horn with wood plug in large end and hardwood stopper.

The warriors carried their guns in majestic beaded buckskin cases. The old ones were simply dazzling pieces of work, with long fringes that swayed in the breeze as the proud owner rode along with one held lightly in the crook of his arm. Some guns also had a beaded sling. A Sioux states that the Crow warriors had such a characteristic way of carrying theirs that they could be identified by the custom at some distance. Crow gun cases could be recognized by the white beaded borders around the other beaded areas. Sioux gun cases were characterized by dark-blue, yellow, and red beaded designs placed on a light-blue background. A cross section of a typical gun case shows it to be in a teardrop shape, and much like the quiver in this regard. The typical Indian pistol holster was shorter than the gun case, had animal drawings on it and quilled fringes. When an Indian gun was placed in its case, it was inserted so deeply as to be virtually covered for protection against weather.

The Indians sometimes made gun belts with cartridge pockets fashioned out of thick rawhide, although few are to be seen in photographs. The belts were worn around the waist, and the warrior's knife, flint, tobacco pouch, awl, etc. were attached to the gun belts. Before the days of cartridge guns, a patch bag containing balls, caps, and grease was carried over the shoulder and under the right arm on a hide loop, as was the large powder horn or the small powder flask made from a buffalo cow horn. A war horn could always be told by its thin sides, for the warrior scraped it down until he could read its contents immediately by holding it up to the light. Horns were fitted with a permanent wooden plug in the large end, and with a hardwood stopper in the small end which was attached by a safety thong. When an emergency charge of gunpowder was required because the warrior was in a hurry he simply poured out enough powder to cover a ball placed in the palm of the hand. Under more leisurely circumstances, a wooden charge-measuring cup made of a plugged reed tube was used. The measuring cup was tied by a short string to the patch bag loop so as to be readily available.

The bow and arrows, lance, knife, tomahawk, and club made up the Indian warrior's total hunting and offensive-defensive arsenal, and this remained the case until he finally obtained enough repeating guns and ammunition to serve his purposes. After a period of diligent practice and experience he could acquit himself with exemplary skill with his handmade weapons, and he held his own in all instances until he was overcome by the White man's numbers and superior armaments.

The only other piece of equipment added to his gear was the buffalo hide shield, which was a medicine item, and in this wise was considered to be more of a protective power than would have been afforded by the thick hide itself.

When a warrior started off toward enemy territory he always carried his full arsenal of weapons, and if mounted on horseback his shield. The enemy warriors he would meet there carried the same weapons, and any contest between them was determined by defensive as well as offensive skills. With good fortune, and as he saw it, divine favor, a warrior would return home with no more than a few bruises or a minor wound. This much is certain, the Plains warriors considered their days in the field before the period of White encroachment to be truly happy ones, and of this they are assuredly the best judges.

# Chapter 21

# SHIELDS

As the eagle's-feather head-dress is the acme of all personal adornment, so the shield is the head and front, the topmost summit of warlike paraphernalia. On it he bestows infinite patience, care and thought. Not only must it be perfect in shape, in fit, in make, but also in its "medicine." He thinks it over, he works it over, he prays over it; to its care and protection he commends his life; to its adornment he elaborates thought, and devotes his time and means; to it he appends his "medicine bag" and the scalps of his enemies; on its front is painted his totem; it occupies a conspicuous but safe place in his lodge, and is hung out every fair day *in front of* his door; it is his shield, his protector, his escutcheon, his medicine, almost his God.[1]

In *Memories of Life Among the Indians,* by James Willard Schultz, the story is told how a Blackfoot named Fox Eyes came to make his shield. It's a superb story, and it touches upon many of the delightful and mysterious parts of shield making.

After several days of fasting, Fox Eyes had a vision experience of "a certain water animal," who had come to be his sacred helper. He returned to camp and shortly thereafter gave a feast, to which he invited several warriors, including some sacred-pipe men who were believed to be especially favored by "Sun."

Fox Eyes explained he now had a secret helper but needed a shield to go to war. Now he wanted to know who would make one for him if he provided the material.

Black Otter offered first, and was chosen for the honor. Fox Eyes promised him two horses to show his gratitude, since, as Schultz explains, shields were the Blackfeet's "most cherished, believed-to-be protective possessions."

The first requirement was golden eagle tail feathers with shiny black tips, so Fox Eyes built his eagle pit, and within ten days' time he had the tail feathers of four eagles. Everyone said this was "wonderfully good luck, since he now had enough to decorate the shield and to make a war bonnet, too." After this he went hunting with Schultz, and killed a buffalo bull. It was an old, old one, "whose once crescent-shaped, smooth, black, sharp horns were now mere rough, pale stubs."

This was the best possible evidence he had been brave: "He has fought many battles and survived them," said Fox Eyes as he and Schultz were removing the

Shield types common to the northern Crow/Sioux area. *Left,* has three stuffed weasels and eagle feathers appended, and duck symbols painted on it. *Right,* has two bear tracks and four directions symbol painted on it, with eagle talon and beaver tail appended.

hide from its neck and shoulders. It was surely a sign that a shield made of his hide would be his powerful protector, and would keep him safe in battles with the enemies of his tribe.

They then took the piece of thick hide to Badger Woman, and she carefully removed its fur, leaving the glossy, brownish-black surface intact. Sometime later, it was handed to Black Otter, and the interesting ceremony of transforming it into a shield began to take place.

For this great occasion Black Otter dressed himself in his finest war clothes: soft buckskin shirt, leggings, moccasins, all of which were beautifully embroidered with multicolored porcupine quill designs. On his head was the stupendous Blackfoot horns-and-ermine-skins warbonnet. His hands and face were painted a dull red, the sacred color. By the side of his lodge the piece of bull hide was stretched and pegged to the ground, and kneeling on it, he began to pray, at the same time starting to cut from the hide a circular piece about four feet in diameter.

"Oh, Sun! Oh, Night Light! Morning Star! Oh, all you Above Ones," he chanted, "Listen and pity us this day. This shield that I am making, give it of your sacred power so that it will keep its owner safe in his encounters with the enemy. Oh, Above Ones! To all of us, men, women, children, give long good life, good health; help us to overcome our enemies who are ever seeking to destroy us."

Meanwhile, several women were heating a number of stones in a little fire, and near it a small pit had been dug in the ground. The women rolled some of the stones into it and covered them with a thin layer of loose earth. Then Black Otter, with the help of three war-clothed friends, laid the circular piece of hide over the pit, and with each of them inserting pegs one after the other into slits that had been cut at regular intervals along its edge, fastened it tightly to the ground. As each of Black Otter's warrior friends drove in his peg, he told of some fight with the foe in which he had been the victor and counted coup. Soon the hide began to shrink from the heat until it bent the pegs toward the center. As fast as they loosened, the three men helpers pulled them, and then drove them in again. Black Otter supervised every step of the work, often feeling of the hide to make sure that it did not burn, and calling for more hot rocks as they were needed.

In about an hour the hide had shrunk to about half its original diameter, "and," says Schultz, "it was at least an inch thick." During the entire process Black Otter prayed frequently, and together with his helpers sang a number of sacred songs. Finally, the shrinking was completed, and Fox Eyes took the hide home and finished making a "beautiful, tail-feathers-shield of it."[2]

Here then is a combination of people involved in a Blackfoot shield's construction. A friend chosen for the honor supervised the shrinking, and the owner finished it. Still others helped, including women.

Black Otter cutting shield hide to prepare it for shrinking.

Fox Eyes and warrior friends shrinking hide over hot stones to increase thickness.

Warrior counting his coups with sticks while holy man paints symbols on front of shield.

A Sioux warrior, however, reported that he secured and prepared the hide himself, and the symbols were applied by a medicine man. A common Sioux practice as this last step was completed was for the warrior to sit before the holy man and recount his coups with small sticks, dropping one for each coup, while the holy man painted on designs, prayed over them, and sang war songs to affix their power permanently. His services in such cases were considered to be worth as many as two fine horses.[3]

Although it could be punctured by a direct blow, a shield struck at an angle was tough enough to deflect lances, arrows, or even a smoothbore ball at mid-range. And so the regal, smoked shield of buffalo bull hide was carried on raids and war parties by almost every Plains warrior. Furthermore, it was highly valued for its medicine power, and it was considered a most sacred and potent possession. Its painted symbols and the items appended to it had resulted from a vision, and in its manufacture and care the warrior bestowed intense selectivity, craftsmanship, and thought.

Paradoxically, to carry an especially fine one in battle was also something of a risk, as the shield-bearer became more conspicuous and a prize coup. Grand boasting was sure to follow a victory over such a foe. And what a sight it was for a mounted warrior to sweep into a fight with his shield feathers and long pendants trailing out like visible lines of speed. The paintings of Russell and Remington, most of all, capture the full effect of the shield and owner at their regal best.

It might be assumed that the medicine power of the shield was contained in the designs painted on it and in its other decorations, but serious consideration of the origin and construction of shields reveals that in the Indian's mind their power came from the sum of every step involved. As they saw it, the completed shield was literally infused with prayer and "power," and this force could be brought to bear as a wall of defense and to radiate destruction at the enemy. The fact is that it worked, perhaps because the enemy believed it too and responded accordingly. Battles were often won or lost simply on a strategy of shield medicines.

The war shield is a perfect example of the mingling of practical experience and holiness in Indian thought. To the Indian mind, not only the shape and properties of the material imparted their protective value, but also the vision, helpers, incantations, and rituals used to sensitize the shield and its cover of elk skin or some other fine material. Shields and covers for any warrior had to be made, or at least considered, by pipe holders or medicine men. Everyone in the

PLATE 25.   RIDES AT THE DOOR—BLACKFEET WARRIOR

tribe knew that dreams or visions had entrusted these men with the holy power required and the ceremonies which must be used, such as purifications, prayers, songs, sacrifices, and rituals with specific symbolisms. The resultant symbols burned into and/or painted on the shields, and painted or beaded or quilled on the covers, as well as the feathers, tassels, and the many other ornaments hung from both, were all talismanic, and when added together gave the shields a cumulative power. It was this assembled power which the warrior believed would preserve him from harm when he carried the shield into battle.

Some shields performed so well they became prophets for war expeditions. A certain Crow war party was led by a man named Mountain Wind, who had a shield of great renown. When they were in sight of the Sioux, Mountain Wind stopped to talk to his medicine before the fight.

The shield had a figure of a man painted in blue on his face. He had large ears and held in his left hand a straight red stone pipe. The figure was in the center of the shield, and it was bordered around its rim with "beautiful eagle feathers that fluttered in the breeze."

Mountain Wind took the shield from its cover, and held it above his head. Then he began to sing a song the others could not understand. Four times he sang it, and ceased. Four times the others responded with the traditional Crow yell. By then Mountain Wind was staggering like a blind man who was dizzy, and he was singing softly to his medicine, his face not toward the enemy, but toward the rising sun. His shield was waving toward the sun like a man's hands when he asked what was going to happen.

The others watched in utter fascination, even forgetting momentarily about the Sioux. Suddenly, Mountain Wind dropped the shield! It fell to the ground face downward. He lifted it as it had fallen, face downward, to the level of his breast, still singing his medicine song, and held it there till an eagle's feather fell fluttering from the shield's edge to the ground. Then Mountain Wind turned the

---

◄ PLATE 26.   A NORTHERN PLAINS CHIEF

The painting is of a mountain chief, and its special aim is to show the unique ancient Blackfoot warbonnet of the tribal leaders. Only these tribes and the Cheyenne made headdresses in the tubular form, with the feathers standing nearly straight up. Of course, each such bonnet was different from all others, but most were, as this one is, laden with ermine tails, ermine skins, and shiny brass tacks.

The warrior holds a leader's staff in his hand to reveal his high place in the tribe. It also shows that his animal helpers are the fox, the golden eagle, and the hawk. The hoop symbolizes the universe and God's eternal nature. A horse and a White soldier carving hangs from his necklace.

shield to see its other side. He saw many Sioux scalps and many horses, but added that one great Crow warrior would not be going home with them. Immediately Long-horse began to sing, telling of his own foreboding dream, and that he was the one who would not return.

The Crows took nine Sioux scalps and all their horses on that raid. Long-horse was the only Crow to die by a Sioux hand![4]

Another story tells of a shield which its owner could roll along the ground and then prophesy by its condition and whichever side was face up upon falling what course to follow and what the result of a raid or battle would be. The impressive thing is that the predictions were so numerous and accurate as to merit everyone's attention and reflection.[5]

In some of the tribes, shields of a common design were carried by members of societies who also used virtually the same war dress, war cries, body paint, horse decorations, and songs. Sioux pictographic drawings reveal their commonly shared society symbols did not always include the shield, but it is said that among the Cheyenne all of the shields were made by one of the societies whose members carried a plain red shield with a buffalo tail hanging from it. These red shields were believed to be particularly powerful, for the pattern was supposed to have been handed down originally by the great prophet, Sweet Medicine, who brought the tribe its sacred medicine arrows. When swung in a circle before the enemy, the red shield bearers were convinced such powers would prevent enemy arrows from hitting either the shields or themselves. If the shields failed to prevent this, it was "obviously" due to some other failure than the shields'.

Designs were usually painted on both the front of the shield and on its soft buckskin cover (or covers). Some of the patterns contained pictures of animals and/or symbols of the elements, such as stars, or lightning, or other natural objects. Some of the designs painted on Comanche shields were lines so located as to serve as a compass to guide the owner on a cloudy day. A certain line was kept pointed at a distant landmark. All of the designs were special helpers given to the shield owner in his vision. Such designs were always applied in accordance with the strict ceremonies and taboos connected with the tribal traditions. And it was accepted that the violation of a single one would destroy the shield's power.

Bear Society members always had a bear on their shields, although an individual other than the society members might also use the symbol as the result of a vision. A drawing of a bear or bear footprint meant that the owner believed it would transfer to him the strength and abilities of that animal whenever they were needed. If a tortoise was included in the pattern, it was because the shield-bearer had been led to believe he would live a long life (that is, long enough to live through most battles—but not till he was toothless!). The tortoise was long-lived, and the warrior had seen that it would move about even though its head was cut off. Special medicines made of the whole or parts of "dream" animals or birds were tied to the shield or placed under the outer cover, and long pendants

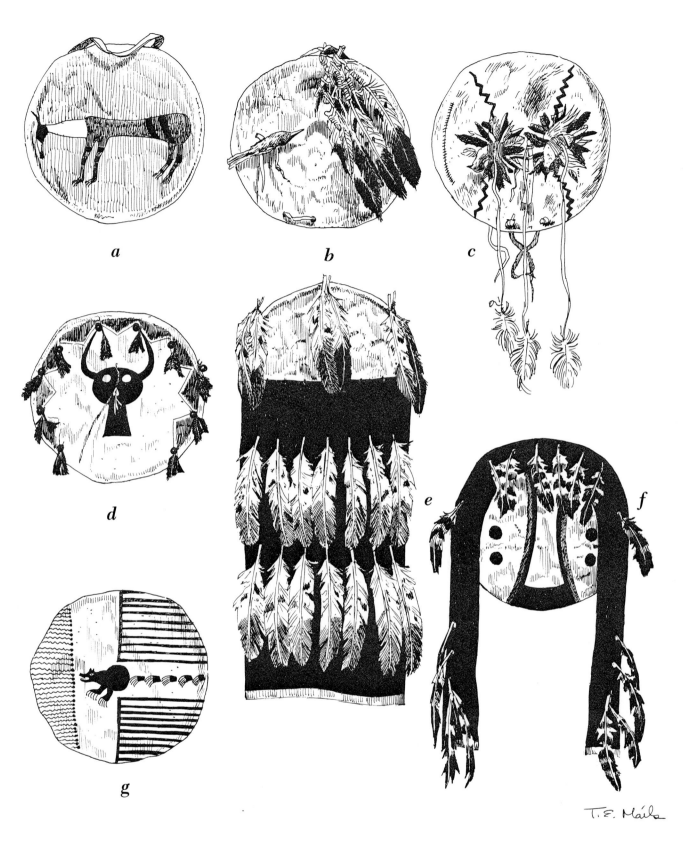

War shields. *a*, Crow shield with antelope symbol. *b*, Crow shield with stuffed bird on left and eagle feathers attached to small wooden stick on right. *c*, Crow shield with two small birds with feathers spread. *d*, Sioux shield with buffalo symbol and bells and clipped feathers around edge. *e*, Sioux shield with banks of eagle feathers attached to trade cloth apron. *f*, Sioux shield with typical trade felt trim to make streamers. *g*, Kiowa shield with bear symbols.

of animal hides, soft buckskin, or blanket cloth, preferably red or blue and decorated with eagle feathers, were fastened to the shield itself. These were supposed to endow the warrior with the courage and abilities of those animals or birds. Naturally, an opponent could read the symbols as well as the owner, and the ensuing engagements became all the more interesting for it.

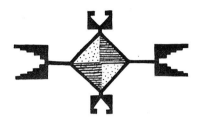

To make the standard shield in use on the Plains, a circular section of hide, approximately forty inches in diameter, was cut from the original piece taken from the buffalo bull. This was slightly more than twice as large as the shield was to be when finished. The average hide, after shrinking, was about seventeen inches in diameter, although they varied from twelve to twenty-six inches. The skin was also shrunk until it was almost twice its original thickness, or a half inch at its thickest point. It is said that "The shield was a good practical shield made from the breast or neck hide of a bull buffalo." The area indicated is under the neck and between the shoulders.[6] But the assertion is made many times that the hide used for the shield actually came from the hump area, which was thick and tough. An Assiniboine clearly affirms this, stating that "shields for warfare were made from the thick hide that covers the hump of the buffalo."[7]

The hide was fastened down with wooden pegs over a round hole in the ground about eighteen inches in diameter by eighteen inches deep. One edge of the hide was left loose, and this was lifted from time to time and red-hot stones were dropped in the hole. Water was poured on the stones until the hot steam caused the hide to shrink to the desired size. The hair was then removed with a stone or bone scraper, and the still soft hide was then pegged down over a small mound of earth. This gave it a dish shape which increased its strength. A circular shape was marked on the hide with a pointed stick which had been rubbed with charcoal, and the edges were trimmed smooth to this pattern. Finally, the shield was laid on a hard surface such as a piece of rawhide, and the wrinkles and dents were pounded with a smooth stone or berrymasher until the surface of the shield was fairly smooth.

A buckskin, rawhide, or other type of sling and a hand loop were then attached to the shield, and it was tested by having the warriors shoot arrows at it from a distance of twenty yards or so. If the arrows bounced back from the hide, leaving it neither penetrated nor injured, the shield was considered fit for use. If not, it was rejected and another was made.[8]

*a*, Arikara shield with buffalo symbol and eagle tail feathers. *b*, Gros Ventre shield with stuffed hawk appended. *c*, circles on buffalo indicate areas reported by Indian authorities from which hide was taken for shields. *d*, tipi with tripod behind for sunning shield, and in which position shield protected rear of tipi through its infused power.

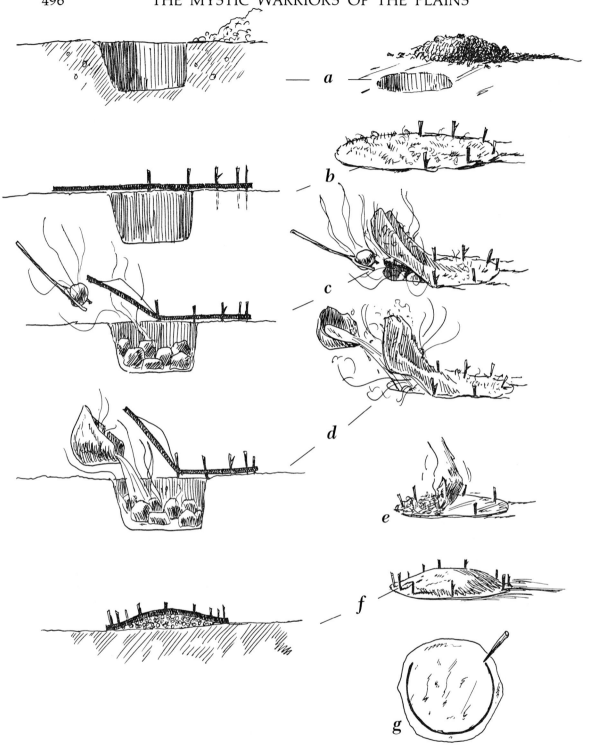

T. E. Máile

Steps in making shield by most common method. *a*, pit for fire. *b*, hide stretched and pegged over pit. *c*, heated rocks added. *d*, water poured on rocks to make steam. *e*, hair removed. *f*, shrunken hide pegged over mound to give dish shape. *g*, marking with charcoal to indicate finished shape.

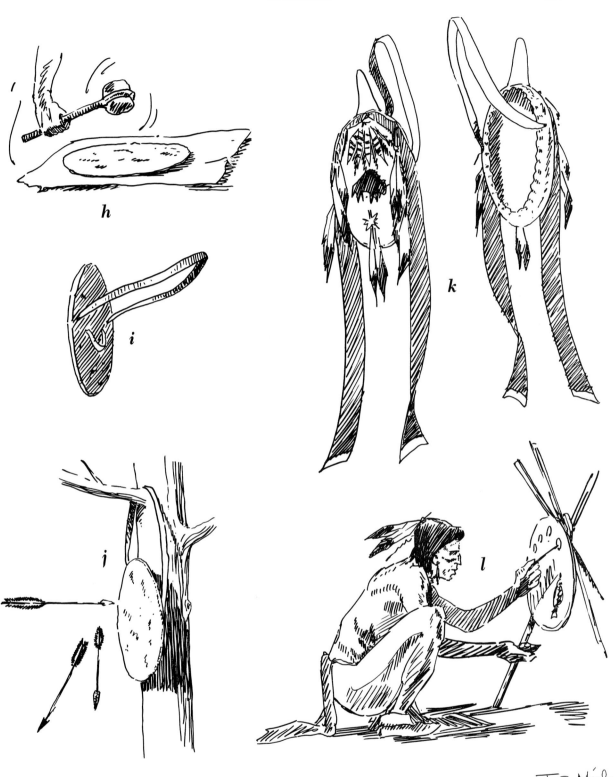

Shield making continued. *h*, pounding hide for final shaping and smoothing. *i*, shoulder loop attached to back of shield through holes in shield. *j*, testing shield. *k*, shield cover, front and back view. *l*, painting symbols on shield proper.

Herman Lehmann relates how the Comanches taught him to ride wild horses, to jump from the ground onto a horse as he raced by and dodge an arrow at the same time. He was taught to crouch close to the neck of the horse so an enemy could not hit him, and how to use the shield to ward off arrows. He was given a shield and placed off about fifty yards. Four braves took bows and blunt arrows and began to shoot at him. He knew what he had to do, for he had seen the performance before. He began moving the shield up and down and from right to left. The arrows poured against it and he managed to ward some of them off with the wavy motion, but torrents of blunt sticks came and he was too slow. One passed just over the shield and struck him in the forehead. He saw stars—not those painted ones on the shield, but real fiery flashes—the arrow downed him, and those who were firing let up the shooting for a time. However, the target practice soon resumed, and he had to keep at it until he had learned how to use the shield. He was knocked down several times before he became adept. "All Indians," he said, "were thus trained."[9]

The decoration of the shield was always accompanied by special ceremonies conducted by medicine men and proven warriors. The cover of soft dressed skin, such as deer or elk, was generally made first. It was painted with a design different from but related by color or substance to that on the shield itself.

The front of the shield was painted after the cover was finished, and other decorations were attached to it, such as feathers, animal skins, birds, etc.

The foregoing was the most common method of making a shield, but there were a number of ways in which hides were shrunk to make shields both among the tribes and within a given tribe. They certainly illustrate the versatility of the Indian craftsmen.

In one method the hide was prepared by staking it down on the bottom of a hole six or eight inches deep and covering it with dirt. A fire was kept burning over it for several days. After this, the hide would be shrunken and very thick. Those relating the method do not explain how the Indian moved his stakes while they were covered with fire and hot dirt. Perhaps the fire could burn down and be removed at regular intervals once the Indian became familiar with the hide's rate of shrinkage. However, since it shrank rapidly, other methods seem easier by far. The pit hole would need to be as large in diameter as the original hide, though, and perhaps if the fire were only placed in the center and could still manage to shrink the hide, the stakes, being outside it, could be more easily reached.[10]

In another method a man about to construct himself a shield dug a hole two feet deep and as large in diameter as he intended to make his shield. In this he built a fire. Over it, a few inches higher than the ground, he stretched the rawhide horizontally over the fire, using little pegs driven through holes made near the edges of the skin. Again, this skin was twice as large as the size of the finished shield. He invited his particular and best friends into a ring to dance and sing

Alternate methods of shrinking hide. *a*, shrinking by layer of heated dirt. *b*, pit fire kept burning. *c*, steaming over hot stones. *d*, covering with thin layer of clay and hot coals. *e*, shrinking by use of heated rocks. *f*, method of making hoop shield, top view, *g*, back view, and *h*, cross section showing hide folded around wood hoop.

Hoop shield details. *a*, method of measuring size of willow hoop. *b*, three fingers' width allowed around hoop to provide for hide to wrap over hoop. *c*, shrinking hide in hot water. *d*, punching holes in softened hide for lacing. *e*, method of lacing hide on hoop. *f*, close-up of lacing detail.

around it until the shrinking was completed, and to petition the Great Spirit to instill power into it. Then he spread glue made by boiling buffalo hoofs and joints in water, which was rubbed and dried in as the skin was heated. Meanwhile, a second man busily drove other pegs inside of those in the ground—as the first were gradually giving way and being pulled up by the contraction of the skin.[11]

In yet another method the rawhide was cut in a disk shape twice the size of the finished shield, and shrunk by steaming over hot stones.[12]

In another variation the hide was covered with a thin layer of clay on which burning coals were placed until the skin was shrunk and hardened.[13]

In a final method, a pit was dug, including an access trough on the side by which cold rocks could be removed and hot rocks added from time to time. The pit was filled with hot rocks and covered by a layer of dirt shaped to the curve the owner wanted his shield to be. Over this the hide was staked, with one edge loose and the pegs being moved in the conventional way as the hide shrunk.[14]

An Arapaho states that he shrunk the hide for his shield by soaking it in water. This may account for the extremely wrinkled surfaces one sees on some shields.[15]

A second and less common kind of Plains shield was made with a wooden hoop for a frame.

The Sioux made it in the following way: A green, three-quarter-inch-diameter willow hoop was bent to a diameter approximately the width of a man's chest. The ends of the hoop were beveled, lapped, and lashed together with sinew. The buffalo hide was soaked in boiling water to shrink it (finished hoop shields were not as thick as the heat-shrunken self-shields which used no hoop). The hide was trimmed to the shape of the round hoop, allowing three fingers width of extra hide beyond the hoop, and holes or slits were punched at regular intervals around the edge of the hide. The hide was then pegged down over a mound of dirt to give it its concave shape. An alternate method of obtaining the shape was to form it by pressing the still soft skin down into a dished-out sand mold. The extra hide was then folded over the edges of the hoop and cross-laced through the slits to the frame. Shield lacings were thongs cut from heavy buckskin. The buckskin sling and hand loops were then attached in the traditional ways and the shield was tested.[16]

Lightweight ceremonial dance shields were often made in this way, with the wooden hoop being removed after the hide had hardened. The back of the shield in such cases was interlaced with a buckskin thong after the manner employed for tightening shield covers.

The Comanches made the regular heat-shrunken shields, but they also made hoop shields by throwing the hide over a fire until it was hot enough to remove the meat. The hide was then worked with round stones until it was soft and sewed onto a rattan or hickory hoop. It was "dished" by stretching it over stakes until it was dry.[17]

Comanche shield from Harvey Collection. *a*, outer cover. *b*, inner cover. *c*, concave shield.

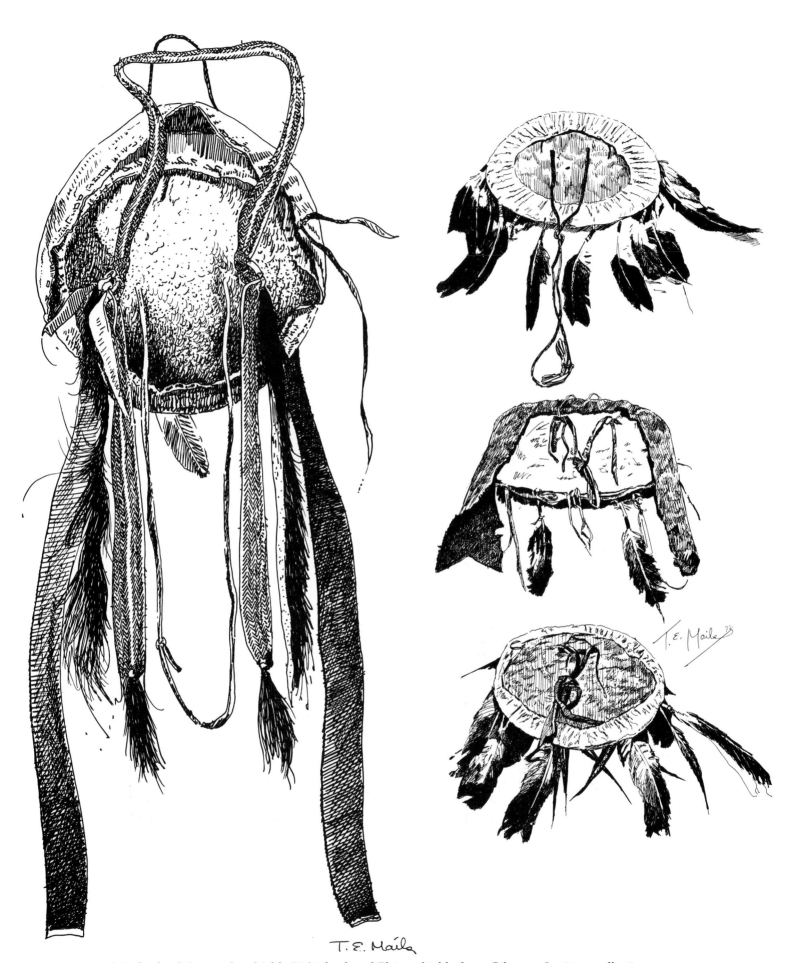

*Left,* back of Comanche shield. *Right,* backs of Plains shields from Gilcrease Institute collection.

To speak of shields and their construction is one thing, to actually see them is another, since a beautifully crafted one is simply stupendous. From the collector's point of view it is regrettable that so many were buried with their owners, and thus deteriorated in the grave or on the burial platforms. Fred Harvey, who assembled one of the finest private collections of Plains and Southwest items ever known, obtained a heat-shrunken Comanche shield which deserves special mention, and it is illustrated in black and white on pages 502–3.

This Comanche shield has not one, but two covers. It is concave, and thus provides a dish or basket to hold its beautiful pendants and array of eagle feathers. It is eighteen inches in diameter, and the total length from the top of the shield to the end of the wool pendants is fifty-two inches. The shield itself is approximately one-half inch thick.

The cap, or outer cover, has an inner circle of black bordered by white, the next area is deep blue, and the outer edge is lemon yellow. The radiating lines are alternately orange and black. A small group of feathers in the center of the cover is a combination of hawk and eagle wing feathers. One large eagle tail feather also hangs from the center and there are two smaller side feathers with breath feathers attached. The outer cap fits over the inside cover like a dust cover on a case. There are metal bells on it—which means it was used for ceremonial dances, and perhaps was not carried into enemy territory, where the noise of the bells would give the owner away.

The inside cover has the greatest number of eagle tail feathers attached to its front at each side, and also two long dark-blue blanket cloth pendants. Its center dishes in to fit the concave shape of the shield itself, and everything hanging on it packs into this dish receptacle so neatly it excites the utmost appreciation. Undoubtedly, this cover was carried to war, pointed toward the enemy to dispel its medicine, and then removed as an actual battle was engaged.

The shield itself was used for the fight. A war sling of buckskin is attached to the back, as is another sling of woven (Mexican origin) woolen material. This second band is four inches wide, and being more comfortable than the narrow buckskin sling was probably used to carry the shield to and from a raid. There are also two long pendant strips of buffalo skin, with hair, attached to the back of the shield.

According to the paintings of Russell, Remington, and Koerner, a warrior carried his shield on foot or horseback in several different ways. Ordinarily the loop of the shield was hung around the warrior's neck, and the shield itself was carried on his back. The quiver was carried horizontally underneath or below it. The shield loop was knotted in front to pull the shield snugly to the back to prevent loss or bouncing while traveling. During engagements, the shield was shifted to where it could be brought into play by the left arm, and raised or lowered to ward off arrows or bullets. Judging by most paintings and photographs, when not carried on the warrior's back, the shield was hung from the saddle cantle

*a* and *b*, diagrams illustrating the advantages of the concave over the convex shield for deflecting arrows. The question as to whether shields could deflect both arrows and rifle balls has never been settled, but it has been stated so many times as to give credence to the idea. Indians did use them for defense against all types of weapons. *c*, *d*, and *e*, methods of carrying shield on shoulder loop.

on the left side of the horse—again, with the loop knotted and the shield pulled snugly to the horse. The left side attachment was not an absolute, however, and some warriors hung them on the right. They were also hung from the pommel, and so were sometimes in front of and underneath the rider's legs.

The loop was usually attached to the back of the shield with its tie on the left back tie point placed a bit higher than the tie point on the right. When carried over the shoulder this allowed the shield design itself to remain straight for the benefit of all who viewed it.

It is commonly believed that the shield front, or side held toward the enemy, was convex. Yet some shields in the Harvey Collection, the Gilcrease Institute, the Southwest Museum, and the San Diego Museum of Man are concave, as was the Comanche shield just mentioned. There are two reasons for this. The first is that a concave shield provided better deflection than a convex one, since an obstacle striking the loosely held shield caused it to yield and turn around the arm. The convex shield, in moving, tended to deflect the arrow or bullet into head or legs, whereas the concave shield provided a lip to help shunt them away. The second was that a concave shield provided a dish or basket into which the numerous feathers and other medicine items could be neatly packed or folded.

Museum shields are seldom smooth and round. Admittedly, some of them may have warped considerably over the years, yet at best they were irregular circles and of a somewhat uneven surface in the beginning. Shrinking and cutting and pounding such a heavy hide obviously had its difficulties and effect.

When not being carried by the warrior, the shield was placed outside the tipi on a sunny day on a tripod at the rear or west side. It was placed there as a bulwark to protect the lodge owner against attack or evil spirits approaching on his "blind" side. Blackfoot tipis often had two tripod racks behind them. One tripod held the shield and the other the medicine bundle. It was, however, equally common to place both on the same tripod. Placing the shield outside was called "sunning the shield," and the Indians believed that it was being further infused with power from the sun. The Kiowas said that anyone violating the taboos concerning the placement and care of shields was subject to certain disgrace and disaster. Drawings and paintings also show tripods of different heights, some not more than five feet, some ten or more feet tall. Photographs hit a mid-point, and are probably the best guide, indicating a tripod of seven or eight feet at its apex.

PLATE 27.   KIOWA MOUNTAIN LION BOW CASE AND QUIVER—  ▶
WEAPON STUDY NO. 1

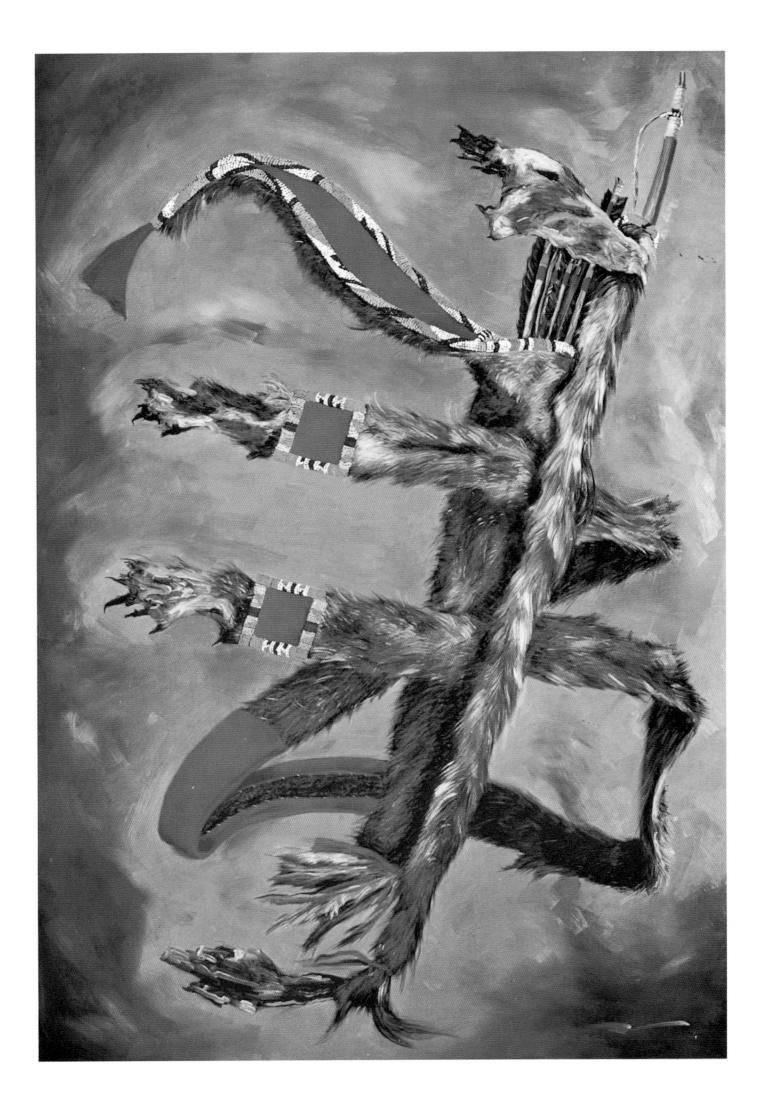

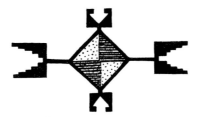

There were four types of shields which were used on the Plains: the dance shield, which was a lightweight version of the war shield; the medicine or holy man's shield, of which several are illustrated and described in the material on medicine; the miniature shield, which was a small copy of a warrior's war shield, and which he sometimes carried on long journeys in place of the war shield; and the war shield.

The war shield was made in three varieties. The least-used variety, and one which has not been described in the previous shield material, was made by stitching four or five layers of flat rawhide together, cutting these in the traditional round shape, and then decorating the front side of the hide with feathers and strips of cloth. A second variety was made by forming the hide around a wooden hoop. Many kinds of hoop shields were constructed, but these called for a thinner and weaker hide than those made by the third means, which was the heat-shrinking process. Most war shields by far were fashioned this way, for the shrinking produced a thick hide and it was easier to press into a concave or convex shape which aided deflection.

Prior to the arrival of the horse, Plains war shields were quite large—often being three feet or more in diameter. These were much too cumbersome for mounted men, though, and so the size was reduced until the average war shield measured only eighteen inches in diameter.

Young men often went as initiates on their first or second raid without a shield. And men who journeyed on foot into enemy territory did not always carry

---

◀ PLATE 28.   PIPE TOMAHAWKS—WEAPON STUDY NO. 2

The pipe on the left was given as a friendship gesture to an Indian chief by the renowned Hudson's Bay Company about 1845. The pipe on the right is attributed to the Shoshone Indians. Its shaft is studded with brass tacks. The flap is 34 inches long and terminates in a section of red trade cloth. It is decorated with ermine, buckskin fringe, and hawk bells. The pipe itself is 24½ inches long.

Methods of carrying and employing shields (after C. R. Russell and Koerner).

heavy shields. But the shield was the final piece of equipment constructed by a young man preparing to take up his full adult responsibilities. He might make several more shields during his active period as a warrior, but the first one, coupled with his personal medicines, gave him the initial protection and confidence he needed to share the full responsibilities of a raid or war party to be carried out on horseback. He would also use the shield for defense if his village was attacked.

Medicine shields were usually covered with the most intriguing appendages and symbols, but the war shields were the truly sumptuous creations. Some of them would rank with the finest artworks of all time—and yet a shield was much more than a piece of art. To the Indian, a shield vibrated with power, and by sunning it, he could continue to draw power from above into it for an indefinite time. Small wonder then it was placed by his side to protect him when he made his final journey into the Mystery Land of the dead.

Crow warrior with full tail bonnet and war shield decorated with eagle tail feathers.

# Chapter 22

# THE BIRTH AND TRAINING
# OF THE BOY

When a boy went to a mountain top to seek a vision, he cried continually throughout his fasting for the Great Spirit to be merciful to him *so that his people might live!*[1]

It is strictly believed and understood by the Sioux that a child is the greatest gift from Wakan' tanka, in response to many devout prayers, sacrifices and promises. Therefore the child is considered "sent by Wakan' tanka," through some element—namely, the element of human being. That the child may grow up in health with all the virtues expected, and especially that no serious misfortune may befall the child, the father makes promises or vows to Wakan' tanka as manifested by the different elements of the earth and sky. During the period of youthful blessedness the father spared no pains to let the people know of his great love for his child or children. This was measured by his fellow men according to the sacrifices or gifts given, or the number of ceremonies performed. In order to have a standard by which this love could be shown, the first thing taken into consideration and adopted was the White Buffalo Maiden, sent to the Sioux tribe by the Buffalo tribe. The impression left upon the people by the Maiden and her extraordinary good qualities were things that were much admired by every parent as a model for his children. This Maiden was pure white, without a blemish—that was the principal desire of the father for the character of his child.[2]

Preparations for the survival and longevity of all Plains warriors began before they were born. During pregnancy, either the mother or one of the grandmothers made two curious quilled or beaded objects, a sand lizard and a turtle. These were gracefully shaped, and finished with horsehair or breath feathers attached to the ends of the four legs. Both animals were revered because they "lived forever" and were so difficult to kill. Their protective power was enlisted early as a guardian and guarantee of the individual's long life. When the child was born, the umbilical cord was cut and placed inside the turtle, packed in tobacco or herbs, while the lizard served as a decoy to lure away malevolent forces. A second use of the turtle was to remind the bearer that his life was a precious gift from his parents, and he had the responsibility to marry and to pass the gift

*Top,* Sioux beaded turtle and sand lizard. *Bottom,* Kiowa woman with child in cradleboard.

of birth and life on to his own children. Such vigilant protection of life was essential to the Indian's sense of well-being in a land of extremes and unknowns. Obviously, the first step toward survival was to turn one's mind in the direction of whatever was necessary to achieve it.

When the child began to walk, the amulet was attached to his clothing to serve as a constant reminder of its purpose. Therefore, a child of five or six was known as a "carry your navel." Sometimes the turtle was put away later on and other times it was kept by the mother. A boy often tied it to the left shoulder of his shirt, and then transferred it to his buffalo-horned headdress if he became a renowned warrior.

It was the duty of one of the father's sisters to make the cradleboard, and the same loving care as was devoted to the turtle was expended upon it, for it was to be a tangible symbol of sisterly respect, and it maintained the vital bond among the members of the family. After the boy grew, the sight of his beautiful cradle became a continual reminder of this. Even the nature of the cradleboard design contributed to the idea. For example, the Kiowas mounted their cradles on two long boards, with the upper ends sharply pointed so as to stick in the ground and thus protect the baby in case of a head-first fall from a horse.

To avoid the problems of overpopulation in a nomadic society, the Indian family was kept small, consisting usually of one to three children being born from three to five years apart—in any case a second not being encouraged until the first could walk.

If difficulties occurred during labor, and a priest had to be called for a medicine rite before a child was born, the child's turtle was decorated with a small design representing a tortoise, which charmed further dangers away. Thus the tortoise revealed an intimate fact about the person's birth, and it became the first of many marks a man would wear to tell the story of his life.

An ancestral name was given to a child at a festive naming rite a few days after birth, and he kept it until a new name was conferred at a special ceremony honoring his first great accomplishment in life.

Where other children had already received the prized family names, the father, or else a great warrior of the tribe invited to perform the naming, named the baby according to a war deed the name-bestower had accomplished. He might also name him after a brave animal or something seen in a dream. While a crier, or village herald, reported the name to the entire camp, a wealthy father, following custom, announced that a horse would be given to a specified poor man. Sometimes it would go to another rich man who could return the favor, but this was considered a bit obvious. At this juncture the friends of the family expressed their wish that the child "might live to have his ears pierced," whereupon the father or grandfather announced through the crier that a certain warrior of note would perform the operation. At this time the tribe vowed to protect the child "until it walked." The ear piercing, which was done with a sharp stick and was very painful, took place during the first Sun Dance to be held after the child was able to walk, and the boy wore earrings from then until he died. In the mind of the Indian, ear piercing played, in fact, a role very similar to Jewish circumcision and Christian baptism.

In evidence of the high regard and love in which some Indian children were held, the Sioux had a wonderful ceremony dating from around A.D. 1800 called the Alo' wanpi, or Hunka. The word "Alo' wanpi" meant "to sing for someone," and "Hunka" was the name applied to children participating in the ceremony. A tribesman of renown was invited by the child's father to perform the rite, and the man who performed it was regarded as a second father by the child involved. He made a solemn vow taking the child under his protection until one or the other had died. And he became like a brother to the man whose child or children he sang over and painted with the Hunka ceremonial stripes. In all the great ceremonies of the Sioux there was not one which bound two men together so strongly as this. The tie was even stronger than natural brotherhood, because the invited man had assumed a responsibility not placed on him by nature.

The Alo' wanpi ceremony was a miniature version of the Sun Dance, but without the torture aspects. A special pipe, an altar, a small tree, and a buffalo skull were used, and the ceremonial articles included an ear of corn, a tuft of white down for the child's hair, and a bunch of shed buffalo hair. The pipe was decorated with woodpecker feathers, for this was a simple, humble bird which stayed by its nest and was seldom seen. The bird was considered appropriate because the Hunka child would be more closely guarded and protected than others, and the girls so consecrated were seldom seen in public until they had grown up. The corn was used because of a Sioux legend about the growth of a beautiful plant—which turned out to be corn. The celebration of this ceremony placed a child in a highly respected position in the tribe. Such a child was regarded as possessing that which would make it nothing but good in every way, and was recognized by all as ranking above an ordinary child.[3]

The care and responsibility of the infant fell to the mother. She was assisted in this by the grandmother, various sisters and female cousins, or an older daughter. An older sister might care in every way for a girl, but she was limited by custom to feeding and baby-sitting a boy.

Boys ran naked a good part of the time, "since children became tired of their clothes and took them off for relief." Apparel was first required around the age of seven, and the degree of nakedness from then on depended somewhat upon the sex of the older children in the family.

The disciplining of small children was almost non-existent. In fact, they were catered to and greatly indulged. Children were not permitted to cry, however, and to prevent it their earliest wants were either immediately satisfied, or they were rocked and cuddled until their desires ceased. Where coddling was ineffectual, the grandmother cried along with the child to "help it." The exception among some tribes was that the noses of older children who continued to cry were held, or else water was poured into their nostrils, until the treatment became so intolerable they quit. After all, a group hiding from its enemies in those days could easily be given away by a crying child. Otherwise, children were "asked," not "told," what to do. Ponderous but entertaining lectures about responsibilities began at an early age, and the children had responded so well by the time they were ten or eleven that admonitions about discipline were no longer necessary.

The use of culture frighteners such as the owl, the medicine man, and (later) the White man were sometimes employed to gain obedience from unruly older boys. Children who could not overcome bed-wetting were threatened by being told they would be fed mice, and the Indians claim it was an effective remedy.

Indian parents and grandparents openly expressed a great love and fondness for their children, and all Indians agree that youngsters were never whipped or handled roughly. Even grown boys who misbehaved were reasoned with until they were able to realize their mistakes.

Indian leaders did recognize that children must be taught, however, "or they will not know anything; if they do not know anything, they will have no sense; and if they have no sense they will not know how to act."[4] So boys were painstakingly instructed in every matter necessary to a fruitful life.

Parents encouraged the qualities of spirituality, pride, respect for elders, conformance to the tribal code of ethics and to the standard rules of etiquette. Every mother sang instructive lullabys which included lessons in morals and bravery. Tribal historians taught history, and other elders gave instructions in national loyalty.

The father-son relationship took on a special warmth when the father presented his son of four years or so with his first bow and arrows, and began instructing him in shooting, hunting, and trailing techniques. Sometimes uncles or older brothers aided in a boy's development.

By the time they were four or five, children had been given their own clothing, utensils for eating, tools for use in their activities, and a separate bed. They had also received fine garments for participating in festivals. They were expected to take care of these and to keep them in order. Careful attention was paid to the selection of playmates, to dress, and to manners, for children were expected to show the reserve and bearing that elevated family pride. Older children who lacked the qualities of neatness, deportment, respect, and self-control were publicly shamed, since scorn served as a social conditioner for every family.

Children's games were educational, and as such played a significant role in their development. Play between girls and boys was common, and received strong encouragement by the parents. Parents made little tipis, travois, and weapons with which the children could imitate the activities of their elders. The entire play scheme became, in fact, the basic pathway over which the child made a smooth adjustment to adulthood. It continued until the age of eleven years or so, when

Nez Percé boy dressed for festival purposes, wearing otter skin dance chest cover, beaded gauntlets, and roach.

a strict separation of the sexes was begun, and a more mature training was introduced.

Speed was a secondary aim in their games. Skill, endurance, daring, and the ability to withstand pain were placed at the top of the list, for each of these developed the qualities necessary for national survival. Therefore, the method of choosing leaders in the games was identical to the method of selecting the ranking men for adult activities. They were chosen in accordance with their demonstrated abilities and their successes in contests.

A young boy's first hunting parties were mimic and communal, although without formal organization. Male children less than ten years of age went rabbit hunting together, and also took other small game such as birds and turtles. This was a gratifying and valuable service, for it furnished the family with a supplementary food supply. At the same time, important hunting techniques were being learned. Each son would employ the methods taught him by his father, observe the tricks and approaches used by other boys, and do some experimenting on his own. Above all, they learned to kill for need, rather than for sport or exhibition. On these hunts, young boys learned the first essentials for becoming good providers, cooperative hunters and skillful trackers, and they also learned the laws of survival.

Screech owls, coyotes, wolves, and birds were common to all parts of the Plains, and boys learned to imitate such special animal and bird calls as were chosen by their tribe to be used for communication with each other while hunting, raiding, or fighting.

Boys ten or more years of age were compelled to take long runs, to go without food and water for long periods of time, to roll in the snow, to dive into icy water, and to stay awake and alert for hours on end. As they grew older they took their runs at noon, when the sun was boiling hot. Later still, they were given sacred sweat baths and made to purify themselves in preparation for war. They learned how to throw the lance, and to dodge arrows by spinning or dropping down, to take advantage of any cover, to shoot rapidly from a crouched position, to be able to ride with only their knees guiding the horse, and to swing the shield so as to give the least possible target to an enemy. Among the Sioux, the eyes of the young men were always fixed on the tribe's sacred water bag stick which would be carried by them when they were invited to go on their first raiding party.

The aspiring warrior was trained never to show cowardice, and any such indication gave him a name others never let him forget. No coward ever became a warrior or leader. So young men were placed in situations which would test their courage and alertness to the limit. Once in a "rare" while there was a failure, a boy who didn't have the stuff in him for war and hunting. For him there was no middle ground; he had to put on women's clothing and live his life as a woman. He was not, however, totally scorned, and now and then one of the failures would become the finest craftsman in his village.

The boy in training. *a*, catching butterflies for agility. *b*, throwing lance for skill. *c* and *d*, swimming, running for endurance. *e*, Sioux youth carrying special water bag stick used by young man on first war raid.

Boy tending horse herd.

Assiniboine elders advised boys to travel on foot as much as possible. "If," they said, "you wish to keep on being a fast runner, you should not ride horses, as your legs will be bowed and your joints will grow fast together."[5] One of the very first lessons a Crow boy experienced was running to catch butterflies. When one was caught, its wings were rubbed on the boy's chest to "borrow" the creature's grace, cunning, and swiftness. Other general advice among the Assiniboines went as follows: "Among our people everyone is expected to marry and raise children. In order to make a success of marriage the father must be a good provider—and that means a good hunter. Look to your equipment and use it skillfully. Study the habits of animals and birds and learn to take them at the right time and in the correct manner. Make your kills neatly and quickly, or else you and your family will have to eat sour meat from exhausted game."[6]

The moment a son was big enough to straddle a horse, his father gave him a colt and some gear. He was carefully instructed in the colt's care and was responsible for its well-being thereafter. As boys grew older, they were assigned the responsibility of caring for their parents' herds. The task was usually done by two or more boys at a time, and it gave them an opportunity to ride to their heart's content. It was also a good way to observe the horses' manners and abilities. Often a boy came to know more about what a certain horse could accomplish than his father did.

The young brave had to learn how to get the most out of a horse, and some of the old warriors said that after a White man had completely exhausted one, an Indian could ride the same animal another twenty miles or more. The boy learned how to ride hour upon hour at the fastest possible speed. He was taught that as one horse grew tired and almost fell, he could leap from the back of that one to the back of another while they were both at full gallop. He must even learn to sleep while riding. Groups would divide into sections while being pursued, one section sleeping hanging over their horses' necks, while the other led them— and drove a stolen herd at the same time. Then when all of the horses were exhausted he still must have enough strength left to run on foot! The training was most demanding, and they had plenty of accidents when they were young, although they insisted "they were always happy," and one can readily see why!

Among the Blackfoot, eminent men would make long speeches to groups of boys, telling them what they ought to do to be successful in life. They would point out that to accomplish anything they must be brave and untiring in war; that long life (beyond sixty) was usually not desirable, that old people always had a hard time. The aged were given the worst side of the lodge and generally neglected. It was much better, while the body was strong and in its prime, while the sight was clear, the teeth sound, and the hair still black and long, to die in battle fighting bravely. The example of successful warriors would be held up to them, and the boys were urged to imitate their brave deeds.

At the time of the annual Blackfoot Medicine Lodge Ceremony, excited boys gathered by the hundreds to see the brave warriors count their coups. A man would get up holding in one hand a bundle of small sticks, and taking one from the bundle, would recount a brave deed, repeating this for each of his coups until the sticks were gone. As soon as he sat down, another man took his place. When the boys saw how respected those men were, they said to themselves, "That man was once a boy like us, and we, if we have strong hearts, may do as much as he has done." Understandably, it was not unusual for enthusiastic boys to steal off from the camp and follow war parties. In such cases they went without the knowledge of their parents and without food or extra moccasins. But aided by sympathetic older men who had done the same thing, they would get to the edge of the enemy's camp, watch the ways of the fighters, learn about going to war, and how to act when on the war trail so as to be successful. They also became acquainted with the country, and were soon equipped to undertake their adult raids.

Bearing all of this in mind, whenever a writer states that Indian boys were "not trained," he means they were not formally trained, since as one follows the course of their growth he soon begins to wonder whether, in fact, any youngster of any land ever had a better preparation for his life and environment. Throughout his early years he was instructed and groomed in religion, ethics, heritage, warfare, raiding, and hunting. Listening, observing, participating in games of skill and fortitude, practicing the techniques of running, swimming, dancing, shooting, riding, trailing, and hunting all equipped him for the proud role of a mystic warrior, and more hopefully, of a leader.

The Crow boy learned early in life that the arenas for achieving success were the fasting place, the raid, and the council of chiefs. Everything in his schooling was designed to make him yearn to begin the series of offices which made him first a war party's helper, then a scout, then a leader of scouts, then a pipeholder, and finally a chief and a head chief. Yet rarely was the progression truly as regimented as the ladder of achievement implied, for an outstanding exploit or a notably powerful vision could land a man almost anywhere on the ladder in a moment.

To become a pipeholder, or "the One Who Owns the War Party," the primary requirement was either a successful vision, which the accredited pipeholders would accept, or the purchase of an acknowledged pipeholder's war medicine bundle. However, a Crow man must also have completed the four prescribed coups even to be eligible for this office. Therefore, the boy's goal was to obtain them, and so he set out to strike an enemy with something held in his hand, to steal an enemy's best horse, to capture an enemy's weapons or medicine, and finally to ride a foe down.

There was always much to dream about, much to prepare for.

At the age of fourteen or fifteen, a promising youth might be invited to join one of the important Warrior Societies. Before he was seventeen, he might steal an enemy's horse or count coup and take a scalp. Often, before he was nineteen, his first Sun Dance would be made. At twenty he might have proven his abilities, holiness, and power sufficiently well to lead a small war party. At twenty-five he might be a chief. At the age of thirty his active warpath days would begin to draw to a close. Hopefully, he would now have many war honors and horses. He might even have two tipis, with a wife or more in each, and several children.

After thirty-five he would devote himself to the hunt, to whatever defensive warfare was required of his village, to spiritual meditations, to becoming a wise and recognized elder, and to intense concern over the future of the tribe. He would constantly substantiate his claims by the material evidence of his past achievements, for much of his time would be spent in encouraging young men to seek the warpath, and by this to perpetuate the system and his own status. Finally, the circle of life which moved along the Sacred Path would be completed, and having become "a child again," he would return to the Father Who gave him birth.

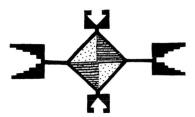

My son, I like to have you come out with me, and travel about over the country. You have no father to teach you, and I am glad to take you with me, and to tell you the things that I know. It is a good thing to be a member of our tribe, and it is a good thing to belong to a good family in that tribe. You must always remember that you come of good people. Your father was a brave man, killed fighting bravely against the enemy. I want you to grow up to be a brave man and a good man. You must love your relations, and must do everything you can for them. If the enemy should attack the village, do not run away; think always first of defending your own people.[7]

Do you know why your relations treat you well? It is because you are a man and must act a man's part. They know that perhaps they may not have you long with them, that at any moment you may be taken away.[8]

Thus far the intercommunity living, religion, arts, and weapons necessary to a boy's basic training have been considered. Now the maturing youth journeys forth to engage the challenging world around him, and those who accompany him discover what a man can accomplish who lives in the very atmosphere of God and nature.

With the exception of the Australian aborigines, no one else has matched the abilities of the Indian-American as a trailer of animals and men, or his ability to survive in a land of challenging extremes. An Indian youth on the Plains may not have had reading and writing and arithmetic to learn, but he had the alphabet and calculations of the wilderness to conquer, and that alone involved the learning of a thousand signs, any combination of which must be read and acted upon immediately in order that he might triumph and live.

By the time he entered his teens, the Indian boy not only saw things non-Indians missed, but he saw them when they were farther away. When he couldn't see them he could put his ear to the ground and find them by their sounds. Beyond that, he could smell almost as well as the wolf. He was always at attention, looking, calculating, and measuring his chances of success. He was honed by his elders until his reactions were sharp and instant. Panic was out. When caught off guard he must automatically spot the enemy, estimate what would happen next, whether

Uncle taking nephew on hunting trip.

he should fight or run, and above all think more of giving warning to others than of saving himself.

The youth in training learned that an incredible number of questions faced a warrior journeying away from his home. For example, what terrain should he follow into or out of unfamiliar country? What should he do when he was about to collapse from want of water while crossing a desert? How would he obtain meat when he found himself with a broken bow or no arrows in a country filled with game? How would he know what tribe of Indians made a certain trail? How many were in the band, what errand were they on, were they going to or coming back from it, how far from home were they, were their horses laden, how many horses did they have and why, how many women accompanied the men, what mood were they all in? How old was the trail, where were the other Indians now, and what did the product of all these answers require of the sign reader? Amazing deductions from such sign reading are recorded, and would have seemed impossible if they were not so routinely faced and solved. A branch floated past him down a stream. A quick look and he would say whether this was a natural occurrence or the work of animals, or of Indians and trappers. Another branch, a bush, or a pebble was out of place along the trail, and he usually knew why. Off on the limits of the plain, blurred by a heat mirage, off against the gloom of distant cottonwoods, between the branches of a tree or in a cleft where a hill and mountain met, there was a split-second movement—and he knew whether man or animals made it, and why those who made it moved. When buffalo were shifting their position downwind or an elk was in an unlikely place or posture, when too many magpies were hollering at once, when a wolf's howl was off key—it always meant that something important was happening and the sign reader should govern himself accordingly.

Even as the Indian's mind was dealing with all of these factors, it was simultaneously performing a more complex judgment still. It was recording the immediate details in relation to past experiences of the country, the route across it, and the weather forecast. A ten-mile trip was always weighed in its relationship to a goal hundreds of miles away, and as such there were economics of time, effort, comfort, and horseflesh to be arranged, and success and survival would certainly depend on how well these were provided for. All this and more required continual checking as the warrior practiced his arts as hunter, soldier, tribal leader, responsible father, and craftsman. The result at the peak of his maturity was an amazing integration of faculties, a fact which soon became more than apparent to those who invaded his country, suffered where he lived comfortably, and died where he had never been in permanent danger.

One of the most unusual and yet needed abilities of the Indian was his natural faculty of direction, heightened, honed, and whetted by instructors and experience. In sheer amazement over the talents of his Indian guide, Captain R. B. Marcy wrote that he could "start from any place to which he had gone by a sinuous route, through an unknown country, and keep a direct bearing back to the place of departure; and he assured me that he never, even during the most cloudy or foggy nights, lost the points of compass. There are very few white men who are endowed with these wonderful faculties, and those few are only rendered proficient by a comparable experience."[9]

Scout tracking enemy.

It was the exalted pipeholder's responsibility to guide the war party under all conditions. So the young Indian with ambition to succeed had to develop an exceptional sense—an instinct—of direction. And he was taught to manage this without the use of a compass. Astounding as it may seem, with a point of destination fixed in his mind, an Indian warrior could go to it as directly in darkness as in daylight, on a calm, cloudy day as well as in bright sunshine, and with the wind shifting regularly so as to blow from different quarters. His instinct could be trusted as absolutely as that of the homing goose, for he relied on what was fixed in his mind by field experience more than he did on celestial bodies or winds or landscape features.

There was no "north" and no "south" to him insofar as traveling was concerned. The Indian spoke of "sunrise" to designate that side of the horizon on which the sun rises, and of the "sunset" on the other side. He had the six ceremonial directions radiating out from any ritual circle he was in in his camp, yet he made little use of these for his journeys since the sun never rose in exactly the same place, and as such would not have been a safe guide.

The same held true for night travel. If it ever occurred to him in ancient days that use might be made of the stars to aid his journey, he dispensed with the idea. For short excursions, say for hunts of just a week or more out from his camp, he simply relied upon his conditioned instinct—not precisely the same incomprehensible something that takes a pigeon to its nest, but very close to it. In all his thirty-three years on the Plains, Colonel Dodge heard of but one instance where an Indian became "turned round," lost, and wandered for several weeks alone before he recovered himself.[10]

However, on long journeys to selected sites the warrior's primary reliance was placed upon his memory of "landmarks" he'd learned himself or been taught by others. As monotonous as the hillocks and valleys of the Plains appeared to the uneducated eye, each had its own distinctive features to him, and once the Indian had seen these, they were never forgotten. A journey into an unknown area was preceded by consultations with warriors who had already visited it, and Whites who listened to the warriors as they gave instructions said it was astonishing to see how clearly the one described and the other comprehended all that was necessary for a successful journey.

Among the Comanches, whenever neophyte braves wished to go on a raid into a country unknown to them, it was customary for some of the older men to assemble the group for instruction a day or two before the start. The youths were seated in a circle, and a bundle of sticks marked with notches to represent days was produced. Commencing with a stick with a single notch, the older warriors placed each stick in succession along a travel line, the end result being a rude map in the dirt which marked the distance to be covered each day. After a stick was placed, the larger rivers and streams which would be encountered on the next day's journey were indicated, as were the hills, valleys, ravines, and hidden water holes in dry countries. Every natural object, especially those which were peculiar or easily remembered, was located and marked. Once a given day's lesson was thoroughly understood, the stick representing the next day's march was used in the same way, and so on to the end of however many days the journey would take. A Comanche raiding party of young men and boys, the oldest being not over nineteen, and none of whom had ever been to Mexico, was known to have started from the main camp on Brady Creek in Texas and gone as far into Mexico as the city of Monterey, solely employing information fixed in their minds and represented by such sticks. Countless journeys such as this were made by groups from all Indian tribes into countries utterly strange to anyone but their elders or ancestors before the trip was made.

A party exploring a country unknown to it, or to others of the tribe, would, if it proved desirable as a hunting ground, set up small piles of stones to indicate the best route to be taken by those who followed. Numerous rock cairns were found on the rough ground of the Laramie plains of Wyoming, in the precipitous canyons of southern Kansas, and in the country north of the North Platte River.

It is believed that the taller ones were built to indicate the location of the trail when the ground was covered with snow.

Society, band, or clan signs were commonly used to mark a trail—not only that others might follow, but so that all might speedily find their way back home when pursued. In the few wooded areas, trees were blazed by notching or peeling off the bark. At times young saplings were bent to the ground in an elbow shape, and instructional items such as straight sticks were tied to them. Tufts of tall grass might be bunched, tied, and bent in the direction of the trail. Piles of stones were also used on occasion where the best trails led up a steep cliff or hill. It is said that some of these stones accumulated because of the custom of the Indian, when approaching a steep grade, of picking up and throwing a stone ahead; an exercise he claimed would keep him from feeling tired.

Each of the Plains tribes had a comparatively well-defined home country which they learned by heart. Every ridge and valley was intimately known. Every shallow rut affording safety in retreat, every water hole, no matter how hidden in rocks or prairie, was indelibly marked in their mind.

Yet even in one's own country the war parties of another tribe might be encountered at any moment, so one always moved cautiously—even when close to his own camp. Sooner or later, those who failed to do so would probably be found dead. So a young man in training learned that a warrior did not walk boldly over the top of a hill, he crept to the crest and peered beyond it to see whether other men were in sight, or how the animals were acting, or else he just sat quietly like a wolf for a long time. In crossing a wide flat, a man on foot or horseback was to bend over and cover himself with his robe so that anyone seeing him from a distance might think he was a buffalo. The boy was taught that White men walked on the ridges where traveling was easy, but the wise Indian always chose the gullies. As one Indian said, "The White people think that because they cannot see Indians, there are none about; and this belief has caused many White people to be killed."

*Left*, scout on horseback wearing buffalo hide to appear like buffalo to anyone watching from a distance. *Right*, scout with wolfskin on head looking for signs of enemy.

A youth in training soon learned to make camp at sunset, to build his fire and eat there, and then to move some distance away in the darkness to a sleeping place in the bushes where he would build no fire. In that way an enemy who watched him make the first camp would be foiled when he tried to take him by surprise.

While he could do so amazingly well, the Indian traveled comparatively little by night. Yet when advancing toward an enemy whom he hoped to surprise, when stealing horses or escaping from too close a pursuit, he overcame his natural distaste for night travel. In the average instance, however, a man on a raid wanted all the light he could get, and a prudent enemy guarded his best horses especially well during the full of the moon in May or June.

Every father or uncle who educated a boy was a strict disciplinarian and a good teacher. When the young man left the tipi in the morning, he would say, "Look closely to everything you see"; and at evening, on his return, he would often question the boy for an hour or so.

He would expect him to know which side of the trees had the lighter-colored bark, and which side had the most regular branches. He would ask him to name all the new birds he had seen during the day. And the boy would name them according to the color of the feathers, or the shape of the bill, or their song, or the appearance and locality of the nest. When the boy made errors, the father or uncle corrected him. There were many such questions about many things, and while a correct reply to all the questions was not immediately necessary, the intent was to make the youngster an observant and good student of nature.

Admonitions always followed the questions. A boy was told to study animals unobserved, since he would learn many of their secrets this way. A father would tell his son that he ought to follow the example of the wolf, for even when he was surprised and ran for his life, the wolf would pause to take one more look at his enemy before he entered his final retreat. The wolf also knew how to endure under the severest conditions. Deer would teach the boy how to withstand thirst for a long time. The hawks gave lessons in how to strike with unerring accuracy. The elk taught gallantry, the frogs watchfulness, the owls night wisdom and gentle ways, the bears strength and the proper use of herbs, the kit foxes cunning, the coyotes how to elude capture, and the crows how to move swiftly to the battlefield. So the boy should take a long and second look at everything he saw.

The father armed his son against the larger beasts by teaching him how to outwit them. He was to be guided by the habits of the animal he sought. A moose or elk stayed in swampy or low land or between high mountains near a spring or lake for thirty to sixty days at a time. Large game moved about continually, except the doe in the spring; it was then an easy matter to find her with her fawn.

Whenever a bear or a wildcat showed signs of attacking him, he must make the animal fully understand that he had seen him and was aware of his intentions. If he was not well equipped for a pitched battle, the only sure way to make one retreat was to take a long, sharp-pointed pole for a spear and rush toward him. No wild beast would face this unless he was cornered and already wounded. He was generally afraid of the common weapon of the larger animals—the horns, and would have learned the hard way that if these were very long and sharp, he dared not risk an open fight. Sometimes, though, a grizzly bear would attack without reason, and the only hope was to get in close and stab him repeatedly in the belly or chest. A boy was also taught that because of certain beliefs about bears, their hide could only be kept by Bear Cultists and medicine men, but any warrior could cut the claws off and wear them as a necklace.

A trainee learned that packs of gray wolves would also attack fiercely when very hungry. But even then their courage depended upon their numbers. One or two of them would never attack a man. Also, the mountain lion would attack savagely when wounded, and tracking one with an arrow in him was a very dangerous business.

The Indian boy learned how to make a number of ingenious traps and snares to capture small animals such as badgers, foxes, coyotes, and skunks—although these were only employed when buffalo were scarce.

The larger animals such as deer and elk were to be hunted mostly in winter, and would be captured through a careful knowledge of their signs. Deer were caught at water holes, or by a knowledge of their bed-ground habits, or by calling them with a calling horn. The Shoshone fathers taught their sons to kill antelope by running them until they dropped from exhaustion. They also learned that white-tailed deer could be caught with rawhide loops placed along their trails through the willows. Winter hunters ran deer into snowdrifts, and the Indian hunters learned to make good use of dogs as bloodhounds and pack animals.

The boy was taught to recognize every animal on the Plains by its tracks, and further still to know by these exactly what it had been doing. A feeding deer moved slowly and wandered about—which was easily confirmed by finding the trodden places where one had eaten. Sand thrown up in piles meant that fawns had been playing. Sharp, spread-out tracks meant that the animal was running full tilt when it passed, and that one should forget about catching it in that vicinity.

No two animals ever left the same trail, and even beyond that, each one at each stage of its life left a trail as distinctive as the creature's appearance. The tracks told what animal it was, when it passed, its size, its mood, its age, and sometimes its sex. So when following tracks, one never walked on them, but alongside to preserve them for further reference.

A Plains science of great consequence was the ability to read an animal's droppings. Once he had acquired this skill, an Indian hunter could tell exactly what species of animal had dropped it, and by the size of the pellets whether it was a large or small specimen of its kind. Piled pellets meant the creature was not being molested at the time it dropped them, while scattered ones showed that it was racing away. The consistency and temperature told the hunter a great

An encounter to be avoided.

A wounded mountain lion was a dangerous prey.

deal about the animal's whereabouts. He could see what it was eating, and look for the source. In winter a still steaming sign meant the game was near. Cold pellets were dropped an hour before, and the animal might already be a mile or so away. Frozen pellets indicated that the game was probably two or more miles distant.

Northern tribes were seldom faced with an acute water problem, but in an arid southern wilderness, shortages could easily become the most serious hazard of all for travelers. Ancient stories attest to the anxiety, the suffering, and the tragedy exacted by a Plains land of little water or widely spaced water holes.

Wherever he was, a first requirement was that by merely looking at the country, a warrior should be able to judge accurately in what direction water could be found and the approximate distance to it. Therefore, he had to be familiar with every grass, shrub, bird, or animal that indicated water in a general way. Even more, he must know the significance of all the vegetation and animal life of a particular country he ranged. By these he often estimated his elevation and his approximate location in relation to familiar landmarks.

A hundred years ago one could have blindfolded and taken an experienced Indian warrior anywhere in the Plains country, then uncovered his eyes so that he could look at the vegetation, and he could have told where he was. The southern mesquite, for instance, had different forms for varying altitudes, latitudes, and areas of aridity. It did not grow far north of where old Toscosa now is in the Texas Panhandle. And while there were many mesquites adjacent to the Canadian River in the Panhandle of Texas, a few miles away one would find only a few lonesome bushes on great sections of land. So an Indian scouting on the Plains was always glad to see a mesquite bush, for in the dry climate it sprang up only from the droppings of an animal, and the only one that ate mesquite seeds was the mustang. After the mesquite seeds were soaked for a while in the bowels of a horse and were dropped, they germinated quickly. The Indian scout knew that undisturbed mustangs rarely grazed out from water more than three miles. Therefore, when a mesquite bush was seen, all he had to do was to locate the direction of the water.

Cottonwood trees always indicated water, and the Indian boy was taught that when he saw a long line of cottonwoods before him, he would know that if there was water the entire length, the foliage of all the trees would be the same dark color. If the water was only in holes, the trees near these holes would be much darker, and it was useless to hunt the length of the line when nature's signs were so clear. Sometimes a tule—a water grass—showed where water had sunk into a bed of heavy wet sand. By riding his horse up and down this bed of sand he could, with luck, cause the water to rise.

When an Indian youth was familiar with every bird of the region, he would know those that watered each day, like the dove, and those that could go without water for a long while, like the Mexican quail. A careful observer could mark the course of the doves as they went off each evening into the breaks to water. But the easiest of all the birds to follow was the dirt dauber or swallow. He flew low and straight, and if his mouth was empty he was going to water. If his mouth had mud in it, he was coming straight from water. The Indian could also watch the animals, and learn from them where water was. Mustangs watered daily, at least in the summertime, while antelope sometimes went for months without a drop. If mustangs were strung out and walking steadily along, they were going to water. If they were scattered, frequently stopping to graze, they were coming from water.

In some southern areas, water was very scarce, and in many places it was extremely bad. In fact, most of it was undrinkable, for it often had a sickening effect. In these areas the Indians sometimes suffered exceedingly from thirst, which suffering was said to be the worst torture of all. At night they tossed in a semi-conscious slumber in which they dreamed of every spring they knew. The restlessness invariably awakened them, leaving them in even more distress. Suffering from thirst caused a strange reaction. Every ounce of moisture was sapped from the flesh, leaving men and animals haggard and thin, so that one could hardly recognize them if they had been deprived for a long time.

Given half a chance, however, the Indians learned how to take care of themselves in such dire emergencies. Placing a small pebble in the mouth would help, a bullet was better, a piece of copper, if obtainable, better yet, and a peeled piece of prickly pear was the best of all. To drink muddy water, a warrior put grass over the surface to strain out the flies or bugs, and sucked the water through it.

Under any and all conditions the Indian boy had to learn to be able to make a fire. He needed it for warmth, and he needed it to cook his food. It is true that some portions of a newly slain animal were eaten raw, such as the liver and some fats, and in emergencies the gall was drunk and the raw lining of the second stomach was eaten, but the common practice was to cook whatever was not to be "jerked" for future use.

Whenever possible, cooking was done in a buffalo paunch, the animal's stomach lining. This served as a kettle or bucket to hold the water for boiling the meat. The paunch was suspended from four green poles, each about five feet long. Small wooden pegs pinned the edges to the poles.

The paunch was washed and half filled with water, and the meat was placed in it. Carefully selected clean stones, chosen for their resistance to cracking or exploding, were piled on a log framework above a fire located to one side of the paunch, heated till they were red-hot, and then dropped one at a time into the paunch. The water was kept at a continual boil, and it cooked the meat in about thirty minutes. The broth made a very good soup, and the kettle itself could be eaten once the primary meal was finished.

When hunters were without poles to hold the paunch, they dug a hole in the ground and placed the paunch in it. For fuel to heat the stones they used

Blackfoot warriors scouting for enemy sign at water's edge.

Tracking and survival signs. *a*, Indian mounting from right side of horse. *b*, tracks at side of hoofprints indicated whether rider was Indian or White. *c*, rock moved indicated someone passed by. *d*, actions of soaring bird revealed person moving below, and bird with mud in mouth was coming from water. *e*, grazing mustang indicated water within three miles, and mustangs walking steadily were moving toward water. *f*, scout peering over crown of hill to avoid being seen. *g*, footprint with fresh insect lines across it indicated man passed by the night before. *h*, animal tracks of deer and wolf.

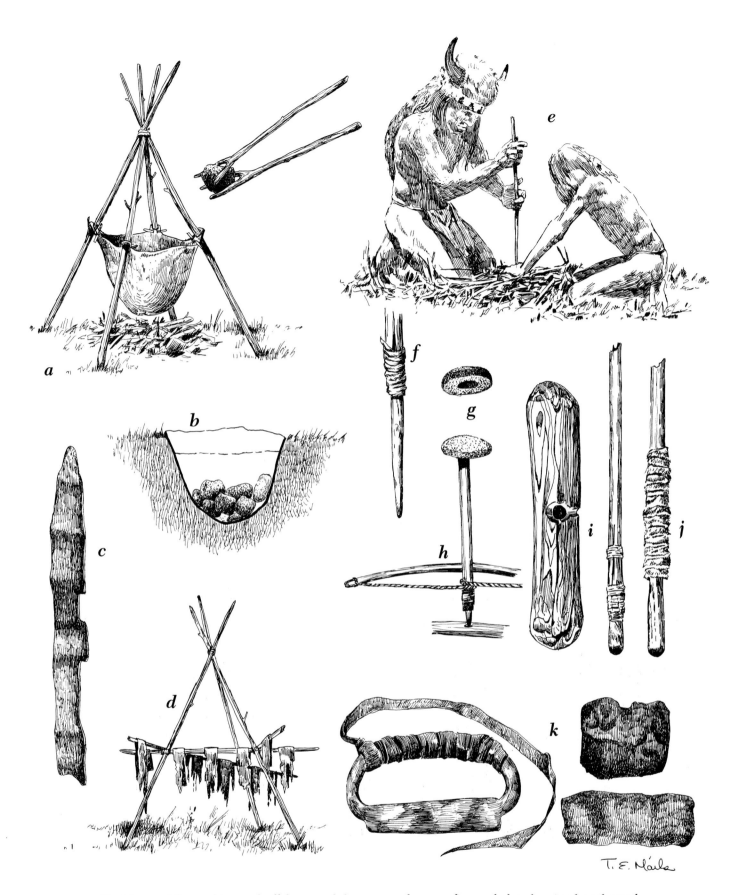

Cooking and fire making. *a*, buffalo paunch hung on poles over fire, and also showing how heated rocks were carried on forked sticks to be dropped in water in paunch. *b*, buffalo paunch used to line pit dug in ground. *c*, meat sliced thin for jerky. *d*, small rack built to dry jerky while traveling. *e*, two men working together to spin fire drill. *f*, Crow wooden drill point. *g*, stone cap to protect hand. *h*, bow drill. *i*, Lehmi Shoshone hearth and drill. *j*, Wind River Shoshone drill. *k*, flints and steel carried by a Sioux warrior.

buffalo chips. These were the prime fuel of the Plains, for they remained dry in the center when wet by rain, they burned slowly, and they made a hot fire with more glow than flame.

To preserve their meat, the Indians "jerked" it. To do this, they cut it into very thin slices, a quarter of an inch or less thick and from one to six feet long. The thin slices were placed on wooden racks and dried in about two days. They were not smoked. Flies were unable to plant their eggs in the thin meat, and so left it alone. In drying, the meat became very hard. It could be eaten in that condition, but was usually cooked before meals taken at home. Warriors on the move ate it without cooking it while they were in enemy country. A small tripod rack was used by war or hunting parties to dry the meat slices. Huge drying racks literally covered the main camp areas during the hunting seasons.

Pemmican was the other best-known type of prepared meat. To make it, jerky was pounded to a fine consistency with a berrymasher. Fresh chokecherries were then pounded to a pulp and mixed with the jerky. Suet was poured on this, and the whole was divided into small cakes which were stored in rawhide cases for future use.

The ancient way of making fire on the Plains was by the "fire stick" friction of wood on wood. The end of a round stick was split, and a hardwood point was inserted in the split and lashed tight. Then the stick, called a "drill," was twirled between the palms of the hands while the turning end spun and ground on another piece of wood called the "hearth." This was done by a single man, or better by two men working in relays. Friction caused the wood to form a hot powder or glowing coal, which was allowed to fall into a tinder. To coax this into a flame the Indian blew softly on it or placed it in a "sling" of grass or strip of bark and swung it back and forth in the air.

An improvement over that method came when the Indian began using a bow with a thong of soft rawhide, which was turned once around the drill stick, and as the bow was run back and forth, the thong spun the stick. The drill stick was held at the top by a cupped-out stone, a piece of wood, or a clamshell to protect the fire maker's hand while he pressed down on it to hold it against the hearth.

It is said that some tribes believed that a spark of fire "slept" only in certain kinds of trees, and only the roots of these were to be used in kindling a flame by friction.

The tinders used were dried wood from decayed trees, frayed inner bark of the cedar, fungi, pounded buffalo chips, or downy feathers of the blue jay. The Blackfoot tribes used a fungus which grows on the birch tree, gathering it in large quantities and drying it so as always to have it available to start their fires. Of course, the flints and steels of the Whites were more sure and provided an instant spark, so at almost their first meeting with the traders the Indians obtained flints and steels and enthusiastically learned how to use them.

In a common method of transportation, fire was carried from camp to camp in a "fire horn." This was a large buffalo horn with its core burnt out, and slung by a buckskin loop over the shoulder like a powder horn. The horn was lined with moist, rotten wood, and the open end had a hardwood stopper or plug fitted to it. On leaving camp in the morning, the man who had the responsibility of carrying the horn took a live coal from the fire and put it in the horn. On this coal he placed a piece of punk, and then plugged up the horn with the stopper. The punk smoldered in this almost airtight chamber, and after the course of two or three hours, the man looked at it, and if it was nearly consumed, put another piece of punk in the horn. The first men who reached the appointed camping place would gather several large piles of wood in different places, and as soon as the one who carried a fire horn reached camp, he turned out his spark at one of these piles of wood. A little blowing and nursing resulted in the blaze which started the fire. All other fires of a village were kindled from this first one, and when the rest of the party reached camp they went to these blazing piles for coals with which to start the fires in their lodges.

If trailing animals had its adventures, even these took on a heightened dimension when the competition was elevated to one between hunter and hunter, skilled man against skilled man—and both were products of the same schoolroom! One could never be certain as to which in any case had the advantage over the other as they traveled on the prairies.

The Indians of one tribe knew that their enemies depended on the same landmarks they relied upon for their own guides, and as they trailed them they might even be able to determine where the others were headed and take a short cut to intercept them. On the other hand, the enemies might turn back and do the same to them.

Boys were taught that by moccasin tracks an Indian tracker *might* determine the identity of the tribe of the man who made them. Nearly every tribe had its own pattern and method of decorating moccasins, so that under ideal conditions it was possible for a skilled Indian scout to tell a man's tribe by a study of their tracks. Captain William F. Drannan, who spent thirty-one years on the Plains and in the mountains, and many of them with Kit Carson, declares that no two tribes cut and made their moccasins alike, and at that time he could tell an Indian by his track—"if he belonged to any tribe he was familiar with." [11] The toe and heel shapes of the various tribes did differ, but all moccasins toed in, and a print could seldom be read without an absolutely clear and crisp track, for the variations were not that great. The Indians themselves were often not able to identify a track they found. They stated that their war parties found some tracks, but "they did not know whose they were." [12]

Travelers also employed tricks to deceive potential pursuers. They usually walked over rough ground, and warriors picked up enemy moccasins from victims whenever they could to wear when they entered that tribe's territory. Some Indians put an animal tail or a heavy fringe at the heel of their moccasins, which was said to obliterate or smear the tracks as the wearer walked along.

An experienced tracker *could* tell whether the man he was after was running

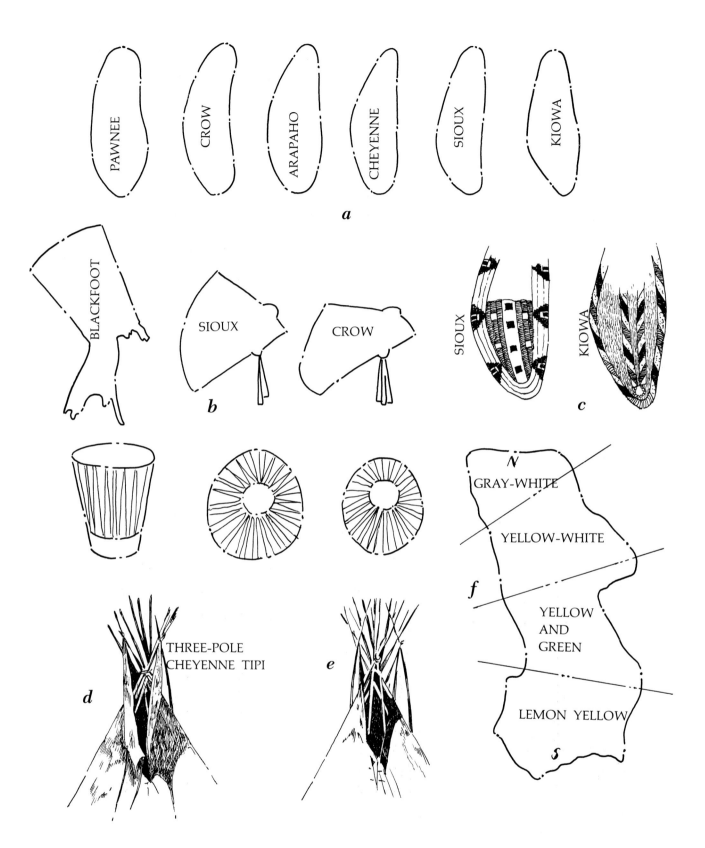

Signs used by raiders to identify enemies from a distance. *a*, footprints of different tribes—from right to left, Kiowa, Sioux, Cheyenne, Arapaho, Crow, Pawnee. *b*, side and back shapes of feathered headdresses—from left to right, Blackfoot, Sioux, Crow. *c*, southern Plains moccasins with strong diagonal pattern, northern moccasins with mountain designs. *d*, three-pole tipi used by Cheyenne. *e*, four-pole tipi used by Crows. *f*, clothing color division of Plains area—from north to south, gray-white, yellow-white, yellow and green, lemon yellow.

or walking. If he was running, only the ball of his foot touched the ground. If the fugitive was trying to throw his pursuer off the trail by walking backward, his steps were of necessity shorter, his heel marks were deeper, and the trained pursuer would notice this.

A young man learned to tell a great deal from the tracks and other evidences of animals, and he was taught to put the same principles to work on the natural objects. If he saw a rock moved from its regular place, he could tell when it was moved by the edges of the dirt, for the wind changed these hour by hour. If he saw a broken twig, a broken blade of grass, or a bit of weed cut off by a horse's hoof, he was able to tell exactly how long it had been withering. It was easy to determine whether a track had been made before or after daylight. A track made during the night would usually be marked with minute insect tracks. Even on desert sands this was true. By bending close to the ground, the scout could observe the tiny insect lines.

The Indian trailer must become alert to everything. If the one he pursued did not leave traces, the trailer still might determine the direction in which other men were going by noting the tracks of animals frightened out of their path. Flocks of birds rising swiftly and sharply showed that someone was moving and frightening them.

When a man was away from home every living thing was watched for any significance attached to its motion or appearance. No movement was too slight for the hunter to ignore, and no sound too meaningless to go unheeded. The soaring maneuvers of any bird were to be looked into. If a man was below an eagle, the bird would either circle over him or turn back and fly the other way. The calls of the prairie cranes were announcers of important weather changes. Herman Lehmann tells how Comanche Indians could forecast the weather by examining the webs of spiders. In dry weather the web was thin, long, and high, but just before a rain the web was low, short, and thick. A croaking frog proclaimed a tiny marsh or hidden spring, and at once called for more caution. Someone might already be there. A distant dust column might reveal an advancing enemy party.

Even the black horned ground beetle, commonly called the tumblebug, was attentively watched. The two horns on the top of the insect's head were movable in all directions, yet they were invariably pointed and held toward a buffalo herd, probably being attracted in that direction by the noise made by stamping hoofs too distant even for sensitive human ears.

If a fugitive tried to cover his tracks by wading up or down a stream, the trailer was taught first to look for the trail on the same side of the water where the other man had entered it. Usually a man would come out of the water on the same side. But there was always the question of whether he had done this deliberately or through force of habit, and so the trailer had to reason out whether he had a cunning or a thoughtless man to deal with. Miscalculations were exceedingly dangerous, for often the pursuer, being outwitted, found himself being pursued or ambushed instead.

A successful warrior's hearing must be sharpened until it was perfect. Reading sounds correctly had much to do with his longevity as a scout, since the enemy was as expert as he at animal and bird imitations. The Indians often used these to locate and orient themselves at night. But it is said that no man's imitation cry of a bird or beast could actually deceive a skilled hunter.

The Indians discovered that the human voice echoes more than any other; in truth, it is almost the only voice which echoes at all.

Of course, on the open plains of northeast Texas, the Indians did not have this advantage because there was nothing to create an echo. But the ancient Indians who were consulted about the mountains, canyons, and broken country agreed that no human could give an exact imitation of the sound of a beast or bird there. A Crow Indian declared that he easily knew when the enemy was gathering in strength. "All night long coyote yelps and wolf howls in the hills indicated that they were closing in." When owls were heard in addition, he knew that Sioux, Cheyenne, and Arapaho were thick about his party "like ants on a freshly killed buffalo hide."[13]

An expert trailer could readily tell whether a pony was carrying anything by the depth of its tracks. Also, the position of the hoofmarks would show whether the pony was walking, trotting, or galloping.

The experienced Indian tracker could tell whether a horse track had been made by a loose horse, a riderless horse being led, or a horse with a man riding him. He could even determine the horse's color. Suppose he was on the hunt for a man he knew to be riding a brown horse. He found the tracks of a horse carrying a man. But was the horse a brown horse? To determine this he simply followed the tracks until he found where the rider had unsaddled his mount to let him graze. When the saddle was taken off, a horse that had been ridden any distance generally fell on the ground. When the tracker found where the one he was trailing had rolled, he examined the dirt or the grass for hairs, found a few, and their color told him whether the horse was brown. Another fact was that no Indian wore boots, so that footprints easily showed whether the rider was Indian or White. The Indian warrior usually mounted and dismounted on the right side of the horse because he carried his weapons in his right hand, and did not then need to throw them across the horse's back. The White man mounted and dismounted on the left side. In considering the absoluteness of always mounting on the right side, an amused old Blackfeet warrior claimed that his horse was trained to receive him from any direction in an emergency—even over the rear end if necessary, since anything else would have accounted for "a heap of dead Indians!"

It was important for the boy in training to be taught how the Indians of different tribes could tell one another apart, and especially how they could tell

Blackfoot warriors Black Bull and Stabs by Mistake searching countryside for sign of enemies.

friend from foe in the haste and fright of an unexpected confrontation, or at the sighting of a distant camp. There were a few definite signs they could go by.

Clear moccasin tracks would be one indication. A second would be the variations in tribal bonnet styles. A third sign would be the difference between the northern and southern moccasin quill or bead designs, with the southern moccasin being recognized by its strong diagonal lines. A fourth help would be the zonal color variations in garments. Northern clothing, such as that of the Blackfoot and Crees, was either a sparkling white with a gray cast, or else painted in a purple range. Next came the Crow-Sioux area. Their garments were white with a yellow cast—or else a smoked, warm beige. After this was the Cheyenne country garments, which were painted a yellow of a stronger nature than their northern neighbors', and finally the southernmost clothing color preference of lemon yellow and green. A last indication would be the difference between tipi pole structures. The Crows, for example, used a four-pole base and the Cheyenne a three-pole foundation upon which the other poles were laid.

Once the basic skills of making and handling weapons, of horsemanship, of hunting, and of survival and tracking had been conquered, a young man was ready to complete his training period by also mastering the techniques of raiding and war for tribal defense and being a member of pipeholders' war parties. Naturally, his exposure to these had been a regular part of his life from childhood, and he had continually imitated everything his father and the other warriors did, doing so by himself or in concert with other boys. Therefore, a youth about to take up the mature responsibilities of manhood did not need to learn the warring skills so much as he needed to practice with other men in order to become an efficient part of his tribe's defense unit.

In warfare and raiding the warrior remained an individual. He was always, in a sense, his own man. He answered to his supernatural helpers in that he conducted himself in accordance with instructions received in visions and dreams. He also developed a special allegiance to his society, and his conduct in the field was governed in part by the club's rules, by its aims, and by his vows to fellow members. Standing over all of this, however, was his responsibility to the band and tribe to defend it against any menace. This meant that besides the practice needed to increase an individual's proficiency with weapons, there must also be society, village, and tribal drills in readiness for those great and sudden emergencies when a large enemy war party attacked his village, or when it became desirable to strike at the enemy in force on their home grounds.

Every band or clan had its camp chiefs and its war chiefs. The latter were men who had earned their positions by superior achievements in battles, and often they were the leading officers of the various men's societies. Each of the war chiefs chose several subchiefs to assist him, and each of these were assigned a certain number of the men of the band. Both the experienced warriors and the trainees were called out for instruction several times a week when the weather was good.

Warriors picking up fallen comrade by use of rope in midst of battle.

The war chiefs agreed in a general way as to what they would try to accomplish. Then each subchief gathered his unit around him and outlined the plan, and they proceeded from there.

The tactical maneuvers of the Plains tribes always presupposed an enemy located in various and strategic places. The war chiefs set the situation for their units, and at a signal sent their mounted warriors speeding toward the enemy positions, racing and circling in such a way as to confuse the enemy regarding their actual strength and plan. Warriors on foot had already mastered the skills of approaching their prey without being discovered, and in maneuvers, it was simply a matter of learning to coordinate their efforts with the other members of their unit. Ambush techniques were also considered and practiced, for this was a favorite method of attack on the Plains.

Drills included training in picking up fallen warriors while riding at top speed, each man practicing until he could do it alone, or better still with another warrior, for two men could do this surprisingly well. If a man was down but still able to move, a rope loop was dropped over his head as the pickup team rode by. While they circled, the downed man slipped his arms through the rope and got to his hands and knees. On the next pass of the pickup team, one man swung down and grabbed the loose end of the rope with his left hand while the other caught the loop with his right hand, and together they hoisted the wounded man and carried him off the field of battle to a safe place. Here, depending upon his condition, they either put him down or else took him up to ride double with them on one of the horses.

The war chiefs signaled their men in several ways: by hand or arm signals— sometimes holding a flag or a lance or a gun or a robe at arm's length; by the use of trade mirrors; or by war whistles made of the bone of an eagle's wing or of a turkey leg bone. It is said that two different sounds could be produced by blowing each end of the whistles. Such whistles made a shrill noise, and were easily heard above the din of battle. At any signal the different units would immediately wheel or turn, attack or retreat as prearranged. As long as the practiced techniques went well in an actual battle, the prepared orders were followed—but if anything went awry, it was every man for himself until a desist or retreat sign was issued, or he decided to leave on his own.

Actually, two kinds or modes of signals were employed on the Plains—those just mentioned which were designed for close-quarter communication, and those designed for signaling over long distances of a mile or more. There were three long-distance methods: body action; action of the signaler in connection with objects, such as a robe or blanket, or a mirror, or a flag or lance, or the direction imparted to a horse; and by smoke or fire or dust. Using any of these means the Indians could signal alarm, anger, a request to come, warnings of danger, defiance, a call to halt, directions, peace, friendship, a question such as "Who are you?" submission, surrender, buffalo discovered, the success of a war party, a camp site, and the implementation of a military drill.

Smoke or mirror signals were used in daytime, with the number of flashes or puffs serving as a kind of Morse code, and fires placed at intervals in rows accomplished the same thing at night. Smoke signals were made by letting the smoke rise in a single column, or by slipping a robe or blanket sideways over a fire made with dry wood and green grass or moss thrown on it. Fire signals were made on high ridges or away from water so that people would know they were not campfires.

Nez Percé warrior using lance to signal to rest of raiding party, 1880.

*a*

*b*

Signaling methods. *a*, using robe or blanket with horse standing still. *b*, robe used in combination with moving horse. *c*, using mirror. *d*, smoke signals.

Warrior looking back to guard against pursuers.

The Indians made horseback signals by riding in certain ways, walking, circling, zigzagging, or racing to indicate their message. Sometimes a warrior just rode into view and away again one or more times. The Omahas had a signal in which two scouts crisscrossed on their horses. Robes and blankets were added to the horseback maneuvers to convey the more complicated messages. Certain signals were given by tossing a balled-up robe into the air a given number of times. Friends were summoned by waving the robe in an outward motion and back again.[14]

Of this much one could be sure, the boy in training learned that all the while a warrior traveled, he must realize that as he watched for others he was being just as intently spied upon. The eyes of the animal world were upon him, and human eyes would often be too. Every so often he must turn quickly to scan the landscape in back of him, and if he had reason to suspect the presence of an enemy scout, he should lay in wait until the enemy watcher was located.

When a young man's training had made him a proficient hunter and neophyte warrior, he was ready to make his first excursions into the enemy war zone. Here he reached the supreme level in his life, and discovered that spirituality and limited warfare were really not as alien as one might think for the natural man.

Painted eagle bone war whistle with beaded pendant and eagle feather.

# Chapter 23

# THE MATURE WARRIOR ON
# THE FIELD OF ACTION

"Yes," he smiled. "I shall always remember my first war-party. I was asked to go
by the man who was to carry the pipe, and I felt so proud I could scarcely keep the
secret to myself. I thought the day very long, and was relieved when at night we rode
silently out of the village with our faces toward the east. We wore only light shirts and
leggings made from the skins of bighorns, and carried nothing except our bows and
shields. War-bonnets and bright colors were hidden away, because they can be seen
easily, and no war-party wishes to be seen. Bonnets were never used by warriors until
all chance of surprise was gone. Then they were brought out, if there was time. Our
bonnets were in rawhide cases and might not be used at all."[1]

We rode all night without seeing our Wolves. Yet I knew, of course, they were out
ahead of us somewhere. I kept looking at every knoll top until we hid away for the
day. Then they came in, looking exactly like wolves.[2]

The Indian boy who lived during the golden age of the Plains people was
trained from infancy to be a warrior. In a sense, his very life was oriented around
the field of conquest. This fact must, however, be prefaced and tempered with
a qualifying note. According to Indian accounts, prior to the advent of the horse
and mobile warfare in the 1700s, there were neither general nor continued disputes
of consequence among the Plains tribes. Once each nation had settled into its
geographic area, it lived on relatively good terms with its neighbors. Most quarrels
were trivial at best, since there were few people, and there was plenty of land
for everyone. Physical confrontations were inconsequential, since defensive skills
could nearly offset the damage which could be done by the old stone weapons.
The greatest losses in early times occurred when one party was surprised from
ambush, or when one side panicked and ran so they could be struck from behind.
If, however, the pursued party rallied and turned to fight, the pursuers usually
drew off at once, well satisfied with whatever they had already accomplished. With
the arrival of the horse, however, raiding and warfare became an intense manner
of life for the entire tribe: the men making the raids, the women helping to prepare

Young warrior challenging enemy.

for their going and receiving them back, the older men aiding with exhortations, advice, and prayers, and the young learning in anticipation of their days to come. Even then casualties were usually light—because the coup, not killing, was what counted.

The Kiowas say they could never understand why the Whites made such a fuss over small fights. Fighting was a man's business—that was the way he earned the respect of his people and was honored by the women. In their eyes there never would have been any serious trouble if the Whites had stayed away and left them alone: "We were happy before they came."[3]

Robert Lowie points out that he learned of no concerted effort by one tribe to oust another from their territory, and that tradition revealed that relatively few wars were fought on a really large scale.[4]

George Grinnell felt that the White people completely misunderstood how the Indians enjoyed their small encounters, that it is impossible for those who live the commonplace, humdrum lives of a civilized community to form any adequate conception of the variety and excitement of the life of a young man who was constantly going on the warpath. He believed that the barest enumeration of the odd circumstances and thrilling occurrences which took place in a single band of a brave, warlike nation would fill many volumes. "Such a recital would present many examples of reckless hardihood almost beyond belief."[5]

A very strong case can be made for White intrusion as the real motivation for some of the deep and lasting antagonisms which came to pass between the Indian tribes during the horse period. The White soldiers and settlers encouraged them to turn against each other, caused territorial shifts or pressures, and kept them in such a ferment over their land losses and cultural interferences that the mood of the Indian underwent a marked change. Where once war was sporadic, it became systematic. Where once it was considered sport, it became a deadly contest of counterthrust and revenge.

There were two types of trips made by the Indian warriors into enemy territory. Some journeys were for the express purpose of making war, but the most common purpose was the horse raid, and the horse alone was *the* target. Raiders rarely attacked enemy villages with the intent to destroy or appropriate other property. They took horses, and in many instances probably retrieved animals already stolen from themselves. Other things were brought home on occasion. After a battle, and time permitting, some of the weapons and apparel of their enemies might be taken as proof of victory.

As a rule, horse raids were stimulated by tribal defense patterns or came about as a reaction to the activities of the enemy. Blackfoot accounts say that most raids "originated in a dream," but the aforementioned causes were undoubtedly the foster parents of the dream itself. In any case, dreams came at all times during the year, and men responded to them by going on raids during all but the impossible parts of the winter. A dream might only provide the impulse to go, but it often included an uncanny prediction of the destination, and even something of what would take place there. Significantly enough, such dreams usually came to men of proven merit, for everyone knew—and was influenced by the fact—that other men were not likely to follow an inexperienced leader into enemy territory.

If a dream inspired confidence, the warrior who had it invited certain men of proven or potential worth to accompany him—the number depending upon the task which confronted them. The invitation could be accepted, or it could

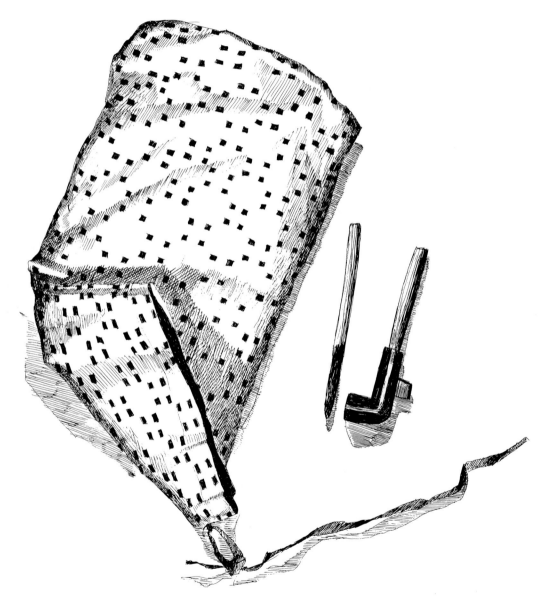

Small pipe of type carried by warrior on raid, with pipe tamper stick. Pipe is 4½ inches long, stone bowl. The tobacco bag is calico, red with small yellow squares.

be declined without embarrassment on the part of one who felt it was not a proper time for him to go. His own dream might warn him off, which was an honorable excuse during those times when raiding was an option. Tribal defense was another matter, and membership in a large war party became the obligation of every warrior within the fighting age bracket of fifteen to thirty-five. A man older than that of a medicine man could turn instead to prayers or to making medicine—as did Sitting Bull during the famous Custer affair. His contribution would be considered as important as the fighting itself, and his prestige would not suffer.

Any raiding party could also include a few men who were not invited— especially young men anxious to get started—yet who would follow the party out and join them some distance after they left the village. These were not always the most desirable traveling mates, but they were acceptable if they were willing to submit to the authority of the party leader.

A noteworthy exception to the normal procedure occurred when certain young men became especially desirous to make a name for themselves, and decided to sneak off during a period of intertribal tensions when the elders felt that it was a time to be more prudent; when the risks and consequences were considered greater than usual. Knowing the mind of the youth from their own neophyte days, the chiefs posted society members around the camp perimeter to watch for young adventurers, and it became an interesting contest to see which could outwit the other as the adventurers attempted to sneak away. "Youth," said the Indian elders, "is like fire, marvellous to behold, but needing to be controlled."[6]

The leader of a raid or a war party became known as the pipeholder, or the one who carried the pipe. If the trip was to be a long and especially dangerous one, he would have been on many raids already, and in most instances would be well acquainted with all the landmarks and water holes in whatever country they might cross. Often the leader would be a war priest, known for his visions and astuteness. Once a man accepted the pipeholder's invitation, his authority became all but absolute, and the party put itself in his hands for preparation and execution from that moment until the day it returned home.

By and large, the approach to raiding and warfare was the same for all tribes, yet each had its peculiarities which, taken in their sum, added luster to the general picture.

Therefore, the following material is drawn from the comprehensive Indian accounts of the Sioux, Blackfoot, Crow, Kiowa, Cheyenne, Assiniboine, and Shoshone tribes. The general sequential pattern of raids will be followed, and the interesting details from each tribe will be inserted whenever they deviated from the norm. The total picture produced will portray more happenings than would take place on the ordinary raid or battle trip, yet each journey would include a significant part of them.

The Indians were always prayerful and careful in their religious observances, but they were never more scrupulous about these matters than when starting on a journey to war. Realizing they were risking their lives, they sought divine assistance and offered sacrifices, such as slices of flesh, in return. In most instances, a priest was asked to lead them in a medicine sweat, and while they were in the sweat lodge, he smoked the sacred pipe and prayed, asking that they might return in safety to their people. While they were away he would continue to pray for their success and welfare, and at intervals would ride about through the camp, shouting out the names of the warriors to make certain they would not be forgotten by the people whom they had gone forth to protect. One should always remember that their warfare was defensive, rather than an exercise for personal glory. The stories told by the Indians make constant reference to the need to protect and preserve the tribe. If it was a revenge raid, men would gash each other's legs to gird and excite themselves for the task. Sometimes a great tribal holy item would be taken along to ensure success. The Kiowas, for example, often took one of their ten sacred medicines. If it got wet at any time, everyone took it as a plain warning to turn back.

There were also mechanical things to be done, and except for the preparation for intertribal wars, these must be carried out in secret or performed casually to prevent unwanted people from learning what was happening and seeking to join the party.

The clothing worn for war parties and horse raids depended upon the nature of the job at hand. On occasion the Indian warriors rode forth bareback and near naked. But they usually were wrapped in a blanket or fully dressed in lightweight shirts and leggings. In summer these prevented sunburn, in winter they were for warmth, and in all instances they guarded the wearer against being scraped by brush, thorns, and rocks. Northern winter gear included the blanket coat called the capote, with red or yellow horizontal stripes, which made it harder for the enemy to see the coat. The finest clothing and regalia, including warbonnets and coup feathers, were carried along on war expeditions, so that time permitting they could be put on before the enemy was engaged. Most of this gear was packed in the familiar parfleche and fringed cylindrical cases and suspended from the saddle. Upon arriving in the vicinity of an enemy village, a war party put on its war clothes, took the saddles off the horses, and left all of the superfluous gear at a carefully chosen place to be picked up after the battle. War clothes were worn as indications to the enemy of a warrior's abilities, and as reminders to the owner of the medicine things he should be thinking of. A Kiowa warrior said that his war clothing was put on so as to prepare him properly for death.

An impressive amount of gear would be taken on a raid, and even more on a war party. Each warrior would provide his share of the equipment, so that between the members of a given group, everything necessary would be available as it was required. There would be rawhide carrying cases and such clothing as fitted the journey; extra bowstrings, carried in the quiver; glue sticks, carried in

Pawnee war leader, back view, wearing painted buffalo robe, buffalo hair rope, otter skin collar with ear of corn and storm eagle hung on collar, and carrying lance and shield.

Warriors scarifying (gashing) legs in fortifying attitudes for revenge raid. Lowie and Ewers reported that hoop medicines were one of the most sacred war medicine bundles carried to war, especially in revenge situations.

the quiver; quirts; a small supply of sinew and awls; war paint bags and shell cups for mixing the paint; extra moccasins, sometimes carried under the covers of the shields; fire-making equipment, the old bow types or flint and steel; jerky and pemmican; the small field pipes, wooden pipe tampers, and tobacco—with pipe bags; personal medicine items, and the special war medicine of the band; robes or blankets, sometimes rolled and strapped across the back infantry-style; bows, and perhaps extra ones for a war party trip, and about twenty arrows per man; knives, usually good-sized multipurpose ones for skinning or battle; shields if riding, but not always carried when on foot—miniature shields or just the large shield covers might be taken instead, clubs and/or tomahawks; lances, a standard weapon for mounted warfare, and certainly not unknown to foot parties either, at least in short, lightweight versions; when guns were taken, the added equipment consisted of powder horns or flasks, and patch bags for bullets or patches and round balls; enemy moccasins to deceive their pursuers; ropes to make war bridles for stolen horses; and snowshoes for rough going in winter.

All of the survival talents the Indian had mastered were called upon each step of the way out to a raid or battle and back, and in its sum, the journey to weaken the strength of the foe became an exercise in consummate skill, especially when one realizes that parties of warriors from all of the tribes were simultaneously on the move over all parts of the Plains, with each party trying to anticipate the moves of the others in its area while it accomplished everything necessary to its own success.

Horse-raiding groups consisted of anything from four to twenty persons, depending upon the dream and estimates of the pipeholder. War parties ranged from fifteen upward to several hundred men, although even a party of one hundred was rare enough to be considered a mean force. Each group of raiders would include a few young men for training purposes, and on occasion a few women to do the cooking, although some wives went along intending to fight. Now and then dogs were taken along as pack animals. They were especially useful in the winter season.

The preferred time for departure was before sunup, so that when the rest of the village arose the adventurers would already be well on their way. Under average traveling conditions, a party on foot would make twenty-five miles per day on the way out, and might increase that pace on the return trip if they were unsuccessful.

A party on horseback would average fifty miles a day on the way toward the enemy, although the distance would vary in some ratio to the problems encountered after it entered enemy territory. Mounted war party members rode an average horse and led their prized war horses behind them, so as to keep these in prime condition for the demanding events ahead.

Some raiding trips were relatively short and were completed in two weeks, while others covered great distances, and the party might be gone from its home

Foot party of warriors on winter revenge raid. State of dress and alertness show they are on border of enemy territory and have dressed for battle. Dogs were often used as pack animals. Old photo by Schultz, *My Life As an Indian,* shows Blackfoot war party in winter dressed as group shown in drawing.

T.E. Mails

Typical gear carried by war and raiding parties. *a*, a rawhide carrying case or two, and clothing as required. *b*, extra bowstrings, carried in the quiver. *c*, war paint bags and shell for mixing. *d*, extra moccasins, sometimes carried in the covered shield. *e*, enemy moccasins to deceive their pursuers. *f*, personal medicine items, and the special war medicine. *g*, fire-making equipment, the old bow type or flint and steel. *h*, jerky and pemmican. *i*, pipe, tamper, and tobacco. *j*, a robe or blanket, sometimes rolled and strapped across the back infantry style. *k*, a shield if riding, but not always carried when on foot. A miniature shield or just the cover might be taken instead.

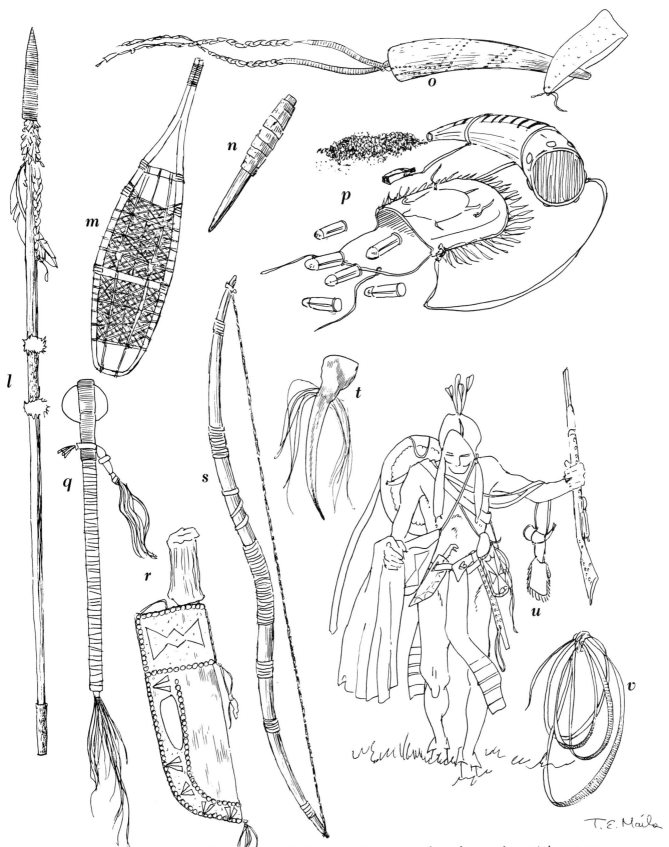

Typical gear continued. *l*, lances, a standard weapon for mounted warfare, and certainly not unknown to foot parties either, at least in short, lightweight versions. *m*, snowshoes for rough going
in winter. *n*, a glue stick, carried in the quiver. *o*, a quirt. *p*, when guns were taken, the added
equipment consisted of a powder horn or flask, and a patch bag for bullets or patches and round
balls (see also *u*). *q*, clubs and/or tomahawks. *r*, a knife, usually a good-sized multipurpose one
for skinning or battle. *s*, a bow, and perhaps an extra one for a war party, and about twenty
arrows. *t*, a small supply of sinew and an awl. *u*, patch bag on leather straps. *v*, a rope to make a
war bridle for stolen horses.

Mounted war party.

camp for several months. Blackfoot accounts tell of ancient war parties which left in the spring of one year and did not return till the summer or fall of the next. Sometimes the Blackfeet traveled all the way into Mexico, and returned with Spanish weapons and horse bits to prove it. Other Plains tribes say their war parties went as far west as the Pacific coast.

In starting out, a war party usually marched in the daytime, but sometimes traveled only at night from the beginning. Occasionally they would make an all-night march across a wide prairie where they might be seen if they traveled during the day. When the parties traveled on foot, the experienced men carried their weapons while the boys in training bore the moccasins, ropes, food, and other equipment. The pipeholder had but little physical labor to perform. His mind was occupied with planning the movements of his party, and he was treated with the greatest respect. The others mended his moccasins, cared for his horses, and gave him the best of the food they carried or prepared.

All along the way the leader would seek to invoke dreams in an attempt to determine where his group would meet the enemy, how far away the foe was, and the size of his party or camp. On the night they reached the borderline area, all would smoke the sacred pipe and meditate upon the contents of the pipeholder's bundle. At this time the leader would pray for specific successes, and the others might make those impressive vows which would lead to their participation in Sun Dances. The men might also make sacrifices of favored possessions or of small slices of flesh, and deposit these on or before the bundle. At the border they also took fresh game, and packed the surplus meat in bags, so that fewer noises would be required later when they were in more dangerous places. They did their best to preserve their pemmican and dried meat for the direst emergencies.

On foot or horseback the war party traveled single file, with the war leader always in front. The experienced warriors came next, and the youngest men last. When the leader stopped, everyone else did the same. His commands were passed by word or hand signals back from one to the other. If ambushed, they went

Sioux warrior praying for success in battle. Adapted from famous statue by Cyrus Dallin, 1913, Boston Museum. Battle gear added.

in all directions, with every man for himself. In enemy territory they remained as close together as wisdom and training dictated.

Shortly after leaving his village, the pipeowner would select at least two experienced young men to serve as scouts. Many of the warriors carried along wolfskins to be used as disguises for this service, and the Crows say that sometimes they daubed themselves with mud to look like wolves. Often, two advance scouts were sent ahead and to either side, and a third one acted as a rear guard.

The advance scouts often traveled by night so as to be at an advantageous lookout point when morning came. Having obtained their information by watching for all of the natural and animal signs, they then met the main body at a prearranged point and reported their findings. Every tribe had its own interesting ritual for this, and each was designed to produce an accurate story. Some kicked a waiting pile of buffalo chips. The main group of a Blackfoot raiding party prepared a pile of sticks for their scouts to kick over. Then the party members scrambled for the sticks, believing each stick recovered represented a horse they would take. A Kiowa scout coming in to report had a straw thrust through his hair "in a traditional manner" by the pipeholder, and as he removed it he told his story. It is said that an arrogant Kiowa leader sometimes pinched a scout hard to make certain he was telling the truth.

As a general rule the scouts and the war party traveled in ravines and coulees, so as to avoid being seen. In large war parties, the leader would often appoint one or more assistants to help lead the party, and these were identified by long, crooked staffs, which were made in the field of green saplings wrapped with fur or cloth.

Few fires were made in enemy country, and the men were careful about their foot tracks. If possible, camps were made in brushy or wooded areas. A typical one-night shelter was made of willow or cottonwood branches bent over after the nature of the sweat lodge. The branches were covered with brush, leaves, and blankets. The Blackfeet, and some of the other northern tribes, made a unique war lodge shelter of trees stacked in a tipi shape and covered with bark and leaves. Both field shelter types were designed to hide the campers and to diffuse the smoke from their fires. The war lodge closest to an enemy village became a base camp, though, and was believed to be an effective fort in case of attack. It was also the storage place for supplies to be used on the way home. Some accounts speak of rock shelters being prepared for the night. They also made excellent defense breastworks.

To cross rivers, the Mandans and the Hidatsas made a wood-frame, hide-covered "bull boat." The Kiowas made a pontoon by wrapping deerskins around a pile of brush and bent willow branches. They even used this makeshift boat to ferry wounded men. The warrior was tied on the bundle and towed across by a swimmer—usually the pipeholder, since he gained prestige according to the number of men returning home with him.

*a*, Wolfskin for war party scout. *b*, wolfskin as collar prepared to be worn by Omaha warrior. *c*, wolfskin worn over shoulders by warrior.

One-night shelter of branches covered with blankets, type used by raiding party.

Northern Plains war lodge made of logs and bark, used as forts and storage houses by war parties.

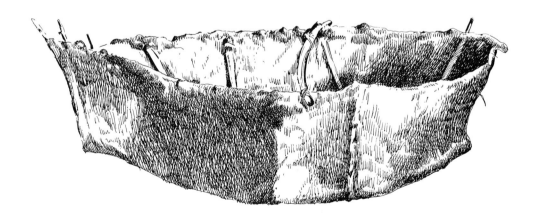

Mandan bull boat made of hide stretched over willow branches, about five feet in diameter.

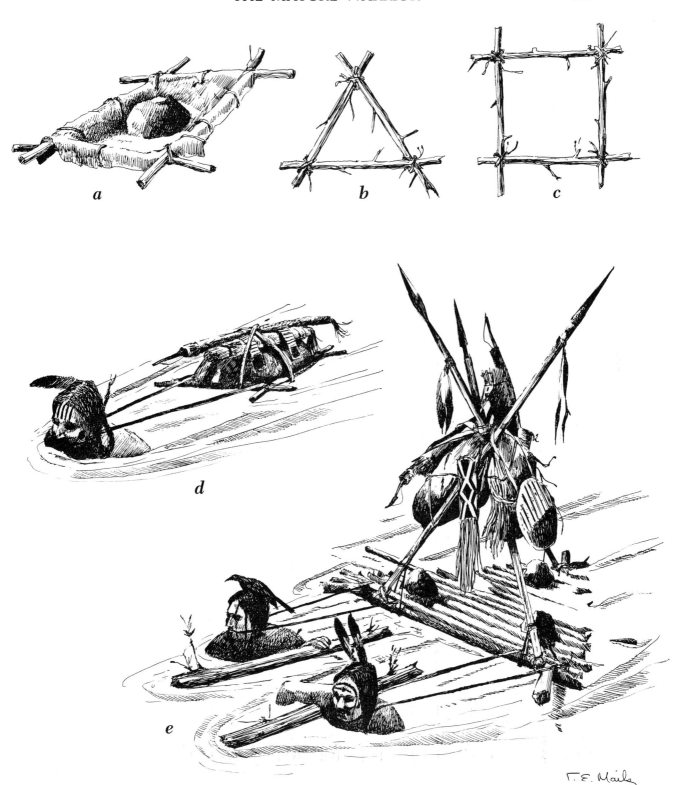

Rafts used to carry goods across rivers and streams. *a*, *b*, and *c*, Crow method of making raft frames with skin tied across to transport small cargoes. *d*, warrior pulling raft by holding towline in mouth. *e*, triangular log raft for large cargoes.

The Crows lashed three sticks together to form a triangle, or four to make a rectangle, then spread a hide across them and tied it to the frame edges to make a raft. A rock was placed in the center as a ballast. To cross deep, swift water they lashed three poles in a triangle and tied other poles across them to make a larger raft. Their guns and spears were then tied on top of the triangle in a tripod form, and the rest of their equipment was hung on this makeshift rack.

An alternate Crow method was to pile up several robes and to run a string around them to form a bundle. A rock ballast and articles to be kept dry were put in the middle. Among the Crows, the towing was done by the horses, or by men holding the towline of the rafts in their teeth.

The Shoshones piled bundles of bulrushes up and lashed them together till they made boats large enough to hold baggage weighing from six to eight hundred pounds.

Some warriors say they shot their arrows across a stream to keep them from getting wet. Swimmers usually crossed on the downstream side of their horses, with one arm hanging over their necks. An alternate method was to hold onto the horse's tail and let the horse pull them.

Some interesting side details of some of the Plains journeys are as follows:

A Kiowa war party, being caught in a place where water was scarce, licked the moisture seeping from some of the rocks in a cave. To climb down from a cliff, they tied their bows to their waists with the bowstrings, so that both hands would be free. Another time they used their bows as poles to help one another up the sides of steep places.

Crows riding down steep hills clung to the manes of their horses, so that even when they slid off they could boost themselves back on. Their water bags were made of buffalo stomachs closed by a drawstring.

Sioux party members always moved on the down side of the wind from animals or enemies. They said that the smell of fire or tobacco, or the sound of a snorting horse, were sure signs of danger. On horse-stealing trips, they rarely attacked a war party, but rather went around them so as to accomplish their primary purpose. One war leader states that he wore enemy clothing so that he would smell like them, and painted and fixed his hair in their manner—although he always wore his medicine underneath all of this!

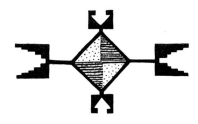

Blackfoot buffalo and war horses picketed at tipis.

T. E. Mails

Warriors driving stolen horses.

T. E. Mails

When a small horse-raiding party had moved some distance into enemy country and came upon fresh tracks that clearly indicated the foe was nearby, the scouts began to look for a village to raid. Once one was discovered, a next-to-last camp was made ten or so miles away from the village, and the next day was spent in preparing for the raid.

Attention was given to weapons and other gear, to painting for battle, and to final prayers and supplications. Finally, the Indians' personal medicines were securely fixed in place. All food and surplus equipment, plus horses if they were riding, were left at the camp in the care of the first-timers, and that night the experienced warriors stripped for action and moved, under cover of darkness, to within sight of the village. This was the real moment of tenseness and excitement.

Ordinarily the pipeholder would scout the area, sometimes even sneaking into the village if a dance was going on. He might also do this if the village was very quiet, and in either case would return to advise the group as to how to proceed.

Some of them always went for the horses picketed at the tipis, since these were the greatest prizes, but while they did this the others cut away a part of the main herd in the pasture area. Depending upon the situation they would get a few animals or a great many; perhaps sixty or more. If no suspicions were aroused they might even lead the first horses off a short distance, hobble them, and return for additional ones. The greater the risk, the better they liked it, and except at the time of the full moon, Plains sentries for some peculiar reason were often notoriously absent—as if to egg them on.

The raiders carried short ropes with them, and led some of the horses away with war bridles made from their ropes. Once they were a safe distance away from the village, they mounted the best horses and herded the others to their base camp. Here they would hastily pick up their gear, the young men, and be

---

PLATE 29.  SHOT IN THE EYE—OGLALA SIOUX ▶

Shot in the Eye wears another of the enthralling buffalo horn bonnets collected by White Bull. The rectangular beaded section has a buffalo's head in the center. The warrior's turtle, with his navel cord enclosed, is tied to the skullcap. The horns are very large, perhaps an unusual size for horned bonnets. Yet they are hollowed and relatively light. A photo of a Sioux Victory Dance taken by Frank Fiske, Custer Album, shows a bonnet with horns as large. H. H. Cross also painted bonnets like this. Remington and Borein saw many bonnets with huge horns and recorded them. Alice Fletcher, *Teton Sioux Music*, BAE Bulletin 61, shows fantastic Sioux bonnets of many kinds—see plates 9, 12, 25, and 69 for examples.

off for a ride that lasted at least two nights and a day before they slept. Pursuit by morning at the latest was inevitable, and they wanted to put as much distance as possible between themselves and the enemy. With so many horses, hiding the trail was almost impossible, and an advantageous head start was their only hope. More than one party was overtaken and badly mauled, and knowing this, they had little rest until the border of their own country was crossed.

The situation with a large war party was somewhat different than with that of a raiding group. A small war party would proceed with the same stealth as the horse-raiding group, but secrecy was out of the question for a large body of warriors. They knew they would be discovered shortly after—or perhaps even before—the enemy country was invaded, yet they took special courage in their medicines and strength. They moved, in any case, against enemy bands, which meant that they would face a force of equal or lesser number than their own. And nine times out of ten that force was on its way to meet them some distance from its village. Ambush was always preferred to an open encounter, and each body, as it approached, would be seeking just such a place and opportunity. Often defensive positions were taken in grass, bush, trees, or a washout. On many occasions rock breastworks were built in preparation for a pitched battle.

Hopefully, the invading body would have time to change into its full war regalia before the forces were enjoined. The Cheyenne say that most of their warriors preferred to dress—to impress the enemy, to take full advantage of their medicines, and to be ready to meet the One-Above in proper attire. Some, though, stripped for action. Those who did painted their bodies extensively, and were certain that their medicine preparations would save them from harm. The Cheyenne warriors had a special way of putting on their warbonnets and feathers, singing appropriate songs and raising the bonnets four times toward the sun, the fourth time putting them on while experienced instructors lectured them as to how to go into the fight.

Upon meeting the enemy in the open, and where all hope of surprise or advantage was gone, the leaders of both sides usually rode out to taunt their

◀ PLATE 30.   ELOTE—JICARILLA APACHE WARRIOR

The Jicarilla, Lipan, Kiowa, and Mescalero Apaches, who lived on the western edge of the Plains, retained a basically Apache culture, yet they adopted many of the habits of the Plains tribes, and made modified adaptations of the Plains dress such as the beaded shirts and leggings, and of the type of warbonnet shown. The painting is adapted from Denver Public Library photographs, 1900, Rose and Hopkins.

opponents, while the main bodies formed long lines behind them. Sometimes the leader's main task was only to hold his young men back and in line. The taunting might go on for hours before mass action began. Once it did, there would first be firing from a distance, and then a mighty clash, with most battle plans forgotten and every man for himself. Each rode in singing his sacred war song, living his medicine to the fullest, and yelling at the top of his lungs to build up his courage.

The Cheyenne say that in a large battle the din was incredible. Horses ran into each other, and some fell and rolled. Clubs, hatchets, and lances were swung in every direction as everyone sought a coup, and the dust was so thick one could hardly see. One of their warriors scalped a member of his own tribe at the exhortation of others before any of them realized who the man was. A Crow, in pulling his gun from its case, accidentally shot his own horse!

Many said they lost all track of time and feeling; that when on foot "their feet hardly touched the ground." Most admitted they were exceedingly afraid, but went in anyway! After all, they had been taught that it was better to die young on the battlefield than to grow old and immobile in the tipi. As a rule, a fighting unit limited itself to a maximum of four passes in one place. After that it shifted its position or abandoned the battle. They did not circle very often, but made a fierce rush at the target, frequently jumping from their horses to fight on foot. Heroes par excellence were made by the rescuing of a fallen comrade, and the leaders in particular made every effort to bring all of their men home.

In relating their stories of battles, warriors did not hide the fact that they were subject to sudden and apparently causeless panics, while at other times they displayed unbelievable valor. Surely their opinions regarding the effectiveness of their medicines had much to do with this, and they were also omen-conscious. If friends began to fall in unexpected numbers, they took it as a clear sign from above to quit and get away, even though they knew that panic reduced their strength and made them easier prey to pursuing tribesmen. After all, they had done the same pursuing themselves. Yet they ran, because their medicine helpers had misfired somehow, or else they had misread their signs, and to stay would be to invite a worse tragedy still.

Generally speaking, losses in even a prolonged engagement involving hundreds of men would be fairly light, with a few being killed and a few more wounded. Everyone knew there would be another day to fight again, and they preserved themselves for it. The Comanches, who were a very large tribe in comparison to others in their area, were experts at this device. They overwhelmed small groups and literally cut them to bits. Yet if a single Comanche fell, they often ran—even when the numerical odds were still heavily in their favor.

The northern tribes were not so quick to do this, but they took any losses as a bad sign, and were glad to find an excuse to call it a day. All experts agree, however, that a badly wounded warrior became an absolute and totally reckless terror. One warrior was seen to fight like a tiger, and then to walk off with two

Warriors in enemy territory dressing and painting on morning of battle.

War leader riding out to challenge and taunt enemy prior to rare mass battle between large groups.

bullets through his body close to his spine, the only effect of which was to cause him to change his gait from a run to a dignified walk.

Wounded men were transported home on a rough travois arrangement. The dead were retrieved if possible, but were often buried on the field in shallow graves or under rocks, the others leaving whatever gifts they could to aid them in their journey to the Faraway Land. At home they would be mourned, but eminently respected. The Blackfoot parties had a unique custom of covering their battlefield dead with the bodies of their enemies. This was said to pay for those who were lost.

If an Assiniboine warrior was wounded, the person who rescued him counted it as a war deed. If a warrior brought back the dead and unscalped body of a comrade at the risk of his own life, that counted too. One who held the enemy off while the main body retreated was a major hero. If he made it back, he was elected to close the final dance in the victory celebration. The Crows mention instances where they covered fallen men with brush and returned later to retrieve their bodies.

Mutilation of fallen enemies was fairly common, with all tribes practicing it to some extent, the Blackfeet and Comanches being the worst. Sometimes a body would be taken home for the women or children to count coup on, sometimes the limbs or fingers were removed, and it was fairly common to collect finger bones, which were made into necklaces to be worn at great festivals. A man who had one on when he fell in battle knew full well, however, what his own fate would be when the enemy found the bones.

Women and children captives were often adopted into the captor's tribe, soon to receive all of the rights and privileges of the camp's members. Yet when taken

War party sweeping in to attack in mid-winter.

Victorious war party returning to home camp.

on a revenge raid they might as easily be killed as a warrior. Men were rarely captured. When they were caught, they were sometimes killed in cold blood, but more often were tortured before being put to death. Now and then a valiant captive would be kept for some time and then released, although his captivity was made exceedingly difficult and he was subjected to constant abuse.

Many a warrior who ran into serious trouble on a raid or war party, but escaped, experienced terrible problems in attempting to make his way home. Sometimes he suffered constantly for want of food or water. Sometimes he nearly froze on the snow-covered prairie, or burned under a merciless sun. And when he finally made it back home, he might still be received as a failure who had shared in a tragic raid.

When the members of an Assiniboine war party arrived within sight of their home camp, they attracted the attention of the village by certain standard signs. If the party had been successful, a member trotted in a zigzag fashion. Then the people ran to greet them and took the scalps, horses, or other objects they had captured. A short dance followed, during which the objects were displayed. Everyone was happy. After that the owners often gave away everything they had taken to whomever they had in mind.

However, some warriors preferred to return to camp unannounced, after which they paraded their captured horses, and the entire camp held a victory dance. If the war party lost one or more members, they first attracted the people's attention, then they threw a robe, rolled into a ball-like shape, high in the air. The robe was thrown once for each member slain. A delegation was sent to meet the party and to obtain the names of the ones killed. The party was then escorted back to camp, and word was sent to the relatives of the slain—who immediately began their plaintive mourning customs.

Crow warriors always blackened their faces when they returned from a successful raid to indicate that any internal fires of revenge had burned out. They also used buffalo blood, mixed with charcoal, to paint symbols on robes wetted with clay to mark the coups which had been counted. Each count enabled them to decorate an area whose size was in proportion to the honor earned.

The Crow party approached their village and spent the night close to it. Early the next morning, they fired off their guns, gave characteristic yells, and thundered toward the camp, setting a grand victory celebration into motion which might last for several days.

The unsuccessful Crow parties did not enter the camp in an auspicious manner. A messenger was sent to a prominent place overlooking the camp to

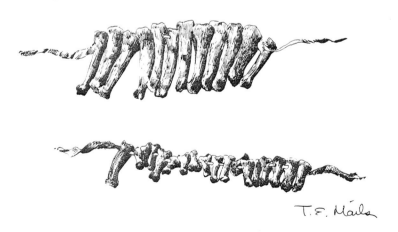

Finger-bone necklace made from fingers taken in revenge raids.

make a robe signal or to fire a gun. When everyone looked, he then lowered a blanket for each man killed, or threw it to one side. He then sat down and waited till the elders came to hear the story. Then the camp went into mourning while the party stayed in the hills for ten days. After this they gathered provisions, made preparations, and left on another raid, seeking success a second time, and a revenge death that could set their own bereaveds' minds at ease.

This was the way of life for the Indian warriors of all the Plains tribes. To them, the swift raids and the miniature wars were part of a very good life in which the days were enjoyed, not measured. As they put it, it was "the time when our hearts sang for joy."

Then the White settlers and army came, first decimating the unprepared Indians by infecting them with epidemics of cholera and smallpox and venereal diseases, and then finishing thousands more off by wars and by starvation through the elimination of the buffalo. Forcing them onto reservations where they were made totally dependent and placed in climates and areas which were unfamiliar to them completed the job of destroying a most commendable life-way.

"Then," said the Indians, "our hearts sank to the ground, and we did not have the strength to lift them up again."[7] The singing and the dancing continued, but the songs and the dances became progressively meaningless and hollow. With the passing of the hunt and the warpath the rich ceremonies built around them lost their force. Nomads need to roam. Buffalo chants need buffalo. Pride finds its strength in usefulness. Crafts only flourish in happy days. Things did happen for the Indians, yet they had no end purpose, no direction, no hope of arrival back at what they believed to be an excellent and worthwhile life.

# Chapter 24

# THE RELOCATION AND
# DECLINE OF THE PEOPLE
# OF THE PLAINS

The white men were not going to disappear; the buffalo would not return; our relatives and friends and heroes of old times would not come back to earth. We must go ahead on the new road we had taken.

Then, more than ever, we needed to carry out our old religious ceremonies, and more than ever the Government was determined to make us discontinue them. The old people were despondent and the young and better educated were confused. It was then that our chief Left Hand went to Agent Stouch to give him a better understanding of our plight. Left Hand, an orator and a leader in all things, made him see that our Man-Above and his God were the same, and that we differed only in the way we worshipped. "Our way," he said, "has come down to us through many generations, and is the only way we know. Among white people there are many ways of worshipping, and many kinds of belief about God. They are all tolerated, but our way is not tolerated. Our children go to school and learn your way and will worship as they are taught. But many of us are old, and can not change our ways. When we die, our way of worship will end. We are so sure that our God and your God are the same that we do not try to take our children away from you; we know your way is good, but we do not understand it. We want you to teach our children your way and let us follow our own. We invite you to come and visit our ceremonies, and to see that they are ancient and reverent and contain nothing harmful.[1]

The Plains Indians tribes of the golden age, which lasted from 1750 to 1875, sprang from several different roots. Some of them were the descendants of farmers and hunters who had lived on the Plains for countless centuries, others descended from ancestors who had come across the great oceans, and some were the offspring of nations which had been forced onto the Plains by the great eastern tribes—who had themselves been pushed westward by White colonization.

The earliest traceable inhabitants of the Plains settled along the major river courses thousands of years ago, and they were farmers who hunted as a sideline. Eventually, the farmers turned more and more to a nomadic way of life, hunting over nearly all of the Plains country for the seemingly endless numbers of buffalo, who by later White estimates totaled sixty million or more.

The Blackfoot tribes were among the most ancient inhabitants of the Plains. Originating in Canada, some of them moved southward and occupied much of Montana. When the first horse was brought to them by a White or Indian trader, they were already pursuing the customs which the horse would enable them to expand in a remarkable way. Present in Montana and Idaho when the Blackfoot tribes arrived were the Flatheads and Nez Percés. East of the Blackfoot, the Gros Ventres and the Arapaho were already moving about in search of buffalo. The Hidatsas were village farmers along the Missouri River in what is now North Dakota. North of them were the villages of the Mandans and the Arikaras. South of them were the stationary Pawnees and the Poncas. Also, a part of the Hidatsa tribe had separated from the rest and moved to the mountain country of the Yellowstone River. Upon arriving there they took the name Crows, ceased following their stationary village habits, and took up a nomadic life of hunting the buffalo on foot. These, then, were the original inhabitants of the Plains.

Next to come to the Plains were the eastern and northeastern tribes who were being forced a step at a time westward by the more powerful eastern nations who had obtained the White man's guns. The first of the dispossessed to arrive from the eastern and northeastern directions were the Plains Crees, the Assiniboines, the Sioux, and the Cheyenne. Except for the ancient Apaches, Kiowas, and Comanches of the extreme south, and whose exact places and times of origin are not known, the aforementioned tribes were the second segment of Indians to arrive on the Plains. It appears that all other tribes making their homes there came later.

By and large, all of these people of the Plains followed a common pattern of life. Their dress and habits were similar, and their spiritual views and pursuits differed very little. They were affected to a considerable degree by the extreme nature of the Plains country in which they lived. The boundless area, the abundant game, and the great gamut of changes in the elements worked their way into the very fabric of the Indian's being, forcing them to impulsive actions at one extreme, and to deepest contemplation at the other. Somehow, in the midst of all this, God was able to encounter the people and to turn them to Himself, so that in time they came to center all things in a monotheistic religion, and whatever they did flowed out from their wellspring of faith.

Because of the way in which the foregoing impressed itself upon some non-Indians, authors frequently caution against going overboard in praising the life-way of the Plains Indians, pointing out that in many of their customs they were something less than the pure and glamorous people they are often said to be. Surely the word of caution is needed, yet it is entirely possible to press too far in the other direction, for the people of the Plains evolved a way of life which manifested praiseworthy secular and religious qualities, and which produced goods comparable in value to the best of the ancient cultures of the world. And, almost incredibly, they accomplished this with the guidance of God and the assistance of little more than two animals, the buffalo and the horse!

The horse, diffused northward into the Plains after 1700 through the Spanish settlements in the areas now known as Texas and New Mexico, offered the tribes a golden opportunity to shift their nomadic way of life into high gear. The tribes divided themselves into bands or clans, and the smaller units struck out on their own to hunt the buffalo, gathering together for a tribal encampment at least once each year, and settling in close proximity to one another in the winter.

Before the horse, families moved their possessions on their backs and with the help of pack dogs dragging small A-shaped pole frame trailers. The Indians built a much larger A frame, which the French called a "travois," to use with the horse, and more and heavier possessions could then be transported from place to place as the tribal bands followed the grazing buffalo herds. At last the Indians could employ a more efficient method of killing buffalo than the laborious piskin or buffalo jump methods. Now they could run the buffalo down at will, and after stripping the hides and cutting up the meat, could carry them back to the main village without difficulty.

Almost immediately, every part of the buffalo was put to a productive use. The meat which was not eaten at once was either cut into thin strips and dried or molded into pemmican. The bones were made into tools, and the hides were fashioned into tipis and into cases for transporting the family possessions. The hides were also made into magnificent robes, headdresses, and shields and the hair into ropes; the skulls became a premium object for religious ceremonies.

For the first time the people of the Plains were able to indulge to the fullest in three wonderful luxuries: in the arts, in raiding and warfare, and in social and religious activities. The time left over from hunting, stocking food, and tanning was now used in part for producing a spectacular array of tools, costumes, and ceremonial items. The principal characteristic of these was found in their simplicity, grace, and mobility. Each item they made was a further development of its natural form. It had a functional shape, texture, and a balanced design and color scheme. Moreover, it was designed to sway with every motion, and to create melodious sounds. It was lightweight—and for the most part collapsible—so as to be easily transported from one place to another. Above all, each item bore a direct relationship to the religious view of its owner, and the qualities stemming from his spiritual manner were brought to bear on every product. In this sense, a Plains product always exhibited some of the life-way and history of its creator. As craftsmen, the Indians achieved outstanding success in three arts: painting—where they produced an effective simplicity in making their pictorial statements; porcupine quillwork; and beadwork with the beautiful beads brought to them by the White traders.

The very means by which the various tribes entered the Plains set the stage for the pattern of existence and survival which came to be the norm for the tribes. Every new arrival forced a reshaping of the territories occupied by the tribes who were already there. As such, in order to maintain any position and the right to their share of the ever migrating buffalo herds, the tribes had no option but to contest with one another—until at last all of the tribes which were to settle on the Plains had arrived. The trouble was that by then the horse and the gun were also there, and every tribe was inexorably drawn into a contest of one-upmanship, of continually seeking to take advantage of any new thing or idea it received in order to hold its own ground; plus of course seeing to it that the other tribes were kept occupied with holding theirs as well.

Within twenty years after the first horses came, enough steeds were available on the Plains to turn the men of the major tribes into mobile striking forces. The Plains warrior became the dominant factor in every tribe, and soon everything in the Plains life-way was centered in him. An arsenal of handmade but sophisticated weapons came into being. The bow and arrow was the primary weapon and hunting instrument, but there was also the lance, knife, hatchet, and club—and eventually the White man's guns. Boys were trained until they could use these weapons with great skill in hunting, and both offensively and defensively in war. They were also trained to hunt and to track animals and men. As the years passed, the men of each tribe developed a social scheme of Warrior Societies, with special costumes, special sacred rites, special customs, and special purposes. The societies served to perpetuate the male's responsibility to become the defender of his tribe, and they also served as the police units for each band or clan. Each boy, as he matured, entered a society, and the society scheme governed his life from that point until he retired to a less active life at the age of forty or so. Young men went off in small groups at regular intervals to raid the enemy horse herds and to make defensive war raids throughout the clement seasons of the year. It was natural that men who fulfilled their responsibility to defend the tribe and band should have a reward for their services. The feathers of the golden eagle were chosen for this purpose, and its feathers served as medals to designate those who

While it has been difficult to maintain, the life-way of the Plains warrior continues. Albert Mad Plume, of the Piegan branch of the Blackfeet, was photographed in the 1930s wearing the fourth edition of a famous painted war shirt named "the Lord's Shirt." The original dated back to 1850. It was fashioned by Bear Chief. When he wore it he "was invisible to the enemy and bullets could not hit him." The original shirt was remade three times by successive owners. In 1930 Albert Mad Plume could only put it on, remember—and dream.

T. E. Mails

struck, or counted, coup in defense of their people. The greatest warriors won enough medals to fashion them into the stunning feathered warbonnets which came to characterize the warriors of the Plains.

The extreme nature of the Plains country combined with the war society structure to produce the other half of the social life of the people. The constant uncertainty which confronted each band and tribe drew them into a mode of life wherein they sought personal protection from the One-Above, and also the comfort and happiness of an interdependent group. Dancing and singing were primary means of personal expression and social intercourse. They were a means of concentrating the heart and mind of the people upon the major events and thoughts in individual and tribal life. Dancing expressed what a man felt and wanted to become, and becoming had a direct link in the Plains scheme to visions, or as the Indians referred to it, "lamenting."

Visions were sought as channels whereby a providential God would send them counsel and helpers. Since everything on earth and in the sky above was believed to be alive, each created thing was the possessor of its own special and desirable qualities, and through the message received in a vision or visions a man could take unto himself, by reflection and imitation, the qualities he needed to survive and to ensure the longevity of his band and tribe. By acquiring all or some part of his vision helpers, and by studying their qualities and habits carefully, a man could obtain medicine or "power." With this power as a protective barrier, he could then go forth to the hunt and war assured of success—or else serene in the knowledge that his power or medicine would warn him off if need be.

In the same way, the holy men and doctors acquired their power to heal and to prophesy through visions, and because vision power was the standard for everyone, the other members of the tribe accepted their guidance as "almost" infallible and their healing abilities as legitimate. The holy men and doctors, while lacking in great degree the educated skills of modern priests, psychologists, and doctors, did indeed work amazing cures from time to time because they learned to apply herbs and to manage the psychology of bringing a patient's faith and will to live to the fore. Above all, the holy men and doctors understood themselves to be tubes through which the One-Above worked. Once they had properly purified themselves, He reached down through them to touch the patient and to accomplish the actual healing.

It was natural that a parallel scheme of purification to become fit vessels for the One-Above's use would take place among the lay people. A system of purification in preparation for all major undertakings was followed by all members of a tribe. For this purpose a ritually built sweat lodge was employed and traditional rituals were conducted within it. Together with the lodge, sacred sage, sweet grass, white clay, steam, smoke, and smoking were used to promote a pure self, or one forgiven and born anew, hence fit for God to work through.

The smoking pipe became a revered instrument for sacred ceremonial purposes. Its straight stem served to epitomize the connection of the Indian with his maker, and its proper use gathered the wisdom of the universe into the midst of those who smoked the pipe in preparation for a discussion of important events. Because they were so spiritually oriented, the Indians also developed a reverent approach to everything that existed. Each step taken during a day was thought to be along a sacred path, and in order to prosper one learned to imitate, insofar as a human being could, the obviously good things of the earth and sky. The sun, which might well be the dwelling place of God, sent light and enlightenment, warmth and growth down to earth. Since it moved in a circular and clockwise direction, the Indians carried out their sacred activities in a circle, and moved in a clockwise direction. A circle symbol also represented the universe and eternity. The other celestial dwellers shared the sun's duties in creation and procreation. Therefore, they too were honored in ceremonies and played their individual part in the governing of human lives. Each celestial object was translated into symbolic form and also appended to the Indian's person by painted designs or quilled or beaded items so as to obtain power and wisdom through one's proximity to the duplicated object.

It was inevitable that a vow and thanksgiving aspect would accompany the religious scheme of the Plains. The warrior believed he had the privilege of divine guidance, therefore he felt free to call upon God at any time for help. Sometimes he did this directly, but more often he sent his plea up to God through his spiritual helpers, which were the objects or animals which had come to him in his vision. Often, he accompanied his plea with personal sacrifices to show his sincerity. Sometimes he presented all or part of a prized possession to God by placing it on a buffalo chip or in a tree, or by casting it into the water—his belief being that as the elements absorbed it, it was transformed into a form which could ascend up to God. Along with the sacrifice he often made a vow that if God enabled him to succeed in what he wished to do, he would make a further sacrifice in thanksgiving—perhaps even the great Sun Dance.

The Sun Dance was a tribal event of considerable magnitude. Sometime during the summer months of each year the bands and clans assembled at an appointed place. Here a great Sun Lodge was built according to traditional rules, and the men who had made their vows fulfilled them by pulling against thongs which secured them by their chests to the Sun Pole, which stood at the center of the lodge, until at last they either pulled or were cut free. Such painful rites were always carried out on behalf of the tribe and because of this all of the people shared in the event, looking upon it as a holy and a joyful occasion. It did relatively little damage to the warriors most directly involved, and the Indians, to this day, are not able to understand why the Sun Dance Ceremony, which was so important to them, vexed the White man so that once he dominated them he forced its abandonment.

The White man, religious as he was, did not comprehend the Indian mode of thanksgiving. He thought it was nothing more than a heathen form of Sun Dance in which the sun was worshiped in a ghastly way. The Indians called it a Sun Dance too, but since its true meaning was as a religious ceremony of thanksgiving for the well-being and longevity of the people, it was a time of unspeakable joy, and more truly *a dance in the sun!* Such tribal meetings had a festival atmosphere, and special times were set aside for sharing gifts and for helping the poor. The sacred rite of ear piercing was enacted with the children, and renowned warriors who had earned new names by feats of valor on behalf of the tribe were given these names by the tribal leaders. When the Sun Dance ended each band and clan went its individual way back to its accustomed hunting area, secure in the knowledge that a good thing had been done to thank their providential God, and warm within over the happiness of renewed fellowships.

It is true that the Indians of the Plains in the years 1750 to 1875 were not able to maintain the standards of hygiene which are common today. It is true that some of their raiding and warfare was not necessary, that greater efforts for peace between the tribes could have been made, and that on occasion the treatment of captives was brutal. It is true that not all of the Plains people were sophisticated or commendably moral. Yet considering their isolation from other civilizations and their great limitation of means, the majority of Plains Indians achieved standards of life and qualities in crafts which deserve the highest possible praise. The last 125 years of their life before the Whites finally pulled a curtain of gloom completely across their life-way and land can indeed be characterized as a golden age, for it was a time of great happiness and productivity. They lived a good life and a natural life. To them, it was also a very genuine life.

---

PLATE 31.   ARAPAHO GHOST DANCER ▶

From the spring of 1890 to early 1891 the Plains Indians participated in a passionate revival which was known as the Ghost Dance. Men and women who danced made themselves magnificently painted "ghost shirts," which were covered with prayer symbols. They expected these to protect them from harm by the Whites. The revival came to a tragic end on December 29, 1890, with the massacre of several hundred Indians by United States soldiers at a place called Wounded Knee in South Dakota.

Curtis photographed the Arapaho warrior shown here, in his studio, wearing his Ghost Dance shirt. It is a painted hide shirt, and is perhaps as beautiful an example as was done. The colors are taken from actual museum specimens. Ghost Dancers did not, as a rule, wear their warbonnets while dancing. However, the man in the Curtis photograph had his on, and is painted that way. He is posed before a Sun Dance enclosure in remembrance of his proudest former days.

Indian children did not have soap, but they were scrubbed inside and outside with morals, ethics, worship, tradition, responsibility, bravery, self-respect and respect for parents, and the group spirit. They learned how to live gracefully, and how to die bravely in the full confidence that a continuation of life awaited them beyond the grave.

Indian children did not have books or a written language, but their parents unfolded the pages of nature for them in a truly marvelous way. In this context they came to appreciate and to make as much as possible of their environment. It can be said that they developed an unusual reverence for life and living, and being so sensitive learned to move with nature, rather than to break in a willful attempt to stand against her. They learned to *cope* with an environment and circumstances which made incessant and seemingly impossible demands upon them. Living in the midst of unusual extremes and constant dangers, the Plains Indians found no reason to concoct strong drugs or drinks, and they did not experience the countless fears, anxieties, and pressures which have driven so many in our generation to materialism, to pleasure seeking, to excessive amounts of drugs and alcohol, to mental distress, and to rebellion.

Yet in the span of a few years, all that the people of the Plains had achieved was gone, wiped out, and so completely that the very next generation of Plains Indians to be born could hardly learn what it really had been like.

Actually, it didn't happen that suddenly. It just seemed as though it did. The decline of the Plains life-way began when the first White man entered their territory. It continued at an accelerating pace thereafter, and finally, when it was all but over, a series of cataclysmic events conspired to slam the door so suddenly that it shook the Indians and their life-way to their very foundations. In fact, it shook their life-way loose from them, so loose that they could hardly catch it again.

French fur traders were in the Plains country by 1700, and by 1750 they had reached the Rockies and had established trade routes along every major northern river. Alexander Mackenzie journeyed to the Canadian Pacific in 1793, and Lewis and Clark made their epic journey across the Plains and to the Pacific coast in 1805. By 1815 the United States government had begun to make what would prove

---

◄ PLATE 32. MOUNTAIN CHIEF—BLACKFEET

Mountain Chief was a noted warrior and leader of the Southern Blackfeet. Picture shows him reflecting upon the rich and happy past of his people. Adapted from photograph by F. A. Rinehart.

to be an unbroken string of broken treaties with the various tribes of the Plains. To their undying credit the Indians at first accepted these as noble documents to be taken at face value. It was not till toward the end they realized that most of the treaties were not worth the paper they were written on. Before 1840 trains of wagons were moving West Coast-bound emigrants across the Plains. Along with them came plagues, whiskey, venereal diseases, provocations, and the first few Christian missionaries. Before long depredations were being committed by both the Indians and the Whites. Soon White military posts were being established to protect the Whites, and this agitated the Indians further still. In 1851 the situation was serious enough to require a great peace council, which was held at Fort Laramie. All agreed to a general peace, but the agreement could not be kept. The constant westward migrations of the Whites caused too many problems for the Indians, and in 1854 open warfare erupted. Soon both the guilty and the innocent were being killed on both sides. Every so often a treaty would be made and would bring a momentary peace. But that was all, for mindless of the agreements, the frontier settlements of the Whites moved inexorably deeper into the Plains. In 1849 the Bureau of Indian Affairs was transferred to the Interior Department from the War Department, and with both now being involved with the Indians, and at loggerheads continually with one another, the Indians suffered more severely still. Indian tribes were imprisoned on reservations, given promises and little else, urged to begin building and farming and conforming to the White man's way, and although some did not try because the new way was so foreign to their life-way, those who did found themselves being moved to a new and more miserable area as soon as anything worthwhile was done. All of them endured periods when they were living in concentration camp conditions, eating roots, tree bark, and dried cornstalks, and sometimes starving by the hundreds because the promised supplies did not arrive. The intervals of peace grew shorter, and the wars became more violent. When gold was discovered first in the Rockies and later in the Black Hills, the Whites came in such a rush that battles were enjoined which led to an inevitable end for the great people of the Plains.

Coupled with the constant wars, the terrible diseases, and the privations of reservation life in terrains much different from their original homelands was the slaughter of the buffalo by White hunters.

The marketing of buffalo hides from the Plains area began about 1764, but only a comparatively few hides were taken before the 1830s. Interestingly enough, the Indians furnished most of the first large supplies of robes, trading them to the Whites in considerable quantities for guns, ammunition, and other useful items. Then in 1860 a German tannery discovered a way to make a fine grade of leather from the buffalo hides, and the rush was soon on. With each hide being worth considerable money, it was not long before more than ten thousand White hunters were on the Plains at one time after buffalo skins—except for the tongue, the rest of the animal was left to rot. The Indians, who were hunting buffalo themselves, nevertheless looked on in stunned displeasure as the wanton slaughter by the Whites continued. Before long they began to fight the hunters, but they were too few and too late and too deprived. By 1873 some parts of the buffalo ranges were entirely empty of buffalo. By 1885 all but a handful were gone from the entire Plains.

Goaded, starved, humiliated, and buffeted about, the Indians finally scored the victory that brought them, somewhat ironically, defeat. In June of 1876 they crushed General Custer at the battle of the Little Bighorn in southeastern Montana. That was too much for forty million Whites to bear, and so the cry went up to crush "once and for all" the terrible savages of the Plains. After that the White troops pursued them without mercy, until finally they were all hunted down and put on reservations or driven into Canada. By now, less than half the Indians who were living when the White-Indian wars began were still alive.

The starvation, the freezing, the diseases, and the whiskey continued. Every slight advance was accompanied by a major setback. There was one brief re-surgence for the Indians—like a match flaring up one last time just before it went out. In January of 1889 a Paiute Indian from Nevada, named Wavoka, had a vision which inspired him to proclaim a sacred Ghost Dance which, when enacted, would return the land and the buffalo herds to the Indians of the Plains. The news came like manna from above to the lamenting and desperate tribes. The dance spread like wildfire, with men and women alike adopting a ghost shirt patterned after one Wavoka had seen in his vision, and which was supposed to protect the wearer from all harm. As the peaceful revival spread, the Whites reacted in alarm. The Indian wars were still fresh in their minds. In fact, they overreacted, for on December 29, 1890, at a place called Wounded Knee, they arrested a band of Minneconjou Sioux who were suspect because of their Ghost Dance activities. Under somewhat disputed circumstances a disturbance began, and several hundred Indian men, women, and children lay dead within a few minutes. Many of them wore Ghost Dance shirts which had been shredded by the White soldiers' guns. That broke the back of the Ghost Dance, and of the Plains spirit. After that there was nothing to do but sink back into the corners of their reservation cells and accept the misery which awaited them.

Oh, and misery it was, of a peculiar kind, for it has not ended to this day.

Repeated and rigorous attempts were made to demolish tribal ties and struc-tures. The White ideal was to pull the Indians into a circumscribed resemblance of the American way of life and quickly assimilate them. The problem was complicated by the fact that most tribes still owned some property that some group of White men never ceased trying to get, and a constant handicap for the Indians beyond the land leeches was the depressing fact that any Indian program was subject to complete change at each turnover in political administration. It is said that the years from 1876 to the 1920s testify to some of the most anguished silent suffering that will ever be related. On one side the Indian children, in those rare times when they were being instructed by the Whites, were being taught to feel shame and contempt for the life-way of their parents. On the other side, abject hunger drove the Indians to groveling beggary. The Bureau of Indian Affairs labored for years under charges of crookedness that no amount of reform could seem to hush. By 1881 the situation was already so notorious that a White woman named Helen Hunt Jackson would write an astounding book called *A Century of Dishonor*, in which she would relate the State Department-documented story of the abysmal treatment of the Indians.[2] Still, it did little more than arouse a ripple of public indignation. Soon it had passed by and was forgotten, and the shameful treatment went on as before.

We can hardly begin to realize how the Plains Indians felt when our ancestors brusquely and unfeelingly ground the substances of their lives into a desolate pulp. One day their hearts sang for joy, one day they danced in the sun, and the next there was no sun, and no reason for song. It was as if they were in the midst of a glorious party, the evening was young, and suddenly the lights went out.

Two quotes, by Frank B. Linderman and George Catlin, men who had the great privilege of living in deepest empathy with the Indians at the crest of their cultural development, sum it up:

Plenty-coups refused to speak of his life after the passing of the buffalo, so that history seems to have been broken off, leaving many years unaccounted for. "I have not told you half that happened when I was young," he said, when urged to go on. "I can think back and tell you much more of war and horse stealing. But when the buffalo went away the hearts of my people fell to the ground, and they could not lift them up again. After this nothing happened. There was little singing anywhere. Besides," he added sorrowfully, "you know that part of my life as well as I do. You saw what happened to us when the buffalo went away."

I do know that part of his life's story, and that part of the lives of all the Indians of the Northwestern plains; and I did see what happened to these sturdy, warlike people when the last of the buffalo was finally slaughtered and left to decay on the plains by skin-hunting white men.

The Indian's food supply was now gone; so too were the materials for his clothes and sheltering home. Pitched so suddenly from plenty to poverty, the Indian lost his poise and could not believe the truth. He was dazed, and yet so deep was his faith in the unfailing bounty of his native land that even when its strange emptiness began to mock him he believed in the return of the buffalo to the plains, until white men began to settle there, their wire fences shutting off his ancestral water-holes. Then a bitterness tempered by his fatalism found a place in the Indian's heart, while a feeling of shame for the white man's wantonness was growing up in my own. The Indian was a meat eater, and now there was no meat. He had followed the buffalo herds up and down the land, or visited the foothills and mountains for elk, deer and bighorn, so that his camps had always been clean. Now, confined to reservations often under unsympathetic agents, his camps became foul, and he could not move them. Twice, in earlier days, white men had brought scourges of smallpox to the Indians of the Northwestern plains, and each time many thousands had died. Now, with the buffalo gone and freedom denied him, the Indian was visited by two equally hideous strangers, famine and tuberculosis. He could cope with neither. His pride was broken. He felt himself an outcast, a pariah, in his own country.[3]

I have viewed man in the artless and innocent simplicity of nature, in the full enjoyment of the luxuries which God had bestowed upon him. I have seen him happier than kings or princes can be; with his pipe and little ones about him. I have seen him shrinking from civilized approach, which came with all its vices, like the dead of night, upon him; I have seen raised, too, in that darkness, religion's torch, and seen him gaze and then retreat like the frightened deer, that are blinded by the light; I have seen him shrinking from the soil and haunts of his boyhood, bursting the strongest ties which bound him to the earth, and its pleasures; I have seen him ('tis the only thing that will bring them) with tears of grief sliding over his cheeks, clap his hand in silence over his mouth, and take the last look over his fair hunting grounds, and turn his face in sadness to the setting sun. All this I have seen performed in Nature's silent dignity and grace, which forsook him not in the last extremity of misfortune and despair; and I have seen as often, the approach of the bustling, busy, talking, whistling, hopping, elated and exulting white men, with the first dip of the ploughshare, making sacrilegious trespass on the bones of the valiant dead. I have seen the skull, the pipe, and the tomahawk rise from the ground together, in interrogations which the sophistry of the world can never answer. I have seen thus, in all its forms and features, the grand and irresistible march of civilization. I have seen this splendid Juggernaut rolling on, and beheld its sweeping desolation; and held converse with the happy thousands, living, as yet, beyond its influence, who have not been crushed, nor yet have dreamed of its approach.

I have stood admidst unsophisticated people, and contemplated with feelings of deepest regret, the certain approach of this overwhelming system, which will inevitably march on and prosper, until reluctant tears shall have watered every rod of this fair land; and from the towering cliffs of the Rocky Mountains, the luckless savage will turn back his swollen eye, over the blue and illimitable hunting grounds from whence he had fled, and there contemplate, like Caius Marius on the ruins of Carthage, their splendid desolation.[4]

Still, it is not within the province of this book to discuss the transition period from 1890 until today, nor to consider to any degree the present state of the Plains Indians. Fortunately, the Indians themselves are at last coming alive in their own defense, and with good sympathy and the help they ask for, they will soon emerge from their sorry state of deprivation. However far the Indians have come in some areas, one might only consider a few current statistics to see the distance they have to go. Compared to the national averages for all Americans in the year 1970: three times as many Indian children die before they are four years old; the average Indian lives twenty-five fewer years; two and one half times as many Indians have mental illness; the suicide rate for young Indians is four times as high, and on some reservations it is several hundred times greater; they are the most poorly educated of any group; unemployment is eight to ten times as great; their high school dropout rate exceeds any other major group.[5] In a message to Congress in July 1970 President Richard Nixon, citing "centuries of injustice," described the American Indians as "the most deprived and the most isolated minority group in our nation."

There is, today, a movement which is pressing hard for self-determination by and for the Indian people. It wants improved education under Indian control for Indian youngsters, education which is suited to their experiences and opportunities. It wants restoration of lands and resources sufficient to provide an economic base for the Indian population. It wants majority control of Indian funds and resources, public as well as tribal. It wants recognition of the Indian culture and way of life as an integral part of America's cultural pluralism. Progress will be made. Considering their rich life-way, the requests are most reasonable, for the people of the Plains and the other Indians of America possess a proud heritage, and one which can make enormous contributions to the rest of the world—which requires their particular contributions rather desperately right now.

A boy growing up today has no way of knowing how good life was, or what life was like, unless he reads about it in books. Even if he should read books about our life, he would miss something. Books could not make him see the sun rising over the land that stretched for miles without fences or roads, or the North Canadian River and the smaller streams winding through that land with trees and brush along their banks and reeds and grass as high as a man's waist in the low places, or feel how friendly the life in our villages was, with children and dogs and ponies outside the tipis, and men and women busy drying meat or beading moccasins or making arrows or dressing skins. But I am an old man who can remember all this from my boyhood, before the white man's government and religion and houses and inventions changed everything. The road of the Arapaho was an old and good one, and we believed it had been traveled since the beginning of the world. Now, though we can no longer travel it, it is a good thing to show how that road once ran before we lost it.[6]

# NOTES

CHAPTER 1

    1. Catlin, *North American Indians,* Vol. I, p. 102

    2. Wissler, *Indians of the Plains,* pp. 154–57

    3. Miller, *The West,* p. 63

    4. Tibbles, *Buckskin and Blanket Days,* p. 69

    5. Spaulding, *On the Western Tour with Washington Irving,* pp. 40–41

    6. Catlin, op. cit., Vol. II, pp. 2–3, 155–57

    7. Denver Art Museum, *Indian Art of the Americas,* p. 43

CHAPTER 2

    1. Dodge, *33 Years Among Our Wild Indians,* p. 240

    2. Devoto, *Across the Wide Missouri,* p. 139

    3. Ibid., pp. 322–23

    4. Linderman, *Plenty Coups,* pp. 118, 206

    5. Dodge, op. cit., p. 248

    6. Wilson, *The White Indian Boy,* pp. 39–40

    7. Linderman, op. cit., p. 118

CHAPTER 3

    1. McClintock, Southwest Museum Leaflet No. 8, pp. 18–30

    2. Ibid., p. 11

    3. Lowie, *The Crow Indians,* p. 173

    4. Fletcher, *Teton Sioux Music,* pp. 314–18

    5. Lowie, op. cit., pp. 181–92

    6. Ibid., pp. 192–97

    7. Omahas, BAE 27th Report, pp. 441–42

    8. Dorsey, *The Cheyenne,* pp. 20–24

    9. Linderman, *Plenty Coups,* pp. 20–22

  10. Lowie, op. cit., pp. 202–6

  11. Ewers, *Indian Life on the Upper Missouri,* p. 133

  12. Linderman, op. cit., p. 53

CHAPTER 4

    1. Seton, *The Gospel of the Redman,* pp. 2–3

    2. Omahas, BAE 27th Report, p. 331. See also McClintock, *The Old North Trail,* Appendices, p. 530

    3. McClintock, *Old North Trail,* p. 334

    4. Henry, *Journal,* Vol. I, p. 325

    5. Catlin, *North American Indians,* Vol. I, p. 96, Vol. II, p. 233

    6. Seton, op. cit., p. 47

    7. Carver, *Travels,* p. 271

8. Dodge, *33 Years Among Our Wild Indians*, p. 58

9. Brown, *The Sacred Pipe*, Preface, pp. 9–10

CHAPTER 5

1. Hassrick, *The Sioux*, pp. 15–16
2. Grinnell, *Blackfoot Lodge Tales*, p. 219
3. Omahas, BAE 27th Report, pp. 199–206
4. John Stands In Timber, *Cheyenne Memories*, p. 44
5. Nabokov, *Two Leggings*, p. 87
6. Denig, *Indian Tribes of the Upper Missouri*, pp. 431–50
7. Ibid., pp. 431–50
8. Grinnell, op. cit., p. 220
9. Longstreet, *War Cries On Horseback*, p. 20

CHAPTER 6

1. Williams, *The Soul of the Red Man*, pp. 45–46
2. Ibid., pp. 47–48
3. Linderman, *Plenty Coups*, p. 79
4. Ibid., p. 78
5. Ibid., pp. 79–80
6. Dorsey, *Traditions of the Skidi Pawnee*, pp. 52–55
7. Linderman, op. cit., pp. 11–13
8. Ibid., p. 80
9. Neihardt, *Black Elk Speaks*, p. 198; Brown, *The Sacred Pipe*, p. 5
10. Fletcher, BAE Report, 1904

CHAPTER 7

1. Bass, *The Arapaho Way*, p. 69
2. Ibid., p. 70
3. Dorsey, *Traditions of the Skidi Pawnee*, p. 20. See also Brown, *The Sacred Pipe*, p. 45
4. Wildschut, *Crow Indian Medicine Bundles*, p. 143
5. McClintock, *The Old North Trail*, pp. 246–50
6. Densmore, *Teton Sioux Music*, pp. 195, 266
7. Ibid., p. 267
8. Ibid., p. 253
9. McClintock, *Old North Trail*, Appendices, pp. 525–28
10. Catlin, *North American Indians*, Vol. I, p. 39
11. Linderman, *Plenty Coups*, pp. 261–65
12. Catlin, op. cit., Vol. I, pp. 39–41
13. Grinnell, *Blackfoot Lodge Tales*, pp. 276–86
14. Point, *Wilderness Kingdom*, p. 16
15. Ibid., see also p. 204
16. Nabokov, *Two Leggings*, p. 204

CHAPTER 8

1. Seton, *The Gospel of the Redman*, pp. 16–17
2. Brown, *The Sacred Pipe*, p. 44
3. Linderman, *Plenty Coups*, pp. 34–43

4. Ibid., pp. 58–65
5. Wildschut, *Crow Indian Medicine Bundles*, pp. 16–17
6. Densmore, *Indian Notes and Monographs*, pp. 180–81
7. Lowie, *The Northern Shoshone*, p. 230
8. John Stands In Timber, *Cheyenne Memories*, p. 114

CHAPTER 9

1. Brown, *The Sacred Pipe*, pp. 136–37
2. Nabokov, *Two Leggings*, p. 203
3. Brown, op. cit., p. 42
4. Ibid., pp. 31–43

CHAPTER 10

1. Brown, *The Sacred Pipe*, p. 74

CHAPTER 11

1. Linderman, *Plenty Coups*, p. 78
2. Ibid., p. 242
3. Dodge, *33 Years Among Our Wild Indians*, pp. 177–78
4. Catlin, *North American Indians*, Vol. I, pp. 89–90

CHAPTER 12

1. Neihardt, *Black Elk Speaks*, pp. 55–56
2. Catlin, *North American Indians*, Vol. I, p. 128
3. Catlin, op. cit., Vol. II. See also Grinnell, *Pawnee Hero Stories and Folk Tales*, pp. 309–10
4. Catlin, op. cit., Vol. I, p. 24
5. Rachlis, *Indians of the Plains*, p. 28. See also J. A. Allen, *The American Bisons, Living and Extinct*
6. Devoto, *Across the Wide Missouri*, p. 134
7. Catlin, op. cit., Vol. II, pp. 65–66
8. Blish, *Pictographic History of the Oglala Sioux*

CHAPTER 13

1. Grinnell, *The Story of the Indian*, pp. 160–61
2. Lowie, *Indians of the Plains*, p. 130
3. Linderman, *Plenty Coups*, pp. 257–58

CHAPTER 14

1. Henry, *New Light on the Early History of the Greater Northwest*
2. Lowie, *Indians of the Plains*, p. 130
3. Royce, *Burbank Among the Indians*, pp. 204–5
4. Omahas, BAE 27th Report, pp. 358–62
5. Henry, op. cit.
6. Brown, *The Sacred Pipe*, p. 110
7. Ibid., p. 123
8. Point, *Wilderness Kingdom*, p. 31
9. Lowie, *The Northern Shoshone*, p. 223

CHAPTER 15

1. Lyford, *Quill and Beadwork of the Western Sioux*, p. 40

CHAPTER 16

1. Catlin, *North American Indians*, Vol. I, pp. 102–3
2. Lowie, *The Assiniboine*, p. 31
3. Lowie, *Indians of the Plains*, pp. 108–9
4. Grinnell, *The Cheyenne Indians*, pp. 29–38
5. Grant, *American Indians Yesterday and Today*, p. 96
6. John Stands In Timber, *Cheyenne Memories*, pp. 51–52
7. Hassrick, *The Sioux*, pp. 171–72
8. Grinnell, *Blackfoot Lodge Tales*, pp. 238–39
9. Ibid., pp. 239–40
10. Salomon, *The Book of Indian Crafts and Indian Lore*, pp. 37–39
11. Hassrick, op. cit., pp. 90–91
12. Dodge, *33 Years Among Our Wild Indians*, pp. 512–22. See also Parkman, *The Oregon Trail*, Heritage, pp. 114–28
13. Catlin, op. cit., Vol. I, pp. 267–69
14. Goodnight, *Cowman and Plainsman*, U. of Okla. Press, 1949
15. Densmore, *Teton Sioux Music*, pp. 77–84
16. Brown, *The Sacred Pipe*, pp. 10–30

CHAPTER 17

1. Bass, *The Arapaho Way*, p. 29
2. Ibid., p. 29
3. Catlin, *North American Indians*, Vol. I, pp. 145–47

CHAPTER 18

1. Catlin, *North American Indians*, Vol. II, pp. 23–24
2. Ibid., Vol. I, pp. 49–51
3. Lehman, *Nine Years with the Indians*
4. Omahas, BAE 27th Report, pp. 351–52
5. Dodge, *33 Years Among Our Wild Indians*, pp. 297–310
6. Catlin, op. cit., Vol. I, pp. 32–33

CHAPTER 19

1. Andrews, *Indians as the Westerners Saw Them*, p. 74
2. Southwest Museum, *Bows and Arrows*, p. 10
3. Lowie, *Indians of the Plains*, pp. 76–77
4. Southwest Museum, op. cit., p. 12
5. Linderman, *Plenty Coups*, p. 17
6. Dodge, *33 Years Among Our Wild Indians*, p. 420
7. Grinnell, *The Story of the Indian*, p. 152
8. Dodge, op. cit., p. 418
9. Linderman, op. cit., p. 17. See also Miller, *The West*, p. 59
10. Pope, *Bows and Arrows*, pp. 62–63
11. Wissler, *Indians of the Plains*, pp. 25–26

12. Dodge, op. cit., p. 417
13. Catlin, *North American Indians,* Vol. I, pp. 103-4
14. Miller, op. cit., p. 6
15. Pope, op. cit., pp. 17-19
16. Salomon, *The Book of Indian Crafts and Lore,* p. 160
17. Southwest Museum, op. cit., p. 13
18. Hassrick, *The Sioux,* p. 198
19. Catlin, op. cit., Vol. I, p. 32
20. Hassrick, op. cit., p. 197
21. Pope, op. cit., pp. 44, 74
22. Southwest Museum, op. cit., p. 13
23. Linderman, op. cit., pp. 40-41
24. Lehman, *Nine Years with the Indians,* pp. 93-94

CHAPTER 20

1. Bass, *The Arapaho Way,* p. 33
2. Catlin, *North American Indians,* Vol. I, p. 236
3. Dodge, *33 Years Among Our Wild Indians,* p. 423

CHAPTER 21

1. Dodge, *33 Years Among Our Wild Indians,* p. 422
2. Schultz, *Blackfeet and Buffalo,* p. 144-54
3. Hofsinde, *Indian Warriors and Their Weapons,* pp. 74-75
4. Linderman, *Plenty Coups,* pp. 279-80
5. Wildschut, *Crow Indian Medicine Bundles,* p. 72
6. Ewers, *The Horse in Blackfoot Indian Culture,* p. 203. See also Catlin, *North American Indians,* Vol. II, p. 241, and Grinnell, *The Story of the Indian,* p. 153
7. Grant, *American Indians Yesterday and Today,* p. 285
8. Salomon, *The Book of Indian Crafts and Indian Lore,* pp. 179-82
9. Lehman, *Nine Years Among the Indians,* pp. 25-27
10. Grant, op. cit., p. 285
11. Catlin, op. cit., Vol. I, p. 241
12. Tunis, *Indians,* p. 100
13. Lowie, *The Northern Shoshone,* p. 193
14. Grinnell, *The Cheyenne Indians,* pp. 187-202
15. Bass, *The Arapaho Way,* p. 33
16. Hassrick, *The Sioux,* p. 199
17. Lehman, op. cit., pp. 25-26. See also Wallace, *The Comanches,* pp. 106-7

CHAPTER 22

1. Brown, *The Sacred Pipe,* p. 57
2. Densmore, *Teton Sioux Music,* p. 70
3. Ibid., pp. 68-77
4. Grinnell, *Blackfoot Lodge Tales,* p. 188
5. Kennedy, *The Assiniboines,* p. 36
6. Ibid., p. 39
7. Grinnell, *When Buffalo Ran,* p. 35
8. Ibid., p. 36

9. Dodge, *33 Years Among Our Wild Indians*, pp. 551–73
10. Ibid., p. 551
11. Drannon, *Thirty One Years on the Plains*, p. 255
12. Linderman, *Plenty Coups*, p. 247
13. Ibid., p. 165
14. Dodge, op. cit., pp. 425–34. See also Grinnell, *By Cheyenne Campfires*, p. 29

## CHAPTER 23

1. Linderman, *Plenty Coups*, pp. 119–20
2. Ibid., p. 120
3. Mayhall, *The Kiowas*, pp. 270–78
4. Lowie, *Indians of the Plains*, pp. 198–204
5. Grinnell, *The Story of the Indian*, pp. 125, 126. Also *Blackfoot Lodge Tales*, pp. 242–43
6. Linderman, op. cit., p. 137
7. Ibid., p. 311

## CHAPTER 24

1. Bass, *The Arapaho Way*, p. 73
2. Jackson, *A Century of Dishonor*
3. Linderman, *Plenty Coups*, pp. 311–12
4. McCracken, *George Catlin*, pp. 15–16
5. Steiner, *The New Indians*, pp. 197–201
6. Bass, op. cit., pp. 1–2

# SPECIFIC SOURCES

## PHOTOGRAPH SOURCES

The source photographs from which most of the adaptations were made for the drawings were taken by the following photographers:

Walter McClintock, Blackfoot.

Edward S. Curtis, Plains, general area.

Frank A. Rinehart, Plains, general area.

Will Soule, southern Plains.

D. F. Barry, northern Plains.

Most of the McClintock photographs are from the Southwest Museum, but some Curtis, Rinehart, and Soule photographs are also from their collection, and have been used with their permission: 22b; 30; 41a; 57; 60; 62; 70 bottom; 168; 221; 239; 274 right; 317; 325a; 342; 343; 389; 392; 395; 451; 480; 481; 495 bottom; 511; 515; 533; 541; 545; 556; 574; 583; plates 9, 20, 22, 23, 25, 26, 32.

Most of the Curtis, Rinehart, and Soule photographs are from the Denver Public Library Collection, and all of the Barry photographs are from that source, and are used with their permission: 26; 45f; 84; 65; 70 top; 144; 164; 172a; 211; 278; 281; 299; 341; 358; 359; 361; 366; 367; 368; 371; 382; 383; 390 center; 402; plates 1, 8, 12, 19, 21, 24, 30, 31.

Items from the Smithsonian Institution or from the book *Teton Sioux Music*, Densmore: 233; 234; 316; 364; 365; 374; 375; 391; plates 2, 3, 4.

Most Crow medicine items are from the book *Crow Indian Medicine Bundles*, Wildschut and Ewers

Items 268; 312; 326; 330; 336 are from the book *Indianer Nordamerikas*.

All other photographs are from sources too numerous and scattered to name, with only one or two photographs being used from each source. Many of the drawings are original, however, although where artifacts are included the pieces are authentic items from collections.

## ARTIFACT SOURCES

The artifacts which are illustrated came from the following sources and are included by their permission:

The Gilcrease Institute, Tulsa, Oklahoma: 63e, c; 84; 228a, c, e; 229; 241a, b, c; 254a, b, d; 272; 273; 281i; 291a, b, c, d, e; 348; 370c; 373c, d; 448; 456a, b; 458b; 459; 460a, g; 467d; 468; 469; 503 right.

The Fred Harvey Collection, Grand Canyon, Arizona: 63a, b; 113; 141; 248; 331b, c, d; 373a; 378a, b; 387; 391g, i; 414f; 433a, b; 434; 435; 457; 458a; 462; 463; 466a; 502; 503 left; 549; plate 27.

The Southwest Museum, Highland Park, California: 83; 454a, b; 487 right.

The Heard Museum, Phoenix, Arizona: 339; 354.

The Museum of the American Indian, New York, New York: 140; 146; 147; 148; 163; 172c, d, f, g; 237.

The Museum of Natural History, New York, New York: 38; 45a; 252c, d; 161a; 171d.

The Denver Art Museum, Denver, Colorado: 255c; 313; 354 right.

Author's collection: 41b; 45c, d; 52; 55b, c, d; 63d; 64a, b, c, d; 98; 99; 102; 111; 116; 120; 121; 126a, b, c; 135; 136; 137; 138; 143; 166a, b, c, d; 224a, f; 231; 232a, e, f; 235; 238 right; 240; 247; 252e, f, g; 258a, b, c, d, e, f; 281j, k, l, m; 331a, e, f; 337 bottom; 340; 350; 352; 353; 370a, b, d; 373b; 378c, e; 379; 381 right; 384; 385; 391h; 394; 433c; 447a, b, c, d; 560b, c, d; 467a, b, c; 470; 478; 479c; 483; 553; 577; plates 6, 15, 16, 29.

# BIBLIOGRAPHY

Allen, Durward L. *Prairies and Plains.* Published in cooperation with the World Book Encyclopedia. McGraw-Hill Book Co., New York, Toronto, London, 1967.

Andrews, Ralph W. *Indians As the Westerners Saw Them.* Superior Publishing Co., Seattle, 1962.

Andrist, Ralph K. *The Long Death; The Last Days of the Plains Indian.* The Macmillan Co., New York; Collier-Macmillan Ltd., London, 1964.

Appell, Claude. *Indians!* Follett Publishing Co., Chicago and New York, 1965.

Bass, Althea. *The Arapaho Way, A Memoir of an Indian Boyhood.* Clarkson N. Potter, Inc., New York, 1966.

Beebe, Lucius, and Clegg, Charles. *The American West, The Pictorial Epic of a Continent.* E. P. Dutton & Co., Inc., New York, 1955.

Belous, Russell E., and Weinstein, Robert A. *Will Soule, Indian Photographer at Fort Sill, Oklahoma 1869–74.* Ward Ritchie Press, Los Angeles, 1969.

Benndorf, Helga, and Speyer, Arthur. *Indianer Nordamerikas 1760–1860, Aus der Sammlung Speyer.* Herausgegeben vom Deutschen Ledermuseum, angeschlossen Deutsches Schuhmuseum, Offenbach a.M., 1968.

Berke, Ernest. *The North American Indians.* Doubleday & Company, Inc., Garden City, New York, 1963.

Bleeker, Sonia. *The Sioux Indians, Hunters and Warriors of the Plains.* William Morrow and Co., New York, 1962.

Blish, Helen H. *A Pictographic History of the Oglala Sioux.* University of Nebraska Press, Lincoln, 1967.

Bowers, Alfred W. *Mandan Social and Ceremonial Organization.* University of Chicago Press, Chicago, 1950.

Brown, Joseph Epes. *The Sacred Pipe.* University of Oklahoma Press, Norman, 1953.

Brown, Mark H., and Felton, W. R. *The Frontier Years, L. A. Huffman, Photographer of the Plains.* Bramhall House, New York, 1955.

Bryant, Will. *Great American Guns and Frontier Fighters.* Grosset & Dunlap, Inc., New York, 1961.

Burbank, E. A. *Burbank Among the Indians.* Caxton Printers, Ltd., Caldwell, Idaho, 1946.

Burland, Cottie. *North American Indian Mythology.* Paul Hamlyn Ltd., Drury House, Russell Street, London WC2, 1965.

Bushnell, David I., Jr. *Burials of the Algonquian, Siouan and Caddoan Tribes West of the Mississippi.* Smithsonian Institution Bureau of American Ethnology, Bulletin 83, 1927.

Buttree, Julia M. *The Rhythm of the Redman.* Ronald Press Co., New York, 1930.

Catlin, George. *Letters and Notes on the Manners, Customs, and Condition of the North American Indians* (Vol. 1 and 2). Ross & Haines, Inc., Minneapolis, 1965.

Chapel, Charles Edward. *Guns of the Old West.* Coward-McCann, Inc., New York, 1961.

Chilton, Charles. *The Book of the West.* Bobbs-Merrill Co., Inc., Indianapolis-New York, 1962.

Cohoe, William. *A Cheyenne Sketchbook.* University of Oklahoma Press, Norman, 1964.

Cole, Philip G. *Montana in Miniature.* O'Neill Printers, Kalispell, Montana, 1966.

Cunningham, Robert E. *Indian Territory.* University of Oklahoma Press, Norman, 1957.

Curtis, Edward S. *Indian Days of Long Ago*. World Book Company, New York, 1918.

————. *The North American Indian.* twenty volumes. The University Press, Cambridge, 1909.

Curtis, Natalie. *The Indians' Book*. Harper Brothers Publishers, New York and London, 1907. Natalie Curtis.

Denig, Edward Thompson. *Five Indian Tribes of the Upper Missouri*. University of Oklahoma Press, Norman, 1961.

————. *Of the Crow Nation*. Smithsonian Institution Bureau of American Ethnology, United States Government Printing Office, Washington, 1953.

Densmore, Frances. *A Collection of Specimens from the Teton Sioux*. Museum of the American Indian, Heye Foundation, New York, 1948.

————. *Teton Sioux Music*. Smithsonian Institution Bureau of American Ethnology, Bulletin 61, 1918.

Denver Art Museum. *American Indian Art Before 1850*. Summer quarterly, 1965.

————. *Elk Antler Roach Spreaders*. Norman Feder.

————. *Indian Art of the Americas*. Winter quarterly, 1960.

————. *Indian Art of the Great Plains*. Fall quarterly, 1956.

DeVoto, Bernard. *Across the Wide Missouri*. Houghton-Mifflin Co., Boston; Riverside Press, Cambridge, 1947.

Dines, Glen, and Price, Raymond. *Dog Soldiers and the Famous Warrior Society of the Cheyenne Indians*. The Macmillan Co., New York, 1961.

Dixon, Joseph E. *The Vanishing Race*. Doubleday, Page & Company, New York, 1913.

Dockstader, Fredric J. *Indian Art in America*. New York Graphic Society, Greenwich, Connecticut, 1962.

Dodge, Colonel Richard Irving. *The Plains of the Great West*. Archer House, Inc., New York, 1959.

————. *Thirty-Three Years Among Our Wild Indians*. Archer House, Inc., New York, 1959.

Donnelly, Joseph P. (translator). *Wilderness Kingdom, Indian Life in the Rocky Mountains: 1840–1847, The Journals and Paintings of Nicholas Point, S. J.* Holt, Rinehart & Winston, New York, Chicago, San Francisco, 1967.

Dorsey, George A. *Traditions of the Skidi Pawnee*. Houghton, Mifflin and Company, Boston and New York, 1904.

Drannan, Captain William F. *Thirty-One Years on the Plains and in the Mountains*. Thos. W. Jackson Publishing Co., Chicago, 1900.

Driggs, Howard, R. *The Old West Speaks*. Prentice-Hall, Inc., Englewood Cliffs, N.J., 1956.

Eastman, Charles A. *Indian Boyhood*. McClure, Phillips & Co., New York, 1902.

————. *The Soul of the Indian*. Houghton-Mifflin Co., Boston and New York, 1911.

Ewers, John C. *Artists of the Old West*. Doubleday & Company, Inc., Garden City, New York, 1965.

————. *Blackfeet Crafts*. U. S. Department of the Interior, Bureau of Indian Affairs . . . Branch of Education, 1945.

————. *The Horse in Blackfoot Culture*. Smithsonian Institution Bureau of American Ethnology, Bulletin 159, 1955.

————. *Indian Life on the Upper Missouri*. University of Oklahoma Press, Norman, 1968.

————. *Plains Indian Painting*. Stanford University Press, Stanford, California, 1939.

————. *The Story of the Blackfeet*. U. S. Department of the Interior, Bureau of Indian Affairs . . . Branch of Education, 1944.

Farb, Peter. *Man's Rise to Civilization*. E. P. Dutton & Co., Inc., New York, 1968.

Frost, Lawrence A. *The Custer Album*. Superior Publishing Co., Seattle, 1964.

Gard, Wayne. *The Great Buffalo Hunt*. University of Nebraska Press, Lincoln, 1959.

Garland, Hamlin. *The Book of the American Indian*. Harper and Brothers, Publishers, New York and London, 1923.

Glass, Paul. *Songs and Stories of the North American Indians.* Grosset & Dunlap, Inc., New York, 1968.

Goldfrank, Esther S. *Changing Configurations in the Social Organization of a Blackfoot Tribe.* University of Washington Press, Seattle and London, 1945 and 1966 (American Ethnological Society).

Grant, Bruce. *American Indians Yesterday and Today.* E. P. Dutton & Co., Inc., New York, 1960.

Grinnell, George Bird. *Blackfoot Lodge Tales and the Story of a Prairie People.* University of Nebraska Press, Lincoln, 1962.

———. *By Cheyenne Campfires.* Yale University Press, New Haven and London, 1962.

———. *The Cheyenne Indians, Their History and Ways of Life.* Cooper Square Publishers, Inc., New York, 1962.

———. *The Indians of Today.* Herbert S. Stone and Co., Chicago and New York, 1900.

———. *Pawnee, Blackfoot and Cheyenne, History and Folklore of the Plains.* Charles Scribner's Sons, New York, 1961.

———. *Pawnee Hero Stories and Folk-tales.* University of Nebraska Press, Lincoln, 1961.

———. *The Story of the Indian.* D. Appleton and Co., New York, 1906.

———. *When Buffalo Ran.* Yale University Press, New Haven; Humphrey Milford, Oxford University Press, London, 1923.

Haines, Francis. *The Buffalo.* Thomas Y. Crowell Co., New York, 1970.

Hamilton, Charles. *Cry of the Thunderbird.* The Macmillan Co., New York, 1950.

Hanson, Irvin W. *101 Frederic Remington Drawings of the Old West.* Color Press, Willmar, Minnesota, 1968.

Hassrick, Royal B. *The Sioux—Life and Customs of a Warrior Society.* University of Oklahoma Press, Norman, 1964.

Heath, Monroe. *Our American Indians at a Glance* (The Great Americans Series, Vol. IX). Pacific Coast Publishers, Menlo Park, California, 1961.

Hewitt, J. N. B. (ed.). *Journal of Rudolph Friederich Kurz.* Smithsonian Institution Bureau of American Ethnology, United States Government Printing Office, Washington, 1937.

Hofman, Charles. *American Indians Sing.* The John Day Company, New York, 1967.

Hofsinde, Robert. *The Indians' Secret World.* William Morrow & Company, New York, 1955.

———. *Indian Warriors and Their Weapons.* William Morrow & Company, New York, 1965.

Horan, James D. *Timothy O'Sullivan, America's Forgotten Photographer.* Doubleday & Company, Inc., Garden City, New York, 1966.

Howard, James H. *The Ponca Tribe.* Smithsonian Institution Bureau of Ethnology, Bulletin 195, 1965.

Hyde, George E. *Indians of the High Plains—From the Prehistoric Period to the Coming of the Europeans.* University of Oklahoma Press, Norman, 1959.

Jackson, Clarence C. *Picture Maker of the Old West, William H. Jackson.* Charles Scribner's Sons, New York, 1947.

Kennedy, Michael S. *The Assiniboines.* University of Oklahoma Press, Norman, 1961.

———. *The Red Man's West.* Hastings House, Publishers, New York, 1965.

LaFarge, Oliver. *A Pictorial History of the American Indian.* Crown Publishers, Inc., New York, 1956.

LaFlesche, Alice, and Francis. *The Omaha Tribe.* Bureau of American Ethnology, Twenty-seventh Annual Report, 1911.

Lamb, E. Wendell, and Schultz, Lawrence W. *Indian Lore.* Light and Life Press, Winona Lake, Indiana, 1964.

Lancaster, Richard. *Piegan.* Doubleday & Company, Inc., Garden City, New York, 1966.

Lance, Chief Buffalo Child Long. *Long Lance.* Cosmopolitan Book Corporation, New York, 1928.

Laubin, Reginald, and Gladys. *The Indian Tipi, Its History, Construction and Use.* University of Oklahoma Press, Norman, 1957.

Lehmann, Herman. *Nine Years Among the Indians—1870–1879.* Von Boeckmann-Jones Co., Printers, Austin, Texas, 1927.

Lewis, Oscar. *The Effects of White Contact upon Blackfoot Culture.* University of Washington Press, Seattle and London, 1966 (American Ethnological Society).

Linderman, Frank B. *Plenty Coups, Chief of the Crows.* University of Nebraska Press, Lincoln, 1962.

Logan, Herschel C. *Cartridges, A Pictorial Digest of Small Arms Ammunition.* Bonanza Books, New York, 1959.

Lowie, Robert H. *The Crow Indians.* Holt, Rinehart & Winston, New York, 1956.

————. *Indians of the Plains.* Natural History Press, Garden City, New York, 1963.

————. *The Northern Shoshone.* American Museum of Natural History, Published by the Order of the Trustees, New York, Jan. 1909.

————. *Robert H. Lowie, Ethnologist, A Personal Record.* University of California Press, Berkeley and Los Angeles, 1959.

Luther Standing Bear. *My People the Sioux.* Houghton-Mifflin Company, Boston and New York, 1928.

Lyford, Carrie A. *Quill and Beadwork of the Western Sioux.* United States Department of the Interior, Bureau of Indian Affairs . . . Branch of Education, 1940.

Maine, Floyd Schuster. *Lone Eagle, The White Sioux.* University of New Mexico Press, Albuquerque, 1956.

Marquis, Thomas. *Custer on the Little Big Horn.* End-Kian Publishing Co., Lodi, California, 1967.

Mason, Bernard J. *The Book of Indian Crafts and Costumes.* The Ronald Press Co., New York, 1946.

Mayhall, Mildred P. *The Kiowas.* University of Oklahoma Press, Norman, 1962.

Maximilian, Prince of Wied Neuwied. *Travels in the Interior of North America.* H. Evans Lloyd, London, 1843.

McClintock, Walter. *The Old North Trail, Life, Legends and Religion of the Blackfeet Indians.* University of Nebraska Press, Lincoln, 1968.

McCracken, Harold. *The Charles M. Russell Book.* Doubleday & Company, Inc., Garden City, New York, 1957.

————. *The Frederic Remington Book.* Doubleday & Company, Inc., Garden City, New York, 1966.

————. *George Catlin and the Old Frontier.* Dial Press, New York, 1959.

————. *Portrait of the Old West.* McGraw-Hill Book Co., New York, Toronto, London, 1952.

McDermott, John Francis. *Seth Eastman, Pictorial Historian of the Indian.* University of Oklahoma Press, Norman, 1961.

McNickle, D'Arcy. *The Indian Tribes of the United States, Ethnic and Cultural Survival.* Oxford University Press, London, New York, 1962, 1964, 1966.

Miles, Charles. *Indian and Eskimo Artifacts of North America.* Henry Regnery Co., Chicago, 1963.

Myrus, Don. *Collector's Guns.* Arco Publishing Co., Inc., 480 Lexington Avenue, New York, 1962.

Nabokov, Peter. *Two Leggings, The Making of a Crow Warrior.* Thomas Y. Crowell Co., New York, 1967.

Neihardt, John G. *Black Elk Speaks.* William Morrow & Company, New York, 1932.

Newcomb, W. W., Jr. *The Indians of Texas—From Prehistoric to Modern Times.* University of Texas Press, Austin, 1961.

Nye, Wilbur Sturtevant. *Bad Medicine and Good, Tales of the Kiowas.* University of Oklahoma Press, Norman, 1962.

————. *Plains Indian Raiders.* University of Oklahoma Press, Norman, 1968.

Paige, Harry W. *Songs of the Teton Sioux.* Westernlore Press, Los Angeles, 1970.

Parsons, John E. *The First Winchester, The Story of the 1886 Repeating Rifle.* William Morrow & Company, New York, 1955, 1960.

Peterson, Harold. *American Indian Tomahawks.* Museum of the American Indian, Heye Foundation, New York, 1965.

————. *American Knives.* Charles Scribner's Sons, New York, 1958.

————. *Pageant of the Gun.* Doubleday & Company, Inc., Garden City, New York, 1967.

————. *The Remington Historical Treasury of American Guns.* Grosset & Dunlap, Inc., New York, 1966.

————. *The Treasury of the Gun.* Ridge Press Books, Golden Press, New York, 1962.

Pope, Saxton T. *Bows and Arrows.* University of California Press, Berkeley and Los Angeles, 1962.

Powell, Peter J. *Sweet Medicine.* University of Oklahoma Press, Norman, 1969.

Raphael, Ralph B. *The Book of American Indians.* Arco Publishing Co., Inc., New York (Do-It-Yourself Series), 1959.

Remington, Frederic. *Frederic Remington's Own West.* Dial Press, New York, 1960.

————. *Pony Tracks.* Harper and Brothers Publishers, New York and London; copyright Harper and Bros., 1895; copyright Miss Emma L. Caten, 1923.

Renner, Fredric G. *Charles M. Russell, Paintings, Drawings and Sculpture in the Amon G. Carter Collection.* Published for the Amon G. Carter Museum of Western Art, Fort Worth, by the University of Texas Press, Austin and London, 1966.

Reusswig, William. *A Picture Report of the Custer Fight.* Hastings House, Publishers, New York, 1967.

Roe, Frank Gilbert. *The Indian and the Horse.* University of Oklahoma Press, Norman, 1955.

Ross, Marvin C. *The West of Alfred Jacob Miller (1837).* University of Oklahoma Press, Norman, 1951, 1968.

Ruby, Robert H. *The Oglala Sioux.* Vantage Press, Inc., New York, 1955.

Russell, Virgil Y. *Indian Artifacts.* Johnson Publishing Co., Boulder, Colorado, 1951, 1953.

Salisbury, Albert, and Jane. *Two Captains West.* Superior Publishing Co., Seattle, 1950.

Saloman, Julian H. *The Book of Indian Crafts and Indian Lore.* Harper and Row, Publishers, New York and Evanston, 1928.

Sandoz, Mari. *Hostiles and Friendlies.* University of Nebraska Press, Lincoln, 1959.

————. *These Were the Sioux.* Hastings House, Publishers, New York, 1961.

Scacheri, Mario, and Mabel. *Indians Today.* Harcourt, Brace and Co., New York, 1936.

Schmitt, Martin F., and Brown, Dee. *Fighting Indians of the West.* Charles Scribner's Sons, New York and London, 1948.

Schoonmaker, W. J. *The World of the Grizzly Bear.* J. B. Lippincott Company, Philadelphia and New York, 1968.

Schulenberg, Raymond F. *Indians of the North Dakota.* Reprinted from *North Dakota History,* Vol. 23, No. 3 and 4, July–Oct. 1956. Published by the State Historical Society of North Dakota.

Schultz, James Willard. *Blackfeet and Buffalo.* University of Oklahoma Press, Norman, 1962.

————. *My Life As an Indian.* Houghton-Mifflin Co., Boston and New York; Riverside Press, Cambridge, 1906, 1967.

————. *On the Warpath.* Houghton-Mifflin Co., Boston and New York; Riverside Press, Cambridge, 1914.

————. *Seizer of Eagles.* Houghton-Mifflin Co., Boston and New York; Riverside Press, Cambridge, 1922.

Serven, James E. *The Collecting of Guns.* Stackpole Co., Harrisburg, Pennsylvania, 1964.

Seton, Julia M. *American Indian Arts, A Way of Life.* The Ronald Press Co., New York, 1962.

Southwest Museum Leaflets, Southwest Museum, Highland Park. Los Angeles, California:

  *Painted Tipis and Picturewriting of the Blackfoot Indians.*
    Walter McClintock.

  *The Blackfoot Tipi.* Walter McClintock.

  *Blackfoot Warrior Societies.* Walter McClintock.

  *Dances of the Blackfoot Indians.* Walter McClintock.

  *Indians of the Plains.* M. R. Harrington.

Spaulding, George F. *On the Western Tour with Washington Irving, The Journals and Letters of Count de Pourtales.* University of Oklahoma Press, Norman, 1968.

Speck, Frank G., and Broom, Leonard, in collaboration with Will West Long. *Cherokee Dance and Drama.* University of California Press, Berkeley and Los Angeles, 1951.

Stands In Timber, John, and Liberty, Margot. *Cheyenne Memories.* Yale University Press, New Haven and London, 1967.

Steward, Julian. *The Blackfoot.* U. S. Department of the Interior, National Park Service, Field Division of Education, Berkeley, California, 1934.

Stirling, Matthew W. *National Geographic on Indians of the Americas.* National Geographic Society, Washington, D.C., 1955.

Strong, Phil. *Horses and Americans.* Garden City Publishing Co., Inc., Garden City, New York, 1939.

Swan, Oliver. *Frontier Days.* Grosset & Dunlap, Publishers, New York, 1928.

Terrell, John Upton. *Traders of the Western Morning, Aboriginal Commerce in Precolumbian North America.* Southwest Museum, Los Angeles, 1967.

Thwaites, Jeanne. *Horses of the West.* A. S. Barnes and Co., South Brunswick and New York; Thomas Yoseloff Ltd., London, 1968.

Tibbles, Thomas Henry. *Buckskin and Blanket Days.* Doubleday & Company, Inc., Garden City, New York, 1957.

Tilden, Freeman. *Following the Frontier with F. Jay Haynes, Pioneer Photographer of the Old West.* Alfred A. Knopf, New York, 1964.

Trenholm, Virginia Cole, and Carley, Maurine. *The Shoshones, Sentinels of the Rockies.* University of Oklahoma Press, Norman, 1964.

Tunis, Edwin. *Indians.* The World Publishing Company, Cleveland and New York, 1959.

Wearin, Otha Donner. *Clarence Arthur Ellsworth, Artist of the Old West.* World Publishing Company, Shenandoah, Iowa, 1967.

Webb, Walter Prescott. *The Great Plains.* Grosset & Dunlap, New York, 1931.

Wellman, Paul I. *Indian Wars and Warriors West.* Houghton-Mifflin Co., Boston, 1959.

Wheeler, Francis Rolt. *The Boy with the U. S. Indians.* U. S. Service Series, Lothrop, Lee & Shepard Co., Boston, 1904.

White, Leslie A. (ed.). *Lewis Henry Morgan, The Indian Journals 1859–62* (Illustrations selected by Clyde Walton) University of Michigan Press, Ann Arbor, 1959.

Wildschut, William. *Crow Indian Medicine Bundles.* Museum of the American Indian, Heye Foundation, New York, 1960.

Wildschut, William, and Ewers, John C. *Crow Indian Beadwork.* New York, Museum of the American Indian, Heye Foundation, New York, 1959.

Wilson, E. N. *The White Indian Boy* (Pioneer Life Series). World Book Co., Yonkers-on-Hudson, New York, 1922.

Wissler, Clark. *Indians of the United States.* The American Museum of Natural History Science Series. Doubleday, Doran & Company, Inc., New York, 1941.

Wright, Muriel. *A Guide to the Indian Tribes of Oklahoma.* University of Oklahoma Press, Norman, 1951.

Wyman, Walker D. *The Wild Horse of the West.* University of Nebraska Press, Lincoln, 1945.

Under the direction of Jay Monaghan. *The Book of the American West.* Julian Messner, Inc., New York, 1963.

By the editors of *American Heritage, the Magazine of History. The American Heritage Book of Indians.* Published by American Heritage Publishing Co., Inc., distribution by Simon & Schuster, Inc., 1961.

# INDEX